The Raw Cotton Trade

European Expansion and Indigenous Response

VOLUME 52

The Raw Cotton Trade

Brazil, Portugal, and Europe during the Industrial Revolution

By

Felipe Souza Melo

BRILL

The open access publication of this book has been published with the support of the Swiss National Science Foundation.

ISSN 1873-8974
ISBN 978-90-04-75755-4
ISBN 978-90-04-75756-1 (PDF)
DOI https://doi.org/10.1163/9789004757561

Library of Congress Control Number: 2026937984

Brill and Koninklijke Brill BV are part of De Gruyter Brill.
www.degruyterbrill.com

Questions about General Product Safety Regulation: productsafety@degruyterbrill.com

Cover illustration: Print from Manuel Arruda da Câmara, *Memoria sobre a cultura dos algodoeiros e sobre o methodo de o escolher, e ensacar* [...], 1799. [*Flor do algodão, estampas 1 e 2*]. The illustration represents the cotton flower in its natural grandeur and on the first day of its appearance. Source: Biblioteca Brasiliana Guita e José Mindlin.

o real não está na saída nem na chegada:
ele se dispõe para a gente é no meio da travessia.

Grande Sertão: Veredas, João Guimarães Rosa

∵

Contents

General Series Editor's Foreword

Over the past half millennium, from circa 1450 until the last third or so of the twentieth century, much of the world's history has been influenced in great part by one general dynamic and complex historical process known as European expansion. Defined as the opening up, unfolding, or increasing the extent, number, volume, or scope of the space, size, or participants belonging to a certain people or group, location, or geographical region, Europe's expansion initially emerged and emanated physically, intellectually, and politically from southern Europe—specifically from the Iberian peninsula—during the fifteenth century, expanding rapidly from that locus to include, first, all of Europe's maritime and, later, most of its continental states and peoples. Most commonly associated with events described as the discovery of America and of a passage to the East Indies (Asia) by rounding the Cape of Good Hope (Africa) during the early modern and modern periods, European expansion and encounters with the rest of the world multiplied and morphed into several ancillary historical processes, including colonization, imperialism, capitalism, and globalization, encompassing themes, among others, relating to contacts and, to quote the EURO series' original mission statement, "connections and exchanges; peoples, ideas and products, especially through the medium of trading companies; the exchange of religions and traditions; the transfer of technologies; and the development of new forms of political, social and economic policy, as well as identity formation." Because of its intrinsic importance, extensive research has been performed and much has been written about the entire period of European expansion.

With the first volume published in 2009, Brill launched the European Expansion and Indigenous Response book series at the initiative of well-known scholar and respected historian, Glenn J. Ames, who, prior to his untimely passing, was the founding editor and guided the first seven volumes of the series to publication. Being one of the early members of the series' editorial board, I was then appointed as Series Editor. The series' founding objectives are to focus on publications "that understand and deal with the process of European expansion, interchange and connectivity in a global context in the early modern and modern period" and to "provide a forum for a variety of types of scholarly work with a wider disciplinary approach that moves beyond the traditional isolated and nation bound historiographical emphases of this field, encouraging whenever possible non-European perspectives … that seek to understand this indigenous transformative process and period in autonomous as well as inter-related cultural, economic, social, and ideological terms."

The history of European expansion is a challenging field in which interest is likely to grow, despite, or perhaps because of, its polemical nature. Controversy has centered on tropes conceived and written in the past by Europeans, primarily concerning their early reflections and claims regarding the transcendental historical nature of this process and its emergence and importance in the creation of an early modern global economy and society. One of the most persistent objections is that the field has been "Eurocentric." This complaint arises because of the difficulty in introducing and balancing different historical perspectives, when one of the actors in the process is to some degree neither European nor Europeanized—a conundrum alluded to in the African proverb: "Until the lion tells his tale, the hunt will always glorify the hunter." Another, and perhaps even more important and growing historiographical issue, is that with the re-emergence of historical millennial societies (China and India, for example) and the emergence of other non-Western European societies successfully competing politically, economically, and intellectually on the global scene vis-à-vis Europe, the seminal nature of European expansion is being subjected to greater scrutiny, debate, and comparison with other historical alternatives.

Despite, or perhaps because of, these new directions and stimulating sources of existing and emerging lines of dispute regarding the history of European expansion, I and the editorial board of the series will continue with the original objectives and mission statement of the series and vigorously "… seek out studies that employ diverse forms of analysis from all scholarly disciplines, including anthropology, archaeology, art history, history (including the history of science), linguistics, literature, music, philosophy, and religious studies." In addition, we shall seek to stimulate, locate, incorporate, and publish the most important and exciting scholarship in the field.

Towards that purpose, I am pleased to introduce volume 52 of Brill's EURO series entitled: *The Raw Cotton Trade: Brazil, Portugal, and Europe during the Industrial Revolution*. Authored by Felipe Souza Melo, this study demonstrates prodigious research, judicious use of evidence, and originality in argumentation. The author employs "commodity chain analysis" to reconstruct late colonial and early modern Brazil's process of growing and trading raw cotton during the Industrial Revolution. The arguments and points made throughout the manuscript are thoroughly documented from evidence gleaned from archives located mainly in Portugal but also in Brazil, Spain, and the United Kingdom. It makes a welcome contribution to our understanding of the role of cotton production during the Industrial Revolution. It shows that the cotton produced in Brazil and exported to Europe via Portugal played a key role in fostering the Industrial Revolution in Great Britain and elsewhere. Introducing a different perspective on the role of cotton in the Industrial Revolution, it often refers to Great Britain and the cotton plantations of the U.S. South but concentrates its analytical focus on centers of production and consumption in Brazil, Portugal, France, Hamburg, and other places in Europe.

The Raw Cotton Trade does not dispute the conclusions of previous contributions or diminish the role of Great Britain as a significant player in the cotton industry. Rather, it "seeks to position Brazil, the Portuguese Empire, and the various merchant communities involved with them in a more prominent position." It makes multiple historiographical interventions: e.g., contributions to Brazilian historiography in detailing the history (and differences) surrounding cotton production in Maranhão and Pernambuco/Northeastern Brazil; revision of Anglo-centric stories of the rise of "king cotton" and the early industrial revolutions; meticulous reconstruction of the mechanics of commercial and distribution networks in early modern Europe (through comparative analysis of Portugal, France, England, Scotland, and Genoa). It makes the argument that without mercantile communities, a transnational perspective, and the economic policy of the Portuguese Empire, the story of one of the most critical cotton suppliers during the industrial revolution cannot be satisfactorily narrated. The EURO series' readers should determine on their own and evaluate this perspective and argument. But they should thank this author for this manuscript.

George Bryan Souza
University of Texas, San Antonio

Acknowledgements

This book is, with some adjustments, my Ph.D. thesis defended at the European University Institute in 2023. It would not have transcended its mundane and rudimentary condition without the stringent and astute oversight of Giorgio Riello. Because he constantly pushed me to think of bolder and more sophisticated arguments and saw things in my text that I could not see, it is Giorgio who is responsible for this book not getting lost in trivialities, which I myself would have fallen prey to, if it were not for his comments, observations, and ever-present guidance.

I also thank Stéphane Van Damme, my first supervisor when I arrived at the EUI, and Regina Grafe, my second reader. The conversations we had in my first year were very important and, in a way, guided me throughout my whole Ph.D.

As if joining a renowned organization like the EUI and receiving mentoring from individuals of Riello's caliber weren't enough, I was also fortunate enough to be able to participate in the Fabric of Profit project at the Paul Bairoch Institute of Economic History as a postdoctoral researcher. I am profoundly indebted to Professor Mary O'Sullivan for inviting me to join her research group. In Geneva, I had the privilege of receiving guidance from Mary and engaging in intellectual discussions with my esteemed colleagues and friends Lorenzo Avellino, Lea Meyer, and Gaia Valenti. During my postdoctoral research, I was able to gather additional data and refine the manuscript.

Maximiliano Menz, my friend and master's supervisor at the University of São Paulo and my Professor during my undergraduate studies at the Federal University of São Paulo, never actually stopped supervising me. I thank him for helping me during my Ph.D. and for the article we wrote together, but mainly for investing so much time and effort in me in the early years of my academic career. If I was admitted to the EUI, it was mainly because of him. Therefore, the realization of this book is also thanks to him.

Diego Martins is a great friend with whom I wrote some articles together with as well as a database. Part of these texts and data were used in this book. He also provided me with original data and information from his research. I wish to thank him for all his help during this journey.

I would like to thank my friends, also supervised by Professor Menz, the historians André Paiva and Gustavo Meira Menino.

Thanks also to Angelo Carrara and Rodrigo Dominguez for the article we wrote together and to Daniel Strum and Jesus Bohorquez for helping me since I was doing my master's degree in São Paulo.

A crucial part of my book depended on the historical sources that Tomás de Albuquerque digitized for me at a time when the COVID-19 pandemic made any kind of trip to the Portuguese archives impossible. I thank him for doing this work.

Special thanks go to the staff at Brill Publishing—George Bryan Souza and Cátia Antunes—who welcomed the initial idea for the manuscript; to the two anonymous reviewers for their valuable suggestions; and to Melissa Allieri for guiding me through the editorial process. This book is published open access thanks to the generous funding of the Swiss National Science Foundation (SNSF). I also thank Kan Wai Min for facilitating this process between Brill and the SNSF.

Thanks to Guillaume Daudin, Giorgio Tosco, Matteo Calcagni, Serge Chassagne, Catia Brilli, Samuel Guicheteau, Gustavo Acioli, Leonardo Marques, Sheryllynne Haggerty, Trevor Burnard, Antonia da Silva Mota, and other scholars whose names I may have forgotten who pointed me to sources and bibliographies. Likewise, I thank the EUI library workers and interns for bringing me all the materials I requested. No less important were the helpful services of the EUI staff. I would like to give a special thanks to Fatma H. Sayed and Sophie Martin for being so good and kind to my many requests.

Thanks to Ana Maria Spariosu and John Ryan for revising the book and making it less painful for those reading it.

Thanks to the examiners Leonor Freire Costa and Cátia Antunes for their comments and suggestions.

I thank my friends Télio Cravo and Augusto Petter for their friendship and our good conversations in Florence.

Last but not least, I thank my family: my parents, Luis and Izabel, for their love, affection, and understanding, and my daughter Natalia, born in the middle of the pandemic, who showed me that there is a—good—life outside of academia. I dedicate this book to her with all my love and affection.

Tables, Maps, Figures, and Flowcharts

Tables

Maps

Figures

Flowcharts

Abbreviations

ACL	Administração Central (*Central Administration*)
AHU	Arquivo Histórico Ultramarino, Lisboa (*Overseas Historical Archive*)
ANTT	Arquivo Nacional Torre do Tombo, Lisboa (*Institute of the National Archives – Torre do Tombo*)
CC	Correspondência com a Corte (*Correspondence with the Court*)
CNL	Cartório Notarial de Lisboa (*Notary Office of Lisbon*)
CU	Conselho Ultramarino (*Overseas Council*)
Cx.	Caixa (*Box*)
Doc.	Documento (*Document*)
F.	Fólio (*Folio*)
FO	Foreign Office
GCGPM	General Company of Grão-Pará and Maranhão
GCPP	General Company of Pernambuco and Paraíba
Liv.	Livro (*Book*)
Mç.	Maço (*Pack*)
NA	The National Archives Kew
N.º	Número (*Number*)
Proc.	Processo (*Process*)
V.	Verso (*Verso*)

Values, Prices, and Conversions

	Réis
Sugar mill in Pernambuco in 1806[a]	16,000,000
Cost of building a big ship (navio) in 1781[b]	20,000,000
Cost of building a medium vessel (galera) in 1796[c]	6,000,000
Cost of building a small vessel (sumaca) in 1792[d]	2,460,000
1 arroba of white sugar in Pernambuco in 1800[e]	1,300
1 arroba of brown sugar in Pernambuco in 1800[f]	632
1 arroba of cotton with seed in 1805 in Paraíba[g]	1,120
1 arroba of ginned cotton in Pernambuco in 1800[h]	6,868
1 arroba of ginned cotton in Maranhão in 1800[i]	6,720
Cotton ginning machine in Maranhão in 1816[j]	800
Cotton ginning machine in Bahia in 1802[l]	39,000
Freight of one arroba of sugar in 1807 (for a trip between Pernambuco and Portugal)[m]	300
Freight of one arroba of cotton in 1807 (for a trip between Pernambuco and Portugal)[n]	1,400
Price of an enslaved person in Guinea in 1783[o]	85,500
Price of an enslaved person in Maranhão in 1783[p]	160,000
Fortune of a big planter in Maranhão in 1805 (José Antônio Gomes de Sousa)[q]	67,042,210
Fortune of a large merchant in Lisbon in 1806 (João Teixeira de Barros)[r]	1,000,000,000

1 bale of cotton = 4.15 *arrobas* in 1796[s]
1 crate of sugar = 42.2 *arrobas* in 1795[t]
1 *arroba* = 32 lb = 14.7 kg[u]
1 *conto* = 1,000,000 *réis*

[a] ANTT, 6º Cartório notarial de Lisboa – Livro de Notas, Cx. 37, liv. 185, f. 57–57v.
[b] ANTT, 7º Cartório notarial de Lisboa – Ofício A, Livro de Notas, Cx. 101, liv. 610, f. 70–71.
[c] ANTT, 7º Cartório notarial de Lisboa – Ofício A, Livro de Notas, Cx. 110, liv. 670, f. 6v–7v.
[d] ANTT, 6º Cartório notarial de Lisboa – Livro de Notas, Cx. 28, liv. 140, f. 42–43v.
[e] Melo, *O negócio de Pernambuco*, 434.
[f] Melo, *O negócio de Pernambuco*, 434.
[g] AHU, ACL, CU, 014, Cx. 47. Doc. 3318.
[h] Melo, *O negócio de Pernambuco*, 441.
[i] AHU, Avulsos Maranhão, Cx. 110, Doc. 8606.
[j] Mota, *A Dinâmica colonial*, 137–39.
[l] Filho, *Uma Comunidade Rural Do Brasil Antigo*, 326
[m] ANTT, Juízo da Índia e Mina, mç. 81, n.º 13, cx. 81.
[n] ANTT, Juízo da Índia e Mina, mç. 18, n.º 8, cx. 142.
[o] Gayoso, *compendio*, 245.
[p] Gayoso, *compendio*, 243.
[q] Mota, *A Dinâmica colonial*, 50.
[r] Pedreira, *Os Homens de Negócio da Praça de Lisboa*, 151.
[s] Melo, *O negócio de Pernambuco*, 157
[t] Melo, *O negócio de Pernambuco*, 163
[u] P. Kelly, *The Universal Cambist*, 245.

Introduction

1 Goals and Scope of the Book

This book offers, for the first time, a comprehensive history of cotton in Brazil, Portugal, and the rest of Europe during the Industrial Revolution. As a result, it tracks the course of Brazilian raw cotton from its cultivation to its transportation across the Atlantic to its consumption and circulation in the key European manufacturing hubs. The significance of Brazilian cotton to European spinners is just one of the reasons for writing this book; another is that Brazilian cotton touches on a number of topics that historiography has failed to place in the same setting, thus failing to give it a wider meaning. The production conditions that differed across Brazil's plantation regions, the relationship between cotton and the slave trade, the trade dynamics from both macroeconomic and microeconomic perspectives that facilitated the transfer of cotton from Brazil to Portugal and subsequently to Europe's spinning centers, along with the particularities of cotton consumption, are themes that occasionally emerge in historiography, yet remain fragmented and lack a cohesive narrative that integrates the central elements surrounding cotton.

When we think about cotton and the Industrial Revolution, what perhaps automatically comes to mind are the slave plantations in the U.S. South and the mechanical inventions in Great Britain. Thus, another reason for writing this book is to present the narrative of cotton during the Industrial Revolution from a different point of view than the conventional and plentiful academic production that we used to.[1] We are aware of the almost perfect symbiosis between the raw materials from the southern United States and the British spinning

1 The literature is huge; see for instance, Harold D. Woodman, *King Cotton and His Retainers: Financing and Marketing the Cotton Crop of the South, 1800–1925* (1968; University of South Carolina Press, 1990); John R. Killick, "Bolton Ogden & Co.: A Case Study in Anglo-American Trade, 1790–1850," *The Business History Review* 48, no. 4 (1974): 501–19; Ronald Bailey, "The Other Side of Slavery: Black Labor, Cotton, and Textile Industrialization in Great Britain and the United States," *Agricultural History* 68, no. 2 (1994): 35–50; Mary B. Rose, *Firms, Networks and Business Values: The British and American Cotton Industries since 1750* (Cambridge University Press, 2000); Walter Johnson, *River of Dark Dreams: Slavery and Empire in the Cotton Kingdom* (Belknap Press of Harvard University Press, 2013); Sven Beckert, *Empire of Cotton: A Global History* (Alfred A. Knopf, 2014); Alan L. Olmstead and Paul W. Rhode, "Cotton, Slavery, and the New History of Capitalism," *Explorations in Economic History* 67 (January 2018): 1–17; Mark Harvey, "Slavery, Indenture and the Development of British Industrial Capitalism," *History Workshop Journal* 88 (October 2019): 66–88; Kassia St Clair, *The Golden Thread: How Fabric Changed History* (Liveright Publishing, 2019).

machinery that commenced circa 1800. But prior to and shortly before that date, numerous sources provided cotton to European spinners, and comprehending these alternative markets remains a subject for further investigation, with this book being an attempt to cover the Brazilian side. Maybe it is worthwhile to recall that the traditional machines revered as the core components of the textile industry—the "spinning Jenny" by Hargreaves, the water-powered spinning frame by Arkwright, and the spinning mule by Crompton—initially processed raw cotton sourced from the Caribbean, South America, and the Levant, and not from the United States.

In short, there are three general goals that I sought to pursue in this book: 1) to seek a more global vision of the history of cotton from Brazil; 2) to provide another perspective of analysis that does not focus on the well-known and well-analyzed trade in cotton from the United States to Britain (although this book also looks in depth at the British side of this history); and 3) to seek to contribute new elements to understand how markets functioned in the early modern period, in dialogue with the literature on globalization and market integration.[2] Contrary to what it may seem, markets are not so easy to understand, as Koray Çalışkan rightly points out when dealing with current markets for cotton. The challenge is perhaps even greater when it comes to old markets. In this sense, the market, or rather markets—far from being something universal as described and wanted by neoclassical economists—deserve to be treated as historical places with particular socioeconomic functions and specific institutions where agents and structures interact.[3] For this to be done, this

---

2 Kevin H. O'Rourke, "The Worldwide Economic Impact of the French Revolutionary and Napoleonic Wars, 1793–1815," *Journal of Global History* 1, no. 1 (2006): 124; Kevin H. O'Rourke and Jeffrey G. Williamson, "When Did Globalisation Begin?," *European Review of Economic History* 6, no. 1 (2002): 23–50; Ronald Findlay and Kevin H. O'Rourke, "Commodity Market Integration, 1500–2000," in *Globalization in Historical Perspective*, ed. Michael D. Bordo et al. (University of Chicago Press, 2003). See also Cátia Antunes, *Globalisation in the Early Modern Period: The Economic Relationship between Amsterdam and Lisbon, 1640–1705* (Aksant, 2004); Cátia Antunes and Karwan Fatah-Black, eds., *Explorations in History and Globalization* (Routledge, 2016).

3 Koray Çalışkan, *Market Threads: How Cotton Farmers and Traders Create a Global Commodity* (Princeton University Press, 2010). See also Neil Fligstein and Luke Dauter, "The Sociology of Markets," *Annual Review of Sociology* 33, no. 1 (2007): 105–28; Amy A. Quark, *Global Rivalries: Standards Wars and the Transnational Cotton Trade* (University of Chicago Press, 2013); on the market as a synonym for the financial market and its great influence on the media and the current public debate, see Maria Lucia de Paiva Jacobini, "O jornalismo econômico e a concepção de mercado: uma análise de conteúdo dos cadernos de economia da Folha de S.Paulo e O Estado de S.Paulo," *Brazilian journalism research* 4, no. 2 (2008): 190–209; Serge Halimi, "When Market Journalism Invades the World," *Le Monde Diplomatique*, May 1, 1997, https://mondediplo.com/1997/05/globalsation3158.

book analyzes a set of actors on specific trade routes: growers in Brazil, and the dealers who traded raw cotton in Brazil, Portugal, and the rest of Europe between the 1750s and 1820s. This period was the time of a higher presence of Brazilian raw cotton in the European markets before being completely overshadowed by U.S. cotton. Brazilian cotton is therefore the item in concern here but so are the individuals who handled it.

In the golden age of Brazilian cotton, at least six of its regions (captaincies in the colonial period that would become provinces after Brazilian political independence in 1822) cultivated the fiber: Maranhão, Pernambuco, Bahia, Pará, Rio de Janeiro, and São Paulo. The first three captaincies, however, concentrated almost 95% of cotton exports to Portugal between 1796 and 1807. At the end of the eighteenth century, they were regions highly dependent on the labor of enslaved Africans but with differing demographic profiles (Map 0.1). The cotton growers were in two essentially different regions. Maranhão, located in Northern Brazil, was a peripheral captaincy in the economy of the Portuguese Empire until the mid-eighteenth century, despite its relevance to the Jesuits and Portugal's geopolitical goals.[4] However, it rapidly advanced by importing substantial numbers of enslaved individuals and making significant investments in extensive cotton and rice plantations. By the close of the eighteenth century, it had become one of South America's wealthiest and dynamic regions. Conversely, a large region historically linked to sugar plantations, inhabited by an affluent rural and commercial elite, also emerged as a vital region for cotton cultivation. In the absence of a more suitable designation, I shall refer to this extensive area, comprising the captaincies of Pernambuco, Paraíba, Alagoas, Rio Grande do Norte, and Ceará, as the Northeast of Brazil. This region can be confused for Pernambuco, as numerous crops from other captaincies were transported via the port of Recife. The captaincy of Bahia exhibited certain characteristics akin to those of the Northeast, though not examined in detail here. Consequently, at its peak, cotton agriculture and commerce were predominantly situated in the North and Northeast of Brazil, which will be the focal point of this book.

Cotton was sent mostly to Lisbon and, to a lesser extent, to Porto. Because of this, the merchant communities that imported and reexported cotton into the Empire's capital are examined in this book. These merchants, nonetheless, engaged in other enterprises that were crucial for comprehending the

4 Rafael Chambouleyron, *Povoamento, Ocupação e Agricultura na Amazônia Colonial* (Editora Açai, 2010); Rafael Chambouleyron, "Conquistas diferentes e de diferentes climas: o Maranhão, o Brasil e a América portuguesa (séculos XVII e XVIII)," *Esboços: histórias em contextos globais* 26, no. 41 (2019): 84–103.

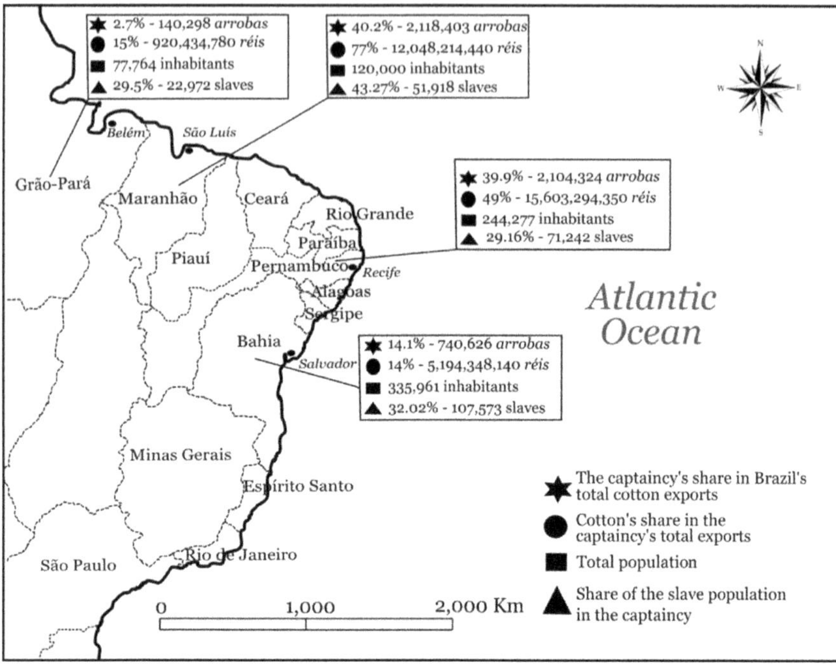

MAP 0.1 *The main cotton-growing regions in Brazil at the beginning of the nineteenth century*
Sources: the export figures, covering the years 1796 to 1807, were taken from José Jobson de Andrade Arruda, *O Brasil no comércio colonial* (Editora Ática, 1980), 204, 224, 244, 262, 368–369. For population data for 1808 see Tarcísio R. Botelho, "A população da América portuguesa em finais do período colonial (1776–1822): fontes e estimativas globais," *Anais de História de Além-Mar*, no. 16 (janeiro de 2015), 96–97. Map prepared by the author.

dynamics of the cotton trade, including the slave trade, the trade in wine and gold, and their interests in tax collection across various regions of Brazil. This book additionally examines the European merchants and markets involved in the importation of Brazilian cotton. During this time frame, France and England were the primary consumers of cotton. Over time, there were numerous alterations concerning the ports of each nation that dominated cotton imports from Portugal. This book explores these ports and their corresponding textile industry. Furthermore, it analyzes the significance of other ports that gained prominence at various times, including Genoa, Hamburg, and Glasgow.

Although the framework and general objectives of this book are new, the ideas that influenced it nevertheless came from diverse sources. Below, I will comment on some of them, starting with the most general aspects of the most recent historiography on cotton. I will then comment on the historiography of Brazilian cotton and, finally, on the current discussion on trade and traders in the early modern period. These subsequent sections of this introduction, therefore, can also be seen as a state-of-the-art, or a brief review of the literature I engaged with throughout the book and some new contributions I bring to the debate.

2 New Perspectives on Raw Cotton

In a way, the cotton revolution that took place in Europe in the second half of the eighteenth century was the culmination of the maritime discoveries of the Portuguese and Spanish at the beginning of the modern era. Maritime expansion brought more Asian cotton textiles to Europe, and land in America was colonized for raw cotton cultivation. Obviously, neither Christopher Columbus nor Vasco da Gama, who entered the history books as the "discoverer" of America in 1492 and the first European to arrive in India by sea in 1498, had the revolutionary potential of cotton in mind. But about 200 years after their achievements, Europeans were so admired by Asian textiles that they spared no effort to produce them in their own countries, and the vast American lands came in handy to provide them with the indispensable raw material, not to mention the supply of enslaved people from African ports.

A lot happened between maritime expansion and the cotton revolution, but European interest in Indian textiles and the desire to copy them were always growing. Asian cotton textiles, due to their washability and color retention, were highly sought after. They were very varied in quality and price, which is why they reached a wide range of the population. Their floral themes were characteristics highly valued by Europeans at a time when the perception of the natural world was undergoing changes. The "branches, leaves, repeating blossoms birds and insects" according to Lemire, "were radiant expressions of nature which charmed and intrigued." A "passion for flowers" was taking place. Perhaps the only equivalent to cotton was silk's floral motifs, but silk was expensive and restricted to the elite.[5]

---

5 Beverly Lemire, "Fashioning Cottons: Asian Trade, Domestic Industry and Consumer Demand, 1660–1780," in *The Cambridge History of Western Textiles.*, ed. David Jenkins (Cambridge University Press, 2002), 493–94, 498, 500–501; see also John Styles, "What Were Cottons for in the Early Industrial Revolution?," in *The Spinning World: A Global History of Cotton Textiles, 1200–1850*, ed. Giorgio Riello and Prasannan Parthasarathi (Oxford University Press, 2009), 307; Giorgio Riello, *Cotton: The Fabric That Made the Modern World* (Cambridge University Press, 2013), 113–15.

However, not everything was all roses. Europe saw numerous conflicts about cotton textiles. Some sectors of society believed that the lightness and color of these textiles corrupted women. They were seen as effeminate luxuries. But the most serious threat to cottons came from wool and silk producers and traders who felt that the import of cotton fabrics was killing their businesses. The dispute in England started in the 1680s and culminated in 1721 with the ban of a significant portion of Asian textiles. France introduced several laws against these textiles between 1681 and 1716. Spain banned them in 1713, and Prussia did so in 1721. Nevertheless, these decorated cotton textiles continued to go to the Netherlands, where they were illegally redistributed to the rest of Europe, and smuggling proved to be difficult to fight. Still, even at the time of the prohibitions, there were always attempts by Europeans to copy Asian textiles, either by simply bringing plain cotton cloths from India and printing them in Europe or by attempting to weave them domestically, frequently mixing linen warp with cotton weft.[6]

At that period, discussions about floral cotton fabrics referred to fine printed calicos,[7] also known as chintz (*indiennes* in French, *estampados* in Portuguese), which is why the desire for these cotton fabrics was called the "calico craze."[8] The 1721 regulation that forbade the creation of calicos in England was repealed in 1736, but a requirement to utilize linen for the entire warp of fabrics was established. Pure cotton calicos were not permitted until 1774.[9] France obtained this authorization somewhat earlier, specifically in 1759. What we can learn about all this is that the history of cotton is closely intertwined with the history of linen. Throughout the majority of the eighteenth century, advancements in the cotton business, primarily in Lancashire, were achieved through the production of blended cotton-linen fabrics known as fustian. These textiles were an effort to replicate the all-cotton fabrics produced in

6 Lemire, "Fashioning Cottons: Asian Trade, Domestic Industry and Consumer Demand, 1660–1780", 502, 504; Serge Chassagne, "Calico Printing in Europe Before 1780," in *The Cambridge History of Western Textiles.*, ed. David Jenkins (Cambridge University Press, 2002), 518.

7 "In England, all white or unprinted cotton cloths are denominated calicoes; but in the United States this term is applied to those only that are printed." See John Ramsay McCulloch, *A Dictionary, Practical, Theoretical, and Historical, of Commerce and Commercial Navigation: Illustrated with Maps and Plans* (Longman, Orme, Brown, Green, and Longmans, 1839), 1: 213.

8 McCulloch, *A Dictionary, Practical, Theoretical, and Historical, of Commerce and Commercial Navigation,* 1: 273; Beverly Lemire, "Revising the Historical Narrative: India, Europe, and the Cotton Trade, c.1300–1800," in *The Spinning World: A Global History of Cotton Textiles, 1200–1850*, ed. Giorgio Riello and Prasannan Parthasarathi (Oxford University Press, 2009), 218.

9 McCulloch, *A Dictionary, Practical, Theoretical, and Historical, of Commerce and Commercial Navigation,* 1:213.

Asia.[10] During the weaving process, linen was highly valued for its suitability as a warp thread. This is mostly due to its superior strength compared to cotton, making it less prone to breakage. This persisted over an extended period until Arkwright's discovery enabled the production of cotton threads that were both durable and affordable, thereby allowing them to replace linen in the warps. Although 100% cotton fabrics existed in Europe prior to Arkwright, the process of creating cotton warps was more time-consuming and required more manpower.[11] It was only with the mechanization of the industry in the mid-1760s that Lancashire was able to compete with the fine Indian calico.[12]

The 1780s saw a logical twofold increase in the demand for raw cotton due to the substitution of linen for cotton in warps.[13] At this juncture, the significance of the American continent, which was previously substantial, becomes even more pivotal. In addition to offering huge tracts of land for cultivating cotton, it also provided cotton species that were extremely suitable for European spinners. *Gossypium barbadense* was a New World plant that yielded long-staple cottons that could be used for warps since the beginning of the eighteenth century and for the spinning machines that were developed in the 1760s. The strength of yarn created from long-staple raw cotton exceeded that of yarn made from short-staple cotton, derived from the two Old World cotton species

---

10 Beverly Lemire, "Transforming Consumer Custom: Linen, Cotton and the English Market, 1660–1800," in *The European Linen Industry in Historical Perspective*, ed. Brenda Collins and Philip Ollerenshaw (Oxford University Press, 2003); Lemire, "Revising the Historical Narrative: India, Europe, and the Cotton Trade, c.1300–1800," 224; Styles, "What Were Cottons for in the Early Industrial Revolution?," 322.

11 John Styles, "The Rise and Fall of the Spinning Jenny: Domestic Mechanisation in Eighteenth-Century Cotton Spinning," *Textile History* 51, no. 2 (2020): 196, 212, 224; "Velvet and the finer thicksets were best made with a cotton warp, and, as the manufacture extended, the use of cotton twist probably in the form of doubled yarn—for warps became more common. Single cotton warps were also used in lighter materials; but the difficulties to be overcome were much greater than in using doubled yarn, and there was a tendency to introduce linen, at least in the cheaper varieties," see A. P. Wadsworth and J. D. L. Mann, *The Cotton Trade and Industrial Lancashire, 1600–1780* (1931; Manchester University Press, 1965), 175.

12 Florence M. Montgomery, *Textiles in America: 1650–1870. A Dictionary Based on Original Documents, Prints and Paintings, Commercial Records, American Merchants' Papers, Shopkeepers' Advertisements, and Pattern Books with Original Swatches of Cloth* (W.W. Norton & Company, 1984), 184–85; Douglas A. Farnie, "Cotton, 1780–1914," in *The Cambridge History of Western Textiles.*, ed. David Jenkins (Cambridge University Press, 2002), 723.

13 Frances Armytage, *The Free Port System in the British West Indies. A Study in Commercial Policy, 1766–1822* (Longmans, Green and Co., 1953), 74.

(*Gossypium arboreum* and *Gossypium herbaceum*).[14] Starting in the 1790s, *Gossypium hirsutum*, a different type of cotton from the Americas, also called upland cotton, emerged. While its fibers were smaller than those of *Gossypium barbadense*, they were still longer than fibers from the Old World. Upland cotton, characterized by a medium fiber length, became the predominant variety of cotton utilized by the European cotton industry from the early nineteenth century till the present. Despite the textile industry's ability to utilize many types of cotton for yarn production, long-staple cotton maintained its market share due to its superior suitability for warps and the production of high-quality yarn and fabrics.[15] As Russell pointed out, the success of the Industrial Revolution in Europe must also be credited to the cultivators in America who for centuries domesticated long-fiber cotton species that could be spun.[16] It was with these threads that not only the calicos industry developed but also the velvet and muslin industries, for example.

Nevertheless, there were distinctions observed between the two New World cotton species (*Gossypium barbadense* and *Gossypium hirsutum*), and within each species, other varieties were also identified. *Gossypium barbadense*, for example, was grown in the West Indies and Brazil, but its attributes differed significantly according to the specific cultivation locations and varieties. Planters at the time were aware of these differences and made efforts to understand the natural and economic characteristics of cotton. In the 1780s, German Julius Philipp Benjamin von Röhr conducted a series of tests using over 30 cotton seeds sourced from various regions worldwide, with a majority of them originating from America. He cultivated them on his property at Saint-Croix, located in the Caribbean, and made notes on their growth and output. From his records, we acquired extensive knowledge regarding the growth and harvesting of cotton. It was evident that during that period, there was a significant focus on developing more efficient varieties of cotton. According to his account, the harvest yields of different cotton species exhibited significant variation. Certain species had the capability to yield two harvests per year, whereas

14 Edmund Russell, *Evolutionary History: Uniting History and Biology to Understand Life on Earth* (Cambridge University Press, 2011), 104; about the botanical, genetic and historical characteristics of cotton species, see C. L. Brubaker et al., "The Origin and Domestication of Cotton," in *Cotton: Origin, History, Technology, and Production*, ed. C. Wayne Smith and J. Tom Cothren (John Wiley & Sons, 1999); C. R. Benedict et al., "Cotton Fiber Quality," in *Cotton: Origin, History, Technology, and Production*, ed. C. Wayne Smith and J. Tom Cothren (John Wiley & Sons, 1999).

15 Edward Baines, *History of the Cotton Manufacture in Great Britain* (H. Fisher, R. Fisher, and P. Jackson, 1835), 311.

16 Russell, *Evolutionary History*, 108, 111.

the majority were only able to produce one. Certain species have a greater propensity to discolor cotton, resulting in the loss of its original white hue. This was also associated with the rainfall that discolored the cotton, hence the need of planting in dry regions. Certain species encountered greater challenges in picking cotton from trees compared to others. Similarly, for certain species, it was easier to separate the seed from the lint. Röhr pointed out that the longer it takes to separate the two, the more expensive cotton tends to become. Most importantly, not only did the type of cotton plant have an impact on productivity but also the soil and climatic conditions.[17]

In the following decades, U.S. planters took things a step further. Eli Whitney had already solved the problem of ginning upland cotton, whose lint was very stuck to the seed. Soon after, planters recognized that it would be crucial to create a variety of cotton that matured faster and was simple to pick. The latest literature indicates that our comprehension of cotton's history during the Industrial Revolution would be significantly limited without a thorough examination of the technological and biological innovations that influenced productivity, including aspects of harvesting, ginning, and other factors impacting agricultural output.[18] These issues were prevalent among planters throughout the American continent, from north to south, to satisfy the demands of European spinners. These aspects largely explain the place and history of different producers in the global raw cotton market.

Lemire, Styles, Russell, and Riello have drawn our attention to the importance of the demand for cotton textiles, the centrality of European desire from Asian textiles, and the quality (and not just the quantity) of raw cotton fibers in the history of industrialization. They, in many ways, provided another perspective on a story that was often told from the supply side, that is, emphasizing machines and technological development in Great Britain. This literature serves as inspiration for this book, which seeks to explore other aspects of cotton not covered by the Anglocentric perspective. The case of Brazilian cotton seems to me to be a good exercise for this, as it was a highly consumed cotton in Europe, and to date, there are no studies that have explored its entire commodity chain. However, there are many studies that do involve cotton, either

17 Julius Philipp Benjamin von Röhr, *Observations sur la culture du coton, rédigées par ordre de S. M. le Roi de Danemarck, pour l'utilité des colonies danoises dans les Indes Occidentales; par J.-P.-B. de Rohr, directeur et inspecteur de l'Agriculture dans l'île de Sainte-Croix, etc. Avec un préface de M. L. D. Philippe-Gabriel Hensler, professeur de médecine, à Kiel. Traduit de l'allemand.* (1793; Imprimerie-Librairie de Madame Huzard, 1807), 69.

18 Alan L. Olmstead and Paul W. Rhode, "Biological Innovation and Productivity Growth in the Antebellum Cotton Economy," *The Journal of Economic History* 68, no. 4 (2008): 1123–71.

directly or indirectly. Therefore, the next section will first seek to position cotton in the historiographical discussion and then discuss the mercantile chain and the debates involving merchants or merchant networks. While doing this, I will also go over some of the book's findings.

3 The Place of Brazilian Cotton in the Historiography

In a seminal work on Brazilian economic history, Simonsen's 1930s publication depicts cotton as an inferior commodity during the colonial period. Despite recognizing its importance to the economy of Northern Brazil and Pernambuco and its growing consumption in European markets, only two pages of his voluminous book were dedicated to raw cotton. To a large extent, the interpretative framework developed by Simonsen, which focused on the Brazilian economy in terms of cycles, helped to erase the role of cotton. According to him, Brazil's economic cycles were associated with various commodities that succeeded one another over time. First came Brazilwood, then sugar, gold, and coffee.[19] However, Simonsen's overly simple scheme overshadowed the role of cotton, which, as this book will show, figured prominently between the decline of gold and the rise of coffee. It is worth noting that Simonsen's cycle scheme is still widely reproduced, perhaps not so much in academic historiography but certainly in textbooks.

Caio Prado Junior correctly positioned cotton at a very favorable time for the economy of the Portuguese Empire, a time when Brazilian agriculture benefited from the absence or decline of products from Saint-Domingue, present-day Haiti. At the same time, he argued that before that, Brazilian cotton emerged thanks to technological developments in spinning in Great Britain, which demanded more raw cotton from Brazilian producers.[20] Although Prado Junior was right regarding the positive impact of the enslaved revolution in Saint-Domingue on Brazil's colonial economy, this book shows how the first exports of Brazilian cotton to Europe, more specifically to France, occurred before the improvements in spinning machines in England. When discussing cotton, as well as other Brazilian products, Prado Junior highlighted the lack of agricultural and technical improvements, lamenting that while the Whitney saw gin machine was in full use in the United States, farmers in Brazil, unwilling to

19 Roberto C. Simonsen, *História Econômica Do Brasil: 1500–1820* (1937; Senado Federal, Secretaria Especial de Editoração e Publicação, 2005), 460, 468, 473–74, 547.

20 Caio Prado Júnior, *Formação do Brasil contemporâneo: colônia* (1942; 6. ed, Brasiliense, 1961), 125.

modernize their techniques, did not adopt the new invention.[21] However, we now know—and this book will go a bit more into this point—that the Whitney gin was designed for medium-fiber cotton and was not appropriate for long-staple cotton from Brazil.[22]

Still according to Prado Junior, similarly to sugar, cotton was a crop that belonged to the world of large-scale plantations.[23] Pereira recently presented a similar argument, claiming that the idea that cotton was a crop for the poor developed throughout the nineteenth century and that this interpretation is inaccurate. Instead, taking the case of Maranhão, from the beginning of cotton plantations until around 1820, Pereira and others pointed out how cotton plantations were controlled by large slave-owning landowners.[24] However, these more recent assessments of the cotton economy were conducted without considering Palacios's findings regarding the cotton economy in northeastern Brazil. According to Palacios, in the Northeast, cotton was planted by poor, free farmers.[25] Given this literature, it is easy to fall into misconceptions and classify the organization of labor in cotton farming as fundamentally dependent on large slave plantations, generalizing the Maranhão model for the rest of Brazil. Or, conversely, we might feel inclined to argue that cotton farming was restricted to poor farmers on the margins of the slave system, generalizing the case of the Northeast to the rest of Brazil. This book seeks to shed more light on the nature of labor modes in cotton farming. By pointing out that there were at least two modes of cotton production, this book already helps clarify the divergent interpretations seen above. But this book goes further. It validates the interpretation that large plantations were the rule in Maranhão but points

21 Prado Júnior, *Formação do Brasil contemporâneo*, 132–33.

22 Assunção had briefly noticed this problem; see Matthias Röhrig Assunção, *De Caboclos a Bem-Te-Vis. Formação Do Campesinato Numa Sociedade Escravista: Maranhão 1800–1850* (Annablume, 2015), 195–96.

23 Prado Júnior, *Formação do Brasil contemporâneo*, 146–47.

24 Thales Augusto Zamberlan Pereira, "Poor Man's Crop? Slavery in Brazilian Cotton Regions (1800–1850)," *Estudos Econômicos (São Paulo)* 48, no. 4 (2018): 623–55; Antonia da Silva Mota and Daniel Souza Barroso, "Economia e demografia da escravidão no Maranhão e no Grão-Pará: uma análise comparativa da estrutura da posse de cativos (1785–1850)," *Revista de História*, no. 176 (January 2017): 1–41.

25 Guillermo Palacios, "Peasantry and Slavery in Brazil: A Contribution to the History of the Free Poor Planters from the General Captaincy of Pernambuco, 1700–1817. Volume II" (Ph.D., Princeton University, 1993), 47; ten years before Palacios' thesis José Ribeiro Júnior was not very clear on this point. Although he argued that the main way of producing cotton in Pernambuco was through large slave-owning properties, he also emphasized smallholders (matutos) as important players in cotton production; see José Ribeiro Júnior, "A Economia Algodoeira Em Pernambuco. Da Colônia à Independência," *Revista Brasileira de História* 1, no. 2 (September 1981): 237–38.

out that small properties in the Northeast, rather than relying on the labor of poor, free men, were actually also based on slave labor, albeit on a small scale, and dispersed throughout the vast area of northeastern Brazil. In other words, small, poor landowners or even tenant farmers might own one or two enslaved people, and this seemed to be the pattern in northeastern Brazil.

There is also controversy in the literature about what exactly triggered cotton exports' surge and what led to their decline. This book offers, I believe, better answers to the first question. For Furtado (and others), the rise of cotton exports was also associated with the British Industrial Revolution, as Prado Junior had also argued. Furtado, however, added the American War of Independence as an event that favored cotton production in Brazil, assuming that the 13 colonies were cotton producers.[26] However, this book will point out that the 13 colonies did not produce cotton. Cotton production in the U.S. for export only took off in the 1790s. In any case, for Prado Junior, the cotton boom in Brazil was "a momentary fever," as it was short-lived and negatively affected by foreign competition.[27] Similarly Furtado referred to the events in Maranhão as "false euphoria."[28]

All of this inevitably leads us to the topic of cotton's decline. For Caio Prado, "the distance from shipping ports and transportation difficulties" suffocated cotton production. Furthermore, "international competition and falling prices eliminated the most disadvantaged regions; leaving only the Northeast and Maranhão, albeit in a mediocre position internationally speaking."[29] For Furtado, it was also international competition that made cotton profitability low in Brazil.[30] Barbosa devoted an entire thesis to analyzing the factors contributing to the decline of Brazilian cotton, ultimately supporting the hypothesis that transportation expenses from the interior to the port were a crucial reason for cotton's inability to compete with other producers around the world. Here, poor farmers played a key role. From the second half of the nineteenth century onward, according to Barbosa, these small producers, lacking economic and political power, could not afford to invest in transportation improvements.

26 Celso Furtado, *Formação Econômica Do Brasil* (1959; Companhia das Letras, 2007), 139; the same idea is in Charles Ralph Boxer, *The Portuguese Seaborne Empire 1415–1825* (Hutchinson, 1969), 193; Manuel Nunes Dias, *Fomento e Mercantilismo: A Companhia Geral Do Grão Pará e Maranhão (1755–1778)* (Universidade Federal do Pará, 1970), 1: 453; José Jobson de Andrade Arruda, "O Algodão Brasileiro Na Época Da Revolução Industrial," *América Latina En La Historia Económica* 23, no. 2 (2016): 168, 171.

27 Prado Júnior, *Formação do Brasil contemporâneo*, 144.

28 Furtado, *Formação Econômica Do Brasil*, 137.

29 Prado Júnior, *Formação do Brasil contemporâneo*, 146.

30 Furtado, *Formação Econômica Do Brasil*, 167.

These improvements, he argued, were being developed for sugar and coffee plantations. Furthermore, unlike the U.S. cotton, Brazilian cotton was more susceptible to crop infestation and lacked good navigable river systems.[31] Barbosa had the merit of examining the domestic cotton trade more closely, and his argument that small producers lacked economic and social power is important for us to think about other cases. But his focus was on the mid-nineteenth century, leaving the history of cotton incomplete. Through econometric methods, Pereira presents the more alternative argument. According to him, the high taxes levied on cotton after 1808 discouraged planters from investing in agricultural improvements to compete in the international market.[32] And in a critical response to Pereira, historians Marquese and Ferraro argued that there were other factors at play, most notably the fact that the slave trade and slavery were negatively affected after the 1820s, escalating the costs of slave labor and consequently increasing expenses for Brazilian cotton planters.[33]

The reasons why Brazil could not find ways to compete are what are truly at stake in the sometimes divergent interpretations, but despite subtle differences, everyone seems to agree that Brazilian cotton could not withstand international competition. This book does not attempt to present new arguments about the decline of Brazilian cotton. It accepts the thesis that U.S. production drove down cotton prices worldwide, including in Brazil, making the cotton trade an unattractive sector from the 1820s onward. However, while quantity is important, it is also essential to highlight that fiber quality and demand played a crucial role. Although long-staple cottons were crucial to feed the new machines at the beginning of the Industrial Revolution, they gradually lost ground to medium-staple cottons from the U.S. What certainly contributed to this shift were improvements in machinery that allowed for blends of different fiber types. Only with improvements in the carding stages (more specifically in the lapping machine) was it possible to mix different fibers (medium and long and sometimes short) in the manufacture of warp yarns, something that probably occurred after 1824.[34] Upland cotton itself became more complex and

31 Luiz Cordelio Barbosa, "Cotton in 19th Century Brazil: Dependency and Development" (PhD diss., University of Washington, 1989), 1–39.

32 Thales Augusto Zamberlan Pereira, "Taxation and the Stagnation of Cotton Exports in Brazil, 1800–60," *The Economic History Review* 74, no. 2 (2021): 522–45.

33 Rafael de Bivar Marquese and Marcelo Rosanova Ferraro, "The Political Economy of Brazilian Cotton in the Age of Industrial Capitalism," in *Colonial Commodities in Historical Capitalism: Brazil for Export*, ed. Gustavo Acioli Lopes et al. (Routledge, 2026).

34 Andrew Ure, *The Cotton Manufacture of Great Britain: Systematically Investigated, and Illustrated by 150 Original Figures, Engraved on Wood and Steel; with an Introductory View of Its Comparative State in Foreign Countries, Drawn Chiefly from Personal Survey* (C. Knight,

gained different gradations, short, medium and long.[35] By the 1850s, the mixture of different types of cotton was well perfected, as pointed out in an article by the Economist.[36] What this book, as a form of hypothesis, suggests is that the golden days of long-staple cotton were over and that the reason for this was also rooted in the way spinning machines were tuned to accommodate the cheap medium-staple cottons increasingly required to make cheaper textiles. Despite this, long-staple cottons of good quality, required for more expensive fabrics, were still in demand throughout the nineteenth century. This market niche helps explain why Brazilian cotton continued to be produced during the first half of the nineteenth century. In fact, when we look at Brazilian cotton exports, quantities decrease slightly after the 1820s but began to grow again in the 1850s, just before the U.S. Civil War.[37]

Brazilian cotton is also a key element in historiography when considering Portugal's political economy in the second half of the eighteenth century. In this context, the General Company of Grão-Pará and Maranhão (GCGPM), a state-sponsored monopoly, emerged, responsible for initiating large-scale cotton production in Maranhão in the late 1750s. It is through this company and its extensive documentation that we have detailed works on the colony's production conditions, credit, slave trade, navigation, and the cotton trade from Maranhão to Portugal.[38] The problem with these works dedicated to the GCGPM, however, is that cotton ends up not being the focus of attention. Furthermore, the narrative of what happened after the monopoly and the productive and commercial conditions during the free trade period, from 1778 onward, are briefly and insufficiently explored. Hawthorne and Assunção, nevertheless, explored more fully the sources of enslaved people and the general conditions of production in Maranhão during and after the GCGPM.[39]

Raw cotton was part of Pombal's protectionist measures to strengthen Brazilian agriculture, thus avoiding dependence on the wealth brought by gold mining. Pombal's policies continued even after his departure from government, resulting in agricultural diversification in Brazil that would be so profitable that it provided the Portuguese Empire with the resources necessary

1836), 2: 2; David J. Jeremy, *Transatlantic Industrial Revolution: The Diffusion of Textile Technologies between Britain and America, 1790–1830s* (The MIT Press, 1981), 287, 292.

35 Olmstead and Rhode, "Biological Innovation".

36 *The Economist, Vol. XV, May 23*, 1857.

37 Stanley J. Stein, *The Brazilian Cotton Manufacture: Textile Enterprise in an Underdeveloped Area, 1850–1950* (Harvard University Press, 1957), 198.

38 See the books by Manuel Nunes Dias and António Carreira cited in this book.

39 Walter Hawthorne, *From Africa to Brazil: Culture, Identity, and an Atlantic Slave Trade, 1600–1830* (Cambridge University Press, 2010); Assunção, *De Caboclos a Bem-Te-Vis.*

to generate a trade surplus with its trading partners, mainly Britain, in the late 1780s.[40] Aware of these shifting circumstances, the British attempted to update the Methuen Treaty,[41] which had, since 1703, provided English wool tariff benefits in Portugal in return for Portuguese wine benefits in England. The treaty did not contemplate cotton fabrics, though,[42] which were then emerging as the most extensively produced commodities in Great Britain and had the potential to mitigate trade imbalances with Portugal. Portugal was reluctant to allow British cottons to enter its territory because it did not want to disrupt its lucrative trade in white cotton cloths brought from India, which were printed in Portugal and then sent to the colonies. No matter how hard they tried, cotton goods were only legally admitted into the Portuguese Empire from 1810 onwards, specifically into Brazil, contributing—to use an idea dear to Manchester—to the British preeminence in Brazil.[43] Thus, the Methuen Treaty reigned supreme for over a hundred years and set much of the economic agenda between Portugal and Great Britain. The Methuen Treaty is often seen, at least since Sideri's work, as one of the most perfect examples of dependency theory, contributing to Portugal's lack of development. Dependency theory, however, is most often used to explain Brazil's position as a colony subordinate to the economic interests of its mother country, Portugal. A clear example of this was the prohibition of textile manufacturing in Brazil, allowing only the production of coarse cottons to clothe enslaved people.[44]

The 1810 treaty was a major turning point in the history of Brazilian cotton. The treaty not only reaffirmed Brazilian raw cotton exports straight to Great Britain but also opened the Brazilian market to British cotton goods. Cotton goods accounted for 40 to 50 percent of all British exports between the early nineteenth century and the middle of the 1840s. As the largest single market for its exports, primarily to Brazil, Hobsbawm argues that it is not unreasonable

40 José Jobson de Andrade Arruda, *O Brasil no comércio colonial* (Editora Ática, 1980), 641–42.

41 Kenneth Maxwell, *Conflicts and Conspiracies: Brazil and Portugal, 1750–1808* (1973; Routledge, 2004), 154–56.

42 Valentim Alexandre, *Os sentidos do Império: questão nacional e questão colonial na crise do Antigo Regime português* (Edições Afrontamento, 1993), 49.

43 Rudy Bauss, "A Legacy of British Free Trade Policies: The End of the Trade and Commerce between India and the Portuguese Empire, 1780–1830," *Calcutta Historical Journal* 6, no. 2 (1982): 81–115; Alan K. Manchester, *British Preeminence in Brazil, Its Rise and Decline. A Study in European Expansion* (1933; Octagon Books, 1964).

44 Sandro Sideri, *Trade and Power: Informal Colonialism in Anglo-Portuguese Relations* (Rotterdam University Press, 1970); Fernando A. Novais, "A proibição das manufaturas no Brasil e a política econômica Portuguesa do fim do século XVIII," *Revista de História* 33, no. 67 (1966): 213–37; Stanley J. Stein and Barbara H. Stein, *The Colonial Heritage of Latin America: Essays on Economic Dependence in Perspective* (Oxford University Press, 1970).

to claim that Latin America saved the British cotton industry in the first part of the nineteenth century. Cotton textiles made up three-quarters of England's exports to Brazil in 1812, and this situation remained almost unchanged in 1835. These textiles would also serve as important commodities to buy enslaved people in African ports, thus gradually replacing the function previously performed by Indian textiles.[45]

Thus far, Brazilian cotton has been addressed almost exclusively from the supply perspective, as illustrated by the existing literature. Arruda was among the earliest, and few, to examine, albeit briefly, the Brazilian cotton trade with Europe.[46] His 1980 publication systematically organized Portugal's trade balances with Brazil and Europe from 1796 to 1811, offering multiple interpretations of their meaning mostly used as a supplement to Fernando Novais's thesis.[47] The best cotton import and re-export figures we have to date come from his research, and among so many important conclusions, Arruda was one of the few to recognize the importance of France to the cotton trade with Portugal. A controversial point in Arruda's argument, however, is that according to him there was a robust industrialization process in Portugal and that Brazilian cotton played a key role in this history, as it provided the raw material for Portuguese spinners. These yarns were transformed into fabrics, these fabrics were printed, and they were mostly sold to the Brazilian market.[48] However, Arruda's interpretative framework is severely compromised when confronted with Pedreira's conclusions, who pointed out how spinning in Portugal was marginal, even though it was protected from foreign competition. What was truly a successful industrial sector was printing, and these primarily used cotton fabrics brought from Asia, which were processed in Portuguese workshops and exported overseas. Considering the entire Portuguese industry, the share of these printed cotton fabrics was the largest between 1796 and 1806.[49] Thus, raw cotton from Brazil contributed little to the spinning industry in Portugal,

---

45 Stanley D. Chapman, *Merchant Enterprise in Britain: From the Industrial Revolution to World War I* (Cambridge University Press, 1992), 6; Eric J. Hobsbawm, *Industry and Empire: The Making of Modern English Society, 1750 to the Present Day* (Pantheon books, 1968), 121; Manchester, *British Preeminence in Brazil*, 97, 314; Bauss, "A Legacy of British Free Trade Policies"; Luís Henrique Dias Tavares, *Comércio proibido de escravos* (Editora Atica, cnpq, 1988), 96; Louise H. Guenther, *British Merchants in Nineteenth-Century Brazil: Business, Culture, and Identity, 1808–50* (Centre for Brazilian Studies, 2004), 33, 42, 47–48, 176.

46 Arruda, *O Brasil no comércio colonial*, 364–71.

47 Fernando A. Novais, *Portugal e Brasil na crise do antigo sistema colonial (1777–1808)* (Hucitec, 1979).

48 Arruda, "O Algodão Brasileiro Na Época Da Revolução Industrial," 182.

49 Jorge Miguel Pedreira, *Estrutura industrial e mercado colonial: Portugal e Brasil (1780–1830)* (DIFEL, 1994), 97, 289, 293, 371.

which was relegated to a mere interim between Brazil's raw material and the spinners in the rest of Europe. Hence the centrality of the Lisbon merchant community for this book, rather than its spinners.

4 Commodity Chain Analysis and Merchants

A significant portion of this book focuses on commerce and traders, and this is largely due to the methodology employed. This book addresses trade through the connections established by people and companies that made it possible for raw cotton to leave South America, pass through Portugal, and be distributed to various European ports. This methodology is called commodity chain analysis, and it is intrinsically linked to the world-systems perspective to demonstrate that capitalism is a global phenomenon and thus not restricted to the nation-state.[50] Commodity chain analysis is, in other words, the act of chasing a commodity from its producers to its consumers, passing through a set of intermediaries. Identifying the people and social sectors that took part in the transfer of the merchandise is the most basic task, but it is equally important to pay attention to how the merchandise is passed from hand to hand. Consequently, traders or intermediaries constitute key players in this book, and a further reason for examining them is that they are frequently overlooked in the global history of cotton.

When we speak of the mercantile community in Portugal, however, we quickly think of the historiography that, once again, gave centrality to the British. Pombal's policies, aimed at nationalizing the Empire's economy, extended to an attack on the British mercantile community in Portugal, traditionally the most powerful foreign community there. As I will show in more detail in due course, some historians have argued that Pombal's plan succeeded, and the British were indeed replaced by Portuguese merchants. Others have argued that Pombal's plan failed. In short, this history has never been satisfactorily explained, and I believe raw cotton is a good commodity to focus on to better understand the changes in the mercantile communities in

50 Terence K. Hopkins and Immanuel Wallerstein, "Commodity Chains in the World-Economy Prior to 1800," *Review (Fernand Braudel Center)* 10, no. 1 (1986): 157–70; Gary Gereffi et al., "Introduction: Global Commodity Chains," in *Commodity Chains and Global Capitalism*, ed. Gary Gereffi and Miguel Korzeniewicz (Praeger, 1994), 2; John Scott, "Commodity Chains," in *A Dictionary of Sociology* (Oxford University Press, 2015); Immanuel Maurice Wallerstein, *The Modern World-System. Capitalist Agriculture and the Origins of the European World-Economy in the Sixteenth Century*, vol. 1 (1974; University of California Press, 2011).

Lisbon. It is possible to anticipate here, though, that the mercantile communities that exported cotton were more diverse, changed over time, and what greatly impacted their composition also had to do with the ports to which they exported cotton from Lisbon. For instance, the English in Portugal dominated exports to the ports of Great Britain, and the Portuguese dominated exports to the ports of France and other parts of Europe.

The notion of market integration, closely associated with trade and merchants, is fundamental to this book. In this context, two fundamental terms seem crucial in the ongoing conversation concerning the economic history of the early modern period: trust and networks. As pointed out by Daniel Strum, trust between traders impacts the integration, complexity, and expansion of markets.[51] And networks, connecting merchants globally, would be the means by which merchants would organize their businesses and connect supply and demand.[52] Thus, for trade to occur, trust between merchants was necessary, and they achieved this through the formation of networks. The literature on merchants is vast, but it seems to me that there are three major theories that are being used at the moment: one that underscores commercial connections within the same cultures as vital, another that highlights connections between different cultures as more relevant, and a third that emphasizes the role of institutions. For the first, trade would occur through relationships between family members, members of the same religion or ethnic group—which would guarantee trust in mercantile activity. The logic behind this was that it was safer to trade with a relative, for example, than with a non-relative. As a result, commercial relations were informal, agreements tended to be verbal, relationships were more cooperative than hierarchical, and third-party mechanisms, such as the state, laws, and courts, were somewhat relegated to the background or even absent.[53] All of this, however, is not necessarily new. There is an old literature that advocated that long-distance trade was possible thanks to kinship relations. This interpretation was probably disseminated by Bernard Bailyn, at least since 1954. For Bailyn, the only possible generalization is the

51 Daniel Strum, "Institutional Choice in the Governance of the Early Atlantic Sugar Trade: Diasporas, Markets, and Courts," *Economic History Review* 72, no. 4 (2019): 1202.

52 Manuel Herrero Sánchez and Klemens Kaps, "Connectors, Networks and Commercial Systems: Approaches to the Study of Early Modern Maritime Commercial History," in *Merchants and Trade Networks in the Atlantic and the Mediterranean, 1550–1800: Connectors of Commercial Maritime Systems*, ed. Manuel Herrero Sánchez and Klemens Kaps (Routledge, 2016), 5.

53 Perhaps the most recent and best example of this is Sophie H. Jones and Siobhan Talbott, "Sole Traders? The Role of the Extended Family in Eighteenth-Century Atlantic Business Networks," *Enterprise & Society* 23, no. 4 (2022): 1092–121.

importance of kinship relations: it was through these relations that generations and generations of merchants expanded their businesses.[54] Regarding long distance trade, he wrote that "commercial ties were best secured by the cement of kinship or long friendship."[55] The importance of kinship networks was also highlighted in the case of the trade between Brazil and Portugal.[56] But between Bailyn's work and the more recent academic productions that emphasize family and ethnic ties as drivers of trade, there is a vast literature that suggests that trade was more likely to bring together different cultures[57] and to be able to mobilize mercantile networks that went beyond empires.[58]

---

54 Bernard Bailyn, "Kinship and Trade in Seventeenth Century New England," in *Explorations in Enterprise*, ed. Hugh G. J. Aitken (1954; Harvard University Press, 1965).

55 Bernard Bailyn, *The New England Merchants in the Seventeenth Century* (Harvard University Press, 1955), 87.

56 Daniel Swetschinski, "The Portuguese Jewish Merchants of Seventeenth-Century Amsterdam: A Social Profile" (Ph.D., Brandeis University, 1979); Júnia Ferreira Furtado, *Homens de negócio: a interiorização da metrópole e do comércio nas minas setecentistas* (Editora Hucitec, 1999). See also the literature review in Daniel Strum, "The Portuguese Jews and New Christians in the Sugar Trade: Managing Business Overseas – Kinship and Ethnicity Revisited (Amsterdam, Porto and Brazil, 1595—1618)" (PhD diss., Hebrew University of Jerusalem, 2009); Leonor Freire Costa, "Comércio e família em Portugal, Séculos XVI–XVIII," in *Sociedade, Família e Poder na Península Ibérica: Elementos para uma História Comparativa*, ed. Juan Hernández Franco and Mafalda Soares da Cunha (Publicações do CIDEHUS, 2010).

57 Philip D. Curtin, *Cross-Cultural Trade in World History* (Cambridge University Press, 1984); Peggy K. Liss, *Atlantic Empires: The Network of Trade and Revolution, 1713–1826* (The Johns Hopkins University Press, 1982).

58 Horst Pietschmann, "Introduction: Atlantic History – History between European History and Global History," in *Atlantic History: History of the Atlantic System 1580–1830: Papers Presented at an International Conference, Held 28 August-1 September, 1999, in Hamburg*, ed. Horst Pietschmann (Vandenhoeck & Ruprecht, 2002); Linda K. Salvucci, "Atlantic Intersections: Early American Commerce and the Rise of the Spanish West Indies (Cuba)," *Business History Review* 79, no. 4 (2005): 781–809; Pierre Gervais, "Neither Imperial, nor Atlantic: A Merchant Perspective on International Trade in the Eighteenth Century," *History of European Ideas* 34, no. 4 (2008): 465–73; Cátia Antunes, "Free Agents and Formal Institutions in the Portuguese Empire: Towards a Framework of Analysis," *Portuguese Studies* 28, no. 2 (2012): 173–85; Regina Grafe, "On the Spatial Nature of Institutions and the Institutional Nature of Personal Networks in the Spanish Atlantic," *Culture & History Digital Journal* 3, no. 1 (2014): 1–11; Cátia Antunes and Amélia Polónia, *Beyond Empires: Global, Self-Organizing, Cross-Imperial Networks, 1500–1800* (Brill, 2016); Klemens Kaps, "Small but Powerful: Networking Strategies and the Trade Business of Habsburg-Italian Merchants in Cadiz in the Second Half of the Eighteenth Century," *European Review of History: Revue Européenne d'histoire* 23, no. 3 (2016): 427–55; Mark Sheaves, "The Anglo-Iberian Atlantic as a Hemispheric System? English Merchants Navigating the Iberian Atlantic," in *Entangled Empires: The Anglo-Iberian Atlantic, 1500–1830*, ed. Jorge Cañizares-Esguerra (University of Pennsylvania Press, 2018).

Yet, whether concentrating on commerce within or between cultures, the role of institutions can easily be overlooked, and trade networks might appear as autonomous entities devoid of outside influences like the state. Therefore, some scholars believe that it is necessary to consider the insights offered by other areas of social science, particularly neo-institutionalism and sociology. Nee and Ingram, integrating both, questioned whether social relationships—or rather, personal ties—can "cement trust between economic actors." They argue that without a third-party enforcer, "there is often no firm basis for deciding whether an acquaintance or friend is trustworthy." This is why neo-institutionalists argue that "formal institutional arrangements and their enforceability are necessary to support informal constraints." The social convention that says "never lend money to a friend" is an example of how personal ties are not by themselves sufficient to ensure compliance with agreements. Personal ties open up space for both trust and distrust. Thus, personal ties alone are not enough, so it is necessary to add the "constraints of the state, law, regulation, contracts, property rights, and organizations."[59] An example of this is the medieval merchants that Avner Greif examined. The Jews of the Maghreb had no third-party mechanisms to monitor their agents. The merchants of Genoa did. That is why the latter flourished, and the former did not, according to him.[60] Another important example of how to nuance the interpretation that places too much emphasis on family, ethnic, and religious networks as platforms where trade flowed without major obstacles is Trivellato's book, which analyzes how trade between different cultures was possible and, in some cases, better than trade practiced within the same group. But Trivellato also had the merit of warning that the role of cross-cultural networks and the role of legal authorities, or the state, should not be seen as universal. In some cases, one might be more relevant than the other. In others, such as that of the Sephardic merchants of Livorno in the seventeenth and eighteenth centuries, internal norms within the group and legal instruments were combined.[61]

The way that all of these merchant network-related issues relate to the Brazilian cotton trade is somewhat unusual and, at the very least, challenges

59 Victor Nee and Paul Ingram, "Embeddedness and Beyond: Institutions, Exchange, and Social Structure," in *The New Institutionalism in Sociology*, ed. Mary C. Brinton and Victor Nee (Russell Sage Foundation, 1998), 22–23.

60 Avner Greif, "Cultural Beliefs and the Organization of Society: A Historical and Theoretical Reflection on Collectivist and Individualist Societies," in *The New Institutionalism in Sociology*, ed. Mary C. Brinton and Victor Nee (Russell Sage Foundation, 1998).

61 Francesca Trivellato, *The Familiarity of Strangers: The Sephardic Diaspora, Livorno, and Cross-Cultural Trade in the Early Modern Period* (Yale University Press, 2009), 3–4; See also Strum, "Institutional Choice".

what the majority of the research has focused on. At the outset, ethnic and cultural distinctions appear to be irrelevant in the Brazilian cotton trade context. Trade between Brazil and Portugal was executed by Portuguese Catholics, and connections were predominantly intra-imperial, suggesting minimal foreign involvement. Conversely, the re-export trade centered in Lisbon encompassed various nationalities. In this instance, cross-imperial networks were more prominent and significant. However, nothing has emerged from the sources or literature that points to conflicts or commercial preferences related to the nationalities or cultures that traded cotton. As I will point out, other factors were more important in shaping the re-export mercantile networks: like treaties, the economic conjuncture, and the political economy of each nation trading with Portugal for Brazilian raw cotton. Much of these conclusions stemmed from the quantitative survey I conducted of the mercantile community that imported and re-exported Brazilian cotton in Lisbon (revealing hundreds and sometimes thousands of people who traded cotton). This can be seen as an alternative methodology to studies of mercantile networks that generally focus on a few merchants and make meticulous use of mercantile correspondence. This book, therefore, approaches mercantile connections from a broader perspective, counting the number of merchants trading raw cotton, paying attention to their nationalities, and attempting to recount parts of the biographies of the main merchants. The Lisbon customs records were essential for this, as were other documents that offer more qualitative details, which I will discuss later.

A more accurate assessment is certainly more difficult when it comes to family or friendship relationships as the foundations of commercial networks. This book has shown some cases of commercial relationships between family members, but this does not mean that the cotton trade was based on this type of commercial strategy. Family relationships also went awry, with family members resorting to courts and other Portuguese state institutions to sue relatives and recover capital. This also does not mean that family networks were irrelevant or inefficient. Friendship ties may have been the basis of many early modern commercial associations, but this did not prevent a hierarchy from existing within this type of commercial organization, as I will show. And even though many merchants were bound by friendship ties, this did not prevent them from resorting to written commercial instruments that could be used in court or by third parties to resolve potential disputes. Relationships between friends were an important part of history, but they do not explain everything regarding the issue of trust. That is why institutions also mattered, and with the exception of smuggling, it is clear that merchants—whether linked by family, friendship, or ethnocultural ties—made use of them. Laws, courts, regulations, commercial treaties, and consuls, not to mention the warfare between the leading European nations that produced a great deal of commercial regulation—all of them had an impact in one way or another—which is impossible to measure—on the performance of merchants and agents in the cotton trade.

A final word about networks, which I have been using throughout this introduction. The concept and application of the term network lack precise definition. Casson, a leading authority on the topic, acknowledges the existence of various network types and emphasizes the necessity of specifying which one is being utilized.[62] But even the most recent historiographical productions tend to treat everything as networks.[63] As a result, the concept loses its explanatory power. Another consequence of the widespread use of the network concept is that it can lead to ignoring other forms of commercial organization. I believe two of them are central to understanding the cotton trade in the early modern period: markets and hierarchies. Grahame Thompson defined them theoretically very well and made the role of networks clear.

Markets depend on dispersed decision-makers who are guided by competitive market prices. For neoclassical economists, the market is based on the interaction between supply and demand and how exchanges generate an equilibrium in prices after a certain amount of time. This balance does not exist for the Austrian school, though. For them, the market is constantly pushing for new products and means of production to be implemented. As a result, the market is always in a "constant state of imbalance." Monopoly is expected as a temporary prize for innovators confronting competition; nevertheless, throughout the early modern period, monopolies arose not from market forces but from political decisions. However, monopolies typically diminish over time. Overall, the market is regarded as a catalyst for coordination and order. That is, the market itself produces an economic order. There is no conscious intervention that guides and governs coordination. In the market, individuals make decisions based on competition and price mechanisms. In this situation, the aggregate of individual actions will culminate in a coordinated outcome, reflecting the Smithian concept of the invisible hand.[64]

Hierarchies, in their turn, are overtly directed and planned. Hierarchy involves clear administration and interference. From this perspective, a

62 Mark Casson, "Networks in Economic and Business History: A Theoretical Perspective," in *Cosmopolitan Networks in Commerce and Society, 1660–1914*, ed. Andreas Gestrich and Margrit Schulte Beerbühl (German Historical Institute London, 2011), 18.

63 Carolyn Downs, "Networks, Trust, and Risk Mitigation during the American Revolutionary War: A Case Study," *The Economic History Review* 70, no. 2 (2017): 509–28.

64 Grahame Thompson, *Between Hierarchies and Markets: The Logic and Limits of Network Forms of Organization* (Oxford University Press, 2003), 24–28, 38.

company can be guided by hierarchical activities: to coordinate their activities, companies need managers to direct operations. To a large extent, the hierarchy involves delegating orders that personnel (or agents) within the firm must follow. Still, firms are being affected by the market, which strongly impacts the type of management that will be employed. Above all, hierarchies involve bureaucracies (to check, supervise, monitor, audit), organizational structure, authority, and power.[65]

Networks borrow some of the characteristics of the coordination mechanisms of hierarchies and markets, and sometimes networks can be mistaken as being a variation of them. However, networks are generally linked to the following attributions: they are composed of informal, mutual-help, or self-help institutional arrangements. Networks tend to be small-scale and local. Furthermore, they are "cooperative forms of social existence." They "organize and regulate themselves in the context of a narrow and sometimes closed network." Finally, they are characterized by attributes such as "reciprocity, moral norms, trust, duty, obligation" and by "solidarity, altruism, and loyalty."[66]

5 Sources

Unlike trade between the United States and England—where sources richly detail the intricacies of production and marketing,[67] perhaps because both countries specialized in the cotton trade, something the Portuguese never did—the sources for Brazilian cotton are far less detailed. This limited our knowledge of more specific aspects of the work of enslaved Africans and the cotton trade within Brazil. Accounting books for cotton plantations in Brazil in the eighteenth and nineteenth centuries have not survived. And the few merchant letters that exist show cotton being treated indifferently from sugar, rice, or hides, for example. As a rule, Portuguese merchants did not specialize in cotton, which is perhaps why they wrote nothing specific about this commodity. To a large extent, the limitations of these sources, or lack of them, made me collect small pieces of information and quantitative data on cotton from different sources scattered throughout various archives that indirectly touched

65 Thompson, *Between Hierarchies and Markets*, 22–24, 39.

66 Thompson, *Between Hierarchies and Markets*, 30, 40.

67 See, for instance, Robert William Fogel and Stanley L. Engerman, *Time on the Cross: The Economics of American Negro Slavery* (Wildwood House, 1976); Killick, "Bolton Ogden & Co."; John R. Killick, "Risk, Specialization and Profit in the Mercantile Sector of the Nineteenth Century Cotton Trade: Alexander Brown and Sons 1820–80," *Business History* 16, no. 1 (1974): 1–16.

upon cotton. Part of the methodology of this research involved organizing the large body of information I collected into a chronological framework to clarify the history of Brazilian cotton. Although the individual sources have limitations, when connected they reveal important aspects of raw cotton production and trade.

Several sources, mainly documents produced by the Portuguese authorities in Brazil, such as governors' reports providing demographic, agricultural production, and trade data for Maranhão and Northeast Brazil, were key to my book. Furthermore, I made use of correspondence between agents of a monopoly company in Maranhão and its principals in Lisbon. I also drew on several customs books from Lisbon, sources that the literature has very little explored. With this last documentation, it was possible to set up the merchant community in Lisbon that imported and re-exported cotton. I also used records from merchants who entered litigation with other merchants in Portugal. Additionally, I drew on notarial records from Lisbon to collect powers of attorney, company charters, contracts, and credit documents involving Brazil and Europe. With these last two sets of records, it was possible to gather qualitative information about how the cotton trade and financing took place.

6 Book Structure

This book is divided into three parts. The first deals with the beginning of cotton cultivation and trade in Maranhão during and after the establishment of the GCGPM. The first chapter analyzes trade, as it was with the capital of a monopoly trading company that the cotton plantations were financed. It explores how financing took place and how colonial growers and merchants sought to disengage themselves from using the services of the monopoly company. The GCGPM was not successful at preventing planters and merchants from exporting more cotton to Portugal than the GCGPM itself in the final years of its monopoly. This is an interesting case of how individuals can break a monopoly without resorting to contraband. The company, however, despite suffering from the defaults of colonial residents, established the economic foundations that would be copied in the period of free trade by the merchants who financed the planters.

The second chapter surveys the conditions of cotton growing after the end of the GCGPM, the intersections between merchants and planters, and the role of the slave trade and the triangular trade in the business of raw cotton towards Portugal. One of the main goals of this chapter is to map the location of the leading cotton-growing regions in Maranhão and explore how their growing conditions, with large plantations, made it more favorable for planters to commercialize their crops overseas. Still, this did not prevent big merchants—who financed the planters—from exporting cotton.

The second part deals with the cotton trade from when it was no longer framed in the monopoly system, that is, from the end of the 1770s. Around this time, the Northeast of Brazil entered the scene as a key fiber supplier. The third chapter considers cotton cultivation in the Northeast and shows how small slaveholders were the main actors in this context. In Northeastern Brazil, several small-scale farmers used a modest number of enslaved people but produced cotton fiber on a scale similar to the few large plantations of Maranhão.

The fourth chapter explores the internal cotton trade, from the Northeast's interior to the Recife port. It shows that small slaveholders could not market their crops over long distances. As a result, they sold their small crops to middlemen who, in turn, sold the cotton to coastal exporters. The farmers' poverty also meant they did not have the resources to gin, bag, and press their cotton. Thus, it was once again necessary for intermediaries (large growers and merchants), who had ginning and bagging machines, to buy the crops from small farmers. In general, farmers in the Northeast were poor; in Maranhão, they were rich.

The fifth chapter will look at the cotton trade from the perspective of traders and financiers in Portugal. By revealing for the first time the merchant community in Lisbon that imported cotton from Brazilian ports, this chapter shows an increasing number of recipients of cotton bales between the 1780s and 1800s. Hundreds of people were interested in this commodity. Most of them were Portuguese. Although foreign merchants were allowed to import from Brazil, they were not very involved in this business. Trade with Brazil was in the hands of the Portuguese. This chapter also analyzes the institutions that ensured—or at least sought to guarantee—the security of trade between Brazil and Portugal. It will delve into some merchants' strategies to minimize commercial risks, like trading with traveling agents, merchant companies, and attorneys. It will also point to Lisbon customs' central role as a place where merchants used to do business. Moreover, formal enforcement mechanisms, like colonial governors and judges, were part of the day-to-day exchanges in the Portuguese Atlantic, with merchants in Lisbon relying on the services of these authorities. The chapter also shows how important the transfer of money from the metropolis was to the purchase of cotton in Brazil. In this context, smuggling was perhaps more observed than before.

The third part of the book considers the cotton re-export trade and the main textile centers in Europe that purchased fiber from Brazil. The sixth chapter goes back to the mercantile groups that re-exported Brazilian cotton from

Lisbon. The French market emerges as the most important early on, between the 1770s and the beginning of the 1780s, and in the final years of the old colonial system, between 1802 and 1807. A detailed analysis of this trade shows how French merchants in Lisbon were practically irrelevant in this business. Those responsible for re-exporting to France were mostly Portuguese merchants. The chapter seeks to explain why this occurred through the historical trajectory of trade between the two nations and how traditional trade relations with England ended up disfavoring France. Genoa, in a way, was also an important port until the beginning of the French Wars. And like with France, trade with Genoa was hampered in the 1790s because of the wars. Genoa used to bring cotton from Portugal, distribute it to the cotton mills in its surroundings, and ship it to Switzerland.

The seventh chapter explores the Franco-Portuguese trade during the French Wars and how Brazilian cotton continued to enter France through neutral navigation and smuggling. Many changes occurred at this juncture. One of the most relevant was the multiplication of French ports that imported cotton. France's main cotton-producing center, Rouen, remained the most important, but the ports of Caen, Cherbourg, and Nantes ended up replacing the traditional port of Le Havre, albeit for a short time. The chapter seeks to explain why these changes took place. It also explores trading conditions after the Continental Blockade and the French invasion of Portugal in late 1807. During much of the wars, Hamburg was a meaningful entrepôt for the illegal trade that linked Portugal and France, but a share of the Brazilian cotton also supplied the German textile industry. With Portugal occupied by the French and the seas practically blocked against Napoleonic France, cotton from Lisbon went to London and was later sent to Rouen, through a system of licenses. There was also an active overland trade in cotton, which passed through Spain to feed the French spinners. Furthermore, this chapter explains how the cotton industry worked in the *Seine-Inférieure*, France's most significant consumer of raw cotton.

England ended up being the leading buyer of Brazilian cotton throughout the colonial period and during the first decades of independent Brazil. The eighth chapter tells how this happened by exploring the historical course of Anglo-Portuguese relations between the seventeenth and eighteenth centuries from the perspective of trade carried out from Portugal. The chapter shows that these dealings were marked by commercial treaties favorable to England and by the strong presence of English factors in Portugal even after Pombal's policies. The British merchant community's interest in Portugal was diverted from the declining gold trade to the promising cotton trade. Wine played a similar role, as marketing connections previously used to trade it were used to exchange the Brazilian fiber.

The ninth chapter departs from the perspective of merchants established in England. It seeks to explain changes in import ports. London was traditionally the central hub between England and Portugal. But during the Brazilian cotton trade, from the 1780s onwards, London gradually lost shares in total imports from the United Kingdom, and Liverpool became the main destination port. However, London was an essential port of entry for cotton that would quickly be sent to the textile centers of Northern England and Scotland. It also functioned as a financier for industries in the north and an important port for shipping cotton goods that would be exported to Portugal and Brazil and other markets. The chapter considers how merchants and spinners in England bought Brazilian cotton and explains how the internal trade in cotton in the North of England worked. Finally, it analyzes how exchanges took place after the opening of Brazilian ports and how the Brazilian market was necessary for the British in the early decades of the nineteenth century.

This book reveals how the rise of cotton production and trade in Brazil were important elements in the economic, social, and political connections of the Portuguese empire and beyond. By tracing the trajectory from Maranhão's plantations to the smallholder economies of the Northeast, and from Lisbon's merchant networks to the re-export flows that supplied the European Industrial Revolution, this book shows how Brazilian cotton was central to the making of the Atlantic economy. It shows not just the different trajectories of Maranhão and the Northeast but also how important merchants, enslaved workers, and imperial systems were in shaping global capitalism. By placing Brazilian cotton at the center of colonial rule, European conflicts, and the rise of new industrial hubs, this book highlights how agriculture and trade routes across the Atlantic were closely connected to the changes that shaped the late 1700s and early 1800s. These connections reveal the complicated series of relationships that influenced economic development and social structures on both sides of the ocean. As the demand for cotton surged, it transformed local economies and had profound effects on the labor systems and social hierarchies within the colonies. This transformation underscored how agricultural practices and commerce were intertwined, highlighting their profound impact on societal dynamics.

PART 1

The Beginning: Monopoly and Agriculture in Maranhão

Introduction to Part 1

Cotton, known by indigenous peoples before Portuguese colonization of South America, was only cultivated and commercially traded with Portugal on a considerable scale beginning in the mid-eighteenth century. The General Company of Grão-Pará and Maranhão (GCGPM) contributed significantly to this. This joint-stock company, supported by the Portuguese state, brought enslaved people and capital to initiate the plantations of cotton and rice, the primary commodities of the North of Brazil. Chapter 1 will explore how the GCGPM worked by highlighting how debtors in Maranhão (merchants and planters) developed ways of not paying the credits back to the company and, on top of that, showing how colonials managed to export cotton outside the monopoly scheme established by the GCGPM in the final years of the monopoly. In addition, it will discuss how the agency relationships between the principals in Lisbon and the managers in São Luís impacted the company's colonial business. The GCGPM laid the foundations for developing a cotton culture in Maranhão, which was based on large production units with a significant number of enslaved Africans throughout the last decades of the eighteenth century and the beginning of the nineteenth century. Chapter 2 focuses on this moment, considering the production and commercialization of cotton after the end of the GCGPM monopoly in 1778. One of its main arguments is that the concentration of cotton plantations in *Ribeira do Itapecuru* positively impacted agricultural productivity. The large-scale plantations, utilizing gangs of enslaved people, prospered by focusing on the cultivation of a particular variety of long-staple cotton that produces a significant amount of lint, surpassing the yield of the cotton varieties grown in Northeast Brazil. Foods like manioc were acquired from adjacent areas in *Ribeira do Itapecuru* and hence did not diminish cotton productivity, unlike in the Northeast. In Maranhão, the wealthy large planters had resources for ginning, bagging, and pressing cotton on their properties. In addition, they had capital and connections that enabled them to export their crops to Portugal and still participate in the Atlantic slave trade. The rich and powerful planters of Maranhão contrasted with the poor—but slaver—smallholders of the Northeast, as will be shown in Chapters 3 and 4.

CHAPTER 1

The Monopoly Trade and How to Get around It

1 Before Cotton Exports

Cotton was a plant known to different indigenous tribes that inhabited the lands of South America, even before the arrival of Europeans. Despite scarce documentary evidence, it is likely that the indigenous people already knew about the process of ginning and weaving cotton fibers. Pero Vaz de Caminha, a member of the group of navigators headed by Pedro Álvares Cabral who docked for the first time in the lands that would later be called Brazil, wrote to the King about the hammocks being produced and the clothes that the natives wore, although without clearly pointing out that such items were made of cotton. Not long afterward, and soon before the Portuguese began a robust policy of colonization of the American lands, travelers who reached Santa Catarina and Pernambuco described in precise detail the use that indigenous populations made of cotton. Other reports by later travelers also pointed to the knowledge and the use that indigenous peoples made of the cotton plant in places as far away as Bahia and Maranhão during the sixteenth and seventeenth centuries.[1]

From the arrival of the Portuguese in the Americas in the early sixteenth century until the middle of the eighteenth century, the cultivation, spinning, and weaving of cotton remained residual activities in the Portuguese economy as a whole. And while external demand remained low, there was no reason for the populations who lived in Brazil to be interested in planting and exporting cotton on a large scale. The products that fulfilled this function and took time and money from colonizers and the work and lives of enslaved Africans were sugar, tobacco, and gold. For more than two centuries, cotton mostly constituted an economic endeavor confined to the home market, conducted by enslaved indigenous people in the peripheral areas of extensive estates run by enslaved Africans in Bahia, Pernambuco, and Rio de Janeiro. The Maranhão

1 John Casper Branner, *Cotton in the Empire of Brazil; the Antiquity, Methods and Extent of Its Cultivation, Together with Statistics of Exportation and Home Consumption* (Government Printing Office, 1885), 9–13.

captaincy in Northern Brazil was the inaugural location for large-scale cotton cultivation and exportation.[2]

Before the 1750s, Maranhão was a poor captaincy composed of a vast indigenous population, sometimes enslaved by religious institutions (more specifically, the Society of Jesus) and other colonists. For a region that never managed to develop sugar plantations, cotton culture and weaving were relatively important activities in Maranhão. Cotton clothes were used as currency as early as 1688. In 1744, raw cotton and cotton cloth production had managed to connect the interests of traders dispersed throughout Maranhão and the neighboring captaincies. It also attracted enslaved women (and their owners), most likely enslaved indigenous women, since the African slave trade was small there. The law prohibiting the enslavement of indigenous people would only come to fruition in the 1750s. Every year, traders from the interior of Piauí used to go to Maranhão to seek cotton cloths to take them to Pará. As a medium of exchange and source of income for enslaved people and their owners, exporting raw cotton outside Maranhão was prohibited. However, the export of cotton cloth was permitted.[3]

Almost ten years later, in 1755, the governor of Maranhão, Diogo da Costa Silva, had a different interpretation of this prohibition. In his opinion, what was spun in Maranhão and exported to Portugal was "so crude that only for candle yarn and lights it is used."[4] But if the ban were to be lifted, it would be possible to convert raw cotton into "fine fabrics," and the tithing taxes would increase.[5] Yet, the interim governor of Pará argued to the contrary. To him and the municipal councilors, if raw cotton were allowed to be exported, poor women and their enslaved workers would enter into "lethal idleness."[6] The freedom to export raw cotton would also significantly decrease the cotton cloths negotiated between Maranhão and the hinterlands. The municipal councilors of São Luís even went so far as to say that the cotton spinning branch was almost the only way enslaved workers and all the other people in the captaincy were employed.[7] One year later, the same governor gave another reason for not exporting raw cotton: the fiber was necessary to manufacture

2 Stuart B. Schwartz, "Colonial Brazil, c. 1580–c. 1750: Plantations and Peripheries," in *The Cambridge History of Latin America. Volume 2: Colonial Latin America.*, ed. Leslie Bethell (Cambridge University Press, 1984), 421–500; Jerônimo De Viveiros, *História do Comércio do Maranhão 1612–1895*, vol. 1 (Associação Comercial do Maranhão, 1954), 31–33.

3 AHU, ACL, CU, 009, Cx. 28, doc. 2880.

4 "tão grosseiro que só para pavios de velas e para luzes se aproveita".

5 AHU, ACL, CU, 009, Cx. 36, doc. 3597.

6 "letal ociosidade".

7 AHU, ACL, CU, 009, Cx. 36, doc. 3603.

cloth for military uniforms.[8] Consequently, the exportation of raw cotton was difficult, leading certain segments of colonial society to prioritize retaining it for local economic activities.

This whole struggle was minor within an equally minor economy. Maranhão was in a marginal position compared to the other captaincies. The economic activities in Maranhão and the Amazon region were defined by extractivism, involving the extraction of natural resources from the Amazon jungle, conducted by indigenous communities and controlled by settlers and religious institutions. In addition to aiming at the religious conversion of the indigenous peoples, Church members also used their labor to raise economic resources. Maranhão remained peripheral for a long time due to many factors, two of which are the most important. First, much of their territory was controlled by indigenous peoples, and the white population was small. Second, the cultivation of sugarcane, or any other cash crop plantation, was made unfeasible by the lack of enslaved Africans and the problems arising from the use of indigenous slave labor.[9] This made agricultural production well below that of other regions of Brazil. It also made it very difficult to develop a class of wealthy planters or merchants who could afford to buy enslaved workers. Consequently, slave traders and ship owners always preferred to dock in Pernambuco or Bahia, for example, to sell captives. Another problem was the risk of transporting enslaved people from the traditional slave market of the Portuguese Empire in West Central Africa—which was very far from Maranhão—because of the high possibility of mortality in the middle passage.[10]

According to the political leaders of the time, mainly Sebastião José de Carvalho e Melo (1699–1782), since 1769 the Marquis of Pombal, and his brother, Francisco Xavier de Mendonça Furtado (1701–1769), who had been governor of the State of Grão-Pará and Maranhão (1751–1759), greater intervention by the Portuguese State was necessary to overcome the economic backwardness of the North of Brazil and to increase tax collection. In the repertoire of economic ideas available to these authorities, few projects were more tempting than creating a monopoly company to solve the region's economic problems.

---

8 AHU, ACL, CU, 009, Cx. 37, doc. 3699. See also Walter Hawthorne, *From Africa to Brazil: Culture, Identity, and an Atlantic Slave Trade, 1600–1830* (Cambridge University Press, 2010), 147.

9 Mortality among the indigenous peoples was high because of European diseases. Traditionally, the indigenous peoples were unaware of or even rejected intensive agriculture, focusing on gathering and hunting activities. Furthermore, in order not to work for the Europeans, they tended to flee into the forest, as they were familiar with the territory.

10 Hawthorne, *From Africa to Brazil*, 28–29, 32, 38, 48–49.

The project was not novel. At least since the beginning of the eighteenth century, governors and members of the city councils in Maranhão and Pará had proposed the creation of monopoly companies to carry out the slave trade and overcome the obstacles caused by using indigenous labor. Notwithstanding these local attempts, the Pombal plan prevailed, which aimed not only to supply the captaincy with enslaved people but also to create a company that would monopolize the route that connected the regions of Grão-Pará and Maranhão with Portugal.[11] Besides, the most general guidelines for developing the region should encourage exportable agricultural production, financed by the company. The General Trade Company of Grão-Pará and Maranhão (GCGPM) was created in 1755 with an initial capital of 480,000,000 *réis*, 90% of which came from shareholders based in Portugal.[12] Two years later, due to pressure from GCGPM members and opinions of the Overseas Council (*Conselho Ultramarino*), the King allowed the export of raw cotton from Maranhão.[13] For a long time, from its beginning until more or less the 1830s, cotton production was concentrated in the lower part of the *Itapecuru* River, and it was done through large slave plantations. Rice, grown alongside cotton, was another key cash crop for export. This was a region very focused on these two cultures. Planting began in the rainy season in January, and the fruits were harvested eight to ten months later, between September and November.[14]

An important institution in the history of cotton in the Portuguese Empire, the GCGPM's actions had an impact that went beyond its monopoly. This chapter relies heavily on records produced by the company, mainly the letters exchanged between Lisbon and São Luís members. Through these correspondences, we can have a clearer picture of how the company worked. They also show how colonial residents circumvent the monopoly by exporting cotton to merchants in Lisbon. Another valuable documentation is the records of colonial and metropolitan authorities on the economic and commercial state of

11 Manuel Nunes Dias, *Fomento e Mercantilismo: A Companhia Geral Do Grão Pará e Maranhão (1755–1778)* (Universidade Federal do Pará, 1970), 1: 121–226; Maxwell, *Pombal: Paradox of the Enlightenment.* See also Rui Manuel Figueiredo Marcos, *As Companhias Pombalinas: Contributo Para a História das Sociedades por Acções em Portugal* (Almedina, 1997); Leonor Freire Costa et al., "Democracia e plutocracia nas companhias coloniais pombalinas, 1757–1777," *Ler História*, no. 82 (June 2023): 82.

12 Alden, "Late Colonial Brazil," 622; António Carreira, *A Companhia Geral do Grão-Pará e Maranhão. (O comércio monopolista. Portugal-África-Brasil na segunda metade do século XVIII)* (Companhia Editora Nacional, 1988), 1: 52.

13 AHU, ACL, CU, 009, Cx. 37, doc. 3699.

14 Hawthorne, *From Africa to Brazil*, 161. The second chapter will deal more extensively with the cotton production process.

Maranhão at the time of the monopoly company. There should be no doubt that the establishment of the GCGPM was a milestone. Still, it should be noted that the good performance of Maranhão matches the aftershocks of the Seven Years' War (1756–1763). This event disturbed the West Indian trade, where there were a large number of cotton growers.[15] With the war, complications arose for the slave trade and other commercial sectors in the French colony because of several port blockades. As a result, freight and insurance rates were rising and French merchants began to reduce investments there.[16] Around this time, in 1759, the authorization to print cotton fabrics in France was restored, likely stimulating the spinning and weaving business,[17] but it is undisputed that the cotton from Maranhão during the GCGPM period predominantly went to Rouen.[18] An additional significant factor elucidates the relative success of the GCGPM. During the Seven Years' War, the French and English became less concerned about Upper Guinea. This facilitated a straightforward access for the Portuguese to the supplies of enslaved labor in that region. The ports of Bissau and Cacheu emerged as the primary suppliers of enslaved individuals to the plantations of Maranhão until at least 1815.[19]

2 The General Trade Company of Grão-Pará and Maranhão and the Beginning of the Cotton Economy

The monopoly of the GCGPM established new foundations that guided the captaincy's financial, commercial, and productive organization that continued after its extinction in 1778. The main traits developed and bequeathed by the GCGPM included 1) the ownership and investment of capital; 2) functional

15 Most of the cotton imported into Rouen came from the French West Indies; see Pierre Dardel, *Navires et Marchandises Dans Les Ports de Rouen et Du Havre Au XVIIIe Siècle* (SEVPEN, 1963), 561.

16 Trevor Burnard and John Garrigus, *The Plantation Machine: Atlantic Capitalism in French Saint-Domingue and British Jamaica* (University of Pennsylvania Press, 2016), 84, 86, 93.

17 Even before that, the French were able to copy Indian muslins with some ease, but they lacked good quality yarn to do so. "King Louis XV, wanting to encourage cotton spinning, decided, in 1756, that bonuses would be granted to spinners who devoted themselves to this type of industry. This measure was intended to increase the number of cotton spinners, and to facilitate the means for weavers to make muslins." See Charles Picard, *Saint-Quentin: de son commerce et de ses industries* (J. Moureau, 1865), 1: 204–5.

18 António Carreira, *A Companhia Geral do Grão-Pará e Maranhão. (O comércio monopolista. Portugal-África-Brasil na segunda metade do século XVIII)* (Companhia Editora Nacional, 1988), 2: 319.

19 Hawthorne, *From Africa to Brazil*, 61.

specialization; and 3) a continuous flow of imports of enslaved labor. The first had to do with the capital of metropolitan shareholders to supply credit to the company's managers in Maranhão that would later be lent to the colonial inhabitants (planters and colonial merchants). After the end of the company, private merchants in Portugal continued to finance merchants based in Maranhão, which, in turn, financed cotton planters. Second, a functional specialization placed planters on one side and merchants on the other, the former being constantly indebted to the latter. In addition to financing the planters, the merchants were primarily responsible for the commercialization of cotton in the Atlantic. The third pillar of Maranhão's economy was the slave trade and slave labor that drove export agriculture. The company established the bases for the slave trade, which would be continued by private merchants in subsequent years, mainly with the regions of Upper Guinea, and to a lesser extent with Angola and other ports in Brazil. The company was also a platform of action for individuals who would persist for a long time in the economic, social, and political life of the captaincy. Among them were colonial debtors (merchants and planters) and the company's administrators, both in the colony and Portugal.

This chapter deals exclusively with the monopoly period, which runs from 1755 to 1778. But before delving into GCGPM's organizational mechanisms, I tried to outline a more general theoretical framework for dealing with monopoly companies in this period, especially looking at relations between the principals in Europe and the agents that governed the company overseas. The principal-agent problem, originally derived from the economic sciences, is a suitable lens of analysis, though other contextual considerations are necessary to explain the Portuguese Empire's reality. For this reason, the second section will point to the specificity of Pombaline companies compared to other monopolistic enterprises. The third section highlights what type of colonial domestic market the monopoly company operated in. The fourth part of the chapter outlines the GCGPM operating plan. The fifth, sixth, and seventh parts explore how planters, merchants, and managers in Maranhão sought to evade the rules imposed by the principals in Lisbon. The chapter concludes by covering the final years of the GCGPM, focusing on the debt collection process and, finally, trying to explain the reasons for the various vicissitudes faced by the company in Maranhão.

3 Monopoly Companies and the Principal-Agent Problem

One of the main purposes of monopolistic joint-stock companies in the early modern history was to overcome market uncertainties and risks. They provided security for shareholders as they promised them a market without competitors and with guaranteed incomes. Above all, monopolistic companies were a form of commercial organization that aimed to circumvent the commercial problems involved in long-distance trades. However, despite being successful on several fronts, those responsible for the companies (the principals) had to face the problem of monitoring the managers overseas (the agents) so that they would ensure the smooth running of the company and protect its capital. Hence, one of the main obstacles was the moral risk that their overseas managers would carry out private business and not fully dedicate themselves to their original obligations. In large part, it was the asymmetry of information that made it possible for managers to trade privately since the principals were unable to monitor their agents fully.[20] Thus, according to economic theory, the relationship between employers and employees, principals, and agents, or any other form of connection that involves hierarchies leads to potential "selfish" attitudes. In this theoretical framework, the agents, like the principals, would be induced to pursue their own benefits.[21]

The GCGPM was no exception to this rule. Both in the company's charters, and throughout its history, specific rules were launched and modified over

20 For agency problems within the organizational structure of companies, see Ann M. Carlos and Stephen Nicholas, "Agency Problems in Early Chartered Companies: The Case of the Hudson's Bay Company," *The Journal of Economic History* 50, no. 4 (1990): 855, 857, and 858; Ann M. Carlos and Stephen Nicholas, "Theory and History: Seventeenth-Century Joint-Stock Chartered Trading Companies," *The Journal of Economic History* 56, no. 4 (1996): 916. For an overview of monopoly companies in the Early Modern Period, see C. E. Walker, "The History of the Joint Stock Company," *The Accounting Review* 6, no. 2 (1931): 97–105; E. L. J. Coornaert, "European Economic Institutions and the New World; the Chartered Companies," in *The Cambridge Economic History of Europe. Vol. IV. The Economy of Expanding Europe in the Sixteenth and Seventeenth Centuries*, ed. E. E. Rich and C. H. Wilson (Cambridge University Press, 1967), 240 and 262–63. To understand monopoly companies as a way of mitigating risks by excluding competition, see Robert Brenner, *Merchants and Revolution: Commercial Change, Political Conflict, and London's Overseas Traders, 1550–1653* (Verso, 2003); Baskes, *Staying Afloat*. For the case of the Portuguese Empire, see Jorge Miguel Pedreira, "A economia política do sistema colonial," in *O Brasil Colonial: Volume 3*, ed. João Fragoso and Maria de Fátima Gouvêa (Civilização Brasileira, 2014), 419–60. For a view of monopoly companies as inefficient precisely because of their protectionist character and because they create barriers to free trade, see S. R. H. Jones and Simon P. Ville, "Efficient Transactors or Rent-Seeking Monopolists? The Rationale for Early Chartered Trading Companies," *The Journal of Economic History* 56, no. 4 (1996): 898–915.

21 On the theoretical conceptualization of the principal-agent problem, see Jensen and Meckling, "Theory of the Firm"; Jean Ensminger, "Reputations, Trust, and the Principal Agent Problem," in *Trust in Society*, ed. Karen S. Cook (Russell Sage Foundation, 2001). See the chapters in Emily Erikson, ed., *Chartering Capitalism: Organizing Markets, States, and Publics* (Emerald, 2015).

time, which tried to reduce the level of agents' opportunism. One crucial point was remuneration: the company paid its managers in the colony through commissions and not fixed wages. This was an incentive for agents to always seek to increase the company's trade. In doing so, they were automatically earning more commissions, not needing to engage in parallel activity to increase their incomes. However, as will be shown, this tactic had an opposite effect than expected, since managers used this policy indiscriminately to sell as much as they could on credit to colonial residents unable to repay the loans.

In addition to commissions as an incentive to avoid cheating, the company stipulated the exchange of information as an instrument to monitor the behavior of agents and for better inspection of company accounts. Although the flow of correspondence was part of the company's daily life, together with the sending of accounting documents to monitor the good progress of business in the colony, the principals in Lisbon had other sources of information for the purpose of supervising or at least to know what their agents were doing. Private merchants and residents reported and complained about the agents' behavior. Also, the governors of Maranhão communicated directly with the principals in Lisbon, accusing colonial managers of bad conduct. They also informed the Secretaries of the Navy and Overseas on these and other matters.

4 The Specificity of Pombaline Companies

The Pombaline companies—including the GCGPM and the General Company of Pernambuco and Paraíba (GCPP)—were created under the reformist impulse of King D. José I's right-hand man, the Secretary Sebastião José de Carvalho e Melo.[22] The two companies differed from monopolistic enterprises of the seventeenth century in that they focused on long-established colonial spaces, which did not require investments in forts and protection against foreigners. They were also unique compared with European monopoly companies because they operated on routes and territories already covered by the old colonial system.[23] Furthermore, the Pombaline companies forbade colonial and metropolitan residents to trade directly with anyone else without the

22 On the more general context of Pombaline reforms, see Boxer, *The Portuguese Seaborne Empire 1415–1825*; Maxwell, *Pombal: Paradox of the Enlightenment*; António Carreira, *As companhias pombalinas: de Grão-Pará e Maranhão e Pernambuco e Paraíba*, 2a. ed. (Editorial Presença, 1983).

23 For the metropolitan exclusivity, see Novais, *Portugal e Brasil*; Arruda, *O Brasil no comércio colonial*; Maxwell, "Pombal and the Nationalization of the Luso-Brazilian Economy"; Harold Edward Stephen Fisher, *The Portugal Trade: A Study of Anglo-Portuguese*

intermediation of the monopolistic companies.[24] The Pombaline companies had jurisdiction over all goods entering and leaving monopoly areas (including the slave trade), in sharp contrast to Companhia Portuguesa das Índias (1628–1633) and Companhia Geral do Comércio do Brasil (1649–1720), which held monopolies on only some, and not all, products.[25] Observing the privileges of the Pombaline companies, compared with other similar enterprises, it appears that an essential feature of the former was their interference in the agricultural sector of the monopoly areas. This also differed from previous companies that the Portuguese, Dutch, and English had created in the seventeenth and eighteenth centuries, which claimed the exclusivity of trade and transport, in specific economic sectors, but not all.[26]

It is worth considering Emily Erikson's argument on how managers of the English East India Company in Asia in the seventeenth and eighteenth centuries conducted private trade—outside the purview of the company—with local populations. Erikson argues that this particular trade within the scope of the British company with Asian ports favored private merchant networks that provided the company's employees with information about local markets. The low asymmetry of information obtained by these agents ended up being used by the monopoly company, making its commercial success feasible. The

Commerce, 1700–1770 (Methuen, 1971); see also George Louis Beer, *The Old Colonial System, 1660–1754*, with unknown library, vol. 1 (The Macmillan Company, 1912).

24 It thus differs from the institutional framework that occurred, for example, in Asian trade, between Indian producers and merchants (Asian or European). Producers, while taking loans from private merchants and the Dutch and English company, could sell their products to merchants with whom they had no debt obligations; see Sanjay Subrahmanyam, "Rural Industry and Commercial Agriculture in Late Seventeenth-Century South-Eastern India," *Past & Present*, no. 126 (1990): 88–89.

25 About Companhia Portuguesa das Índias, see A. R. Disney, *A Decadência Do Império Da Pimenta. Comércio Português Na Índia No Início Do Século XVII* (Edições 70, 1981), 128–29. About Companhia Portuguesa das Índias and its relations with private traders, see James C. Boyajian, *Portuguese Trade in Asia Under the Habsburgs, 1580–1640* (Johns Hopkins University Press, 2008), 106–27. About Companhia Geral do Comércio do Brasil, see Leonor Freire Costa, *O transporte no Atlântico e a Companhia Geral do Comércio do Brasil, 1580–1663* (Comissão Nacional para as Comemorações dos Descobrimentos Portugueses, 2002), 1: 508–86. Among the examples of monopolistic companies that did not monopolize all products is the West India Company, which handled trade between Pernambuco and the Netherlands; see Pedro Puntoni, *A mísera sorte a escravidão africana no Brasil holandês e as guerras do tráfico no Atlântico Sul, 1621–1648* (Hucitec, 1999), 81.

26 For a monopolistic company that looked after one specific economic sector, such as the slave trade, see the case of the Royal African Company; see Robin Blackburn, *The Making of New World Slavery: From the Baroque to the Modern, 1492–1800* (Verso, 1998).

agents' decentralized opportunism in pursuing their own interests ended up favoring the company's centralism and, therefore, the principals.[27]

The brief allusion to this interpretation is sufficient to demonstrate the need to examine monopoly companies by taking into account the local specificities in which they operated. In the case of the English East India Company analyzed by Emily Erikson, the agents' opportunism was anchored in the trade within a region with no territorial monopoly. In this scenario, the monopoly concerned only the ocean routes that connected Asia with the respective European nations. Furthermore, the company was not worried about directly financing the productive sectors, nor being in charge of economic areas such as the slave trade. Other companies, like the one the Portuguese themselves started to negotiate with Asia and later the Companhia Geral do Brasil, also had more modest claims in terms of economic branches to manage. Pombaline companies were different from these experiences, as they tried to cover many economic sectors. Therefore, despite being smaller companies in terms of capital, the Pombaline companies had larger claims and scope than other monopolistic ventures in Asia, for instance. These factors had consequences in the interaction of the companies' monopoly policies and the existing configurations of the colonial market.

5 The Configurations of the Colonial Market

The GCGPM was part of a project to develop an economically unattractive region whose main obstacle was the lack of labor force.[28] A monopoly company seemed to be an excellent plan to regulate, without the interference of private agents and their sometimes-disparate interests, the poorly developed region of the Amazon. The GCGPM solved the problem of slave labor by activating the slave trade routes more intensely than before and, on top of that, fostered cotton exports. This was achieved in a colonial market occupied by planters and merchants, with the latter usually financing the former. The figure of the planter assuming commercial functions was also present and was one of the most important ones in Maranhão. These were wealthy planters who financed other producers. Thus, Maranhão, like other places in colonial Brazil,

27 Erikson, *Between Monopoly and Free Trade*. See also Julia Adams, "Principals and Agents, Colonialists and Company Men: The Decay of Colonial Control in the Dutch East Indies," *American Sociological Review* 61, no. 1 (1996): 12–28.

28 Lúcia Lima Rodrigues, Alvaro Ricardino, and Sofie Tortelboom Aversari Martins, ""Corporate Governance Regulations": A New Term for an Ancient Concern? The Case of Grão Pará and Maranhão General Trading Company in Portugal (1754)," *Accounting History*, 2 November 2009.

quickly developed into an economy made up of creditors (merchants and rich growers) and debtors (planters). The reliance of planters on the credit of merchants and wealthy planters was a constant factor. In the absence of a better expression, we can call this separation between planters and merchants, or between creditors and debtors, the configuration of the colonial market. These were structures prior to the establishment of the company that remained, were reinforced by its policies, and that lasted for a long time after the monopoly ended. The metropolitan exclusivity system and the high dependence on African slave labor were other traits of the colonial market.

Around the second half of the eighteenth century, the colonial population grew considerably and, at the same time, developed more complex forms of economic interaction. The domestic market and mercantile groups residing in the central Brazilian markets had already performed important economic functions, which were an essential vector for internal and external exchanges with Brazil. Colonial populations were able to do business in the territories of Portuguese America. Very often they developed their own business strategies while using credits from other individuals who were located in Portugal and other parts of the Empire.[29]

Thus, when the Pombaline companies were established to operate in trade between Brazil and Portugal, they would have to insert themselves within a market structure already in progress. The GCGPM would have to deal with the overseas business occupied by former mercantile groups, something with which the company members did not have so many problems. Still, they would also have to deal with groups residing in the colonies, a task that proved to be a great challenge. The next sections will deal exclusively with this last point, explaining how the GCGPM interacted with the residents in Maranhão and how the company's managers in the colony had difficulty dealing with the economic configurations set up by planters (debtors) and traders (creditors). More specifically, the chapter analyzes how the theoretical model of the principal-agent problem interacts with a concrete historical situation, namely

29 For studies on the colonial internal market, among many, see Guillermo Palacios, "Peasantry and Slavery in Brazil: A Contribution to the History of the Free Poor Planters from the General Captaincy of Pernambuco, 1700–1817. Volumes I" (Ph.D., New Jersey, Princeton University, 1993); João Luís Ribeiro Fragoso, *Homens de Grossa Aventura: Acumulação e Hierarquia Na Praça Mercantil Do Rio de Janeiro, 1790–1830* (1992; repr., Rio de Janeiro: Civilização Brasileira, 1998); Angelo Alves Carrara, *Minas e currais: produção rural e mercado interno em Minas Gerais 1674–1807* (Juiz de Fora: UFJF, 2007); Júnia Ferreira Furtado, *Homens de negócio: a interiorização da metrópole e do comércio nas minas setecentistas* (São Paulo: Editora Hucitec, 1999); Antonia da Silva Mota, "A Dinâmica Colonial Portuguesa e as Redes de Poder Local Na Capitania Do Maranhão" (Ph.D. diss., Recife, Universidade Federal de Pernambuco, 2007).

that of the structure of the Brazilian colonial market vis-à-vis the company's monopolistic policies.

6 The GCGPM Operating Plan in Maranhão

Throughout the GCGPM's period of monopoly, raw cotton figured as its main export commodity. The captaincy of Maranhão was responsible for most of the fiber production, while the captaincy of Grão-Pará was accountable for a much lower portion. The company's performance, from 1755 onwards, favored the substantial entry of enslaved African labor in a way never seen before, partly breaking the almost total dependence that the regions of Northern Brazil had on indigenous compulsory labor. Cotton production and slavery traced parallel paths and the GCGPM was crucial in coordinating the two activities. The members of the company's Board (*Junta*) in Lisbon made up the decision-making center from which orders, credits, and goods departed to carry out business with Maranhão. In the colony, the Administration agents (*Administração*) were responsible for following the guidelines of the principals in Lisbon, who would ensure the smooth running of the company and the management of debts and capital (Tables 1.1 and 1.2).

TABLE 1.1 The GCGPM board members in Lisbon

Board in Lisbon			
1756	1760	1768	1772
Rodrigo de Sande e Vasconcelos	José Francisco da Cruz	Inácio Pedro Quintela	Inácio Pedro Quintela
Manuel Ferreira da Costa	Manuel Ferreira da Costa	Anselmo José da Cruz	Anselmo José da Cruz
Antônio dos Santos Pinto	José Rodrigues Caldas	Francisco José Lopes	Francisco José Lopes
João Francisco da Cruz	Paulo Jorge	Joaquim José Estolano de Faria	Joaquim José Estolano de Faria
Bento José Alvares	José Luís Serra	Manuel Inácio Ferreira	Manuel Inácio Ferreira
Domingos de Bastos Viana	Dâmaso Pereira	João Roque Jorge	João Roque Jorge
	Caetano Jerônimo	Silvério Lima Serra	Silvério Lima Serra
	Manuel Eleutério de Castro	José Ferreira Coelho	José Ferreira Coelho

TABLE 1.1 The GCGPM board members in Lisbon (*cont.*)

Board in Lisbon			
1756	**1760**	**1768**	**1772**
Estêvão José de Almeida João de Araújo Lima	Domingos de Vilas-Boas *Advisers:* Dr. José Rodrigues Estêves José Rodrigues Bandeira Inácio Pedro Quintela	Domingos Lourenço *Advisers:* José Rodrigues Bandeira Manuel Ferreira da Costa José Rodrigues Caldas	Domingos Lourenço *Advisers:* José Rodrigues Bandeira Manuel Ferreira da Costa José Rodrigues Caldas

Source: Carrera, *A Companhia Geral do Grão-Pará*, 1, 240–241. Table prepared by the author.

TABLE 1.2 The GCGPM administration in Maranhão

Bernardo Rodrigues de Lima	Bonifácio José Lamas
Joaquim Barbosa de Almeida	Luís António Ferreira de Araújo
José Vieira da Silva	Marçal Inácio Monteiro
Miguel José Caetano	João Paulo Diniz
Francisco Pereira Vicente Ferreira da Costa	Joaquim José Ferreira de Souza
António Botelho de Almeida	

Source: Carrera, *A Companhia Geral do Grão-Pará*, 1, 256. ANTT. CGGPM. Copiador de cartas para o Maranhão, livro 230, f. 238, 264–265. Table prepared by the author.

The productive and commercial organization of cotton in Maranhão had its initial roots in the purchase of enslaved people and goods on credit by the planters. Captive labor and products were advanced to the planters through GCGPM administration agents, and the company hoped to recover the credit through the crops that the planters would deliver to them in the future. The crops could be sold in three ways:

1. The planters could send cotton at their own risk to some representative in Portugal. Still, they should pay freight to the company and commissions to private representatives in Lisbon.

2. Similarly, planters could also send cotton at their own risk through the GCGPM, but they should also pay commissions and freight to the company, in addition to other charges.
3. Finally, the planters simply sold the crops to the company's managers in São Luís, thus avoiding trading risks in the metropolis and the risks of overseas shipping.[30]

Regardless of the sort of commercialization, planters were to pay the company the debts they had contracted initially in the form of enslaved people and goods. The company expected they would commit to paying them back in the form of tropical goods, like cotton and rice. The process should take place this way; however, the mercantile organization within the monopoly region and the dishonest strategies of Maranhão residents (including GCGPM managers) posed several obstacles to the company's plans.

7 Illicit Practices within the Monopoly Region

The bet that the inhabitants of Maranhão would pay their debts with the crops of their plantations quickly proved to be full of pitfalls. As early as 1760, a very peculiar obstacle that would cause extreme discomfort in the company's financial health began to worry the Lisbon Board: the explicitly prohibited practices of planters who commercialized cotton which was not produced on their own lands. This activity indicated that indebted planters with the GCGPM were not supplying cotton to settle debts but were instead selling fiber to third parties, including different planters and merchants. In turn, these third parties sold the cotton either directly to the company's management in Maranhão or at their own risk to the Board in Lisbon.[31]

However, it was not until 1766, when the Board in Lisbon notified the Administration in São Luís of the fraud, that major measures were implemented to combat these abuses. The Board ordered the Administration to give preference to cash payments in the sale of goods to Maranhão residents. They also ordered that only in the last instance could the Administration sell products on credit. These were measures to guarantee prompt cash payments. Also, sales on credit

30 ANTT. CGGPM. Copiador de cartas para o Maranhão, livro 230, f. 7, April 11, 1760. See also the Institution of Companhia Geral do Grão-Pará and Maranhão in Carreira, *A Companhia Geral do Grão-Pará e Maranhão*, 2: 27.

31 ANTT. CGGPM. Copiador de cartas para o Maranhão, livro 230, f. 4, February, 1760. AHU, ACL, CU, 013, Cx. 51, Doc. 4663. Carreira, *A Companhia Geral do Grão-Pará e Maranhão*, 1: 170–71.

could only be made through obligations signed by buyers (planters and people who shipped colonial goods), a contract in which interest would be incurred. Merchants, or those who were not planters, would not be charged interest, and they would have up to six months to pay for the purchases they made.[32] A year later, in the knowledge that the debts of the residents of Maranhão had reached about 390,000,000 *réis*, the Board took firm action and expressly forbade the Administration to sell on credit to those who had not paid their debts.[33] In 1768, they recommended, once again, that the Administration only sell in exchange for money or in exchange for goods. Credit sales would only be allowed to shopkeepers, but they could only borrow goods after paying off the old debts. Besides, if the payment of debts had been stopped for more than a year, shopkeepers should be charged.[34] These measures had no effect, since the debts of the residents had increased by 1769. This made the Board in Lisbon suspect, in fact, that the 488 debtors in Maranhão were not safe payers as guaranteed by the Administrators of Maranhão. The Board's remedy, though, was the same as before: to charge debtors and to only sell on credit to those who had paid previous debts.[35]

During much of the monopoly period, planters sold cotton directly to the GCGPM Administration, who, in turn, sent the fiber to the Lisbon Board. In other words, the colony residents preferred not to take any chances in the transatlantic commercialization of the product. But, as already mentioned, this did not mean that the company was receiving payment of the debts. In the final years of the monopoly, namely post-1774, residents of Maranhão improved their efforts to circumvent the company's controls. They began to prominently engage in shipments at their own risk, either legally, dispatching fibers from their own plantations, or illicitly, once again calling on third parties to avoid paying debts. The GCGPM and Maranhão residents' cotton shipment trajectory is depicted in Figure 1.1. During the period, the GCGPM was responsible for the dispatch of 198,827 arrobas (72.4%) and residents for 75,727 arrobas (27.6%).[36]

Thus, the relation between credit (in the form of enslaved people and goods), cotton trade, and payment of debts to the GCGPM involved three options that were intertwined at some points in the company's history. First, a process worthy of attention included illicit practices: indebted planters sold cotton to

32 ANTT. CGGPM. Copiador de cartas para o Maranhão, livro 230, f. 115.
33 ANTT. CGGPM. Copiador de cartas para o Maranhão, livro 230, f. 132.
34 ANTT. CGGPM. Copiador de cartas para o Maranhão, livro 230, f. 142.
35 ANTT. CGGPM. Copiador de cartas para o Maranhão, livro 230, f. 160–161.
36 Carreira, *A Companhia Geral do Grão-Pará e Maranhão*, 1: 198.

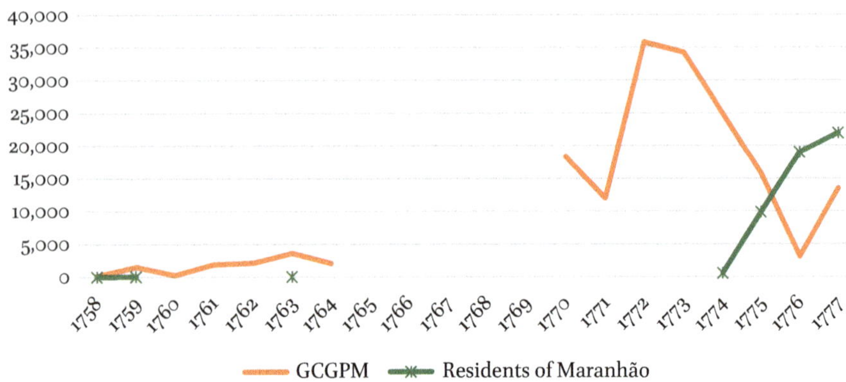

FIGURE 1.1 Export of cotton (in arrobas) by the GCGPM and by residents of Maranhão, 1758–1777
Source: Carreira, *A Companhia Geral do Grão-Pará e Maranhão*, Vol. 1, 225–226, 261. Figure prepared by the author.

private merchants or wealthy planters so as not to settle debts with the company. This was also encouraged because the company's management was reluctant to pay planters promptly with cash.[37] Merchants and wealthy planters, on the other hand, paid producers immediately in cash. Second, another illicit practice happened when indebted planters used non-indebted third parties in the colony to sell cotton to the Administration with their names. Indebted planters also used the names of third parties to send cotton to the Company's Board in Lisbon at their own risk. Although slightly different, this was also a way of getting around the payment of debts. Third—an option that initially had nothing to do with the debt issue—was the practice of residents in Maranhão sending cotton directly to the Board in Lisbon. By shipping at their own risk, planters and merchants in Maranhão could get better prices than if they sold directly to the company's Administration.

Options 1 and 2 probably took place during almost the entire monopoly period. Option 3 only occurred in the last three or four years of the company, as shown in Figure 1.1, when residents began to export more cotton than the GCGPM itself. However, it was possible for options 2 and 3 to mix, since planters and indebted merchants could send cotton at their own risk to Lisbon so as not to deliver the fiber to the Administration. If they offered the cotton to

37 The governor of Maranhão in 1775 complained to the GCGPM Board that the company's administrators did not pay planters in cash and complained to the Marquis of Pombal about the lack of money in the captaincy. ANTT. CGGPM. Copiador de cartas para o Maranhão, livro 230, f. 228.

the Administration, probably part or all of it would be confiscated to pay old debts. Flowchart 1.1 seeks to make these different processes clearer, taking into account the licit and illicit cotton marketing practices.

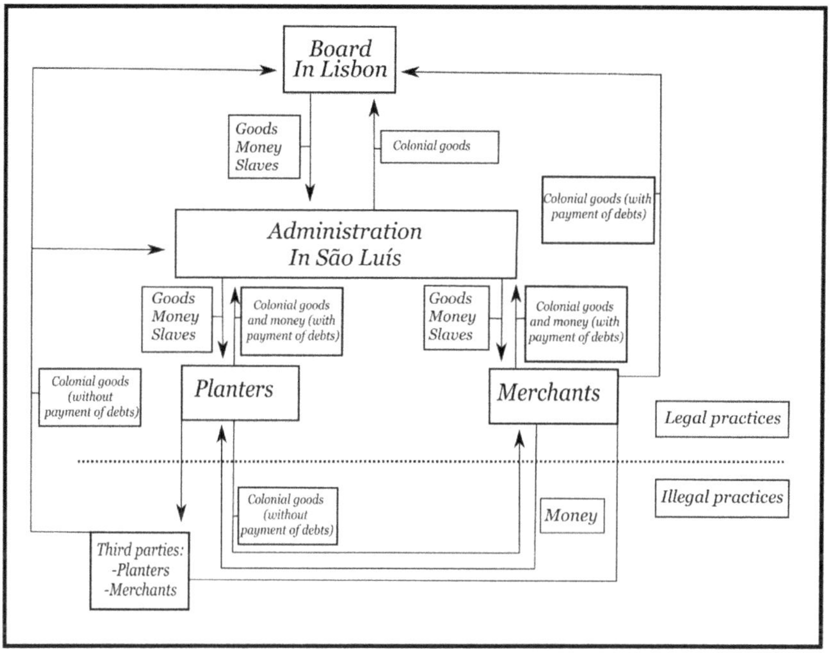

FLOWCHART 1.1 Credit and indebtedness chains during the GCGPM period
Note: This flowchart is divided into two parts. The upper part shows the legal flow of trade that was supposed to take place between the GCGPM and the residents of Maranhão. In the legal flow, the Board in Lisbon sent goods, money, and enslaved people to the Administration in São Luís, who sold them, on credit, to planters and colonial merchants. The latter paid their debts through colonial goods such as cotton, rice, and money. The second (bottom) part of the flowchart illustrates illegal trade practices. These practices were carried out by planters and merchants who—instead of delivering cotton and rice to the Administration in São Luís and paying off their debts—sold the crops to third parties. The latter sent the crops to the GCGPM. Money was an essential element in this flow. Large merchants and planters used it in the colony to buy crops from farmers indebted to the GCGPM, who carried out these deals precisely because they were paid promptly in cash. If they sold directly to the GCGPM, they would not be paid immediately. In addition, the value of their crops would be deducted to pay off debts. Flowchart prepared by the author.

The increase in shipments from the inhabitants of Maranhão to Lisbon occurred simultaneously with favorable cotton prices in the global market. The United States War of Independence impacted the cotton trade in the Caribbean, which was a major cotton producer at the time, resulting in increased prices in Europe. Simultaneously, a factor that prompted residents in Maranhão to ship cotton at their own risk was their attempt to evade paying debts to the GCGPM and the objective of securing more favorable prices for their cotton during this advantageous moment.[38] In any event, the residents of Maranhão sought the aid of representatives in Lisbon, typically referred to as attorneys (procuradores), although they were, in reality, merchants. Utilizing the GCGPM correspondence book (*copiador de cartas*), we can ascertain additional details regarding shipments undertaken by residents in Maranhão. In these letters, members of the GCGPM notified the residents of Maranhão that their cotton bales had been sold in auctions and delivered to the attorneys in Lisbon, detailing the proceeds from their sales and who (residents or attorneys) was receiving the money. In total, 244 letters (or 244 shipments) were exchanged with residents in Maranhão, between 1774 to 1778. The vast majority of them (238 letters) cover the period from 1776 to 1778. Considering all these years, we now know that 108 residents in Maranhão sent 8,596 bales of cotton at their own risk to Lisbon, which gave them a profit of 321,336,497 *réis*.

How did residents in Maranhão receive these profits? There were two ways: 1) After the cotton was sold in Portugal in the auctions held by the GCGPM, the profits could be transferred to the Administration in Maranhão, and the managers paid the residents. Between 1774 and 1778, 63,907,390 *réis* (proceeds from the sale of 1,635 bales of cotton from 27 owners), were transferred directly to Maranhão through this option; 2) Cotton owners in Maranhão appointed an attorney in Lisbon to receive money from sales made by the GCGPM Board. This type of negotiation involved at least 47 attorneys in Lisbon who received 241,849,466 *réis*, proceeds from the sale of 6,535 bales of cotton. In other words, 75% of the profits from cotton sales were—momentarily or not—in Lisbon, while 20% went directly to Maranhão. Due to gaps in the source itself, information on the remaining 5% is missing (Table 1.3).

It is difficult to pinpoint the exact reasons why the revenues from the sale of cotton in Lisbon were not distributed directly to the residents of Maranhão. Three hypotheses come to mind, though. The first is that they could have had a kind of checking account with the attorneys in Lisbon. This could have been a way to have capital in Portugal to do other business. The second hypothesis is that residents in Maranhão could have been indebted to the attorneys in Lisbon, and allowing the attorneys to receive the profits from cotton sales could have been a way to pay off debts. The third hypothesis is that both residents in

38 For complaints from residents of Maranhão about cotton prices paid by the company, see AHU, ACL, CU, 013, Cx. 42, Doc. 4151 and Cx. 50, Doc. 4897.

TABLE 1.3 Destination of profits from cotton sales in Lisbon, 1774–1778

	Cotton sale value (in *réis*)	Bales
For residents in Maranhão	63,907,390 (20%)	1,635
For attorneys in Lisbon	241,849,466 (75%)	6,535
Profit destination not reported	15,579,641 (5%)	426
Total	**321,336,497 (100%)**	**8,596**

Source: ANTT. CGGPM. Copiador de cartas para o Maranhão, livro 230. Table prepared by the author.

Maranhão and attorneys in Lisbon were together part of the same company. Aside from these strictly economic relationships, associations between inhabitants in Maranhão and attorneys in Lisbon were held by family ties. Perhaps the most significant were the negotiations between the Belfort family. Lourenço Belfort (1708–1777), who had lived in Maranhão for many years, was in Lisbon in the late 1770s. He was the attorney for his daughter Maria Madalena Belfort and his son Antônio Belfort, who were cotton growers on lands that belonged, or used to belong, to their father. Sibling negotiations also took place. Alexandre da Serra Freire in Maranhão negotiated with his brother in Lisbon, Francisco da Serra Freire. Antônio Gomes Pires in Maranhão did the same with his brother in Lisbon, José Gomes Pires.

The tithing collector, trader, and planter José Gomes da Silva was the largest cotton exporter in the last years of the monopoly. By receiving tithing taxes on cotton bales, he was able to centralize many crops. Possibly because he shipped huge amounts of cotton at his own risk, the Board in Lisbon began to suspect that the bales were not his but that of indebted planters. The Board warned the governor about the rumor that "many residents" in Maranhão used the name of José Gomes to send crops to their "attorneys" in Lisbon, thus "exempting themselves" from paying their debts to the company.[39] In a direct letter to José Gomes, the Board notified him that they knew what he was doing. José Gomes was reminded that such a practice was forbidden and classified as contraband.[40] According to the estimates of the Board, third parties who sent tropical products without paying the debts to the company shipped 107,600,000

39 ANTT. CGGPM. Copiador de cartas para o Maranhão, livro 230, f. 264.
40 ANTT. CGGPM. Copiador de cartas para o Maranhão, livro 230, f. 265.

réis in 1775, 186,000,000 *réis* in 1776, and 224,000,000 *réis* in 1777. Together, the amounts reached 517,600,000 *réis*.[41]

Cotton owners in Maranhão were required to sign an "obligation" to the GCGPM, stating that the harvests sent were from their crops. On several occasions, the Board explicitly warned that it was "forbidden" for someone else to buy cotton and rice from others and send them to Lisbon, a concern directly related to the collection of residents' debts.[42] Yet, according to the governor, the measure failed to consider a critical aspect of Maranhão's internal trade. In 1776, he wrote that this rule harmed traders who exercised the fundamental function of buying cotton in distant lands and took the fiber to the GCGPM Administration in São Luís. Besides, small planters who did not have the resources to gin, clean, and transport their cotton pieces ended up selling the fiber to individuals who could, such as wealthy planters and traders. The poorest planters always sold their crops (ranging from three to ten arrobas per planter) to third parties (to neighboring planters or to traders), as the poor did not have resources. And these poor planters were many since the governor reminded that "the poor are always more than the rich." Without the rich, the governor argued, small planters would not be encouraged to grow cotton.[43]

8 The Money Problem

Another factor that contributed to the non-payment of debts and also to the increase in direct cotton shipments from residents in Maranhão was the Administration's payment policy, which refused to pay the cotton owners promptly in cash. This favored planters to sell all or part of their crops to third parties (traders and big planters), who paid the growers quickly with cash. Then, these third parties, who were also debtors to the company, paid off their debts with the delivery of cotton from indebted planters. The latter consequently remained in default.

Theoretically, the remedy would have been for the GCGPM to pay indebted planters with money, thus encouraging them to hand over their cotton crops to the company and not to third parties. The Administration in Maranhão, though, argued that the problem was the lack of cash in the colony. Despite sending money in 1771, the Board in Lisbon warned that it was only for encouraging rice culture or for things indispensable to increase trade "and not for

41 Carreira, *A Companhia Geral do Grão-Pará e Maranhão*, 1: 289.
42 ANTT. CGGPM. Copiador de cartas para o Maranhão, livro 230, f. 274–275.
43 "os pobres sempre são mais que os ricos," see AHU, ACL, CU, 013, Cx. 50, Doc. 4873.

the Administration's house to be like a bank of commerce to provide money to any resident."[44] Loans, however, were allowed, as long as they were made with moderation and prudence. According to the Board, the Administration was always asking the members of Lisbon to send cash because the colonial branch lent without caution, failing to observe the fundamental use of money, which was to buy the residents' crops. Most loans were made to merchants and, while these loans were taking place, the Administration still sold goods on credit. These two factors contributed to the colony's debt, reaching 609,578,515 *réis* that year.[45]

Even so, in 1775, the Board sent 10,102,000 *réis* in cash to Maranhão. This money was only to buy cotton and rice from planters who were not indebted to the Administration. The Board also asked the governor for help prohibiting other people from shipping tropical goods that were not from their own plantations to the Kingdom. It was a clear gesture that Lisbon members did not entirely trust the Administration to carry out such a task. According to the Board, it was very harmful for the GCGPM and the indebted planters to deliver tropical commodities to planters who "had the facility to ship" crops of producers who did not have these means, as the latter ended up receiving lower prices for their crops.[46] The accusation was that the planters themselves (the wealthiest and most influential) managed to centralize the production of other smaller planters. When selling directly to large planters, the crops of small producers suffered a price reduction, a compensation for them being paid promptly in cash. Only in December 1776 did the governor report that the amount of money sent to Maranhão satisfied the needs of the residents.[47]

Therefore, some merchants and planters in the colony took advantage of this situation, while others were harmed. This was probably the case for a group of traders headed by Francisco Xavier de Carvalho, Pedro Lamagnère, António Belfort, Lourenço António dos Santos, and José Salgado de Mascarenhas. In April 1777, they wrote to the Secretary of State of the Navy and Overseas Affairs, Martinho de Melo e Castro, complaining about the procedures adopted by the company's Administration. According to them, the managers were responsible for the "decline of commerce and agriculture in this state."[48]

---

44 "e não para que a casa dessa Administração seja como um banco do comércio para se fornecer dinheiro a qualquer morador".

45 ANTT. CGGPM. Cartas aos administradores do Maranhão, livro 215, f. 39–41.

46 "tinham a facilidade de carregar." ANTT. CGGPM. Copiador de cartas para o Maranhão, livro 230, f. 239.

47 ANTT. CGGPM. Copiador de cartas para o Maranhão, livro 230, f. 287–288.

48 "decadência que se achava reduzido o comércio e a agricultura deste Estado," see AHU, ACL, CU, 013, Cx. 51, Doc. 4917.

The claim can be considered fair since the Administrators could indeed favor some groups in Maranhão. Yet, it is worth recalling a warning from the Board itself that responded to complaints about a lack of imported goods in Maranhão. In 1772, the Board said that the shortage was because of the bad and irresponsible sales that the Administration made. Administrators sold on credit to anyone, when in fact they were supposed to sell for money. Credit sales were not a problem, but they should only have been made to trusted people. However, the Board also implied that the residents who complained about the lack of goods were the same who got products from the Administration and did not pay for them.[49] This was probably the case for the merchant Francisco Xavier de Carvalho, who was indebted to the company in 1779. At some point, people like him were probably prevented from buying on credit at the company's headquarters. This, again, encouraged debtors to resort to third parties.

9 The Opportunism of the Administration

Undoubtedly, all these tricks made by the residents (both merchants and rich planters) did not exempt the Administration from responsibility, which also practiced a series of arbitrary and irresponsible commercial operations. In large part, what contributed to the non-payment of the colonial debts was the careless performance of the managers. The company's managers, to show that they were interested in selling goods from Europe, and enslaved migrants from Africa, ended up selling their goods to people who did not have the necessary conditions to honor payments.[50] This was facilitated by the commission rates they received. The commissions of administrators in the colony were higher, from 4% to 8%, when compared with the commissions of the Board in Lisbon, which varied from 2% to 4%.[51] This may mean that it was more challenging to do business in Brazil than in Portugal, so the percentage was higher. Equally, this was perhaps a way for the company to try to match the commission earnings in the colony (which had lower-priced goods based on which the

49 ANTT. CGGPM. Cartas aos administradores do Maranhão, livro 215, f. 67–68.

50 Carreira, *A Companhia Geral do Grão-Pará e Maranhão* (1988), 1: 283–84. On January 31, 1776, the Board wrote to administrators in Maranhão that they should only sell on credit "to people established in commerce and insured and with credit" (a pessoas estabelecidas no comércio e seguras e abonadas). They forbade them to sell on credit to priests and widows, as they were people "unfit for trade" (inabilitadas para o comércio). They said that it was "scandalous" (escandaloso) for a priest, Aires Antônio Rodrigues, to be a debtor of 21,284,707 *réis*, a debt that was never reduced but always increased.

51 Carreira, *A Companhia Geral do Grão-Pará e Maranhão*, 1: 189.

commission would be calculated) with those in the metropolis (with higher commodity prices because of travel costs). Regardless of the situation, the more sales they made, the more commissions managers earned.

Another problem was dishonesty itself. Management deliberately registered entries that did not exist in the account of hypothetical debtors and also listed an undue interest in their accounts. Also, the Maranhão Administration supplied goods and enslaved workers to people who could transport them outside the company's jurisdiction, where debt collection would be virtually impossible. Other than that, the Board repeatedly asked for lists of debtors, and the administrators always delayed or did not send them.[52] In 1772 the Board wrote the following to the Administration: "due to the lack of clarity we find in the accounts that you send us, there are several doubts that move us to ask so many other questions that you must answer to us."[53] This quote clearly illustrates how the colonial managers conveyed ambiguous information to the principals in Lisbon. On another occasion, the Board wrote that "it is not possible to find a greater defect in an administration that governs the capital of others than the lack of true records and the exact regulation of all accounts in which the administrators must show their fidelity."[54] The complaint was related to the lack of correct deeds, and this was a constant criticism by the Board, not only regarding debts but also other matters, such as the sale of European goods and the shipping of colonial commodities.

Opportunism, together with constant problems in the exchange of information, caused the Board to intervene directly to replace the members of the Administration in Maranhão. On May 31, 1775, the Board complained directly about the company's administrator in Maranhão, João Paulo Diniz. They said he took care of his private interests more than the interests of the company. He was accused of facilitating smuggling and embezzlement, in addition to being called inept and "incoherent in his letters." So, they decided to fire him. They handed over the position to Joaquim José Ferreira de Souza, for whom João Paulo Diniz was to be accountable.[55]

---

52 Carreira, *A Companhia Geral do Grão-Pará e Maranhão*, 1: 284.

53 "Da pouca clareza que achamos nas contas que nos remetem, procedem várias dúvidas que nos movem a fazer outras tantas perguntas a que vosmicês nos devem responder …"; see ANTT. CGGPM. Cartas aos administradores do Maranhão, livro 215, f. 72.

54 "Não é possível que se possa encontrar maior defeito em uma administração que rege o cabedal alheio do que a falta de verdadeiros assentos e a exata regulação de todas as contas em que os administradores devem mostrar a sua fidelidade," see ANTT. CGGPM. Cartas aos administradores do Maranhão, livro 215, f. 65.

55 "Incoerente em suas cartas," see ANTT. CGGPM. Copiador de cartas para o Maranhão, livro 230, f. 238.

This did not prevent further amendments. In May 1776, the Board wrote to the governor that the company's managers in Maranhão were careless, negligent, and silent and that "they have very badly served this company so far."[56] The Board, with the consent of Pombal, had decided to change the Administration once again. Luís Antônio Ferreira de Araújo and Marçal Inácio Monteiro would take the place of directors José Vieira da Silva and Bonifácio José Lemos, who should be accountable to the Company's Accounting Department.[57] In September 1777, the Board complained to the governor that the debts in Maranhão had increased, while exports of tropical goods were growing. They regretted that the Administration continued to lend recklessly and to look out more for their personal gains than for the interests of the company. They mentioned the case of José Vieira da Silva who had joined the company's management in debt and who at that time was not only "debt-free but still opulent and enormously wealthy."[58] The Board decided to fire him. Still, he should have been accountable, but like other administrators, he was not. The Board interpreted this as proof that he was doing business with the company's capital for his own benefit and that he hid his accountability because he had lent goods and money to inexperienced and unreliable residents. The Lisbon members, again, asked the governor to press for the administrators to deliver the accounts.[59]

Martinho de Melo e Castro himself, Secretary of State for the Navy and Overseas, ordered the governor of Maranhão, Joaquim de Melo e Povoas, to request the payment of debts from José Vieira da Silva and, if not, to confiscate his assets. After that, José Vieira da Silva—gathering all the documents, accounts, and papers—should go to the Kingdom to account, together with his partner, Bonifácio José Lamas, of his activities at the time when they were administrators of GCGPM in Maranhão. Their administration had lasted from 1770 to 1775. José Vieira da Silva had six months to organize the accounts before going to Lisbon.[60] According to GCGPM members in Lisbon, the practice of calling agents (regardless of where they were) to account for their "greatest companions" in Portugal had already been provided for by law since 1594.[61] Vieira da Silva ended up having his assets confiscated by governor Joaquim de Melo e Póvoas in 1778 after an investigation was carried out against him due to poor management in the company.[62] However, in June 1780, the GCGPM

56 "Tão mal até agora tem servido esta companhia".
57 ANTT. CGGPM. Copiador de cartas para o Maranhão, livro 230, f. 264–265.
58 "Desempenhado mas ainda opulento e grandemente abastado".
59 ANTT. CGGPM. Copiador de cartas para o Maranhão, livro 230, f. 264–265.
60 AHU, códice 598, f. 12–12v e 13.
61 AHU, códice 598, f. 13v.
62 ANTT. CGGPM. Copiador de cartas para o Maranhão, livro 230, f. 312–313. Carreira, *A Companhia Geral do Grão-Pará e Maranhão*, 1:287.

Board approved the accounts of Bonifácio José Lamas and José Vieira da Silva, certifying that they served the Company "with all zeal and truth." Melo e Castro then asked the governor to stop confiscating José Vieira da Silva's assets.[63]

In February 1778, the Board informed the governor that Queen D. Maria I had extinguished the monopoly of the GCGPM and thanked the governor for his efforts to assist the company throughout the period, asking, once again, for his assistance in charging the indebted residents. They declared that shipments of products to the captaincy were ceasing and that they would only concern themselves with recovering capital from the hands of debtors. The Board took the opportunity to communicate that it was firing managers Marçal Inácio Monteiro and Luís Antônio Ferreira de Araújo since they were more interested in personal gains than in the good of the company. In the future, both would be accused of robbing the company by judge Miguel Marcelino Veloso e Gama in 1778, in a process that lasted until 1783. Marçal, however, continued to cause problems in the captaincy when he was accused of disturbing public peace in 1784 by Governor José Teles da Silva.[64] All these cases show how conflicted the relationship with the GCGPM agents in the colony was.

10 The End of the Monopoly and Debt Collection

The termination of the GCGPM monopoly is intrinsically connected to Pombal's exit from the government and the political movement aimed at reversing his actions. Martinho de Melo e Castro, one of the few allies of Pombal who remained in the new government of D. Maria I, was one of the people in favor of the monopoly's continuation. One of the opponents of the extension of the monopoly was Marquis of Angeja. The option for the extinction of the company's monopoly prevailed.[65] The detailed reasons for the end of the monopoly are still uncertain. Still, the justification certainly involved the complaints of residents in the colony that denounced the practices that they considered extortion on the part of the GCGPM, namely because of debt collections. Furthermore, according to them, the company sold European products at high prices and bought tropical products at low prices. Another reason for ending the monopoly was certainly the opposition of other merchants who sought to occupy a space that would eventually be empty with the end of the monopoly.

63 "com todo o zelo e verdade"; see AHU, códice 598, f. 17v, f. 188v–189.

64 ANTT. CGGPM. Copiador de cartas para o Maranhão, livro 230, f. 334–335. AHU_ACL_CU_009, Cx. 52, Doc. 5020. Cx. 57, Doc. 5321. Cx. 60. Doc. 5515. Cx. 64, Doc. 5688.

65 Kenneth Maxwell, *Conflicts and Conspiracies: Brazil and Portugal, 1750–1808* (1973; Routledge, 2004), 62.

It is also necessary to keep in mind that The General Trade Company of Pernambuco e Paraíba (GCPP) faced problems similar to GCGPM. The complaints from its residents, together with pressure from other merchants, certainly strengthened the chorus for ending the monopolies established by Pombal. The GCGPM had its monopoly ended in 1778 and the GCPP in 1780.

The end of the monopoly, however, did not mean the end of the GCGPM. The enterprise would still have to conclude past negotiations and charge debtors, most of them in Maranhão. To do this, the Board needed a survey with the names of the indebted residents, indicating whether they were able to pay the debts. The elaboration of such a list was a challenge because the managers in Maranhão were late in doing the survey, due to apparently opportunistic attitudes. But the list of debtors in Maranhão eventually ended up being made and was sent to Lisbon in May 1779. A very revealing scenario emerges from its data regarding the economic activities of the captaincy (Table 1.4). Total debts, excluding interest, totaled 322,410,664 *réis*. Of the 420 debtors, the list gives the occupations of 319. The planters, by far, were the most numerous, as well as their debts, which were the largest compared to the other indebted residents. Merchants were a significant group on the debtors' list but no less remarkable than individuals directly linked to the GCGPM, such as clerks and administrators. Planters could also own tanneries, so they were sometimes classified as "manufacturers." Some military personnel were certainly planters, although the documentation ignores this. The field "without classification" is made up of several debtors who were no longer alive, and many had gone bankrupt. Of

TABLE 1.4 Social sectors indebted to the GCGPM in Maranhão, 1779

Social sectors	Number of people	Debts (*réis*)
Company administrators	4	12,625,975
Company clerks	7	7,911,865
Merchant-planter	5	4,777,704
Manufacturer and planter	4	40,242,154
Planter	183	136,608,333
Merchant	24	22,184,455
Military	29	15,145,237
Without classification	101	54,816,530
Other social sectors	63	28,098,411
Total	**420**	**322,410,664**

Source: AHU, ACL, CU, 009, Cx. 54, Doc. 5123. Table prepared by the author.

the 420 debtors, 30 had already died, some leaving assets or having heirs who could help pay the debts that added up to 20,662,515 *réis*. Of the 420, 21 were bankrupt, leaving debts of 5,048,215 *réis*. In this field, we can also find one of the biggest debtors, the governor of the captaincy, Joaquim de Mello e Póvoas. The "other social sectors" indebted to the GCGPM were made up of priests, magistrates, carpenters, sailors, etc.

This list is crucial since it provides us with a kind of census of the population of planters and merchants in the captaincy, even though not all residents of Maranhão were indebted to the GCGPM. It is also important data because many of the debtors in 1779 were active economic agents during the time of the monopoly and would be essential figures in the time of free trade.

If we would try to trace the evolution of debts in Maranhão, we would see that 1779 was not the year with the highest values. As far as it is possible to know (and here it is unknown whether the total debt included interest), the indebtedness of the residents of Maranhão toward the GCGPM followed the trajectory shown in Table 1.5.

TABLE 1.5 Debts of residents of Maranhão to the GCGPM, 1767–1786

Year	Debts (*réis*)
1767	390,000,000[a]
1771	609,578,515[b]
1776	400,000,000[c]
1779	322,410,664[d]
1784	171,470,396[e]
1786	135,272,282[f]

Notes and sources:

a ANTT. CGGPM. Copiador de cartas para o Maranhão, livro 230, f. 132.

b ANTT. CGGPM. Cartas aos administradores do Maranhão, livro 215, f. 39–41.

c ANTT. CGGPM. Copiador de cartas para o Maranhão, livro 230, f. 276–277.

d AHU, ACL, CU, 009, Cx. 54, Doc. 5123.

e AHU, ACL, CU, 009, Cx. 61, Doc. 5563.

f AHU, ACL, CU, 009, Cx. 64, Doc. 5729, Cx. 67, Doc. 5844 e Cx. 68, Doc. 5939. During the years 1784, 1785 and 1786, the company managed to recover part of the debts; respectively the company was repaid in 15,241,433 *réis*, 12,674,236 *réis* and 8,282,445 *réis*. Therefore, at the end of 1786, there were 135,272,282 *réis* in debts in Maranhão that the company had not yet managed to collect. Table prepared by the author.

Despite the considerable embezzlement regarding unpaid debts, this did not hamper shareholders' profit margins. Carreira states that in 69 years (1755 to 1824), shareholders "received not only the capital invested but also 242.2% dividends—this in the worst case."[66] Two questions are immediately brought up by this fact: would profits have increased if there had been fewer frauds and reckless behavior? Did the company's accounting anticipate such losses and remedy them by augmenting profit margins on sales and purchases in both the colony and the metropolis? A comprehensive examination of the GCGPM accounting records may reveal the compelling case of a company that has incited considerable discontent while consistently achieving profitability and markedly enhancing the economic performance of a previously marginalized region.

11 Explaining the Company's Problems

Just as important is the question of why the residents of Maranhão did not cooperate with the company. Since there is no simple answer to this, it is wiser to explore a few hypotheses. One of the GCGPM's problems was that it prohibited the monopoly territory from doing business with merchants residing in other places, such as Rio, Bahia, and African ports. In the short term, this action favored the captaincy's economy, since the company restricted investments directly in the monopoly space, benefiting the economic groups there. Subsequently, these policies became unpleasant since colonial residents could not capitalize on their income in any way other than through the company's intermediation, which controlled prices and regulated credit lines, rates, and payment times as it wished. This explains, to some extent, why the colonials developed practices to evade the control of the company, such as the planters in Maranhão using third parties (wealthy planters and traders) either to not pay the debts to the GCGPM or to get better prices or better payment terms.

Another part of the explanation of the company's problems was probably rooted in its organizational framework. Few managers controlled a market volume and dealt with a considerably high number of customers. Two administrators in Maranhão managed and collected the debts of 488 debtors in 1767.[67] Although the number dropped to 420 debtors in 1779, the number of managers remained the same.[68] In addition, these managers had other obligations,

66 "receberam não só o capital investido, como também 242,2% de dividendos – isto na pior das hipóteses." Carreira, *A Companhia Geral do Grão-Pará e Maranhão*, 1: 304–5.

67 ANTT. CGGPM. Copiador de cartas para o Maranhão, livro 230, f. 160–161.

68 AHU, ACL, CU, 009, Cx. 54, Doc. 5123.

with their time also being devoted to tasks not linked to debt collection, such as taking care of the entry and exit of goods and enslaved people for a captaincy that held about 47,000 people.[69] These points are relevant when taking into account the contribution of organizational theorists with the maxim "the smaller the decision-makers"—in this case, the managers—"the less information they can process."[70] With this in mind, it is noteworthy that each manager in Maranhão was responsible for handling loans and debt collections for almost 244 people.[71] Theoretically, these organizational structures, composed of few members (both in Lisbon and São Luís), would reduce the information asymmetry among those responsible for the company.[72] At the same time, there was a mismatch between the members at both ends of the Atlantic, precisely because of the low processing of information by colonial managers.

Because of its large size—a large monopoly company that covered vast geographical areas, with a large number of customers and a considerable range of economic branches to manage—the small number of managers was probably unable to handle processing all of the operations. These operations touched on the slave trade, investments, and incentives in the productive sector. They also lacked the necessary management skills to deal with the market scenario that the colonial residents themselves developed to face the payment of debts owed to the company. This, however, does not mean that managers' dishonest and obscure attitudes should be excluded from the analysis. It just means that they must be placed within the economic scenario in which they were interacting, taking into account the configurations of the colonial market.

12 Conclusion

After analyzing the functioning of the GCGPM in Maranhão, the first obvious conclusion that emerges is that the residents did not cooperate with the company, and neither did the colonial managers. Despite the existence of merchants based in the colony, some planters actively participated in the export

---

69 Dauril Alden, *Royal Government in Colonial Brazil, with Special Reference to the Administration to the Marquis of Lavradio, Viceroy, 1769–1779* (University of California, 1968), 497.

70 Erikson, *Between Monopoly and Free Trade*, 78.

71 The number of debtors (488) in 1767 was divided by the managers (2) of the company in Maranhão.

72 This is a hypothesis presented by Angélica de Vasconcelos Silva when she analyzed the monopoly company for Pernambuco; see Angélica de Vasconcelos Silva, "Closing Doors (1780–1813): The Liquidation Process at General Company of Pernambuco and Paraíba" (PhD diss., Universidade de São Paulo, 2016), 134.

circuits of their cotton crops. The figure of the third party, who could be a wealthy planter or a merchant, emerges as a tactic in order not to pay the debts to the GCGPM. That is why planters associated themselves with other planters and merchants to circumvent the payment of debts. Excluding the opportunistic behavior of its managers, one of the major obstacles for the company was the presence of private merchants in the colonial regions. But suppressing them was unthinkable, as they were crucial to transport the crops of small producers to the port of export.

At the same time that residents were developing strategies for not paying their debts, colonial managers resorted to shady practices for their own benefit or to favor people close to them. As demonstrated, the company's Lisbon-based principals attempted to curb the opportunism of colony managers through a series of layoffs, but, ultimately, these actions were insufficient. However, the fact that the administration had inappropriate attitudes for the majority of the company's existence and that there were no effective policies in place to stop malpractice is evidence that the poor performance of the Maranhão agents was caused by more than just the agency's issues. If it were just agency problems, layoffs and incentives for managers would have probably had a more positive effect.

The chapter demonstrates that it is not enough just to consider the opportunistic behavior of colonial managers to understand the tortuous path followed by the company. Although these agents' attitudes had a considerable weight in the company's management, the company's performance was based on how colonial residents used the company's institutional loopholes, as well as on explicitly illicit attitudes, both to get better prices for their tropical products and to avoid paying debts. The crucial point about the GCGPM was not just an exercise in monitoring agents and providing incentives for them not to cheat. To fully understand how the company worked, it is necessary to take into account the existence of a series of local circumstances that were out of the control of managers in Maranhão and, above all, out of the control of the principals in Lisbon.

Notwithstanding its tumultuous history, it was through the GCGPM that the cultivation and exportation of cotton first originated in Maranhão, and afterward across Brazil. Following the dissolution of the GCGPM monopoly, the financing of growers through enslaved people and the interactions between merchants and planters via credit and debit relationships continued practically unchanged.

CHAPTER 2

The Golden Age of Cotton Growing in Maranhão and Its Elite

1 Growing Locations and Expansion

Maranhão was historically sparsely populated, with a limited enslaved African workforce, and no staple commodity to drive the economy as sugar did in other regions of Brazil. This may appear paradoxical, yet the captaincy's ability to yield substantial cotton, with consistent growth rates until the early nineteenth century, is largely attributable to its underdevelopment. As pointed out by Caio Prado Júnior, Maranhão grew out of nothing,[1] which meant that it possessed a kind of idle capacity that could be tapped. However, this does not imply that Maranhão's economy was irrelevant prior to cotton cultivation. Until the mid-eighteenth century, the workforce consisted of indigenous populations subjected to compulsory service regimes. Although small, production was targeted at the international market; the region produced *drogas do sertão* and cocoa. At the same time, its economy was somewhat isolated: Maranhão was poorly linked with the rest of Portuguese America while enjoying direct trading connections to Lisbon.[2] Still, from the 1750s onwards, the massive importation of enslaved people and the arrival of Portuguese landowners and slavers, all supported by the new political economy implemented by Pombal, completely changed its demographic structure. Its old precarious division of labor favored a small group of planters to undertake commercial functions, exporting their cotton crops and getting actively involved in the slave trade. In short, growers in Maranhão owned large plantations and could also be long-distance traders and slave traders. Simultaneously, merchants constituted a class primarily oriented toward commercial endeavors and played a vital role in providing planters with capital and enslaved laborers. In the absence of alternative credit institutions, such as banks, merchants became essential in supporting the cotton economy. At the onset of the nineteenth century, the three classes (merchant-planter, merchant, and planter) coexisted, occasionally

1 Prado Júnior, *História Econômica do Brasil*, 82.

2 Chambouleyron, "Conquistas diferentes e de diferentes climas"; Chambouleyron, *Povoamento, Ocupação e Agricultura na Amazônia Colonial*. See also John Hemming, *Red Gold: The Conquest of the Brazilian Indians* (Harvard University Press, 1978), 451, 477.

© 2026 THE AUTHOR(S) | HTTPS://DOI.ORG/10.1163/9789004757561-005

engaging in conflict. But compared to growers in Northeastern Brazil, the other Brazilian region that produced large amounts of cotton (which will be covered in chapters 3 and 4), the growers in Maranhão had a lot more power. The planters in Maranhão had many enslaved people, land, and great political power. In addition, they had connections in Portugal to trade their cotton crops. Cultivators in the Northeast lacked all this.

This chapter will explore the fundamental elements that explain the emergence and development of cotton culture in Maranhão after the monopoly of the GCGPM was ended: slave labor, the specialization of cotton cultivation in specific areas, the type of fiber grown and the wealth of the planters. Since wealthy planters were able to export their crops, this chapter will occasionally deal with commercial matters. A deepening of the exchanges between Maranhão and Portugal, though, will be fully addressed in Chapter 5.

The European industry's demand for raw cotton, coupled with difficulties in trade with the West Indies and the GCGPM's investments in enslaved labor and capital, propelled Maranhão's growth in the latter half of the eighteenth century. However, significant internal factors contributed to the expansion of the cotton economy. The geographical positioning of the plantations in Maranhão, the organization of labor among enslaved people, and the kind of cotton cultivated were pivotal for keeping high productivity levels.

If someone was to invest in cotton cultivation in Brazil in this period, they would probably look for land between the Itapecuru and Mearim rivers (Map 2.1). Since the beginning of the seventeenth century, the Portuguese were aware of the potential of the soil in the valley between these two rivers, mainly because of the tropical heat and abundant rainfall. It was not until the mid-eighteenth century, though, that farmers and merchants started cash crop plantations. Due to the valley's fertility, most of the cotton production in Maranhão originated from there. The Parish *Nossa Senhora do Rosário da Ribeira do Itapecuru* (66 kilometers from the port of São Luís) alone produced 87% of all the cotton exported by Maranhão in 1802.[3] However, some areas on the upper Mearim River, south of São Luís, and Alcântara and Guimarães, west of the capital, though smaller, were also suitable for growing cotton. Appropriate arable lands were utilized in the upper region of the Itapecuru River, particularly in Caxias, located 360 kilometers south of São Luís. This expansion occurred slightly later, yet by the early 1820s, Caxias generated over 50% of the total

3 For Parish data, see AHU, ACL, CU, 009, Cx. 134, Doc. 9861. Hawthorne, *From Africa to Brazil*, 27–29; for exports, see Diego de Cambraia Martins and Felipe Souza Melo, "Cotton Exports from Brazil, 1758–1815 Dataset" (European University Institute, HEC, 2022), https://cadmus.eui.eu/handle/1814/74724.

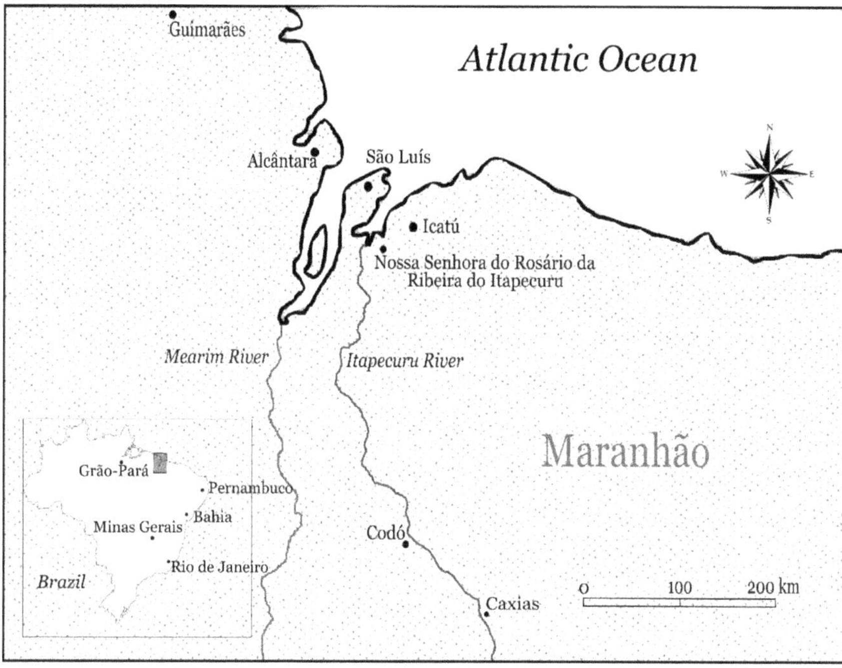

MAP 2.1 Cotton-growing areas in Maranhão at the beginning of the nineteenth century
Sources: This map is based on Raimundo Jose de Sousa Gayoso, *Compendio historico-politico*, 99–100, 162–64, 179; Pereira, "The Cotton Trade and Brazilian Foreign Commerce," 84–88. Map prepared by the author.

cotton output in the captaincy. In 1853/54, Itapecuru and Caxias comprised 74% of Maranhão's cotton production.[4] Despite growing some cotton, Alcântara, Guimarães, and Icatú focused on planting manioc, potatoes, corn, and beans.[5] Thus, the captaincy developed a specialization in cotton cultivation encompassing a few of its areas.

Rice was another important commercial crop. The benefit of rice was that it could be grown on most of the soil of the captaincy and could be planted

4 Pereira, "The Cotton Trade and Brazilian Foreign Commerce," 87; see also Francisco de Assis Leal Mesquita, *Vida e morte da economia algodoeira do Maranhão: uma análise das relações de produção na cultura do algodão, 1850–1890* (Universidade Federal do Maranhão, 1987); Johann Baptist von Spix and Carl Friedrich Philipp von Martius, *Viagem Pelo Brasil (1817–1820)* (1828; Senado Federal, 2017), 2: 358.

5 Matthias Röhrig Assunção, *De Caboclos a Bem-Te-Vis. Formação Do Campesinato Numa Sociedade Escravista: Maranhão 1800–1850* (Annablume, 2015), 32–33, 177.

side by side with cotton plants.[6] Cotton spacing between plants was a crucial factor for growers because it had a direct effect on food production. Such a feature was not limited to Maranhão. In Camamú, located on the southern coast of Bahia, cotton seeds were sown at distances of eight feet (2.43 meters). Due to the considerable distance, farmers intercropped food crops like corn and beans among the cotton plants to prevent land from remaining idle.[7] In Paraíba (where cotton was cultivated for Europe under the name *Pernambuco*), a farmer deemed it more suitable to plant at a distance of 14 feet (4.26 meters) apart. However, when planting in the backlands, he also suggested spacing plants six to eight feet (1.82 to 2.43 meters) apart.[8] A 1798 document reported that in Pernambuco, cotton plants were placed 15 feet (4.57 meters) apart.[9] This was unfeasible on the sugar cane plantation, as the canes were cultivated in close proximity to one another. To cultivate food for the sugar plantation, it was essential to grow crops in a separate location. Furthermore, manioc was especially suited to regions of the Northeast where sugar was not grown because of its exceptional durability under drought and capacity to flourish in unfavorable soil conditions. Farmers would not plant cheap manioc in places where they could plant valuable sugar cane.[10] Rice, though, was particularly important for feeding Maranhão. Between the seventeenth and eighteenth centuries, rice was increasingly associated with the diet of enslaved migrants and was second only to manioc. Animal protein constituted another food for enslaved people, and large planters who owned land with cattle could sacrifice animals to feed their enslaved workers with meat.[11] Rice was an essential commodity for Portugal as well. With wheat prices rising in Europe and the demand for rice to accompany fish dishes on Catholic holy days, Portugal increasingly encouraged rice cultivation in its colonies. Maranhão ended up

---

6 Antonio Bernardino Pereira do Lago, *Estatistica historica-geografica da Provincia do Maranhão oferecida ao Soberano Congresso das Cortes Geraes, extraordinarias, e constituintes da monarchia portugueza* (Academia Real das Sciencias, 1822), 46; Hawthorne, *From Africa to Brazil*, 161.

7 Bettencourt, *Memória Sobre a Plantação Dos Algodões, e Sua Exportação: Sobre a Decadencia Da Lavoura de Mandiocas, No Termo Da Villa de Camamú, Comarca Dos Ilhéos, Governo Da Bahia ...*, 14.

8 Câmara, *Memoria sobre a cultura dos algodoeiros*, 29.

9 AHU, ACL, CU, 015, Cx. 202\Doc. 13809.

10 Schwartz, *Sugar Plantations in the Formation of Brazilian Society*, 436; Stuart B. Schwartz, *Slaves, Peasants, and Rebels: Reconsidering Brazilian Slavery* (University of Illinois Press, 1992), 67.

11 Hawthorne, *From Africa to Brazil*, 143–44, 166–68.

being Brazil's leading producer, primarily because of the incentives and financing of the GCGPM.[12]

The growth of cotton and rice exports was based on the enlargement of arable areas. This development did not occur without serious problems for the environment and the indigenous populations, not to mention the inhumane conditions of the work performed by enslaved Africans. The way the land was prepared—slash-and-burn or *coivara*—its use, and fallow led producers to seek new ground for planting. Thus, the growth of Brazilian agricultural productivity was based on using new (more fertile) lands and abandoning old lands (which were losing their fertility over time).[13] Although this process took time to take on large proportions—Codó, for example, only began to be populated in 1840[14]—planters in Maranhão were "land-hungry," as Hawthorne pointed out.[15] An indication of this is the granting of *sesmarias* (royal land grants): about 95 grants of *sesmarias* (each with 50 square miles) were given to planters by King Dom José I, between 1750 and 1777. In the last 25 years of the eighteenth century, around 505 *sesmarias* were granted. Hawthorne succinctly encapsulated this process: "with capital from Lisbon and labor from Africa, planters fully exploited the lands around them. With no thought for long-term consequences, whites pressed blacks to clear jungles as fast as they could and to reclear them as soon as possible."[16] The maximum dimensions of a *sesmaria* donation were three leagues in length and one league in width; however, an individual could possess several large portions of it. The *sesmarias* themselves were of low value, at least in the period when the Crown was still donating them. But even so, legal disputes over land in Itapecuru were not uncommon. Once given by the Crown, the land could be sold by the owner or even rented out.[17] This expansion, however, clashed with the local indigenous populations. Around 1822, Lago noted that "on the S. Raymundo farm, belonging to Colonel

12 Hawthorne, *From Africa to Brazil*, 148; Arruda, *O Brasil no comércio colonial*, 395–96.

13 Lago, *Estatistica historica-geografica da Provincia do Maranhão*, 55–56; Prado Júnior, *Formação do Brasil contemporâneo*, 129–31; Maria Yedda Leite Linhares, "Pecuária, alimentos e sistemas agrários no Brasil (séculos XVII e XVIII)," *Arquivos do Centro Cultural Calouste Gulbenkian*, no. 34 (1995): 585–99; Hawthorne, *From Africa to Brazil*, 157–60.

14 Assunção, *De Caboclos a Bem-Te-Vis.*, 37.

15 Hawthorne, *From Africa to Brazil*, 160.

16 Hawthorne, 160; see also Sven Beckert et al., "Commodity Frontiers and the Transformation of the Global Countryside: A Research Agenda," *Journal of Global History* 16, no. 3 (November 2021): 435–50.

17 Mota, "A Dinâmica Colonial," 43–44, 55–56, 60; Guillermo Palacios, "Peasantry and Slavery in Brazil: A Contribution to the History of the Free Poor Planters from the General Captaincy of Pernambuco, 1700–1817. Volume II" (Ph.D., New Jersey, Princeton University, 1993), 385.

Manoel José Marques, 6 leagues into the Itapecuru River, the wild Indians killed 10 blacks, and mortally wounded four: these examples are frequent."[18] A little earlier, Koster pointed out that the large plantations in Maranhão were in danger because of attacks by indigenous peoples.[19]

As in the Northeast of Brazil, there were large planters and merchants in Maranhão who could centralize the harvest of other producers and small traders. The big ones in Maranhão could also lend money to small traders—or middlemen—to buy cotton. There were also those Portuguese who migrated to Maranhão only for a short time. They acquired enslaved workers, tools, and land and could even employ an overseer. They could make a fortune for a while and then return to Portugal. With so much migration, legal disputes were constant between planters over land in Itapecuru.[20]

2 The High Productivity of Enslaved People

Other aspects that explain the growth of the cotton culture lie in the demography of an underpopulated captaincy, the organization of slave labor, and the type of fiber grown there. We know that the captaincy's low population density was rapidly increased by the forced migration of thousands of enslaved people. This transfer was so successful that between 1777 and 1821, Maranhão held a slave labor force of around half its total population (Table 2.1), making this region a special case when considering all of Brazil, whose enslaved population comprised about one-third of all inhabitants.[21] The proportion of enslaved workers in the *Ribeira do Itapecuru* was even bigger. In 1803 enslaved people accounted for 84% (10,710 enslaved) of the region's population.[22] However, by the mid-1830s, significant demographic changes occurred: captive

18 "na Fazenda S. Raymundo, pertencente ao Coronel Manoel José Marques, 6 legoas para dentro do rio Itapecurú, os indios selvagens, lhe mataram 10 pretos, e feriram mortalmente quatro: são frequentes estes exemplos." Lago, *Estatistica historica-geografica da Provincia do Maranhão*, 58.

19 Henry Koster, *Travels in Brazil* (Longman, Hurst, Rees, Orme, and Brown, 1816), 171.

20 Mota, "A Dinâmica Colonial," 44, 75, 78–79.

21 For Brazilian demographic data, see Tarcísio R. Botelho, "A População Da América Portuguesa Em Finais Do Período Colonial (1776–1822): Fontes e Estimativas Globais," *Anais de História de Além-Mar*, no. 16 (January 2015): 79–106.

22 Raimundo Jose de Sousa Gayoso, *Compendio historico-politico dos principios da lavoura do Maranhão: suas producçoens, e progressos, que tem tido até ao prezente, entraves que a vão deteriorando; e meios que tem lembrado para desvanece-los, em augmento da mesma lavoura, e sem prejuizo do real patrimonio ...* (P.N. Rougeron, Impressor, 1818), 164.

TABLE 2.1 Number of enslaved people and the total population of Maranhão, 1763–1850

Years	Enslaved people	Free	Total
1777			47,410[a]
1780	23,541 (46.8%)	26,804 (53.2%)	50,345[b]
1798	36,877 (46.7%)	41,817 (53.1%)	78,694[c]
1808	51,918 (43.3%)	68,082 (56.7%)	120,000[d]
1821	84,534 (55.4%)	68,100 (44.6%)	152,634[e]
1835	49,953 (37.9%)	82,115 (62.1%)	132,068[f]
1850	96,716 (38.3%)	156,353 (61.7%)	253,069[g]

Sources:

a AHU, ACL, CU, 009, Cx. 52, D. 5014.

b Tarcísio R. Botelho, "A População Da América Portuguesa Em Finais Do Período Colonial (1776–1822): Fontes e Estimativas Globais," *Anais de História de Além-Mar*, no. 16 (January 2015): 100.

c Antonia da Silva Mota and Maísa Faleiros da Cunha, "No âmago da africanização: pessoas negras e de cor nos mapas populacionais do Maranhão colonial (1798–1821)," *Revista Brasileira de Estudos de População* 34, no. 3 (2017): 470.

d Botelho, "A População Da América Portuguesa," 96–97.

e Mota and Cunha, "No âmago da africanização," 470.

f Botelho, "A População Da América Portuguesa," 97.

g Tarcísio R. Botelho, "A população brasileira em 1850: uma estimativa," *Revista Economia e Políticas Públicas* 7, no. 2 (2019): 151. Table prepared by the author.

work declined sharply, causing the enslaved population to fall to less than 38% of its total inhabitants.

Data on *Nossa Senhora do Rosário da Ribeira do Itapecuru,* the central cotton-growing parish in Maranhão, provides valuable information about the number of planters and the average number of enslaved workers they owned (Table 2.2). The parish was responsible for 87% of Maranhão's exports and, additionally, it produced 165,788 arrobas of rice, 61% of total exports in 1802. Here we have a ratio of 31.5 enslaved workers per farmer (a total of 340 farmers), with each slave producing 18.8 arrobas of cotton. Although we do not have the production data, it is possible that the parish followed these patterns between 1803 and 1805.[23] This parish performed very efficiently (at least when compared with the Brazilian Northeast), with high productivity per enslaved

23 For 1802, see AHU, ACL, CU, 009, Cx. 134, Doc. 9861 and for exports see Melo and Martins. "Cotton Exports from Brazil, 1758–1815 Dataset." For data between 1803 and 1805, see Gayoso, *Compendio historico-politico*, 164.

TABLE 2.2 Demographic data from *Ribeira do Itapecuru* and estimates of the enslaved population employed in cotton cultivation in Maranhão

***Ribeira do Itapecuru* in 1802**[a]

Farmers	Slaves	Slaves per farmer	Arrobas of cotton	Arrobas per slave
340	10,740	31,5	202,316	18,8

Estimated number of slaves needed to produce the 277,028 annual averages of cotton arrobas exported in the 1800s[b]

First estimate (1802)	One slave – 18,8 arrobas of cotton[c] 14,735 slaves – 277,028 arrobas of cotton
Second estimate (1812/1813)	One slave – 12 arrobas of cotton[d] 23,085 slaves – 277,028 arrobas of cotton

Number of enslaved workers employed in cotton cultivation in Maranhão: 14,735 to 23,085 (27% to 44% of its total enslaved population in 1808)[e]

Notes and sources:
a AHU, ACL, CU, 009, Cx. 134, D. 9861.
b The annual averages were drawn from Melo and Martins. "Cotton Exports from Brazil, 1758–1815 Dataset."
c Based on data from the Ribeira do Itapecuru in 1802.
d Gayoso, *Compendio historico-politico*, 263–64.
e For demographic data, see Table 2.1. Table prepared by the author.

worker. Based on data from *Ribeira do Itapecuru* in 1802 and data presented by Gayoso in 1812–13, Table 2.2 also estimates how many enslaved people were needed to produce 277,028 arrobas of cotton, which was the annual average exported by Maranhão in the first decade of the nineteenth century. These estimates suggest that Maranhão necessitated about 14,000 to 23,000 enslaved workers to grow cotton, which meant between 27% and 44% of its total enslaved population in 1808.

According to Mota and Barroso, drawing on post-mortem inventories between 1785 to 1824, the vast majority of slave owners in Ribeira do Itapecuru owned more than 20 enslaved people, with a third of the farmers having more than 100 captives.[24] Therefore, the pattern of slave ownership in Maranhão

24 Antonia da Silva Mota and Daniel Souza Barroso, 'Economia e demografia da escravidão no Maranhão e no Grão-Pará: uma análise comparativa da estrutura da posse de cativos

was high and it is reasonable to assume that planters in Maranhão, precisely because of their large plantations, brought into play a labor organization based on slave gangs that augmented slave productivity.[25] In the early nineteenth century, Henry Koster—an English merchant in Brazil—noticed that "there exists at St. Luiz a great inequality of ranks; the chief riches of the place are in the hands of a few men who possess landed property to a great extent [and] numerous gangs of slaves."[26] Also linked to economies of scale, plantations in Maranhão should have a greater presence of overseers. Small properties, like those in Northeastern Brazil—which I will deal with in the next chapter—could not afford complex and optimizing ways of organizing labor and the presence of supervisors, because of the low amount of labor per production unit and because the farmer himself acted as an overseer.[27]

Maranhão also benefited from a spatial division of labor. The main cotton-producing region, Ribeira do Itapecuru, produced and consumed 18,477 *alqueires*[28] of manioc flour in 1802.[29] However, it was too little, and according to Gayoso, the Ribeira was not a place that produced a lot of manioc.[30] This supports the hypothesis that Ribeira was a place that specialized in cash crop plantations—although the rice it produced could be consumed by its inhabitants. Overall, it depended on other producers—probably located in Guimarães and Icatú—to be fed.[31] We could also assume that, with larger plantations, it was cheaper to buy food from other places. In Maranhão, the lack of manioc flour was rare, at least during most of the period covered here. In 1792, its

(1785–1850)," *Revista de História*, no. 176 (January 2017): 14; Pereira, "Poor Man's Crop?," 636.

25 For gangs, see Fogel and Engerman, *Time on the Cross*, 203–4; Robert William Fogel, *Without Consent or Contract: The Rise and Fall of American Slavery* (W. W. Norton & Company, 1989).

26 Koster, *Travels in Brazil*, 171–72.

27 Jacob Metzer, "Rational Management, Modern Business Practices, and Economies of Scale in the Ante-Bellum Southern Plantations," *Explorations in Economic History* 12, no. 2 (1975): 124; David Beck Ryden argued that the cotton farms on the island of Carriacou, in the West Indies, presented positive economies of scale in planting. See David Beck Ryden, ""One of the Finest and Most Fruitful Spots in America": An Analysis of Eighteenth-Century Carriacou," *The Journal of Interdisciplinary History* 43, no. 4 (2013): 567.

28 1 alqueire was equal to approximately 13 liters; see Luis Seabra Lopes, "Sistemas Legais de Medidas de Peso e Capacidade, do Condado Portucalense ao Século XVI," *Portvgalia* XXIV (2003): 155. A different source indicates that 1 alqueire was equivalent to 1 bag; see Antonio de Moraes Silva, *Diccionario Da Lingua Portugueza – Recompilado Dos Vocabularios Impressos Ate Agora, e Nesta Segunda Edição Novamente Emendado e Muito Acrescentado, Por Antonio de Moraes Silva* (Typographia Lacerdina, 1789), 105.

29 AHU, ACL, CU, 009, Cx. 134, Doc. 9861.

30 Gayoso, *Compendio historico-politico*, 223.

31 For the cultivation of manioc in Maranhão, see Assunção, *De Caboclos a Bem-Te-Vis.*, 183–84.

governor reported that the culture of manioc flourished like the cultures of cotton and rice.[32] The production of manioc flour was so abundant in Maranhão that even exports were possible. Apparently, the first moment of difficulty was in 1799 when the governor declared that he would not be able to send manioc flour to Portugal because the quantity was barely enough to supply the colony.[33] Yet, in 1801 and 1821, Maranhão was producing manioc not only to feed its population but also to be exported.[34] The food supply crisis in 1816–19, in turn, affected the capital of São Luís more than the cotton-growing areas of *Ribeira do Itapecuru*.[35] And based on reports from the 1810s, Caio Prado Júnior—while admitting that Maranhão suffered from a lack of food, as farmers were mostly interested in planting cotton—argued that the region's enormous rice production helped circumvent the scarcity problems.[36] Wide and severe food supply crises reached Maranhão only in the 1820s and 1830s.[37]

The type of fiber grown and harvested there certainly had an impact on boost cotton exports. The size of the cotton staple in Maranhão was smaller compared to that of the Northeast.[38] And the longer the staple, the longer the picking.[39] In theory, Brazilian cotton varieties would follow this rule. Therefore, the high productivity of enslaved workers in Maranhão compared to the Northeast can also be attributed to the harvesting of shorter fibers, even though Maranhão fiber was large when compared to other fibers from the West Indies, for example. Another reason associated with the inherent characteristics of the cotton plant was that despite both Maranhão and Northeast cotton being of the *Gossypium barbadense* species, they exhibited varying levels of productivity. According to the accounts of German explorers Spix and Martius, the

32 AHU, ACL, CU, 009, Cx. 80, Doc. 6775.

33 AHU, ACL, CU, 009, Cx. 102, Doc. 8250.

34 Assunção, *De Caboclos a Bem-Te-Vis.*, 469–70.

35 Matthias Röhrig Assunção, "Exportação, mercado interno e crises de subsistência numa província brasileira: o caso do Maranhão, 1800–1860," *Estudos Sociedade e Agricultura* 14 (2000): 47.

36 Prado Júnior, *Formação do Brasil contemporâneo*, 159.

37 Assunção, "Exportação, mercado interno," 48; see also Assunção, *De Caboclos a Bem-Te-Vis.*, 258–68.

38 Pereira, "The Cotton Trade and Brazilian Foreign Commerce," 65; Gayoso, *Compendio historico-politico*, 312.

39 Historians observed this association when they compared the act of picking long fibers, such as Sea Island cotton, with the median fibers of upland cotton; see Kenneth M. Stampp, *Peculiar Institution: Slavery in the Ante-Bellum South* (Vintage, 1956), 46; Olmstead and Rhode, "Biological Innovation," 1131. See also Philip D. Morgan, "Task and Gang Systems: The Organization of Labor on New World Plantations," in *Critical Readings on Global Slavery*, ed. Damian Alan Pargas and Felicia Roşu (Brill, 2017).

production of one pound (0.45 Kg) of ginned cotton in the Northeast required four pounds (1.8 Kg) of seed cotton, whereas in Maranhão, three pounds (1.3 Kg) were sufficient. Put simply, the cotton tree in Maranhão exhibited higher productivity compared to its counterpart in the Northeast.[40]

Thus, what explains Maranhão's exceptional performance was a combination of factors: the low demographic density in the early 1750s helps to explain the large number of enslaved people in the captaincy and the concentration of plantations in the hands of a few white owners. The cultivation of a specific cotton plant certainly helped to increase productivity. This last factor, together with the specialization of cotton cultivation in Ribeira do Itapecuru and the employment of gangs of enslaved people, were different from those elements present in the Northeast. The case of the Northeast will be dealt with in the next chapter, but it is important to make it clear that one of the main causes that limited its productivity was the fact that cotton and food were grown on the same plots of land by free poor farmers who used few enslaved people. They were not rich like the Maranhão farmers, who could buy food from elsewhere. Furthermore, this configuration impacted the commercial circuit: the wealthy planters in Maranhão were able to export their crops and became involved in the slave trade. Small growers in the interior of the Northeast had no way of participating in these businesses.

A further factor that influenced productivity was technology. Ginning was arguably one of the most critical processes in the cotton production chain; the labor intensity involved in separating the seeds from the lint and the quality of the remaining fiber significantly influenced the final cost of the product. The processes of bagging and pressing were also important. Despite possessing substantial wealth, rich planters and merchants in Maranhão refrained from investing in improvements that would improve the cotton economy, opting instead for the traditional way of acquiring more land and enslaved people. Consequently, developments in ginning, bagging, and pressing were of minimal interest to the wealthy residents of Maranhão. Gayoso asserts that cotton ginning was performed manually until 1795;[41] however, he may be overstating this claim, as planters prior to that time likely possessed knowledge of ginning machines. It can be determined from various sources that enslaved workers operated a famous mechanism featuring two cylinders that rotated in opposing directions: one cylinder facilitated the passage of fiber, while the other retained the seed. This gin was called *jaboty* but also had other names in Brazil. In Pernambuco and Bahia, for example, it was called *bolandeira* and *roda de*

40 Spix and Martius, *Viagem Pelo Brasil (1817–1820)*, 2: 359.

41 Gayoso, *Compendio historico-politico*, 313.

mão. This machine most likely originated in South Asia or the Middle East in the sixth century; it was called *Churka* (Figure 2.1), and in the twelfth century, it was present in much of the Indian subcontinent. It was based on the "roller system" as opposed to Eli Whitney's famous "system based on a cylinder filled with wire teeth" invented in the 1790s.[42] Since the seventeenth century, the roller gin could be found in Brazil, where it was used in the sugar mills and to prepare manioc.[43] It was not until the end of the eighteenth century that it was adopted to gin cotton. Of course, this machine was subject to adaptations, and its functioning could vary. Sometimes it required two enslaved workers, one to move the cylinders, either through a handle or by large wheels, and another worker to pass the cotton between the cylinders. In the British West Indies, all this work was done by a single person, as enslaved people could move the cylinders with their feet.[44] There were about 500 *jaboty* machines in 1820 in Maranhão, and they could gin two *arrobas* of cotton a day.[45]

The roller gin was used in the ginning process across Brazil and while it was not as productive as the saw gin, it was a better machine for long fibers from the Northeast and Maranhão. The use of the saw gin was absent in Brazil; for a long time, its use was basically restricted to upland cotton in the USA.[46] Whitney's ginning machines were only set up in Maranhão after 1835, when planters were starting to plant upland cotton. Both devices had their problems, though. With the *jaboty*, fragments of the seeds were often broken and mixed with the fiber, which resulted in dirty pieces of cotton. This required more cleaning work for the enslaved workers. Conversely, Whitney's machine "did not preserve the entire fiber length," resulting in an inferior quality of cotton.[47] There was not much that could be done about ginning. During the time period

42 Riello, *Cotton*, 50; see also Angela Lakwete, *Inventing the Cotton Gin: Machine and Myth in Antebellum America* (Johns Hopkins University Press, 2003).

43 Francisco Augusto Pereira da Costa, *Anais Pernambucanos. Vol. VII.* (FUNDARPE, 1983), 238; Lycurgo de Castro Santos Filho, *Uma Comunidade Rural Do Brasil Antigo: (Aspectos Da Vida Patriarcal No Sertão Da Bahia Nos Séculos XVIII e XIX)* (Ed. Nacional, 1956), 275.

44 Câmara, *Memoria sobre a cultura dos algodoeiros*, 63–64; Koster, *Travels in Brazil*, 367.

45 Assunção, *De Caboclos a Bem-Te-Vis.*, 195.

46 Stampp, *Peculiar Institution*, 46; Karen Gerhardt Britton, *Bale o' Cotton: The Mechanical Art of Cotton Ginning* (Texas A&M University Press, 1992), 39; Lakwete, *Inventing the Cotton Gin*, 176; Assunção, *De Caboclos a Bem-Te-Vis.*, 195–96; Mesquita, *Vida e morte da economia algodoeira*, 113; Luiz Cordelio Barbosa, "Cotton in 19th Century Brazil: Dependency and Development" (PhD diss., University of Washington, 1989), 51–52; Koster, *Travels in Brazil*, 367; Gorender, *O Escravismo Colonial*, 138–39.

47 Assunção, *De Caboclos a Bem-Te-Vis.*, 195–96; Mesquita, *Vida e morte da economia algodoeira*, 113; Barbosa, "Cotton in 19th Century Brazil," 51–52; Koster, *Travels in Brazil*, 367; Carvalho, *Ascensão e Crise Da Lavoura Algodoeira*, 116–17.

FIGURE 2.1 The Churka in India and an old cotton gin in Brazil
Source: The image on the left is an Indian churka. The image on the right is an old cotton gin in Cuiabá, Mato Grosso (no date). Sources: James Talboys Wheeler, *Hand-Book to the Cotton Cultivation in the Madras Presidency* (Virtue bros. & co., 1863), 16–17; Sérgio Buarque de Holanda, *Caminhos e Fronteiras* (1956; Companhia das Letras, 2001), 126–27.

covered in this book, there was simply no technology that could gin cotton more effectively than the roller gin.

Bagging, in turn, was expensive because it required a large amount of cloth. Maranhão had, around the end of the 1810s, 230 looms that made coarse fabrics not only for the clothes of enslaved people but also for making bales. They were looms that were most likely located inside the plantations. After that came the pressing process, which was done by the enslaved worker "who put himself inside the sack and pressed the cotton in the bottom with the strength of his feet and weight." It was a degrading process for the worker because of the heat and inefficiency: it took an enslaved worker a whole day to bag and press 100 kg of cotton. It was not until around 1820 that large planters began to use presses.[48]

Cotton was ginned in Maranhão because the cost of labor was lower there than in Portugal. And since the owner of the cotton (in Brazil or Portugal) was the person who paid for the freight, he pressed (or asked someone to do it for him) the bales in the colony precisely to save on transatlantic shipping. According to Mota, planters' inventories claimed to have "ginning mills and bagging looms." In 1816, for instance, Pedro Miguel Lamagnère had eight

48 Assunção, *De Caboclos a Bem-Te-Vis.*, 196; Lago, *Estatistica historica-geografica da Provincia do Maranhão*, 64.

cotton ginning machines, each worth 800 *réis*. He also had "two cloth weaving looms," each costing 2,000 *réis*. Yet, Postmortem inventories show that bagging in Maranhão was done without machines. It was only in the second decade of the nineteenth century that tools for "bagging" and a "cotton press" were adopted.[49] The first cotton press in the city of São Luís was only installed in the late 1810s.[50]

These cotton processing stages and their machines were also found in the Northeast. Yet there were a handful of traders who managed to monopolize the ginning and bagging process, making them a very important group for the history of cotton. Gayoso, a planter in Maranhão, stated that the distances from the plantations to the port varied between five and 29 kilometers.[51] Bales of cotton in the Northeast had to be transported over much greater distances. I will elaborate on these points in the section dedicated to the Northeast. The important thing to keep in mind here is that in Maranhão, the planters themselves did the ginning, bagging, and pressing on their plantations, even if it was an archaic and inefficient process.[52] They did so because they had large plantations with many enslaved workers. In contrast, the small farms in the Northeast of Brazil, with their few slaves and capital, favored the development of intermediaries who owned gins and presses.

3 Wealthy Planters and Their Trade Links

Once the productive aspects of cotton are covered, it is possible to look more carefully at the agrarian elite that most benefited from the economic boom and how they commercialized their crops. Planters and merchants in Maranhão could send cotton to Portugal in two ways: at his own risk to an agent in Portugal, or to a merchant in Portugal who asked for cotton. In the latter case, the risk belonged to the merchant in Portugal, and the planter or merchant in Maranhão worked only as an agent. The merchants in Portugal, through their nearest connections within the marketplaces of Lisbon and Porto, knew who the trusted planters and merchants were in Brazil. At the beginning of the nineteenth century, this knowledge of the most reputable men was perhaps

49 Mota, "A Dinâmica Colonial," 137–39.
50 Viveiros, *História do Comércio do Maranhão 1612–1895*, 1: 242.
51 Gayoso, *Compendio historico-politico*, 287.
52 In the 1810s, ginning cotton cost at least 200 réis per arroba. The bagging was 320 réis per bale. And the freight from the plantation to the port could reach 460 réis per bale; see Gayoso, *Compendio historico-politico*, 287.

common, so much so that lists of merchants in the different marketplaces of the Empire were published in the Lisbon Almanach. Some editions of this periodical provided extensive lists of traders in the main Portuguese ports around the world.[53] In the 1805 edition, there is a list of 32 merchants in Maranhão. Through it, it is possible to glimpse part of the mercantile group that exported cotton and its links with cotton cultivation and the slave trade. Of the total, it was possible to obtain information on 23 of them: at least nine were landowners in Maranhão, and the others were only merchants or merchants with military titles who possibly owned land (Table 2.3).

From the list, some of the key names linking plantations in Brazil, cotton merchants, and the slave trade emerge. One of them is Ricardo Nunes Leal. He was based in Lisbon, and at least since 1774, he had been in Maranhão buying

TABLE 2.3 Merchants and planters in Maranhão in 1805

Merchant	Merchant
Antônio José Basto	Joaquim José de Siqueira
Antônio José Gonçalves Cascaes	João Bento de Brito
Antônio José Meireles*	João Ignacio de Figueiredo
Antônio Pinto Machado Lobo	José da Costa Oliveira
Antônio Rodrigues de Miranda*	José Gonçalves da Silva*
Aureliano Antônio Florêncio	José Joaquim Ferreira Neto
Balthazar Pereira Viana	José dos Santos Henriques Castelão
Caetano Alberto da Rocha	Luis da Rocha Compasso*
Caetano José Teixeira*	Luis Nogueira de Sousa
Custódio Barbosa de Carvalho	Luis Manuel da Fonseca Morato
Custódio Gonçalves Bastos	Manuel Álvares da Silva Bastos*
Fernando Antônio da Silva	Manuel José Avelino
Francisco José da Costa	Manuel João Correa de Sousa
Francisco José de Souza	Manuel José Ribeiro da Cunha
Joaquim Clemente Duarte	Mathias João Teixeira
Joaquim José Gomes*	Ricardo Nunes Leal*

Source and notes: Almanach de Lisboa de 1805, 505–512. *Merchant and planter. I determined that some of these merchants were also planters through some AHU and ANTT documents. Table prepared by the author.

53 See, for instance, *Almanach de Lisboa de 1805*, 505–512.

enslaved workers, probably drawn to the colony because of the GCGPM. He was in debt to the company and worked as its clerk in 1779. By 1783, however, he was regarded as a reputable man of business. In addition to having three houses, he had a rice mill and a plantation with more than 80 enslaved workers who grew plenty of rice and cotton.[54] In 1796, Leal described himself as a grower of uncultivated lands, owner of many enslaved people, and a notable vassal who promoted agriculture and commerce.[55] To some extent, part of Leal's time in Maranhão revolved around the activity of getting land. In 1788, he, along with Joaquim Antônio de Launé, Feliciano dos Santos, Manuel Antunes do Rosário, Manuel José Marques Guimarães, Manuel Rodrigues Mina, and Bernardo José dos Santos, owned more than 700 enslaved workers. They possessed land in Itapecuru and were disputing over some of it with another farmer, José de Carvalho, who had just under a hundred enslaved workers.[56] In 1789, Leal along with Feliciano dos Santos were in conflict over land in the Itapecuru forest with Antônio da Cunha Sanches and his attorney Antônio José de Brito. At that point, there were lands in Itapecuru that, despite having owners, were not adequately demarcated or cultivated.[57] Apparently, a good argument for getting land from the Crown was to show the possession of a large number of enslaved people. Still, in 1789, Leal owned a square league near the Itapecuru River.[58]

At the end of his life, when he wrote his will in 1810, Leal left a reasonably detailed account of his possessions. In addition to his various properties in the city of São Luís, he had "three slave plantations in *Ribeira do Itapecurú*": the *Livramento* plantation with half a league in front and one in the back, the *Goanaré* with a square league, and the *Nossa Senhora do Rosário* in Caxoeira Grande, also with a square league. He had a farm—though not a plantation—in Ribeira do Itapecuru, also called Goanaré. He also owned land in Mearim, some in partnership with the heirs of Feliciano dos Santos and others still in the process of being shared with the heirs of Antônio da Cunha Sanches. In addition to all of that, he had a few cattle on the lands of Maracú. Leal, however, did not bear all the risk nor receive all the profit from these undertakings, as he was in a partnership with João Bento de Brito "in half of all businesses, crops, and cattle ranches."

54 Dias, *Fomento e Mercantilismo: A Companhia Geral Do Grão Pará e Maranhão (1755–1778)*, 1: 483–84. See also AHU, ACL, CU, 009, Cx. 54, Doc. 5123 and Cx. 60, Doc. 5495.

55 AHU, ACL, CU, 009, Cx. 92, Doc. 7604.

56 AHU, ACL, CU, 009, Cx. 73, Doc. 6272.

57 AHU, ACL, CU, 009, Cx. 74, Doc. 6389.

58 AHU, ACL, CU, 009, Cx. 73, Doc. 6324.

In previous years, Leal had partnered with José Xavier Faustino Ramos (with a quarter interest) and Joaquim José de Santiago (also with a quarter interest) in a shop in São Luís. When writing his will, he had another partnership with Joaquim José de Santiago, who was interested in a third of the profits. The capital of the company belonged entirely to Leal. His indigo factory, formerly owned by the GCGPM, was used for ginning rice in 1796.[59] Leal's interests also touched on ocean voyages and African coasts. He owned a third on the ship *Príncipe Atelante*, with partner Jerônimo José de Carvalho, one of the main importers of cotton in Lisbon (Appendix A). In 1810 this vessel was authorized to sail from Maranhão directly to Liverpool.[60] Leal no longer had a partnership with the partners of the ship *Asia*, but he still expected to receive some profits from this negotiation. He had accounts with several residents of Angola regarding shipments of enslaved Africans.

Leal, a Portuguese, was one of the leading slave traders in Maranhão, and, as pointed out, someone looking to expand his lands—nothing better for exemplifying the typical colonizer. When he died, part of his capital stayed in the colony, while the other was remitted to Portugal. As he had no children, he left all his assets to his three nephews, sons of his brother Antônio Rodrigues Leal: Ricardo, Alexandre, and Lourenço. In addition, he left legacies in money (113,400,000 *réis* in total) to various people and religious institutions. A good portion of his fortune ended up going to several of his sisters and nieces (58.2%), some in Portugal, and, in some cases, the inheritance intended to serve as a dowry for their marriages. Another part of Leal's wealth was distributed to several of his friends and acquaintances in Maranhão.[61] The case of Ricardo Nunes Leal is an example of the trajectory of the first men who ventured into the cotton business in Maranhão. His arrival in the colony was closely linked to the GCGPM. The resources provided by the company (its capital, enslaved workers, and agricultural tools) attracted many immigrants who wanted to become landowners.

Maranhão was a new agricultural frontier, drawing even naturalized Portuguese Europeans.[62] Perhaps because of the low population density, the first settlers, including those who arrived in Maranhão before the foundation of the GCGPM, ended up taking on various occupations, including combining mercantile activity (as well as the slave trade) with that of cultivation. One of

59 AHU, ACL, CU, 009, Cx. 92, Doc. 7604.

60 AHU, ACL, CU, 003, Cx. 40, Doc. 3199.

61 For the will of Ricardo Nunes Leal see ANTT, Feitos Findos, Juízo da Índia e Mina, Justificações Ultramarinas, Brasil, mç. 13, n.º 13.

62 Mota, "A Dinâmica Colonial," 17.

the most famous was Lourenço Belfort, mentioned in Chapter 1. In the first half of the eighteenth century, when some merchants and farmers in Maranhão were profiting from the cotton that was woven into cloth in the colony, Belfort was one of the few who opposed this measure. He exported a few bales of raw cotton in 1759, arising the wrath of some villagers profiting from the cotton weaving, causing him to flee to Portugal. Still, he quickly returned to Maranhão and became one of the prominent cotton planters during and after the GCGPM.[63] His family, along with others associated with him, had a significant influence on the economic, political, and social life of Maranhão until the mid-nineteenth century. Lourenço Belfort, however, arrived in Maranhão well before the foundation of the GCGPM. He was born in Dublin in 1708, moved to Portugal where he became Portuguese, and migrated to Maranhão. It is not known when he arrived in Brazil, but it was certainly before 1739, the year in which he appears in the sources participating in the slave trade of indigenous people. He and Antônio Gomes de Sousa were the first pioneers who began to settle in the lands of Ribeira do Itapecuru. There, Belfort established large-scale cotton and rice plantations and even had a cotton bale press machine. His other business was cattle, as he was one of the main traders in Maranhão dealing with hides. His fortune enabled him to buy urban buildings in São Luís. Belfort's influence extended to the political and military fields as well. He was made a councillor in the same city and achieved one of the highest military ranks, that of *mestre de campo*. He was also a cotton merchant with the famous Paulo Jorge in Lisbon as his attorney and agent.[64] Paulo Jorge had been a member of the GCGPM Board in 1760. At the same time, he purchased a great amount of cotton through the company's auctions to reexport it to France. In addition, Paulo Jorge also participated in the slave trade from Lisbon.[65]

Antônio Belfort was the most important son who succeeded Lourenço; although his sister Maria Madalena had a very interesting trajectory: a widow at an early age, she managed to run the business herself. Antônio increased the land he had inherited from his father through requests for *sesmarias*. Like many wealthy people in the colony, he became a councillor and tax farmer.[66] But perhaps the secret of the Belforts—as well as of other affluent

63 Hawthorne, *From Africa to Brazil*, 147.

64 Mota, "A Dinâmica Colonial," 21, 23–26, 101.

65 Carreira, *A Companhia Geral do Grão-Pará e Maranhão*, 1: 240–41; Diego de Cambraia Martins, "A Companhia Geral de Comércio Do Grão-Pará e Maranhão e Os Grupos Mercantis No Império Português (c.1755 – c.1787)" (PhD diss., Universidade de São Paulo, 2019), 260–61; Maximiliano M. Menz, *Senhor Da Morte: Capitalismo, Guerra e Tráfico de Escravos. Portugal, Angola e Brasil (1640–1771)* (HUCITEC, 2024).

66 Mota, "A Dinâmica Colonial," 103.

families in the colony and Europe—lay in the family alliances and the benefits derived from them. They helped each other either through political favors, as they had vacancies in the São Luís council, or strictly in the economic field: they could finance activities in the agricultural sector of their relatives, friends, and acquaintances through generous loans or donations, sales, and purchase of land. Lourenço Belfort, for instance, married one of his sisters-in-law to Antônio Gomes de Sousa, another wealthy settler. They had a son named José Antônio Gomes de Sousa. Again, like his father, he prospered: he had received several *sesmarias*, raised cattle, cultivated cotton, and rice, was a councilor in São Luís, and was the tax farmer for one of the central taxes of the captaincy, the collection of tithes from Itapecuru and Mearim. In 1787, already *mestre de campo*, he claimed to have more than 200 enslaved workers and to be one of the wealthiest men in Maranhão.[67] The Belfort family also allied themselves through some marriages with Pedro Miguel Lamagnère, a descendant of a Frenchman who settled in Maranhão in the first half of the eighteenth century. Lamagnère was also an influential landowner. At the beginning of the nineteenth century, he owned eight plantations with 267 enslaved people.[68]

Lamagnère had a son, Pedro Nolasco, who, in addition to owning *sesmarias* in Maranhão requested by his father,[69] was also a merchant in Lisbon participating in the slave and cotton trade. He held a company together with his brother, which went into bankruptcy because of the losses caused by the war against the French and Spanish in 1801. Through a judicial process, it is possible to see that the brothers had a very active business with Brazil, mainly with Maranhão. Adding up all their active debts (which amounted to 76,885,791 *réis*), 29,258,766 *réis* referred only to the debts (including goods and enslaved people) that several residents in Maranhão owed to them. In second place were bill debts (14,979,245 *réis*) which were owed by residents in London. The creditors of the Nolasco brothers were all Portuguese: Eusébio de Souza, Nicolau Joaquim das Merces, Nogueira e Companhia, Joaquim José Torcato de Barros, Francisco de Paula Nogueira, and Caetano José Pacheco. The brothers' connection with Maranhão crossed commercial borders. They had "property of noble houses built in the city of Maranhão,"[70] another in the village of Alcântara, and a farm with a lime factory and attached houses, movable assets that totalled 30,900,000 *réis*. They also owned a ship, the *Nossa Senhora do Rosário, São Macário*, which sailed between Maranhão and Lisbon. In addition, the brothers

67 Mota, "A Dinâmica Colonial," 28.
68 Mota, "A Dinâmica Colonial," 28–29, 42, 73.
69 Mota, "A Dinâmica Colonial," 28–29, 42, 73.
70 "propriedade de casas nobres edificadas na cidade do Maranhão".

had business in Bissau, most likely to carry out the slave trade. There, José da Silva Cardoso and João Lucas Cordeiro were their correspondents, owing 3,937,513 *réis* and 1,947,050 *réis* respectively.[71] Long before, in 1789, the brothers were very active in the business with Bissau, constantly shipping goods there, as reported by the Lisbon customs records and the powers of attorney they granted in the Lisbon notary offices.[72]

The wealth of these planters, who marketed their crops, was determined by the size of their land and the quantity of enslaved individuals they possessed or could organize to work on their plantations. Antonia da Silva Mota organized the list of *sesmarias* granted to the main families of Maranhão: Belfort, Gomes de Sousa, Lamagnère, and Vieira da Silva. Between 1771 and 1819, there were 58 concessions, a good part of them in Ribeira do Itapecuru, encompassing three leagues in length by one in width. The land gained through donation could later be put on the market by the recipients and their families. Of the 26 postmortem inventories referring to the Ribeira do Itapecuru, none of the owners had less than seven enslaved workers. It was customary for most of them to have more than 30 enslaved people on their plantations.[73]

Additional examples elucidate this process with greater clarity. Upon José Vieira da Silva's arrival in Maranhão around 1760 to serve as an agent for the GCGPM, he took the opportunity to acquire an extensive *sesmaria* in Ribeira do Itapecuru. He spent many years in the captaincy and his son, Luis Antonio Viera da Silva, born in Portugal, inherited and expanded his father's business, becoming Captain General of the Itapecuru region.[74] Still, with the increase in population, it is very likely that immigrants started with commerce and then moved on to agriculture. José Gonçalves da Silva (see Table 2.3) is an example. He was a debtor to the GCGPM in 1779 (classified as a merchant) and was one of the largest debtors in Maranhão in 1794. He had started as a merchant, including trading in slaves, and later migrated to rural investments, including cotton plantations with gins. Bento Gonçalves da Silva, his brother, seems to have done the same thing, as the two were partners.[75] It is possible that José Gonçalves da Silva got land and enslaved workers through the debts that the planters of Maranhão owed him. Unable to pay José Gonçalves da Silva with cotton and rice crops, planters were forced to hand over land, enslaved people, and equipment to him. In 1811, he owned several properties and about

71 ANTT, Feitos Findos, Conservatória Geral do Comércio, cx. 53, mç. 12, no. 7.

72 ANTT, Alfândega de Lisboa, Casa da Índia, liv. 315, f. 38 and ANTT, 10º CNL – cx. 25, liv. 134, f. 14v–15.

73 Mota, "A Dinâmica Colonial," 39–41, 43, 56.

74 Mota, "A Dinâmica Colonial," 29–30.

75 AHU, ACL, CU, 009, Cx. 54, Doc. 5123 and AHU, CU, 009, Cx. 84, Doc. 7093. Mota, "A Dinâmica Colonial," 83, 85–87.

250 enslaved workers. In his will, just for his partnership with his brother, he left 111,000,000 *réis*, and Silva would send another good amount of money to relatives in Portugal. According to Mota, José Gonçalves da Silva was the biggest businessman in Maranhão at that time. In second place was Antônio José Meireles, known for being a slave trader and who left a fortune of 370,000,000 *réis*.[76]

Most planters did not live in rural areas, though, but chose to live in their mansions in São Luís. "Almost two-thirds of the farmers in Maranhão were absentees," according to Mota. The fact that they lived in the capital favored them to participate more in the export business to market their crops. Residence in the city also came from the fact that these big planters were councilors.[77] For this reason, overseers were central in Maranhão: there were 102 of them in 1803.[78] A share of these rich merchant-planters were also holders of military titles. Like others in Brazil, and not just in Maranhão, rich men sought to insert themselves into political and military circles, whether in search of prestige and to raise their social status or merely to increase their economic power. Being councilors, for instance, allowed them to lay down political rules that could benefit their group.[79] Likewise, members of military orders in Brazil were exempt from paying the tithe. That is why many asked for titles and honors of this type, and because of this, the Crown was reluctant to grant them.[80] Having a military post in the colony also had crucial social implications. The militia, far from being solely responsible for the task of military defense, was an institution that sought to overcome and discipline the colonial populations. To exercise social control, militia members had to be wealthy and distinguished. They were people who benefited from the colonial system, and it was in their interest to maintain that order. Moreover, the militia positions gave them even more "prestige and power."[81] Perhaps because of this social, political, and economic prestige, these individuals became trusted merchants for investors and principals in Portugal. Their social standing earned them a good reputation in the eyes of merchants across the Atlantic. With their social position, political influence, and economic resources, these members of the colonial elite, to

76 Mota, "A Dinâmica Colonial," 83, 86–90, 93.

77 Mota, "A Dinâmica Colonial," 62–63, 69–70, 128–29.

78 Gayoso, *Compendio historico-politico*, 164.

79 On municipal councils in colonial Brazil see, Charles Ralph Boxer, *Portuguese Society in the Tropics: The Municipal Councils of Goa, Macao, Bahia, and Luanda, 1510–1800* (University of Wisconsin Press, 1965).

80 Schwartz, *Sugar Plantations in the Formation of Brazilian Society*, 275.

81 Nanci Leonzo, "As Instituições," in *Nova História Da Expansão Portuguesa. O Império Luso-Brasileiro, 1750–1822. Volume VIII*, 1a. edição, ed. Joel Serrão et al. (Editorial Estampa, 1986), 325.

some extent, made it possible to circumvent agency problems in long-distance trade.[82]

Planters with a lot of capital, like those who managed to be big tax farmers, had investments in Lisbon. The rural owner Bernardino José Pereira de Castro, with 37 enslaved workers on a plantation in Itapecuru, was a shareholder in a textile factory in Lisbon.[83] Some merchant-planters could even move to Portugal and run their business from there. Again, Lourenço Belfort when in Lisbon around 1776 received cotton from his son Antônio Belfort and his daughter Maria Madalena Belfort who lived in Maranhão.[84] This is also the case with Colonel Aires Carneiro Homem Souto Maior. He was a planter in 1779 and owed 5,302,762 *réis* to the GCGPM. He lived in Lisbon for a few years, where, among other things, he tried to sell cotton from his plantations in Maranhão to merchants based in Lisbon. The deal essentially involved the presence of attorneys and representatives in colonial marketplaces. In 1790, Carneiro Homem, with "an established house, goods, and farms on the Itapecuru River," agreed on a deal with the merchant resident in Lisbon, José Antônio Pereira, a well-known slave trader who also did business with Asia.[85] Carneiro Homem promised that his attorneys in Maranhão, Filippe Marques da Silva and Francisco Felix Carneiro, would deliver cotton ("500 arrobas of good quality cotton [...] from the Colonel's own crop")[86] to the attorney and correspondent of Antônio Pereira, the merchant Antônio José de Seixas, who, as we have seen, worked as a debt collector for partners in Lisbon as well. The Colonel was actually simply selling cotton to Pereira. But if cotton did not reach Pereira by the end of the same year, the Colonel would have to pay him with interest.[87]

4 Slave Trade and Slave Traders

Much has been said so far about the slave trade and some major slave dealers in Maranhão. But how exactly did the slave trade connect with the cotton trade?

82 Jesús Bohorquez, "Globalizar el sur: la emergencia de ciudades globales y la economía política de los imperios portugués y español: Rio de Janeiro y La Habana durante la era de las revoluciones" (PhD diss., European University Institute, 2016), 320–35.

83 Mota, "A Dinâmica Colonial," 77.

84 ANTT. CGGPM. Copiador de cartas para o Maranhão, livro 230, f. 256 and 283.

85 About José Antônio Pereira see J. Bohorquez and Maximiliano M. Menz, "State Contractors and Global Brokers: The Itinerary of Two Lisbon Merchants and the Transatlantic Slave Trade during the Eighteenth Century," *Itinerario* 42, no. 3 (2018): 403–29.

86 "500 arrobas de algodão em pluma de boa qualidade [...] da própria lavoura do Coronel".

87 ANTT, 6º CNL – Cx. 27, Liv 132. f. 61–61v.

Evidently, the sources of slave labor were a crucial element for the growth of the cotton economy. To a large extent, what happened in Maranhão during the height of cotton exports was a continuation of the patterns initially established by the GCGPM. Between 1756 and 1777, through the monopoly company, 9,799 Africans arrived in São Luís: 89.5% of them came from Guinea and 10.5% from Angola. From the end of the monopoly in 1778 until the end of the slave trade in the mid-nineteenth century, Maranhão, with some variations, continued this pattern of importing enslaved Africans, with Guinea figuring as its primary source of labor and Angola in second place. Pernambuco and Bahia were crucial suppliers of enslaved workers to Maranhão, re-exporting the captives that had come from Angola and *Costa da Mina* (Gold Coast) (Map 2.2). Between 1780 and 1820, Maranhão imported 63,184 enslaved Africans, an average of 1,541 workers per year disembarked in São Luís.[88] The slave trade dropped drastically from 1815 onwards when Portugal, under pressure from the British, prohibited its nationals from continuing the trade with Guinea.[89]

The prominent planters of Maranhão were not only interested in the cotton trade but also in the slave trade. This is what this set of documents shows us: several primary sources that list vessels that unloaded enslaved Africans in São Luís bring important information about almost 30,000 enslaved people and the connections between slave ships and those that carried cotton. Of the 27,118 enslaved people who arrived between 1781 and 1797, it is possible to know the ports of origin for 25,516. Of the 171 slave voyages that landed in São Luís, most came from Brazilian ports (Pernambuco and Bahia with 77 voyages) and the ports of Guinea (Bissau and Cacheu also with 77 voyages). Angola, with nine voyages and other smaller ports, made up the rest. Despite the share of re-export trade from the ports of Brazil, the ports of Guinea supplied the most enslaved workers to the plantations in Maranhão (Table 2.4).

By sorting out the origin of the enslaved Africans into two big blocks, it is clear that most of them came from Guinea (53%), which is widely known.[90] However, the part of the enslaved people brought from other parts of Brazil (Pernambuco and Bahia) and Angola constituted a considerable part of the workers transported to Maranhão (44%), a fact that historiography tends

88 Daniel B. Domingues da Silva, "The Atlantic Slave Trade to Maranhão, 1680–1846: Volume, Routes and Organisation," *Slavery & Abolition* 29, no. 4 (2008): 487. For the numbers of slave imports, see "Trans-Atlantic Database," Slave Voyages, https://www.slavevoyages.org/voyage/database.

89 Hawthorne, *From Africa to Brazil*, 2–3.

90 Dias, *Fomento e Mercantilismo: A Companhia Geral Do Grão Pará e Maranhão (1755–1778)*, vol. 1; Carreira, *A Companhia Geral do Grão-Pará e Maranhão*, vol. 1; Silva, "The Atlantic Slave Trade to Maranhão, 1680–1846"; Hawthorne, *From Africa to Brazil*.

MAP 2.2 The slave ports of Africa in the eighteenth century
Source: This map is based on Hawthorne, *From Africa to Brazil* and David Eltis, *The Rise of African Slavery in the Americas* (Cambridge University Press, 1999). Map prepared by the author.

not to pay much attention to. In terms of sales, Guinea's share was slightly higher, 58%, while that of Pernambuco, Bahia, and Angola was 39%.

According to the governor of Maranhão, re-exports from Brazilian ports consisted of enslaved Africans rejected by farmers (*escravos de refugo*) in Pernambuco and Bahia because of their poor health. They were enslaved workers who, despite being cheap, were sold for cash in Maranhão, which took money out of the captaincy. In 1785, the governor estimated that each vessel (usually *sumacas*)[91] from Pernambuco and Bahia took about 8,000,000 to 10,000,000 *réis* in cash from Maranhão. This money was crucial to buy cotton and rice

91 About the sumaca, see Evaldo Cabral de Mello, *Um Imenso Portugal. História e Historiografia* (Editora 34, 2008), 188–201.

TABLE 2.4 Origin of enslaved people arriving in Maranhão, 1781–1797

Origin	Enslaved people	Total sales (*réis*)	Vessels	Price per enslaved person (average)
Guinea				
Bissau	7,365	1,044,516,000	43	141,357
Cacheu	4,868	651,851,700	28	133,552
Guinea	1,192	118,961,300	6	97,071
Total	**13,425**	**1,815,329,000**	**77**	
Pernambuco, Bahia, and Angola				
Pernambuco	3,962	479,566,500	46	116,141
Bahia	3,754	427,790,000	31	114,568
Angola	3,616	305,554,660	9	85,456
Total	**11,332**	**1,212,911,160**	**86**	
Others				
Mozambique	371	59,360,000	1	160
Costa da Mina	184	29,440,000	1	160
Rio Grande do Norte	138	16,442,000	3	117,238
Malagueta	40	4,400,000	1	110
Aracati	13	1,430,000	1	110
Tapajé	13	1,187,000	1	91,308
Total	**759**	**112,259,000**	**8**	
TOTAL	25,516	3,140,499,160	171	

Sources: AHU, ACL, CU, 009: Cx. 58, Doc. 5353, Cx. 59, Doc. 5432, Cx. 61, Doc. 5562, Cx. 64, Doc. 5730, Cx. 67, Doc. 5843, Cx. 68, Doc. 5938, Cx. 70, Doc. 6112, Cx. 73, Doc. 6292, Cx. 75, Doc. 6429, Cx. 77, Doc. 6567, Cx. 79, Doc. 6718, Cx. 81, Doc. 6868, Cx. 84, Doc. 7042, Cx. 86, Doc. 7178, Cx. 89, Doc. 7404, Cx. 93, Doc. 7680 e Cx. 97, Doc. 7887. Table prepared by the author.

as the number of goods imported from Portugal was not enough to make the exchanges.[92] The higher price paid to enslaved people coming from Guinea than to those coming from Brazilian ports is shown below (Figure 2.2), also drawn from the vessel lists.

But who were the slave exporters, how did they trade, and what was the relationship between the slave trade in Africa with the cotton trade from Brazil?

92 AHU, ACL, CU, 009, Cx. 66, Doc. 5832; see also Hawthorne, *From Africa to Brazil*, 127.

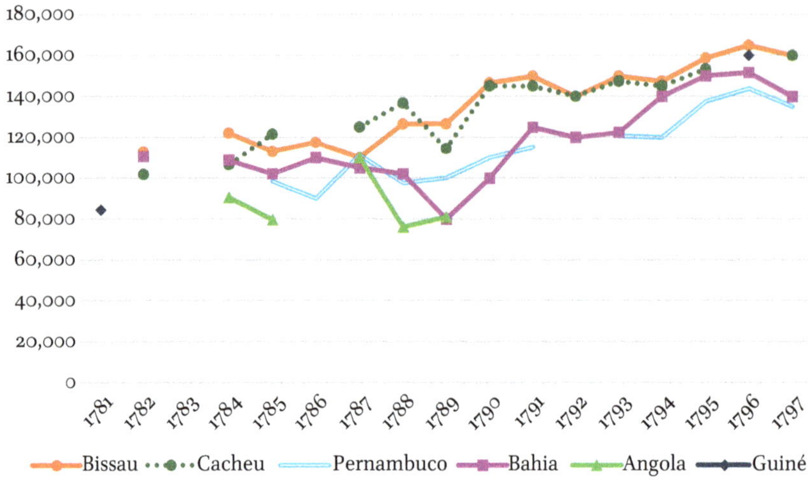

FIGURE 2.2 Prices of enslaved Africans in Maranhão, 1781–1797
Sources and notes: the same as in Table 2.4. Prices are in *réis*. Figure prepared by the author.

Most vessels that went to Upper Guinea (namely to the ports of Bissau and Cacheu) were Portuguese. They brought cloth, iron, weapons, gunpowder, rum, tobacco, and other items to exchange for enslaved Africans.[93] Access to supplies of enslaved people was relatively easy for the Portuguese, although this was not always the case. At the time when France and England came into conflict during the Seven Years' War (1756–1763), diminishing their interest in Upper Guinea, the Portuguese could participate extensively in the slave trade in the region.[94]

Conflicts between communities in the coastal area of Upper Guinea produced most of the enslaved who were later sent to Maranhão. According to Hawthorne, "slave production was not controlled by any one state or a single set of elites. Rather, slaves were captured during myriad small-scale raids launched by bands of young men, kidnappings carried out by 'evil-doers' from widely scattered places, and witchcraft trials conducted within countless communities." Still according to Hawthorne, although they filled the GCGPM vessels, the enslavement of people in the region did not have a negative impact on the demographics of these communities (contrary to what Walter Rodney

93 Hawthorne, *From Africa to Brazil*, 2.
94 Hawthorne, *From Africa to Brazil*, 61.

and Boubacar Barry claimed).[95] The production and sale of enslaved people proved necessary for them for at least two reasons. First, these communities ended up engaging with slave traders in order not to be enslaved. Second, selling enslaved people was a way for these communities to obtain iron, an essential item to produce weapons (both to enslave and to fight against the enslavers), and tools for agricultural work.[96]

People or communities immediately tried to get rid of the enslaved people once they were in their control because, in addition to the expenses of providing food and keeping an eye on them to prevent them from escaping, the captives might organize and rebel. Usually, sales were made to merchants who frequented the rivers in the region. They self-identified as Portuguese and had Christian names. Still, despite that, they were "Luso-Africans – brown-skinned, African-born children, grandchildren, and great-grandchildren of Portuguese men and local African women." At the same time, "others were black African 'converts' to Christianity." These merchants were called *moradores* (residents), and they were the ones who made the connection between the rural communities that produced enslaved people and the merchants on the coast, such as ship captains and the GCGPM agents. Like the slave-producing communities, *moradores* sought to sell the enslaved Africans as quickly as possible.[97]

Although it had a monopoly, the GCGPM still had to compete with the illegal trade of the French and English, so agreements with the "residents" that guaranteed the delivery of enslaved people to the monopoly company were essential. A well-known system consisted of these agents of the GCGPM lending goods to *moradores* who, in turn, promised to pay the debts with the delivery of enslaved people. In the hands of the company, the enslaved were gathered in barracoons and waited until they had reached an adequate number to fill the vessels. Ship delays, and insufficient numbers of captives to fill the vessels, resulted in suffering for the enslaved people chained in the barracks. With the end of the GCGPM monopoly, *moradores* took control of the slave trade. They concentrated the enslaved people in the barracoons in Bissau and Cacheu and waited to make agreements with the ship captains. These, in turn, "had little incentive to purchase sick and unhealthy slaves. They might take some at a discount to fill out shipments, but if slaves abounded in port, they could choose

95 Walter Rodney, *A History of the Upper Guinea Coast, 1545–1800* (1970; Monthly Review Press, 1980); Boubacar Barry, *Senegambia and the Atlantic Slave Trade* (1988; Cambridge University Press, 1998).

96 Hawthorne, *From Africa to Brazil*, 64–65; for GCGPM exports of iron and other goods to Guinea and Bissau, see Martins, "A Companhia Geral de Comércio Do Grão-Pará e Maranhão".

97 Hawthorne, *From Africa to Brazil*, 100, 109.

TABLE 2.5 Portuguese merchants in Bissau and Cacheu, 1805

Merchant	Port
Antônio Carlos Gavino	Bissau
Antônio José Carlos	Bissau
Bento Rodrigues Souza	Bissau
Domingues da Veiga	Bissau
João Lucas Cordeiro	Bissau
Joaquim Pedro Genieux	Bissau
José da Silva Cardoso	Bissau
Lourenço da Veiga	Bissau
Manuel Carvalho de Alvarenga	Cacheu
Maria dos Passos	Cacheu
Maria da Silva	Cacheu
Pascoal Pereira da Silveira	Cacheu

Source: *Almanach de Lisboa de 1805*, 505–512. Table prepared by the author.

those they thought most likely to survive the passage to Amazonia [Maranhão e Pará] and most likely to fetch high prices."[98] Around the beginning of the nineteenth century, few major Portuguese merchants were in Upper Guinea. Most of them, eight in total, were in Bissau, and half of that was in Cacheu (Table 2.5). Despite being few, they exported enslaved Africans in a volume higher than that achieved by the GCGPM.[99]

Other slave traders figured as important links between Upper Guinea and Maranhão. The governor of Bissau, Inácio Xavier Baião, was one of the biggest slave dealers in the 1790s who sent enslaved Africans to Maranhão. Likewise, Thomas da Costa Ribeiro came to dominate the business in 1807 and 1808. Other important slave dealers at the same time were Joaquim António de Mattos and Caetano José Nozolini. The Luso-African João Pereira Barreto and his sons João Pereira Barreto and Antônio Teixeira Barreto were important merchants after the prohibition of the slave trade in the North of the Equator in 1815. They were based in Cacheu but also had properties in Maranhão, where they sent the enslaved people. Later, one of the family members—Honório Pereira Barreto—would also become a major slave trader in 1858 and Portuguese governor in Guinea. The slave trade, however, was not only controlled

98 Hawthorne, *From Africa to Brazil*, 109–15.

99 For exports of enslaved people, see https://www.slavevoyages.org/voyage/database.

by big merchants. Small traders also participated in the business by borrowing goods to be paid in enslaved people. A native of Portugal, Manuel Antônio Claudino, had a series of debts with merchants regarding the slave trade. Before 1805, he owed "unnamed amounts" to José Bento Garcia in Lisbon, to Thomas da Costa Ribeiro himself in Bissau, and to the ship captain João Rodrigues Bicho, who used to take enslaved Africans to Maranhão on the vessel *Santo Antônio Vitorioso*.[100]

The capital employed to run the slave trade in Upper Guinea came largely from merchants based in Portugal. The way this happened should not be too complicated. In 1798, the slave trader Antônio José Carlos in Bissau advised the merchant Antônio Esteves Costa in Lisbon that for the business to go well, it was necessary to send good merchandise from the Metropolis. Through their sales, enslaved people would be easily bought.[101] Even after the opening of Brazilian ports in 1808, the Portuguese were still deeply engaged in the slave trade, as recorded by the British consul in Maranhão, Robert Hesketh, in 1821.[102] Thus, to find out who were the merchants interested in the slave trade with Upper Guinea, it is necessary to see who was sending goods from Lisbon. This is possible thanks to the Lisbon customs documentation (Table 2.6).

Table 2.6 shows that major Lisbon merchants were involved with Guinea and quite possibly with the slave trade. For that, they also needed agents in Maranhão to sell the enslaved migrants and send goods, such as cotton, as a payment. In 1797, for example, João Roque Jorge in Lisbon was directly involved in the slave trade. He had a correspondent in Maranhão, José Gonçalves da Silva, who received enslaved Africans from Bissau. Silva was one of the largest traders in Maranhão who had "four large plantations" with 400 enslaved workers.[103]

The lists of vessels that unloaded enslaved migrants in São Luís provide more data on the merchants who were receiving the captives. These merchants were classified as consignees and were responsible for selling the enslaved, although they could also be the owners. Sales, both during the time of the GCGPM monopoly and during free trade, were mainly through auctions.[104] Between 1781 and 1797, more than 90 merchants and ship crew members were responsible for receiving and organizing the sales of 25,743 enslaved people (out of 27,118 transported in 185 voyages). The share of merchants was greater, but even so, the large number of ship crews in the slave trade, especially captains, is noteworthy. Of the 25,743 imported enslaved people, the crews of the vessels were responsible

100 Hawthorne, *From Africa to Brazil*, 116–19.

101 Hawthorne, *From Africa to Brazil*, 116–19.

102 Pereira, "Poor Man's Crop?," 643.

103 AHU, ACL, CU, 009, Cx. 93, Doc. 7702 and Cx. 96, Doc. 7859.

104 Hawthorne, *From Africa to Brazil*, 129, 131.

TABLE 2.6 The largest merchants in Lisbon who exported to Guinea, 1782–1806

1782		1789		1792	
Name	**Value**	**Name**	**Value**	**Name**	**Value**
Society of the Islands of Cape Verde, Bissau, and Annexes	17,901,911	Antônio Lourenço Marques	4,421,911	Bernardo Clamousse & Co.	5,966,711
José Félix Rodrigues	870,000	Bernardo Clamousse & Co.	2,638,267	João Roque Jorge	2,500,000
Francisco Paliart	628,267	Pedro Nolasco Gaspar & Brothers	2,164,867	João Teixeira de Barros*	2,114,333
Jacome Ratton	623,200	João Batista Gemioux	842,489	Antônio Lourenço Marques	1,236,200
Francisco José Gomes	262,689	Marcos José de Matos	739,556	Joaquim Pedro Genioca	1,082,289
Manuel Rodrigues de Sá Viana	260,711	João Roque Jorge	600,000	João Batista Ginox	972,578
Antônio José Silva	90,467	Hack and Comos	366,000	José Antônio Correia	896,533
Antônio José Lourenço	36,000	Joaquim José Ferreira de Almeida	325,244	Pedro Nolasco Gaspar e Irmão	658,533
José Francisco da Cruz	16,333	Manuel Caetano Barrabino	241,222	Francisco Xavier Fernandes Nogueira*	620,422
Manuel José	12,800	Joaquim dos Santos Rosas	234,844	Manuel Ferreira de Araujo	600,000
Total of the first 10	**20,702,378**	Total of the first 10	12,574,400	**Total of the first 10**	**16,647,600**
Total of all 14 exporters	**20,735,422**	**Total of all 38 exporters**	**14,671,244**	**Total of all 55 exporters**	**21,071,667**

1799		1806	
Name	**Value**	**Name**	**Value**
Francisco Xavier Fernandes Nogueira*	4,130,060	Luis Gonçalves Teixeira de Barros*	5,982,433
Marcos José de Matos	966,000	José Antônio Correia & Co.	4,738,733
Antônio Florêncio	650,400	Lourenço Lassence	3,944,600
Antônio Esteves Costa*	605,500	Antônio Simões da Costa*	3,764,833
João Teixeira de Barros*	600,000	Bernardo Clamousse & Co.	3,531,283
Bernardo Clamousse & Co.	551,400	Antônio Xavier*	2,403,867
José Álves Viana*	536,400	Stichling & Co.	1,927,200
Manuel Antônio Basto	497,200	Ricardo Clamousse	1,809,567
Manuel Joaquim Batista and José Antônio dos Santos Bento	398,640	Anhlenge [...]& Co.	1,464,000
João José Dias	276,760	José Bento Garces*	1,174,200
Total of the first 10	**9,212,360**	**Total of the first 10**	**30,740,717**
Total of all 33 exporters	**10,918,840**	**Total of all 85 exporters**	**43,317,367**

Notes and sources: The values are in *réis*. Sources: Arquivo Nacional Torre do Tombo (ANTT), "Alfândegas de Lisboa, Casa da Índia." For the year 1782, see books 138, 290, 288, 250, 249, 248, 247, 246, 139, 289, 140, and 141. For 1789, see books 192, 193, 194, 195, 196, 311, 312, and 313. For 1792, see books 133, 132, 131, 95, 94, and 97. For 1799, see books 44, 45, 104, 162, 215, 407, 409, and 412. For 1806, see books 284, 106, 348, 517, 189, 207, 511, 329, 534 and 484. [...] – illegible name. *Main cotton importers in Lisbon (Appendix A). Table prepared by the author.

for trading 8,710 enslaved (34% of the total), with the overwhelming majority in the hands of the captains (8,415), and the rest in the responsibility of pilots and ship masters. Merchants established in Maranhão were responsible for selling the remaining 17,033 enslaved migrants (66%) (Table 2.7).

Of the 185 voyages that brought 27,118 enslaved migrants and generated sales of 3,316,237,160 *réis* in São Luís, 88 were made through the triangular trade.[105]

TABLE 2.7 The consignees who sold enslaved people in Maranhão, 1781–1797

Consignees	Enslaved people	Consignees	Enslaved people
Unknown ("several", "miscellaneous", "owner", "private")	2,767	Miguel Cotrim*	313
		José Teixeira Pinto	301
		Antônio José de Guimarães	292
Ricardo Nunes Leal	1,937	GCGPM	284
Antônio José de Seixas	1,725	Jacinto José Ferreira*	281
Caetano José Teixeira	1,444	Inácio José*	260
José Gomes	1,293	Mestres	252
Antônio José Roberto	1,018	José Antônio de Moraes*	233
Manuel Pereira Neves*	859	José das Neves Leão*	231
Antônio Bernardo Garrett	809	João Antônio Taboas*	221
Antônio José de Sousa	705	Joaquim dos Santos Rosa*	214
Feliciano dos Santos	641	João Vicente da Silva Basto	212
Antônio José Gonçalves Cascaes	627	Joaquim Lazaro Madeira*	211
Gregório Dias Madeira*	555	Manuel Rodrigues Ferreira	200
José Ferreira da Rocha*	494	Manuel Caetano da Fonseca	198
Manuel Lopes Trindade	484	GCGPM and Francisco de Sales Silva*	193
José Gonçalves da Silva	431		
Francisco José de Melo*	386	José de Azevedo Santos* e a diversos	190
Francisco de Sales Silva*	369		
Domingos Antônio Ribeiro*	340	João Gonçalves da Silva	185
Francisco da Silva Falcão*	330	Francisco Pereira Abrão*	184

105 In Williams' words, the triangular trade began when "the slave ship sailed from the home country with a cargo of manufactured goods. These were exchanged at a profit on the coast of Africa for Negroes, who were traded on the plantations, at another profit, in exchange for a cargo of colonial produce to be taken back to the home country." Eric Williams, *Capitalism and Slavery* (1944; University of North Carolina Press, 1994), 51–52; see also David Eltis, *The Rise of African Slavery in the Americas* (Cambridge University Press, 1999).

TABLE 2.7 The consignees who sold enslaved people in Maranhão, 1781–1797 (*cont.*)

Consignees	Enslaved people	Consignees	Enslaved people
Administradores do novo contrato	171	Manuel Munis*	68
		José Félix do Espírito Santo*	58
José de Azevedo Santos*	168	Manuel Francisco*	58
Isidoro Álves*	165	Manuel Luis de Almeida*	57
João Coelho de Souza	164	Raymundo José da Silva Gayoso	57
GCGPM and others	146		
Francisco Antônio Pinto Cardoso*	146	Ricardo Nunes Leal e ao Novo Contrato	54
Manuel Martins Marques*	134	José Joaquim de Souza*	53
Feliciano dos Santos*	127	Antônio da Mota*	52
José Antônio Dias*	126	Gregório José Inácio*	50
José do Carmo Simões*	120	Inácio Xavier Baião	50
Antônio de Sousa	114	Pilotos	43
José Gonçalves dos Santos	114	José Antônio dos Santos*	42
José Joaquim*	112	Luis da Silva*	41
Andre Joaquim de Lima*	110	Manuel Cordeiro	38
José Antônio de Basto	104	Manuel Monteiro*	38
José Francisco da Silva*	100	Alberto José Lopes*	37
Antônio Francisco Maia*	95	Antônio Pereira da Silva	36
Manuel Álves da Silva Basto	89	José Antônio Franco*	34
Jacinto José Teixeira	87	Domingos José Pinheiro*	33
Domingos Antônio Chaves* e a particulares	85	Joaquim Ribeiro Duarte*	14
		João Manuel de Carvalho	13
Manuel Gonçalves Rosa*	83	José dos Santos Franco*	13
João Coelho	81	José Francisco de Lemos *	13
Antônio Francisco Branco*	80	Francisco Félix de Souza*	12
José Gonçalves Chaves	80	João Belfort	10
Manuel Fernandes da Porsiuncula*	73	Domingos Antônio Lopes*	8
		Manuel Martins*	7
José Joaquim da Silva Rocha	72		
João Antônio* e a particulares	71	**93 Consignees**	**25,743**
Isidoro Martins*	68		

Notes and sources: *ship captain. For the sources, see Table 2.4. Table prepared by the author.

These triangular voyages took 16,764 enslaved Africans to Maranhão, which represented 62% of imports, generating sales totalling 2,091,268,660 *réis*. In other words, the triangular trade vessels were responsible for 63% of the total enslaved people sold in Maranhão. Still, it was not through triangular navigation that the bulk of colonial goods arrived in Portugal. Through other lists that recorded exports of cotton and rice from Maranhão to Portugal (Table 2.8), it is possible to know that the 88 vessels of the triangular trade returned to Lisbon carrying 1,677,263,457 *réis*. In contrast, the rest of the other trips that linked São Luis and Portugal totalled 327 and transported 9,775,405,331 *réis*. That is, 85% of the goods sent to Portugal from Maranhão had nothing to do with the

TABLE 2.8 Exports from Maranhão to Portugal, 1781–1797

Year	Vessels	Cotton	Rice	Total (*réis*)
1781	24	54,421	171,564	459,762,808
1782	17	51,739	147,596	561,646,036
1783	22	49,756	164,519	544,980,691
1784	22	56,744	150,118	375,760,904
1785	28	48,612	282,299	566,558,664
1786	23	61,184	258,247	610,405,123
1787	28	73,736	304,341	673,671,086
1788	26	63,363	368,780	687,736,788
1789	25	77,089	295,966	513,536,459
1790	20	61,253	196,693	471,031,064
1791	25	76,134	328,797	596,881,483
1792	25	90,218	281,079	816,366,852
1793	24	81,413	192,219	819,706,088
1794	23	105,738	315,112	722,322,771
1795	36	180,025	419,381	1,352,723,110
1796	31	145,632	311,736	1,091,985,150
1797	16	75,323	195,404	587,593,711
Total	415	1,352,380	4,383,851	11,452,668,788

Notes and Sources: cotton and rice are in arrobas. AHU, ACL, CU, 009, Cx. 58, Doc. 5353, Cx. 59, Doc. 5432, Cx. 61, Doc. 5562, Cx. 64, Doc. 5730, Cx. 67, Doc. 5843, Cx. 68, Doc. 5938, Cx. 70, Doc. 6112, Cx. 73, Doc. 6292, Cx. 75, Doc. 6429, Cx. 77, Doc. 6567, Cx. 79, Doc. 6718, Cx. 81, Doc. 6868, Cx. 84, Doc. 7042, Cx. 86, Doc. 7178, Cx. 89, Doc. 7404, Cx. 93, Doc. 7680, and Cx. 97, Doc. 7887. Table prepared by the author.

famous triangular navigation. The total cotton carried by them was 198,082 *arrobas* (out of 1,352,380 *arrobas*), while the total rice transported by them was 633,659 *arrobas* (out of a total of 4,383,851 *arrobas*). That is, the central system to buy tropical goods was through selling goods and money coming directly from Portugal.

The largest consignees of enslaved migrants in Maranhão linked with the triangular voyages were merchants residing in São Luís. Together they were responsible for the sale of 13,777 enslaved people (82%). The rest was left to the ships' crews: 2,985 enslaved people (18%). Excluding some merchants not specified by the sources, only nine slave dealers and the GCGPM (out of a total of 38, including vessel crews) received half of the enslaved Africans imported between 1781 and 1797 (Table 2.9). Therefore, merchants residing in São Luís were more important to the triangular navigation than ship crews. This may have something to do with credit. Credit sales took time to pay off, hence the need for local agents to collect debts. This was different, for example, from the re-export trade carried out by Pernambuco and Bahia, which sold enslaved workers in Maranhão mostly for cash.

TABLE 2.9 Consignees in Maranhão linked to the triangular trade, 1781–1797

Consignees	Enslaved people
Ricardo Nunes Leal	1,839
Various	1,699
Antônio José de Seixas	1,409
José Gomes	1,293
Caetano José Teixeira	1,244
Antônio José Roberto	1,018
Without classification	796
GCGPM	623
José Ferreira da Rocha (ship's captain)	494
Manuel Lopes Trindade	484
Antônio Bernardo Garrett	465
Feliciano dos Santos	464
Total	**11,828**

Sources and notes: see Table 2.4. "Various" and "Without classification" are unnamed merchants. Table prepared by the author.

While triangular navigation was not directly important to the cotton trade, it was indirectly so. Since enslaved people carried out the vast majority of Maranhão's export cultivation, even the vessels that carried out direct navigation between São Luís and Portugal benefited indirectly from triangular navigation, which was the main way for enslaved Africans to enter Maranhão. In the end, the profit from selling enslaved migrants in Maranhão was distributed, in the form of cotton and rice, in the hundreds of vessels that sailed to Lisbon. This can be roughly calculated, by the way. The sale of 25,516 enslaved people between 1781 and 1797 generated a fortune of 3,140,499,160 *réis*. Along with the enslaved workers already inhabiting the colony, they produced another even greater fortune of 11,452,668,788 *réis* in cotton and rice.

Although they were men of importance in the economic and social life of the colony, these great consignees in Maranhão were merely links to larger chains of merchants stationed in Portugal and Africa. Antônio José de Seixas is a case in point. When Manuel de Souza, captain of the vessel *Rainha dos Anjos*, the master of the same vessel João Batista Ferreira, and crew member José Ribeiro were heading to Luanda, they took with them 32,000,000 *réis* in merchandise. This was the capital of the company that creditors had provided. The sale of these goods would be at the partners' own risk, and they would not be able to work as commission agents for other merchants. After the goods were sold, the profits would be shared equally. Still, the negotiation did not end in Angola. The sales proceeds would be transformed into bills, enslaved people, or wax and have to be sent to Pernambuco, Maranhão, or Pará. Enslaved Africans exported to Brazil would be entirely at the company's risk, and one of the partners would be obliged to accompany the cargo of enslaved Africans during the Atlantic crossing. In Pernambuco, José Joaquim Jorge would manage the negotiation and in Maranhão, Antônio José de Seixas.[106]

Once we know who the leading suppliers of goods to Guinea were (Table 2.6.) and the merchant-planters who sold the enslaved people in Maranhão (Tables 2.7 and 2.9), it would be relevant to know who were the merchants in Lisbon receiving payments in cotton. Lisbon customs data reveal the merchants in Portugal that were importing cotton. Some of them were the same ones who were sending goods to Guinea.[107] However, a few partnerships are sufficient to illustrate Lisbon's connections to the slave and cotton trade and merchant-planters' importance in Maranhão.

106 ANTT, 10° CNL, Cx. 25, liv. 134, f. 52v–53v.

107 I will not analyze them here as I will deal specifically with Lisbon's cotton importers in Chapter 5.

As revealed by Diego Martins, the end of the GCGPM monopoly "temporarily disorganized the slave trade." Between 1778 and 1780, the number of enslaved people exported from Upper Guinea to Brazil drastically decreased. The solution was to create a Portuguese company with commercial privileges to revive the slave trade. In many respects, this new company performed the same functions as the GCGPM. It was named "Society of the Islands of Cape Verde, Bissau, and Annexes," which, among many functions and privileges, had the exclusive right to trade and transport enslaved people from the ports of Guinea but did not have a monopoly on trade between Maranhão and Portugal.[108] The new company started in 1781 and ended in 1786. Diego Martins' estimates pointed out that during this period, the new company was responsible for 64% to 70% of the voyages that transported enslaved people from the Upper Guinea region to the Amazonian ports (São Luís and Belém).[109] The triangular journeys of the new company's vessels were a relevant way of transporting cotton from Maranhão to Lisbon. Wealthy Lisbon merchants formed the "Society" and included Anselmo José da Cruz, Geraldo Venceslau Braamcamp de Almeida Castelo Branco, João Roque Jorge, João Rodrigues Valle, and João Lourenço Peres. All of them, in one way or another, were involved in other lucrative ventures linked to the Empire: tax farming was one of the most important, but they were also shareholders in companies set up by Pombal, traded in various lucrative products, such as diamonds and tobacco from Brazil, and some had experience in the slave trade from Lisbon.[110]

Later, some of them continued to trade in enslaved people and cotton. João Roque Jorge—son of the aforementioned Paulo Jorge (slave dealer, a prominent merchant in Lisbon, and with commercial connections in Maranhão with the Belfort's planters)—was perhaps one of the most important among them. In 1797, João Roque Jorge was directly involved in the slave trade from Lisbon. He had a correspondent in Maranhão, José Gonçalves da Silva, who received enslaved people from Bissau. Silva was one of the largest traders in Maranhão, who had "four large plantations" with 400 enslaved people.[111] Francisco Paliart and Jacome Ratton were also active in the slave trade in the Guinea region in the 1780s and 1790s.[112] They figured as major exporters of goods to

108 Martins, "A Companhia Geral de Comércio Do Grão-Pará e Maranhão," 154–59.
109 Martins, "A Companhia Geral de Comércio Do Grão-Pará e Maranhão," 163, 165–66.
110 Martins, "A Companhia Geral de Comércio Do Grão-Pará e Maranhão," 159–60; Pedreira, "Os Homens de Negócio Da Praça de Lisboa," 155–67.
111 AHU, ACL, CU, 009, Cx. 93, Doc. 7702 and Cx. 96, Doc. 7859.
112 Martins, "A Companhia Geral de Comércio Do Grão-Pará e Maranhão," 169.

Upper Guinea (Table 2.6) and were also important cotton merchants in Lisbon, importing it from Brazil and re-exporting it to European ports.

Another important partnership that made the link between Portugal, Africa, and Brazil was the one established by Bernardo Clamousse and Caetano José Teixeira. Bernardo Clamousse & Company was one of the biggest suppliers of goods to the Guinean markets and one of the leading cotton importers based in Portugal.[113] His attorney was Caetano José Teixeira, an influential member of the group of wealthy men from Maranhão.[114] Caetano was a plantation owner,[115] but perhaps he was best known for his ventures in the slave trade. Like most of the slave dealers in Maranhão, his business was towards Guinea. In 1801, he was involved in the slave trade with the region.[116] In 1806, together with Antônio Xavier (a major exporter to Guinea and one of the key cotton importers in Lisbon, Table 2.6 and Appendix A), he owned the brigantine called Nossa Senhora da Vitória e Santo Antônio (made in the United States) whose master was Ricardo José de Sá. The vessel had a passport authorizing it to travel from Lisbon to Guinea and from there to Maranhão to finish the trip in Lisbon later. In 1809, Caetano presented himself as the sole owner of the vessel, which remained with the same master. On that occasion, the ship would leave São Luís for Liverpool, pass through Lisbon on its way back, and end the journey in Maranhão.[117] Caetano was also a merchant linked to the slave trade through other ports in Brazil. By 1801, he and João Pedro Esteves were engaged in the slave trade with Pernambuco, buying enslaved people cheaply there and reselling them at "excessive prices in Maranhão."[118] Between 1817 and 1818, his vessel *São Pedro de Águia*—that also belonged to his son Honório José Teixeira—traveled to Angola to load enslaved Africans, stopping in Rio de Janeiro, which points to Caetano's connection with the slave traders in Southeast Brazil. The vessel left Angola in October 1819 and headed for Maranhão. However, "the slaves revolted and killed almost all the whites during the voyage. Two pilots and some sailors survived. Later dominated by a Spanish ship, with about 300 slaves having died, [the vessel] returned to Angola to collect more slaves

113 ANTT, Feitos Findos, Juízo da Índia e Mina, mç. 7, no. 14, cx. 273.

114 AHU, ACL, CU, 009, Cx. 75, Doc. 6495.

115 AHU, ACL, CU, 009, Cx. 81, Doc. 6882.

116 Mariléia dos Santos Cruz et al., ""Exma. Sra. D. Maria Firmina Dos Reis, Distinta Literária Maranhense": A Notoriedade De Uma Professora Afrodescendente No Século XIX," *Notandum*, no. 48 (n.d.): 160.

117 AHU, ACL, CU, 009, Cx. 155, Doc. 1113 and Cx. 158, Doc. 11370.

118 Cruz et al., "Exma. Sra. D. Maria Firmina Dos Reis, Distinta Literária Maranhense," 160.

and then proceeded to Maranhão."[119] When he died—also in 1819—Caetano's properties, including his lands, plantations, and his 2,000 enslaved workers, were estimated at 600,000,000 or 800,000,000 *réis*.[120]

5 Commercial and Agricultural Changes after the Opening of Brazilian Ports

While an individual could assume the roles of planter and merchant, a fundamental reality disrupted this integration: the volatility of cotton prices in the colony meant that these were two separate groups with conflicting interests. It appears that the situation of growers in Maranhão changed substantially in the 1810s. The mercantile class had already gained prominence in commercial activities, and the presence of English merchants after 1808 contributed to this. They began to sell goods on credit to planters who paid their debts in gold, silver, or cotton at prices stipulated by the English. Many Portuguese merchants, disadvantaged in exports and imports of goods, ended up turning to the services of monetary loans to planters. Repayment of debts involved the delivery of cotton, or rice, which necessarily diminished the share of growers in the transatlantic trade.[121]

The excessive indebtedness of the planters, pointed out by Lago in 1822 as one of the causes that hampered the development of the cotton culture, partly explains the lack of capital for investments in technologies to respond to American competition. Another explanation lies in planters' dependence on slave labor and conspicuous consumption. When cotton prices rose and planters made good profits, the only way to expand the business they knew—or were willing to risk—was by purchasing more enslaved workers and land. Another part of the capital was spent on buying luxury goods such as French silks and

119 "O navio pertencente a Caetano José Teixeira do Maranhão, entre 1817 e 1818 viajou do Rio de Janeiro para Angola a recolher escravos. Em outubro de 1819 seguiu para o Maranhão. Durante a viagem os escravos revoltaram-se e mataram quase todos os brancos. Ficaram vivos 2 pilotos e alguns marinheiros. Dominado depois por um navio espanhol, tendo morrido cerca de 300 escravos, voltou a Angola para recolher mais escravos seguindo depois para o Maranhão." ANTT. Feitos Findos, Juízo da Índia e Mina, Justificações Ultramarinas, Brasil, mç. 341, n.º 11 and mç. 45, n.º 3.

120 Biblioteca Nacional, Hemeroteca digital, Imperio do Brasil: Diario da Camara dos Deputados (RJ) – 1826, número 56, 901. Caetano's influence was such that in 1815 he had been creditor of the late Aires Carneiro Homem de Souto Maior. Caetano was trying to collect the debt through Aires' heirs who resided in Lisbon; see ANTT, Feitos Findos, Juízo da Índia e Mina, Justificações Ultramarinas, Brasil, mç. 113, no. 12.

121 Assunção, *De Caboclos a Bem-Te-Vis.*, 255–57.

English cotton fabrics.[122] Indeed, the most important capital for a cotton plantation was its enslaved workers (unlike sugar plantations, where the means of production, tools and utensils were their most expensive elements).[123] Manuel Coelho de Souza—born in the Azores and established in Maranhão around 1790—grew cotton, manioc, and sugarcane in Guimarães. When he died in 1843, he left a fortune of more than 90,000,000 *réis*. His assets were largely comprised of enslaved workers (111 slaves worth 41,600,000 *réis*, representing 45.6% of his total assets). His land was only worth 5,000,000 *réis* or 5.4% of his assets. The rest of his possessions consisted of houses, warehouses, farms, cotton gins, and other items.[124] However, this scenario would change drastically in a few years. According to U.S. Treasury Department reports, the capital invested in Brazil's cotton plantations was much greater than that invested in the U.S' cotton plantations in 1791. Ten years later, though, the United States was investing 60% more than Brazil.[125]

Although indebted to merchants and despite having diminished their overseas trade connections, planters were still central figures in the colony. A British man traveling through Brazil in the second half of the 1830s noted that "the more wealthy people who reside here [in Maranhão] are the owners of cotton plantations."[126] A little before that, in 1817, another English traveler recorded that the richest in Maranhão were those who had large plantations and, at the same time, performed the function of merchant.[127] Such was the wealth of Maranhão that the captaincy had the highest per capita income in Brazil at the end of the colonial period.[128] Yet it was a wealth concentrated in the hands of a few planters.[129]

Shortly before the independence of Brazil in 1822, there were 54 commercial houses owned by nationals (that is, Portuguese) in Maranhão and four foreigners. The most important among the Portuguese was that of *Antonio Jose*

---

122 Assunção, *De Caboclos a Bem-Te-Vis.*, 255–57.

123 On sugar plantations, see Antonio Barros de Castro, "Escravos e senhores nos engenhos do Brasil: um estudo sobre os trabalhos do açúcar e a política econômica dos senhores," *Estudos Econômicos (São Paulo)* 7, no. 1 (1977): 177–220; Vera Lúcia Amaral Ferlini, *Terra, trabalho e poder: o mundo dos engenhos no Nordeste colonial* (Brasiliense, 1988); Frédéric Mauro, *Portugal, o Brasil e o Atlântico, 1570–1670*, vol. 1 (1983; Editorial Estampa, 1997); Schwartz, *Sugar Plantations in the Formation of Brazilian Society*.

124 Assunção, "Exportação, mercado interno," 185.

125 Barbosa, "Cotton in 19th Century Brazil," 150.

126 George Gardner, *Travels in the Interior of Brazil: Principally Through the Northern Provinces, and the Gold and Diamond Districts, During the Years 1836–1841* (Reeve Brothers, 1846), 552.

127 Koster, *Travels in Brazil*, 171.

128 Arruda, *O Brasil no comércio colonial*, 648–55.

129 Mota, "A Dinâmica Colonial," 53.

Meirelles Ferreira & Company, and among the foreigners was that of Robert Hesketh, the British consul in Maranhão.[130] Yet, according to Gayoso, there seemed to be a particular alliance between Portuguese and British merchants to control the price of cotton. Writing in 1813, Gayoso stated that after 1808 the number of growers increased and the number of buyers/exporters decreased, causing the price of cotton to fall. Intentionally, Portuguese and British merchants "coordinated" to restrict competition and thus set cotton prices the way they wanted. They made, in Gayoso's opinion, a monopoly and stipulated low prices that the planters had no choice but to pay. Cotton production continued to grow, but buyers were few from 1808 onwards.[131]

In 1822, contemporaries like João Antonio Garcia de Abranches and the governor of Maranhão, Pinto da Fonseca, criticized the monopolistic practices of foreigners for detrimental effects on the merchants and producers of Maranhão, while also cautioning about the increasing indebtedness of farmers. The relationship between merchants and planters was crucial, as the expansion of cotton cultivation became possible by merchants' financing. However, two moments seem to have contributed to damaging this relationship. First, there was a drop in the price of cotton from 1814 onwards, which harmed planters. Second, with the Independence movement, the planters saw a good opportunity to break off relations with the Portuguese "oppressors" in São Luís, not paying their debts. During this time, many military and militia members in Maranhão had Portuguese origins, and because of these ties, they were reluctant to accept the Independence imposed by Rio de Janeiro, even if part of the recruits leaned to the side of the patriots. Moreover, part of the elite residing in São Luís and Ribeira do Itapecuru monopolized political power and prevented Maranhão from adhering to Independence immediately. Yet, they were soon confronted by patriotic troops from Ceará and Piauí and later by the fleet of the English Lord Cochrane.[132] In the end, this elite gave in, and Maranhão was one of the last provinces to adhere, on July 28, 1823, to the Independence Movement that had been engineered in the Southeast in September 1822. In this new government, some important families, like the Belforts, played an active role in the political transition from colonial-Maranhão to Maranhão-part-of-the-Brazilian-nation-state. Thus, the colonial elite—those linked to

130 Lago, *Estatistica historica-geografica da Provincia do Maranhão*, 64; James Henderson, *A History of the Brazil* (Longman, 1821), 447.

131 Gayoso, *Compendio historico-politico*, 257, 259–60.

132 England supported and helped Brazil militarily to gain independence from Portugal, and Cochrane's role was fundamental in suppressing opponents. See Luís Antônio Vieira da Silva, *História Da Independência Da Província Do Maranhão, 1822–1828* (1862; Companhia Editora Americana, 1972), 177–94.

the plantations in Itapecuru and with houses in São Luís—first paid allegiance to Portugal. But due to confrontations and losses, they chose to join the cause of Independence. Even though one of the goals of Independence was the separation from Portugal, Emperor D. Pedro I soon began to have a policy of safeguarding the interests of the Portuguese elite in Brazil. After a period of turmoil, they recovered their "riches and offices."[133] Even so, it is important to note that most of the rich whites in Maranhão were Portuguese, including the landowners. But some of them also had debts with merchants, mostly Portuguese. In this case, the Independence in Maranhão can be seen as a tactic to evade debt payments. But it is undeniable that the cotton elite of Maranhão—different from the growers in Northeastern Brazil, as I will show later in the book—had solid ties with Portugal that ended up delaying Maranhão's adherence to the Independence Movement. For Marcelo Cheche Galves, indebtedness as a factor that explains the political independence of the regions of Brazil from Portugal is something ignored by historiography.[134]

As for the slave trade, it became practically irrelevant after the 1820s in Marahão, which has been attributed to external pressures to end the traffic and also due to the very crisis of the plantation economy. In Ribeira do Itapecuru, with soil exhaustion and land division by the heirs of the families, the plantations were decreasing in size. Large plantations became rarities, and small and medium-sized properties took over the agricultural landscape of the valley between the Itapecuru and Mearim rivers. At this time, plantation areas began to see their enslaved workers being replaced by peasants. Still, some planters sold their land and managed to take their enslaved workers to other unexplored agricultural frontiers in Maranhão.[135]

6 Conclusion

The economic foundations established by the GCGPM were largely maintained and deepened in the years following the end of its monopoly in 1778. Big merchants and planters continued to finance the cotton culture, which was largely based on the work of thousands of enslaved people forcibly transferred from

133 Matthias Röhrig Assunção, "Elite Politics and Popular Rebellion in the Construction of Post-Colonial Order. The Case of Maranhão, Brazil (1820–41)," *Journal of Latin American Studies* 31, no. 1 (1999): 4, 9, 12, 15.

134 Marcelo Cheche Galves, ""Ao Público Sincero e Imparcial": Imprensa e Independência Do Maranhão (1821–1826)" (Ph.D., Universidade Federal Fluminense, 2010), 40, 117, 181.

135 Assunção, "Elite Politics and Popular Rebellion in the Construction of Post-Colonial Order. The Case of Maranhão, Brazil (1820–41)," 6.

the slave ports in Africa to North Brazil. Because it was an underdeveloped and marginal region, demographically speaking, planters tended to accumulate a lot of land, work, and capital in Maranhão. They also leaned heavily into the commercial sector, allowing them to export their cotton crops to Lisbon. These large merchant-planters enjoyed high social status, participated as protagonists in colonial political life, and held military posts. They were wealthy men who actively participated in the slave trade. Although in constant decay, their social and economic power extended until the mid-nineteenth century.

The elements that made up the wealth of these planters help explain the high productivity of their plantations. Because they held so many resources, mainly enslaved people and land, they were able to establish large plantations with a gang-based organization of work. These large production units tended to be concentrated in the fertile Itapecuru region. They practically specialized in cash crop plantations, such as cotton and rice, and depended on food supplies (manioc, mainly) from other neighboring areas. Land expansion and the acquisition of more and more enslaved workers were the only ways that the opulent planter-merchants of Maranhão found to face the increasing demand for cotton in Europe. The type of cotton cultivated in Maranhão enhanced productivity by yielding a greater quantity of lint compared to other cotton plants in Brazil, but improvements in the cleaning, bagging, and pressing phases remained, in essence, archaic.

In many respects, the configuration of the cotton economy in Maranhão differed from what was happening in the other major Brazilian region engaged in cotton. In the Northeast, the small properties of poor slave owners, who did not have political, economic, and social power, were mainly responsible for the growth of the cotton economy in a much wider geographic area than Maranhão. The following two chapters will deal with the cultivation and domestic trade of cotton in this part of Brazil.

PART 2

The Entrance of the Northeast and the Colonial Free Trade

Introduction to Part 2

The cotton cultivation and trade in Northeast Brazil (encompassing the captaincies of Pernambuco, Alagoas, Paraíba, Rio Grande do Norte, and Ceará) radically differed from that of Maranhão. The cotton cultivation in the old sugar region of Pernambuco—the main captaincy of the region—was since the beginning of the eighteenth century articulated with the agricultural work of the small poor farmers. The geographic expansion of the sugar economy along the coast of the Northeast is key to explaining the development and growth of these cotton farmers. For a long time, they orbited around sugar mills and cane plantations, providing them with food. However, when cash crop prices increased (as with tobacco in the first half of the eighteenth century and with cotton from the 1770s onwards), this sector of the colonial society not only decreased food production but also made use of enslaved people on its small properties. Far from being rich rural landowners able to sell their crops to Portugal and engage in the slave trade, these small slaveholders in the Northeast were poor and without political influence. In this instance, merchants on the coast, primarily in Recife, conducted the transatlantic cotton trade, with a number of middlemen linking the coast and the Northeast's interior. Chapter 3 will briefly explore the peculiar development of the sugar economy in the Northeast and how it paved the way for the emergence of cotton culture until approximately the 1770s. It will also deal with the elements that sustained the growth of the cotton economy (from the 1780s onwards), contrasting it with what happened in Maranhão. Chapter 4 provides a detailed description of the internal cotton trade in the Northeast. Chapter 5 analyzes the overseas trade between 1780 and 1820, encompassing both the Northeast and Maranhão, a period in which both were in a free trade regime.

CHAPTER 3

The Precarious Sugar Expansion and Changes in the Agrarian Structure Brought by Cotton

1 The Sugar Background and the Emergence of Cotton

The framework for understanding the economic history of the Northeast, particularly regarding sugar and cotton, is rooted in the repercussions of the war against the Dutch in the mid-seventeenth century. This extensive historical digression is essential as the emergence of small cotton farmers is rooted in the historical evolution of the sugar economy. Otherwise, one gets the impression that cotton started to be planted in the Northeast solely due to external factors, that is, according to the demand of the industrial revolution. Therefore, one of the objectives of this section is to show the internal conditions—which were different from Maranhão—that made cotton cultivation grow in the Northeast.[1]

In the first half of the eighteenth century, Pernambuco was in second place as the captaincy that most exported sugar in Brazil, behind Bahia and ahead of Rio de Janeiro. It was a different picture a hundred years earlier, when it took first place and Bahia second.[2] The change in position coincides with the war against the Dutch that ended in 1654, when many sugar mills were destroyed during the conflict, opening space for Bahia and Rio de Janeiro to fill the void left by Pernambuco. The recovery of Pernambuco took a while, and when sugar production resumed growth—most likely towards the end of the seventeenth century—the social relations between merchants and planters, the two main sectors that led the sugar economy, had changed. The consequences of the Dutch presence in the Northeast, directly or indirectly, helped to distance the mercantile sector from the productive sector. This political and economic tension eroded cooperation between the two groups, leading to a lack of trust and a decrease in merchants' capital to finance planters. The disharmony between these communities made the lack of capital a pressing issue in the

1 This section draws on Felipe Souza Melo, *Financiando o Negócio de Pernambuco: Produção Colonial, Comércio Ultramarino e a Economia Do Transporte No Atlântico Português (Século XVIII)* (Hucitec; ABPHE, 2021), Chapter 1.

2 Mircea Buescu, *História Econômica Do Brasil. Pesquisas e Análises* (APEC, 1970), 66; see also Evaldo Cabral de Mello, *O Bagaço da Cana* (Penguin, 2012).

mid-eighteenth century, facilitating the entry of a monopoly company that, henceforth, would inject new credits into the region: the General Company of Pernambuco and Paraíba (GCPP).

The period of restoration of the Luso-Brazilian presence and the territorial reconfigurations caused by the conflict against the Dutch made the delimitation of properties in Pernambuco uncertain. The *querela dos engenhos* (quarrel of the mills), in the words of Evaldo Cabral de Mello, was the clash between the old landowners, who had lost their properties during the conflict, and the new owners. The quarrel that encompassed property and debt issues (mainly those left by the Luso-Brazilians to the Dutch) had to wait for Portugal's peace negotiations with the United Provinces, which only happened with the second Treaty of the Hague in 1669, in which the means were agreed to pay the debts left to the WIC (Dutch West India Company). The negotiations that ended the disputes took place between 1672 and 1678. The lack of definition of properties, although temporary, must have reduced the productivity of the sugar mills. In addition, the war caused physical damage to properties, which further delayed the reconstruction of Pernambuco's productive chains, despite the metropolitan effort to grant tax exemptions to those who would rebuild the destroyed sugar mills.[3]

But certainly, one of the most important legacies was the immaterial heritage that the war imposed on the relations between merchants and planters. Subsequent to this event, the "nobility of the land"—a designation employed by the sugar mill proprietors and cane cultivators to refer to themselves—asserted that the responsibility for the triumph over the Dutch belonged solely to them. The Portuguese Crown, according to this "nobility," did not help at all. In their version, Portugal was actually indebted to the Pernambuco inhabitants because once the war was won, at the cost of their "blood, lives, and properties," the colonists chose to return to the Portuguese, discarding joining another foreign nation.[4] Thus, "the desired reward for the good services rendered to the Crown should materialize in tax benefits, honorary rewards and political

3 Evaldo Cabral de Mello, *Olinda Restaurada: guerra e açúcar no Nordeste, 1630–1654* (Editora 34, 2007), 318–19, 329–30, 360, 364, 366; see also Wolfgang Lenk, *Guerra e Pacto Colonial. A Bahia Contra o Brasil Holandês (1624–1654)* (Alameda, 2013); Cátia Antunes, ed., *Pursuing Empire: Brazilians, the Dutch and the Portuguese in Brazil and the South Atlantic, c.1620–1660* (Brill, 2022).

4 Evaldo Cabral de Mello, *Rubro Veio. O Imaginário Da Restauração Pernambucana* (Alameda, 2008), 94, 101–3, 107.

positions."[5] However, in the years following the war, Pernambuco faced some political and economic pressure from Portugal. As defined by treaties, Portugal had to pay some compensation to the Netherlands for having retaken Pernambuco. Yet, part of these payments was requested from the colonials in Pernambuco. In addition, fiscal privileges and guaranteed public positions to the colonizers were ended. From then on, the interference by Lisbon would be more severe. Taxes, previously collected regionally, began to be administered by the metropolis. Although not very recurrent in the documentation, protests against excessive taxes were part of the complaints.[6]

In the view of the colonial aristocracy of Pernambuco, the Portuguese were also recurrently associated with the figure of the merchant who extorted sugar producers through loans aimed at financing their plantations. Credit worked through loans in goods and enslaved workers supplied by merchants to sugar mill owners and cane growers, who, in turn, would pay these commitments with the income from the upcoming sugar harvests.[7] This was a common practice in the colonial marketplaces of Brazil and the West Indies.[8] Yet, due to the tension between producers and traders, this relationship had unique consequences in Pernambuco: it generated and fostered a situation of chronic indebtedness, debt executions, and capital shrinkage.

The situation was further aggravated by the global sugar market prices. Until the end of the seventeenth century, Brazilian sugar found no competitors, but from that date onwards, West Indian producers emerged. Very quickly, due to the high supply of sugar to Europe, prices dropped significantly, affecting producers in Brazil and merchants in colonial ports and Portugal. At the same time, more cultivators in continental America and the Caribbean demanded enslaved Africans, driving up the price of labor. The discovery of gold in Minas Gerais at the beginning of the eighteenth century dealt another blow to

5 George Félix Cabral de Souza, *Elites e Exercício de Poder No Brasil Colonial: A Câmara Municipal Do Recife, 1710–1822* (Editora UFPE, 2015), 45.

6 Mello, *Rubro Veio. O Imaginário Da Restauração Pernambucana*, 92, 119–20; Evaldo Cabral de Mello, *A Fronda dos Mazombos: Nobres Contra Mascates, Pernambuco, 1666–1715* (Editora 34, 2003), 50. See also AHU, ACL, CU 015, Cx. 8, Doc. 743.

7 Vera Lúcia Costa Acioli, *Jurisdição e conflitos. Aspectos da administração colonial: Pernambuco, século XVII* (EDUFPE, 1997), 30.

8 Schwartz, *Sugar Plantations in the Formation of Brazilian Society*; Fragoso, *Homens de Grossa Aventura*; Richard Pares, *Merchants and Planters*, Economic History Review Supplement, 4 (Cambridge University Press, 1960); Richard S. Dunn, *Sugar and Slaves: The Rise of the Planter Class in the English West Indies, 1624–1713* (University of North Carolina Press, 1973); Lowell Joseph Ragatz, *The Fall of the Planter Class in the British Caribbean, 1763–1833: A Study in Social and Economic History* (1928; Octagon, 1977).

Pernambuco's troubled sugar sector, further increasing the already costly slave labor.[9] All this impacted both Pernambuco and Bahia, but the latter captaincy performed better than the former, responding more effectively to the crisis. As I argue, the reason for this lies in the different relationship between the mercantile and productive sectors that in Pernambuco shaped the scope of loans and debt foreclosures.

There were two possible directions for this relationship. In one instance, when the debt was not fulfilled (creditors were not fully reimbursed), it rendered the return on initial investments uncertain or delayed. This created a lack of trust among the merchant group. Conversely, when debts were foreclosed, the productive sector suffered. Debt collection could happen in a couple of ways. One less detrimental aspect for sugar mill owners and cane cultivators was that traders required crop yields as collateral for loans. However, contingent upon the magnitude of the harvest owed, producers may lack the capital for launching future crops. A more detrimental method involved creditors seizing debts by confiscating properties: tools, mills, oxen, other assets, and enslaved laborers. Merchants frequently appropriated planters' properties due to the sugar price crisis. Due to low sugar prices, merchants might opt to retain the goods or the enslaved individuals instead of the sugar.

The strategy of sugar mill owners and cane growers was to appeal to the authorities in Portugal to issue a kind of moratorium obliging merchants to only execute debts referring to part of the crops and not the properties and other capital goods such as enslaved workers. These moratoriums were called *provisões*, which meant provisional law. Many other planters across Brazil asked for the same privilege. Yet, Pernambuco received more *provisões* than Bahia. This indicates a relaxation in debt enforcement, that is, producers were getting what they wanted. However, these determinations were often disregarded by the law officers in favor of the creditors, which made the debtors request more *provisões* from the king and ministers in Lisbon. Thus, the very fact that there were many of these *provisões* also suggests that some part of the creditors' income was sacrificed in respect of royal decision; that is, the Portuguese State authorities were also interested in protecting colonial growers.[10]

---

9 Charles Ralph Boxer, *The Golden Age of Brazil, 1695–1750: Growing Pains of a Colonial Society* (University of California Press, 1962), 24, 26, 43; on the gold trade, see Bill M. Donovan, "Commercial Enterprise and Luso-Brazilian Society During the Brazilian Gold Rush: The Mercantile House of Francisco Pinheiro and the Lisbon to Brazil Trade, 1695–1750" (PhD diss., Johns Hopkins University, 1990), 246–50; Leonor Freire Costa et al., *O ouro do Brasil* (Imprensa Nacional-Casa da Moeda, 2013), 153–80.

10 For more on these moratoriums, see Melo, *Financiando o Negócio de Pernambuco*, 54–63; see also Breno Almeida Vaz Lisboa, "Engenhos, açúcares e negócios na Capitania de

Yet, enforcement on producers' assets appeared to be an ongoing strategy. The words that repeatedly appear in these *provisões* were that the mills and plantations were "dismantled" or "disassembled" (*desfabricados* or *desmontados*). The lack of primary sources makes knowledge of this process impossible. However, what happened in Bahia helps us understand the relationship between indebtedness and fragmentation of plantation ownership. When the owner wanted to sell his sugar mill, he registered the debts he had in the notary offices and used his mill as collateral. A mill could have more than ten creditors, for example. When unable to pay the debts, the owner probably had to give up the mill or parts of it. The task of dividing the various debts among the multiple creditors made the fragmentation of property an alternative for investors to recover capital and/or for the owner to keep part of his property.[11] This was mainly due to the price of sugar. Most likely, if the price were high, the creditors would not resort to taking the properties but would demand payments in sugar. It happened, however, that, in times of high sugar prices, the producer looked for buyers other than his creditors,[12] a practice to get better prices and avoid paying debts. This was mainly done because merchant-creditors bought sugar from producer-debtors at discounted prices.

The Pernambuco planters were highly susceptible to indebtedness for the simple fact that they did not have their own credit and because they depended on intermediaries—the merchants—to buy their crops. In Bahia, this also occurred, but in Salvador, there was greater cooperation between merchants and planters. For reasons not worth delving into here, the sharp separation between producers and traders was profound in Pernambuco but not in

Pernambuco (c.1655– c.1750)," *CLIO: Revista de Pesquisa Histórica* 32, no. 1 (2014): 196–214; Ana Lunara da Silva Morais, "Senhores de engenho e lavradores de cana-de-açúcar da capitania de Pernambuco: Conflitos e direitos de propriedade, América portuguesa, século XVIII," *Historia Agraria* 83 (April 2021): 73–95. For Bahia, see Russell R. Menard, "Law, Credit, the Supply of Labour, and the Organization of Sugar Production in the Colonial Greater Caribbean: A Comparison of Brazil and Barbados in the Seventeenth Century," in *The Early Modern Atlantic Economy*, ed. John J. McCusker and Kenneth Morgan (Cambridge University Press, 2001). For the possible historical and anthropological reasons for the state and rulers to employ means to ease and even cancel the debts of agricultural producers, see David Graeber, *Debt: The First 5,000 Years* (Melville House, 2011), 65, 217; Michael Hudson, *The Lost Tradition of Biblical Debt Cancellations*, Research Paper Presented at the Hentry George School of Social Science (1992), https://michael-hudson.com/wp-content/uploads/2010/03/HudsonLostTradition.pdf.

11 Rae Jean Dell Flory, "Bahian Society in the Mid-Colonial Period: The Sugar Planters, Tobacco Growers, Merchants, and Artisans of Salvador and the Recôncavo, 1680–1725" (PhD diss., University of Texas at Austin, 1978), 38, 74, 84.

12 José Antônio Gonsalves de Mello, "Nobres e Mascates Na Câmara Do Recife, 1713–1738," *Instituto Arqueológico, Histórico e Geográfico Pernambucano* 53 (1981): 113.

Bahia.[13] Indebtedness was also common in the British West Indies. Still, from 1732, after a law passed by the British Parliament, creditors gained legislative advantages to foreclose on the property of their colonial debtors. According to Jacob Price, this law increased credit for the colonies.[14] Apparently, the trade in tropical goods (especially sugar and tobacco) was also experiencing difficulties in other parts of the Atlantic. In Pernambuco, creditors—who were in the colony but who could work with capital from investors in Portugal—were collecting debts from producers. Still, producers in Portuguese America had the advantage of having moratoriums that, although not always efficient, gave them some security.

Over the long term, it became likely that the Pernambuco sugar mills were dismantled and divided up, with various buyers acquiring them. This made their number grow and expand to the extreme south and extreme north of the traditional sugar-producer centers of Recife and Olinda. It can be argued that this was a means of evading assessments by merchant-creditors in Recife and a specific response by producers in America to the general sugar price crisis mentioned above. These sugar mills in the Northeast of Brazil, however, ended up employing few enslaved people and producing lower quality sugars. Additionally, the price of Pernambuco sugar was lower than that of other Brazilian regions. Thus, to reduce the risks, the new owners of the seized properties may have chosen to fragment their sales to various sugar mill owners and cane growers. It is also possible that the merchants ventured into managing the sugar plantation. Another possibility is to look at the scenario from the producers' point of view: resorting to small productive units (including few enslaved workers) with little capital was an alternative for planters to go through future and frustrating debt settlements. This seems to have been the solution found: the multiplication of small sugar mills scattered throughout the stretch seacoast of the Brazilian Northeast, poorly capitalized, working with a small number of enslaved people, with low productivity, and producing low-value sugars.

Table 3.1 shows a clear growth in the number of sugar mills, interrupted by the Dutch occupation between 1630 and 1654. Unfortunately, there is no further information on the number of productive units after 1780. Still, the growth continued, as in 1802, the construction of new mills was prohibited, except

13 Mello, *A Fronda dos Mazombos*, 129–31, 135–136; Menard, "Law, Credit, the Supply of Labour, and the Organization of Sugar Production in the Colonial Greater Caribbean".

14 Jacob M. Price, "Transaction Costs. A Note on Merchant Credit and the Organization of Private Trade," in *The Political Economy of Merchant Empires. State Power and World Trade, 1350–1750* (Cambridge University Press, 1991), 296.

TABLE 3.1 Sugar mills and their productivity in Pernambuco, 1570–1780

Year	Working	Not working	Total	Arrobas	Arrobas/mill
1570[a]			24		
1580[b]			66		
1584[a]			60		
1587[a]			53		
1591[c]			63	378,000	6,000
1612[a]			122		
1620[b]			150		
1622[c]			119	544,072	4,572
1623[d]			135	659,069	4,881
1627[a]			140		
1630[e]			150	396,000	2,640
1638[f]	149	51	200	125,114	839
1639[g]			122	182,336	1,494
1640[h]	166	46	212	197,428	1,189
1655[i]			109		
1710[j]			246	430,500	1,750
1749[l]	234	46	280	573,166	2,449
1751[m]	232	43	275	474,129	2,043
1761[n]	268	40	308	509,907	1,902

Notes and sources:

a Buescu, 1970, 66 (I added the Pernambuco, Itamaracá, and Paraíba sugar mills).
b Costa, *O transporte no Atlântico*, 2000, 13.
c Schwartz, *Sugar Plantations*, 1986, 168.
d Mello, *O bagaço da cana*, 2012, 35.
e for the number of sugar mills, see Mello, *Olinda Restaurada*, 2007, 319; for production, see AHU, ACL, CU, 015, Cx. 9. Doc. 873.
f Puntoni, *A mísera sorte*, 1999, 78.
g Lisboa, *Engenhos, açúcares e negócios*, 2014, 197.
h Puntoni, *A mísera sorte*, 1999, 85.
i Lisboa, *Engenhos, açúcares e negócios*, 2014, 197.
j Antonil, *Cultura e opulencia do Brazil*, 1711, 96.
l for the number of sugar mills, see Informação geral da capitania de Pernambuco em 1749, 1908, 477–478; for production, see Morineau, *Incroyables gazettes et fabuleux métaux*, 1985, 153.
m for the number of sugar mills, see Schwartz, 1986, 562, for production, see Morineau, 1985, 153.
n for the number of sugar mills, see AHU, ACL, CU, 015, Cx. 95. Doc. 7501, for production, see AHU, ACL, CU, 015, Cx. 95. Doc. 7502 and 7503.

TABLE 3.1 Sugar mills and their productivity in Pernambuco, 1570–1780 (*cont.*)

Year	Working	Not working	Total	Arrobas	Arrobas/mill
1763[o]	268	40	308	210,306	784
1777[p]			369	252,981	685
1780[q]			390	245,414	629

o for the number of sugar mills, see BNRJ, Mapas Estatísticos de Pernambuco, 1763, BN, 03,01,038; production for this year was discovered through several vessel loading lists at the AHU.

p for the number of sugar mills, see Ferlini, *Terra, trabalho e poder*, 2003, 158; production for this year was discovered through several vessel loading lists at the AHU.

q for the number of sugar mills, see AHU, ACL, CU, 015, Cx. 136, Doc. 10156; production for this year was discovered through several vessel loading lists at the AHU. Table prepared by the author.

with the governor's permission. In 1818, Pernambuco surpassed the mark of 500 mills.[15] Nevertheless, it should be noted that, even though the overall number was increasing, the productivity per mill was declining. For example, with 135 mills in 1623, Pernambuco produced much more than the 390 mills in 1780.

Despite the adversities and the loss of productivity of the sugar mills, sugar exports increased throughout the century (Figure 3.1). This growth, therefore, was based on small productive units, little capitalized and dispersed along the coast. This was the way Pernambuco faced the sugar price crisis. What happened in Pernambuco was not intensive growth, as in Bahia, but extensive growth, something noted by Frédéric Mauro.[16] As I will show in the next sections, the proliferation of sugar mills and sugarcane cultivators along the Northeast coast is the key to explaining the inland expansion of small slave cotton cultivators from the 1770s onwards.

In addition to the low productivity, the sugar mills in Pernambuco produced sugars of lower value than those in Bahia. Antonil, around 1710, wrote that Bahian sugar was worth 175 to 204 *réis* per arroba more than Pernambuco sugar.[17] In 1731, an anonymous report stated that the planters of Pernambuco

15 Costa, *Anais Pernambucanos. Vol. VII.*, 69, 299.

16 Mauro, *Portugal, o Brasil e o Atlântico, 1570–1670*, 1: 258.

17 André João Antonil, *Cultura e opulencia do Brazil, por suas drogas e minas, com varias noticias curiosas do modo de fazer o assucar., Obra de André João Antonil* (1711, 1837), 100, http://digital.bbm.usp.br/handle/bbm/7461.

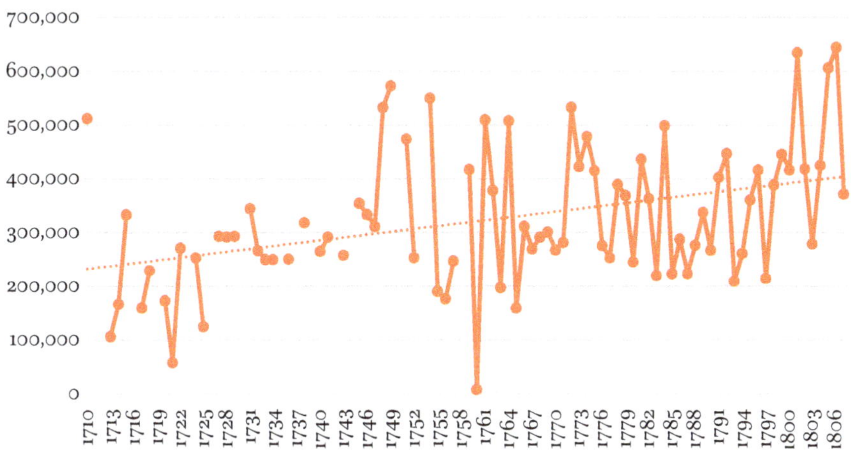

FIGURE 3.1 Sugar exports from Pernambuco, 1710–1807
Notes and sources: Exports and trendline are in arrobas. This chart is based on various vessel cargo lists and other sources. For more details, see Melo, *financiando o negócio*, 69. Figure prepared by the author.

adulterated sugars, giving them artificially high prices, and recommended that sugars be lowered from 100 to 200 *réis* in relation to those in Bahia.[18] The following year, King João V complained about the sugars that came from Pernambuco, saying "that in batches of 100 and 200 crates [...] it seems that the worst are chosen among the lowest."[19] In 1737, a group of merchants in Lisbon recommended fixing sugar prices for all markets in Brazil. All types of sugar from Bahia would have an advantage of 50 to 150 *réis* over sugars from Pernambuco, Paraíba, and Rio de Janeiro.[20] In 1751, King José I even decreed that Bahian sugar should be 100 *réis* higher than all types of sugar in Pernambuco.[21] Some 50 years later the scenario had not changed: between 1796 and 1807, the sugars from Pernambuco (white and brown) were the lowest in value traded in Lisbon.[22]

Because of decapitalization, sugar mills and cane farms worked with little slave labor. Some evidence points to this, as in 1675 when the king warned the residents of Paraíba to keep the indigenous people in their villages, as he had

18 AHU, ACL, CU, 015, Cx. 42, Doc. 3767.

19 "que em partidas de 100 e 200 caixas senão acha uma fina, antes parece que se escolhem as piores entre as mais inferiores [...]," AHU, ACL, CU, 015, Cx. 44, Doc. 3940.

20 Alberto Lamego. AL-050-012.

21 Antonio Delgado Silva, *Collecção da legislação Portugueza desde a ultima compilação das ordenações: Legislação de 1750 a 1762* (Typ. Maigrense, 1830), 1: 39.

22 Arruda, *O Brasil no comércio colonial*, 360–61, 375–76.

come to know that "the Indians of the villages of my administration" were used as servants in the cultivation of cane and the sugar mills "due to the lack of capital to buy slaves from Angola."[23] In 1704, Recife municipal officers asked King Pedro II that sugarcane growers be allowed to employ at least three enslaved workers per property and not six as was the law, which, according to them, was already being disobeyed by the sugar mill owners.[24] The opinion of the governor of Pernambuco, Duarte Sodré Pereira Tibão, in a letter to King João V in 1733, also indicated that the sugarcane plantations and even the sugar mills worked with a number of enslaved people below what was required by law.[25]

The new inventions and methods of growing cane and producing sugar proposed by the colonial inhabitants also provide information about the number of enslaved workers employed in the sugar units. In 1696, Antônio Carvalho Guimarães mentioned that the mills in Pernambuco worked with eight enslaved people.[26] In 1757, Judge João Rodrigues Colaço, with the support of Governor Luís Diogo Lobo da Silva, spoke of a method that would reduce the number of enslaved workers per mill, which at the time was eight, and would go down to four.[27] An inventor named José Antônio da Costa came up with an idea to reduce the number of enslaved workers per mill and got the approval from Governor José César de Meneses to disseminate the plan in 1783. According to José Antônio da Costa, the mills worked with six enslaved people, and with the new invention, it would be possible to work with three.[28] The following year, another invention by Bernardo José Cardoso ensured that if the mills worked with "four oxen and two blacks," they would produce much more than the mills that "currently" are run with at least "eight beasts and four negroes."[29]

These small fragments of historical records point to the small number of enslaved workers in the sugar production units. They, in a way, are endorsed by other sources that cover broader aspects of Pernambuco's economy. In the 1750s, more than 60% of the enslaved Africans who arrived in Recife were sent to Rio de Janeiro, probably because they could not be sold in the Northeast. Demographics point in the same direction.[30] In 1763, the enslaved population

---

23 "os índios das aldeias de minha administração," "pela falta com que se achavam [os engenhos e lavouras] de cabedais para comprarem escravos de Angola," AHU, Códice 256, f. 14v.

24 AHU, ACL, CU, 015, Cx. 21, Doc. 1967.

25 AHU, ACL, CU, 015, Cx. 44, Doc. 4004.

26 AHU, ACL, CU, 015, Cx. 17, Doc. 1711.

27 AHU, ACL, CU, 015, Cx. 83, Doc. 6913.

28 AHU, ACL, CU, 015, Cx. 146, Doc. 10688.

29 AHU, ACL, CU, 015, Cx. 152, Doc. 11023.

30 AHU, ACL, CU, 015, Cx. 136, Doc. 10156.

of Pernambuco (and its neighboring captaincies) comprised only 23% of its total population.[31] Population lists discriminating captives and free people are rare for Pernambuco. But neighboring Paraíba, for example, had a share of enslaved people for 1798, 1799, and 1802 that was around 22.3%, 22.5%, and 20.9%, respectively.[32] Sirinhaém, 77 kilometers south of Recife, a classic sugar producing region, had in 1788 only 36.5% of enslaved people.[33] This all points to the great importance of the free population of the Northeast, which made the share of the enslaved population below the average of the whole of Brazil (about a third of the population of Brazil were enslaved workers in the middle of the eighteenth century).[34]

The scattering of sugar mills and cane fields along the Northeastern coast is partly connected to the conflict between merchants and planters. Being away from creditors—usually in Recife—was a way for sugarcane growers and mill owners to avoid paying debts. Yet, it is also possible that sugar plantations were dispersed precisely because of soil exhaustion in old plantation areas.[35] In any case, the distribution of sugarcane plantations in the Northeast until the 1770s can be seen in the map below (Map 3.1). Through it, it is possible to see that in 1774, about 55% of the mills were far from the traditional sugar regions of Recife, Olinda, and Igaraçu, which also had the benefit of being close to the port.

From 1760 onwards, the GCPP did something that merchants were reluctant to do: finance cane farmers and sugar mill owners. It is unnecessary here to retrace the company's operating process in detail. It suffices to point out that the sugar economy grew because of the company's capital and the organization of overseas transport. Still, the indebtedness of the sugar sector increased. The place of cotton growing in this scenario of sugar growth was modest.[36] Before the GCPP, the governor of Pernambuco noticed the presence of a large population composed of free poor workers, suggesting to the Portuguese authorities that they would be instrumental in the cotton culture.[37] Around 1772 and 1773,

31 BNRJ, Mapas Estatísticos de Pernambuco, 1763, BN, 03,01,038.

32 AHU, ACL, CU, 014, Cx. 35, Doc. 2510, Cx. 36, Doc. 2617, and Cx. 41, Doc. 2890.

33 AHU, ACL, CU, 015, Cx. 178, Doc. 12472. Schwartz, *Sugar Plantations in the Formation of Brazilian Society*, 350.

34 Botelho, "A População Da América Portuguesa".

35 The archaic and soil-damaging methods that were used at the time possibly facilitated soil exhaustion; see Warren Dean, *With Broadax and Firebrand: The Destruction of the Brazilian Atlantic Forest* (University of California Press, 1995).

36 Melo, *Financiando o Negócio de Pernambuco*, 80–99, 150–70, 265–84.

37 Palacios, "Peasantry and Slavery in Brazil, Volume I," 92–93.

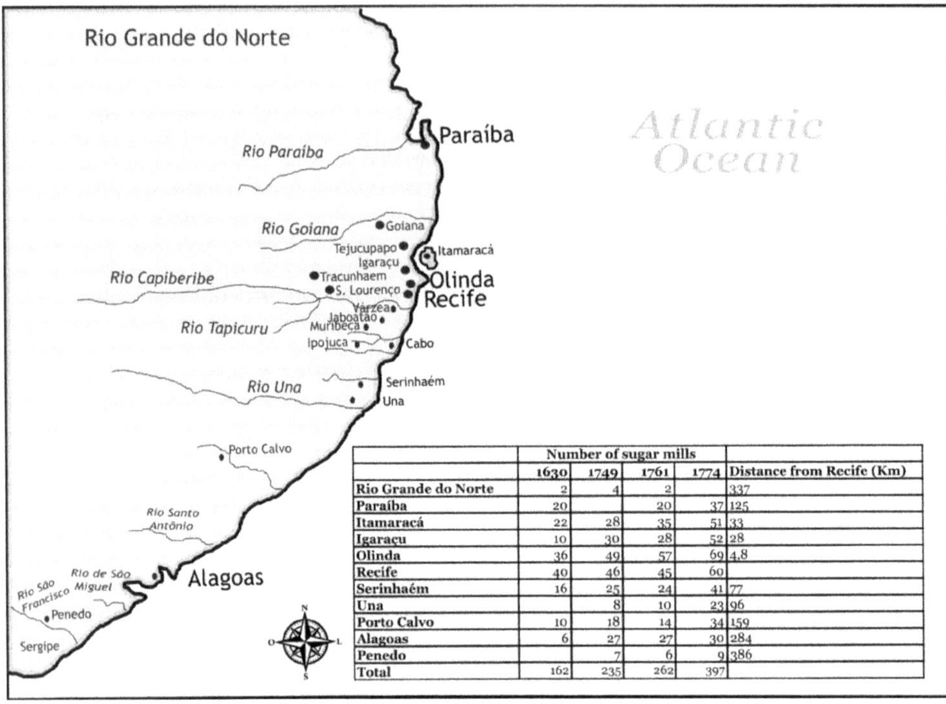

	Number of sugar mills				
	1630	1749	1761	1774	Distance from Recife (Km)
Rio Grande do Norte	2	4	2		337
Paraíba	20		20	37	125
Itamaracá	22	28	35	51	33
Igaraçu	10	30	28	52	28
Olinda	36	49	57	69	4,8
Recife	40	46	45	60	
Serinhaém	16	25	24	41	77
Una		8	10	23	96
Porto Calvo	10	18	14	34	159
Alagoas	6	27	27	30	284
Penedo		7	6	9	386
Total	162	235	262	397	

MAP 3.1 Distribution of sugar mills in Northeastern Brazil, 1630–1774
Source: Evaldo Cabral de Mello, *O Bagaço da Cana* (Penguin, 2012), 319; "Informação Geral Da Capitania de Pernambuco, 1749 – Anais Da Biblioteca Nacional Do Rio de Janeiro, Volume XXVIII" (1906), 477–78; "Ideia Da População Da Capitania de Pernambuco, e Das Suas Anexas, Extensão de Suas Costas, Rios e Povoações Notáveis, Agricultura, Número Dos Engenhos, Contratos, e Rendimentos Reaes, Aumento Que Estes Tem Tido, Etc, Etc, Desde o Ano de 1774 Em Que Tomou Posse Do Governo Das Mesmas Capitanias o Governador e Capitam General Jozé Cezar de Menezes," *Anais Da Biblioteca Nacional Do Rio de Janeiro, Volume XL*, 1918, 1–112. AHU, ACL, CU, 015, Cx. 95.Doc. 7501, February 15, 1761. Map prepared by the author.

members of the GCPP in the colony even reported on cotton cultivation. But after that, almost nothing is known.[38]

What triggered cotton production in the Northeast had little to do with the encouragement of government bodies or deliberations from the GCPP. Likewise, the stimulus was not linked to the port blockade of British colonies in North America due to the American War of Independence. This is because, until around 1780, the biggest supplier of cotton to Europe was the West Indies. According to Charles Boxer and Manuel Nunes Dias, Brazil's cotton exports to Britain increased as a result of the U.S. War of Independence. This assumption

38 ANTT. Copiador de Pernambuco. No. 1 – liv. 382. CGPP. 1759–1773, f. 250v–251 e 268.

is incorrect for two reasons, though. First, at that time, the United States had an insignificant role in the cotton export market. Furthermore, a significant portion of the Brazilian cotton was exported to France rather than Britain.[39] Three factors can be raised to explain the growth in cotton production and exports in the Northeast: first, the damage caused to Caribbean plantations by a strong hurricane in 1780; second, the maritime blockades to the ports of the West Indies (this was a factor linked to the War of Independence of the 13 colonies but which had no connection with their cotton production). It was not until the English defeated Spanish and French forces in 1782 that trade was normalized;[40] third, the European demand—namely the British because of the breach of Arkwright's patent and the invention of the mule, which must have doubled the need for raw cotton—for cotton was so high that it further favored the entry of yet another producing region into the world market.[41] Still, the external context found a favorable social and economic arrangement in Northeastern Brazil conducive to the growth of cotton cultivation and trade.

2 Free Poor Farmers and Their Enslaved People

It is in the general context of the dispersion of sugar plantations across the Northeast and the precarious—but constant—growth of sugar production throughout the eighteenth century that the challenge arises of explaining not only the emergence of free poor farmers but also why they were the main responsible for cotton cultivation. There is still room for interpretation, but I believe that the reason for the emergence and interest of these farmers in cotton lies in the troubled development of the sugar economy associated with population growth. The increase in sugar production was to be followed by the supply of food, which poor farmers traditionally took care of. As the forest zone—roughly speaking, the coast—was the perfect place for sugarcane cultivation, it resulted that food production and free poor men ended up being pushed to the interior, which was also a favorable place for cotton cultivation. The role of these small farmers was to feed not only the agro-export sector but

39 Boxer, *The Portuguese Seaborne Empire 1415–1825*, 193; Dias, *Fomento e Mercantilismo: A Companhia Geral Do Grão Pará e Maranhão (1755–1778)*, 1: 453. My guess is that the two historians extended the conclusions about rice to cotton. In the case of rice there was indeed an impact of the American Revolutionary War on Brazilian rice exports.

40 Thomas Ellison, *The Cotton Trade of Great Britain: Including a History of the Liverpool Cotton Market and of the Liverpool Cotton Brokers' Association* (Effingham Wilson, Royal Exchange, 1886), 81–82; Palacios, "Peasantry and Slavery in Brazil, Volume II," 15.

41 Baines, *History of the Cotton Manufacture in Great Britain*, 214.

also other sectors not linked to the sugar economy, since there was constant demographic growth in the Northeast. The supply task also extended to the livestock sector, which not only supplied meat for the domestic market and hides for export but also helped to expand economic activities further into the captaincies of the Northeast.

The free poor farmers, however, did not only aim to meet the demands of the sugar economy. At times they turned to the production of tobacco, a much-needed commodity to carry out the slave trade. And when cotton prices soared in the 1770s, they seriously engaged in this culture. No one better than Guillermo Palacios has studied in-depth the emergence and historical course of this group of workers, which is why a large part of this section will draw on his work. The only—but crucial—disagreement I have with Palacios' interpretation is his defense that peasants were non-slavery. According to him, peasant labor was an alternative to slave labor in cotton cultivation in the 1770s. Palacios argued that these peasant smallholdings grew markedly between 1760 and 1817 thanks to cotton and that they did not use enslaved people. Cotton cultivation helped develop the peasant class precisely because it was based on free labor and endangered agriculture based on slavery.[42] Palacios further argued that peasants were being persecuted by the slaveholder class, who wanted to get peasants back to producing cheap food. They were also under attack by the Portuguese state, which targeted peasants to fill in the military enlistment. The state's response was to ban cotton cultivation for those who did not have a certain number of enslaved workers, reinforce enlistment, and confiscate peasant lands. The consequence of this was the migration, from 1799, of peasants from the coast to the interior of the Northeast.[43] I do not disagree with much of the factual information and historical chronology that Palacios has provided, and I will make use of it. However, I will demonstrate through new data that peasants were always using enslaved workers. In other words, being a peasant in colonial Brazil did not prevent the use of enslaved people. The very term peasant in this scenario is problematic, though, and some historians are more cautious about its use when referring to colonial Brazil.[44] Free poor farmers, instead, seem to be a less inconvenient classification.

---

42 Palacios, "Peasantry and Slavery in Brazil, Volume II," 47.

43 Palacios, "Peasantry and Slavery in Brazil, Volume I," xxi.

44 See, for instance, Schwartz, *Slaves, Peasants, and Rebels*; Gustavo Acioli Lopes, "O Saco de batatas colonial? Considerações sobre o uso do conceito de campesinato na historiografia do Brasil colônia," *Clio – Revista de Pesquisa Histórica* 1, no. 29.1 (2011).

My main argument—and differently from Palacios' interpretation—is that there was a large number of enslaved people in Northeastern Brazil who were not employed in the sugar sector and who were being used by free poor farmers on their small properties to grow cotton. We can glimpse a gross dimension of the enslaved population deployed in these two crops by means of a simple cross-multiplication. Let us take intervals of six years, thus avoiding possible distortions of years that have had good or bad harvests and also assuming that the enslaved population remained the same for the period. Let us consider that all the 39,219 enslaved people that Northeast Brazil held in 1763 produced 1,338,651 arrobas of sugar between 1763 to 1768 (a period in which no cotton was exported). We could then estimate that to make the 2,838,949 arrobas of sugar between 1805 to 1810, proportionally, a total of 83,173 enslaved people would be required (59% of the total enslaved population). Subtracting this last figure from the total enslaved population of 1808 (150,429), we would have a remainder of 58,975 enslaved workers. Supposedly, that would be the number of enslaved people (41% of the total enslaved population) employed in cotton culture, which produced 1,133,608 arrobas between 1805 to 1810.[45] Yet, these proportions are clearly overestimated since enslaved people also worked in other economic activities, such as cattle raising, food crops, domestic work, etc. Apart from that, groups of free people also worked with sugar and cotton crops. However, right from the start, we realize that the Brazilian Northeast had an impressive number of enslaved people not deployed in sugar culture.

Demographic and parish data for Northeastern Brazil help to improve these estimates and still point to a less efficient performance than Maranhão, especially when we consider the low productivity of enslaved workers. Table 3.2 puts together general data for the whole Paraíba in 1798 and five of its parishes in 1805 that did not produce sugar but only cotton and food. Paraíba was one of the main captaincies that cultivated the fiber. Between 1798 and 1805, it produced 298,960 arrobas, which meant 29% of all cotton exported from the Northeast. In an exceptional year, such as 1798, this share reached 66%.[46]

45 For demographic data, see Table 3.3. For sugar and cotton data, see Melo and Martins, "Cotton Exports from Brazil, 1758–1815 Dataset." Unfortunately, there is no demographic data that informs the share of the slave population between the years 1763 and 1808. For this reason, I made calculations considering that the slave population did not change in a period of six years close to these dates (1763 to 1768 and 1805 to 1810). The six-year period was a random choice, but the results would not change dramatically even if I had chosen four, five, or ten years.

46 For cotton production in Paraíba, see Table 3.5. For exports from the Northeast, Melo and Martins, "Cotton Exports from Brazil, 1758–1815 Dataset".

TABLE 3.2 Demographic data from Paraíba and estimates of the enslaved population employed in the cultivation of cotton in the Northeast

Paraíba in 1798[a]

Farmers	Slaves	Slaves per farmer	Arrobas of cotton	Arrobas per slave
6,317	8,032	1,2	54,532	6,7
Five parishes in Paraíba that did not produce sugar in 1805[b]				
3,213	4,394	2,4	32,276	7,34

Estimated number of enslaved workers needed to produce the 177,146 annual averages of cotton arrobas exported in the 1800s[c]

First estimate (1798)	One slave – 6,7 arrobas of cotton[d] 26,439 slaves – 177,146 arrobas of cotton
Second estimate (1805)	One slave – 7,34 arrobas of cotton[e] 24,134 slaves – 177,146 arrobas of cotton
Third estimate (1798–1805)	One slave – 6,2 arrobas of cotton[f] 28,571 slaves – 177,146 arrobas of cotton
Fourth estimate (1817)	One slave – 6 arrobas of cotton[g] 29,524 slaves – 177,146 arrobas of cotton

Number of enslaved workers employed in cotton cultivation in the Brazilian Northeast: 24,134 to 29,524 (16 to 20% of its total enslaved population in 1808)[h]

Notes and sources:
a AHU, ACL, CU, 014, Doc. 2510.
b Martins and Melo, "Reassessing the productivity."
c The annual averages were drawn from Melo and Martins, "Cotton Exports from Brazil, 1758–1815 Dataset."
d AHU, ACL, CU, 014, Doc. 2510.
e Average drawn from five parishes in Paraíba that did not grow sugar: Vila Real de São João, Vila de Pombal, Vila Nova de Souza, Vila Nova da Rainha and Pilar; see Martins and Melo, "Reassessing the productivity."
f Average drawn from 46 parish records in Paraíba, see Martins and Melo, "Reassessing the productivity."
g Louis-François de Tollenare, *Notas dominicaes tomadas durante uma residencia em Portugal e no Brasil nos annos 1816, 1817 e 1818* [*Notes dominicales: prises pendant un voyage en Portugal et au Brésil en 1816, 1817 et 1818*] (Empreza do Jornal do Recife, 1905), 115. Tollenare wrote in 1817 that a captive in Pernambuco could harvest 20 arrobas of cotton but without detailing whether it was cotton with or without seeds. It is very likely that it was with seeds, which would give six arrobas of ginned cotton per slave, a numerical figure practically identical to my numbers (6,2) extracted from the parishes of Paraíba. If Tollenare was instead referring to 20 arrobas without seeds, this would mean that the slaves would have had to harvest 66,6 arrobas of seeded cotton, an excessively high number, not even reached by Maranhão.
h For demographic data, see Table 3.3. Table prepared by the author.

Both the general data of Paraíba and that of the five parishes present a pattern of slave ownership and cotton production per enslaved worker well below the figures found for the *Ribeira do Itapecuru* in Maranhão. Farmers had 1.2 to 2.4 enslaved people, and each slave was able to produce 6.7 to 7.34 arrobas of cotton per year. This contrasts radically with the number of enslaved workers per grower in Maranhão, which reached a ratio of 31.5. In other words, cotton farms in the Northeast employed few enslaved people while those in Maranhão employed many. These figures, together with data from 46 parish records (including parishes that produced cotton and sugar) and data provided by Tollenare for Pernambuco in 1817, are used to estimate the number of enslaved workers needed to produce cotton across the Northeast. Table 3.2 shows that the Brazilian Northeast required between 24,134 and 29,524 enslaved workers to grow cotton, which meant between 16 and 20% of its total enslaved population in 1808. These figures are not far from the reality since Versiani and Vergolino estimated that 28% of Pernambuco's slaves resided in areas suitable for cotton cultivation in 1827.[47]

The numbers in Paraíba, in turn, are similar to the broader pattern of slave ownership that could be more commonly found throughout Brazil, with a dispersion of slave ownership across small and medium farms. According to Schwartz, sugar production units in Brazil were far from being a "great latifundium." In Bahia, for instance, about 57% of the cane farmers had less than ten enslaved workers, and 24.5% had less than five in 1817. In Minas Gerais, between 1718 and 1804, "slave owners with one to four slaves predominated" in mining activities.[48] Based on hundreds of inventories produced in the hinterlands of Pernambuco, Versiani and Vergolino concluded that the pattern of slave ownership there was 8.1 enslaved workers per farmer between 1770 to 1887, with more than half of the owners having five or less than five enslaved people.[49]

The excessive number of farmers in Paraíba, the small pattern of slave ownership, and the low production per enslaved workers enable the classifying of growers in Northeast Brazil as free poor farmers, not large rural owners. Yet, there was a consistent slave trait in the practice of small shareholders in the hinterlands of Northeast Brazil. As Schwartz argues, the fact that they were

---

47 Flávio Rabelo Versiani and José Raimundo Oliveira Vergolino, "Posse de escravos e estrutura da riqueza no agreste e sertão de Pernambuco: 1777–1887," *Estudos Econômicos (São Paulo)* 33, no. 2 (2003): 360.

48 Stuart B. Schwartz, "Patterns of Slaveholding in the Americas: New Evidence from Brazil," *The American Historical Review* 87, no. 1 (1982): 69, 71, 73, 75.

49 Versiani and Vergolino, "Posse de escravos," 361–62.

poor did not prevent them from acquiring captive labor. Owning enslaved people was an "extremely common and accessible form of investment" for Brazilian society as a whole, "including people of humble circumstances."[50] To some extent, the voluminous and constant trade of enslaved Africans to Brazilian ports made it an "accessible asset" for large portions of the colonial population.[51]

Unlike Maranhão, the Northeast was one of the main sugar producers in Brazil and, for a long time, developed a massive and frequent slave trade with African ports. For having to supply the sugar industry and cotton crops simultaneously, the numbers of enslaved Africans imported to Pernambuco are even bigger than those of Maranhão. Between 1780 and 1820, about 139,471 enslaved migrants landed at the port of Recife (and were then sold to the neighbouring captaincies of Alagoas, Paraíba, Rio Grande do Norte, and Ceará), an average of 3,400 slaves per year.[52] Therefore, the Northeast received more than twice as many enslaved Africans as Maranhão. The captives' origins were also different. Between 1781 and 1785, 98% of the enslaved migrants came from Angola, and the rest from Costa da Mina. Between 1801 and 1851, Angola still dominated, sending around 83% of the captives, seconded again by Costa da Mina. Recife was America's fifth or sixth largest port for the slave trade.[53] Koster, in the 1810s, commented on the moment when the enslaved were gathered in Recife for sales shortly after disembarking from the slave ship: "The males wear a small piece of blue cloth round their waists, which is drawn between the legs and fastened behind; the females are allowed a larger piece of cloth, which is worn as a petticoat; and sometimes a second portion is given to them, for the purpose of covering the upper parts of the body."[54] Lady Maria Callcott (also known as Mary Graham), on her travels to Brazil in the early 1820s, portrayed the enslaved similarly in the engraving of her book and even indicated how the enslaved were repressed by sword-wielding officers (Figure 3.2). It is worth remembering that a significant portion of the enslaved people (about 4,000) who arrived in Maranhão in the 1780s and 1790s most likely came from Angola,

50 Schwartz, "Patterns of Slaveholding in the Americas," 73, 75, 76, 79.

51 Nuno Palma et al., "Slavery and Development in Nineteenth Century Brazil," *Capitalism: A Journal of History and Economics* 2, no. 2 (2021): 384.

52 See "Trans-Atlantic Database," Slave Voyages, https://www.slavevoyages.org/voyage/database.

53 David Eltis and Daniel B. Domingues da Silva, "The Transatlantic Slave Trade to Pernambuco, 1561–1851," in *Extending the Frontiers: Essays on the New Transatlantic Slave Trade Database*, ed. David Eltis and David Richardson (Yale University Press, 2008), 119–20, 122.

54 Koster, *Travels in Brazil*, 416.

FIGURE 3.2 Gate & slave market at Pernambuco, 1824
Source: Lady Maria Callcott, *Journal of a Voyage to Brazil: And Residence There, During Part of the Years 1821, 1822, 1823* (Longman, Hurst, Rees, Orme, Brown, and Green, 1824).

as they arrived in northern Brazil after being re-exported through Pernambuco (Table 2.4).[55]

Also distinct from Maranhão, the most relevant shipowners responsible for shipping enslaved migrants to Recife were merchants based in Brazil. Yet these vessels were essentially just businesses for freight earnings. Brazilian goods, mainly *cachaça*, were not enough to buy enslaved people in Luanda and Benguela. The bulk of the captives transported by these vessels from Brazilian traders had been purchased through goods sent by merchants and investors in the metropolis, through a bilateral trade between Portugal and Angola. In short, the transport was done by the "Brazilians," while trade was the responsibility of the Portuguese.[56] During most of the eighteenth and early nineteenth centuries, Pernambuco brought enslaved Africans mostly from Luanda. Rio de Janeiro and Bahia dominated captive purchases in Benguela and Costa da

55 Joseph C. Miller, *Way of Death: Merchant Capitalism and the Angolan Slave Trade, 1730–1830* (University of Wisconsin Press, 1988), 323–24.

56 Miller, *Way of Death*, 324–26, 453.

Mina, respectively.[57] Between the 1780s and 1810s, with sugar and cotton prices rising, enslaved migrants arriving in the Northeast did not need to be sold—as before—to mining regions. As a result, Recife became one of the leading destinations for enslaved people exported by Luanda in 1810.[58]

This massive importation of enslaved people was reflected in the demography of the Northeast: the number of enslaved was very large when compared to the number of enslaved in Maranhão, for example. But unlike Maranhão, the share of enslaved workers in the Northeast—less than one-quarter of the overall population, and a proportion that remained at the same level for 45 years, from 1763 to 1808—was much smaller than the share of its free inhabitants (Table 3.3).

TABLE 3.3 Number of enslaved people and the total population of Northeast Brazil, 1763–1850

Years	Enslaved people	Free	Total
1763	39,219 (23.13%)	130,363 (76.87%)	169,582[a]
1782			367,431[b]
1808	150,429 (22.61%)	515,030 (77.39%)	665,459[c]
1835	151,726 (18.62%)	663,016 (81.38%)	814,742[d]
1850	293,027 (17.80%)	1,352,622 (82.20%)	1,645,640[e]

Sources and notes:

a Biblioteca Nacional do Rio de Janeiro, Mapas Estatísticos de Pernambuco, 1763, BN, 03,01,038 (this document does not provide data on Rio Grande do Norte).

b "Ideia Da População Da Capitania de Pernambuco." Anais Da Biblioteca Nacional Do Rio de Janeiro, Volume XL, 1918, 98–110.

c Botelho, "A População Da América Portuguesa," 96–97.

d Botelho, "A População Da América Portuguesa," 97.

e Botelho, "A população brasileira em 1850: uma estimativa," 151. Table prepared by the author.

57 Miller, *Way of Death*, 488.

58 Miller, *Way of Death*, 492–93, 525. For more on the slave trade and slavery in Pernambuco, see Marcus J. M. de Carvalho, *Liberdade: Rotinas e Rupturas Do Escravismo No Recife, 1822–1850* (Editora Universitária da UFPE, 2010); Débora de Souza Leão Albuquerque et al., "Financiamento e Organização Do Tráfico de Escravos Para Pernambuco No Século XIX," *EconomiA* 14, no. 1A (2013): 211–25; Maximiliano M. Menz, "A Companhia de Pernambuco e Paraíba e o Funcionamento Do Tráfico de Escravos Em Angola (1759–1775/80)," *Afro-Ásia*, no. 48 (December 2013): 45–76; Gustavo Acioli Lopes, *A Fênix e o Atlântico: a Capitania de Pernambuco e a Economia-Mundo Europeia* (Alameda Editorial, 2018); George Félix Cabral de Souza, "Comerciantes de Escravos Em Pernambuco (c. 1660 – c. 1760): Aproximação a Um Grupo Mercantil Colonial," *CLIO: Revista de Pesquisa Histórica* 37, no. 2 (2019): 2.

This was perhaps noticeable to contemporaries, as it made Koster feel that a transition to free labor in Pernambuco would not be so dramatic.[59] Thus, the large numbers of free inhabitants explain the low percentage of enslaved people among the total population. The size of the total population is a decisive element in understanding the agricultural economy of the Northeast, mainly because its ramifications impacted the patterns of slave ownership, food cultivation, and cotton output.

3 The Unlikely Dispute between Cotton and Sugar and the Geographical Expansion of Cotton Cultivation

One may well infer that the Northeast of Brazil would have produced much more cotton than Maranhão precisely because of its higher number of enslaved workers. However, during the period spanning 1780 to 1813, Maranhão and Pernambuco exported a total of 8.5 million arrobas of cotton: Maranhão was responsible for 57% of exports while the Northeast shipped the remaining 43%. Quantities increased significantly each decade, but in all of them, Maranhão overtook Pernambuco. The best performance in the Northeast was in the 1790s, when it exported 46%. In the 1800s, Maranhão and Pernambuco shipped 61% and 39% of total exports respectively. Still, in the 1800s, the annual average of cotton exported by the Northeast was 177,146 arrobas, whereas, for Maranhão, it was 224,257 arrobas.[60] Thirty years later, the scenario had changed: between 1839 and 1849, the annual average of cotton exported by the Northeast was 382,661 arrobas (57%), while in Maranhão, it was 286,697 (43%).[61]

Therefore, even though the Northeast had more enslaved workers than Maranhão, it ended up producing slightly less cotton than the latter for a long time. Following Beckert, Bernardes, and Andrade's reasoning, this would lie in the competition between the cotton and the sugar sector for slave labor and land. According to them, this competition was won by sugar.[62] However, I have

59 Koster, *Travels in Brazil*, 451–52.

60 Martins and Melo, "Cotton Exports from Brazil, 1758–1815 Dataset".

61 These figures do not include Rio Grande do Norte; see Frederico Leopoldo Cesar Burlamaqui, *Monographia do algodoeiro* (Typ. de N.L. Vianna e filhos, 1863), 94–98. See also Sebastião Ferreira Soares, *Notas estatísticas sobre a produção agrícola e carestia dos gêneros alimentícios no Imperio do Brasil* (Typ. Imp. e Const. de J. Villeneuve e Comp., 1860), 266.

62 See Beckert, *Empire of Cotton*, 94–96, 105, 109; Denis Bernardes, *O patriotismo constitucional: Pernambuco, 1820–1822* (Editora Hucitec, 2006), 115, 117; Manuel Correia de Andrade, *A Terra e o Homem no Nordeste* (Brasiliense, 1963), 143.

already pointed out how the large region of the Northeast held a number of enslaved people sufficient to produce cotton and sugar. Hence, a dispute over slave labor between these two crops is unlikely. The land arguments also do not provide a satisfactory argument. Sugar and cotton were essentially different crops, requiring distinct climates and places. Sugarcane plantations tended to be scattered over the humid areas near the coast, while cotton was planted in the dry hinterlands.[63] Furthermore, they required different soils. Tomás José de Melo, governor of Pernambuco, wrote in 1798 that sugar needed land with liquid clay, without the slightest sign of sand. For cotton, land mixed with sand was necessary,[64] and Tollenare asserted in 1817 that the proper land for cotton was that with equal mixtures of sand and clay.[65] In terms of capital, it was cheaper to cultivate cotton than sugar. However, the planters may have been discouraged from investing in cotton and instead opted for sugar for other reasons. The planters of cotton reaped enormous profits in good years, but they often experienced disappointments, according to Koster, a British merchant in Pernambuco from 1808 to 1816. Sometimes a whole crop is ruined because of the grub, the caterpillar, rain, or severe drought. Conversely, these obstacles did not affect sugarcane.[66]

Arguably, the coexistence with sugar might have slowed the speed and volume of cotton exports from Pernambuco. Yet, this did not prevent both cultures from growing, at least until the 1820s (Table 3.4). Moreover, cotton surpassed sugar in Northeastern Brazil when we focus on monetary values (in millions of *réis*) between 1780 and 1807.[67] As for Paraíba, the situation was even more favorable for cotton since it outstripped sugar both in volume and value (Table 3.5). In sum, cotton and sugar production in Northeastern Brazil were in full swing at the turn of the nineteenth century.[68]

The main cotton-producing areas tended to be located far from the coast and from the areas most favorable for sugarcane plantations. In its

---

63 AHU, ACL, CU, 015, Cx. 159, Doc. 11475 and Cx. 202, Doc. 13809. Koster, *Travels in Brazil*, 366–67.

64 AHU, ACL, CU, 015, Cx. 202, Doc. 13809.

65 Louis-François de Tollenare, *Notas dominicaes tomadas durante uma residencia em Portugal e no Brasil nos annos 1816, 1817 e 1818* [*Notes dominicales: prises pendant un voyage en Portugal et au Brésil en 1816, 1817 et 1818*] (Empreza do Jornal do Recife, 1905), 113.

66 Koster, *Travels in Brazil*, 368.

67 Felipe Souza Melo and Diego de Cambraia Martins, "Reassessing the Productivity of Enslavement on Large-Scale Plantations and Small Farms in Brazilian Cotton Production (c. 1750 – c.1810)," *Historical Research* 96, no. 272 (2023): 205.

68 Pernambuco's economic growth can also be seen through tax collection, see Daniele Ferreira da Silva, "Colonialismo e fiscalidade na capitania de Pernambuco (1770–1793)" (Master's thesis, Universidade Federal de Pernambuco, 2011).

TABLE 3.4 Cotton and sugar exports per decade from the Northeast, 1771–1830

Decades	Cotton	Sugar
1771–1780	1,532	3,774,216
1781–1790	344,227	3,134,936
1791–1800	973,516	3,648,784
1801–1810	1,771,459	4,596,213
1811–1820	2,304,254	5,101,631
1821–1830	1,907,866	9,555,501

Sources and notes: For the period 1771–1810, see, Melo and Martins, "Cotton Exports from Brazil, 1758–1815 Dataset." For 1811–1830, see Soares, *Notas estatísticas sobre a produção agrícola*, 266. Exports are in arrobas. Table prepared by the author.

TABLE 3.5 Cotton and sugar production and number of enslaved people employed in Paraíba, 1798–1805

Year	Cotton	Sugar	Enslaved people
1798	54,532	37,376	8,032
1799	46,664	27,576	11,392
1800	27,380	30,828	11,713
1801	52,284	14,708	10,637
1802	23,056	9,520	9,295
1804	26,676	9,252	9,463
1805	68,368	14,564	10,077
Total	**298,960**	**143,824**	

Sources and notes: sugar and cotton are in arrobas. See, AHU, ACL, CU, 014, Doc. 2510, 2617, 2711, 2764, 2890, 3273, and 3318. Table prepared by the author.

beginnings—at the end of the 1770s—cotton cultivation could be found in Penedo, 400 kilometers from Recife. But shortly afterward, it was planted in the areas North and West of Recife, some of them deep into the hinterland. The distances between these regions to the port of Recife varied considerably. São Lourenço da Mata, for instance, was only 20 kilometers from Recife, but fertile soils were also found in remote places like Fortaleza, more than

600 kilometers from the capital. The cotton farms in Paraíba, responsible for 29% of the Northeast's production between 1798 and 1805, were about 117 kilometers away from the export port.[69] Most of the cotton from the Northeast was transported to the port of Recife in Pernambuco to be shipped to Europe. After 1808, and especially after Brazil's independence in 1822, Recife ceased to concentrate exports, although it remained the main port in the region. Yet, the share of cotton production of each captaincy (provinces after independence) in total exports from the Northeast does not appear to have changed in the following four decades. Between 1839 and 1849, Pernambuco was the largest producer, exporting 43% of cotton from the Northeast. Paraíba exported 28%. Alagoas and Ceará, respectively, accounted for 21% and 8%.[70] Map 3.2 put together 32 cotton-growing areas in the Northeast at the beginning of the nineteenth century. Remarkably, Northeastern Brazil had a more diffuse distribution of cotton farms when compared to Maranhão, where most of the plantations were concentrated in the *Ribeira do Itapecuru*.

The expansion of cotton to the South and Southwest of Pernambuco was obviously facilitated by the "generous policy of *sesmarias* distributions." Between 1770 and 1820, large portions of land were divided into parishes and villages in the interior of the Northeast. There were, for example, "1,097 *sesmarias* granted in Paraíba between 1698 and 1797–448 of them during the long government of Jeronimo Jozé de Mello e Castro, at which time the expansion of cotton began."[71] In this expansion and land transfer, some farmers amassed a good portion of land and enslaved workers. Antônio dos Santos Coelho da Silva, in Cimbres, was one of them. He was considered one of the richest cotton planters in Pernambuco, but he was also reputed to be a "land usurper and burglar."[72] However, although we can find more examples like this, they were the exception to the rule, as the general scenario in the Northeast was made up of small properties of poor farmers who held a small number of enslaved people. The expansion of cotton to the interior of Pernambuco was a process where farmers occupied lands that belonged to indigenous groups. This expansion made parishes grow in the interior of the Northeast, which soon became villages. Atalaia, whose population was primarily indigenous, was practically occupied by free poor farmers and their cotton farms.[73]

69 For cotton production in Paraíba, see Table 3.5. For exports from the Northeast, see Melo and Martins, "Cotton Exports from Brazil, 1758–1815 Dataset".

70 Burlamaqui, *Monographia do algodoeiro*, 94–98. There is no data for Rio Grande do Norte.

71 Palacios, "Peasantry and Slavery in Brazil, Volume II," 254–55, 376.

72 Palacios, "Peasantry and Slavery in Brazil, Volume II," 257.

73 Palacios, "Peasantry and Slavery in Brazil, Volume II," 244, 246, 248. For the economic and political-administrative foundations of the seizure of lands from indigenous populations in the Northeast, see Elba Monique Chagas da Cunha, "O Diretório dos Índios como

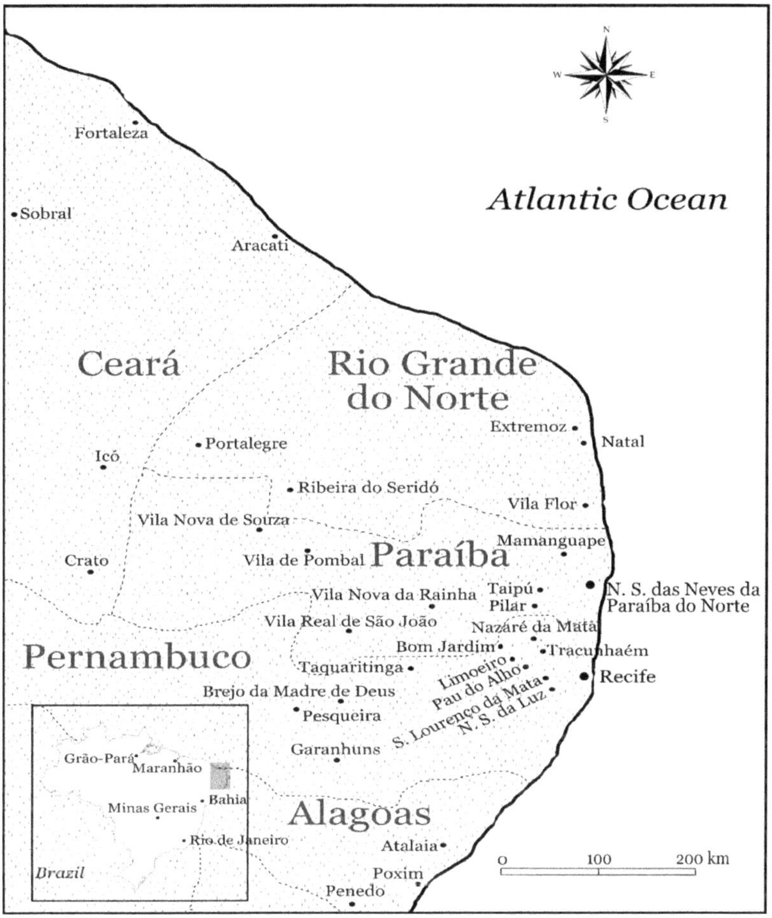

MAP 3.2 Cotton-growing areas in the Northeast (early nineteenth century)
Sources: This map is based on the following works and historical records: Guillermo Palacios, "Peasantry and Slavery in Brazil: A Contribution to the History of the Free Poor Planters from the General Captaincy of Pernambuco, 1700–1817. Volume II" (Ph.D., Princeton University, 1993), 22, 23, 260; Maria Sylvia Porto Alegre, "Vaqueiros, agricultores, artesãos: origens do trabalho livre no Ceará Colonial," *Revista de Ciências Sociais* 20/21 (1989): 14–15; Flávio Rabelo Versiani and José Raimundo Oliveira Vergolino, "Posse de escravos e estrutura da riqueza no agreste e sertão de Pernambuco: 1777–1887," *Estudos Econômicos (São Paulo)* 33, no. 2 (2003): 361; Thiago Alves Dias, "Dinâmicas Mercantis Coloniais: Capitania Do Rio Grande Do Norte (1760–1821)" (Master's thesis, Universidade Federal do Rio Grande do Norte, 2011), 227–28; Luís dos Santos Vilhena, *Recompilação de Notícias Brasílicas Contidas Em Três Cartas* (Salvador, Bahia, 1802), 7–12v; Felipe Souza Melo and Diego de Cambraia Martins, "Reassessing the Productivity of Enslavement on Large-Scale Plantations and Small Farms in Brazilian Cotton Production (c. 1750 – c.1810)," *Historical Research* 96, no. 272 (2023): 193–221. See also AHU, ACL, CU, 015, Cx. 159, Doc. 11475. Map prepared by the author.

Thus, the period between the 1770s and the 1810s marked the growth of the cotton economy in the Northeast. So far, I have tried to show that this growth was sustained by the small property of the poor slaveholders. The dispersion of these small cotton properties in the hinterlands (Map 3.2) was undoubtedly connected with the dispersal of the mills throughout the Northeast coast (Map 3.1). The poor farmers who grew food and orbited around the sugar economy began to penetrate the hinterlands of the Northeast. The reasons for this can be twofold: the land and climate in the interior were more favorable for cotton cultivation. But, as Palacios argued, another explanation can be attributed to the persecution that small cotton growers suffered from the sugar aristocracy and the state. The first aimed to get small farmers to stop producing cotton to produce cheap food. The Portuguese state, in turn, wanted the small farmers to stop farming to enlist in the army. This persecution drove the farmers further and further away from the coast.[74]

4 Cotton and Food Productivity

The development of the cotton economy, however, had a negative impact on food production. Free poor farmers who used to produce enough food at reasonable prices for the sugar sector and other sectors of society began to reduce their production because they were also growing cotton. The subsistence crisis only emerged when prices and scarce quantities of food began to affect the urban populations of Recife and Olinda around 1785. Whereas the first cotton exports started in the second half of the 1770s, in less than ten years, cotton managed to shake the fragile balance between the export economy and domestic food supply in the Northeast.[75] To remedy this, in Paraíba and Pernambuco in 1782 and 1786, the governors passed laws stipulating that only those with more than six enslaved workers could plant cotton (and sugar and tobacco, for that matter). This, according to Palacios, was to prohibit free poor farmers from growing cotton and to go back to growing food to feed slave plantations.[76] As with sugarcane at the beginning of the eighteenth century, orders like this do not seem to have had any effect.[77] Despite the law, smallholders continued

projeto de "civilização" portuguesa para os sertões pernambucanos," *Revista Latino-Americana de História- UNISINOS* 3, no. 12 (2014): 85–116.

74 Palacios, "Peasantry and Slavery in Brazil, Volume I," xxi.

75 Palacios, "Peasantry and Slavery in Brazil, Volume II," 23, 39.

76 Palacios, "Peasantry and Slavery in Brazil, Volume II," 24, 36.

77 AHU, ACL, CU, 015, Cx. 21, Doc. 1967.

to grow cotton. They also never stopped growing food. Yet, the productivity of both declined.

Growing both cotton and food was not necessarily a problem. The renowned Paraíba farmer Manuel Arruda da Câmara, who wrote a cotton cultivation guide towards the close of the eighteenth century, went so far as to suggest that farmers combine cotton with other crops like corn, beans, and manioc. The cotton plants flourished substantially after harvesting food. In addition, this method also provided food for the farmer.[78] Plus, rationally speaking, there was a lot of room between the cotton plants, so it would have been a waste not to plant anything in that space. However, the food crops suffered as a result of this practice of growing cotton alongside them. This was because the cotton was occupying space that was previously reserved for food. Food productivity dropped as a result of this. Furthermore, in theory, these small-scale farmers would produce most of their own food rather than relying on the market. This seems to be something that other places have noticed. Following Gavin Wright's argument, the smaller the farm, the larger the number of acres allocated to food production.[79] In contrast to Maranhão, the Northeast lacked a distinct specialization in cotton, as cotton cultivation coexisted with food crop production in the same regions. The Northeast lacked substantial production units that enabled cotton plantation owners to procure food externally. Finally, the Northeast did not produce significant quantities of rice, which could alleviate food scarcity issues. Although it was an export commodity, rice was also widely consumed by the inhabitants of Maranhão.[80] In turn, rice was not so crucial to feed Pernambuco according to Koster in the 1810s.[81] The Northeast as a whole probably produced large quantities of food, certainly much more than Maranhão. In annual averages, between 1798 to 1805, only Paraíba produced 138,331 *alqueires* of manioc flour and was still able to export a small amount to the captaincy of Pernambuco.[82] However, even the great production of staples in Northeast Brazil was not enough to end the constant food supply crises.[83]

78 Câmara, *Memoria sobre a cultura dos algodoeiros*, 30.

79 Gavin Wright, *The Political Economy of the Cotton South: Households, Markets, and Wealth in the Nineteenth Century* (W. W. Norton & Company, 1978), 55–56, 66.

80 Hawthorne, *From Africa to Brazil*, 146–48.

81 Koster, *Travels in Brazil*, 381.

82 Sources: the same as in Table 3.5.

83 The droughts of the period, mainly in 1791, also contributed to the scarcity of food; see Mariely de Albuquerque Mello Felipe, "E a natureza os entregou ao jogo dos tempos: a seca de 1791 na capitania de Pernambuco e suas anexas" (Master's thesis, Universidade de São Paulo, 2020). Further explanation on the relationship of small farmers and food production can be found in Maria Yedda Leite Linhares and Francisco Carlos Teixeira

The productivity of cotton is also influenced by the limited scale of production units and by laborers switching between food and cotton cultivation. Yet, the distinctive features of plants play a significant role in this matter: it is very likely that the type of cotton cultivated in the Northeast further exacerbated the low productivity in the region. Although cotton from Maranhão and the Northeast was of the same variety (*Gossypium barbadense*), the cotton tree planted in Maranhão was more productive than the tree in Pernambuco.[84] Moreover, the picking phase likely influenced productivity. The process of picking the long and fine fiber typical of the Northeast may require more time compared to the shorter fiber cotton from Maranhão. This was particularly true for Sea Island cotton (long fiber), which was more challenging to harvest compared to the shorter staple varieties of Upland cotton.[85]

Be that as it may, the case of Northeastern Brazil highlights the crucial role of poor farmers who used to produce food but had switched to cotton. In 1797, the governor of Pernambuco noted that the lack of manioc flour coincided with the increase in cotton output.[86] In 1801, the Governing Board that administered Pernambuco wrote that the problem was related not only to manioc flour but also beans, corn, and rice, which in turn had a negative impact on poultry farming. According to the Board, it was the "ambition" of sugar mill owners and cane and cotton farmers that led to the lack of basic foodstuffs. The problem was widespread, but it affected more those who were not involved in the agricultural sector. Sugarcane and cotton farmers held a privileged position because they could dedicate part of their workforce to growing food that would be consumed by their own workers or traded regionally between neighboring farms and parishes. Still, the constant complaints suggest that little was destined for the market, which explains the high prices and paucity of food in marketplaces across Northeast Brazil. Despite pointing to sugar cane and cotton farmers as being guilty of the food shortages, the Board was very clear in underlining that those mainly responsible were cotton farmers, since

Silva, *História da agricultura brasileira: combates e controvérsias* (Brasiliense, 1981); Evaldo Cabral de Mello, *A Outra Independência: o federalismo pernambucano de 1817 a 1824* (Editora 34, 2004).

84 Spix and Martius, *Viagem Pelo Brasil (1817–1820)*, 2:359.

85 Olmstead and Rhode, "Biological Innovation," 1131; John Hebron Moore, "Cotton Breeding in the Old South," *Agricultural History* 30, no. 3 (1956): 95; John Hebron Moore, *The Emergence of the Cotton Kingdom in the Old Southwest: Mississippi, 1770–1860* (Louisiana State University Press, 1988), 85; Pereira, "The Cotton Trade and Brazilian Foreign Commerce," 65.

86 Palacios, "Peasantry and Slavery in Brazil, Volume II," 23, 24, 318. See also AHU, ACL, CU, 015, Cx. 202, D. 13809.

many of them stopped growing the staple foods—as they had historically been doing—to grow the fiber.[87] In Paraíba, the same thing happened as early as in 1787.[88] Pernambuco solved the problem of lack of food by importing it from other regions of Brazil. In 1823, a report by the customs administrator of Recife still pointed out that the lack of manioc flour was due to cotton cultivation, but that scarcity was being circumvented by high imports from Bahia, Rio de Janeiro, and Rio Grande do Sul. This last region also sent meat to the Northeast, which, affected by serious droughts, saw its livestock drop drastically. Food purchases could be made in cash. That is why much money was leaving Pernambuco for other regions.[89] This phenomenon is closely connected with overseas trade. Pernambuco was one of the captaincies in Brazil that received the most money from Portugal. As will be explained in Chapter 5, goods alone were not enough to barter for or buy cotton. Due to the high price of the fiber, merchants in Portugal sent gold to merchants in the colony to purchase cotton, including gold that belonged to the British.

5 Conclusion

Unlike Maranhão, which was scarcely explored and had a low population density, the Northeast of Brazil had already been occupied for about two hundred years when cotton took off between the 1770s and 1780s. This chapter sought to trace the historical elements that enabled it to become a prominent culture in the large region commanded by Pernambuco. Small farmers—and not big planters, as in Maranhão—played a key role here. Feeding the sugar mills on the coast and other colonial inhabitants for a long time, free poor farmers grew more and more cotton as fiber prices rose because of the demand of the industrial revolution in Europe. The way they did this was by employing enslaved people on small properties. But, unlike Maranhão, farmers were

87 AHU, ACL, CU, 015, Cx. 230, Doc. 15543.

88 AHU, ACL, CU, 014, Cx. 30, Doc. 2178.

89 For the customs report, see Evaldo Cabral de Mello, *Frei Joaquim do Amor Divino Caneca* (Editora 34, 2001), 21; for the droughts in the Northeast and the reduction in livestock, see Felipe, "E a natureza os entregou ao jogo dos tempos"; Melo, *Financiando o Negócio de Pernambuco*. On food imports, see Larissa Virginia Brown, "Internal Commerce in a Colonial Economy: Rio De Janeiro and Its Hinterland, 1790–1822" (PhD diss., University of Virginia, 1986). Perhaps this is a good opportunity to point out that, as far as I have been able to find out, droughts have not had an impact on cotton production, at least not for the period and regions covered by this book.

not concentrated in a specific region; instead, they were spread across various regions of the interior of the Northeast.

Contrary to what is generally argued, the growth of cotton cultivation had no adverse consequences on the sugar economy or vice versa. The cotton and sugar sectors were not disputing enslaved people and land, and both crops increased in quantitative terms. But very quickly, cotton cultivation harmed a fundamental sector of the colonial economy: the cultivation of food, mainly manioc. This raised the prices of essential foodstuffs, causing them to be scarce. These were the most damaging consequences of the cotton boom that shook the fragile subsistence economy of the Northeast.

Moreover, this chapter highlighted crucial factors that contributed to the increase in raw cotton productivity. In addition to a specific variety of cotton plant grown in the Northeast, the mixture of food crops with cotton and the less productive work of small properties bring to light other elements to understand the work of enslaved people and the impacts of this on their productivity.

CHAPTER 4

From the Field to the Bale: the Cotton Trade in the Interior of the Northeast

1 The Poverty of the Farmer and the Presence of the Trader and the Middleman

A significant conclusion derived from the Northeast case is the social standing of cotton growers in relation to those in Maranhão. It is important to note that the planters in Maranhão were regarded as the wealthiest individuals in the captaincy during the 1830s.[1] Conversely, the French vice-consul in Pernambuco, Boilleau, wrote in 1826 that few cotton growers were wealthy in Northeastern Brazil. Most were poor, in debt, and living in penury. They were repeatedly exploited by traders who "speculated on their misery": they advanced resources to growers who promised them their crops in the future.[2] If landowners in Maranhão owned mansions in São Luís and left their cotton plantations in the care of overseers, small landowners in the Northeast most probably only left their farms to sell their crops. They could sell their crops to local merchants or large farmers, who would head to the coast to sell the cotton to the merchants/exporters. The great planters in Maranhão were part of broader mercantile connections that even allowed them to participate in the slave trade. The small farmers were far from being slave dealers, although they used slave labor. Another shortcoming of the small farmer was that he probably could not afford the cost of ginning, bagging, and pressing the cotton. It can be concluded from this that the grower in Maranhão was more likely to market the crop already processed in his large plantations, while the grower in the Northeast did not. Therefore, economically speaking, the small farmer was in a disadvantaged position compared to the farmer in Maranhão. In the social and political sphere, the same thing happened: while the planter in Maranhão acquired military posts and participated in political life in the city council of São Luís, the small farmers in the Northeast were geographically far from political decisions and, following Palacios, were being persecuted by the state.

1 Gardner, *Travels in the Interior of Brazil*, 552.

2 Denis Bernardes, "Notícia Sobre a Cultura Do Algodoeiro Na Província de Pernambuco Pelo Chancelier Boilleau (1826)," *Revista Do Instituto Arqueológico, Histórico e Geográfico Pernambucano*, LI (1979): 310.

The expansion of cotton cultivation in the Brazilian Northeast revealed the profound vulnerability of small farmers, whose dependence on intermediaries grew as production moved from the interior to the coast. Unlike in Maranhão, where planters retained a degree of autonomy, intermediaries in the Northeast consolidated their importance by ginning, bagging, and compressing bales, and at times even exporting them. These traders not only linked dispersed producers to coastal markets but also exercised tight control through credit networks, monopolies, and the sale of European goods and enslaved people. Their dominance, however, was contested—by rival merchants, by itinerant Portuguese agents who offered better conditions, and, ultimately, by the farmers themselves, who bore the weight of poverty and distance. Merchants from Lisbon, whose investments interconnected the region with transatlantic trade networks, were prominent in these transactions. By the early nineteenth century, this dependency fueled resentment: the Portuguese began to be seen less as partners and more as unwanted creditors and monopolists, especially as England replaced Portugal as the principal destination for Northeastern cotton.

The precarious situation of cotton farmers in the Northeast affected their options for the commercialization of their crops. Small growers usually did not have warehouses, so they tried to sell their crops as quickly as possible after harvesting. Câmara, a farmer in Paraíba at the end of the eighteenth century, also wrote that storing was a danger as the accumulated cotton attracted a large number of rats. In addition, the manual ginning process was the most labor-consuming, encouraging them to sell seed cotton to dealers or large farmers with gin machines.[3] At first, these machines were located near Recife, but later they entered the hinterlands, and by the 1810s, they were concentrated in Una, Tracunhaém, Pau d'Alho, Nossa Senhora da Luz, São Lourenço, Limoeiro, Bom Jardim, and Taquaritinga. It was also possible to find machines that bagged in these regions. After that, the cotton went to Recife (Map 3.2).[4]

Despite the fact that there are no historical sources for the regions that are being discussed here, a farmer in Bahia provides evidence of how this trade took place.[5] In Rio de Contas, in the outback of the captaincy, near the bor-

---

3 Palacios, "Peasantry and Slavery in Brazil, Volume II," 56–57; Câmara, *Memoria sobre a cultura dos algodoeiros*, 62; Koster, *Travels in Brazil*, 366. Through hundreds of inventories, Versiani and Vergolino pointed out that the inhabitants of the interior of Pernambuco had very few cotton gins. "On average 0.3% of the total" had these machines between 1770 and 1887; see Versiani and Vergolino, "Posse de escravos," 377.

4 Palacios, "Peasantry and Slavery in Brazil, Volume II," 246, 258–59, 317–18.

5 Bahia cotton staple was shorter than Pernambuco's. Furthermore, the cotton from Pernambuco was stronger than that from Bahia. Between 1796 and 1807, Bahia was Brazil's third

der with Minas Gerais, farmer Antônio Pinheiro Pinto grew cotton like other farmers in the region. And like many others, Pinto was a "mediocre" grower. His property could yield only 200 arrobas of cotton a year. Yet, Pinto successfully played the role of a cotton trader and intermediary. He advanced money and tools to farmers in the region, who promised him cotton crops in the future. In good years, he bought up to 1,200 arrobas of ginned cotton to sell to exporters in Salvador, the capital of Bahia. Pinto was responsible for the transport costs to the port (almost 500 kilometers to Salvador). Once, Pinto personally participated in the journey. In 1809, he recorded in his ledger that the transport was carried out by a troop of 63 donkeys, with each animal carrying six arrobas of cotton. Pinto also delegated the work of going to Salvador to his trusted employee, Luís, to sell the cotton at a fixed price. On other occasions, as in 1819 and 1820, Pinto resorted to the services of transporters and paid for the freight to transport the cotton to the coast. Pinto already had buyers at the export port ready to receive the cargo. For Pinto, it was more advantageous to use his capital to buy and sell cotton than to take risks in planting and harvesting activities.[6] However, even the commercialization of cotton was risky and costly, so only farmers with sufficient capital could play the role of intermediary between producers in the interior and exporters on the coast.

A farmer like Pinto charged both for ginning and pressing.[7] The method of ginning was through a water-powered machine with two cylinders that rotated in opposite directions, similar to the *churka*. While in Maranhão, it was commonly called *jaboty*, in Bahia, it was known as *bolandeira*. Its use in Brazil dates back to at least 1618. However, it was not until the end of the eighteenth century that it was used to gin cotton. Pinto's machine had been built in 1802, and he paid 39,000 *réis* for it. It was also used to "grate manioc and crush the corn."[8] Yet, it was not uncommon then for people to still carry out the fiber cleaning process by hand alone. As early as 1799, cotton bales were pressed on the Pinto

largest cotton exporter (see map 1). Bahia used to export 24,440 bales of cotton a year between 1813 and 1816 and shipped over 36,000 bales in 1818. The vast majority of the cotton went to Liverpool in 1818; see James Henderson, *A History of the Brazil* (Longman, 1821), 343, 345. Cotton from Bahia was very similar to cotton from Maranhão; see James Butterworth, *A Complete History of the Cotton Trade: Including Also, That of the Silk, Calico-Printing, & Hat Manufactories; with Remarks on Their Progress in Bolton, Bury, Stockport, Blackburn, and Wigan, to Which Is Added, an Account of the Chief Mart of These Goods, the Town of Manchester* (Manchester: J.W. Leake, printer, 1823), 51.

6 Filho, *Uma Comunidade Rural Do Brasil Antigo*, 270, 277.

7 Filho, *Uma Comunidade Rural Do Brasil Antigo*, 275.

8 Filho, *Uma Comunidade Rural Do Brasil Antigo*, 326.

farm using a very simple press, which was made up of two large pieces of wood, with screws that tightened one against the other.[9]

Antônio Pinheiro Pinto's clientele consisted of acquaintances, friends and relatives. Neighboring farmers who sold cotton to Pinto owned enslaved workers as these captives also sold cotton to Pinto. They did this to buy their freedom in the future.[10] Pinto could pay the cotton owners with cash, but also—when he did not have cash on hand—he could pay them with goods, such as groceries, fabrics, hardware, cattle, and horses. He traded all that for cotton. They were essentially bartering operations, which got around Pinto's lack of cash.[11] What Pinto practiced between the end of the eighteenth century and the beginning of the nineteenth century was something common. We can trace it back to the sugar economy of the seventeenth century and the way the GCGPM financed the cotton planters in Maranhão. The amounts given to Pinto were always small, as cotton cultivation in the region was a "subsidiary." If the farmer failed to deliver the cotton promised to Pinto, he would have to pay him in cash. The cash value to be delivered would be an estimate of what the cotton would be worth on a given date.[12] Pinto did not demand papers proving the debt obligations in most of the negotiations between him and the cotton growers. In most cases, he simply noted the loans (advances) he had made in his ledger, and in a few cases, he required the cotton growers to provide a "credit paper." Thus, in most cases, the debtor's word was enough, and legal proofs were needed for a few cases.[13]

Pinto's cotton, bagged and pressed on his farm, was perhaps easier to sell on the coast. In contrast, small growers who wished to sell their crops directly on the coast—sometimes not bagged and pressed—could face serious problems with baggers and pressers between the hinterland of the Northeast and Recife. These small growers, called *matutos*, faced with the precariousness of institutions in Recife, ended up being deceived by the baggers and pressers

9 Filho, *Uma Comunidade Rural Do Brasil Antigo*, 275.

10 As Koster wrote, it was easier for enslaved people to buy their freedom through cotton growing than through sugar cane. Cotton required almost no capital, expenses were low, and the enslaved person could sell it directly to the merchant. Also, cotton was worth much more than sugar. However, for enslaved people the purchase of freedom should not have been so fast and easy. In 1801, Antônio Manuel, a "brown man" living in Maranhão, wrote to the Prince Regent in Portugal about the many enslaved people in Maranhão who wished to buy their freedom from their masters. The price of freedom would be the one at which the slave was valued; however, the masters demanded "exorbitant sums," making manumissions unfeasible. See, AHU, Códice 599, f. 112. Henry Koster, *Travels in Brazil* (Longman, Hurst, Rees, Orme, and Brown, 1816), 436. See also Claudia Dale Goldin, "The Economics of Emancipation," *The Journal of Economic History* 33, no. 1 (1973): 66–85.

11 Filho, *Uma Comunidade Rural Do Brasil Antigo*, 281, 283–84.

12 Filho, *Uma Comunidade Rural Do Brasil Antigo*, 272, 276.

13 Filho, *Uma Comunidade Rural Do Brasil Antigo*, 285.

and their agents—known in the sources as *atravessador* (middlemen)—who paid them prices well below those quoted in the market. These middlemen offered cash advances to the *matutos* to pay for their extended stay in the city. In the meantime, they postponed the deal to tire the *matutos* and thus bargain for lower cotton prices. Apparently, it was only in 1819 that this problem was resolved. That year, the governor of Pernambuco ordered that the current price of cotton be more clearly communicated to the public by displaying the figures in the customs building to avoid "misleading the farmers."[14]

However, before that date, the action of these baggers/pressers was even harming other traders. In 1804, there were six owners of cotton bale presses that, according to Palacios, practically monopolized the cotton trade. They had "a good number of agents" who "deceived" cotton sellers on the roads between the interior and the port of Recife. Furthermore, these middlemen made it difficult or prevented other traders from buying cotton from the growers. Because of this, a conflict arose between Recife's pressers and traders in the same year. In 1808, the number of pressers increased to eight, but 32 merchants in Recife still accused the pressers of monopolistic practices. José Tavares Gama was one of the traders who complained against the monopoly of the pressers. But, according to Palacios, he also had monopolistic goals since he asked for privilege in 1809 to be solely responsible for pressing the cotton that passed through the public press in Recife for 20 years.[15] This was nothing new. In 1804, one of the monopolists of the cotton pressing business was José Maria de Vasconcelos e Bourbon, who received that year the privilege for ten years of using his invention to gin and press cotton, which was much more efficient than the others existing in the captaincy.[16] There were efforts to create a public press to circumvent the monopoly of baggers, but these last ones managed to undermine these initiatives. In this scenario of middlemen and monopolists, there was also the figure of the *almocreve*, the one who drove the pack animals from the interior to the coast. According to Palacios, he also bought cotton and went to the port to sell it. His activity, however, could be confused with that of the *atravessador*.[17]

Perhaps because of the existence of many intermediaries between producers and exporters, there seemed to be a more significant concern in the Northeast with the modernization of the ginning, pressing, and bagging processes than in Maranhão. Nobody better than the farmer Manuel Arruda da

14 Palacios, "Peasantry and Slavery in Brazil, Volume II," 67, 330; See also José Ribeiro Júnior, "A Economia Algodoeira Em Pernambuco. Da Colônia à Independência," *Revista Brasileira de História* 1, no. 2 (September 1981): 239–40.

15 Palacios, "Peasantry and Slavery in Brazil, Volume II," 328–30.

16 AHU, ACL, CU, 015, Cx. 251, Doc. 16832.

17 Palacios, "Peasantry and Slavery in Brazil, Volume II," 66–67, 132.

Câmara in 1799 described the attempts to improve the machines used to process raw cotton. According to him, there were six types of gins in Pernambuco, but only two were really important. The first and least complicated was called *roda de mão* (hand wheel): the well-known machine with two rolls that moved in opposite directions. Two people were needed to do the work: one in charge of turning the rolls by means of a wheel and the other in charge of passing the cotton in the rolls (Figure 4.1). If these workers started work at 6 in the morning and finished at 6 in the afternoon, they could gin six *arrobas* of seed cotton, which was an *arroba* and a half of ginned cotton. Other more skilful people were able to gin eight *arrobas*, resulting in two *arrobas* of clean cotton. It was a machine that left the "workers entirely fatigued." The task of turning the wheel, however, could be done by animals. This was the most widespread invention, both in the Northeast and Maranhão, and, as we have seen, several small variations in its function could exist.[18]

Large planters and traders who handled large quantities of cotton, such as Câmara, used another machine that was more complex but more productive. It consisted of a set of eight hand wheels, as in the image above, but instead of being moved by enslaved workers, they were connected to four wheels which

FIGURE 4.1 Cotton gin, hand wheel type, in 1799
Source: Câmara, Manuel Arruda da. *Memoria sobre a cultura dos algodoeiros.*

18 Câmara, *Memoria sobre a cultura dos algodoeiros*, 63–64.

in turn were connected to a giant wheel that could be moved by both water and animals (Figure 4.2). In one day, it could gin 128 *arrobas* of cotton with seeds, which yielded 31 *arrobas* seedless.[19]

Bagging was another labor-intensive process. One bale contained 4 to 4.5 arrobas of cotton (equivalent to 60–67 kilos).[20] According to Câmara, without the help of machines, a worker could only bag one bale a day. Such was the intensity of the work that enslaved people sometimes refused to bag the

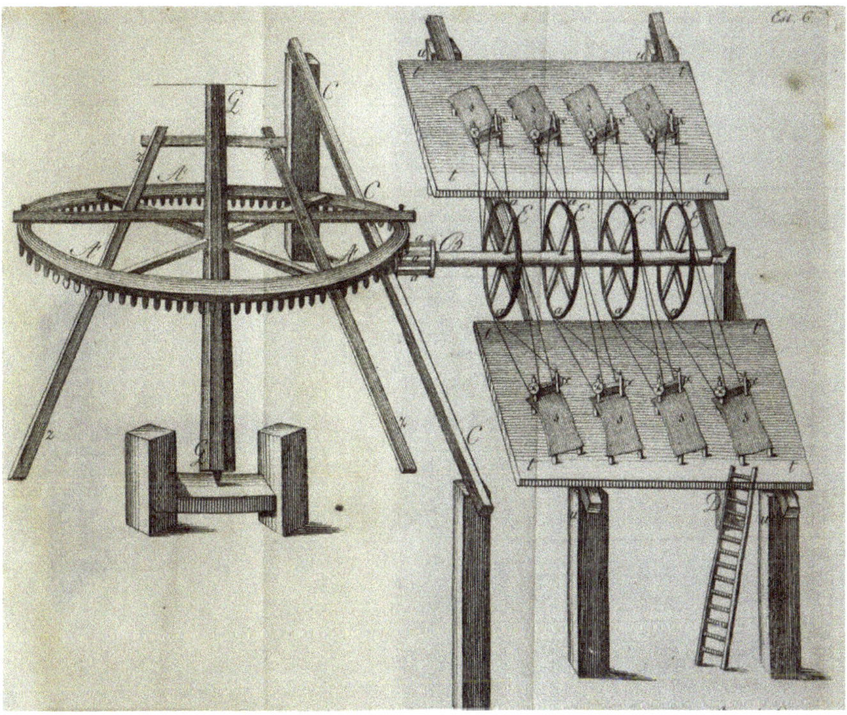

FIGURE 4.2 Machine with a set of eight gins in 1799
Source: Câmara, Manuel Arruda da. *Memoria sobre a cultura dos algodoeiros.* References to the scale of this invention are few. Câmara only reported that the four wheels (marked in the figure as EEEE) are each six palms (45.7 centimeters) in diameter and are 23 palms (175.2 centimeters) apart from each other.

---

19 Câmara, *Memoria sobre a cultura dos algodoeiros*, 66–73.

20 The amount of cotton in Brazilian bales was lower compared to U.S. bales. For example, between 1800 and 1810, a bale of cotton in the U.S. weighed 112 kilos, and 121 kilos in 1824. In northeastern Brazil, between 1786 and 1806, a bale had no more than 4.15 arrobas of cotton (about 60 kilos); see Luiz Cordelio Barbosa, "Cotton in 19th Century Brazil: Dependency and Development" (PhD diss., Washington, University of Washington, 1989), 170; Felipe Souza Melo, *Financiando o Negócio de Pernambuco: Produção Colonial, Comércio Ultramarino e a Economia Do Transporte No Atlântico Português (Século XVIII)* (São Paulo: Editora Hucitec, 2021), 113.

cotton. The fiber owner then had to pay someone for the job, around 240 *réis* per bale in Paraíba. This was likely true since Gayoso in Maranhão recorded that bagging costed 320 *réis*.[21] With these problems in mind, Câmara invented his bagging machine (Figure 4.3). It could not only bag 20 bales a day but

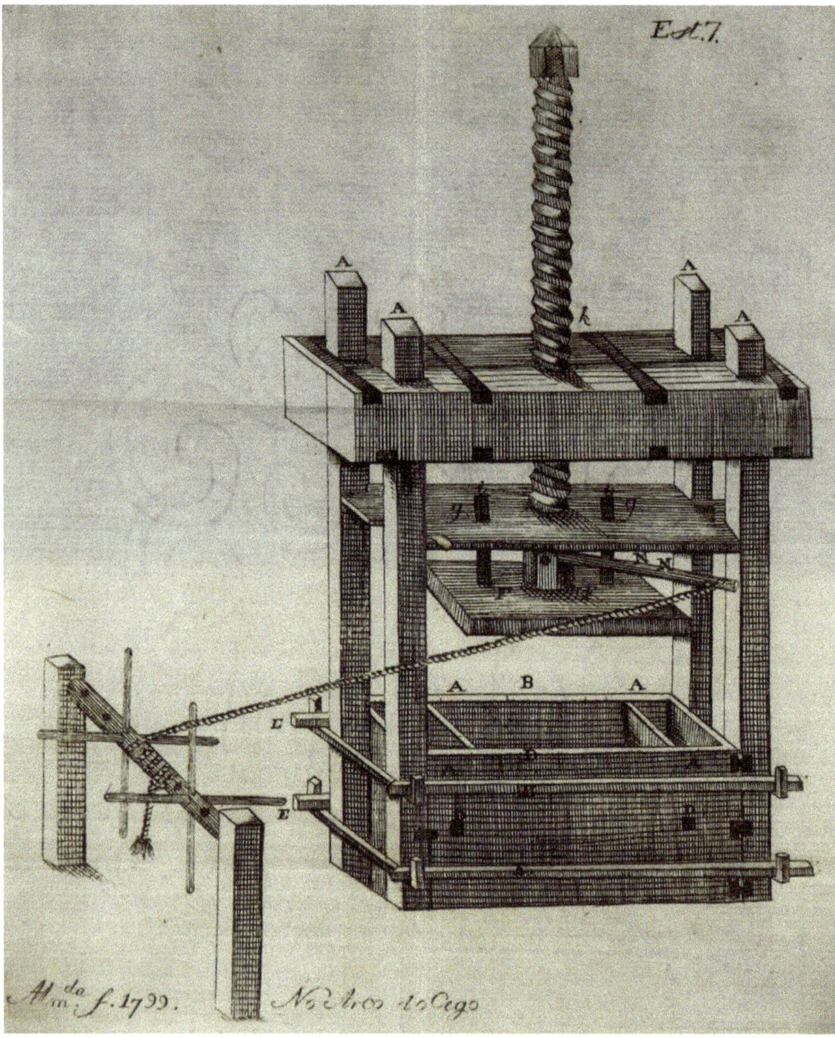

FIGURE 4.3 Bagging and pressing machine in 1799
Source: Câmara, Manuel Arruda da. *Memoria sobre a cultura dos algodoeiros*.

21 Câmara, *Memoria sobre a cultura dos algodoeiros*, 73–74, 77; Gayoso, *Compendio historico-politico*, 287.

also compressed the cotton. Both men and animals could move the machine. Other benefits of the bagging device developed by Câmara were that, unlike the manual method, the fibers did not break, the cotton was in a quadrangular shape, perfect for being transported by horses, and very convenient to be stored on ships for transatlantic transport. The cloth used for bagging in Câmara's machine could be the most ordinary, as the new invention did not require resistant and more expensive fabrics, as was the case with manual bagging. The device should not have cost more than 12,000,000 *réis*. Câmara mentioned that there were not many machines like his in use, but he believed that it would become popular because he had sent models of his invention to other people.[22]

But according to the reports of the French vice-consul in Pernambuco, Boilleau, in 1826, it seems that Câmara's predictions were still far from being fulfilled. Talking about cotton ginning, Boilleau still described it as a manual process. Growers and traders had even tried to use a machine made by the English, but because it broke the fiber, they continued to gin the cotton manually. The vice-consul was probably referring to the American Eli Whitney, inventor of the saw gin. In fact, most likely the farmers and traders of Pernambuco—and perhaps Maranhão—had tried to use the saw gin during its earlier diffusion and perhaps they were not as averse to modernization as we like to think. Yet, both Pernambuco and Maranhão grew long-staple cotton—despite the first being longer than the second—and saw gins were not suitable for this type of fiber but only for medium-staple ones.[23] Still according to Boilleau the initial pressing was also done manually, as it involved boards that compressed the cotton when stepped on by the "blacks." The transport of cotton was carried out on the backs of horses and was carried out in caravans where the drivers—with "bizarre" aspects, according to Boilleau—were usually armed (maybe like the gunman drawn in Koster's book in 1816: Figure 4.4). But the transport could also be done by sea and rivers in rafts. Perhaps it was the precariousness of the machines and the difficulty of installing more efficient models that helped the pressers to gain so much prominence in the cotton trade, to the point of monopolizing it, according to some accounts. After the bales arrived in Recife, the cotton was inspected to check its quality. Then the cotton was sold to the pressmen. Dealers never bought it directly from the grower, according to Boilleau, although this was not necessarily so, as I will explain below. But even so, the pressing was still very imperfect, and it was as if the bales were not pressed.

---

22 Câmara, *Memoria sobre a cultura dos algodoeiros*, 77–80.

23 Britton, *Bale o' Cotton*, 39; Lakwete, *Inventing the Cotton Gin*, 176; Assunção, *De Caboclos a Bem-Te-Vis.*, 195–96; Gorender, *O Escravismo Colonial*, 138–39.

FIGURE 4.4 Cotton transporter in Pernambuco in the 1810s
Source: Koster, Henry. *Travels in Brazil*. London: Longman, Hurst, Rees, Orme, and Brown, 1816.

To him, due to private interests and ignorance, hydraulic machines were never used to compress the bales.[24]

2 Buying the Bale and Shipping It

Under normal conditions—leaving aside monopolists and *atravessadores*—there were merchants, including small ones, who traveled through the interior of the Northeast and bought cotton from producers, whether large or small, peasants or slavers.[25] The action of these merchants was supported by the credit advanced by the rich wholesale merchants of the coast. From the exporter's point of view, the domestic cotton trade is best illustrated by the example of Bento José da Costa. Some of his commercial transactions help to understand the cotton bales' journey from the Northeast's interior to the main export port, Recife. Born in October 1759, in the region of Vila Real in Braga,

24 Bernardes, "Notícias Sobre a Cultura Do Algodoeiro," 308–9.
25 Palacios, "Peasantry and Slavery in Brazil, Volume II," 65.

Northern Portugal, Bento José da Costa only appeared in the colonial territory in September 1786, when he was 27 years old. Almost nothing is known about him from when he settled in Recife until 1799. What is known is that, on that last date, Bento José owned a sugar mill and was the tithe tax farmer for the captaincy of Ceará. In the following year, he auctioned off the right to collect tithes from the parishes of Cabo, Ipojuca, Alagoas, and Penedo for 56,180,000 *réis*. By 1799, he was already classified as "one of the main traders in this marketplace [Recife]." He had vessels that not only connected Pernambuco with Portugal but also made trips to the United States and Spain. The life trajectory of Bento José da Costa repeats a pattern identified for a long time by historiography: a Portuguese who tried to make a living, through commerce, in the colonial territory.[26] Successful, at the age of 40, he was already identified as one of the leading traders in Recife and a major slave trader in the early nineteenth century.[27] Through the information in his bookkeeping journal, a record of expenditure and receipts of money and goods from his business house between September 1786 and October 1789, it is possible to know that Bento also had a brother in Acaraú, Ceará, called Antônio José da Costa.[28] In one consignment, his brother sent him more than 1,000,000 *réis* of goods (cotton, leather, and soles) in two boat trips. These goods were part of a debt that Antônio had with Bento of almost 3,000,000 *réis*. Antônio had taken goods on credit from Bento in January and February 1788 and only started paying him in April 1789.

Many other traders in the colony were his clients: 27 shopkeepers, 24 merchants, a few with military ranks, and many others without that sort of classification. None of them were sugar mill owners or cane growers, which points to the importance of intermediary mercantile agents who connected the goods of a wholesaler such as Bento and the final consumers, including sugar and cotton producers. Quite possibly, these shopkeepers financed the productive sector through credits and goods that wholesalers initially provided.

26 Jorge Miguel Pedreira, "Brasil, Fronteira de Portugal: Negócio, Emigração e Mobilidade Social (Séculos XVII e XVIII)," in *Do Brasil à Metrópole, Efeitos Sociais (Séculos XVII–XVIII). Anais Da Universidade de Évora, n. 8–9*, ed. Mafalda Cunha (1998); Leonor Freire Costa, "Entre o Açúcar e o Ouro: Permanência e Mudança Na Organização Dos Fluxos (Séculos XVII e XVIII)," in *Nas Rotas Do Império. Eixos Mercantis, Tráfico e Relações Sociais No Mundo Português*, ed. João Fragoso (EDUFES, 2006); Maximiliano M. Menz, "Domingos Dias da Silva, o último contratador de Angola: a trajetória de um grande traficante de Lisboa," *Tempo* 23, no. 2 (2017): 383–407.

27 Albuquerque et al., "Financiamento e Organização Do Tráfico," 220.

28 Instituto Arqueológico Histórico Geográfico Pernambucano (IAHGP). Códice 169 – Diário de escrituração de Bento José da Costa – 1786–1792.

In three years of activity, what came out of Bento's commercial house totalled 128,061,242 *réis* (381 operations). Bento provided goods and lent money to a total of 134 people. Most lived in Recife (61), but their clients were also in Ceará (mainly in Acaraú and Curu), Rio Grande do Norte (in Açú), Bahia, Goiana, Maranhão, Paraíba, Pau do Alho, Ponte do Alho, Peba (São Francisco River), and also in Lisbon and Porto. When Bento released money from his commercial house, he did so to pay other merchants' bills or as a direct loan. These operations, which totalled 44 transactions, totalled 1,564,103 *réis*. Colonial goods sent to Portugal reached 43,593,894 *réis* in 75 operations. But the bulk of what came out of Bento's house were goods sold in the colonial territory: 246 operations totalling 61,199,287 *réis*.

In turn, what went into Bento's house totalled 94,403,033 *réis* (269 operations). Colonial goods were responsible for 28 operations, totalling 5,920,733 *réis*, and non-colonial goods accounted for 44, totalling 52,043,324 *réis*. The inflow of money was the most significant, representing 185 operations totalling 32,739,593 *réis*. That is, although Bento's sales were in the form of goods, the payments he received were mostly in cash. Colonial goods, as a form of payment, were not very representative. This draws attention to the importance of having enough cash in the colony to carry out the exchanges. Money, therefore, was this merchant's preferred way of recouping the initial investments in goods he had made. With money in hand, he purchased colonial goods. This explains why the outflow of money to Portugal was small (just over 1,000,000 *réis*) and that the outflow of colonial goods was greater (over 43,000,000 *réis*). The presence of much cash passing through this merchant's hands should not come as a surprise. Pernambuco was the region of Brazil that received the most gold from Portugal, because to buy cotton, the main product of the captaincy at that time and the most expensive, merchants needed to bring gold from abroad to carry out the exchanges. Only the goods imported from Portugal were not enough.[29] Barter, therefore, tended to be rare. Instead, credit and debit operations took place that required bookkeeping so that creditors

29 This part about Bento José da Costa is based almost entirely on my article; see Felipe Souza Melo, "A movimentação comercial de um negociante em Pernambuco no final do século XVIII: o diário de escrituração de Bento José da Costa," *Faces da Historia* 5, no. 1 (2018): 179–97. Among Brazil's products, such as sugar, hides, rice, and cassava, cotton was the most expensive. The reason for it being more expensive than the others was more related to the high demand for the raw material than to its production costs, since cotton was relatively cheap to grow.

and debtors knew, even if roughly, the state of their finances and who they should charge or pay.[30]

How did the Atlantic cotton trade from Brazil work? The records left by Bento do not shed much light on this route, but a merchant in Pernambuco, whose name it is not possible to identify, did so in two ways: he sent cotton (and other goods) at his own risk or worked in exchange for commissions for major merchants. When this merchant sent goods at his own risk, he sent them to his correspondent in Lisbon, *Manuel de Souza Freire & Co*. On one occasion, the merchant in Pernambuco sent 33 bales of cotton (worth 809,000 *réis*) to Souza Freire on May 26, 1803. On December 17, 1804, the cotton was sold in Liverpool for 1,118,625 *réis* after deducting the expenses. And finally, on January 8, 1805, the unknown merchant received the sales invoice from Souza Freire. It took more than a year and a half to complete the deal, and he made a profit of 369,626 *réis*, with a return of 38%. But this is an extreme case, perhaps because it involved shipping the cotton out of Portugal. In most of the negotiations at the expense and risk of this merchant, the completion of sales in Portugal took much less time, approximately four to six months. Still, this is a good example illustrating how merchants stationed in the colony were able to access markets outside Portugal.[31]

On other occasions this unknown merchant worked as an agent for different merchants. In 1806 and 1807, Manuel Francisco Regadas and Antônio de Queiros Monteiro Regadas, also from Pernambuco, ordered the unknown merchant to send bales of cotton to Manuel de Souza Freire.[32] The unknown merchant also had contacts with Angola, which points to his involvement as an intermediary in the slave trade. On different occasions between 1806 and 1807, Manuel Gomes de Araujo, Joaquim Pedro Alexandrino, Antônio Nunes de Matos, and Agostinho Álves de Niza, residents of Angola, asked him to ship bales of cotton to Manuel da Cruz, one of the main importers of cotton in Lisbon (Appendix A).[33] Once the goods were purchased, an agent such as this merchant paid expenses, such as travel costs (carts and cranes), storage (such

30 William T. Baxter, "Observations on Money, Barter and Bookkeeping," *The Accounting Historians Journal* 31, no. 1 (2004): 129–39; Graeber, *Debt*; Angelo Alves Carrara, "O crédito no Brasil no período colonial: Uma revisão historiográfica," *Varia Historia* 36, no. 70 (2020): 15–51.

31 IAHGP, códice 171, f. 93–94. About commissions in Brazil, see also Donovan, "Commercial Enterprise and Luso-Brazilian Society During the Brazilian Gold Rush," 258–59.

32 IAHGP, códice 171, f. 206, 214, 237, 239.

33 IAHGP, códice 171, f. 192, 193 e 241.

as warehouses), taxes, and the freight of the overseas travel. After adding up all these costs (which were borne by the principal), this agent calculated his commission, which in the case of the unknown merchant was almost always 3%.[34] It was a fixed amount, meaning the commission income varied according to the size of the agent's trades. Bento José da Costa also worked as a commissioner when he sent cotton at the behest of a Lisbon merchant, Manuel da Fonseca Silva.[35]

What was the most important way of doing business, at his own risk or as a commission agent? Considering everything this unknown merchant traded, not just cotton, it is possible to answer part of this question. From September 1801 to November 1807, this merchant made 172 commissioned trades, which netted him more than 10,000,000 *réis*. The average with commission earnings was 60,000 *réis*, with a maximum of 1,220,364 *réis* and a minimum of 1,600 *réis*. The commissioner's activity took up most of his working hours since the negotiations he carried out on his own account amounted to only 43 operations. However, it was in these trades carried out at his own risk that this merchant could obtain the most outstanding returns.[36] In total, for six years, this merchant invested more than 68,000,000 *réis* in shipments to Portugal, Angola, Paraíba, and Maranhão,[37] achieving a return of more than 12,000,000 *réis*. The average of his profitability was 18%, with trades that yielded, at most, 109% of profit and, at least, a loss of 16%. In fact, only five out of 43 operations at their own risk resulted in losses.

In six years, he got more than 60,000,000 *réis* to make trades at his own risk. So much capital could not have come only from his commission earnings, which stood at 10,000,000 *réis*, more or less, in the same period. He could have well had other businesses that the source does not mention, or he could simply have saved considerable sums of money during his lifetime. But another hypothesis is credit. There were residents in the colony—small merchants, civil servants, and even producers—who had no transatlantic connections and when they wanted to send goods abroad, they did so through merchants familiar with these circuits. A merchant with contacts could gather various types of capital, large or small, in the form of goods. The other part of the explanation lies in the fact that this merchant could receive credits (money) from several

---

34 IAHGP, códice 171, f. 85, 86, 91.

35 IAHGP, códice 169, f. 23.

36 Adding up all the merchants in the kingdom with which this unknown merchant had contacts, both to work as a commissioner and to carry out transactions at his own risk, they came to the number of 49.

37 He even sent, at his own risk, two slaves to São Luís, to his correspondent Luis da Rocha Compaso. AHGP, códice 171, f. 105.

different merchants in Recife, Portugal, or even from other marketplaces in Europe. A case from the Lisbon notary offices helps clarify this last case. In 1800, José da Silva Maine, a resident in Pernambuco, had received from several Lisbon creditors the large amount of 26,805,879 *réis*, most in the form of bills (*letras*) and a small part in goods. Maine undertook to satisfy creditors "as he could" by sending goods exclusively to them. The interesting thing about this obligation contract was that all shipments Maine would make from Pernambuco would be at his own risk, with the creditors exempting themselves from any responsibility. It is a case that sets precedents, as it means that not every merchant in Recife—or elsewhere in colonial Brazil—who sent goods "at his own risk" worked with his own capital. The same happens when one considers the metropolitan merchant, who could gather goods and credits from various agents to do business with Brazil. The intermediary between Maine and the creditors was one of the big traders in Lisbon, and one of the largest importers of Brazilian cotton, Bento José Pacheco.[38]

Thus, it was very likely that investors in Portugal would send capital to merchants/exporters in the Northeast, and these, in turn, would finance shopkeepers and cotton growers. The prominent role of merchants as the main responsible for financing and marketing cotton crops was something that had occurred since the beginning of the cotton economy, and merchants were also pivots in the financing and commercialization of sugar.

3 Mercantile Control over Growers

The big difference between the approaches of merchants regarding sugar and cotton was monitoring. Cotton merchants had greater control over production chains because they financed a sector with virtually no political and economic power, not to mention the monopolistic practices of bagging and pressing. Conversely, those connected with sugar production were a traditionally powerful group with greater leeway to evade mercantile control. This was further complicated by the fact that the capital for cotton farming was small compared to the capital required by the sugar industry. Therefore, the cotton growers' social position was radically different from that of cane growers and sugar mill owners.[39]

38 ANTT, 10° CNL, Cx. 36, liv. 190, f. 130v–131.

39 This paragraph summarizes some core hypotheses that have been drawn from the primary sources discussed so far and from other records and secondary literature. On the social power of sugar producers, see Daniel Strum, *O Comércio do Açúcar: Brasil, Portugal*

As an illustration, the merchants took away the means to demand better conditions for business from the small cotton growers, who were, once again, devoid of political power. In the early 1790s, some merchants in Pernambuco wrote that cotton growing was carried out "by part of the poor men" and was supported by "the trader's industry and risk." These same merchants intended to persuade the Queen that a donation of 30 *réis* per arroba of cotton, charged from the growers for the construction of a hospital in Pernambuco, was unfair since it would only penalize cotton cultivation and leave the sugar planters and other traders exempt from such a burden. Yet, these traders were not showing solidarity with the cotton farmers. They knew that the tax burden would fall on them too. But even so, the cotton merchants did not think it was fair that only a share of "society" contributed with the tax, particularly the poorest part since the rest of the population would benefit from the hospital. They said the donation should be offered "by the richest and most powerful, the sugar mill owners and some of the country's great traders." And they continued to criticize the rich old men, in what is perhaps one of the most unmistakable signs of how cotton carved out an entirely new social distinction in Pernambuco, saying that they were "individuals whose wealth and large assets are only shown for the ostentation of demarcated luxury, almost always ruined by the patrimony of their children and the good customs of their families, [...] rich men, prodigals of poor sweat, and greedy even of the superfluous that superabounds in their riches, driven either by shameful flattery or by an excess of avarice and inhumanity."[40] Table 4.1 lists the names of the 67 merchants in Pernambuco who were interested in cotton and who spoke for the growers. They were probably the main financiers of the cotton culture; some were simple local traders, others were big wholesalers and exporters.

---

e Países Baixos, 1595–1630 (Versal, 2012), 362; Melo, *Financiando o Negócio de Pernambuco*, chapter 1. See also the article by Ribeiro Júnior, which highlighted the importance of intermediaries in the cotton trade in Pernambuco; Ribeiro Júnior, "A Economia Algodoeira Em Pernambuco," 241.

40 "indivíduos cuja riqueza e grandes cabedais só se mostram para a ostentação de demarcado luxo, quase sempre arruinados do patrimônio de seus filhos e dos bons costumes das suas famílias, [...] homens ricos, pródigos de suor pobre, e avarentos ainda do supérfluo que lhes superabunda das suas riquezas, levados ou de uma vergonhosa lisonja ou de um excesso de avareza e desumanidade [...]." ANTT. Junta do Comércio, mç. 10 (cx. 38) Correspondência recebida das autoridades ultramarinas. It is an undated document, but the idea of building the hospital is probably from 1792, according to some documents from the AHU.

TABLE 4.1 Cotton traders in Pernambuco in the early 1790s

Name	Name	Name
Alexandre José de Araújo	Francisco Lopes Porto	José Bras Duarte
Anastácio da Silva Guimarães	Francisco Nunes Correia	José de Sani
Antônio de Souza Barroso	Gervásio Francisco Soares	José dos Santos Ormur
Antônio José da Silva Porto	Gervásio José de Mendonça	José Fernandes da Cunha
Antônio José Pires	Jerônimo Francisco dos Reis Guimarães	José Gomes Ferreira
Antônio José Quaresma	João Alemão de Campos	José Joaquim da Silva Sacotto
Antônio Marques da Costa Soares	João Antônio Gomes	José Joaquim Jorge
Bento Pereira Salgado	João Bernardo Madeira	José Porfírio de Freitas
Custódio José Ribeiro dos Santos Guimarães	João Crisóstomo da Fonseca e Silva	José Ramos Chaves
Daniel da Silva Queiros	João de Deus Pires Ferreira	Lourenço Pereira Bernardes
Domingos Antônio Pereira	João do Rego Falcão	Manuel Antônio Ferreira
Domingos Gomes da Silva Vasconcelos	João Gomes de Melo	Manuel de Matos Simoens
Euzébio Joaquim Damazio Porto	João Lourenço dos Santos	Manuel José Ferreira
Francisco Branco	João Pereira da Silveira	Manuel José de Liveira e Jacomo
Francisco de Oliveira Antunes	João Pereira de Brito	Manuel José de Sergras
Francisco de Oliveira Gomes	Joaquim José de Moura	Manuel José Duarte Guimarães
Francisco de Paula Pinto	Joaquim Rodrigues Pinheiro	Manuel José Francisco Barros
Francisco de Souza Rego	Joaquim Silveira de Aguiar	Manuel José Gonçalves do Vale
Francisco José Peixoto de Freitas	Joasé Antônio Soares	Manuel Martins Pereira Monteiro
Francisco José Ribeiro Coelho	Joquim Ribeiro de Brito	Manuel Pinto de Souza
	José Alemão de Cisneiros	Nuno Antônio Rodrigues Lima
	José Álvares da Silva	Pedro Rodrigues Lima
	José Antônio dos Anjos	Tomás Lourenço da Costa
		[...]Bento Furtado de Mendonça

Source: ANTT. Junta do Comércio, mç. 10 (cx. 38) Correspondência recebida das autoridades ultramarinas. [...] – illegible name. Table prepared by the author.

Although the supplicants were very explicit in their intentions against new taxes and directly confronted members of the sugar aristocracy, part of the mercantile group in Table 4.1 was also made up of sugar mill owners, and it seems evident that there was always a presence of capital from Portugal in the hands of these colonial merchants. Between the 1780s and 1790s, for example, João Crisóstomo da Fonseca e Silva appears in the sources at the same time as a cane grower, sugar mill owner, and merchant.[41] In 1785, he worked as the attorney for investors in Lisbon who asked him to collect a series of debts from Manuel Rodrigues Sete.[42] In the same year, though, Silva was a debtor who was being charged by the merchant in Lisbon, Antônio Martins Bastos, for a certain amount of vinegar that he had sent him to sell in Pernambuco.[43] His main contact in Portugal was perhaps his brother Manuel da Fonseca e Silva, with whom he had a company that had been established in the early 1780s.[44]

Antônio José Quaresma offers an even more complete example of how the capital governing mercantile relations with Pernambuco could have come from Portugal. He probably knew Brazil reasonably well, as he was the pilot of a vessel doing business to Pernambuco in 1783–84.[45] But it was only later that he would establish himself in the Northeast of Brazil. In 1787 he went to Pernambuco on the ship *Nossa Senhora do Livramento e Santo Antônio*, of which João Felix Borralho was captain. This trip, together with the first shipment of goods to Recife, marked the beginning of the company he had made with Francisco Malaquias da Cunha, a merchant established in Lisbon. The partner in Lisbon would subscribe to all the capital, and the partner on the way to Recife would only contribute with "his agency and work." Both would share profits and losses. Annually the partners had to exchange the accounting books with each other. The partner in Lisbon could do business outside the partnership but not the partner in Pernambuco. Quaresma "will be obliged to ask for the goods and everything else he finds best-selling and useful so that the Lisbon partner can send them to him." The dissolution of the company would take place after four years when the partners would pay all their debts, and the Lisbon partner would recover his initial capital. Only after that would they share the profits "which God has been pleased to give to this society in an equal share, or pay equally the losses if any." Antônio José Quaresma made Francisco Malaquias da Cunha his attorney to represent him in Lisbon during the time he would be in Pernambuco. Soon after he arrived in Recife, Quaresma not only became one of the leading cotton traders but an influential colonial merchant in the early nineteenth century.[46]

---

41 ANTT, 10º CNL, Cx. 30, liv. 164, f. 103. AHU, ACL, CU, 015, Cx. 207, Doc. 14139, Cx. 158, Doc. 11423, and Cx. 223, Doc. 15104. See also Souza, *Elites e Exercício de Poder No Brasil Colonial: A Câmara Municipal Do Recife, 1710–1822*, 575–795.

42 ANTT, 10º CNL, Cx. 21, liv. 114, f. 12v–13.

43 ANTT, 10º CNL, Cx. 30, liv. 164, f. 103.

44 ANTT, Junta do Comércio, Registo Geral, Liv. 122, f. 137–140v.

45 ANTT, Feitos Findos, Juízo da Índia e Mina, mç. 40, n.º 5, cx. 227.

46 AHU, ACL, CU, 015, Cx. 270, Doc. 18008.

The company between Cunha and Quaresma is just one of several other partnerships between Lisbon merchants. In a survey of 94 mercantile companies registered in the Lisbon notary offices, it was discovered that what happened between Cunha and Quaresma exemplified a kind of rule that the other companies followed. In total, these companies were established by 196 individuals: 98 partners in Portugal and 98 in Pernambuco, an average of two people per partnership (Table 4.2.). They were made up of businessmen, merchants, grocers, clerks, tax farmers, goldsmiths, bakers, coachmen, tinkers, cooks, customs officers, ship captains, sea pilots, carpenters, caulkers, cake sellers, surgeons, priests, and owners of shipyards. The partners in Lisbon contributed most of the capital. In total, they subscribed to 216,116,924 *réis* (73.02%), most of which consisted of goods. Those who traveled to Pernambuco (40) or who were already there (7) 8 invested 79,825,769 *réis* (26.98%). Together, all capitals totaled 325,012,999 *réis*.[47] Among several different rules, a clause appears in most companies' agreements: if a company should close, after the subscribed capital has been recovered, the profits and losses would be equally divided between the partners. Of the 94 contracts, 87 stipulated this rule (92.5%). The other companies would split the gains and losses unequally, but always with the metropolitan partner having the largest fraction. In many cases, merchants in Lisbon resorted to company contracts to guarantee the exclusive services of an agent in the colony. Of all the agreements, 57 (60.6%) prohibited the partner in Pernambuco from doing business outside the company, and five contracts (5.3%) allowed this. Still, the profits from these businesses would go to the partnership. Only 20 companies (21.3%) freed up colonial partners to have other businesses.[48] The reason for these contractual restrictions was linked to the capital composition of the companies. Whether from members in Lisbon or Pernambuco, the companies' initial funds could come from loans. Some companies clarified that they were registering contracts with notaries to produce legally admissible evidence for their creditors, enabling them to file lawsuits to recover their capital eventually. Thus, it was common for companies to first commit to paying their creditors before sharing profits and losses. Even if they started with their own resources, companies could opt for credits from other individuals during the course of their activities.[49]

---

47 This is the sum of the capital of all companies, even those that did not distinguish between what belonged to the merchant in Lisbon and that of Pernambuco, so it is a greater value than the sum of the capital divided between the merchants in Lisbon and those in Pernambuco.

48 Twelve contracts did not inform whether the colonial partner could do business outside the company or not.

49 For more on trading companies, see Melo, "Hierarquias mercantis no Atlântico Português".

TABLE 4.2 Companies that traded between Lisbon and Pernambuco, 1784–1807

Date	Partner in Lisbon	Partner in Pernambuco
07/1784	Antônio José dos Santos Rodrigues	Bento José dos Santos Rodrigues
03/1785	Antônio José dos Santos Rodrigues	Francisco Nunes Correa
10/1785	José Francisco Campos	Manuel José de Cerqueira
11/1785	Manuel José da Cruz e Silva	Antônio José da Silva
12/1785	Francisco de Souza	Francisco de Andrade
10/1786	José Bento de Araújo*	Manuel José Ribeiro
10/1786		José Antônio Soares e João Rodrigues de Carvalho
10/1787	Antônio Pires Marinho*	Nuno Antônio Rodrigues Lima
11/1787	Francisco Malaquias da Cunha*	Antônio José Quaresma
11/1787	José Pereira da Silva	José Pedro Machado
02/1788		Domingos Caetano e João Antônio de Freitas
08/1788	José Antônio Soares da Rocha	Lourenço José Lisboa
11/1788	Antônio Martins Portela e Camilo João de Queiros	Daniel da Silva Queiros
04/1789		João Francisco Lucas e Manuel da Silva Soares
04/1789	José Anacleto*	José Joaquim Jorge
08/1789	João Manuel Álves	José Francisco Belem
11/1789	José Quintino	João Rodrigues Salazar
04/1790	Manuel de Miranda Correa*	Manuel Rodrigues de Aguiar
08/1790	Antônio José dos Santos Amorim*	João Lourenço dos Santos e Gervásio José de Mendonça
09/1790	José Antônio Barbosa	José Bernardes
10/1790	Correia, Viana e Companhia*	Manuel Xavier Faustino Ramos
05/1791	João de Deus Pinto	José Dias de Andrade e Gregório Rodrigues de Perim
10/1791	Antônio Lopes Ferreira e Manuel Ribeiro dos Santos	
07/1792	José Quintino	João Rodrigues Salazar
07/1792	Raimundo da Silva*	José Felipe dos Santos
09/1792		João Raposo e Manuel Inácio Ferreira*
02/1793	Geraldo Van Egmond Fauvareq	Luis José Soares
05/1793	Antônio Esteves Costa*	Antônio Rodrigues da Cunha Viana
05/1793	Mateus Vaz Corvello	Manuel Moniz de São Pedro
07/1793	Manuel Francisco Lavra*	Amaro Branco

TABLE 4.2 Companies that traded between Lisbon and Pernambuco, 1784–1807 (*cont.*)

Date	Partner in Lisbon	Partner in Pernambuco
10/1793	Manuel dos Santos da Cruz e Domingos da Costa	
04/1794	José Fernandes de Matos* e Bernardo Pereira de Souza	Manuel José Duarte Guimarães*
12/1794	Januário José Gorjão	João Raposo
12/1794	Manuel de Souza Lobo*	Jerônimo Lourenço da Silva
12/1794	João Fernandes dos Santos	Antônio Veloso
01/1795	José Tavares*	Antônio José da Rocha
01/1795	Joaquim José Vasques*	Manuel Inácio Garraxo
02/1795	José Domingues Lima	José da Fonseca Guimarães
05/1795	Januário José Gorjão	Francisco Marques Brandão
05/1795	Pedro Gonçalves Chaves	Pedro da Costa Virgulino
05/1795	Francisco José Pereira de Oliveira*	José Tavares da Gama
07/1795	Manuel José Machado*	Manuel da Fonseca
10/1795	José Fernandes de Matos*	Antônio do Couto
12/1795	José João Gonçalves	Francisco de Paula Carrilho
02/1796	Antônio Carlin	Silvestre Cardoso da Fonseca
02/1796	Felipe José Rodrigues de Aguiar	João Antônio Gonçalves Maduro
07/1796	José Manuel da Cunha Oliveira*	Manuel Ribeiro do Couto
11/1796	José Bento de Araújo*	Álvaro Gonçalves
11/1796	José Rodrigues	Domingos da Costa
01/1797	João José	Manuel Lourenço
01/1797	Manuel da Silva Franco	José de Matos Girão
01/1798	Ângelo Gonçalves Aires	José Bento Moreira
01/1798	Joaquim José de Almeida*	Antônio Ferreira
10/1798	Antônio Rodrigues da Cunha Viana	Manuel Rodrigues da Cunha
11/1798	Francisco Bernardo de Faria e Companhia	Antônio Afonso Duarte
11/1798	Bento Pacheco	João Teixeira
04/1799	José Inácio Mendes	José Pacheco
05/1799	Francisco José Teixeira	Joaquim Martins e Antônio José da Costa
09/1799	João da Silva e Bento Pacheco	João Teixeira
09/1799	Francisco José Nunes	Teotônio Simões dos Reis
12/1799	Antônio Domingues	Luis Marques da Silva
12/1799	Manuel Pedroso	Jacinto Pedro Antunes
12/1799	João Antônio	Jacinto Pedro Antunes
12/1799	Luis Antônio Rodrigues Sete*	Manuel Rodrigues Ferrão

TABLE 4.2 Companies that traded between Lisbon and Pernambuco, 1784–1807 (*cont.*)

Date	Partner in Lisbon	Partner in Pernambuco
02/1800	Manuel Lopes Teixeira	Antônio José Teixeira Delgado
06/1800	João Fernandes	José da Costa
07/1800	Antônio José Maria	Manuel do Nascimento
01/1801	Luis José de Brito	Sebastião de Outorelo
01/1801	Francisco Antônio Lago	José Pinto
02/1801	Pascoal José Fernandes	Antônio Estevão dos Santos
10/1801	Fernando José Rodrigues	Bernardo Coelho da Costa
06/1802	Manuel Joaquim Martins	Manuel de Jesus e Souza
07/1802	Manuel Francisco Lavra*	José Francisco Mindello
07/1802	Manuel Caetano Veloso de Castro da Silveira Maia	José Veloso da Silveira
07/1802	Tomás Antônio Ferreira Carros	Antônio José Brandão
09/1802	Luis José de Brito	Joaquim Anacleto Pires Oldemberge
01/1803	Manuel Ribeiro da Silva*	Jacinto José Dias de Carvalho
02/1803	Manuel Pires	José Vicente Álves e Antônio José Nunes
04/1803	José Rodrigues	Martinho Francisco Pereira
07/1803	Manuel Gonçalves	Bertolo Gonçalves
12/1803	Manuel José Barbosa Braga	José Afonço de Faria
01/1805	Manuel José Mendes Guimarães	Basílio Gonçalves Ferreira
01/1805	Francisco Xavier Martins	Basílio Gonçalves Ferreira
03/1805	Antônio José Pinto da Cruz	Antônio Ramos Belo
04/1805	Rafael Antônio	João Antônio de Souza
09/1805	Félix José Antônio Viana*	Joaquim Antônio Batista
12/1805	Fernando de Souza Machado*	José Ferreira Gomes
01/1806	José Fernandes de Matos,* José Francisco de Matos e João Francisco de Matos	Domingos José Martins Vieira
07/1806	Luis Martins de Paula	José de Ayrella Jardim
08/1806	José Maria de Almeida	Francisco José da Costa Guimarães
09/1806	Antônio Raimundo da Silva	José Correia
10/1806	Manuel Gonçalves Meira	Francisco Xavier Gonçalves
02/1807	Dionísio Cornel e Antônio Ferreira Soares	
07/1802	José Tavares*	Manuel da Fonseca

Source: Melo, "Hierarquias mercantis no Atlântico Português," 33–38. *Main cotton importer in Lisbon (Appendix A). Table prepared by the author.

Table 4.2 identifies 24 merchants who were part of the leading cotton importers in Lisbon (Appendix A). They also participated in other businesses, like Antônio Esteves Costa, who joined in the slave trade with Guinea (Table 2.6), and Antônio José dos Santos Amorim, an important cotton re-exporter to European ports (Appendix B).

These merchants, especially those who invested and went to Pernambuco, were obviously taking advantage of a favorable scenario for business. There was a space left by the extinct monopoly of the General Company of Pernambuco and Paraíba, and the good prices of cotton (and sugar after 1793) attracted more and more Portuguese traders and investors. As early as 1783,[50] Francisco Nunes Correia, already stationed in Pernambuco, made a company with his brother-in-law in Lisbon, Antônio José dos Santos Rodrigues. The person who represented Francisco Nunes Correa was his attorney in Lisbon. The initial capital belonged entirely to Rodrigues. The partnership could not dissolve before eight years, but it could in case one of the partners acted in bad faith. The partnership would start with the first shipment transported by the *Santo Antônio Voador* vessel. Antônio José dos Santos Rodrigues had already sent his brother-in-law "several shipments of goods," which totalled 23,483,662 *réis*. Francisco Nunes Correa's job—who did not bring in any capital to the company but only "his industry" and "administration"—was to sell the goods for "cash and on credit to people of notorious credit and probity for the best and highest price that time and the state of the land [i.e., the market] allow, provided, however, that the credit sales are in moderation and for limited times, so that he [Correa] can make prompt shipments of his products, so that the cashier of this city of Lisbon does not suffer vexation by the creditors of the society."[51] Francisco Nunes Correa became a merchant very interested in cotton, as evidenced by the complaint he signed against new taxes in the early 1790s (Table 4.1). Even in 1805, he was one of the leading merchants in Recife and a potential contact for merchants and investors who read the Lisbon Almanach.[52]

Daniel Rodrigues Grijó, despite not being on the lists above, became an important figure in the history of the cotton trade. His interest revolved around the activity of outfitting ships, including getting loads of cotton to fill his vessels. He got into trouble with a judge in Pernambuco in 1791, who even had

---

50 The company's charter is from 1785, but the partners had been trading since 1783.

51 "dinheiro de contado e fiadas a pessoas de notório crédito e probidade pelo melhor e mais alto preço que o tempo e estado da terra permitir, contanto, porém, que as vendas fiadas sejam com moderação e por tempos limitados, afim de que possa fazer prontas remessas dos seus produtos, para que não padeça o caixa desta cidade de Lisboa vexames pelos credores da sociedade." ANTT, 2° CNL, Cx. 132, liv.626, f. 88v–90.

52 *Almanach de Lisboa de 1805*, 505–512.

him arrested, and was criticized by the governor who said that he did not even deserve the title of a merchant, as he was nothing more than an agent. Yet, Grijó was raised as an attorney for the cotton merchants from Pernambuco in the 1790s to negotiate with His Majesty, in Lisbon, with the "honor of kissing the royal hand," so that the idea of creating a new tax on the fiber would be abandoned. The reason for returning to Portugal was his excessive debts in Pernambuco, according to the governor. On that occasion, probably between 1796 and 1807, he became a solicitor for Recife merchants in Lisbon.[53]

4 Monopolies, Trade Conflicts, and Revolution in Pernambuco

By the end of the 1790s, a consensus was being formed that there were many de facto monopolies in Pernambuco. I mentioned earlier how there was dissatisfaction on the part of merchants in Recife with cotton baggers/pressers. But it so happens that merchants themselves were accused of being monopolists. This occurred not only in the sale of European goods but also in the slave trade. For example, José Porfírio de Freitas, one of the cotton traders (Table 4.1), was accused of being a monopolist in Pernambuco in 1799. Before that, though, he owed money to merchants established in Lisbon.[54]

We cannot rule out the bad faith of the traders in this scenario, but it is important to note that the low supply of goods could negatively impact the reputation of colonial merchants. The problem was that the quantity of imported goods was insufficient to buy tropical goods, hence perhaps the strong impression that there were monopolies happening. As the governor of Pernambuco, Tomás José de Melo, bluntly stated in 1798, "our current imports are much smaller than exports. The Kingdom's goods are not enough to exchange the country's products [of Pernambuco]."[55] This was as true for 1798 as it was ten years before. The same governor provided data in 1788 that clearly showed exports were much greater than imports.[56]

At the same time, the employment of *comissários volantes* (itinerant Portuguese traders who worked as agents between Portugal and Brazil) in the 1780s

53 Maria Beatriz Nizza da Silva, *Elites Pernambucanas Do Fim Do Período Colonial* (São Paulo: Editora Singular, 2018), 190–93; Melo, *Financiando o Negócio de Pernambuco*, 300, 339–40. See also AHU, ACL, CU, 015, Cx. 207, Doc. 14139.

54 Melo, *Financiando o Negócio de Pernambuco*, 231.

55 AHU, ACL, CU, 015, Cx. 199, Doc. 13653 and APEJE. CC. 09, f. 2–2v.

56 APEJE. CC. 03, f. 14v–15.

was another commercial strategy that impacted colonial merchants. Sending goods from Portugal to Brazil through these itinerant agents could be a more advantageous practice—than, for instance, sealing ties with merchants in Brazil—as they were able to enter the productive circuits by advancing goods and money to the cultivators, achieving more profitable exchange conditions. It was a good strategy for the metropolitan merchants as the whole commercialization process was faster. Furthermore, upon returning to the metropolis, the itinerant trader would have to give an account to his principal. At the same time, it was a negotiation with benefits to the itinerant trader, who would not have to stay in the colony for too long. These agents caused distress in the mercantile community of Pernambuco, though. In 1797, officials from the Recife council wrote that itinerant agents came from Portugal to Pernambuco with passports issued by the Board of Trade in Lisbon with the excuse of collecting debts. But what they actually came to do was trade and, according to the councillors of the same city, unfairly: the *comissários* went to the hinterlands and bought cotton from the growers, causing prices to increase for merchants established in Pernambuco.[57] Almost ten years earlier, Governor Tomás José de Melo had criticized this practice precisely because it harmed colonial merchants.[58] Catharine Lugar concluded the same for Bahia. In Salvador, resident merchants complained about the *comissários* because they performed unfair competition since they had no costs to "maintain stores or extend credit to build a clientele."[59] In Maranhão, in the 1780s, itinerant agents were important traders who unsettled the already established merchants.[60]

Yet, the general feeling was that the merchants established in Pernambuco were Portuguese with ties to Portugal. This belief prevailed until the final moments of colonization. Furthermore, the Portuguese were the individuals associated with the monopolies. There was also the feeling that they were the only owners of the capital and, recurrently, the people who collected the debts. However, one of the links that kept the old colonial system in place was the relationship that existed between the "native aristocracy" and the merchants, who were frequently Portuguese. These relationships gradually deteriorated over the course of time. They deteriorated by the foreclosure of debts by sugarcane growers and planters and the issuance of various moratoriums in favor of

57 Palacios, "Peasantry and Slavery in Brazil, Volume II," 132.

58 AHU, ACL, CU, 015, Cx. 162, Doc. 11607.

59 Catherine Lugar, "The Merchant Community of Salvador, Bahia, 1780–1830" (PhD diss., State University of New York at Stony Brook, 1980), 145. Complaints against *comissários volantes* appear in Rio de Janeiro as well; see Maxwell, "Pombal and the Nationalization of the Luso-Brazilian Economy".

60 AHU, ACL, CU, 009, Cx. 73, Doc. 6284.

the colonial aristocracy (see chapter 3). They also wore down during the GCPP monopoly, where sugar mill owners and cane growers once again found themselves heavily indebted, this time to a company made with capital from investors in Portugal.[61] The last sign of exhaustion was when a group of merchants monopolized some trades in the captaincy, such as the slave trade and the sale of goods imported from Europe. The figure of the *atravessador*, known for selling dearly to the colonial inhabitants and buying their agricultural products (including cotton) cheaply, was also associated with Portuguese merchants. These relations degenerated in 1817 when the people of Pernambuco made a revolution, of which one of the objectives was to eliminate the Portuguese domain.

Pernambuco was already looking for political autonomy even before the Independence of Brazil in 1822, and cotton had a central place in this anti-colonial revolution.[62] When the Portuguese Crown settled in Rio de Janeiro, it found itself in great need of money, but it could not increase its revenue by raising import taxes that would hurt the English in Brazil and the treaties signed with England. The Crown, though, raised funds by increasing taxes on agricultural production in several regions of Brazil, including Pernambuco's sugar and cotton. The fight against the "fiscal voracity of Rio," to use the words of Evaldo Cabral, was part of the agenda of the Pernambuco insurgents in 1817 and another revolution that took place in 1824.[63] Yet, there was a crucial difference between cotton and sugar in this context. After 1808, most cotton went straight to England. Sugar, in turn, was still exported in large quantities to Portugal and then re-exported to the main markets of Hamburg and Italy. In addition, Portuguese merchants in Recife financed the sugar plantations, marketed the crops, and even supplied enslaved workers to sugar mill owners and cane growers. Because it was exported to England, cotton depended a lot on English merchants in Pernambuco. Sugar, being shipped to Portugal, still depended on Portuguese merchants, so the planters and cane growers were still leaning toward the Portuguese monarchy. Those interested in cotton

61 José Ribeiro Júnior, *Colonização e monopólio no nordeste brasileiro: a Companhia Geral de Pernambuco e Paraíba, 1759–1780* (1976; HUCITEC, 2004).

62 Carlos Guilherme Mota, *Nordeste 1817: Estruturas e Argumentos* (Perspectiva, 1972), 16–17, 21–23, 27.

63 Mello, *A Outra Independência*, 29–30; on the negative effects of taxes on the Brazilian cotton economy and its loss of competitiveness in the world market, see Thales Augusto Zamberlan Pereira, "Taxation and the Stagnation of Cotton Exports in Brazil, 1800–60," *The Economic History Review* 74, no. 2 (2021): 522–45; Rafael Cariello and Thales Zamberlan Pereira, *Adeus, senhor Portugal: crise do absolutismo e a Independência do Brasil* (Companhia das Letras, 2022), 36.

had more reason to be frustrated with the Portuguese than those interested in sugar. So much so that rural support for the 1817 revolution in Recife came from the residents who inhabited the cotton regions.[64] Not coincidentally, the insurgency took place during a recession, when cotton prices, both in Pernambuco and Maranhão, were falling from 1813 to 1821, possibly because of the end of the wars in Europe.[65]

But in general, the opening of Brazilian ports in 1808 and the English presence in Pernambuco met the context of dissatisfaction of the colonists with the Portuguese. The British were no longer interested in making agreements with Portuguese traders, and neither were the farmers, who wanted to get rid of colonialism. Some traders from Pernambuco—although some of them had Portuguese origins—were no longer interested in doing business with Portugal. Therefore, they supported the insurrection.[66] Contrary to what happened in Maranhão, where planters suffered from the monopolistic schemes of the English and Portuguese,[67] in Pernambuco, it seems that the English managed to keep their reputation clean. According to Koster, after 1808, the British merchants even ended the monopoly of the Recife merchants, who sold everything at exorbitant prices.[68] Koster himself was in Recife during the events of 1817. He even acted as an intermediary between the Portuguese government and the insurgents. Around 1817, English merchants already lent goods to Pernambuco traders to go inside the captaincy to sell them. At that time, the British Consul John Lempriere, fearing the negative impacts of the revolution, wrote to officers in England about the importance of having a good relationship with the insurgents to facilitate not only trade but also the collection of debts that Pernambuco had towards the English merchants in Recife.[69] Paraíba, due to its large cotton production, also had some foreign merchants. But even in the late 1810s, Paraíba sent its cotton bales to Recife to export. By 1828, there were already five English commercial houses and a French one in Paraíba. Yet, some of them worked with capital from English firms in Recife to buy cotton. Overall, Pernambuco's connection with England was strong. The high cotton exports to England made Pernambuco not so much averse to the English as the merchants and the rural elite in Bahia and Rio de Janeiro, who detested the British agenda of ending the slave trade.[70]

64 Mello, *A Outra Independência*, 57, 60; Mello, *Frei Joaquim do Amor Divino Caneca*, 21, 24.
65 Mota, *Nordeste 1817*, 16–17, 21–23, 27.
66 Mota, *Nordeste 1817*, 18.
67 Gayoso, *Compendio historico-politico*, 259–60.
68 Koster, *Travels in Brazil*, 145.
69 Mota, *Nordeste 1817*, 39–40, 59.
70 Mello, *A Outra Independência*, 33, 60.

In the years leading up to Brazil's Independence in 1822, Pernambuco and Maranhão chose different political paths. While in Pernambuco, in 1817 and 1824, autonomist ideas and attitudes were fostered, that is, neither linked to Rio nor to Portugal, in Maranhão—which took a long time to join Brazil—the idea of "fidelity to the Portuguese Empire" remained against the political decisions taken in Rio de Janeiro.[71]

5 Conclusion

The economic vulnerability of cotton farmers in the Northeast led to the rise in importance of intermediaries who moved cotton bales from the interior to the coast. These intermediaries were significantly more important in the Northeast than in Maranhão, consistently accumulating capital to gin, bag, and compress the cotton bales. Occasionally, they also functioned as exporters. Nevertheless, a group of merchants appeared to prioritize commerce with Lisbon, while another concentrated on domestic trade. Chains of credit, in turn, linked the two groups together: the capital that the large coastal wholesalers lent to the internal traders could be used to buy cotton from the small farmers. Perhaps the huge number of farmers dispersed across the vast region of the Northeast favored the crucial role of intermediaries. Without them, the large exporters on the coast would have more difficulty buying cotton from an infinity of sellers spread over a vast region. And the sellers themselves, because of their poverty, were in an unfavorable position to travel great distances to sell their small crops.

Traders in the Northeast, in general, exercised much greater control over small cotton farmers, much more compared to the relationships they had with sugar producers. Even in Maranhão, the planters were at least strong enough to export their crops, or parts of them. But even though they exercised control over the small slaveholders in the Northeast, these merchants did not fail to come into conflict with each other. Sometimes some merchants managed to exercise a monopoly on the bagging and pressing of cotton bales. Monopolies also emerged on the sale of European goods and the sale of enslaved people. At times, colonial merchants were threatened by itinerant agents (*commissários*) from Portugal who could obtain better conditions for purchasing raw cotton.

In one way or another, it seemed that the capital of the residents of Portugal was the most relevant in the negotiations with the Northeast of Brazil.

71 Galves, "Ao Público Sincero e Imparcial," 16, 21.

This, to some extent, was true. What demonstrates this was the share of subscribed capital in commercial companies formed between 1784 and 1807: most of the investments belonged to merchants established in Lisbon. There was also the feeling that the Portuguese were the main creditors of the captaincy. This feeling surfaced and was used politically in 1817, 1822, and 1824. In these final years of colonization, the Portuguese were increasingly seen as undesirable creditors, intermediaries, and monopolists, especially for the inhabitants of the Northeast who dealt in cotton, whose primary market was now England and no longer Portugal.

CHAPTER 5

A Business for Many: Cotton Importers in Lisbon and the Transatlantic Cotton Trade

1 A Multitude of Importers

The expansion of cotton cultivation in Maranhão and Pernambuco, driven by rising prices, access to land and enslaved labor, and the intensification of trade and transport services, transformed these regions into promising centers for growers, merchants, and agents. In Lisbon, the number of cotton importers increased between the 1780s and 1806, reflecting the growing importance of the commodity in transatlantic commerce. Although the market was technically open to all, including small importers and foreign traders, participation remained limited. Foreign merchants, while not legally excluded, rarely captured a significant share of the business. The risks of dealing with agents overseas, the difficulties of collecting debts, and the organizational focus of foreign houses on European trade made deep involvement in Brazilian cotton unattractive.

Portuguese merchants, by contrast, were able to consolidate their position. Without forming a strict oligopoly, they centralized imports by leveraging credit networks and capital flows between Lisbon and the colony. Cotton, therefore, moved through a system that relied not only on market opportunities but also on webs of credit, personal ties, and the intermediation of customs officials and dispatchers who facilitated transactions in Lisbon. The economic development generated by this trade created substantial wealth in Brazil, but it also exposed the fragility of mercantile relationships. Agency often broke down, disputes emerged even among relatives, and courts proved ineffective, forcing governors and authorities on both sides of the Atlantic to step in as arbiters.

At the same time, the circulation of credit and goods reinforced asymmetries between Brazilian producers and Portuguese merchants. Planters and traders in Maranhão and Pernambuco frequently relied on advances and credit from Lisbon, indebting themselves to their metropolitan counterparts. This pattern, already established under the General Company of Grão-Pará and Maranhão, persisted into the free trade period. Rising cotton prices further complicated matters, making imported goods difficult to afford and requiring regular remittances of money to the colony. Smuggling helped cover these deficits, revealing the porous boundaries between legal and illegal commerce. In this context, the cotton trade offers a window into both the opportunities and the tensions of free trade in the late colonial period, where wealth, risk, and conflict were inextricably linked.

A major milestone in the history of Brazilian cotton was the commercial opening of Maranhão from 1778. After more than 20 years, cotton planters and merchants (both in the colony and in the metropolis) were able to sell and trade their products without a monopoly company in the way. In the decades before 1778, the GCGPM had increased cotton production and exports, but the growth rates achieved in the following decades were much higher than in the monopoly years. The rapid economic development of Maranhão drew the attention of potential planters, merchants, and agents who wished to make wealth in the colony. What was experienced after the end of the monopoly was the entry of new economic actors, sharing the prosperity and disputing with the old economic actors who had been engaged in cotton production in Maranhão for years. Conversely, the end of the GCPP monopoly in 1780 did not have such an impact on trade, since during its monopoly, Northeast Brazil exported very little cotton. In any case, the end of both monopolies coincided with an exceptional growth in cotton exports in Maranhão and the Northeast.[1] Both were linked to the wider context of the 1780s, which experienced an exponential rise in demand for raw cotton in Britain due to the replacement of linen with cotton in warps, specifically as a result of the breaking of Arkwright's patent and the development of the mule.[2] From the point of view of Lisbon residents, the end of the monopolies meant new markets. Table 5.1 shows for the first time the number of importers in Lisbon receiving cotton from Brazil between the 1780s and 1806.

Table 5.1 was prepared using information from the Lisbon customs books. This is a central collection for the study of the cotton trade. Before going deeper into its data, a brief presentation of this documentation is necessary. All those who received merchandise from outside Portugal had to declare their names to customs officials stating that they had removed goods from the building. In addition, these owners were obviously required to pay the tax. As not all merchants had the time to go in person to the customs place, they allowed third parties to remove the goods from the building. All this information—name of the owner, name of the third party, the quantity removed, value of the goods and the value of the tax—was registered in the Lisbon customs books, a collection of books that extend from the middle of the eighteenth century to the

1 For export figures, see Martins and Melo, "Cotton Exports from Brazil, 1758–1815 Dataset".
2 With reference to the rise in demand, see Baines, *History of the Cotton Manufacture in Great Britain*, 214; Armytage, *The Free Port System*, 74.

TABLE 5.1 Merchants and cotton imports into Lisbon, 1782–1806

Years	Total merchants	Import duties*	Main cotton importers**
1782[a]	384	6,583,762	13 merchants – 3,264,445
1789[b]	620	17,342,916	30 merchants – 8,666,392
1792[c]	750	26,993,501	34 merchants – 13,435,190
1799[d]	949	28,636,348	50 merchants – 14,397,945
1806[e]	1,339	90,137,920	74 merchants – 45,266,519

Sources: Arquivo Nacional Torre do Tombo (ANTT), "Alfândegas de Lisboa, Casa da Índia":
a books 223 and 291.
b books 314 and 315.
c books 129 and 130.
d books 408, 410, and 411.
e book 1,475.
Notes: * Import duties, in *réis*, paid at customs in Lisbon. Except for 1806, the cotton tax was levied on 3% of its value. The latter was based on an administrative price from Lisbon customs which, in turn, was multiplied by the arrobas. The customs books, however, did not report the cotton arrobas, limiting themselves to giving only the number of bales. In 1806, the tax collection method changed: the tax was fixed at 200 *réis* per arroba of cotton. Although it is possible to estimate the amount of arrobas per bale (approximately five arrobas per bale, but this proportion could vary), I chose to base this table on taxes charged, as this was the only standard indicator for all years, and it is the method that probably generates fewer distortions between one year and another. Unfortunately, none of the books informs the origin of cotton; therefore, it is not possible to discover through this documentation the shares of Maranhão, the Northeast, Bahia, and other regions of Brazil.
** The leading cotton importers were considered to be all those who, together, paid more than half of the total import tax each year. See tables in Appendix A for their names. Table prepared by the author.

nineteenth century. Figure 5.1, a fragment of a page from the Lisbon customs books, illustrates what was said.

I also used the customs books that recorded cotton exports from Portugal to the various European ports. I will deal with this trade in Chapter 6, but it is relevant to point out that 37 import books and 245 export books were used, totaling 282 books that span 27 years, from 1780 to 1807. Due to their large number and the limited time to collect and treat them, I chose to carry out a sampling that was based on the available knowledge about the trade in cotton re-exports.[3] I have limited quantifications in the following years and for the following reasons (Table 5.2):

3 Like any record, customs books present challenges, problems, and limitations. First, they are an extensive source which makes the work of collecting information exhaustive and

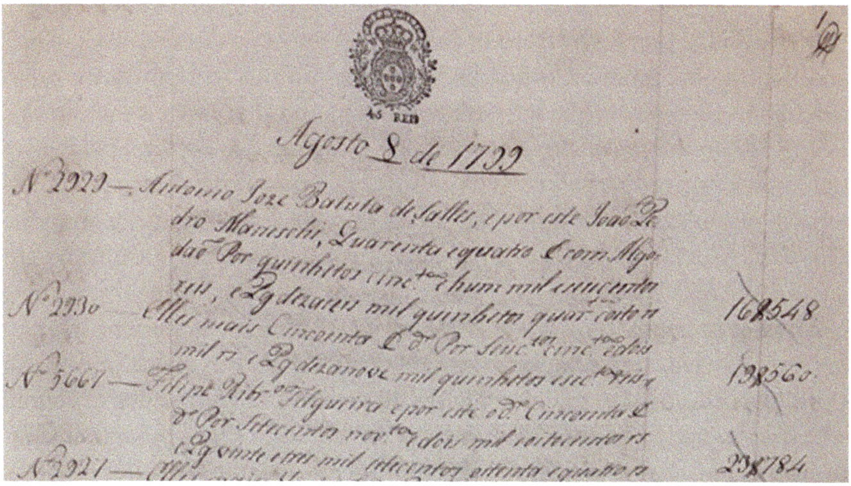

FIGURE 5.1 Copy of an excerpt from the Lisbon customs books
Source: ANTT, Alfândegas de Lisboa, Casa da Índia, book 410.

TABLE 5.2 Year for data collection from Lisbon customs books

Years	Justification
1782	Initial period of cotton exports from Brazil, where France probably dominated imports from Portugal[a]
1789 and 1792	Solidification of the cotton business. France and England probably competed for the raw cotton market.
1799	Period of wars, where France is no longer in the cotton business in Portugal[b]
1806	Period where France and England severely dispute the cotton market in Lisbon. In fact, France imports more cotton than England.[c]

Sources:
a Carreira, *A Companhia Geral do Grão-Pará e Maranhão*, vol. 2, 319.
b Arruda, *O Brasil no comércio colonial*, 370–71.
c Arruda, 370–71. Table prepared by the author.

time-consuming. Second, they have their flaws, as I noticed that the merchants' names were not registered in a standardized way. Also linked to the lack of standardization, customs officials could omit or forget (probably because of the work hours and the large volume of records they were supposed to create) to inform about whether the merchants who removed the cotton from customs belonged to any company, father and son association, or another form of partnership. Imported cotton was most of the time registered in bales and not in a unit of measure (which was the "arroba"), making it difficult to know precisely how much cotton each merchant received at customs. Third, because they only have names and

Prior to being sold, cotton was subject to a tax at the customs (*Casa da Índia*), which specified that each arroba of cotton from Brazil was valued at 3,200 *réis*, and that the tax imposed would be 27% based on this administrative price. In addition, there were extra minor charges amounting to 1,000 *réis* each arroba, as well as the expense of shipping the goods from Brazil to Portugal (which, up until 1796, could not surpass 800 *réis* per arroba). Typically, the buyer of the cotton was responsible for covering the cost of shipping, rather than the importer. This helps to explain why there are so many lawsuits aimed at collecting freight debts in the ANTT. Importers failed to pay freight costs, prompting ship owners or captains to pursue buyers who acquired goods from the importers. In order to be reexported, cotton incurred an additional tax known as the *Imposto do Consulado*. This tax was calculated based on the value of each arroba of cotton, which was set at 3,000 *réis*. The *Consulado* tax was set at 5% of this administrative price, and again it was the responsibility of the buyer to cover this expense, not the importer.[4] Yet, importer and buyer could be the same person.

The Lisbon customs data shows hundreds of importers in Lisbon, constantly growing in number between the 1780s and 1806, interested in Brazilian cotton. In Liverpool, there were hundreds of cotton importers between the 1760s and 1840s, but their number tended to decrease over the period.[5] Yet, like Liverpool,[6] in Lisbon only a small number of merchants (from 13 to 74) were able to import more than half of the cotton in each year (Table 5.1 and Appendix A). The Lisbon customs books also reveal the economic and social composition of importers in Lisbon. Although these numbers are likely inflated, and the cause may be due to the non-standard way the clerks recorded the entries,[7] Table 5.3

---

numbers, and nothing more, a qualitative analysis of trade becomes impossible. Such information, however, can be found in other registries.

4 For taxes, see The National Archives Kew FO 63/15. For shipping, see Felipe Souza Melo, "The Fleet System and the Troubled Shipping Institutions in the Portuguese Atlantic (Seventeenth and Eighteenth Centuries)," *Colonial Latin American Review* 32, no. 3 (2023): 362.

5 R. S. Fitton and A. P. Wadsworth, *The Strutts and the Arkwrights, 1758–1830: A Study of the Early Factory System* (Manchester University Press, 1968), 346; D. M. Williams, "Liverpool Merchants and the Cotton Trade, 1820–1850," in *Liverpool and Merseyside: Essays in the Economic and Social History of the Port and Its Hinterland*, ed. John Raymond Harris (Frank Cass and Company, 1969), 187. See also Arthur Redford, *Manchester Merchants and Foreign Trade, 1794–1858* (Manchester University Press, 1934).

6 Stanley D. Chapman, *The Cotton Industry in the Industrial Revolution* (1972; Second Edition, Macmillan Education, 1987), 39.

7 I suspect there was not a very well-established criterion in Lisbon customs for registering merchants and their companies. For example, for clerks, the merchant Manuel de Souza Freire could be the same as Manuel de Souza Freire & Co., so they sometimes added *Co.* after names, and sometimes not.

TABLE 5.3 The economic and social composition of cotton importers in Lisbon, 1782–1806

	1782		1789		1792		1799		1806	
	Nº	%	Nº	%	Nº	%	Nº	%	Nº	%
Merchants	358	88.7	571	89.2	685	79.7	876	91.2	1,184	86.3
Companies	4	0.7	24	9.6	39	12.5	36	6.8	82	7.8
Women (not counting widows)	6	0.4	10	0.6	10	0.3	5	0.1	16	0.4
Widows			2	0.2	1	0.1	4	0.2	17	1.5
Father-son association	2	0.1	7	0.3	10	6.6	11	0.8	31	3.0
Sibling association							6	0.6	6	1.1
Society of the Islands of Cape Verde, Bissau, and Annexes	1	0.2	1	0.2	1	0.5	1			
Religious (priest, friar, etc.)	9	1.9	5	0.1	2		9	0.1	2	
GCGPM administrators	1	7.6			1					
GCPP administrators	1	0.3			1	0.3	1	0.1	1	
Ship managers	2	0.1								
Total	384	100	620	100	750	100	949	100	1,339	100
Non-Portuguese first and last names	7	7.4	61	13.1	35	6.2	63	7.4	89	3.8
Portuguese first and last names	377	92.6	559	86.9	715	93.8	886	92.6	1,250	96.2
Total	384	100	620	100	750	100	949	100	1,339	100

Sources and notes: Nº = total number of merchants. % = percentage of import tax paid at customs in Lisbon. The sources used to put this table together were the same as those used in Table 5.1. Table prepared by the author.

shows that the bulk of the business was conducted by merchants who worked as sole traders: together they imported 79 to 91% of the cotton. Companies (a partnership between two or more merchants) were the second major means by which merchants in Lisbon obtained cotton. Other forms of mercantile organization, such as what was left of the Pombaline companies, were marginal. The presence of women in trade, including widows, was also minimal.

Table 5.3 contributes to a new perspective on mercantilism and the effectiveness of the exclusive colonial policy (*pacto colonial* or *exclusivo colonial* in Portuguese, or *exclusif colonial* in French).[8] Through it, we can better measure whether foreigners were managing to get around the Portuguese colonial exclusive or not. The answer is affirmative as foreign names appear in official import records.[9] Yet, they did not import significant quantities of cotton. Moreover, non-Portuguese names did not necessarily imply that the merchants were, in fact, foreign. Therefore, the figures in Table 5.3 are overestimated. We can illustrate this with the example of the merchant Jacome Ratton. Born in France, he was naturalized Portuguese in 1762 and classified in 1788 as a Portuguese trader.[10] Bernardo Clamousse, the largest importer of cotton with a non-Portuguese name in 1789 (see Appendix A), was classified as a Portuguese dealer.[11] Also, these merchants with non-Portuguese names used to import cotton in partnership with merchants who were Portuguese. In 1789, Melish & Devisme, British traders in Lisbon and one of the largest cotton exporters in Lisbon (Appendix B), participated together with the Portuguese merchant João de Oliveira Guimarães in some cotton imports from Brazil which totaled 3,121,200 *réis*. Yet, in his own negotiations, Guimarães was responsible for importing 9,272,000 *réis*. Thus, one of the strategies of foreign merchants to access the Brazilian raw cotton markets was to associate with Portuguese merchants.

There are additional indications suggesting that foreigners were granted permission to trade or, at the very least, to partake in the goods from Brazil. First, the Portuguese legislation made it clear that foreign merchants, even those who did not have naturalization, could own shares in Pombaline

8 The exclusive system presupposes that trade between the mother country and its colonies will be carried out by its subjects, and therefore prohibited for foreigners; see Beer, *The Old Colonial System, 1660–1754*, vol. 1; Dorothy Burne Goebel, "The "New England Trade" and the French West Indies, 1763–1774: A Study in Trade Policies," *The William and Mary Quarterly* 20, no. 3 (1963): 332–72; Novais, *Portugal e Brasil*; Alain Clément, ""Du bon et du mauvais usage des colonies": politique coloniale et pensée économique française au XVIIIe siècle," *Cahiers d'économie Politique* (Paris) 56, no. 1 (2009): 101–27.

9 Even in the gold trade, the presence of foreigners in trade with Brazil was permitted according to Shillington and Chapman. "Foreign nations, indeed, such as the French and Dutch, might, and did trade with Brazil. Indeed, in 1716, the Portuguese ambassador in England declared that it was a matter of indifference to his master what nations traded to Brazil, since all returns must be made in gold. But as far as the Portuguese government could control trade, all goods for Brazil must pass through Portugal, and all the rich returns must be made to the mother country; once there, the whole aim of the Portuguese government was to keep this so-called wealth at home." Violet Mary Shillington and Annie Beatrice Wallis Chapman, *The Commercial Relations of England and Portugal* (G.Routledge & sons, 1907), 248–49.

10 *Almanách: para o anno ... 1788* (Typog. da Academia Real das Sciencias, 1788), 205–13.

11 *Almanách*, 205–13.

companies.[12] Second, on March 12, 1773, King Dom José granted Luís Baudovin of Rouen his charter of privileges. The "privileges, graces, exemptions and prerogatives"[13] given to him and the French nation in Portugal were many, but two directly touched commercial activities. He could "negotiate, deal, sell, buy at the prices he wanted, for himself, his overseers and servants, all kinds of merchandise" and have "his goods dispatched right away at Customs."[14] Nothing in the charter of privileges restricted him from trading with Brazil or receiving goods from there.[15] In the case of the Italians, it was no different. Each of these merchants had to ask his consul for a letter of privilege to trade. This charter was based on the authorizations of the King of Portugal, who could veto some benefits and assign others.[16] Thus, permissions to negotiate with Brazil varied from case to case. Merchants of other nationalities also had privileges in Portugal, including the English who even had the right to establish trading houses in Brazil.[17] In reality, the law prohibiting foreign merchants from dealing with Brazil had to do with foreign vessels that tried to trade without touching ports in Portugal. Since the beginning of the overseas expansion at the end of the fifteenth century, the Portuguese kings prohibited the trade of foreigners with the Portuguese colonies. These laws remained in force until the end of the colonial period in the early nineteenth century, though at times they were openly disregarded—for instance, in the sixteenth century, when foreigners traded directly between Brazil and Europe without passing through Portugal. Overall, however, commerce between Portugal and its colonies was carried out primarily by Portuguese vessels. Yet it is important to note that while navigation offered limited opportunities for foreigners, the financing of agricultural

12 Antonio Delgado Silva, *Collecção da legislação Portugueza desde a ultima compilação das ordenações: Legislação de 1763 a 1774* (Typ. Maigrense, 1829), 2:361.

13 "privilégios, graça, isenções e prerrogativas".

14 "negociar, tratar, vender, comprar pelos preços que quiser, por si, seus feitores e servidores, todos os gêneros de mercancia" e ter "suas fazendas logo nas Alfândegas despachadas".

15 ANTT, Feitos Findos, Juízo da Índia e Mina, mç. 35, n.º 22, cx. 35.

16 Catia Brilli, "La Nación Genovesa de Lisboa y Sus Cónsules En El Último Cuarto Del Siglo XVIII," in *Los Cônsules de Extranjeros En La Edad Moderna y a Principios de La Edad Contempóranea* (Ediciones Doce Calles, 2013), 215–16.

17 Vítor Ribeiro, "Privilégios Dos Estrangeiros Em Portugal (Ingleses, Franceses, Alemães, Flamengos e Italianos)," *História e Memórias Da Academia Das Sciências de Lisboa* XIV (1922): 229–84; Richard Lodge, "The English Factory at Lisbon: Some Chapters in Its History," *Transactions of the Royal Historical Society* 16 (1933): 213–15; Maxwell, "Pombal and the Nationalization of the Luso-Brazilian Economy," 613; Shaw, *The Anglo-Portuguese Alliance*, 15.

production often depended heavily on credit provided by foreign merchants operating in Portugal.[18]

Foreigners were also prohibited from owning vessels carrying legal trade between Portugal and Brazil. In 1782, Martinho de Melo e Castro reminded the Board of Trade in Lisbon about this. He warned that the ownership of vessels should only belong to "Portuguese vassals, with no subjects from other nations in it."[19] He wrote this because he had discovered that foreign merchants possessed some ships. He cautioned the Board to exercise greater diligence in the investigation and to prevent further continuation of this matter.[20] Yet, despite his concern, the ownership of the merchant navy, at least in the case of trade with Pernambuco, was almost entirely in the hands of Portuguese merchants.[21]

Despite the freedom granted to foreign merchants in Portugal to engage in trade with Brazil, they generally refrained from doing so. They could even take part in financing the trade, but negotiating directly with agents and merchants in Brazil could be risky. Part of the capital that foreigners employed to fund merchants who traded with Brazil from Lisbon was made up of money and merchandise from merchants in England, France, Italy, and Germany. Collecting the debts of these Portuguese in Portugal was easier and faster than sending someone to collect debts in Brazil. The Portuguese likely dominated this section of the trade due to their advantageous conditions for monitoring and collecting debts in Brazil. Knowledge of the language, Portuguese informal rules and laws, colonial markets, and agents and correspondents who lived in Brazil were elements that, in theory, favored the Portuguese and discouraged foreigners. Besides, foreign merchants were probably already overwhelmed with their re-export duties.[22] Likewise, re-exports tended to be a more profitable business than imports. Foreigners were in Portugal because their correspondents in Europe needed reliable agents. This, to a large extent, was due to the Portuguese economic structure: Portugal was a monarchy characterized

18 Rodrigo Ricupero, "O estabelecimento do Exclusivo Comercial Metropolitano e a conformação do Antigo Sistema Colonial no Brasil," *História (São Paulo)* 35 (2016): 5–6, 8–9, 10, 12. See also Novais, *Portugal e Brasil*, 91, 176–81. "Aviso para se extrair uma cópia autêntica do alvará de 5 de Outubro de 1715, que proíbe a entrada dos navios estrangeiros nos diferentes portos do Brasil, e ser remetida à Secretaria de Estado do Negócios da Marinha." ANTT, Arquivo do Arquivo, Avisos e Ordens, mç. 5, n.º 36, 1801.

19 "vassalos portugueses, sem que neles tenham parte sujeitos de outras nações".

20 ANTT, Junta do Comércio, Registro Geral, Liv. 121, f. 7.

21 Melo, *Financiando o Negócio de Pernambuco*, 324–40.

22 As I will show in the next chapter, the merchant population that re-exported cotton was smaller than the one that imported.

by limited industrialization and reliant on the manufactured goods of other European nations.

Table 5.3 (and Appendix A) shows many people, whether large wholesalers and financiers or small shopkeepers in Lisbon who were interested in Brazilian cotton. This challenged the interpretation that sees the existence of an oligopoly set up by the metropolitan bourgeoisie to control prices in the colony.[23] This argument becomes practically pointless when we are faced with such a large mercantile population dealing with imports in Lisbon. In addition, these importers in Lisbon would have to coordinate with a large number of merchants and agents spread across Brazil's marketplaces so that they could export products also at oligopolistic prices.

Still, what explains so many Portuguese importers being interested in Brazil? A hypothesis elaborated in 1800 by an anonymous writer claimed that trade with Brazil required "little intelligence," "little work," and its profits were "huge." As a result, merchants "do not want to risk their capital in another kind of trade, which they do not know, and in which, consequently, the profit is uncertain for them."[24] This is also the reason why the Portuguese were not meaningful players in trade with Europe, which was more complex, as it required knowledge of double-entry bookkeeping and was riskier because of competition. Jacome Ratton corroborated this in the early nineteenth century. He considered the creation of the *Aula de Comércio* (commerce class or trade school) in 1759 to be of paramount importance. Before it, only three merchant houses in Portugal—composed of Portuguese in association with foreigners—were well known abroad: Bandeira and Bacigalupo, Bom and Ferreira, and Emeretz and Brito. They were well regarded because they possessed knowledge of double-entry bookkeeping, the weights and measures, foreign currencies, and exchange rates. The establishment of the *Aula* was essential as it not only prepared individuals for employment in accounting offices within the Kingdom and its colonies but also equipped them for positions with trading companies. Besides bookkeeping, the *Aula* instructed in French, the prevailing business language of the era.[25] This certainly gave greater international projection to Portuguese traders.

---

23 For this argument, see Novais, *Portugal e Brasil*, 251. See also Pierre Gervais, "Capitalism and (or) Age of Commerce: The Peculiarities of Market Exchange in the Early Modern Era," *XVII–XVIII. Revue de La Société d'études Anglo-Américaines Des XVIIe et XVIIIe Siècles*, no. 77 (December 2020).

24 Novais, *Portugal e Brasil*, 252–54.

25 Jacome Ratton, *Recordações de Jacome Ratton sobre ocorrências do seu tempo, de maio de 1747 a setembro de 1810. 2. ed. revista cuidadosamente por J.M. Teixeira de Carvalho* (Imprensa da Universidade, 1920), 191.

Yet, merchants in Lisbon probably could not control and centralize imports as they did not have the organizational structure to do so. In addition, no law or regulation prevented anyone from participating in trade with Brazil, contrary to what happened in the Spanish Empire.[26] This resulted in the emergence of numerous small merchants, including individuals whose primary income was not derived from trade, who imported modest quantities of cotton. Nonetheless, cotton could be sold, while still within customs, to a big wholesaler. Consequently, the major merchants were unable to monopolize imports; however, they certainly possessed the means to centralize cotton purchases in Lisbon.

However, the success of the cotton trade—measured by the constant growth of imports in Lisbon—was also accompanied by setbacks and disagreements between financiers, merchants, and agents. It is precisely by studying the typical and atypical conditions of commercial relations regarding cotton that we can picture new elements that contribute to a better understanding of markets and commercial history in the early modern period. Furthermore, we can better access how the Brazilian cotton trade was radically different from the classic cotton trade between the U.S. South and England. Since its inception, the latter trade was between two independent nations, and despite commercial and financial complexities, the business tended to be direct and had few intermediaries.[27] In its golden years, Brazilian cotton had to pass through Portugal, so the number of intermediaries tended to increase. Moreover, investors in Lisbon, whether foreign or national, were also ever-present figures in the cotton trade. In the United States, it seems that planters had greater control over the marketing of their crops, including employing agents in Liverpool.[28]

26 Costa et al., "Social Capital and Economic Performance," 7. See, for example, Manuel Bustos Rodríguez, *El Consulado de cargadores a Indias en el siglo XVIII (1700–1830)* (Editorial UCA, 2017).

27 Buck, *The Development of the Organisation of Anglo-American Trade, 1800–1850*; Woodman, *King Cotton and His Retainers*; Killick, "Bolton Ogden & Co."; Killick, "Risk, Specialization and Profit"; Douglas A. Farnie, *The English Cotton Industry and the World Market, 1815–1896* (Clarendon Press; Oxford University Press, 1979); Douglas A. Farnie, "The Role of Merchants as Prime Movers in the Expansion of the Cotton Industry, 1760–1990," in *The Fibre That Changed the World: The Cotton Industry in International Perspective, 1600–1990s*, ed. Douglas A. Farnie and David J. Jeremy (Oxford University Press, 2004); Aldous and Coyle, "Examining the Role of a Private-Order Institution in Global Trade".

28 Michael M. Edwards, *The Growth of the British Cotton Trade, 1780–1815* (Manchester University Press, 1967), 111–12; Nigel Hall, "Liverpool's Cotton Importers c. 1700 to 1914," *Northern History* 54, no. 1 (2017): 79. A comparison of the Portuguese Empire's forms of commodification with the British and French West Indies would be more appropriate. Until about 1800, the islands in the Caribbean were the leading growers competing with Brazilian cotton. However, information on the production and trade of West Indian cotton is very scarce. According to Ryden, cotton from the British West Indies sold in England was owned by the planters. Yet, a portion of the cotton exported from the British

In Brazil, the figure of the small colonial trader who bought crops from producers was always present, especially in the Northeast. This trader was an intermediary between the producer and the merchant on the coast. The latter could be in a company with a partner in Lisbon or just send cotton to merchants who placed an order with him. In Maranhão, the planter tended to export directly to Lisbon, but some colonial merchants bought their crops and exported the cotton. In both cases, the pieces of cotton could be merely orders from merchants established in Lisbon. In Portugal, cotton changed hands once again to be exported. It was usually sold to another merchant (Portuguese or foreign) who had connections to other parts of Europe.

All of this indicates, as Pierre Gervais argued, that early modern markets were largely controlled by intermediaries rather than by supply and demand dynamics, beyond the influence of producers and consumers.[29] This was even more true in the case of the Brazilian cotton trade. But given the existence of so many intermediaries, it is doubtful that they had, for example, controlled prices at will. It was not by chance that there was such a large presence of intermediaries in commerce in general in the early modern period. According to James Farr, middlemen who traded long distance tended to make more profits than if they invested in manufacturing or agriculture.[30] The cotton and the credit flow that supported the cotton trade in the Portuguese Atlantic can be visualized in the Flowchart 5.1.

How, then, did a trade with so many intermediaries work? The answer can be found in a description of the specificities of the Brazilian cotton trade. Whether through small or large importers, a long chain of credit supported the Brazilian (or Portuguese) cotton trade. Creating ways to make safe trade through travelling agents or companies, reacting to the bad faith of commercial partners on the other side of the Atlantic, appointing attorneys to collect debts, and appealing for help from colonial and metropolitan institutions were fundamental traits that permeated the commercial life of financiers and merchants in Lisbon and of agents and correspondents in Brazil. Likewise, Lisbon's customs, far from being just a place for collecting taxes, also proved to be an

islands in the Caribbean was actually grown in Saint-Domingue, so colonial merchants also accounted for an important share of cotton exports from the British West Indies; see Ryden, "One of the Finest and Most Fruitful Spots in America," 552; Barbara Gaye Jaquay, "The Caribbean Cotton Production: An Historical Geography of the Region's Mystery Crop" (Ph.D., Texas A&M University, 1997); Ragatz, *The Fall of the Planter Class in the British Caribbean, 1763–1833*, 39,122, 204, 371; Seymour Drescher, *Econocide: British Slavery in the Era of Abolition* (University of Pittsburgh Press, 1977), 56–86.

29 Gervais, "Capitalism and (or) Age of Commerce," 1.

30 James R. Farr, *The Work of France: Labor and Culture in Early Modern Times, 1350–1800* (Rowman & Littlefield Publishers, 2008), 126.

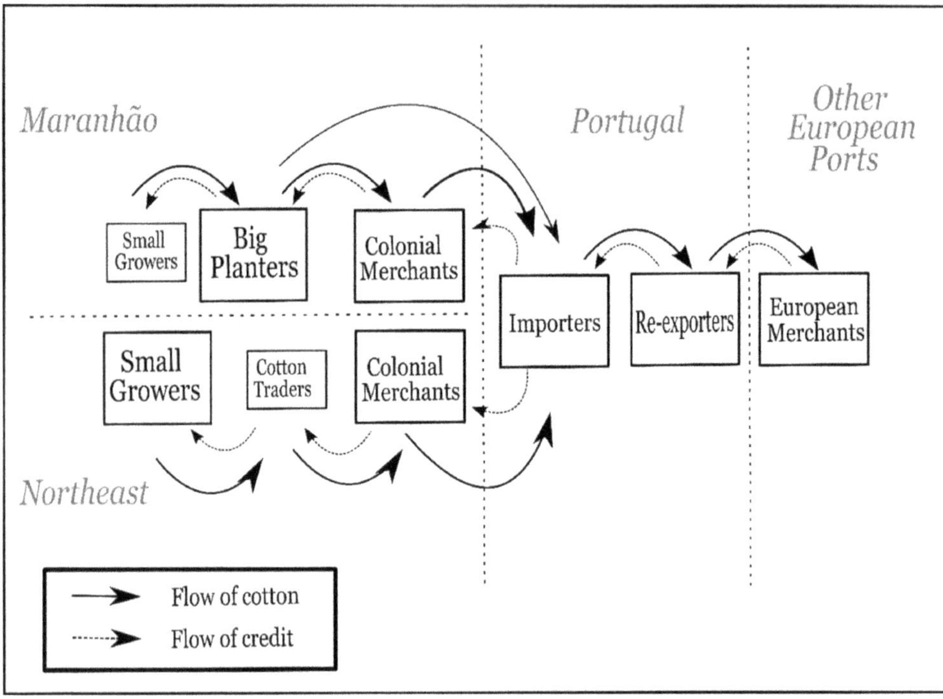

FLOWCHART 5.1 Cotton and credit flows between Brazil, Portugal, and other European ports
Notes and sources: This flowchart is based on Quark, *Global Rivalries*, 41, 71, and also on information contained in this chapter and Chapters 2 and 4. Credit was equal to goods, money, and bills. This flowchart is a simplification of a trade that could take other forms. For example, the flow of credit could go in the opposite direction, that is, from the colony to Europe. Still, according to the literature and the primary sources I worked with, it seems to me that this flowchart represents the most recurrent form and flow of cotton trade and the credits used to buy it. Flowchart prepared by the author.

important institution for the cotton trade since it stored and centralized the cotton that was sold and bought by small and large merchants outside it. The following three sections will explore these points.

2 Travelling Agents

The Lisbon customs books (Table 5.3 and Appendix A) show how the cotton trade touched various layers of Portuguese society. The way in which small importers operated was through small remittances of credit, in the form of goods, to Brazil. The credit was expected to be repaid with colonial goods. What is known about this small trade came to us through the powers of attorney records to collect debts registered in Lisbon's notary offices. The owners of the properties went to the notaries to give power of attorney to individuals who travelled to Brazil or resided there so that they could recover the goods. Probably, the creditor did this after having won the case in some court in Portugal. In Brazil, prosecutors could resolve the contentions amicably or judicially. Sometimes, when the debtors became insolvent, the guarantors were charged. Specific powers of attorney to collect debts may mean that the attorney going to Brazil was also conducting other business. The clauses of the power of attorney documents are very general, covering other economic operations. Besides, it would not be worth someone crossing the Atlantic merely to collect a single debt. All those who played the role of attorneys, ship captains, supercargoes, and seamen could be termed as traveling agents, or *comissários volantes* (already mentioned in Chapter 4).[31] On their initiative or at the behest of others, they raised credit in Portugal (in the form of goods, bills, or money), went to America, made exchanges, and returned to Portugal with tropical goods. A rough and very conservative estimate points out that individuals linked to the seamanship of the vessels performed around 39,000 commercial operations between Recife and Lisbon between 1780 and 1807.[32]

The record of the performance of travelling agents emerges in contracts of obligation, also registered in the notary offices of Lisbon, like when Pedro Antônio Martins—servant of the prominent merchant Francisco Hermano Vanzeller—made an agreement with the sailor Francisco Antônio Gonçalves en route to Pernambuco. He lent him the amount of 270,390 *réis* in goods. In Recife, the goods were supposed to be sold for money, and Pedro warned that he did not want his agent to make sales on credit. With the money in hand, Gonçalves would buy the available tropical goods, which would be sent to Martins, who would bear the risk.[33] Gonçalves should not make sales on credit, as Martins probably knew about the inconveniences of recovering these debts if the debtors did not honor the payments. Still, leaving outstanding credits and debts in Portugal and Brazil was something likely to happen to vessel captains. They were constantly making trips between the marketplaces of Portugal and Brazil and therefore had more opportunities to recover the credits.

31 "Supercargoes were usually to oversee voyages with uncommon shipping conditions: many stops and changeable itinerary, long laytime, large consignments, and so on. Their remuneration often included a share in the profits or commissions. In the former case, the agent would also share any losses." Strum, "Institutional Choice," 1209.

32 Melo, *Financiando o Negócio de Pernambuco*, 181–82.

33 ANTT, 10º CNL, Cx. 37, liv. 199, f. 29v.

João Ferreira Loures, for example, captain of a merchant vessel that operated between 1784 and 1792 on the Pernambuco route, had a series of debts and credits with the people in Brazil and Portugal. In 1789, his creditors in Lisbon were large merchants, such as Francisco Higino Dias Pereira and the English Melish & Devisme. Some of his debtors in Pernambuco were sugar mill owners, but nothing prevented him from having links with cotton merchants.[34] Yet, it is important to make clear that despite the critical role of colonial indebtedness, this does not mean that all the cotton that went into the hands of small importers in Lisbon reached them through foreclosures carried out by prosecutors. What the powers of attorney indirectly show is that small shipments of goods were necessary for small importers in Lisbon. Individually they imported little cotton but taken together their share was substantial.

Travelling agents could raise some capital from the colonial merchants as well. The governor of Maranhão, Fernando Pereira Leite de Foios, in 1789, wrote a few lines about these small itinerant merchants. By that time, he reported that "the plethora of travelling agents, smugglers, middlemen and monopolists who defiantly flooded the captaincy"[35] was ending. But he warned that some merchants based in Maranhão actually "supported" the travelling agents, as they lent them goods. The risks of these sales were high, but they were covered by the huge profits that the travelling agents made from colonial products. Their strategy was to buy cotton from enslaved Africans and indigenous peoples, something that the governor disapproved of since these were quantities of cotton that, in his opinion, had been "extorted from the masters."[36] The cotton was bagged and shipped by those salesmen who worked on a commission basis, under "foreign" marks. This was not done by planters "so as not to lose the reputation of their goods."[37] The term "extorted" may indeed be an overstatement by the governor. It was common for enslaved people, for example, to have their own small fields where they could cultivate small amounts of cotton. Although not a simple process, some planted cotton, which generated income that, after many years of saving, could be used to buy their freedom.[38]

There was an apparent solidarity between some merchants based in Maranhão and the travelling agents. The governor explained this by writing that the

34 ANTT, 7º CNL – Ofício A, Cx. 105, liv. 640, f. 57–58v.

35 "a infinidade de comissários volantes, contrabandistas, atravessadores e monopolistas que insolentemente inundavam a capitania".

36 "extorquidos de seus senhores".

37 AHU, ACL, CU, 009, Cx. 73, Doc. 6284.

38 See AHU, Códice 599, f. 112. Henry Koster, *Travels in Brazil* (Longman, Hurst, Rees, Orme, and Brown, 1816), 436.

merchants established in Maranhão were, at the beginning of their careers, "travelling agents, members of the crews of the merchant ships,"[39] and that they became grocers (*quitandeiros* which were the tenders and tavernkeepers) and later merchants themselves, some very rich and with enrolments at the Trade Board in Lisbon. "These men absorb[ed] most of the fruits of this colony," he argued, and even lent large sums to planters to buy enslaved workers.[40] However, three years after this report by the governor, 13 merchants from Maranhão would claim the exact opposite: the travelling agents were still active in their small businesses in the captaincy and harming the activity of resident merchants.[41]

They pointed out that "an infinity of sailors, and people of other orders, flood the streets of this city loaded with goods of all kinds to sell them through the doors."[42] These sailors and other small sellers did so despite various laws that prohibited it. The merchants asked for action against "such vendors"[43] because they ultimately felt they were facing dishonest competition. On the merchants established in Maranhão, as in any other part of Portuguese America, taxes were levied on the sales of their goods, and they still had to pay "excessive rent" to maintain their houses of commerce and wages to their clerks, charges that "vendors" did not suffer. These merchants established in Maranhão asked the minister in Lisbon, Martinho de Melo e Castro, to "take the necessary steps to suppress such a hateful custom" of these "idle adulterators of commerce."[44] Traveling agents also asked the Crown for *sesmarias*. Not long after, they sold the land at a good profit. This also generated discontent among merchants and farmers in Maranhão.[45]

In fact, several laws sought to curb the activity of travelling agents and sailors. The first and most important was enacted by the Marquis of Pombal. According to the legislation, the travelling salesmen were people "with little capital" and "ignorant" in the activity of commerce, according to the law that restricted their businesses in 1755. They took "large quantities of goods, which

39 "comissários volantes, saídos das equipagens dos navios".

40 "Estes homens absorvem a maior parte dos frutos desta colônia," see AHU, ACL, CU, 009, Cx. 73, Doc. 6284.

41 AHU, ACL, CU, 009, Cx. 79, Doc. 6746.

42 "infinidade de marinheiros, e gente de outras ordens, inundam as ruas desta cidade carregados de fazendas de todos os gêneros para as venderem pelas portas".

43 "semelhantes vendilhões".

44 "dar as providências necessárias afim de suprimir tão odioso costume" and "ociosos adulteradores do comércio," see AHU, ACL, CU, 009, Cx. 79, Doc. 6746.

45 AHU, ACL, CU, 009, Cx. 154, Doc. 11057.

they take on credit without rules, nor limits" for themselves,[46] and when they arrived in Brazil, they were unable to sell them, which is why they fled to the hinterlands, damaging "public faith" and the "private interests of dealers [creditors]."[47] For that reason, the travelling salesmen were prohibited from going to Brazil. The "masters, officers, and sailors of merchant ships," and royal ships were also banned from doing this type of trade.[48] This legislation was clear in restricting these individuals' commercial activities, with the justification that they were defaulting on their creditors. However, the law can also be understood as a way of reducing competition during a difficult time for overseas business. At that time, the long economic depression caused by the reduction of gold production in Minas Gerais was beginning to take shape. Still, in 1755, the monopolistic company was created for Maranhão and Grão-Pará, and in 1759 a similar company was established for Pernambuco and Paraíba. The restriction of traveling agents and the creation of monopolies were strategies to diminish competition, likely to favor certain merchant groups while boosting their profit margins.

Despite banning travelling agents in 1755, the King issued a new law in 1756, allowing sailors, masters, and vessel officers to carry certain goods from Portugal to Brazil and from Brazil to Portugal. Yet, they were all products of little value, and cotton, sugar, and tobacco were not included.[49] Already in 1760, the King reinforced the siege against travelling salesmen. According to the law of March 7 of that year, the travelling salesmen were still going to Brazil, with false certificates, or even none. They circumvented the law by declaring that they came to Brazil with goods from other merchants or returned to Portugal with money and gold. To remedy this, the king declared that the Boards of Inspection (*mesas de inspeção*) in Brazil should issue "certificates" in the same way that the Board of Trade did in Lisbon. Only with certificates could passports be issued to return to the Kingdom, and for that the Boards of Inspection should send the documents to the Board of Trade. When the vessels returned to Lisbon, the General Judge of Commerce (*Conservador Geral do Comércio*) would have the names in hand and would proceed against those travelling agents or dealers who did not have their names on the list. He could jail them for six months, and they would still have to pay a fine of 800,000 *réis*. Travelling

46 "grossas partidas de fazendas, que tomam sobre credito sem regra, nem medida." See Silva, *Collecção da legislação Portugueza desde a ultima compilação das ordenações*, 1:404.

47 "fé pública" and "interesses particulares dos negociantes".

48 "mestres, oficiais e marinheiros dos navios mercantes," see Silva, *Collecção da legislação Portugueza desde a ultima compilação das ordenações*, 1: 404.

49 Silva, *Collecção da legislação Portugueza desde a ultima compilação das ordenações*, 1: 456–58.

salesmen's goods could not be seized, as this would harm creditors.[50] In 1788, the Queen extended a little more the catalogue of products that sailors could take and bring from Brazil. But this new list also did not include cotton, sugar, and tobacco.[51] These laws were very rarely enforced. There always seemed to be a certain relaxation of the authorities that allowed the kind of trade carried out by travelling agents and sailors.

Traveling merchant-commissioners were perhaps a more promising type of agency due to the more profitable business they could do, the speed with which they did it, and because they were more monitorable by their principals (see Chapter 4). Indeed, according to Jacob Price, taking long-distance trade in the North Atlantic as a case, the metropolitan merchant had the advantage of supervision when sealing agreements with ship captains, crew, and itinerant agents. Sooner or later, these agents should return to their home ports. Yet, he acknowledges that this might not be the most flexible form of agency. In fact, for a metropolitan merchant it was cheaper to make agreements with agents domiciled overseas than to send someone there, as in the latter case he would have to pay for his residence and pay him even when he did not do business. With a correspondent established in the colony, the merchant only spent resources when he wanted to carry out occasional trade.[52] More recent research on Brazil's gold trade during the eighteenth century has highlighted the role of itinerant agents as mitigators of information asymmetry and as being more trustworthy than traders resident in Brazil. Furthermore, these traveling merchant-commissioners also monitored resident agents and transmitted information to principals in Lisbon. As a result, "traveling agents contributed to reduce transaction costs in the entire system." They would be a private-order institution that bypassed the deficient and sometimes nonexistent public-order institutions.[53]

It is hard to deny the most beneficial attributes of traveling merchant-commissioners: carrying out business quickly and returning to Lisbon to report to their principals. Their efficiency is not in dispute here. However, the relationship between itinerant agents and colonial merchants had moments of friction in the second half of the century, and monitoring of the former

50 Silva, *Collecção da legislação Portugueza desde a ultima compilação das ordenações*, 1: 726–27.

51 Antonio Delgado Silva, *Collecção da legislação Portugueza desde a ultima compilação das ordenações: Legislação de 1775 a 1790* (Typ. Maigrense, 1828), 3: 531–32.

52 Price, "Transaction Costs. A Note on Merchant Credit and the Organization of Private Trade," 279–80.

53 Costa et al., "Social Capital and Economic Performance," 12, 16–18. See also Costa et al., *O ouro do Brasil*, 169.

over the latter may be a complex hypothesis to demonstrate. The Portuguese authorities' own attitude was to eliminate itinerant agents, which leads us to wait for more studies to find out why precisely the Portuguese state prohibited the activities of traveling merchant-commissioners despite their efficiency. The assumption that there were no other mechanisms—except for itinerant agents—to monitor long-distance trade is also difficult to sustain. The following section will show how company contracts were important instruments that limited the leeway of partners residing in Brazil. Moreover, it is highly probable that courts influenced this situation, although assessing their significance and efficacy poses challenges. While contemporary literature on the Brazilian gold trade highlights the inefficiency of the colonial courts, it neglects to address the functions of the courts in Portugal and the involvement of attorneys (whether based in Brazil or visiting) in recovering debts from agents located in foreign ports. Similarly, the governors and other officials in the colony who assisted in debt collection should not be overlooked.

3 Companies and State Authorities

Although they did not monopolize imports, the wealthy merchants in Lisbon were the biggest importers of cotton. Despite being rich and influential, they needed agents and correspondents in Brazil. Regardless of their strength, they used others' capital to trade and were often in conflict with their trading partners across the Atlantic. The difference in credit chains between small and large importers in Lisbon differed more by the amount of capital and goods than by the quality of the connections. Yet, because they dealt with large quantities, big Lisbon importers tended to seal informal agreements with reputable colonial merchants or even enter into formal mercantile arrangements, such as through trading companies with merchants in the colony or merchants who were migrating there.

Antônio José dos Santos Amorim, one of the biggest importers in Lisbon (see Appendix A), was a key merchant in the history of cotton and illustrated well the mercantile strategy of large merchants when dealing with the cotton trade. He engaged in business with Pernambuco and Maranhão and, on top of that, was a major re-exporter (see Appendix B). Details about his biography are few, but he was a shareholder in the GCPP in the 1770s.[54] In the final years of the GCGPM's monopoly, Amorim worked in Lisbon as an attorney for the tithe

54 ANTT, Feitos Findos, Conservatória da Companhia Geral de Pernambuco e Paraíba, mç. 15, n.º 1, cx. 19.

tax farmer in Maranhão, José Gomes. Amorim's task was to receive and sell the cotton.[55] Soon after the end of the monopoly, he owned a vessel that operated between Lisbon and São Luís.[56] In 1782 he was one of the leading merchants who exported cotton to Rouen.[57] In 1786 and 1787, he owned a few ships that carried cotton and rice from Maranhão. One of the merchants carrying cotton on Amorim's vessels was another major cotton importer, Mateus Poitier.[58] Amorim's interests went beyond shipping and trade. At the end of the eighteenth century, he had an insurance company called *Esperança* with Manuel Francisco Carvalhal, Carlos Francisco Prego, and Camilo João Queiros.[59]

It seems like Pernambuco was the center of his commercial interests in the 1790s, and he partnered with João Lourenço dos Santos and Gervásio José de Mendonça, who were directly involved in the cotton trade with small producers (Table 4.1). The company established between them—like many others formed for dealing with Brazil—provided ample benefits to the partner in Portugal and imposed a series of restrictions on the partners in the colony. Partners in Pernambuco could not receive or sell goods from other people unless they had the partner's authorization in Lisbon. They could only buy goods from the colony to send to their partner in Lisbon. They were not allowed to purchase goods from Portugal. Partners in Pernambuco could not be tax farmers and could not be guarantors of anyone. One of their specific tasks was to correspond with Amorim, informing him about what was being exported so that he, in Lisbon, could insure the goods. The company was supposed to operate for four years. In the end, profits and losses would be divided into three equal parts. In addition, the partners also had the right to receive their sales and purchase commissions: Amorim would receive 3% for both purchases and sales, and Santos and Mendonça would receive 5% for sales and 3% for purchases.[60] According to a power of attorney, though, it seems that the company's end did not occur amicably. In 1796, Amorim sent a solicitor, Manuel Gomes dos Santos (one of the most prominent merchants in Pernambuco), to charge the two partners.[61]

As should be clear by now, for major financiers and merchants in Lisbon, the custom of appointing attorneys to collect debts in Brazil was as important as

55 ANTT, Companhia Geral do Grão Pará e Maranhão, Cartas para o Maranhão, no. 230, f. 258 and 267.
56 ANTT, Feitos Findos, Juízo da Índia e Mina, mç. 14, no. 28 cx. 381.
57 See Appendix B.
58 ANTT, Feitos Findos, Juizo da Índia e Mina, mç. 12, no. 10, cx. 199.
59 Pedreira, "Os Homens de Negócio Da Praça de Lisboa," 346.
60 ANTT, 10º CNL, Cx. 26, liv. 141, f. 50–51v.
61 ANTT, 10º CNL, Cx. 31, liv. 171, f. 19.

forming commercial companies. Amorim was far from being an isolated case. In 1790, Francisco da Fonseca Lemos—another prominent cotton importer in 1782 (see Appendix A)—ordered ship captain Carlos José de Araújo Santos, who was on his way to Pernambuco, to collect two debtors. He sent along a "requisition and enforceable letter" endorsed by Judge Dom José Francisco de Noronha, who presided over the court of *India e Mina*, one of the courts in Lisbon that dealt with commercial disputes. As attorney-in-fact, the captain of the vessel was authorized to enforce in Pernambuco the decision made in the Lisbon court, including collecting the debtors' assets.[62] In that case, resorting to the commercial court was necessary. Yet, dozens of company charters make explicit that the use of the courts was a resource that the partners should not use or only use as a last resort. What should prevail were the agreements brokered by private arbitrators appointed by the partners.[63] According to Craig Muldrew, in England, the use of the courts was more of a strategy to threaten the debtor and make them pay than a means to actually reach the final consequences: the plaintiffs initiated the litigation, but the cases were rarely judged. This may mean that people utilized the courts to force a deal outside of them.[64]

Recovering debts in Brazil directly affected the credit chains of merchants in Lisbon. The case involving the Lisbon merchant Antônio José Coutinho reveals how the extension of commercial credit from Lisbon worked, how it reached Maranhão, and how critical it was to collect debtors. Due to the delay of his ship docked in the port of São Luís—the ship *Santo Antônio Resoluto*, which had been in Maranhão for 15 months—Coutinho "was reduced to the sad situation of not being able to pay [his creditors] right away and completely with the punctuality that he always used to."[65] His 13 creditors wrote that Coutinho always dealt with his business with "good faith," "fairness," and "truth."[66] He owed 18,372,550 *réis*, and his signed agreement specified that he would pay the creditors within five years. At the end of each year, he had to pay 20% of the total debt. Coutinho mortgaged his assets as a guarantee. The plan was for the debts to be paid in full by 1795. In the meantime, between 1790 and 1795, Coutinho could not be sued, nor could his assets be collected by his creditors, unless he failed to pay one of the annual instalments. Creditors had access to the list of his assets, creditors, and debtors. One of his creditors was

62 ANTT, 6º CNL, Cx. 27, liv. 135, f. 75v–76.

63 Melo, "Hierarquias mercantis no Atlântico Português," 15.

64 Craig Muldrew, "Credit and the Courts: Debt Litigation in a Seventeenth-Century Urban Community," *The Economic History Review* 46, no. 1 (1993): 27.

65 "achava reduzido a triste situação de não poder pagar desde logo e inteiramente com a pontualidade que sempre costumou".

66 "boa fé," "lisura" e "verdade".

the English merchant João Bulkeley (one of the biggest cotton exporters in Lisbon, see Appendix B). Coutinho was also a creditor: several people throughout Brazil owed him 24,135,000 *réis*. One of them was the slave trader Alberto José Lopes in Maranhão (Table 2.7) and the merchant José João Gonçalves in Pernambuco.[67] Therefore, debt collection was central for Coutinho and creditors in Lisbon and Brazil. If Coutinho went broke, he would certainly leave others at a loss.

The case of Amorim and Coutinho shows a hierarchical organization: investors and principals in Lisbon with capital circulating in Brazil and with agents following their orders, even if these agents eventually defaulted or acted in bad faith. This hierarchical organization was actually a pattern. Most of the merchant companies formed in Lisbon to trade with Pernambuco were composed of credits from Lisbon merchants.[68] For Maranhão, the situation seems to be the same. In 1788, Guilherme Francisco da Silva and José Francisco da Silva agreed on a six-year commercial partnership contract. The first was a businessman, and the second was a vessel pilot. The surnames indicate that, most likely, they were related. Both started the company in Lisbon by taking loans from city creditors. In the future, the credits and sea loans that they withdrew could only be signed by the company and not by the partners separately. Profits and losses would be divided equally. If one of the partners died, José Joaquim Ferreira would continue the negotiations in Maranhão and hand them over to Joaquim José das Mercês in Lisbon. Partners could not buy properties without each other's knowledge.[69] The contract did not specify which one was going to Maranhão. But it is known that a certain José Francisco da Silva, in 1796, requested a piece of land near the Itapecuru River. He called himself a trader and asked for permission to establish a crop in the region.[70] He was also a slave trader (Table 2.8). Almost certainly, José Francisco da Silva moved to Maranhão and settled there for many years.

Contracts like the above that restrict the agent's room for maneuver in the colony, family connections, courts, and solicitors were sometimes insufficient. Some commercial partnerships that came into conflict appealed to government officials in Portugal and Brazil to resolve their disputes. These are cases that concern partners in Brazil that simply ceased communications with partners in Lisbon, or that, in fact, acted in bad faith and poorly managed the capital of the principals. They also involve cases of heirs trying to collect assets and

---

67 ANTT, Feitos Findo, Juizo da India e Mina, Mç 52, n 7, cx. 239.
68 Melo, "Hierarquias mercantis no Atlântico Português".
69 ANTT, 6º CNL, Cx. 27, liv 132. f. 61–61v.
70 AHU, ACL, CU, 009, Cx. 90, Doc. 7457.

capital overseas from deceased relatives. In many cases, the partners and heirs resorted to the aid of figures such as governors, Secretaries of the Navy and Overseas, and even of the Queen and the Regent. These authorities sometimes pressured the *ouvidor* (the colonial judge) to take care of resolving the dispute in a more active way.

This becomes clear when we look at the firm called *Luís Cipriano Rebelo e Companhia*. In 1799, the company that was managed in Lisbon by Luís Cipriano Rebelo and José Antônio Ferreira Viana was trying to charge the partner in Maranhão, João Antônio Ferreira Viana. To this end, they asked the Secretary of State for Navy and Overseas, D. Rodrigo de Sousa Coutinho, to request the help of the governor of Maranhão. The governor should convince the debtor to pay the Lisbon partners' attorney in Maranhão, the merchant Antônio José de Seixas.[71] In other cases, the governor's action should be more investigative and even punitive. Antônio Florêncio, a merchant from Lisbon, had a clerk in Maranhão, João José Teixeira. In 1797, Antônio accused his clerk of having "spoiled the capital that he entrusted to him, failing to account for the merchandise that was sent to him, nor for the money that it was supposed to produce."[72] Rodrigo de Souza Coutinho requested the governor to investigate the matter, and if he discovered that the clerk had acted in "bad faith" to have him arrested.[73] Similarly, Manuel Francisco Monteiro de Brito in Lisbon argued that he was the creditor of Manuel José Esteves in Maranhão. Thus, in 1800, Souza Coutinho and the Regent asked Governor D. Diogo de Souza to investigate the case. If the debt was proven, the governor should seek to resolve the dispute without the "delays of the court."[74] However, the governor's treatment should be restricted "within the limits of the laws of Justice."[75]

The authorities also acted to facilitate debt collection. In 1799, Alberto Garcia da Silveira sent his clerk, Baltazar Pereira Viana, to the captaincy of Maranhão, to establish a business house for seven years with all the necessary capital. Although the company charter did not require the sending of balance sheets, until that time (in 1805), the clerk had not been accountable to Alberto. Therefore, he asked for permission to go to Maranhão to deal directly with Viana. The Viscount of Anadia, Secretary of State for the Navy and Overseas,

---

71 AHU, Códice 599, f. 47v and AHU, ACL, CU, 009, Cx. 108, Doc. 8499.

72 "estragado o cabedal que ele lhe confiou, não dando conta da fazenda que se lhe remeteu, nem do dinheiro que ela deveria produzir".

73 AHU, Códice 598, f. 200v–201.

74 "delongas do foro".

75 "dentro dos limites das leis da Justiça," see AHU, Códice 599, f. 93.

asked Governor Francisco de Melo Manuel da Camara to assist Alberto in the captaincy.[76]

Even the Regent of Portugal, through authorities in the colony, sought to mediate the process of recovering capital from investors in the metropolis. Some dealers in Lisbon and Maranhão were creditors to Captain Manuel Rodrigues Ferreira, owner of "one of the biggest business houses"[77] in Maranhão. In addition, he was a tax farmer that had won the right to collect tithes from the captaincy. Yet, he owed more than 44,000,000 *réis* to the Royal Treasury (*Real Fazenda*). He had fallen ill, with "a great disturbance of the head and the use of reason."[78] Malicious people, knowing about Manuel Rodrigues Ferreira's illnesses, bought his goods for half the price they were worth; others asked for money and bills. Probably to avoid paying the debts, Manuel Rodrigues Ferreira fled to his farms in the hinterlands of the captaincy. These farms were worth about 160,000,000 *réis*. The value of the farms was enough to pay both creditors and the Royal Treasury. The plan then was to try to recover what was due to the Crown and to the creditors. In order to manage assets and settle debts, in 1796, the Regent delegated the administration of Manuel Rodrigues Ferreira's business house to José Gonçalves da Silva, Ricardo Nunes Leal, Caetano José Teixeira (all three were wealthy merchants, planters, and slave traders; see Tables 2.3 and 2.8), and to Manuel Rodrigues Ferreira himself, only if he was in good health[79] or, if not, to his sons. The administrators should take an inventory of Manuel's assets and hand it over to the *ouvidor*. The administrators should collect all of Manuel's debts and income and pay the *Fazenda Real* first and then pay the creditors. They should not suffer any kind of impediment to comply with what the Regent had determined.[80]

Even companies formed in Brazil asked for credit in Lisbon and needed the help of state institutions and authorities to recover the capital that had been compromised or lost. João Antônio de Miranda, who was going to Lisbon and subscribed to all the capital, and José dos Santos Ribeiro who remained in Pernambuco, established a company, registering it in one of the notary offices in Recife. Between 1794 and 1802, goods shipped to Pernambuco totaled 70,939,003 *réis*, whose sales yielded a profit of 1,017,623 *réis* (1.43%). Colonial goods sent to Lisbon between 1795 and 1802 amounted to around 60,750,050 *réis* and generated a profit of 13,694,912 *réis* (22.54%). These numbers prove

76 AHU, Códice 599, f. 166.
77 "de uma das maiores casas de negócios".
78 "uma grande perturbação da cabeça e do uso da razão".
79 "estivesse restituído de entendimento".
80 AHU, Códice 598, f. 185v–186v.

two things. The first is already known: in both flows, there were profits, but profits from sales in the metropolis were much more significant than profits in the colony. The second is that, probably, this was a very poorly managed company, since after adding the profits of Recife and Lisbon together, they comprised 14,712,535 *réis*. However, losses were deducted from all this profit, which amounted to 13,528,538 *réis*, leaving only 1,183,997 *réis* of net profit over the course of eight years of partnership. The reason for the bad management, according to the partner in Lisbon, lay in the bad faith of his partner in Pernambuco who, still in 1807, owed 12,350,621 *réis* to the company and even owed another 1,219,949 *réis* to him, Miranda, for private business outside the company. Because of these disputes, which his partner in Pernambuco insisted on not settling, Miranda appealed to Prince Regent D. João so that he could summon the governor of Pernambuco and a judge to "take away his [Ribeiro's] capital."[81] Miranda asked for urgency in the request since he was in debt with creditors in Lisbon, and as he was the only one in the company to contribute with capital, all loans made were on his account. He recalled that "the funds with which this company ran"[82] were always his and his creditors.[83]

Heirs also sought to recover the capitals of the deceased through the aid of the authorities. The French-born merchant, Mateus Poitier, one of the main cotton importers in Lisbon (Appendix A), had business with Maranhão. When he died in Lisbon, his wife Maria Luisa da Madre de Deus Poitier asked for help from Rodrigo de Souza Coutinho and the governor of Maranhão, in 1797, to end the business that the deceased had in the captaincy.[84] But sometimes, recovering the capital of the dead could be a challenge. When Lourenço Belfort died in Lisbon in 1784, the Orphans' Court (*Juízo dos Órfãos*) was responsible for dividing the inheritance for his offspring. Lourenço had been one of the most influential planters and traders in Maranhão for many years (as seen in Chapters 1 and 2). However, the completion of Lourenço's inventory was compromised because the attorneys and agents in Maranhão did not deliver the list of the deceased's assets. Belfort's widow returned to Maranhão to try to resolve this issue, but she did not have success as she was "enmeshed and deceived" by the "attorneys and agents."[85] Much later, in 1792, Martinho de Melo e Castro, asked the newly arrived governor, D. Fernando Antônio de Noronha, to help the Belfort family in this matter. The governor should inform the family about

---

81 "arrancar-lhe o cabedal".
82 "os fundos com que girou esta sociedade".
83 AHU, ACL, CU, 015, Cx. 269, Doc. 17903.
84 AHU, Códice 598, f. 202.
85 "enredada e enganada" and "procuradores e agentes".

the situation of the deceased merchant's business house with all accuracy, "seeking to avoid and destroy the frauds and baffles with which the assets of the miserable orphans are so often ruined."[86]

4 Lisbon Customs and the Case of Bento José Pacheco

As with other commodities, customs played a crucial role in the cotton trade. After arriving from Brazil, the cotton was stored and taxed at *Casa da Índia*, the Lisbon customs house that handled the cotton. From the moment of its arrival from Brazil until its sale, whether for export or to the warehouses of merchants established in Lisbon, more negotiations could take place. Bento José Pacheco, one of the biggest importers (see Appendix A), entered into an agreement with other traders that illustrates the fundamental position of customs for the cotton market in Lisbon. The deal placed Bento José on one side and João Pedro de Abreu Lima, dispatcher of the *Casa da Índia* and Isidoro Cardoso Maia, a dealer, on the other. Bento José Pacheco promised to deliver to João Pedro de Abreu Lima and Isidoro Cardoso Maia 2,000 arrobas of cotton from Pernambuco for the price of 340 *réis* per *arrátel*. The delivery should occur between June 7, 1788, and November of the same year. Even if the cotton was priced on the market at a much higher value, Bento José would still have to send the cotton to the other two contractors. By the time they received the cotton, they should "pass bills," to pay Bento José Pacheco in 50 days. The two could not reject Bento's cotton if there was "a big price drop." Cotton was to be received outside the *Casa da Índia*, but if the two buyers wanted to leave the cotton in the *Casa*, the risk would be only theirs, with Bento relieving himself of any responsibilities. If there were any doubts about the price and quality of the cotton, two private judges would be called from each party to inspect the merchandise. All the cotton that came from Pernambuco in the name of Bento was to be delivered to the two buyers and to no one else until the sum of 2,000 arrobas was fulfilled.[87] Yet, the contractors again entered into another agreement. On September 11, 1788, Bento had already delivered 441 arrobas. But as the price of cotton had dropped, and Lima and Maia "sacrificed themselves to considerable loss," they begged Bento to return the cotton to the *Casa da Índia*. The expectation was for the price of cotton to rise. But it seems that this did not happen. The new contract stipulated that the two would pay Bento

86 "procurando evitar e destruir as fraudes e chicanas com que tantas vezes se arruínam os bens dos miseráveis órfãos," see AHU, Códice 598, f. 144v–145.

87 ANTT, 6º CNL, Cx. 25, liv 124, f. 52v–53v.

1,000,000 *réis*, up to four months after the date of the notary contract. By that time, they had paid 376,000 *réis*.[88] In short, what Bento accomplished, through the institution of customs, was an advance sale.

This case brings to light not only market mechanisms but also the preoccupation that economic actors had concerning price fluctuations in the market. It also tells us how the customs institution and the role of dispatchers were crucial in the sale of goods of Brazilian origin in the Lisbon marketplace. Merchants generally did not personally go to the customs house to pay taxes and move the goods. They left this task to third parties, also known at the time as "dispatchers from the House of India" (*despachantes da Casa da Índia*), who were also traders.[89] In 1789, of all cotton that left customs, 95.89% passed through the hands of 74 *despachantes*. Of these, only the first two were responsible for collecting almost half of all the cotton. Ten years later, the situation had changed. In 1799, the total number of dispatchers had been reduced drastically; there were 23, but despite this decrease, they increased their share in the cotton that left customs, concentrating 98.71% of the total dispatches. Of the 23, only the first two were responsible for more than half of the total cotton that left customs that year. In other words, easily more than half of all cotton that came from Brazil passed through the hands of only two people. Table 5.4 gathers information on the main cotton dispatchers at customs in Lisbon.

A particular case from the judicial proceedings in Lisbon effectively exemplifies the role of dispatchers. In 1791, Joaquim José Pereira (the largest cotton dispatcher in 1789) was being sued by the British business house, Daniel Bowden and Sons (one of the biggest cotton exporters in Lisbon to European ports).[90] Daniel Bowden and Sons had bought 14 bags of cotton (from Pernambuco) from Antônio Alves Ribeiro Lima in 1789, free of freight and other rights. It was customary for importers, in this case, Lima, to pay freight and duties. This was done at the same time that the goods were in customs, and the person responsible for this work was the dispatcher, in this case, Pereira. It turns out that Pereira had not paid the freight and duties, and the owner of the vessel (which was Antônio Alves Ribeiro Lima himself) in which the pieces of cotton were transported charged the British firm for the 14 bags loaded. For this reason, British traders filed a lawsuit against Joaquim José Pereira to make him pay the freight and duties. To sue the dispatcher, the British dealers gave a power of attorney to the Portuguese Manuel Esteves to represent them.[91] In short, because they had privileged knowledge of cotton arrivals, dispatchers

88 ANTT, 6º CNL, Cx. 26, liv. 126, f.10–11.
89 ANTT, Feitos Findos, Juízo da Índia e Mina, mç. 38, n.º 9, cx. 225.
90 See Appendix B.
91 ANTT, Feitos Findos, Juízo da Índia e Mina, mç. 38, no. 9, cx. 225.

TABLE 5.4 The cotton dispatchers, 1782–1806

Year	1782	1789
Total number of dispatchers	41	74
Main dispatchers	1º Caetano José Beja	1º Joaquim José Pereira
	2º José Joaquim de Almeida	2º José Lescura Banher
	3º Matias José Rodrigues	3º Antônio Bernardo Cardoso Peçanha
	4º Joaquim José Domingues	4º José Antônio Castanheira
	5º Antônio José Rosa	5º João Pedro de Abreu Lima
	6º Joaquim Raimundo de Azevedo	6º Joaquim Inácio Potiers Lamas
Year	**1792**	**1799**
Total number of dispatchers	33	23
Main dispatchers	1º Antônio Bernardo Cardoso Peçanha	1º Antônio Bernardo Cardoso Peçanha
	2º José Álves Vilela	2º José Álves Vilela
	3º José Lescura Banher	3º José Lescura Banher
	4º Joaquim José Pereira	4º João Pedro Manesch
	5º João Álves Vieira	5º João Álves Vieira
	6º José Antônio Castanheira	6º Manuel Teixeira de Carvalho
Year	**1806**	
Total number of dispatchers	26	
Main dispatchers	1º Antônio Bernardo Cardoso Peçanha	
	2º Antônio José da Silva	
	3º João Pedro Manesch	
	4º Joaquim José Primavera	
	5º José Álves Vilela	
	6º Rocha	

Notes and sources: see Table 5.1 for the sources. The main dispatchers were those who together removed more than 90% of the cotton in each year. Table prepared by the author.

were essential links that more easily united the interests of importers and buyers in Lisbon.

Bento José Pacheco, who effectively illustrated the function of the customs institution in the cotton trade at the beginning of this section, also provides interesting information regarding the nature of his trade relations with Brazil. A quick glance at his biography reveals the specific evolution of his relationship with Pernambuco. Son of Domingos Pacheco and Quitéria de Moura, he was born in the Parish of São Miguel, Archbishopric of Braga, Northern Portugal, in 1751. From his birth until the end of the 1770s, it is not possible to know more about his biography. Apparently, his trajectory toward the top of the hierarchy of businessmen in Portugal was fast. Bento José Pacheco was part of the group of big merchants who claimed the right to collect several taxes in Portugal and Brazil (such as the tax on tithes, Brazilwood, tobacco, soap, salt, whale fishing, olive oil, etc.), from 1777 to 1807 as well as from 1807 to 1822. Between 1790 to 1822, according to Jorge Pedreira, Bento José Pacheco was part of the "elite" of the 60 big merchants in Lisbon.[92]

Bento's interest in cotton started from before 1789. In 1784, together with José Mendes de Fonseca, Bento owned a chintz print manufacturing company in Alcântara, Lisbon's suburbs. He even declared that he lived in his factory in 1787.[93] Yet, in 1793, he leased his factory to others.[94] It was also in 1787 that the first instance of Bento's interest in Brazilian raw cotton appeared, as he began to formalize contacts with a family of traders, the Aguiars: Manuel Rodrigues de Aguiar, José Esteves de Aguiar, and Joaquim Pereira de Aguiar, all residents in Pernambuco. Bento gave powers of attorney for these merchants to represent him on the other side of the Atlantic.[95]

To do business with Pernambuco, Bento used not only representatives but also family connections and company contracts. He had a brother in Pernambuco, Manuel Antônio de Moura, with whom he most likely did business. It is certain, however, that Bento used his brother's services in April 1790 to end a merchant company that he had started a year earlier with merchant Francisco Xavier de Souza. Bento put an end to the company because Souza was not fulfilling the conditions of the partnership.[96] Add to that the fact that Moura and Souza were also, at the time, engaged in a trading company. Apparently, this

92 Pedreira, "Os Homens de Negócio Da Praça de Lisboa," 172, 189.

93 It is unlikely that Bento used the cotton he imported from Brazil in his factory since he had a printing factory. Yet, he might have had it sent to be spun and woven in the country.

94 Carlos Guimarães da Cunha, *Negociantes, mercadores e traficantes no final da monarquia absoluta: a burguesia mercantil em Portugal, dos anos finais do século XVIII até ao início da Revolução Liberal* (Edições Colibri, 2014), 101.

95 ANTT, 6º CNL, Cx. 21, liv. 104, f. 66–68v and 2º CNL, Cx. 134, liv.635, f. 15.

96 ANTT, 3º CNL, Cx. 152, liv. 711, f. 53–53v.

strategy of asking his brother to charge Souza did not work. A year later, in April 1791, Bento asked his already known representative, Manuel Rodrigues de Aguiar, and a new attorney, Francisco Branco,[97] to recover his credits not only from his former partner, Souza, but also from his brother, Moura.[98] These examples show us again that family relationships and contractual relationships were not flawless.[99] Later, in 1797, Bento would also enter into friction with the Aguiars (namely with Manuel Rodrigues de Aguiar, who was José Esteves de Aguiar's uncle, both residents in Pernambuco, and also with Julião Gervásio de Aguiar, Manuel's nephew and resident in Lisbon). Bento filed a lawsuit against them for a debt of 10,788,429 *réis*.[100] These cases point to the fact that even the most successful merchants in Lisbon, such as Bento, could face mishaps in relation to their agents.

As a prestigious figure in Lisbon's marketplace, Bento also acted as a link between Portuguese investors and overseas agents. In 1800, he brokered an obligation contract between a merchant in Recife, José da Silva Maine, and several creditors in Lisbon. Maine had received a large sum of more than 26 million *réis*. Maine undertook to pay creditors with shipments of colonial goods, promising to send the commodities exclusively to them. Bento José Pacheco's role was to centralize the interests of creditors and make the connection with Maine. Bento José was, therefore, a broker, a figure with the necessary social capital and information to connect the interests of economic actors between the two points of the Atlantic.[101]

Bento also partnered with merchants in Lisbon to access businesses that touched Brazil, Portugal, and other European ports. Together with his partner, Agostinho de Oliveira Guimarães, they were two of the biggest shipowners that made the route between Pernambuco and Lisbon in the 1790s and the first seven years of the nineteenth century.[102] The two also owned a vessel that made a trip between Rio de Janeiro and Lisbon in 1798.[103] Bento José Pacheco, together with his partners, Teotônio José da Silva and Pedro Xavier Ferreira, concluded—at a public hearing in Lisbon—the right to collect the tax on

97 Francisco Branco was a cotton trader; see Table 4.1.

98 ANTT, 10° CNL, Cx. 27, liv. 144, f. 97–97v.

99 The case of a merchant established in Lisbon, Francisco Pinheiro, trading with Brazil in the first half of the eighteenth century, also highlights the pitfalls of trade based on family ties; see Donovan, "Commercial Enterprise and Luso-Brazilian Society During the Brazilian Gold Rush," 268–69.

100 ANTT, Feitos Findos, Juízo da Índia e Mina, mç. 3, no. 15, cx. 269.

101 ANTT, 10° CNL, Cx. 36, liv. 190, f. 130v–131. Obligation contract for the year 1800. Unfortunately, the contract does not contain the names of creditors.

102 Melo, *Financiando o Negócio de Pernambuco*, 324–40.

103 ANTT, 7° CNL – Ofício A, Cx. 112, liv. 680, f. 39v.

tithes in São Paulo (Southeast Brazil) for the three years of 1804–1807.[104] At the beginning of the nineteenth century, Bento José Pacheco (together with Marcos José de Matos and Francisco José de Almeida) had a certain reputation for negotiating with the French.[105] Bento also had contacts in Gothenburg and Portsmouth, in 1813.[106]

His commercial journey included an increase in family enterprises and investments within the insurance sector. He had a commercial company with his sons, whose date of foundation is unknown. Around 1798, the firm *Bento José Pacheco & Sons* imported tobacco from Bahia.[107] And sometime around 1797, the company owned 50% of the capital of the aforementioned cotton printing factory.[108] In 1808, the firm, together with other partners, won the right, once again by auction, to collect two other taxes in the city of Lisbon: that of the fruit (auctioned for 34,050,000 *réis*) and that of the toll (auctioned for 20,100,000 *réis*).[109]

At some point in his commercial activity, Bento participated in insurance companies. One of them, *Bom Conceito*, which also included Joaquim José de Barros and José Diogo de Bastos, had a remarkable capital of 400,000,000 *réis*. The company *Bento José Pacheco & Sons*, together with Francisco Antonio Cordeiro and João Antonio Almeida, had an insurance company called, very suggestively, Sossego Comum (Common rest). He also took part in other kinds of insurance that did not involve the companies in which he had capital invested.[110]

Bento contributed to the financial resources of the Portuguese State, possibly to establish his social standing and distinguish himself among his peers. In 1797, he was part of the group of "the main and most distinguished merchants in the marketplace of Lisbon" that lent money to the State for the construction of the royal navy hospital.[111] Likewise, he contributed money to the Portuguese State to end the risks at sea. Algerian corsairs were an almost constant danger to the Portuguese merchant navy. In 1813, they requested a certain amount of money from the Portuguese government to stop attacks on ships. As the government did not have the resources at the time, it chose to invite Portugal's biggest traders to contribute. Bento was one of them, who assisted

104 AHU, ACL, CU, 023-01, Cx. 54, doc. 4144, São Paulo Alfredo Mendes Gouveia.
105 Pedreira, "Os Homens de Negócio Da Praça de Lisboa," 335.
106 Cunha, *Negociantes, mercadores e traficantes*, 213.
107 AHU, ACL, CU, 005, Cx. 93, doc. 18282, Bahia Eduardo de Castro e Almeida.
108 Pedreira, "Os Homens de Negócio Da Praça de Lisboa," 247.
109 Cunha, *Negociantes, mercadores e traficantes*, 133–35.
110 Pedreira, "Os Homens de Negócio Da Praça de Lisboa," 346–47.
111 Pedreira, "Os Homens de Negócio Da Praça de Lisboa," 178–79.

with 2,000,000 *réis*.[112] In addition, as early as December 1807, when the French invaded Portugal, they asked the merchants for a loan and the firm *Bento José Pacheco & Sons* provided 7,500,000 *réis*.[113]

Bento's relations with Brazil were relatively strong and continuous, at least since the 1780s. He was interested not only in cotton from Pernambuco but also in tobacco (and most likely in sugar) from Bahia, in business with Rio de Janeiro and tax collection in São Paulo. But it was perhaps in Pernambuco where his main interests resided. The transfer of the Portuguese Court to Rio de Janeiro and the cessation of colonial exclusive in 1808 likely prompted Bento and his family to consider relocating to the tropics. In April 1810, his wife, Caterina Francisco Pacheco, and the couple's daughters (Marina, Henriqueta, and Guilhermina) had moved to Pernambuco to be with José Bento Pacheco, son of the couple and also a merchant. The couple's other son, Joaquim José Pacheco, would accompany his mother and sisters on the trip. In September of the same year, Bento José Pacheco asked the Portuguese authorities for a passport to do the same and reunite with his family in Brazil. Probably Bento did not make the trip, because while he was still in Lisbon he asked the King, in July 1811, for a license for his whole family to return to Portugal because of "dangerous diseases" in Pernambuco.[114] His son, José Bento Pacheco, possibly stayed in Pernambuco since he was trying to return to Lisbon in 1816, "seriously ill."[115] Even after the end of exclusive system in 1808, Bento José Pacheco still sent vessels to Pernambuco and Bahia.[116] One of the last pieces of information about him was an authorization to send one of his ships to this last port in 1821.[117]

5 Colonial Debts and Money

One of the means—perhaps the main one—to trade with Maranhão and Pernambuco was to send goods to these places. It was through the sale of imported goods that cotton was bought. However, the quantity of goods exported by Portugal to these two Brazilian captaincies was not enough, and the merchants found themselves in need of sending cash across the Atlantic

112 Cunha, *Negociantes, mercadores e traficantes*, 178.
113 Cunha, *Negociantes, mercadores e traficantes*, 111.
114 AHU, ACL, CU, 015, Cx. 274, Doc. 18319.
115 AHU, ACL, CU, 015, Cx. 274, Doc. 18650.
116 AHU, ACL, CU, 015, Cx. 274, Doc. 18726, Cx. 255, Doc. 17592 and Cx. 255, Doc. 18095.
117 AHU, ACL, CU, 015, Cx. 255, Doc. 18523.

to buy cotton. Observing the flow of this form of credit—money—reveals important aspects of the cotton trade between Portugal and Brazil.

Data allows an estimate of the extent of the credit that supported the cotton economy and its transatlantic trade. In spite of the changes brought about by the end of the monopoly in Maranhão in 1778, crucial patterns of productive, commercial, and financial organization, inherited from the times of the GCGPM, carried over. One of the most relevant was the debt chains. Merchants in Portugal lent capital (which could take the form of goods) to merchants in Maranhão, who, in turn, financed cotton planters. The governor of Maranhão, Fernando Antônio de Noronha, explained this very well in one of his letters to the Secretary of State for the Navy and Overseas, Martinho de Melo e Castro. In 1794, the governor wrote that after the GCGPM was extinguished, the mercantile community of Maranhão ("the body of commerce in this state" according to him)[118] lent to the colonists "the sums necessary for the culture of the lands, for the purchase of slaves, tools, furniture, food, clothing and other facilities."[119] The colonizers' debts (in fact only forty-one colonizers) totaled 1,255,600,381 *réis* (Table 5.5). It was "public trust" and "good faith"[120] that made creditors lend to residents. Creditors should treat cultivators, who were debtors of "a commendable compassion,"[121] with special consideration. Farmers, being directly affected by natural events, such as floods, insects, and sterilities, were at greater risk of seeing the value of their plantations decrease in value.[122] The Englishman Henry Koster met many of Maranhão's most prestigious dealers and planters when he was there in the 1810s. Among them, there was José Gonçalves da Silva and Simplício Dias da Silva, two of the biggest debtors who appear on the list drawn up by the governor in 1794. The first was very rich and had a cotton plantation with 1,000 to 1,500 enslaved workers. The second was the sub-governor of Parnaíba.[123] Debt, however, did not only affect producers. Ricardo Nunes Leal, an important planter but also a key merchant and slave trader, was listed as one of the largest debtors. But what perhaps catches our attention the most in Table 5.5 is the size of these residents' debt compared to the debts accumulated during the time of the GCGPM monopoly. At the height of the debt, in 1771, the residents of Maranhão owed more than 600 million *réis* to the monopoly company (Table 1.5). In 1794, they—including the

118 "O corpo do comércio deste Estado".

119 "as somas necessárias para a cultura das terras, para a compra dos escravos, ferramentas, móveis, víveres, vestuários e outras comodidades".

120 "confiança pública" and "boa fé".

121 "uma louvável comiseração".

122 AHU, ACL, CU, 009, Cx. 84, Doc. 7093.

123 Koster, *Travels in Brazil*, 174.

TABLE 5.5 Debts of the inhabitants of Maranhão in 1794

Names	Debts	Names	Debts
Simplício Dias da Silva	199,000,000	José Joaquim Teixeira	10,731,146
GCGPM	142,311,623	Bernardo Rodrigues Lima	9,942,400
Caetano José Teixeira	142,000,000	João Bento de Brito	9,475,000
Seixas, e Gomes e Companhia	130,000,000	João Francisco Vieira Guimarães	8,000,000
José Gonçalves da Silva	71,190,728	Manuel de Almeida	8,000,000
Ricardo Nunes Leal	70,000,000	José de Oliveira e Souza	7,500,000
José Gomes	58,687,000	Antônio Rodrigues de Miranda	6,000,000
José Joaquim da Silva Rosa	52,000,000	Manuel José Pinto Guimarães	6,000,000
Antônio José de Seixas	41,799,983	Caetano Francisco Domingues	5,281,571
Antônio José Gomes Cascaes	36,000,000	Domingos Dias Castelo	5,000,000
Antônio José de Souza	35,022,580	Gil Gomes Feio	4,702,000
Manuel Álves da Silva Basto	28,348,790	José Francisco Pereira	4,483,000
Antônio José Basto	22,235,640	Manuel Rodrigues da Costa	4,282,729
Antônio José Roberto Gaspar	22,000,000	Manuel Pereira das Neves	4,270,000
Manuel José Avelino	19,400,000	Bernardo Pinto	3,200,000
Manuel João Honorato	14,747,800	Policarpo José Xavier	3,200,000
Antônio Gonçalves de Seixas	13,851,641	Luis da Rocha Compasso	2,870,000
João José Teixeira	13,400,000	João Inácio Pinto de Figueiredo	2,800,090
Manuel Barbosa de Carvalho	12,100,000	José Martins de Carvalho	2,680,000
José Luis Machado	10,913,780	Agostinho Inácio Rodrigues Torres	1,422,880
João Gonçalves dos Santos	10,750,000	**Total**	**1,255,600,381**

Source: AHU, CU, 009, Cx. 84, Doc. 7093. The debts are in *réis*. Table prepared by the author.

GCGPM—had doubled this last figure. This indicates not only the importance of credit for cotton production and trade but also how it has augmented considerably in 20 years.

Although residents in the colony, these creditors still had close ties with the mercantile communities in Portugal. The governor also warned not to disregard the debts that these commercial houses (shopkeepers) in Maranhão had "contracted with the Metropolis."[124] There were exceptions to this rule, but in general, the colonial merchants were financed by the Portuguese capital, and they in turn financed the planters. In 1791, the capital allocated to cotton

124 AHU, ACL, CU, 009, Cx. 84, Doc. 7093.

plantations in Brazil, not only considering Maranhão, was approximately tenfold that invested in plantations in the United States of America, but by 1801, the United States had invested 60% more in its plantations compared to Brazil.[125]

Intimately linked to credit, a constantly overlooked element that can be used to explain Brazilian cotton is the money sent from Portugal to Brazil. To better understand the role of money, it is necessary to look at trade between Brazil and Portugal from a macroeconomic perspective and one of the best explanations was given by the Secretary of the Navy and Overseas, Martinho de Melo e Castro, to the newly appointed governor of Maranhão, D. Fernando Antônio de Noronha, where he sought to explain the problems derived from the trade balance between Maranhão and Portugal. From this emerges a very concrete scenario of how credit, in the form of money, played a significant role in the Atlantic cotton trade.[126]

On July 14, 1792, Martinho de Melo e Castro wrote that among all the regions of Brazil, Maranhão was the one that had achieved "the greatest and fastest progress,"[127] with cotton and rice leading as the most important plantations of the captaincy. Other goods were also produced but of lesser value, such as leather (*couros em cabelo, atanados* and *vaquetas*), parsley, and *goma* (a by-product of manioc flour). But it was cotton and rice that the secretary would look at, to make clear to the new governor the situation of the captaincy's trade balance concerning Portugal and African ports. To this end, he took the year 1790 as an example. That year, Maranhão exported 471,031,064 *réis* to Portugal. The Portuguese ports, in turn, exported 146,651,075 *réis* to Maranhão. These last exports should be considered as payment for the products that came from Maranhão to Portugal. In addition, 1,411 enslaved migrants (from Bissau and Cacheu, Gold Coast, Bahia, and Pernambuco) entered Maranhão. Sold at different prices, enslaved people generated 192,630,000 *réis*. There was no reason to believe that the captaincy's production was consumed in other parts of Brazil or even in African ports. Hence, the destination of Maranhão's productions was Portugal, where tropical goods had "the most certain and ready consumption."[128]

---

125 Barbosa, "Cotton in 19th Century Brazil," 150; Beckert, *Empire of Cotton*, 119.

126 Melo e Castro held a central position in the Portuguese administration as secretary of the Navy and Overseas. He received information from different parts of the Empire, through letters from governors, magistrates, city councillors, the military, bishops, and all sorts of residents from different parts of Brazil, Africa, and Asia. His position had the benefit of centralizing a reasonable amount of information, so he was able to have a panoramic view of the Empire and greater clarity of its connections.

127 "os maiores e mais rápidos progressos".

128 "o mais certo e pronto consumo".

Upon realizing that Maranhão sent more to Portugal than Portugal sent to Maranhão, Melo e Castro said that the Kingdom was indebted to its colony, something that contradicted the assumptions of the political economy of the time. For Melo e Castro, the colonies being indebted to their metropolises "is the largest, and it can be said, the only advantage that Capitals derive from their Colonies."[129] But apparently, that was not what was happening with Maranhão. Even when he considered that part of the slave trade vessels belonged to men based in Portugal and that they sold enslaved workers in exchange for tropical products to sell cotton and rice in Portugal later, Melo e Castro concluded that what entered Maranhão was not enough to pay for what came out.[130] Adding up what was imported from Portugal, plus the value of enslaved migrants coming from African ports and Brazil, everything added up to 339,281,075 *réis*. By subtracting this last figure with exports from Maranhão, the secretary concluded that the Northern captaincy had a surplus of 131,749,989 *réis* with the rest of its trading partners. The question that bothered Melo e Castro was how Portugal covered this deficit of 131,749,989 *réis*.

After examining the situation with "some diligence,"[131] Melo e Castro concluded that Portugal covered deficits in goods by sending money to Maranhão (to be more precise, in coins). Official figures said that Portugal had exported 76,981,953 *réis* in cash to Maranhão. Yet, this was still not enough to cover deficits, which is why Melo e Castro was "quite sure" that "considerable sums" of currency transported by merchant ships, and "without a manifesto,"[132] were entering Maranhão, even though he did not estimate how much precisely. Thus, taking into account the remittances of currency, the secretary concluded that, in fact, what was happening was that Portugal had surpluses with Maranhão, and not the other way around as he had initially suspected. This was not an exclusive phenomenon only involving Maranhão. Pernambuco (which received 487,003,200 *réis*), Bahia (211,000,000 *réis*) and Paraíba (47,320,000 *réis*) were also important destinations for the Portuguese currency in 1791. These were the official figures, but it was certainly a larger amount when we consider the unreported shipments. Melo e Castro limited himself to classifying this whole situation as an "inconvenience."[133]

But what were the origins and reasons for such a scenario? Melo e Castro considered that what caused this situation, mainly the deficits of European

129 "é a maior, e pode se dizer, a única vantagem que as Capitais tirão das suas Colônias".
130 AHU, Códice 598, f. 90–92.
131 "alguma diligência".
132 "toda a certeza," "somas consideráveis," and "sem manifesto".
133 "inconveniente," see AHU, Códice 598, f. 92v–93 and 122v.

goods in the colonies—not considering the remittances of money—was, first, the increase in prices in the colonies. Sugar and tobacco were priced high in Rio de Janeiro, Pernambuco, and Bahia. This required more European goods to buy these tropical products. Second, what caused deficits in the trade balance was smuggling in the captaincies of Brazil.[134]

Maranhão did not produce tobacco and sugar but produced rice and cotton that were expensive commodities. Cotton, for example, was by far the most expensive agricultural product exported by Brazil. Rice, however, was almost entirely consumed in Portugal, with little left to be re-exported to the rest of Europe. Until more or less 1772, cotton was not widely produced in Maranhão because its low selling price did not gain the attention of planters. It was only with the efforts of Governor Joaquim de Melo Povoas and the GCGPM that a reasonable price was found to be given to the planter. The price of cotton purchased from producers, at that time, was between 3,200 to 3,400 *réis* per arroba. The price included cotton that had already been cleaned. This price set by the company, according to Melo e Castro, was good for the planter and suitable for the production, since exports had not stopped growing. However, when the company's monopoly was abolished in 1778, cotton prices increased and began to vary from 4,300 to 4,500 *réis* per arroba. Surprising as it may seem, Melo e Castro did not consider these prices excessive.[135] According to Carreira, in fact, cotton prices rose. Most likely, the rise accompanied the appreciation of the commodity in the markets of Lisbon and England.[136]

To remedy the problems arising from the trade balance, what was left was the classic subject of smuggling. One of the reasons why Portugal was unable to pay for trade with Maranhão—and consequently had to send money to cover the differences—was because of the clandestine shipments to the northern captaincy. Melo e Castro was outraged. For him, since the captaincy had grown tremendously, both in population and in economic terms, it did not make sense for exports of European goods to the captaincy to have decreased in that way. For him, it was contraband, which should correspond to three times more than the amounts that Portugal legally exported to Maranhão, that explained the situation. Smuggling, he recalled, took place through vessels that left Portugal, but "mainly" by those that left African ports and Brazil, that took enslaved migrants to Maranhão. Some ships could also access Maranhão through coasts and coves, without entering the port of São Luís, where customs were located.

---

134 AHU, Códice 598, f. 93v.

135 AHU, Códice 598, f. 96–96v.

136 Carreira, *A Companhia Geral do Grão-Pará e Maranhão*, 2: 225–26.

Was Melo e Castro correct in his interpretation of Maranhão's economy? Probably yes, especially when it came to currency. Four years after Melo e Castro's "instruction," Governor Fernando Antônio de Noronha estimated that the currency in circulation in the captaincy was equivalent to one-third of its agricultural products. Thus, if in 1796 the captaincy produced 840,614,510 *réis* in agricultural products, it was a sign, according to him, that there should have been 280,204,836 *réis* of currency in circulation in Maranhão. This included copper coins (worth 5, 10, 20, 40 *réis*), silver (80, 160, 300, 320, 600, 640 *réis*) and gold (1,000, 2,000, 4,000 *réis*).[137] Pernambuco should have faced similar problems. On two occasions, at least, in 1788 and 1798, its governor reported that there were not enough European products to be exchanged for cotton, which was very expensive, so the use of gold to make the trade was recurrent.[138] Later, between 1802 and 1807, Maranhão and Pernambuco would be the two captaincies in Brazil that received the most money from Portugal. Pernambuco received 2,354,000,000 *réis* while Maranhão received 980,000,000 *réis*.[139] Not coincidentally, they were the Brazilian regions that most exported cotton. Furthermore, the figures that Melo e Castro provides to demonstrate that there was an increase in the price of cotton, during and after the monopoly, coincide with the official prices recorded in the GCGPM accounting books.[140] Once in the colony, money tended to circulate in Brazilian marketplaces. It was shown in Chapter 3 that the cotton crop reduced food production in Pernambuco. This made the captaincy import food from elsewhere, and the related payments were made in cash.[141] In Maranhão, in turn, money was sent to Pernambuco and Bahia in exchange for enslaved people as seen in Chapter 2.[142]

6 Contraband

The second point made by Melo e Castro was the illicit trade. This is a controversial issue among academics. Smuggling is one of the central arguments of Fernando Novais' famous thesis according to which smuggling was crucial to undermining the entire system of colonization set up by the Portuguese.

137 AHU, ACL, CU, 009, Cx. 93, Doc. 7684.

138 For the governor's account in 1788, see APEJE. CC. 03, f. 14v–15. For a similar account of the same governor in 1798, see AHU_ACL_CU_015, Cx. 199, Doc. 13653.

139 Valentim Alexandre, *Os sentidos do Império: questão nacional e questão colonial na crise do Antigo Regime português* (Edições Afrontamento, 1993), 68.

140 Carreira, *A Companhia Geral do Grão-Pará e Maranhão*, 2: 225–26.

141 Mello, *Frei Joaquim do Amor Divino Caneca*, 21.

142 AHU, ACL, CU, 009, Cx. 66, Doc. 5832.

With the expansion of industrial production in Europe, mainly in England, the ideal scenario would have been the enlargement of consumer markets in the Americas. However, these markets were protected by the metropolitan exclusivity or the old colonial system.[143] Thus, his interpretation posits European industrial development as dependent on colonial markets. British industrialization was based on the exploitation of its colonies but also on efforts to penetrate the Portuguese and Spanish colonies. Along with the British expansion, political changes were taking place in Portugal that indirectly favored smuggling practice. With the nationalization policy put in place by Pombal, the British lost their share in legal trade from Lisbon with America. Prior to Pombal, the presence of English merchants, namely interested in gold from Brazil, was notorious. But with Pombal's restrictions, the English began to concentrate their efforts more towards the illicit trade, as they were being targeted by political measures that undermined their business within the legal mechanisms of Portuguese overseas trade.[144] According to Maxwell, Pombal sought to promote Portuguese traders, with the aim that they would be able to accumulate capital to compete with foreign traders in businesses that touched Portuguese-Brazilian trade.[145] In other words, at the exact moment when the industrialization process in England required the opening of more consumer markets for the purchase of its products, Portugal, owner of one of the largest colonies in America, tried to hinder the entry of English products in overseas markets.[146] Perhaps the best illustration of this is the ban on importing cotton fabrics from Britain, which was only lifted with the 1810 Treaty.[147] Portugal aimed to bypass English goods by establishing its own industry and sought to undermine the business activities of English merchants engaged with Brazil by founding two monopoly companies, one for Maranhão and another for Pernambuco. Coincidentally or not, these would be the two most important regions that would produce cotton.

It is complicated to assess whether this policy of challenge the English was, in fact, effective or whether it was only nationalist rhetoric. Novais' argument—and Jobson Arruda's as well—is that, once access to Brazilian markets had been hampered, the English first forced an indirect intervention

143 Novais, *Portugal e Brasil*, 114–15, 178–79, 197. See also Beer, *The Old Colonial System, 1660–1754*, vol. 1.

144 Novais, *Portugal e Brasil*, 121, 123.

145 Maxwell, "Pombal and the Nationalization of the Luso-Brazilian Economy," 623.

146 Novais, *Portugal e Brasil*, 123.

147 Rudy Bauss, "A Legacy of British Free Trade Policies: The End of the Trade and Commerce between India and the Portuguese Empire, 1780–1830," *Calcutta Historical Journal* 6, no. 2 (1982): 81–115.

to gain access to Portuguese American markets. This was done through smuggling. And the record of Portugal's trade balances with their colonies since 1796, in fact, shows the officials' concern with the problem of illicit trade.[148] By the way, for Novais, and also for the officers who took care of making the trade balances, the Portuguese industry was failing precisely because of smuggling.[149] Second, the British pushed for direct intervention to gain immediate access to Portuguese American markets through military interference. This refers to the English Navy escort that accompanied the Portuguese Court to Rio de Janeiro in late 1807. This event took place, of course, during the context of the war against the French. However, right at the beginning of the following year, Portugal opened Brazilian ports to friendly nations, including England, and a few years later allowed the entry of British cotton textiles into the Portuguese Empire. Thus, it was no longer necessary for England to depend on Portugal's intermediation to access Brazilian products and markets. The opening of ports to friendly nations had a more pragmatic reason: since Portugal was taken over by the French and colonial production needed to be shipped, opening the ports was, at first, a temporary decision. However, it would prove to be a definitive policy a few years later. This is the moment when the metropolitan exclusivity started to break down.[150] The coup de grâce coincided with Brazil's independence in 1822, when ties with Portugal broke and a new alliance with the English materialized. Obviously, there was criticism from Portuguese traders who experienced the end of the metropolitan exclusivity. Still, the decision was defended and celebrated by the most liberal—and anti-mercantilist—figures of the time.[151] In the end, Brazil gave up its economic dependence on Portugal and exchanged it for dependence on England.[152] Raw cotton and cotton goods were key elements that linked the interests of the two nations.

Still, even if the Pombaline policy was effective, it is difficult to prove that the increase in British smuggling caused the end of the metropolitan exclusivity. Jorge Pedreira, although agreeing that the Pombaline policy of getting rid of

148 Novais, *Portugal e Brasil*, 185–86; Arruda, *O Brasil no comércio colonial*.

149 Novais, *Portugal e Brasil*, 185–87.

150 Ricupero, "O estabelecimento do Exclusivo Comercial Metropolitano e a conformação do Antigo Sistema Colonial no Brasil," 2.

151 Ricupero, "O estabelecimento do Exclusivo Comercial Metropolitano e a conformação do Antigo Sistema Colonial no Brasil," 2.

152 On the influence of the English and the process of Brazil's independence, see Manchester, *British Preeminence in Brazil*; Roderick J. Barman, *Brazil: The Forging of a Nation, 1798–1852* (Stanford University Press, 1988); Cariello and Pereira, *Adeus, senhor Portugal*.

the British was successful,[153] provides a different and more nuanced interpretation. His arguments deserve to be listed here but with some caveats. He does not believe that the British resorted to smuggling to overcome the obstacles imposed by Portuguese mercantilism. Nor does Pedreira endorse smuggling as responsible for the end of the old colonial system. First because, even after 1808, products from Portuguese industry continued to be consumed considerably in Brazil. Thus, Brazil was necessary for Portuguese industrialization before and after 1808. Second, the source that both Novais and Arruda worked with—the reports of the superintendent who oversaw contraband and the person responsible for making the trade balances—should be used with caution. As an officer charged with suppressing smuggling and being paid for it, Pedreira argued that he could have been overstating his reports to prove that contraband was a serious matter and that his job was needed.[154] Although one could also argue the complete opposite—because he denounced contraband and pointed to its growth over the years, the superintendent could have been accused of failing in his duties.

Be it as it may, Pedreira also casts doubt on the reports of the superintendent who fought smuggling, as he was more concerned with the smuggling carried out by the Portuguese. This illicit trade did not directly involve foreigners. The superintendent's concern was with tax evasion and with the decline of the Portuguese industry, and not with a supposed breakdown of the metropolitan exclusivity. Pedreira's third argument involves the tremendous growth of foreign vessels that visited the Brazilian coast in the late eighteenth and early nineteenth centuries. For Novais and Arruda, this was a strong indication that smuggling was taking place, but for Pedreira, these vessels could not be just warships that sought a safe harbor.[155] Similarly, the increase in smugglers' seizures and confiscations may be a sign, not that smuggling was growing (as Ernst Pijning argued)[156] but rather that enforcement over illicit trade was effective. Pedreira's fourth argument is that English smugglers did not have much to buy in Brazil. For the smuggler, it was not enough to just sell products; it was also crucial to buy them. And what could be purchased in Brazil, since sugar was already supplied in abundance by the English colonies in the West Indies? Raw cotton would be the only product that the English would be interested

153 Jorge Miguel Pedreira, "From Growth to Collapse: Portugal, Brazil, and the Breakdown of the Old Colonial System (1750–1830)," *Hispanic American Historical Review* 80, no. 4 (2000): 841.

154 Pedreira, "From Growth to Collapse," 851, 853, 855.

155 Pedreira, "From Growth to Collapse," 855–56.

156 Ernst Pijning, "Controlling Contraband: Mentality, Economy and Society in Eighteenth-Century Rio de Janeiro" (PhD diss., Johns Hopkins University, 1997).

in exchanging for smuggled products. But even considering cotton, Pedreira claims that it would not be enough. Fifth, the British overestimated the Brazilian market after 1808. Pedreira mentions that British merchants who invested in direct trade with Brazil experienced many losses.[157] But Pedreira takes Rio de Janeiro as an example and does not deal with Maranhão or Pernambuco, colonies whose main product was cotton, an expensive product that required a lot of merchandise and money to be bought, as I showed in the previous section. Pedreira's sixth statement is that the commercial connections between Portuguese and Brazilians were strong and more robust than the precarious connections of smugglers with Brazilians' accomplices, so the business ties between Portugal and Brazil did not break with the events of 1808. In conclusion, what Pedreira claims is that Brazil did not have a solid demand, so the influx of smuggled goods should not have had such a huge impact, and even if it did, it would not have been the cause for the collapse of the old colonial system.[158] According to Pedreira, the end of the *old colonial system* should not be interpreted as a slow process of erosion of commercial structures caused by the expansion of the Industrial Revolution and smuggling. The cause, for him, was in the sudden military conflict that made France invade Portugal. This completely changed the commercial structure that had linked Portugal and Brazil for centuries.[159]

Melo e Castro's instruction to the newly appointed governor at the onset of the 1790s did not have the power to foresee the events of the early decades of the nineteenth century. Neither was he equipped with an economic theory that would make him see contraband in the terms presented by academics of the twentieth century. However, Melo e Castro does not mention the smuggling by foreigners, only that by Portuguese vessels, which can help validate Pedreira's argument. On the other hand, an account written after 1808 points out how the English and Portuguese merchants joined forces to monopolize cotton prices in Maranhão.[160] Similarly, those interested in cotton in Pernambuco had more connections with English merchants than with Portuguese merchants on the eve of the 1817 revolution.[161] These facts corroborate the interpretation of Novais and Arruda, which highlighted the English interest in Brazil. In any event, the key component of Melo e Castro's story is his ability to

157 Pedreira, "From Growth to Collapse," 858–59. See also C. H. Lee, *A Cotton Enterprise, 1795–1840: A History of M'Connel & Kennedy Fine Cotton Spinners* (Manchester University Press, 1972), 51–52.

158 Pedreira, "From Growth to Collapse," 860.

159 Pedreira, "From Growth to Collapse," 863–64.

160 Gayoso, *Compendio historico-politico*, 257–60, 262, 267.

161 Mello, *A Outra Independência*, 57, 60; Mello, *Frei Joaquim do Amor Divino Caneca*, 21, 24.

clearly explain how the economy and trade involving Maranhão and its other trading partners operated. His conclusions can largely be applied to the situation in Pernambuco, particularly considering the significance of currency in cotton procurement.

7 Conclusion

What can the case of cotton trade from Brazil in the free trade period teach us? The increase in cotton prices, the possibility of obtaining land, and slave labor in Brazil, added to the intensification in trade and transport services made Maranhão and Pernambuco promising places for growers, merchants, and agents. In Lisbon, the number of cotton importers grew between the 1780s and 1806. The transatlantic cotton market was open to everyone, including small importers and foreign traders in Portugal. The postulate of the old colonial system that prohibited foreigners in colonial businesses was something that, in a way, happened in the cotton trade between Brazil and Portugal. Yet it did not happen because of regulations but because of the specific conditions of the colonial market. Foreigners were even allowed in colonial businesses and actually imported cotton; however, they imported very little. My hypothesis is that they did not increase their share in this trade because it was too risky—it was necessary, for example, to monitor agents and correspondents overseas and, on top of that, deal with deadbeats—and the organizational structure of foreign merchants was already concentrated on trade with Europe. Although open, only a few Portuguese merchants tended to centralize the market of cotton imports but without creating an oligopoly. They could bring large amounts of cotton because they had most likely exported large amounts of credit (merchandise, bills, and money) to the colony. They also tended to centralize purchases in Lisbon, buying cotton from small importers inside or outside Lisbon customs. In this sense, the customs office in Lisbon and the dispatchers—intermediaries who paid the taxes and moved the cotton to its owners—were essential for those interested in the fiber coming from Brazil.

The economic development generated by the growth of cotton cultivation and exports created tremendous wealth for Maranhão and Pernambuco, which involved cooperation between different types of economic actors. But at the same time, this did not prevent a series of disputes and agency relationships did not work in several different situations. The cases I showed point to the fact that personal and family relationships failed since even relatives were targets of accusations of mismanagement of capital and commercial companies. Furthermore, courts could not function effectively. In these cases, the governors and authorities in Lisbon and Brazil emerged as facilitators of conflict resolution and enforced court decisions. However, these partial conclusions are based on documentation that precisely records complaints and requests assistance from the authorities for conflict resolution. Indeed, many other businesses did not face serious problems during their activities. Be that as it may, the act of collecting debtors went beyond agency relationships, as the collection of debts, or not, impacted many other members of the mercantile and financial community.

An essential feature in this trade seems to have been the different associations merchants in Brazil made with merchants in Portugal. The use of travelling agents was recurrent, and their action certainly favored small importers in Lisbon. On the other hand, companies tended to have more capital and handle a larger volume of goods. In one way or another, merchants in Maranhão and Pernambuco recurrently received credits from merchants in Portugal, consequently making them indebted to the merchant community in Lisbon. This was the pattern of credit flows, for instance, that the captaincy of Maranhão experienced during the GCGPM period. Free trade, to no small extent, repeated this same pattern. This relationship, however, was burdened with friction. Sometimes, colonial merchants defaulted or simply mismanaged the capital of the principals and investors in Portugal. The actions of governors, secretaries of state, and attorneys, among others, were apparently central to recovering capital. Largely, the increase in cotton prices made it difficult to buy imported products in Maranhão and Pernambuco. Imports were not enough to buy exports. For this reason, remittances of money to the colony were recurrent. Smuggling, in turn, should cover the rest of the deficits related to legal imports.

PART 3

The Cotton Re-Export Trade and the European Textile Centers

Introduction to Part 3

The golden age of Brazil's cotton exports coincides with the beginning of the European industrialization, particularly concerning the textile industry of England and France, the two main countries engaged in cotton manufacturing. It is also a period that coincides with the Revolutionary and Napoleonic Wars (1793 to 1815), a turbulent time from a political and economic point of view. Despite the relevance of Brazilian raw cotton to the textile industry, more needs to be known about the basic aspects of its trade. We do not have, for example, information on the main ports that purchased Brazilian cotton during this brief period of time. Likewise, little is known about the cotton merchants (both in Portugal and in the rest of the European ports) and how the fiber was sold in a period of high demand but also of high risk and instability due to military conflicts. These will be the topics addressed in this part of the book. The following four chapters seek to explain how the cotton trade between Portugal and the rest of Europe took place. To do so, it relies on the export records of Lisbon customs books. Through them, it was possible to develop two datasets: the ports of destination for Brazilian cotton and the exporters based in Lisbon. The sixth chapter provides an overview of the data extracted from the Lisbon customs books. It also seeks to examine the primary buyers of Brazilian cotton at the beginning of the trade: mainly France but also—to a lesser extent—the port of Genoa. The seventh chapter takes a fresh look at the troubled trade between Portugal and France during the Revolutionary and Napoleonic wars. Chapters 8 and 9 deal with the cotton trade between Portugal and England.

CHAPTER 6

Export, Exporters, and the Cotton Trade to France and Genoa, the Early Years

1 An Overview of the Cotton Re-Export Trade and Its Merchants

In 1806, shortly before Napoleonic France invaded Portugal and made the old colonial system collapse, Brazilian cotton reached twenty-eight European ports (Appendix C). Thirty-three years earlier, when Brazilian cotton was still in its early years, exports only reached five ports. In 1773, Brazil fed the European textile industry with a modest amount of 32,882 arrobas,[1] and by 1806 these were 449,851 arrobas (Table 6.1). Contrary to what one might imagine, the English ports were not the biggest cotton buyers on these two dates. The Brazilian cotton exports to Europe begin with France as the leading buyer and also end with France in 1806. In addition, many other ports bought Brazilian cotton throughout the period (Map 6.1). Still, England was Brazil's biggest cotton buyer via Portugal when considering the entire period. From 1808 onwards, Brazil began to send more and more cotton directly to England, although small quantities still went to Portugal and other European ports.[2]

At first, the chronology of Brazilian cotton re-exports differs from what we know about the links between the slave plantation, cotton, and industrialization in Europe. It is commonly claimed that cotton production, based on enslaved Africans' labor, was in some way activated by the process of industrialization

1 Carreira, *A Companhia Geral do Grão-Pará e Maranhão*, 2: 319–21.

2 For overviews of the period, see Thomas Southcliffe Ashton, *The Industrial Revolution, 1760–1830* (1948; repr., Oxford University Press, 1968); Phyllis Deane, "The Industrial Revolution in Great Britain," in *The Fontana Economic History of Europe. The Emergence of Industrial Societies, Part One*, ed. Carlo M. Cipolla, vol. 4 (Harvester Press, 1973), 161–227; Pat Hudson, *The Industrial Revolution* (1992; repr., Hodder Arnold, 2005); Jeff Horn, *The Path Not Taken: French Industrialization in the Age of Revolution, 1750–1830* (MIT Press, 2006); Paul Bairoch, "L'économie Française Dans Le Contexte Européen à La Fin Du XVIIIe Siècle," *Revue Économique* 40, no. 6 (1989): 939–64; Denis Woronoff, "L'industrialisation de La France de 1789 à 1815 Un Essai de Bilan," *Revue Économique* 40, no. 6 (1989): 1047–59; François Crouzet, "Les Conséquences Économiques de La Révolution Française: Réflexions Sur Un Débat," *Revue Économique* 40, no. 6 (1989): 1189–1203; O'Rourke, "The Worldwide Economic Impact of the French Revolutionary and Napoleonic Wars, 1793–1815".

MAP 6.1 Importers of Brazilian cotton in Europe, 1760s–1810s
Sources: Appendix C. Labourdette, *La Nation française à Lisbonne*, 392–93, 534. Chapman and Chassagne, *European Textile Printers*, 163–64, 241. Carreira, *A Companhia Geral*, vol. 2, 319–21. Bergeron, *Banquiers, Négociants et Manufacturiers*, 239–41. Poitrineau, *Les Relations Économiques Franco-Espagnoles*, 283, 287–88, 290. Heckscher, *The Continental System*, 177, 274–75. Crowhurst, *The French War on Trade*, 18. Macedo, *O Bloqueio Continental*, 58. Map prepared by the author.

in England.[3] However, according to Carreira[4] and the Lisbon customs books (Table 6.1), the first years of the cotton economy in the Portuguese Empire were to feed markets that were not mainly English. The French, between the duration of the GCGPM monopoly until the mid-1780s, were the primary buyers of

3 Furtado, *Formação Econômica Do Brasil*, 139; Barbosa, "Cotton in 19th Century Brazil"; Beckert, *Empire of Cotton*, 93–94.

4 Carreira, *A Companhia Geral do Grão-Pará e Maranhão*, 2: 319.

TABLE 6.1 Export of cotton from Lisbon, 1782–1806

Years	Total merchants	Total cotton exports	Main cotton exporters*	First port	Second port	Third port	Fourth port	Other ports
1782[a]	73	75,996	9 merchants – 45,908	Rouen (49.10%)	Genoa (32.92%)	London (9.19%)	Havre-de-Grâce (7.97%)	5 other ports (0.8%)
1789[b]	140	178,930	10 merchants – 117,940	Liverpool (31.80%)	London (28.61%)	Rouen (21.07%)	Genoa (13.99%)	13 other ports (4.53%)
1792[c]	105	253,090	10 merchants – 170,226	Liverpool (64.88%)	London (10.58%)	Genoa (10.22%)	Rouen (8.18%)	8 other ports (6.15%)
1799[d]	155	293,840	10 merchants – 163,972	Liverpool (49.77%)	London (24.23%)	Greenock (19.52%)	Hamburg (2.57%)	15 other ports (3.91%)
1806[e]	291	449,851	18 merchants – 224,664	Liverpool (27.47%)	Cherbourg (18.33%)	Nantes (17.69%)	Caen (13.03%)	24 other ports (23.48%)

Sources: Arquivo Nacional Torre do Tombo (ANTT), "Alfândegas de Lisboa, Casa da Índia":

a books 138, 290, 288, 250, 249, 248, 247, 246, 139, 289, 140, and 141.

b books 192, 193, 194, 195, 196, 311, 312, and 313.

c books 133, 132, 131, 95, 94, and 97.

d books 44, 45, 104, 162, 215, 407, 409, and 412.

e books 284, 106, 348, 517, 189, 207, 511, 329, 534, and 484.

Notes: exports are given in arrobas. *The leading cotton exporters were considered to be all those who, together, exported more than half of the total each year. See tables in Appendix B and C. Table prepared by the author.

Brazilian cotton in Lisbon. In the same period, Genoa was also a significant buyer. England began to be an important market for Brazilian cotton in the mid-1780s, and Liverpool was not a port of destination in 1782, with London importing cotton from Portugal. Yet, at this time, London accounted for as little as 10% of the cotton Portugal exported that year. Rouen and Genoa were instead the leading cotton buyers. Seven years later, England surpassed both, importing around 60% of cotton in Lisbon, with almost equal percentages destined for the London market (28.61%) and the Liverpool market (31.80%). Nevertheless, Rouen and Genoa were still important markets representing, respectively, 21% and 14% of exports from Lisbon. These numbers indicate two things: first, during the 1780s, England grew as an export destination, and it appears that London and Liverpool were equally important markets. At the same time, Rouen and Genoa declined in relative, though not in absolute, terms. Second, by the end of the 1780s, there was a certain equilibrium in the destinations of cotton exports, with four ports among the leading players.

The 1790s are a complex and unclear period concerning data and commercial relations between France and Portugal. Official figures from the Portuguese balance of trade registered that France imported nothing from Portugal between 1796 and 1799.[5] Data collected from Lisbon customs books for 1799 also points in the same direction: at least at an official level no cotton was exported to French ports that year (Table 6.1). Furthermore, in 1798, no vessel that left the port of Lisbon declared that it was going to France.[6] It is possible to conjecture that the impact of the revolutionary wars that began in 1793 put an end to Portuguese-French commercial relations. Theoretically, negotiations would only resume with the Peace of Amiens in 1802. However, the French consul in Lisbon drew up a list of exports from Portugal that detailed cotton as a traded commodity in the 1790s.[7] This indicates that, despite the war, Brazilian cotton was still reaching France, entering the country mostly via neutral vessels.[8] It was natural that this should happen: with the loss of Saint-Domingue, France could not afford to lose Portuguese supplies. Although trade continued

5 Arruda, *O Brasil no comércio colonial*, 370–71.

6 Joaquim Veríssimo Serrão, *História de Portugal. Volume VI. O Despotismo Iluminado, (1750–1807)* (Editorial Verbo, 1982), 428.

7 Jorge Borges de Macedo, *O Bloqueio Continental: Economia e Guerra Peninsular* (Gradiva, 1990), 195–97.

8 Miguel Dantas da Cruz, "Neutral Shipping and the Portuguese Economic Relations with the Atlantic World (1793–1814)," in *Neutres et Neutralité Dans l'espace Atlantique Durant Le Long XVIIIe Siècle (1700–1820). Une Approche Globale. Neutrals and Neutrality in the Atlantic World during the Long Eighteenth Century (1700–1820). A Global Approach*, ed. Éric Schnakenbourg (Editions Les Perséides, 2015); about neutrals, see Lance E. Davis and Stanley L. Engerman, *Naval Blockades in Peace and War: An Economic History since 1750* (Cambridge University Press, 2006), 4.

with Portugal, albeit indirectly, France continued to import cotton from the Levant.[9]

The relative decline of France and the commercial influence of England in Portugal appear to have occurred in the 1790s. Just three years—from 1789 to 1792—were enough for Liverpool to become the leading export destination (64.88%), followed well behind by London (10.58%) and Genoa (10.22%). Rouen, which ten years earlier had been the primary market, represented just over 8% of exports in 1792. Portuguese trade balances report that between 1796 and 1799, England imported 78% of all cotton exported by Portugal, followed by Hamburg with 16% and Italy (probably Genoa) with 5%.[10] Table 6.1 provides a detailed view of this period. In 1799, Greenock joined Liverpool and London as ports in Great Britain importing Brazilian cotton: together, the three concentrated 93.52% of exports from Lisbon.

In a way, 1799 marks the apogee of England as an importer of cotton from Portugal during the period when Brazil was still a colony. However, from 1800 to 1807, France returned with much more strength than in the 1780s. Admittedly, 1800–1 seem weak from the point of view of exports to France according to the official Portuguese trade statistics. Still, even before the Peace of Amiens, contacts between Portugal and France formally resumed. From 1802 to 1807, commerce returned full swing. During this period, France bought 1,536,604 arrobas of cotton from Portugal, a quantity slightly higher than that purchased by England (1,513,576 arrobas). After France (46%) and England (46%), Italy (3%), Netherlands (2%), and Hamburg (1%) were the main importers of cotton from Portugal.[11] Instead of Rouen, what Table 6.1 shows are the ports of Cherbourg (18.33%), Nantes (17.69%), and Caen (13.03%) as the main French ports for Brazilian cotton in 1806. At this juncture, maritime transport to Le Havre and Rouen was jeopardized by the British navy, prompting a diversion of shipping to alternative ports in France. Liverpool predictably came in first with 27.47%, and the other Great Britain ports played a marginal role, including London (4.05%), which lagged behind Greenock (4.91%).

---

9 Ouvrage collectif, *La Révolution en Haute-Normandie: 1789–1802* (Editions du P'tit Normand, 1988), 130; The use of neutral vessels was nothing new. During the War of Spanish Succession (1701–1714) and the War of Austrian Succession (1740–1748), trade with France was carried out with neutral ships or with Portuguese-flagged ships themselves; see Jean-François Labourdette, *La Nation française à Lisbonne de 1669 à 1790: entre Colbertisme et libéralisme* (Fondation Calouste Gulbenkian, Centre culturel portugais, 1988), 332, 334; Robert Lévy, *Histoire économique de l'industrie cotonnière en Alsace: étude de sociologie descriptive* (Librairie Félix Alcan, 1912), 56–58.

10 Arruda, *O Brasil no comércio colonial*, 370–71.

11 Arruda, *O Brasil no comércio colonial*, 370–71.

From the perspective of European ports that received cotton from Lisbon, this period was volatile, and changes occurred recurrently. This is a conclusion that we can easily extend to the merchant community. Considering its size, how it was structured, and their nationality, the composition of the merchant community in Lisbon who exported cotton changed greatly over twenty-four years (from 1782 to 1806). Table 6.2 shows the most prominent exporters during those years.

Overall, the number of cotton exporters was visibly smaller than that of merchants importing cotton from Brazil. In 1789, for example, 620 people in Lisbon

TABLE 6.2 Main cotton exporters from Lisbon, 1782–1806

Year	Merchants	Nationalities
1782	Antônio José dos Santos Amorim	Portuguese
1789	Arnaldo Henrique Metzener & Son	German
1792	Bellinge & M.e Mahon	English
1782	Bento José da Costa	Portuguese
1799 and 1806	Bernardo Henrique Metzener & Co	German
1782	Boaventura Feliz	Portuguese
1782 and 1789	Bonifácio José Lamas	Portuguese
1806	Bras Francisco Lima	Portuguese
1789	Camilo Pereira Soares Laroche	Portuguese
1789, 1792, 1799, and 1806	Carret, Koster & Co	English
1789 and 1792	Daniel Bowden & Son	English
1792	Devisme & Co	English
1806	Philippe Roussac	French
1806	Francisco Anastacio Antunes	Portuguese
1792, 1799, and 1806	Halford Gonne & Co	English
1799	Houston & Lindt	Unknown
1782	Hulse & Co	Unknown
1792 and 1806	Jacob Dohrman & Co	Dutch
1806	Jacome Ratton & Sons	Portuguese
1799	João Benton	English
1806	João Bulkeley & Son	English
1789	João Daniel de Bruyn & Jautard	Dutch/French
1799 and 1806	João Dowel M(e) Mahon	English
1799	João Pedro Manesch	Portuguese
1782	Joaquim de Souza Fonseca	Portuguese

TABLE 6.2 Main cotton exporters from Lisbon, 1782–1806 (*cont.*)

Year	Merchants	Nationalities
1782	Joaquim Pedro Quintela	Portuguese
1806	José Antônio dos Santos	Portuguese
1806	José Diogo de Bastos	Portuguese
1782	José Gonçalves	Portuguese
1806	José Henriques Pinheiro	Portuguese
1789 and 1792	Lefevre, Dittmer & Co	French/Hamburger
1792	Luis Stephens & Co	English
1806	Manuel Teixeira Basto	Portuguese
1782	Marcos José de Matos	Portuguese
1799 and 1806	Mayne & Brown	English
1789 and 1792	Melish & Devisme	English
1806	Offley Sealy & Son	English
1799	Parkers & Co	English
1806	Pirro Freitas e Silva	Portuguese
1792 and 1799	Ricardo Sealy & Co	English
1806	Thomas F. Dipson & Co	English
1789 and 1792	Thomas March & Co	English
1789	Widow Frenenlet	French

Sources and notes: See tables in Appendix B. This table shows the main cotton exporters in the years 1782, 1789, 1792, 1799, and 1806. Some of them appear in more than one year. For merchant nationalities see: The British Historical Society of Portugal, List of British Merchants in Lisbon 1788–1791, Report: HA 10, 1946–1950, 663 and The British Hospital, Lisbon, 1793, Report: HA 7 by A. R. Walford, 1943, 436–441. All names are taken from the Lisbon Almanach from 1788, 1789, 1790, 1791, and 1794. See also Labourdette, *La Nation française à Lisbonne*, and Cunha, *Negociantes, mercadores e traficantes no final da monarquia absoluta*. Table prepared by the author.

received cotton from Brazil, while 140 carried out exports.[12] For each exporter, therefore, there were 4.4 importers. Some of these merchants, both importers and re-exporters, had commercial offices close to each other, even on the same street, and were established in regions close to the main buildings that touched commerce, such as the customs house and the Board of Trade. The geographic proximity between traders was an element that certainly helped to facilitate exchanges. Furthermore, they were served by several notary offices to seal agreements among themselves (Map 6.2 and the information below).

12 For the number of cotton importers, see Table 5.1.

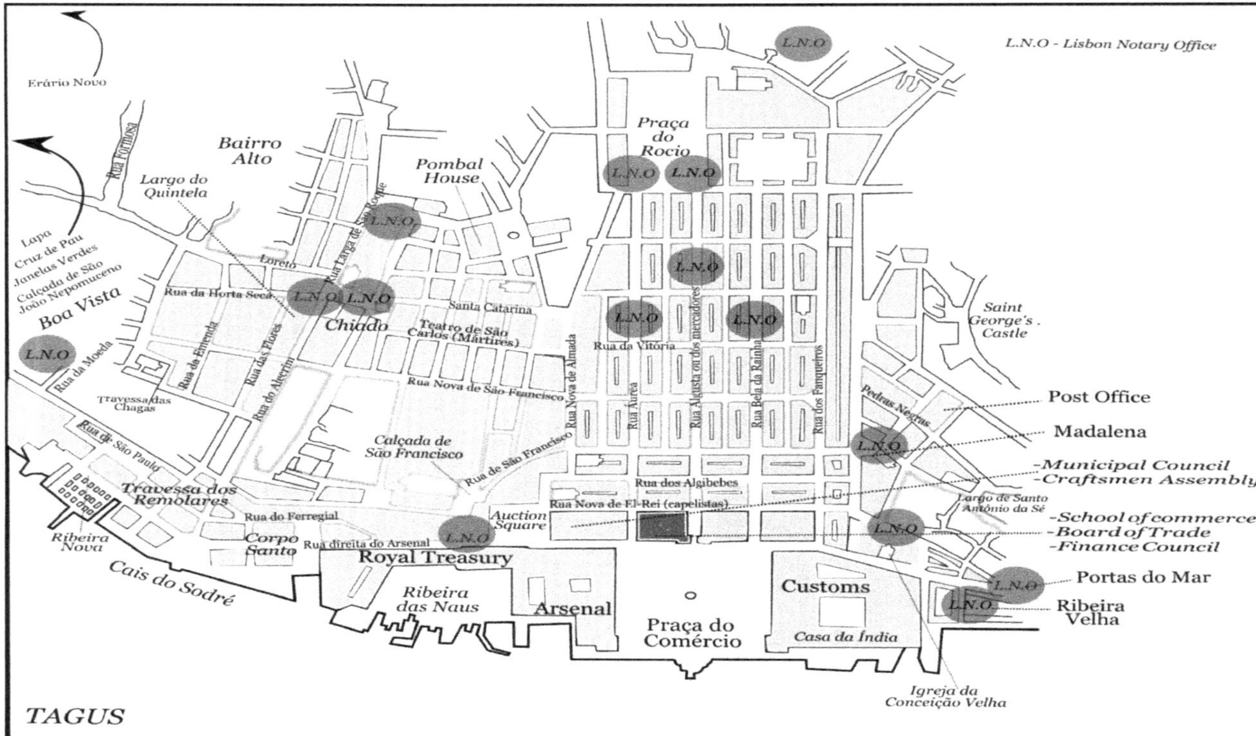

MAP 6.2 Residence of merchants and some important places for trade in Lisbon

Sources and notes: This map is based on the following historical maps: *Planta da Cidade de Lisboa Novamente edeficada della Ruina que padeceó no Terramoto do Primeiro de Novembro del Anno 1755*, Biblioteca Nacional de España and *Plano geral da cidade de Lisboa em 1785, Francisco D. Milcent*, Biblioteca Nacional de Portugal. All the main merchants listed in Appendices A and B were cross-referenced with the lists of merchants and their addresses reported by the Lisbon Almanachs (1788, 1800, and 1805 editions). For many of them, it was not possible to find information about their residences; a few others lived in places not covered by the map above. The approximate location of the Lisbon notary offices was taken from the information provided by the Lisbon Almanach of 1805. Map prepared by the author.

Boa Vista
Francisco José Pereira de Oliveira (import.)
Calçada de São Francisco
Felipe Ribeiro Figueiras (import.)
Calçada de São João Nepomuceno
Jacob Dohrman & Co (reexport.)
Chiado
Antônio José Ferreira (import.)
Corpo Santo
Antônio Esteves Costa (import.)
João Dowel M(e) Mahon (reexport.)
Cruz de Pau
Lefevre, Dittmer & Co. (reexport.)
Erário Novo
Widow Frenenlet (reexport.)
Janelas Verdes
José Antônio Pereira (import.)
Lapa
Mayne & Brown (reexport.)
Largo de Santo Antônio da Sé
José Gonçalves Macieira (import.)
Largo do Quintela
Joaquim Pedro Quintela (reexport.)
Loreto
Caetano Cordeiro de Araujo Feio (import.)
José Gonçalves (reexport.)
Mártires
Bonifácio José Lamas (reexport.)
Moeda
Antônio Simões da Costa (import.)
Bernardo Clamousse & Co. (import.)
Manuel Pinto da Silva (import.)
Pedras Negras
Antônio Francisco Machado & Co. (import.)
Policarpo José Machado (import.)
Portas do Mar
Thomas F. Dipson & Co. (reexport.)
Ribeira Nova
João Bulkeley & Son (reexport.)
Manuel de Souza Lobo (import.)
Marcos José de Matos (reexport.)
Ribeira Velha
Antônio José dos Santos Amorim (import.)
Miguel Pereira Guimarães (import.)
Rua Augusta
Manuel Joaquim Rebelo (import.)
Rua Aurea
José da Silva Ribeiro (import.)
José Lopes de Abreu (import.)
Thomas March & Co (reexport.)
Antônio Pires Leal (import.)
Rua da Emenda
Manuel de Miranda Correa (import.)
Manuel de Souza Freire & Co. (import.)
Rua da Horta Seca
José Antônio dos Santos (reexport.)
José Dioníssio Pereira (import.)
Rua das Flores
Antônio José Batista de Sales (import.)
João Antônio de Almeida (import.)
José Álves Branco (import.)
Rua do Alecrim
Cristovão Manuel Digues (import.)
Jerônimo José de Carvalho (import.)
Manuel José Machado de Sampaio (import.)
Rua dos Algibebes
Antônio Henriques Castelão (import.)
Rua dos Capelistas
Camilo Pereira Soares Laroche (reexport.)
Rua dos Fanqueiros
Carret, Koster & Co. (reexport.)
Paulo Jorge (import.)
Pirro Freitas e Silva (reexport.)
Rua Formosa
Devisme & Co. (reexport.)
Jacome Ratton & Sons (reexport.)
João Teixeira de Barros (import.)
Melish & Devisme (reexport.)
Rua Larga de São Roque
Antônio Martins Pedra (import.)
Francisco José Bandeira (import.)
Rua Nova de Almada
Francisco Hermano Vanzeller (import.)
Rua Nova de São Francisco
Arnaldo Henrique Metzener & Son (reexport.)
Bernardo Henrique Metzener & Co. (reexport.)
José Álves Viana (import.)
Rua Nova Del Rei
Luis Stephens & Co. (reexport.)
Rua Nova do Ferragial
Bento José da Costa (reexport.)
Halford Gonne & Co. (reexport.)
Bento José Pacheco (import.)
Francisco Xavier Fernandes Nogueira (import.)
João Antônio Vieira Caldas (import.)
Santa Catarina
Mateus Poitier (import.)
São Paulo
Marcos José de Matos (import.)
Teatro de São Carlos
José Diogo de Bastos (reexport.)
Travessa das Chagas
Joaquim José Vasques & Co. (import.)
Travessa dos Romolares
Bellinge & M.e Mahon (reexport.)
Daniel Bowden & Son (reexport.)
Vitória
Joaquim José de Almeida (import.)

Yet, one characteristic that both importers and exporters shared was the hierarchical organization of commerce, with few merchants concentrating much of the cotton that was traded. Furthermore, Tables 6.1 and 6.2 show that while France was a key market for cotton, French merchants in Lisbon were marginal in the export business. The English and Portuguese were the main protagonists in this trade. However, a more complex scenario emerges when we break down these data. Table 6.3 shows that companies (probably formal associations that involved written contracts and that were planned to last for a few years) and partnerships (probably informal associations, made for one-off exports and that were not intended to last long) became increasingly important: despite starting timidly in 1782, they accounted for the majority of shipments in 1789, 1792, and 1799. Though of lesser importance (except 1792), associations between fathers and sons and widows who shipped also constituted companies, as they involved more than one member. Another important mode of commercial organization was merchants who exported without any kind of association: merchants were crucial in 1782, dropped in importance in 1789, 1792, and 1799, but came back with strength in 1806. When we look at the names and surnames of these merchants, it can be seen that, in the beginning, the Portuguese predominated, lost strength in 1789, 1792, and 1799, but returned with greatness in 1806. In such manner, this overview of Portuguese and non-Portuguese names and surnames anticipates one of the conclusions of the analysis by leading exporters: in the beginning, the Portuguese dominated the cotton export trade, lost ground in the middle years, and came to be important again in 1806.

As seen in Chapter 5, the Portuguese controlled trade with Brazil. However, the low participation of foreigners in the import trade was not necessarily linked to laws (such as the metropolitan exclusivity) that prohibited them from doing business with Brazil. On the contrary, they were actually allowed to do so (Table 5.3). One of the hypotheses that can explain the limited interest of foreigners in cotton importation is that they were fully engaged in the re-export trade. A further important conclusion to be drawn from Tables 6.2 and 6.3 is that the Portuguese were not structurally excluded from the re-export business. Their importance depended on the ports it traded with and on external contexts, such as wars. As seen in Tables 6.1 and 6.3, there were many individuals in Lisbon exporting cotton. But only a few contributed to most of the shipments (Table 6.2). Table 6.4 provides an overview of the 43 principal merchants who exported cotton in Lisbon. The business tended to be led by the English (with 16 merchants exporting more than 50% of the total), followed by the Portuguese (18 merchants exporting almost a quarter of the cotton) and merchants of other nationalities, who together shipped nearly a quarter of the

TABLE 6.3 The economic and social composition of cotton exporters in Lisbon, 1782–1806

	1782		1789		1792		1799		1806	
	Merchants	Exports	Merchants	Exports	Merchants	Exports	Merchants	Exports	Merchants	Exports
Companies and partnerships	11	13,022	48	121,441	45	188,127	54	219,226	54	132,215
Associations between fathers and sons	3	895	3	5,343	4	34,254	9	3,160	8	26,200
Widows			2	9,369	5	6,247	2	2,642	3	4,990
Merchants	59	62,079	87	42,781	51	24,460	90	68,811	226	286,446
Total	**73**	**75,996**	**140**	**178,934**	**105**	**253,088**	**155**	**293,839**	**291**	**449,851**
Non-Portuguese first and last names	30	19,749	87	155,824	77	241,957	113	265,235	80	177,156
Portuguese first and last names	43	56,247	53	23,110	28	11,131	42	28,604	211	272,695
Total	**73**	**75,996**	**140**	**178,934**	**105**	**253,088**	**155**	**293,839**	**291**	**449,851**

Sources and notes: See tables in Appendix B. Exports are given in arrobas. Table prepared by the author.

total: two Frenchmen, two Germans, a Dutchman, a Hamburg-French association, a French-Dutch association, and two merchants whose nationality it was not possible to identify.

Table 6.4 shows that the Portuguese did not control the trade of one of the main goods of their empire. About 75% of the cotton shipped from Lisbon to Europe was exported by non-Portuguese merchants, with the British leading the way. But the Portuguese still managed to be the second most important nationality, larger than French merchants, whose market was the second (and sometimes the first) destination for Brazilian cotton. Therefore, what appears to be intriguing is the marginal position of French merchants in Lisbon in the raw cotton export trade.

The low incidence of associations between merchants of different nationalities seems to endorse Carrere's reports that foreigners in Lisbon socialize very little among themselves and with the Portuguese community. In social terms, foreigners and Portuguese were quite separate groups.[13] In economic terms, this can be seen in the cotton export trade. Still, further research is needed to

TABLE 6.4 Nationalities of the main cotton exporters in Lisbon, 1782–1806

Nationalities	Exporters	Cotton	% cotton
English	16	364,932	50.49
Portuguese	18	178,123	24.65
French/Hamburger	1	61,378	8.49
German	2	51,309	7.10
Dutch	1	17,441	2.41
French	2	15,813	2.19
Dutch/French	1	10,688	1.48
Unknown	2	23,026	3.19
Total	**43**	**722,710**	**100**

Sources and notes: See tables in Appendix B. Cotton is given in arrobas. For merchant nationalities see: The British Historical Society of Portugal, List of British Merchants in Lisbon 1788–1791, Report: HA 10, 1946–1950, 663, and The British Hospital, Lisbon, 1793, Report: HA 7 by A. R. Walford, 1943, 436–441. All names are taken from the Lisbon Almanach from 1788, 1789, 1790, 1791, and 1794. Labourdette, *La Nation française à Lisbonne* and Cunha, *Negociantes, mercadores e traficantes no final da monarquia absoluta*. Table prepared by the author.

13 Joseph-Barthélemy-François Carrere, *A Picture of Lisbon, Taken on the Spot: Being a Description Moral, Civil, Political, Physical and Religious, of That Capital; with Sketches of the Government Character and Manners of the Portuguese in General* … (Printed for Henry Colburn, 1809), 38–42.

have a more precise dimension of the role of foreign credit in financing the economic activities of the Portuguese and other foreigners.

Comparing the destination of cotton with the nationalities of the exporters, it is evident that the French and Italians did not dominate the raw cotton trade to their own countries (Table 6.5). The Italians simply did not participate

TABLE 6.5 Cotton exports and nationality of major exporters, 1782–1806

Exports to Great Britain			Exports to France			Exports to Italy		
Nationalities	**Exports**	**%**	**Nationalities**	**Exports**	**%**	**Nationalities**	**Exports**	**%**
English	353,319	73	Portuguese	127,820	79	Portuguese	13,279	27
German	49,000	10	French/Hamburger	13,096	8	Unknown	9,045	18
French/Hamburger*	36,878	8	French	9,982	6	French/Hamburger	8,192	16
Portuguese	18,014	4	English	3,980	2	English	7,487	15
Unknown	13,854	3	Dutch/French	3,833	2	French	4,986	10
Dutch	9,997	2	Dutch	2,845	2	Dutch	2,740	6
Dutch/French	4,431	1	German	456	0	Dutch/French	2,424	5
French	845	0	Unknown	127	0	German	1,620	3
Total	486,338	100		162,139	100		49,773	100

Exports to Antwerp, Amsterdam, and Rotterdam			Exports to Hamburg		
Nationalities	**Exports**	**%**	**Nationalities**	**Exports**	**%**
Portuguese	16,728	94	French/Hamburger	2,897	64
Dutch	781	4	Portuguese	1,581	35
French/Hamburger	315	2	Dutch	19	0
			English	9	0
Total	17,824	100		4,506	100

Sources and notes: Appendix B. The total here is slightly smaller than the total in Appendix B, as it does not include ports such as Livorno and general designations such as "north" in the calculation.
* A company formed by merchants from Hamburg and France. Table prepared by the author.

in this business, at least not directly and substantially. It was the Portuguese, French, and English who exported the most to the Italian markets. French merchants in Lisbon fared better than Italians but still far worse than what might be expected: they accounted for only 6% of exports to France. The Portuguese dominated this branch of commerce with 78% of shipments, followed by a Hamburg-French association (8%) and by French merchants (6%). Portuguese merchants once again supplied the markets of Antwerp, Amsterdam, and Rotterdam. The Germans were more engaged in trade with Hamburg, followed by the Portuguese (35%). Examining these branches of the raw cotton trade, the participation of Portuguese merchants was substantive, especially considering exports to France. In contrast, exports to Great Britain were dominated by the English factory in Lisbon (73%), and to a much lesser extent by different nationalities, with the Germans in second place (10%) and the Portuguese with just 4%.

However, when we look at each year of the sample, we see that the Portuguese dominated exports in 1782 (Table 6.6). The English grew a lot in the 1780s, but in 1788 there still seemed to be a fair competition between them and the Portuguese, Germans, French, French-Hamburg, and French-Dutch associations. Three years later, in 1792, and towards the end of the decade, in 1799, the British indeed dominated the cotton reexport market in Lisbon, accounting for more than 70% of exports. In 1806, however, the English decreased significantly in exports, being overtaken by Portuguese merchants who were the most significant exporters that year, responsible for more than 50% of shipments. The

TABLE 6.6 The percentage of Brazilian cotton exported from Portugal by merchants' nationalities

Years	1782	1789	1792	1799	1806
English		43.01	77.95	70.16	29.74
Portuguese	80.02	8.78		4.57	55.02
French/Hamburger		29.3	15.89		
Dutch/French		9.12			
French		6.87			3.46
German		2.93		16.82	8.7
Dutch			6.17		3.09
Unknown	19.98			8.45	
Total	100	100	100	100	100

Sources: Appendix B. Table prepared by the author.

official return of France as a cotton buyer seems to have favored the Portuguese merchant community and does not seem to have been taken advantage of by the French merchant community in Lisbon.

In essence, both from a general point of view (Table 6.1) and from the perspective of the leading merchants (Tables 6.5 and 6.6), the 1780s started very favorably for the Portuguese mercantile community. Still, they were gradually overtaken by other nationalities, mainly by the English. The 1790s seemed to be the zenith for the English merchant community in Portugal, as they did not see serious competition in the cotton export business. The year 1806 appears to bring back the competition experienced in the 1780s.

The significant presence of foreigners in Lisbon was attributed to the financial and maritime vulnerabilities of the Portuguese. Due to the significant demand for capital and maritime services, the Portuguese granted foreigners commercial treaties and legal rights nearly equivalent to those afforded to their own citizens.[14] In this regard, the English were the most privileged among foreigners. France presented a distinct situation. In contrast to England, Portugal lacked a commercial treaty with France. This adversely affected the French mercantile community in Portugal. Despite the treaty signed between France and Portugal in 1667, the Portuguese frequently neglected its stipulations as a form of reprisal for the repercussions of the War of Spanish Succession and the Seven Years' War. It looked as if no treaty existed between the two nations. Perhaps because they invaded Brazil, the Dutch were not very welcome in Lisbon, and the merchants of Hamburg and Genoa did not have powerful states to support them.[15] All this favored the British merchants. Yet, there were ups and downs in the British merchant community in Lisbon. Their performance was linked to the economic trajectories of Portugal and Brazil, the economic policies that involved the apparent "anti-British" feeling of Pombal, and the political and military conflicts between France and England that impacted the community of foreign merchants in Portugal. For the English case, both its ports of destination and its Lisbon-based merchants were essential elements in the history of Brazil's cotton exports.

In the case of France, the importance of its ports is undeniable, but it is evident that its merchants in Portugal were negligible in the cotton trade (Tables 6.2 and 6.5). Furthermore, the commercial treaties and the wars

14 Harold Edward Stephen Fisher, "Lisbon as Port Town in the Eighteenth Century," in *I Porti Come Impresa Economica: Atti Della "Diciannovesima Settimana Di Studi, "2–6 Maggio 1987*, ed. Simonetta Cavaciocchi (Le Monnier, 1988), 721–22.

15 Lodge, "The English Factory at Lisbon," 223; Labourdette, *La Nation française à Lisbonne*, 46–47, 364.

from 1793 onwards were political decisions and events that compromised the Portuguese-French commercial contacts, harming cotton shipping and the French mercantile community in Lisbon. I will consider the trade with England in Chapters 8 and 9. In the remainder of this chapter, I explore the trade with France (and, to a lesser extent, with Genoa) who, chronologically, started the cotton trade with Portugal and were the two most important locations during the early years.

2 Commercial Conditions between Portugal and France

The French case presents an interesting paradox of a foreign merchant community that took slight advantage of a business vital to the economy of its home country: the raw cotton trade. Broadly speaking, the marginal position that the French mercantile community in Lisbon reached towards the end of the eighteenth century was a continuation of what had been taking place since the beginning of the century. What caused the weakness of French trade in Portugal was linked to two diplomatic and economic factors. First, Portugal had a much more beneficial relationship with England because of commercial complementarity. The Methuen treaty of 1703 is the best example of this: Portuguese wines were exchanged for English woollen fabrics. At the same time, Brazilian gold paid for another part of the imports that came from England. Portugal had nothing like this with France. Although France found a small market for its products in Portugal, the Portuguese had little to offer in return, a situation that would change with the Brazilian cotton in the late eighteenth century. Second, there was a political and diplomatic tie between England and Portugal that was very difficult for France to break. The French consuls in Portugal pointed out several other factors that undermined the growth of the French mercantile community: weaknesses in French trade and shipping, the high prices of French products, the French's lack of adaptation to the foreign market, the obstacles raised by Portuguese legislation, and the shortcomings of French commercial houses.[16]

If English merchants in Lisbon were identified as members of the "English factory," French merchants were best known for being part of the "French nation." It was actually an identification applied to the French in any foreign port. The members of the "nation" were regarded as "simple agents of the houses of commerce of their Kingdom" of origin. The head of the French nation

16 Labourdette, *La Nation française à Lisbonne*, 453.

was the consul, who was also a "Commissar of the King" of France, which made the French nation in Lisbon a group framed under the power of the French King.[17] However, the consul would also have to swear allegiance to the King of Portugal, as many of his determinations would have to pass through the Portuguese authorities.[18] Officially, France gained the right to have a consul and vice-consul in Portugal a little later than other nations. While England had the right to its consul in 1654 and the Dutch in 1661, France only won theirs in 1667. Although this was formalized by treaties taking place in these years, the presence of foreign consuls in Portugal preceded these dates.[19] The task of the French consul, in general, did not differ from the obligations of the other consuls: "to protect the commerce of France and the subjects of the King who do it," "to ensure the proper functioning of French navigation in Portugal," "to protect the captains of ships," and "to resolve any difficulties that could arise between the French ships and the Portuguese authorities."[20] He was also an informant who, in addition to notifying ministers in France about the situation of Portugal's internal policy, also reported to them the number of vessels arriving and leaving Lisbon and the goods they carried.

The consuls had the help of the vice-consuls. The latter's function was to assist French ships, both on arrival and departure, accompanying the captains to the various customs offices to declare their cargo and payment of port fees. As no captain spoke Portuguese, the vice-consul acted as an interpreter. One of the most critical vice-consulates in Portugal was Porto, commanded by the important Clamouse family.[21] One of the family members, Bernardo Clamouse, moved to Lisbon, where he was classified as one of the wealthiest merchants in Portugal and even had a cotton industry.[22] He was also involved in supplying goods to carry out the slave trade on the coast of Guinea and was one of the biggest importers of cotton in Lisbon (Table 2.7 and Appendix A). His cotton supplier was probably Maranhão, since he had commercial contacts with the wealthy planter, cotton merchant, and slave trader Caetano José

17 Labourdette, *La Nation française à Lisbonne*, 21, 45.

18 Labourdette, *La Nation française à Lisbonne*, 168–69.

19 Labourdette, *La Nation française à Lisbonne*, 141; Ribeiro, "Privilégios Dos Estrangeiros Em Portugal (Ingleses, Franceses, Alemães, Flamengos e Italianos)".

20 Labourdette, *La Nation française à Lisbonne*, 195, 198.

21 Labourdette, *La Nation française à Lisbonne*, 144, 150.

22 Pedreira, "Os Homens de Negócio Da Praça de Lisboa," 190, 366; Nuno Daupias d' Alcochete, "As Casas de Morada de Bernardo Clamouse," *Boletim Cultural Da Câmara Municipal Do Porto* 17, nos. 1–2 (1954): 221.

Teixeira.[23] Daniel Gildemeester, the Dutch consul in Lisbon, also had contacts with Genoa, serving as a sort of agent working for Genoese investors in 1784.[24]

The French consul served as both a political and intelligence agent for the French government, occasionally engaging in similar tasks as French ambassadors in Portugal. In addition to his political role in negotiating commercial treaties, the ambassador also supplied the French authorities with economic and commercial information. In one instance, Ambassador Bombelles expressed his esteem for Martinho de Melo e Castro in his diary, commending him for his efforts in expanding cotton production in Brazil. In another instance, he documented his journey through Portuguese villages renowned for their production of cotton textiles.[25]

The French private courts were another institution that made commerce happen without much friction. Their function was to provide the French with an institution where they would be treated on an equal footing with the Portuguese. The private court consisted of an establishment that sought to protect the nation's private properties, just as the judge conservator did with the English factory. The French judge conservator, like the English one, was Portuguese. He was chosen by the members of the French nation in Lisbon, but his approval depended on the King of Portugal. It was an important function and one that had to be carefully assigned to the right person: care should be taken not to choose an incompetent judge or even one not daring to defend the French cause.[26]

Yet, although counting on the presence of the institutions of the consulate, the special courts, and the figure of the ambassador, the French did not have the same benefits established in commercial treaties as the English. Supposedly, the French in Portugal should have enjoyed all the privileges that, for example, the English and the Dutch benefited from. This was written in a treaty of 1667 that greatly benefited France. But the Portuguese often denied the French these privileges, as the effects of the War of Spanish Succession and the Seven Years' War had—according to the Portuguese—made the deliberations of 1667 expire. The Portuguese ministers said that this issue would be

23 ANTT, Feitos Findos, Juízo da Índia e Mina, mç. 7, no. 14, cx. 273. AHU, ACL, CU, 009, Cx. 75, Doc. 6495, and Cx. 81, Doc. 6882.

24 Catia Brilli, "Coping with Iberian Monopolies: Genoese Trade Networks and Formal Institutions in Spain and Portugal during the Second Half of the Eighteenth Century," *European Review of History: Revue Européenne d'histoire* 23, no. 3 (2016): 465.

25 Marquis de Bombelles, *Journal d'un ambassadeur de France au Portugal, 1786–1788* (Presses universitaires de France, 1979), 260, 303.

26 Labourdette, *La Nation française à Lisbonne*, 45, 57–62; on the judge conservator of the English, see Shaw, *The Anglo-Portuguese Alliance*, 82–92.

settled only with a commercial treaty between Portugal and France. This was, however, used as a kind of threat by the Portuguese, as they would only make a treaty if the French gave them advantages for the products exported by Portugal. According to Labourdette, the closest commercial agreement reached between France and Portugal in the eighteenth century was Pardo's 1778 Portuguese-Spanish treaty, which benefited France. Shaw mentions a French-Portuguese trade treaty in 1783 but without going into detail about its clauses.[27] What seems certain is that the French mercantile community in Lisbon was weakened, and this was due to following circumstances.

The members of the "French nation" did not equal the total number of French people living in Lisbon. Theoretically, only long-haul merchants, or prominent businessmen, could be classified as nation members and thus be entitled to all its benefits. But big French commercial houses were rare in Lisbon, especially in the first half of the eighteenth century, so small merchants, shopkeepers, and artisans were admitted as nation members. Arriving at a number of French people in Lisbon is difficult, but a rough estimate suggests that they were around 1,000 in 1745 and between 6,000 and 8,000 in the 1780s. Many did not deal in commerce but instead worked for ministers, ambassadors, and great lords. Some were cooks or worked in hotels, and others worked making wigs and jewellery.[28] The number of merchants of the French nation reached forty-seven in 1783 and a number slightly more than this in 1787.[29] It was a somewhat smaller merchant community than the English one, with about fifty-nine members in 1794.[30]

However, it was not in the size of the French mercantile community in Portugal that its weakness lay. The great obstacle to exchanges between Portugal and France was that Portugal did not have much to offer France for its manufactured products. There was a complementarity of exchanges when Portugal exported sugar to France, but this was lost from the second half of the seventeenth century onwards.[31] This was reflected in the balance of trade: France achieved surpluses in its trade with Portugal in the overwhelming majority of the years between 1716 and 1779.[32] But from the 1780s onwards, the high French

27 Labourdette, *La Nation française à Lisbonne*, 46–47, 364; Shaw, *The Anglo-Portuguese Alliance*, 154.

28 Labourdette, *La Nation française à Lisbonne*, 22, 41–43.

29 Labourdette, *La Nation française à Lisbonne*, 677.

30 Fisher, "Lisbon, Its English Merchant Community and the Mediterranean in the Eighteenth Century," 24.

31 Labourdette, *La Nation française à Lisbonne*, 379–80.

32 Labourdette, *La Nation française à Lisbonne*, 638–40.

demand for raw cotton and tobacco from Brazil caused the trade balance to be inverted, and Portugal began to have trade surpluses with France.[33]

Although they were marginal on cotton exports to France, the French merchant community was crucial to their country's textile imports for a long time. This branch of commerce, however, was the target of Pombal's policy. It was clear to the French consuls that, by the late 1760s, British trade in Portugal was in decline. It was so decaying that the British trade level fell to the French level. As there was no increase in French exports in relation to British exports, the consul concluded that industrialization was taking place in Portugal, mainly through woollen fabrics. Another hard blow to English interests was the Treaty of Paris of 1763. Before that, English goods were smuggled into Spanish America through the Colonia del Sacramento (northern bank of the River Plate). But with the treaty, England lost that entrepôt, and the Colonia was closed to smuggling. At the same time, some French textiles, "of good quality and at a good price," managed to enter Portugal under the false name of "Dutch textiles." It was a form of smuggling since the "pragmatics of 1698" prohibited the entry of all woollen fabrics but made exceptions for textiles from England and the Netherlands. The Portuguese authorities were aware of this illicit trade, but they turned a blind eye to it for a long time. In 1771, Pombal made it difficult and banned the entry of these French cloths and fabrics, mostly silks and woollens. At the same time, the importation of hats from France was also forbidden. The French consul argued that Pombal banned French manufactures at the request of the English as a form of compensation for having lost contraband with the Colonia del Sacramento. After these bans, French manufactured goods never recovered. Overall, French exports to Portugal declined especially between the period of the United States War of Independence and 1789.[34] Of the products imported by Portugal between 1772 and 1774, England accounted for 48.7%, while France, even behind Italy and Germany, accounted for just 10.5%. Despite the ban on imports of some textile manufactures, textiles were yet the most significant goods that France sent to Portugal between 1775 and 1790. But with the decline of trade in French products, French merchants in Portugal began to be interested in goods from other parts of Europe, such as Germany, Italy, and even England.[35]

33 Labourdette, *La Nation française à Lisbonne*, 344, 386; Pierre Leon, "Structure du commerce exterieur et evolution industrielle de la France a la fin du XVIIIe siècle," in *Conjoncture économique, structures sociales: Hommage à Ernest Labrousse*, ed. Fernand Braudel (Mouton, 1974), 412–14.

34 Labourdette, *La Nation française à Lisbonne*, 340–44.

35 Labourdette, *La Nation française à Lisbonne*, 344–45.

The consuls attributed the loss of market in Portugal to the transfer of labor. In addition to his proper mercantile function, the French consul also exercised a special role that, it seems, did not concern the English consuls: he tried to prevent the migration of French workers to Portugal. The migration of these French-trained personnel usually specialized in manufactures was believed to help Portuguese industrialization, undermining the import of French goods.[36] For example, a cotton dyer from Rouen had arrived in Lisbon in 1774, and the Portuguese authorities made sure that he landed without being harassed by the French consul. According to the consul, "the French manage the King of Portugal's sheets and hat factories. It is a French stylist who governs the fabrication of fabrics here." The migration of French workers made Portuguese manufactures prosper and, because of that prosperity, French imports and products were being banned. As the Portuguese industry had an almost constant growth since Pombal, "the recruitment of workers was, therefore, on the agenda."[37]

Another interesting example is Luis Paliart, French by origin but who had become a Portuguese merchant and Portuguese consul in Rouen in 1783. The French consul in Lisbon accused him of being one of the "evil Frenchmen," as Paliart helped French workers to go to Portugal to work in factories. The Portuguese Roque Jorge was also named as a merchant who helped transport Swiss and French textile workers to Portugal. In 1783/84, he owned a vessel transporting workers to the cotton factory in Torres Novas that belonged to Joseph Laborde and his Swiss partner Henrique Meuzon; the latter was also a clerk (commis) for the English house *Purry, Devisme, and Company*. Le Bourgeois, a Portuguese merchant and consul in Le Havre helped to put workers on the vessel. He worked as an agent for Roque Jorge, an important merchant who supplied goods to be exchanged for "blacks in Angola." Thanks to the French consul in Portugal, we know that he carried out this trade to benefit French and Swiss cotton merchants and manufacturers established in Portugal.[38] Roque Jorge had experience with the French market as he had been his father's agent in that country.[39] He also knew Brazilian cotton like no one else, since he had participated in the management of the GCGPM in Lisbon (Table 1.1). Until

36 Labourdette, *La Nation française à Lisbonne*, 213.

37 Labourdette, *La Nation française à Lisbonne*, 227, 230; See also Rómulo de Carvalho, "O Recurso a Pessoal Estrangeiro No Tempo de Pombal," *Revista de História Das Ideias*, Tomo I (1982): 91–115.

38 Labourdette, *La Nation française à Lisbonne*, 231–34.

39 Martins, "A Companhia Geral de Comércio Do Grão-Pará e Maranhão," 261.

the end of the century, he was well engaged in the slave trade with Guinea (Table 2.7) and obtained cotton from Maranhão.[40]

Later, Henrique Meuzon would renew the same industry mentioned above with other partners. The contract signed at the notary's office in 1789 informs that this was a chintz factory working with a huge amount of capital: 100 *contos de réis*. Meuzon, described as the "dealer," subscribed 60 *contos* and the other partner, also Swiss, David Suabe, designated as the "master manufacturer," subscribed 40 *contos*. Others also participated in the company: a man named Barthelomi Juge, contributed a fifth of the capital of the society that was incorporated in Henrique Meuzon's capital. Henrique would receive 720,000 *réis* annually to provide houses in Lisbon, their gear, and their clerks. David Suabe would be paid 480,000 *réis* annually. To a large extent, this was a family business, as the partners' brothers would work in it: Luis Meuzon and Jacob Suabe.[41] From consular correspondence, we also know that the Frenchman Knusly had a cotton factory in Portugal. In 1783, the French merchant Bonífas brought, through a French ship leaving Rouen, hare and rabbit skins to be used in the hat industry in Portugal. Similarly, Gabriel Milliet, a hat maker, had beaver skins shipped from France for his industry in Portugal.[42] Henrique Paliart de Clamousse had lived in France and learned there a new way of dyeing cottons red. In 1801, he asked to set up a dyehouse in or around Lisbon using the techniques he learned in France.[43]

Some of the aforementioned examples illustrate how the slave trade involved consular authorities in France, French textile laborers, and Portuguese and French merchants. It is also necessary to comprehend French interest in Brazilian tobacco in this context. Along with sugar, tobacco was an essential commodity for French importers in the late seventeenth and early eighteenth centuries. Similarly, tobacco had the same fate as sugar: it lost space in the French market due to other producers in America; sugar began to be produced in the French West Indies, and English American tobacco supplanted Brazilian tobacco.[44] Brazilian tobacco regained momentum in the 1760s and early 1770s, as the French were trying to disentangle themselves from paying England

40 Martins, "A Companhia Geral de Comércio Do Grão-Pará e Maranhão," 159–160. See also AHU, ACL, CU, 009, Cx. 93, Doc. 7702 and Cx. 96, Doc. 7859.

41 ANTT, 6º CNL, Cx. 27, liv. 132, f. 26v–28v.

42 Labourdette, *La Nation française à Lisbonne*, 232, 234.

43 ANTT, Alfândega de Lisboa, Casa da Índia, liv. 1841. Registo das leis, ordens, condições dos contratos e fábricas, 38–38v.

44 For these matters, see Robert Louis Stein, *The French Sugar Business in the Eighteenth Century* (Louisiana State University Press, 1988); Jean-Baptiste Nardi, *O fumo brasileiro no período colonial: lavoura, comércio e administração* (Brasiliense, 1996), 337–43.

for tobacco brought from English America. They saw Brazilian tobacco as an option, and the famous merchant Jacome Ratton became interested in this trade, but the inferior quality of Brazilian tobacco created obstacles for the business to grow. It was around this time and until the early 1790s that Brazilian tobacco was loaded—clandestinely—onto French ships in Lisbon to be traded for enslaved Africans in the Guinea Coast.[45] Of the 34 ships that left Lisbon for Guinea in 1789, 26 were French vessels that carried tobacco in Portugal, six were English, and two were Portuguese.[46] A key merchant who linked the French and the slave trade was José Rodrigues Bandeira, owner of one of the biggest tobacco exporting houses, member of the Board of Trade and the GCPP. However, Rouen and Le Havre were not the main French ports engaged in the slave trade through Lisbon. In order of importance, the ports of La Rochelle, Nantes, Bordeaux, St Malo, and, finally, Le Havre were the most interested in Brazilian tobacco.[47] Likewise, in Costa da Mina (Bight of Benin), tobacco and textiles were crucial for the slave trade. The Dutch who controlled the castle of São Jorge da Mina required the vessels to go there to bring 10% of tobacco to trade in enslaved people. At the same time, merchants in Brazil brought tobacco directly from America, more specifically from Bahia. In addition to acquiring enslaved Africans, they also exchanged tobacco for English and French manufactured products. This trade brought manufactured goods into Brazil without paying taxes, hindering direct trade between Portugal and Brazil. Thus, the slave trade was also a way found by merchants to bring European textiles into Brazil outside the traditional Portugal-Brazil circuit.[48]

3 Cotton Exports and Navigation until c. 1790

The history of Brazilian cotton toward France occurs in the general context described above. Commerce had already started before in small quantities but would gradually increase over the years. Since at least 1739, Le Havre and Rouen—respectively the most important port and textile center in France—imported cotton from Lisbon, but it was not until 1766 that the volume of Portuguese cotton exports increased. From 1728 to 1776, Rouen's biggest cotton

45 Labourdette, *La Nation française à Lisbonne*, 344, 387, 389–90.

46 ANTT, Junta do Comércio, mç. 310, cx. 620 – Relações de entrada e saída dos navios do porto de Lisboa (see Appendix D).

47 Labourdette, *La Nation française à Lisbonne*, 421–22.

48 Arruda, *O Brasil no comércio colonial*, 322; Pierre Verger, *Fluxo e Refluxo Do Tráfico de Escravos Entre o Golfo Do Benin e a Bahia de Todos Os Santos Dos Séculos XVII a XIX* (1968; 3ª edição, Corrupio, 1987).

suppliers were the French West Indies, but imports from the Levant were also important.[49] For most of the time, Rouen received cotton through the port of Le Havre. But it was possible for cotton from the West Indies to reach Rouen via Nantes and cotton from Brazil via Marseille.[50] Yet, it is safe to say that Marseille was the most important port bringing cotton from the Levant, both in periods of peace and during the French wars (1793–1815).[51]

The growth of Brazilian cotton on the French market must have been related to the growing use of Hargreaves' spinning jenny, invented in England in 1764. In 1771, the first jenny was brought to France and ten years later its number exceeded 1,200 machines. The specificity of the spinning jenny was that it was very suitable for making fine yarn for wefts. Its implementation in France was problematic, though, as French spinners depended heavily on short-fiber cotton brought from the Levant not suitable for the spinning jenny. In 1779, cotton from Maranhão, Cayenne, and, to a lesser extent, from Saint-Domingue and Martinique allowed French spinners to use the spinning jenny to make yarn for cotton velvets, for example.[52] In 1785, a French encyclopedia reported that Maranhão cotton was dirty, because of the seeds that remained, but "the softness of the wool gives it a spinning that is as smooth and as fine as possible; & the resulting fabric has more softness and reflects colors more vividly than when it is made from any other cotton."[53]

It is difficult to determine exactly why France absorbed such large quantities of cotton from Portugal. However, considering that France controlled the small island of Saint-Domingue—the leading cotton producer in the Americas at the time—and that France was also the largest importer of cotton from the Levant, it makes sense that Brazilian cotton would flow there, given its role as Europe's principal cotton importer. Merchants from Amsterdam, Rotterdam, and Hamburg, for instance, went to Rouen to purchase raw cotton. With a large consumer market in France and its colonies, the French textile

---

49 Dardel, *Navires et Marchandises*, 316, 561; Labourdette, *La Nation française à Lisbonne*, 394.

50 Dardel, *Navires et Marchandises*, 314–16, 321 See also ANTT. Companhia Geral do Grão Pará e Maranhão, liv. 22, f. 47.

51 *Nouveau Dictionnaire d'histoire naturelle, appliquee aux arts: Principalement à l'Agriculture et à l'Economie rurale et domestique*, VI (Crapelet, 1803), 327; Lévy, *Histoire économique de l'industrie cotonnière en Alsace*, 56–58.

52 Styles, "The Rise and Fall of the Spinning Jenny," 196, 219–20; R. L. Hills, "Hargreaves, Arkwright and Crompton. Why Three Inventors?," *Textile History* 10, no. 1 (1979): 120; Edouard Delobette, "Ces Messieurs du Havre. Negociants, commissionnaires et armateurs de 1680 a 1830" (Ph.D., Université de Caen, 2005), 219.

53 Jean-Marie Roland de la Platière, *L'art du fabricant de velours de coton précédé d'une dissertation sur la nature, le choix et la préparation des matières et suivi d'un traité de la teinture et de l'impression des étoffes de ces matières* (Moutard, 1780), 4.

industry employed many workers spinning cotton, and by the mid-eighteenth century, protectionist measures were introduced to limit the re-export of raw cotton.[54] It is not unlikely that they made use of Brazilian cotton for its high quality in order to produce fine yarns, as Roland de la Platière observed in 1780 with reference to Maranhão cotton,[55] which was probably used primarily for weft production. Until about 1780, the French spinning industry was relatively strong,[56] but it began to lose ground due to two main factors: mechanization in England—especially after Arkwright's innovations—and the Treaty of Eden in the mid-1780s.[57] The shift of Brazilian cotton exports from France to England coincided with these developments.

Cotton from Portugal was benefited, as it paid the same rights as cotton coming from the French colonies. It was something that bothered the French consul in Lisbon, who claimed that this should not exist since the Portuguese placed a series of restrictions on cotton cloths imported from France.[58] In terms of sales strategy, they differed. From 1770 until 1775, the GCGPM opted not to sell cotton in Lisbon, instead choosing to transport it directly to Rouen. In Rouen, the GCGPM held a dominant position on cotton sales, allowing them to set prices at elevated levels. While the company benefited from this, it adversely affected French dealers in Lisbon who were unable to participate in the cotton trade and receive commissions. However, during the remaining years of the monopoly, the firm employed another approach to market its products: with the arrival of cotton from Maranhão, the GCGPM conducted auctions to facilitate its sale. This allowed merchants from Lisbon to seize control of the commodities that were mostly being sent to Rouen. Regardless of whether the company or the merchants were responsible for the exports, the exportation of cotton was accompanied by the exportation of fruits, namely oranges and lemons, which were harvested in the suburbs of Lisbon. It was

54 Dardel, *Navires et Marchandises*, 214; Pierre Dardel, *Commerce, Industrie et Navigation a Rouen et au Havre au XVIIIe siècle: rivalité croissante entre ces deux ports, la conjoncture* (Société libre d'émulation de Seine-Maritime, 1966), 108, 119, 142; William M. Reddy, *The Rise of Market Culture: The Textile Trade and French Society, 1750–1900* (Cambridge University Press, 1984), 24, 26, 53.

55 Roland de la Platière, *L'art*, 4.

56 Wadsworth and Mann, *The Cotton Trade and Industrial Lancashire, 1600–1780*, 193–208.

57 Oscar Browning, "The Treaty of Commerce Between England and France in 1786," *Transactions of the Royal Historical Society* 2, no. 4 (1885): 349–64; J. Holland Rose, "The Franco-British Commercial Treaty of 1786," *The English Historical Review* 23, no. 92 (1908): 709–24; Léon Cahen, "Une Nouvelle Interprétation Du Traité Franco-Anglais De 1786–1787," *Revue Historique* 185, no. 2 (1939): 257–85; Marie Martenis Donaghay, "The Anglo-French Negotiations of 1786–1787" (Ph.D. diss, University of Virginia, 1970).

58 Labourdette, *La Nation française à Lisbonne*, 390.

among the limited number of Portuguese products that were sent to both France and England.[59] Fruits were Lisbon's most important exports, with the obvious exception of goods originating from the colonies. In the year 1786, more fruit was shipped to England than wine and olive oil added together.[60] Fruit exports remained until the beginning of the nineteenth century.

Two of the most prominent cotton bidders at the GCGPM auctions in Lisbon were Paulo Jorge and his son, the aforementioned João Roque Jorge. Between 1765 and 1777, they bought cotton for around 148 *contos de réis* from the GCGPM. They had close relations with the Pombaline companies, as they were deputies of the GCGPM[61] and shareholders of the GCPP.[62] They were members of the elite of Lisbon's dealers and tax farmers.[63] These traders' interest in foreign markets was perhaps facilitated by the exceptional trajectory of Paulo Jorge, who had worked in Amsterdam in the first half of the 1760s selling goods such as leather and cocoa, and by the merchant network he built in the Netherlands. His connection with the governor of Angola in the second half of the 1760s suggests his participation in the slave trade from Lisbon.[64] By the end of the eighteenth century he had also been a merchant of Brazilian diamonds.[65] His son, João Roque Jorge, also sought to work in European markets. By the mid-1770s, he was in France and had built a merchant network that comprised merchants in St. Petersburg and Amiens. In Paris, he was receiving cotton sent by his father from Lisbon and probably used his contacts in Rouen, the merchants Guillier Pere and Sons and Joseph Champion, to sell it.[66] With the end of the GCGPM, João Roque Jorge, together with other merchants from Portugal, founded a company that specialized in the slave trade from Guinea (Cape Verde and Bissau) to Maranhão and Grão-Pará. Thus, João Roque Jorge and his company, which lasted from 1780 to 1786, were responsible for carrying a portion of the enslaved Africans who cultivated cotton in Maranhão, and it was very likely that they acquired cotton in exchange for the enslaved

59 Labourdette, *La Nation française à Lisbonne*, 386, 390–91. I am grateful to Diego Martins for providing me with some information that helped me in the preparation of this paragraph.

60 NA, FO 63/11.

61 Carreira, *A Companhia Geral do Grão-Pará e Maranhão*, 1: 83, 241.

62 Felipe Souza Melo, "O Negócio de Pernambuco: Financiamento, Comércio e Transporte Na Segunda Metade Do Século XVIII" (Master's thesis, Universidade de São Paulo, 2017), 541.

63 Pedreira, "Os Homens de Negócio Da Praça de Lisboa," 161.

64 Martins, "A Companhia Geral de Comércio Do Grão-Pará e Maranhão," 260.

65 Harry Bernstein, *The Brazilian Diamond in Contracts, Contraband, and Capital* (University Press of America, 1988), 63, 161.

66 Martins, "A Companhia Geral de Comércio Do Grão-Pará e Maranhão," 261.

people sold.[67] Another major cotton buyer from the GCGPM was Anselmo José da Cruz. At a very young age he had been sent to Genoa by his brother to be instructed in the mercantile trade. On returning to Portugal, he ended up becoming one of the principal merchants in Lisbon: he was a shareholder in the two Pombaline companies for Brazil, he was also the tobacco tax farmer for many years, and together with Roque Jorge, he was a partner in the company for the slave trade in Cape Verde and Bissau. Foreign firms and merchants also took part in the GCGPM's cotton purchases: the English Purry, Mellish, and Devisme, the French brothers Paulo Bonifas and Auriol Bonifas, and the Dutch merchant Ludero Illius & Co.[68]

The GCGPM established a commercial framework, from which subsequent merchants derived advantages after the company's dissolution. The French in Lisbon seldom engaged in this enterprise. The Portuguese controlled the majority of cotton exports to France (Table 6.5). Some foreign merchants connected to the GCGPM continued to export cotton in large quantities after 1778, such as the English Mellish and Devisme. But the end of the monopoly also saw the entry of new merchants. One of the central figures in 1782 and 1789 emerged from the world of the GCGPM: Bonifácio José Lamas. Both Lamas' father and grandfathers were sailors, and his father even became a captain of merchant ships. Lamas had a similar trajectory: he started working as a vessel pilot but managed to be promoted to the position of the GCGPM administrator in Bissau, a position he held between 1765 and 1768.[69] Back in Lisbon, he was identified as a businessman who financed negotiations with Brazil.[70] In 1769, still unmarried, he was appointed as administrator of the GCGPM in the Cape Verde Islands.[71] Shortly after, he was in Maranhão, already married, and with a son named Felix Potier Lamas. The latter would become a judge and would die in Mozambique at the beginning of the nineteenth century.[72] Furthermore, Bonifácio José Lamas had been the administrator of the GCGPM in Maranhão between 1770 and 1775, together with José Vieira da Silva. The two had gotten

67 The merchants who together with Roque Jorge established a company for the slave trade were Anselmo José da Cruz, Geraldo Venceslau Braamcamp de Almeida Castelo Branco, João Rodrigues Valle e João Lourenço Peres; see Martins, "A Companhia Geral de Comércio Do Grão-Pará e Maranhão," 262.

68 Martins, "A Companhia Geral de Comércio Do Grão-Pará e Maranhão," 268, 273, 279, 281.

69 Carreira, *A Companhia Geral do Grão-Pará e Maranhão*, 2: 272.

70 He gave "dinheiro a risco para os Brasis".

71 ANTT, Mesa da Consciência e Ordens, Habilitações para a Ordem de Cristo, Letra B, mç. 7, no. 5.

72 ANTT, Conselho da Fazenda, Justificações do Reino, Letra D, mç. 4, no. 4.

into trouble with the company, having to prove that they had not harmed the company's coffers; they were found not guilty in the end.[73]

After the GCGPM ended, Lamas imported cotton directly from Brazil in small quantities[74] but exported it in large quantities. This means that the way Lamas obtained cotton was through purchases in Lisbon from other merchants. In 1787, for example, he had bought 12 bales of cotton from João Lopes Martins de Figueiredo. The latter, however, had not paid the freight and costs of unloading the cotton in Lisbon, and for that reason, Lamas was suing him in court to pay these fees.[75] Having worked on the mercantile arrangements that the GCGPM had created, it was natural that Lamas would export more to France than anywhere else in 1782. Rouen was his primary market, but it is also noteworthy that he was one of the two merchants who more often sent cotton to London. Yet, seven years later, he shipped nearly equal amounts to both markets (see Appendix B). Shortly before he died in 1793, Lamas, who owned a shop in Lisbon, still traded with England and France, mainly in indigo and fabrics.[76]

Another important merchant who exported to France, Marcos José de Matos, had an unusual trajectory compared to other merchants: his family did not deal in commerce, and it does not even seem that he was trained for it. But despite this, he was not only a major cotton exporter but also a wealthy merchant who had business in different parts of the world. Born in Óbidos, he lived in Lisbon and was known for being a wholesaler. In 1784, at the age of forty, he was classified as "one of the richest of this marketplace," trading various goods in Portugal and abroad and owning ships.[77] But before being successful in business, he had been a barber in Lisbon with his own shop and then a surgeon, a profession he practiced for a long time.[78]

Marcos' example is also unusual, as he was one of the few merchants who imported cotton from Brazil and reexported it to Europe in large quantities, at least in the early 1780s (see Appendices A and B). He obtained cotton from Maranhão and Pernambuco and established connections in the latter market by granting powers of attorney to individuals there to collect debts from his two

73 AHU, códice 598, f. 17v, f. 188v–189. See chapter 1.
74 According to Lisbon customs book import data.
75 ANTT, Feitos Findos, Juízo da Índia e Mina, mç. 27, no. 13, cx. 214.
76 Pedreira, "Os Homens de Negócio Da Praça de Lisboa," 325. ANTT, Conselho da Fazenda, Justificações do Reino, Letra D, mç. 4, no. 4.
77 "um dos abonados desta praça".
78 ANTT, Mesa da Consciência e Ordens, Habilitações para a Ordem de Cristo, Letra M, mç. 30, no. 35.

debtors in 1794: Manuel Ferreira Viana and Pedro Antônio Le Roy.[79] But it was perhaps in Maranhão where his primary source of raw cotton was. Soon after the end of the GCGPM monopoly, Marcos José de Matos was already receiving cotton from there. In 1779, his cotton came on the *Santa Ana e São Joaquim* vessel owned by António José dos Santos Amorim, another major cotton exporter in 1782 (Appendix B). As Marcos had not paid the freight and unloading fees, Amorim filed a lawsuit against him.[80] In 1791 Matos was accused of the same thing: he owed the payment of freight for goods that came from Maranhão, including cotton, to João Francisco Lima, captain of the *Santa Rita e Santíssimo Sacramento* vessel.[81] It is also known that between 1793 and 1795, he was receiving goods from Maranhão.[82]

His interests lay in the slave trade, which opened up two sources of profit for him: he could obtain cotton from Brazil or, at the very least, benefit from its freight rates. In 1795, his vessel, *Nossa Senhora da Piedade e Santo Antônio*, whose captain was João da Rocha Bastos, left for Bissau and carried 233 enslaved people there, of which 216 arrived alive in Maranhão on December 24. The human cargo was worth approximately 34,560,000 *réis* (each enslaved worker quoted at 160,000 *réis* in Maranhão) and was consigned to Antônio José Gomes Cascais. The vessel left Maranhão on April 8, 1796, loaded with cotton, rice, and other tropical goods, totalling 24,955,650 *réis* and weighing 125 tons. It docked in Lisbon on June 18.[83] It was possible that Marcos ordered part of the cotton cargo, but he certainly profited from the freights of his vessel on the three legs of the triangular trade.

At least since 1790, Marcos was interested in negotiations with Asia. He owned a ship—which sank—that made a trip to Macau that year.[84] On another occasion, he received from the German Bernardo Henrique Metzner & Co., one of the largest cotton exporters in 1799 and 1806 (Appendix B), a shipment of iron that would be used, as capital, in trade with Asia.[85] Once,

---

79 ANTT, 3º CNL, Cx. 154, liv. 723, f. 77–77v and liv. 726, f. 56v–57.

80 ANTT, Feitos Findos, Juízo da Índia e Mina, mç. 14, no. 28 cx. 381.

81 Feitos Findos, Juízo da Índia e Mina, mç. 55, no. 3, cx. 242.

82 Cunha, *Negociantes, mercadores e traficantes*, 194, 196.

83 Marcos José de Matos is appointed as owner of the vessel in ANTT, Feitos Findos, Juízo da Índia e Mina, Justificações Ultramarinas, África, mç. 19, no. 10, cx. 34. Information on the cargo of slaves and goods exported from Maranhão are in AHU, Maranhão, cx. 89, doc. 7404 e Cx.93, Doc. 7680. See also https://www.slavevoyages.org/voyage/database. Eduardo Frutuoso et al., *O Movimento Do Porto de Lisboa e o Comércio Luso-Brasileiro, 1769–1836* (Comissão Nacional para as Comemorações dos Descobrimentos Portugueses, 2001), 449.

84 ANTT, Feitos Findos, Juízo da Índia e Mina, mç. 68, no. 16, cx. 255.

85 Pedreira, "Os Homens de Negócio Da Praça de Lisboa," 353.

however, his dealings with Asia directly interfered with his other affairs. By 1802, José Gomes Loureiro had provisionally won a lawsuit against Marcos. The sentence was the embargo of Marcos' goods in Lisbon customs (in the *Casa da Índia* to be more specific), including 400 bales of cotton. The problem was linked to sea loans drawn in Goa on a voyage made by Marcos' vessel. While in Goa, the supercargo of the ship Rodrigo José Loureiro, cousin of José Gomes Loureiro, had drawn two sea loans (over eleven *contos de réis*) on Marcos José de Matos. However, Marcos refused to pay the bill. The case was dragged through the courts for a few years, but that was enough to thwart Marcos' negotiations and bother his correspondents and creditors.[86]

This is another example that demonstrates the important role of Lisbon customs as an institution that intervened in the transfer of goods. A similar case was that of the widow Lefranc and Sons in 1792, merchants from the French nation. They intended to embargo some cotton bales because of an unpaid sea loan, written in 1790, by Manuel Fernandes da Porciúncula and José Inácio Batista. The debtors had received the amount in cash (1,367,810 *réis*) and went to Pernambuco. The debtors ended up staying there, and according to the widow and sons, there was a "possibility of not returning." As the debtors did not have real estate in Lisbon, the widow Lefranc and Sons asked for an embargo on 35 bales of cotton that were in customs. They were bales sent by the debtors in Pernambuco to a man named Simão Rodrigues in Lisbon.[87]

Marcos' cotton export business was focused on the Rouen market, and almost all the cotton he shipped went there in 1782. His relationship with France would remain for a long time, as even in 1811/1812, he was trading there and to Malta, Gibraltar, and Sicily.[88] Like other merchants in Lisbon, he also had an interest in the industry, but in this case not in cotton. In 1805, together with Antônio Martins Bastos, he owned a factory that made ivory combs.[89] One of the exciting things about Marcos' case is that it shows that the most prominent cotton exporters did business with each other: Amorim offered Marcos shipping services, and the German Metzner lent him capital.

In the 1780s, the French did not take the place left by the GCGPM. In fact, French merchants were not even that relevant within the GCGPM's commercial arrangements. As early as 1778, the French consul in Lisbon reported that the cotton trade between Portugal and France was carried out by the

86 ANTT, Ministério do Reino, mç. 853, proc. 4.

87 ANTT. Feitos Findos, Juízo da Índia e Mina, mç. 82, no. 19, cx. 82.

88 Cunha, *Negociantes, mercadores e traficantes*, 212; Pedreira, "Os Homens de Negócio Da Praça de Lisboa," 335.

89 Pedreira, "Os Homens de Negócio Da Praça de Lisboa," 364.

Portuguese and their agents, also Portuguese, in Rouen.[90] In 1782, for example, no Frenchman figured as a leading exporter in Lisbon (see Appendix B). The only leading Frenchmen who traded with the GCGPM, the Bonifas brothers, somehow became faded figures in commerce, although they probably had a more active participation in shipping, as I will point out. In 1789, however, a French widow and two French firms associated with other foreigners achieved good export performances. The most important was the firm Lefevre, Dittmer and Co., which comprised the Frenchman Claude François Crespin Le Fèvre and the Hamburger Jacques Dittmer. The two also formed a company with Philippe Roussac, who would be one of the few Frenchmen in 1806 to export large quantities of cotton (see Appendix B). Little is known about these firms and the biographies of their members, but Lefevre, Dittmer and Co. were well connected with both the French and English markets and shipped cotton to Genoa and Hamburg in both 1789 and 1792 (see Appendix A).[91]

The widow Frennelet even exported a lot of cotton to France, but her biggest shipments went to Genoa. Originally named Ines Després Lélue, daughter of the Portuguese Quitéria Ferreira and the French merchant Jean Després Lélue, who died before 1770, she had married in 1769 in Lisbon with the merchant born in Amiens, Natal Grabiel Frennelet (or Noël Gabriel Frennelet).[92] She had four children before her husband wrote his will around 1775, leaving his wife in charge of his business and his children, when they would reach the age of majority. A third of the merchant's goods would be destined for his children. Natal had a foreign business clerk and bookkeeper, Mauricio Hely, and a Portuguese business clerk and bookkeeper, José Paulo de Azevedo.[93] They were supposed to assist Ines in the business after his death. Natal seemed very engaged in the French community living in Lisbon, a natural occurrence since he spent at least 12 years in Portugal from 1764 to 1776, during which time he exchanged correspondence with his father, also a merchant, in Amiens. Around 1765, he wrote that two-thirds of the woollen fabrics consumed in Portugal came from England and another one-third came from Amiens. The Frennelet family had plans to increase the production of these fabrics to overcome the English competition and asked the consul for help in relaxing some of the regulations that prevented business growth. Through his testament we can see that he interacted in other social circles, since his will requested the delivery of 50,000

90 Vitorino Magalhães Godinho, *Prix et monnaies au Portugal: 1750–1850* (Armand Colin, 1955), 338.

91 Labourdette, *La Nation française à Lisbonne*, 534, 537.

92 Labourdette, *La Nation française à Lisbonne*, 689.

93 ANTT, 7° CNL – Ofício A, Cx. 110, liv. 667, f. 88v.

réis to be distributed to "men and women in this city, for once only." He also gave 50,000 *réis* to the Irish religious monks of Lisbon. Moreover, although one of the witnesses to his will was a Frenchman, the merchant João Batista Viozem, he also had five other witnesses, all of Portuguese nationality. Among them was Manuel Rodrigues de Sá Viana, who became a merchant dedicated to the slave trade with the port of Angola in the late 1780s and also with interests in Maranhão at the beginning of the nineteenth century, and Francisco Higino Dias Pereira, one of the major shipowners who operated on the route between Pernambuco and Lisbon in the same decade of 1780.[94] Besides his business in Portugal and with the rest of Europe, Natal was also a shareholder of the GCPP.[95] His business with Brazil was thus continued by his wife and perhaps even expanded.

In 1780, Ines Després Frennelet, or the widow Frennelet, won a claim in one of the courts of Lisbon—"juízo da ouvidoria da alfândega de Lisboa"—against her debtor, Antônio José Marques Guimarães, who lived in Maranhão. To make the debtor pay, the widow gave a power of attorney to the Reverend João Pedro Gomes who was to go to Maranhão that same year.[96] That is, Frennelet, as a foreigner, not only had direct contact with the colonial market of Brazil but also obtained verdicts in her favor from the Portuguese courts. It would not be the only time. Much later, in 1796, she gave a power of attorney to Nicolau Rodrigues dos Santos, in Pernambuco, to collect the debts of her borrower, José Paulo de Azevedo.[97]

Still, overall, the French community was very weak in terms of cotton exports, and this was somehow reflected in the shipping sector. The number of French vessels that docked in Lisbon somewhat stabilized during the eighteenth century but with a slight upward trend: around 40 to 60 vessels a year between 1717 and 1732 and approximately 50 to 70 vessels a year between 1763 and 1791. But compared to the navigation of other nations, the French took only a tiny part of the transportation: they represented 10% of all ships that entered Lisbon between 1763 and 1791. French navigation was always weak

94 For Natal Gabriel Frennelet's will, see ANTT, Feitos Findos, Registo Geral de Testamentos, liv. 306, f. 151v–152v. Manuel Rodrigues de Sá Viana appears, through the customs books of Lisbon, as one of the largest exporters of European goods to Angola. He also appears in the Lisbon Notary offices as a member of some mercantile companies for trade with Angola. Apparently, he had business with Maranhão; see ANTT, Feitos Findos, Juízo da Índia e Mina, mç. 26, no. 12, cx. 26. About Francisco Higino Dias Pereira, see Melo, "O Negócio de Pernambuco"; Labourdette, *La Nation française à Lisbonne*, 375–77, 675.

95 AHU, ACL, CU, 015, Cx. 139, Doc. 10311 de 1781.

96 ANTT, 7º CNL – Ofício A, Cx. 100, liv. 604, f. 75v–76.

97 ANTT, 7º CNL – Ofício A, Cx. 110, liv. 667, f. 88v.

in Portugal, generally losing to the English, Portuguese, and Dutch. It is true that English navigation lost strength during the American War of Independence. It fell from 64.6% of the vessels in Lisbon in 1775 to 24.1% in 1784. During this period, French navigation in Lisbon gained some strength, but it was the Portuguese with their neutral navigation that took most advantage of the opportunities. After the conflict, "the English somewhat re-established the situation, as shown by the numbers from 1788 to 1791, but without returning to the previous status quo: now they have to count on the competition of a Portuguese merchant marine that maintains the positions acquired during the war." In addition, there was competition from their former American colonists, and due to the return of Dutch shipping. "As for French shipping, which had managed to keep itself in second place during the period of wars, it declined in the two years following 1789: it was in fourth place, not only behind the English and Portuguese but also the Dutch." After 1790, it was surpassed by the Americans.[98] As I will show in the next chapter, Portuguese, American, and Scandinavian vessels would be crucial for carrying cotton from Portugal to France during the Revolutionary and Napoleonic Wars.

To a large extent, the deficiencies and weaknesses of French shipping in Portugal related to the very weakness of trade between the two nations. The preponderance of English navigation and commerce further complicated this scenario. Proportionately, French trade and shipping were four to five times smaller than English trade and shipping.[99] The consuls attributed the French navy's faults to several factors, including the deployment of low-tonnage ships, the presence of numerous and undisciplined personnel, and the appointment of officers who displayed either negligence or excessive showiness. Consequently, the duration of voyages increased, resulting in higher costs and causing frustration among merchants who suffered financial losses due to the delays. In addition, the freight expenses were significantly greater compared to those of other rival international ships.[100] French navigation was hindered by two additional problems. Initially, the lack of capability in French shipbuilding hindered the sale of ships. In order to facilitate the Portuguese colonial trade, it was necessary to have ships with a capacity ranging from 300 to 400 tons. Nevertheless, the French vessels passing around the Portuguese coastline had a maximum weight of only 100 tons. Consequently, when the Portuguese required to acquire vessels, particularly during times of conflict, they procured English ships. Furthermore, Labourdette argues that the French navy's

98 Labourdette, *La Nation française à Lisbonne*, 415–16; Costa, "Relações Económicas Com o Exterior".

99 Labourdette, *La Nation française à Lisbonne*, 427–28.

100 Labourdette, *La Nation française à Lisbonne*, 430, 432–33.

inferiority held back its ability to establish robust convoys, similar to those of the British and Dutch navies.[101] This likely resulted in increased expenses for merchants in terms of ensuring adequate protection.

Notwithstanding this "commercial weakness," ambassadors and consuls constantly complained that part of the navigation to France was being done by the English and Dutch merchant marines.[102] French consuls were particularly distressed when French merchants used foreign vessels to bring goods to France. One of the consuls, in 1784, pointed out that the Frenchman Jautard, associated with the Dutchman De Bruyn, used a Dutch vessel to trade with France. On another occasion, the same company chartered a Portuguese ship to take cotton to Rouen. The Frenchman Laborde, one of the owners of a cotton factory in Lisbon, traded with France using a Portuguese vessel. The consul said that many pieces of cotton sent to France were shipped on foreign vessels by French merchants and those of other nationalities. He also complained that the French nation in Portugal was too "miserable," that "the commercial establishments in France did not trust it," and that the French nation in Portugal corresponded "only with Portuguese or foreigners." Furthermore, for the consul, "good business is in the hands of our naturalized Portuguese expatriates, or the subjects of the Queen [of Portugal] to whom almost all our ships are consigned, when they do not belong to them."[103]

From the consul's perspective, what was at stake was the "lack of patriotism" of the French who, "considering only their particular interests, give preference to foreign ships" to carry their goods. In addition, French legislation further harmed the shipping industry. Since 1681, a law was in force prohibiting French merchants in Lisbon from owning vessels. According to the consul, it was an "absurdity" because while this occurred, the presence of foreign ships in French ports was tolerated.[104] Yet, there were merchants—namely the Portuguese naturalized as La Roche, Paliart or Ratton, or even Portuguese like Roque Jorge—who unofficially owned French vessels and left them in the name of other merchants who resided in France. Louis Paliart, a former French merchant in Lisbon who became Portuguese and later Portuguese consul in Rouen, owned a vessel, the *Saint-Antoine*, which had been previously owned by the French merchant Bonifas, who had gone bankrupt in Lisbon around 1783.[105] Table 6.7 shows other partnerships between merchants in France (mainly in

101 Labourdette, *La Nation française à Lisbonne*, 430, 432–33.

102 Labourdette, *La Nation française à Lisbonne*, 427–28.

103 Labourdette, *La Nation française à Lisbonne*, 444–45.

104 Labourdette, *La Nation française à Lisbonne*, 432–33, 445.

105 Labourdette, *La Nation française à Lisbonne*, 447.

TABLE 6.7 Vessels that sailed between Lisbon and Rouen, 1783–1792

Vessel	Correspondent or owner in Rouen	Correspondent or owner in Lisbon	Number of trips	Active years
Alerte	Madame Fournier and Bournisien	Gabriel Milliet and Jacome Ratton	26	1783–1791
Télémaque	Le Jeune	Gabriel Milliet	4	1783–1784
Mariane Chérie	Bournisien	Jacome Ratton	7	1789–1791
Le Deux Soeurs	Darcel	Delante e Costa	12	1783–1791
Nouvelle Alliance	Le Bourgeois	Julien Guillot	15	1783–1790
Portugaise	Darcel	Philippe Bonifas	4	1783–1788
St Antoine	Louis Palyart	Philippe Bonifas	6	1783–1788
Tage	Darcel	Roque Jorge	6	1784–1787
Union	Darcel	Roque Jorge	8	1783–1790
Ville de Lisbonne	Lézurier	La Roche	5	1783–1787
Jeune Dragon	Dupont	François Palyart	2	1784
Jeune Lucienne	Louis Palyart		4	1785–1786
Bonne Union		Le Quen (Lequen)	5	1783–1787
Constant	Joncourt	Le Quen (Lequen)	4	1784–1786
Diligence	Gontier and Pontève	J. M. Mazza	8	1787–1792
Belle Mariane	Gratien Audebert from Tours	Cassou e Carrère	10	1787–1791
Deux Frères	Beau from Morlaix	François Palyart, Helly and La Roche	12	1784–1791
St Jean Baptiste	Mazurier from St Malo	Monié and Dujardin	11	1785–1792
Trois Amis	Le Mège from Roscoff	François Palyart	2	1784
Trois Amis	Desseaux and Cohic	La Roche	2	1788–1789
Total			153	

Source: From Labourdette, *La Nation française à Lisbonne*, 425–426. Table prepared by the author.

Rouen) and Portugal between 1783 and 1792: at least 20 vessels made 153 trips between Lisbon and Rouen.

Although the table above does not specify which of them were the owners and their agents, the majority of the owners were in Lisbon, according to Labourdette.[106] Yet, according to Dardel, of the vessels outfitted in Rouen

106 Labourdette, *La Nation française à Lisbonne*, 427.

that returned to the same port between 1782 and 1792, those that went to Lisbon and returned were the most numerous when compared to other destinations. This gives an idea of how cotton from the Portuguese colonies was important to France and how the French were organizing ships to trade cotton with Portugal.[107] Table 6.7 also helps to clarify that the group that dealt with exports during the GCGPM period was different from the group that would operate in the early 1780s. Still, from the perspective of shipping, there seems to have been a certain continuity. Roque Jorge was a big exporter in the days of the GCGPM and appeared repeatedly offering transport services in the 1780s. The same thing happened to the Frenchman Bonifas. Ratton, who did business with the GCGPM[108] and became one of the largest cotton exporters in 1806 (Appendix B), did not perform as a great player in the meantime. However, in the 1780s he organized many trips for his ships.

4 The Cotton Trade with Genoa

In some respects, the cotton trade between France and Portugal resembles the cotton trade with Genoa. The Genoese, and Italians in general, were a weak merchant community in Lisbon.[109] Writing in 1784, Rodrigo de Souza Coutinho noted that the trade balance was typically favorable to Portugal in its commerce with Italy. The bulk of the trade was carried out between Portugal and Genoa. The Italian market consumed part of what Portugal and its colonies offered. In return, Portugal had access to the products that the Italian ports brought from the Levant and the textile productions made in Italy and Switzerland. According to Coutinho, Genoa paid for its imports with silk (raw and manufactured) and with cash. The main Brazilian product imported by Italy between 1796 and 1808 was still sugar. In fact, the second biggest buyer of sugar from Portugal was Italy, second only to Hamburg. But in second place, cotton was the article most exported to Italy. Shipping was handled by other nations, which is why neither the Portuguese nor the Genoese profited from freight. Trade was mainly carried out by the Genoese and their commissioners. However, the Portuguese also actively participated in this commerce. Coutinho regretted that transactions with Italy were unlike the trade England and France had with Portugal. According to him, England and France benefited, as they had their own ships to trade and had good consuls and national merchants who acted in Portugal

107 Dardel, *Navires et Marchandises*, 686.
108 Ratton, *Recordações*, 181.
109 Brilli, "La Nación Genovesa de Lisboa," 221–22.

as factors (agents).[110] The Lisbon customs books do not indicate the Italians as major exporters, so, likely, the exporters in Lisbon were only sending orders placed by merchants in Genoa (Table 6.5).

Overall, "the Genoese nation had remained competitive regardless of its consuls."[111] This was largely due to the dissatisfaction that Genoese merchants had with them. These latter were more concerned with their private business than their consular duties. As a result, most Genoese in Portugal used foreign ships (with Genoese captains) to send goods to Genoa. They did this in order not to pay consular fees. Yet, the Genoese consul had other sources of income: he was a merchant and a particular merchant with "private prerogatives." In the last quarter of the eighteenth century, the Genoese consul in Lisbon was the merchant Pietro Badano. In the 1780s, Badano exported various colonial goods, including cotton. He sent them to Pietro Garibaldi in Genoa. In one of his letters, he wrote that he did not have direct access to American markets but that he bought products in Lisbon, either from the GCPP, from other merchants in the city, or bought them in "sales/auctions"[112] from *Casa da Índia*. But according to Badano, much of what arrived in Lisbon from Brazil was already "commissioned" to the British and Hamburgers. Pietro Badano also negotiated with Giacomo Filippo Durazzo. Durazzo, however, did not like Badano's services and started doing business with other Genoese in Lisbon, such as Giuseppe Salomone, who was secretary to the Genoese merchant Giuseppe Murta.[113]

The Durazzos, who also traded with Cadis, did not have branches in Iberian markets, kinship ties, or company contracts. Instead, business took place through "trust networks and business collaborations."[114] At first, the Durazzos tried to contact Genoese agents in Lisbon to do business. However, according to Brilli, because they already had many commercial contacts in Genoa, Lisbon agents could not open "space for new arrivals." At some point, the Durazzos got a correspondent in Lisbon, the small intermediary Salomone. He informed the Durazzos that trade between Portugal and Genoa was not exclusive to the Genoese. Among the most famous Genoese in Lisbon that traded with their homeland were Giuseppe Murta and "a certain Canale." Among the Portuguese, the most notable was "Joaquim Pedro Quintela, Paulo Jorge, the

110 Rodrigo de Souza Coutinho, *Textos Políticos, Económicos e Financeiros, 1783–1811. Tomo I* (Banco de Portugal, 1993), 103; For data for 1796 and 1808, see Arruda, *O Brasil no comércio colonial*, 308–58.

111 Brilli, "La Nación Genovesa de Lisboa," 221–22.

112 "remates".

113 Brilli, "La Nación Genovesa de Lisboa," 217–20.

114 Brilli, "Coping with Iberian Monopolies," 460.

Da Cruz family, and the Bandeiras."[115] The Durazzos tried to contact Paulo Jorge, but he did not even reply. They then tried Quintela, who declined to accept negotiations with them, as he "already had many agents for the distribution of merchandise" but was willing to make investments in sea loans for the Genoese. The Durazzos even received cotton from Lisbon, which Vincenzo Mazziotti, the Neapolitan consul in Lisbon, had sent. It was a partnership that did not last long because Mazziotti did not like the services of the Durazzos, who sold the goods for meager prices in Genoa.[116] The Italians' preference for negotiating with Paulo Jorge and Anselmo José da Cruz was understandable. The first was descended from a Milanese merchant,[117] and the second, when very young, had been trained in the art of commerce in Genoa.[118] Both were Portuguese merchants who purchased large quantities of cotton from the GCGPM in the late 1770s.

Be that as it may, the Italians were practically insignificant in Lisbon as cotton exporters (Table 6.5). In general, the Portuguese were the major exporters. However, with the decline of French manufactured goods in Portugal, the French merchant community in Lisbon began to trade with other parts of Europe, including Genoa.[119] It was the case of the widow Frennelet (Appendix B). It was also the case with the French-Dutch firm João Daniel De Bruyn and Jautard. Through it, we can see how Brazilian cotton reached Switzerland. This company, according to Labourdette, was one of the wealthiest French houses in Portugal, not only trading for France but also owning ships.[120] Its exports also involved London, Liverpool, and Genoa. Once, a negotiation with this last port was frustrating for the company, not because of the mercantile agents but because of the changes in the economic policy of France. In the mid-1780s, the French began to worry about competition from other nations. By that time, cotton from Brazil was already travelling in large quantities to England and Genoa. In 1785, a Danish ship was carrying cotton from Portugal to the Netherlands for the first time. And it even happened that the English bought cotton in the ports of Normandy.[121] As a result, and to further encourage its textile industry, France issued a law on October 10, 1785, that directly affected the raw cotton trade: the ban on imports of products made from

115 Brilli, "Coping with Iberian Monopolies," 464.
116 Brilli, "Coping with Iberian Monopolies," 465–66, 477.
117 Brilli, "Coping with Iberian Monopolies," 464.
118 Martins, "A Companhia Geral de Comércio Do Grão-Pará e Maranhão," 268, 273, 279, 281.
119 Labourdette, *La Nation française à Lisbonne*, 344–45.
120 Labourdette, *La Nation française à Lisbonne*, 531, 535.
121 Dardel, *Navires et Marchandises*, 278.

cotton. This specific law affected the distribution of Brazilian cotton: exports of raw cotton from Lisbon to Genova were reduced. Genoa was the gateway for raw cotton to reach Switzerland. And from Switzerland, the cotton textiles made their way to France. The new law prevented textiles from reaching France. Soon after the law was enacted, De Bruyn and Jautard had to send the cotton (originating from Maranhão) that was in Genoa to Rouen. As a result, they lost money: around 1,200,000 *livres tournois* on commissions. The client of De Bruyn and Jautard who gave up on buying raw cotton was the house Portalès, in Neuchâtel, which was a rich and important company that sent several cotton goods to France. The 1785 law also caused Lisbon to be flooded with cotton fabrics from India, as they could no longer go to France.[122] This negotiation involving De Bruyn and Jautard reveals at least two important things. First, one of the leading export firms in Lisbon carried out negotiations in which they were mere agents and not the principals, that is, they only took orders. Second, those running the negotiation were manufacturers in Switzerland who had access to Brazilian cotton through a French-Dutch firm in Lisbon that shipped cotton to Genoa.

At the same time, Genoa and the Lombardy region were booming in the cotton fabric industry then. In 1775 it was not so important, but already in 1807, it was the most significant industry in Liguria.[123] Portugal was a crucial supplier of raw materials for this expanding cotton industry. In Pombal's time, for example, the main items imported by Genoa were leather and cotton from Brazil.[124] Between 1781 and 1789, 2,349 ships entered the port of Genoa. Of these, 1,245 came from the Atlantic, the North Sea, and the Baltic. Portugal was the most important within that last group.[125]

During this period, cotton occupied more and more space on the ships leaving Lisbon for Genoa. The fiber sometimes came from Lisbon aboard

122 Labourdette, *La Nation française à Lisbonne*, 392–93, 534.

123 Luigi Bulferetti and Claudio Costantini, *Industria e commercio in Liguria nell'età del Risorgimento (1700–1861)* (Banca commerciale italiana, 1966), 112–13, 297.

124 Carlo Baudi di Vesme, "Il Portogallo Nell'epoca Di Pombal (1755–1777) Secondo Alcune Relazioni Contemporanee Con Un Excursus Sui Rapporti Tra Il Portogallo e Genova Nel Medesimo Periodo," in *Genova, La Liguria e l'oltremare Tra Medioevo Ed Eta' Moderna – Studi e Ricerche d'archivio*, ed. Raffaele Belvederi, III (Pubblicazioni dell'Istituto di scienze storiche, Università di Genova, 1979), 405–6.

125 Bulferetti and Costantini, *Industria e commercio in Liguria*, 164–65; about the port of Genoa, see Luisa Piccinno and Andrea Zanini, "Genoa: Colonizing and Colonized City? The Port City as a Pole of Attraction for Foreign Merchants (16th-18th Centuries)," in *Reti Marittime Come Fattori Dell'integrazione Europea (Atti Della Settimana Di Studio Datini)*, ed. Giampiero Nigro (Firenze University Press, 2019).

Dutch ships. From the 1770s to 1786, the highest-priced cotton in Genoa was Pernambuco, followed by Maranhão and Pará.[126] According to Niephaus, "Swiss companies' branches [in Genoa] were heavily involved in cotton imports" from Lisbon. Soon after, they re-exported the cotton to their home country.[127] But a lot of the cotton from Lisbon was forwarded to Lombardy through firms in Genoa. There were at least nine merchants and companies that imported cotton between 1773 and 1786 and sent them to Lombardy. The firms Zellweger & Zürcher, Giovanni Battista Rossi, Bertrand, Ricard & Bramerel, and Filippo Dunant brought cotton directly from Lisbon.[128] As late as 1790, "Lisbon was Genoa's main source of leather, sugar, cotton, tobacco, and pepper."[129]

Since the Middle Ages, Genoa has imported cotton (from North Africa, Sicily, and Calabria) and produced textiles from the fiber, namely fustian. However, imports by English and Dutch West Indian companies from the beginning of the seventeenth century dealt a severe blow to the Italian cotton industry. Yet, because of the "passion for printed cottons"—the *indiennes*—at the beginning of the eighteenth century, the cotton industry gained strength in Italy and displaced silk production.[130] From the second half of the eighteenth century, cotton began to be used to produce the *mezzari*. Fashionable among Genoese women—as well as the *indiennes*—the *mezzari* was a large cotton cloth used to cover women's heads and shoulders.[131] According to Gallo, the growth of the cotton industry at the end of the eighteenth century is linked to the foreign business class in Genoa.[132] Foreigners—entrepreneurs and artisans—were instrumental in renewing and expanding the cotton industry in Liguria at the end of the century. "Their business goals were focused on

126 Heinz-Theo Niephaus, *Genuas Seehandel von 1746–1848: die Entwicklung der Handelsbeziehungen zur Iberischen Halbinsel, zu West- und Nordeuropa sowie den Überseegebieten* (Böhlau, 1975), 43–44.

127 Niephaus, *Genuas Seehandel von 1746–1848*, 43.

128 Niephaus, *Genuas Seehandel von 1746–1848*, 44, 297–98, 305, 307, 329.

129 Niephaus, *Genuas Seehandel von 1746–1848*, 107, 284.

130 Marzia Cataldi Gallo, *Mezzari and the Cotton Route. I Mezzari e La via Del Cotone.* (San Giorgio Editrice, 2007), 9–10; Marzia Cataldi Gallo, "Tessuti Genovesi: Seta, Cotone Stampato e Jeans," in *Atti Della Società Ligure Di Storia Patria, Nuova Serie, XLIV/2*, ed. Dino Puncuh (Società Ligure di Storia Patria, 2004), 321; on the cotton industry in Italy in the Middle Ages, see Maureen Fennell Mazzaoui, *The Italian Cotton Industry in the Later Middle Ages, 1100–1600* (Cambridge University Press, 1981).

131 Gallo, "Tessuti Genovesi: Seta, Cotone Stampato e Jeans," 321, 326.

132 Gallo, *Mezzari and the Cotton Route. I Mezzari e La via Del Cotone.*, 16.

technological renewal and the local production of high-quality products."[133] The cotton industry became the most important textile production in Liguria. Despite this, most of the yarn produced was hand-spun. The finest yarns were sent to Switzerland. The mechanization of the cotton industry in Genoa only occurred after the end of the Napoleonic era.[134] The products of the Genoese textile industry were exported to Portugal and then made their way to the colonies. The Genoese also imported products from Marseille and re-exported them to Lisbon. The goods of the Swiss textile industry (from Zurich, Geneva, and Basel) were largely exported via Genoa: knitwear, socks, linen, cotton, and printed calico textiles were shipped to different parts of Europe, including Portugal.[135]

When Liguria was under French influence after 1796, it appears that several of its industries—including cotton—were impaired to the detriment of the French. On top of that, by 1808, English naval forces were putting obstacles in the way of Genoa's export trade. By this time, Genoa was getting cotton from the Levant, which entered Italy through Trieste. With the blockades, obtaining raw materials became expensive and complicated. Exports of cotton goods similarly became difficult. However, both continued to grow over the period.[136] Genova, which in 1782 received 32.4% of Portugal's cotton exports, dropped to 14% in 1789 and 10.2% in 1792. However, imports remained at the same level of 25,000 arrobas of cotton in these three years. Subsequently, Genoa's involvement in the cotton trade becomes ambiguous; however, it is probable that the city continued to import cotton from Portugal, as general trade statistics indicate for Italy.[137]

5 Conclusion

Unlike the import trade, cotton re-exporters were a much smaller group and mostly made up of foreigners. However, this composition changed during the period. After the monopolies of the Pombaline companies ended, the

133 Gallo, "Tessuti Genovesi: Seta, Cotone Stampato e Jeans," 327; Bulferetti and Costantini, *Industria e commercio in Liguria*, 73.

134 Bulferetti and Costantini, *Industria e commercio in Liguria*, 73, 87, 99–100, 101.

135 Niephaus, *Genuas Seehandel von 1746–1848*, 87–88, 89, 93–94.

136 Bulferetti and Costantini, *Industria e commercio in Liguria*, 261, 277–78, 309.

137 For trade between Portugal and Italy, see Arruda, *O Brasil no comércio colonial*, 370–71; for the context of the French invasion, see Stuart Woolf, "L'impact de l'occupation Française Sur l'économie Italienne (1796–1815)," *Revue Économique* 40, no. 6 (1989): 1097–117.

Portuguese dominated exports. Yet, from the mid-1780s until the eve of the end of the old colonial system, the British were, by far, the main ones responsible for exporting Brazilian cotton. Then, in the final years, the English withdrew from the country, fearful of a French invasion of Portugal. As a result, in 1806, the Portuguese became the main re-exporters of cotton. The destination of exports also differed significantly during the period. Initially, from the years of the GCGPM monopoly until the mid-1780s, Brazilian cotton found its primary market in Rouen and, to a lesser extent, in Genoa. From the mid-1780s until the beginning of the nineteenth century, however, the British managed to displace these destinations by buying most of the cotton in Lisbon and sending it to ports in Britain, mainly to Liverpool.

Foreigners worked within a slightly different commercial and institutional framework than the Portuguese and their trade with Brazil. Trade between Brazil and Portugal depended heavily on associations between merchants on both ends of the Atlantic through commissions, attorneys, traveling agents, and commercial companies. However, there was no clear rule regulating this trade, and it ended up being allowed for anyone. Cotton re-exporters also made use of these arrangements, but they also relied on their consuls as heads of foreign trade in Portugal. The consul was the link between his home state and the merchants abroad, and, in a way, he sought to organize and meet the needs of his merchants. Similarly, these foreign merchants had special courts, which gave them better legal guarantees that their rights and property would be preserved. Commercial treaties, or the lack of them, and good diplomatic relations were other vital elements that governed the commercial activities of foreigners.

The histories of the two nations dealt with in this chapter—the French and the Genoese—are similar in some respects. Both were weak merchant communities in Lisbon and had no good, if any, commercial treaties. Consequently, their merchant communities in Lisbon exported little cotton. There are many reasons for these weaknesses, but competition with the British, with better treaties and a long history of commercial cooperation with Portugal, was crucial in displacing Italians, French, Dutch, and Hamburg from the cotton re-export trade. The Portuguese were, after all, the second-largest community exporting cotton to France and Genoa. The good performance of the Portuguese in Rouen was probably a legacy left by the commercial structures of the GCGPM that the merchants copied from the late 1770s until the late 1780s. Portuguese exporters probably took advantage of the trade with Genoa because it was a route that did not have a commercial treaty and perhaps because of the lack of the strong figure of a consul and a national state to support the Genoese merchants.

In the 1790s, France and Italy experienced a drastic change in how they imported cotton. The effects of the Revolutionary and Napoleonic wars constrained the already fragile commercial links between Portugal and Rouen and Genoa. These trades, which were already complicated, would become even more complex with the series of events in the 1790s.

CHAPTER 7

The Troubled French Trade from the 1790s Onwards

1 The Loss of Saint-Domingue and the Revolutionary Wars

In 1784, when the consul wrote that French merchants in Portugal were "miserable,"[1] it was still too early to foresee the profound deteriorations in French foreign trade in the 1790s that would, more than in 1784, harm the French merchants in Portugal.[2] Except for the firm Lefevre, Dittmer & Co. (a partnership between a Frenchman and a merchant from Hamburg) in 1792 and Philippe Roussac in 1806 (see Appendix B), the French ceased to be significant players in the cotton export trade in Lisbon from 1790 onwards. According to the customs books, Rouen dropped to 8.2% of Lisbon's cotton exports in 1792 (Table 6.1), and from 1796 to 1799, both the customs books and the balances of trade show that France did not import anything from Portugal.[3] Furthermore, no French vessel set sail from Lisbon in 1798 and 1799.[4] Thus, official data show a bleak scenario for the Brazilian cotton trade towards France during the 1790s. However, this all contrasts with data collected by the French consul in Lisbon in 1806–7, which shows that France was receiving cotton from Portugal during the 1790s.[5] In fact, it is between 1796–1800 that the peak of cotton exports to France happens before the Treaty of Amiens in 1802 (Table 7.1).

Consequently, trade between France and Portugal occurred through unofficial channels, utilizing neutral vessels and contraband. However, the cotton trade situation was already quite complex for France, even prior to the conflicts of the 1790s. The cotton industry experienced a period of decline, attributed to the 1786 Treaty of Eden, which facilitated the introduction of cheap British textiles into France.[6] Henderson mentions the euphoria of the Committee of Fustian Manufacturers in Manchester: " … We are unanimously of opinion that

1 Labourdette, *La Nation française à Lisbonne*, 444–45.
2 Gavin Daly, "Merchants and Maritime Commerce in Napoleonic Normandy," *French History* 15, no. 1 (2001): 27.
3 Arruda, *O Brasil no comércio colonial*, 370–71.
4 Serrão, *História de Portugal. Volume VI. O Despotismo Iluminado, (1750–1807)*, 428. Almanach de Lisboa … ano 1800, 515.
5 Macedo, *O Bloqueio Continental*, 195–97.
6 Browning, "The Treaty of Commerce Between England and France in 1786"; Rose, "The Franco-British Commercial Treaty of 1786"; Cahen, "Une Nouvelle Interprétation Du Traité Franco-Anglais De 1786–1787"; Donaghay, "The Anglo-French Negotiations of 1786–1787".

TABLE 7.1 Cotton exports from Portugal to France, 1775–1805

Year	Livres tournois	Year	Livres tournois
1775	1,290,795	1791	
1776	679,475	1792	655,669
1777	769,093	1793	
1778	1,440,555	1794	2,018,084
1779	1,499,973	1795	15,500
1780	4,212,750	1796	8,453,695
1781		1797	946,627
1782	2,532,007	1798	1,259,042
1783		1799	2,407,095
1784		1800	7,991,429
1785		1801	13,808,148
1786	1,376,000	1802	9,505,786
1787	2,410,500	1803	16,364,070
1788	2,367,800	1804	21,222,111
1789	3,047,900	1805	8,652,324
1790	1,222,369		

	Average
1776–1780	1,720,369
1786–1790	2,084,914
1796–1800	4,211,578

Sources: 1775–1782: Labourdette, *La Nation française à Lisbonne*, 642. 1786: Godinho, *Prix et monnaies au Portugal*, 361. 1787–1805: Macedo, *O bloqueio continental*, 195–197. Table prepared by the author.

the commercial treaty … will be highly beneficial to the cotton manufacturers of this town and neighborhood." Meanwhile, in France, the feeling was that the treaty had been extremely harmful: "it is said that in Normandy alone 4,000 manufacturers are begging on the streets of Rouen."[7] Recovery was interrupted by the slave revolution in Saint-Domingue (1791), which destroyed one of the

7 W. O. Henderson, "The Anglo-French Commercial Treaty of 1786," *The Economic History Review* 10, no. 1 (1957): 108–9.

primary sources of raw cotton for the French industry. Shortly after that, the French Wars (1793–1815) increased commercial risks and created obstacles to the circulation of goods for about 22 years. Yet, one positive aspect of the conflict is that the Treaty of Eden was annulled in 1793, and France enacted steps to safeguard its textile sector against foreign competition.[8]

When the French executed Louis XVI in 1793, Britain declared war on France. At the beginning of the conflict, one of the few weapons of the French revolutionaries (with little military or naval strength) against their enemies was to close their internal market to English goods. British retaliation came with the blockade of the French coast imposed by the strongest British navy. As a result, Le Havre and Rouen were most of the time accessible only via neutral vessels. Their trade volume decreased, and this situation continued throughout the years of the revolutionary wars. Yet, because of the closure of the French internal market and the protectionist measures imposed by the revolutionary government, the period of wars saw the cotton industry in Rouen develop. Therefore, French shipping suffered for years but not the cotton industry. The development of the domestic market offset the collapse of French exports.[9]

With all these problems, it is imperative to ascertain the process by which raw cotton was transported to France. This chapter primarily aims to elucidate this phenomenon. It is probable that there was a rise in imports from the East, with much cotton from the Levant being brought to the ports of Genoa, Leghorn, Trieste, and Marseille and then being transported to Normandy.[10] At that time, Portugal's neutrality policy was leaning more towards the English side, and, therefore, in theory, the Portuguese-French commercial relations would be compromised. But overall, and especially considering the loss of Saint-Domingue, France could not afford to lose Portuguese suppliers as well. So, the

8 About the end of the Treaty of Eden and France's protectionist measures, see Alan S. Milward and S. B. Saul, *The Economic Development of Continental Europe 1780–1870* (1973; Routledge, 2013), 267.

9 Arruda, *O Brasil no comércio colonial*, 338; Cruz, "Neutral Shipping and the Portuguese Economic Relations with the Atlantic World (1793–1814)," 317; Ouvrage collectif, *La Révolution en Haute-Normandie*, 131. Rouen not only lost in terms of navigation but was also deprived of the important business of the slave trade, in which its mercantile elite actively participated; see Gavin Daly, *Inside Napoleonic France: State and Society in Rouen, 1800–1815* (Ashgate, 2001), 32–33, 37; Woronoff, "L'industrialisation de La France de 1789 à 1815. Un Essai de Bilan," 1049; Milward and Saul, *The Economic Development of Continental Europe 1780–1870*, 263; for an overview of blockades during the French wars, see Davis and Engerman, *Naval Blockades in Peace and War*, 25–52.

10 Ouvrage collectif, *La Révolution en Haute-Normandie*, 130; Lévy, *Histoire économique de l'industrie cotonnière en Alsace*, 57–58; Eli F. Heckscher, *The Continental System: An Economic Interpretation* (Clarendon Press, 1918), 182–83.

main way Brazilian cotton went to France was via neutral vessels and smuggling, mainly using the ports of Cherbourg, Caen, Nantes, and Hamburg. This was not a strategy exclusive to the Franco-Portuguese trade. U.S. ships were crucial in supplying France during the war, transporting goods from the West Indies and cotton from the American South, and offering insurance services.[11] U.S. cotton, though, arrived in Rouen via Bordeaux.[12]

Between 1787 and 1791, 503 ships from France entered Lisbon, but only 19 entered between 1791/92 and 1799/1800. Until 1801, the Scandinavians and the North Americans transported goods in their neutral vessels between Portugal and France and, in a way, replaced the French in shipping services.[13] Neutral vessels were also important to negotiations with Hamburg. Yet, they were not a guarantee of completely safe transportation. British vessels could seize neutral ships if they believed they were engaging with the enemy. Simultaneously, the countries at war employed strategies to circumvent the blockades by carrying various neutral flags and raising the one deemed suitable. Moreover, they brought papers that could be purchased, certifying that the vessel was a neutral one.[14]

At the beginning, the English even banned neutral navigation to France, but in 1794 it was resumed. Even so, merchants felt that trade was stagnant. This situation led some trading houses in France to move to Hamburg and Ostend in 1795. Hamburg increasingly became an important port as it allowed neutral navigation, mainly from the U.S. shippers, and it was very unlikely that the British would interfere in the negotiations since they also traded with the German port. Before and after the French Revolution, France was Hamburg's

11 Jeanne Chase, "War on Trade and Trade in War: Stephen Jumel and New York Maritime Commerce (1793–1815)," *Bulletin Du Centre d'histoire Des Espaces Atlantiques* 4 (1988): 119, 124–25; Paul Butel, "Revolution and the Urban Economy: Maritime Cities and Continental Cities," in *Reshaping France: Town, Country, and Region during the French Revolution*, ed. Alan I. Forrest and Peter Jones (Manchester University Press, 1991), 41; Silvia Marzagalli, "Establishing Transatlantic Trade Networks in Time of War: Bordeaux and the United States, 1793–1815," *Business History Review* 79, no. 4 (2005): 811–44.

12 Daly, *Inside Napoleonic France*, 181.

13 For the years 1788, 1790, and 1798, see Serrão, *História de Portugal. Volume VI. O Despotismo Iluminado, (1750–1807)*, 428. 1799: Almanach de Lisboa ... ano 1800, 515. 1801: Carl Israel Ruders, *Viagem em Portugal, 1798–1802* (Biblioteca Nacional, 2002), 1:271. 1803 and 1804 (from January to October): Almanach de Lisboa ... ano 1805, 587–588. See Table 6.7. for the vessels that sailed between Lisbon and Rouen (1783–1792).

14 Cruz, "Neutral Shipping and the Portuguese Economic Relations with the Atlantic World (1793–1814)," 324–26; see also Anna Cornelia Clauder, *American Commerce as Affected by the Wars of the French Revolution and Napoleon, 1793–1812* (1932; Augustus M. Kelley, 1972); Edmond Buron, "Statistics on Franco-American Trade, 1778–1806," *Journal of Economic and Business History*, 1932, 571–80.

most important trading partner.[15] After Revolutionary France invaded the Netherlands in 1795, Hamburg seized their banking and trade connections, making the port even more connected with England. The commercial growth experienced, together with Hamburg's neutrality policy, significantly increased the number of foreign ships passing through that port in the 1790s. Furthermore, because of its river network and roads, Hamburg was an important point for accessing other European markets, supplying them with raw cotton.[16] Between 1806 and 1814, cotton from Pernambuco, for example, could be found at fairs in Leipzig, one of the centers of the European cotton trade.[17]

From the 1780s, Germany was also growing in terms of manufacturing. A quarter of the calico spinning machines in Continental Europe were in Saxony in 1815. Furthermore, the German textile industry was known for the high quality of its fabrics.[18] Yet it is perhaps due to Hamburg's conditions of carrying out neutral trade—and not so much by its demand for raw material—that Portugal's cotton exports grew towards the German port. The quantities exported between 1796 and 1814 varied a great deal. According to the Lisbon customs books, 7,554 arrobas were shipped in 1799, making Hamburg the fourth main port that bought Brazilian cotton (Appendix C). It was a small amount, but in other years Hamburg bought significant amounts of fiber. According to official trade balance figures, in 1800, for example, Hamburg imported more cotton than England from Portugal. Between 1796 and 1801, Hamburg was the second leading port for Brazilian cotton.[19] However, the bulk of this cotton was likely going to France, and, to a lesser extent, to supply the German textile industry.[20]

At the time of the Peace of Amiens, it was clear to the French that colonial products would only reach France via U.S. neutral vessels. The British did

---

15 Patrick Crowhurst, *The French War on Trade: Privateering, 1793–1815* (Scolar Press, 1989), 9–11; Butel, "Revolution and the Urban Economy," 42; Katherine Aaslestad, "Paying for War: Experiences of Napoleonic Rule in the Hanseatic Cities," *Central European History* 39, no. 4 (2006): 646.

16 Crowhurst, *The French War on Trade*, 9–11; Butel, "Revolution and the Urban Economy," 42; Aaslestad, "Paying for War," 646.

17 Heckscher, *The Continental System*, 177, 274–75.

18 Adelir Weber, "Relações comerciais e acumulação mercantil: Portugal, Hamburgo e Brasil entre a colônia e a nação" (Ph.D., Universidade de São Paulo, 2008), 183–84; See also Heckscher, *The Continental System*, 302–6.

19 Arruda, *O Brasil no comércio colonial*, 370–71; Weber, "Relações comerciais e acumulação mercantil," 643.

20 See also Chase, "War on Trade and Trade in War," 124–25; Jean Mistler, "Hambourg Sous l'occupation Française: Observation Au Sujet Du Blocus Continental," *Francia* 1 (1973): 451–66.

not interfere, as they did not want a war against the United States, and the British themselves had a share in the trade between the American colonies and France through American neutrals. At the beginning of the nineteenth century, much cotton from Georgia and Louisiana, "cheap and in abundance," was being transported by North American neutrals to Amsterdam and was distributed to the markets of northern Europe through the various channels of the Continent. Ports such as Hamburg, Altona, and Tönning functioned in the same way.[21] Similarly, goods from Lisbon and Porto were sent to the neutral ports of Hamburg, Emden, Amsterdam, and Ostend. For French manufacturers and merchants, it was "easier and cheaper" to buy in these neutral marketplaces than to pay for illegal trade direct from Portugal and then pay overland transport fees in France. A merchant in Nantes called Bourcard offered several kinds of cotton—including Brazilian—to firms in Aarau (*Saxer et Cie.*) and Lenzburg (*Hunerwadel Frères*) in Switzerland. In this case, cotton arrived in France via American vessels, which stopped in Lisbon and headed to the ports of the English Channel and the North Sea.[22]

Until 1800, American and Scandinavian neutrals brought tropical products, including cotton, to France relatively easily. They only had to carry false papers declaring that the transported merchandise would be delivered in a neutral or English port. Counterfeit papers were one of the tools for doing business in warfare. At the end of the eighteenth century, document printing was relatively accessible, but verification mechanisms were less common. Supposedly, neutral ships could only trade between two neutral ports. Still, many called at a belligerent port, and British maritime patrols could not know whether the goods were coming from or destined for a neutral port or whether they were belligerent goods. This occurred with trade between the neutral Hamburg and Lisbon, a route on which vessels could stop at French ports. This type of trade occurred until the implementation of the Continental System in 1806.[23] As the ports of Le Havre and Rouen were, most of the time, blockaded by the British, it is quite possible that ports like Nantes, Cherbourg, Caen, and even Bayonne were the most recurrent stopovers for the neutrals. Brazilian cotton

21 Crowhurst, *The French War on Trade*, 16.

22 Crowhurst, *The French War on Trade*, 18; for more on commercial relations between Portugal and the United States during the war period, see Cristina Moreira and Jari Eloranta, "Importance of "Weak" States during Conflicts: Portuguese Trade with the United States during the Revolutionary and Napoleonic Wars," *Revista de Historia Economica – Journal of Iberian and Latin American Economic History* 29, no. 3 (2011): 393–423.

23 Crowhurst, *The French War on Trade*, 33–35.

also arrived in France via England. This happened between 1810 and 1812, but it is perfectly possible that it occurred before.[24]

The details of how the raw cotton trade was carried out toward France between the start of the wars in 1793 and the Peace of Amiens are still unclear. However, negotiations involving the famous businessman Christophe-Philippe Oberkampf in France may help to clarify some issues. His trade was in cotton cloth from England, not raw cotton, though it was a trade that could very well be applied to other goods. From 1795, Oberkampf, with the help of French and Swiss intermediaries and merchants, managed to bring in white cotton cloth from London (which the British brought in through the East India Company). This strategy was so successful that it lasted for ten years. A friend of his, a Genevan in London, sent the cloth to Genevans in Altona or Hamburg. Then, onboard neutral ships, the goods were sent to Rouen or Le Havre. They came in the name of a certain Theodore Rivier, said to be from Geneva, which was a false name, as, in fact, the goods were from Oberkampf. From 1797 onwards, Hamburg (through the trading house of the Huguenots Chapeaurouge) was the link between England and the Oberkampf factory in Jouy. Oberkampf even married one of his daughters to a shipowner's son from Le Havre, who also worked as an agent for the merchants of Hamburg. With peace in 1802, Oberkampf resumed contact with his Manchester cotton textile supplier, Charles-Friederich Brandt, although cotton prices were high at the time. As the war continued in 1803, Oberkampf made arrangements with a Huguenot firm in London (Wiss of Ripley & Riviers). They would send cotton textiles to Oberkampf via Rotterdam or Hamburg.[25] These examples show that smuggling goods between England and France was possible and hard to prevent, and that Hamburg was an important entrepôt for trade between the two countries in times of war.[26] Therefore, it is likely that part of the Brazilian cotton officially going to England ended up arriving in France through these illicit negotiations. It is even plausible that the cotton that was going to Hamburg was actually

---

24 Frank Edgar Melvin, *Napoleon's Navigation System: A Study of Trade Control during the Continental Blockade* (D. Appleton and company, 1919), 263, 304, 327–28.

25 Stanley D. Chapman and Serge Chassagne, *European Textile Printers in the Eighteenth Century: A Study of Peel and Oberkampf* (Heinemann Educational: Pasold Fund, 1981), 161–62; for more information about Oberkampf, see Serge Chassagne, *Oberkampf: Un grand patron au siècle des Lumières* (1980; Aubier, 2015).

26 On Hamburg as an important port for smuggling, see Silvia Marzagalli, *Les Boulevards de La Fraude: Le Négoce Maritime et Le Blocus Continental, 1806–1813: Bordeaux, Hambourg, Livourne* (Presses universitaires du Septentrion, 1999).

destined for French merchants. In both cases, neutral shipping was important for France to be supplied with raw cotton and other goods.[27]

2 The End of the Peace of Amiens and the Role of the Ports of Cherbourg, Caen, and Nantes

The beginning of the nineteenth century witnessed, if only for a short time, the emergence of the ports of Cherbourg, Caen, and Nantes as the leading importers of Brazilian cotton and the virtual disappearance of Le Havre and Rouen. Traditionally—as shown in Chapter 6—it was through the Rouen-Le Havre complex that most of the exchanges between Portugal and France took place during the eighteenth century, unlike in the seventeenth century when Marseilles was the most important French port for Portuguese trade, importing mainly Brazilian sugar.[28] Before c.1790, Rouen and Le Havre were heavily dependent on the Atlantic economy: they had contacts with the West Indies, northern and southern Europe, the Americas, and Africa. The most important partners were the Caribbean islands, mainly Saint-Domingue, the Iberian states, the Netherlands, England, and Germany. But the weight of the colonies and the slave trade was enormous. For example, in 1790, about 80% of the ships that entered Le Havre came from the French colonies in the Caribbean (Saint-Domingue, Martinique, and Guadeloupe) and the African Coast (Coast of Guinea and Angola), bringing the profits from the slave trade. The most significant product imported by Rouen was raw cotton, but it also imported sugar and tobacco and re-exported it to northern Europe. Rouen's main exports were textiles manufactured in Normandy, Paris, and Picardy, destined for the markets of the French Caribbean. Many business houses in Rouen had representatives in Le Havre, and many of the ships that entered Le Havre actually had Rouen as their destination. As a result, much of what entered Le Havre was owned by the merchants of Rouen.[29]

27 Silvia Marzagalli, "Le négoce maritime et la rupture révolutionnaire: un ancien débat revisité," *Annales historiques de la Révolution française*, no. 352 (June 2008): 186, 190.

28 Labourdette, *La Nation française à Lisbonne*, 418; see also Stein, *The French Sugar Business in the Eighteenth Century*.

29 Daly, "Merchants and Maritime Commerce in Napoleonic Normandy," 30–31; Daly, *Inside Napoleonic France*, 25; Labourdette, *La Nation française à Lisbonne*, 418; Philippe Dupré, "Les Difficultés Économiques Des Ports de La Manche Pendant La Révolution et l'Empire: L'apport Des Archives de La Marine," *Les Normands et La Mer XXVè Congrès Des Sociétés Historiques et Archéologiques de Normandie, Communauté Urbaine de Cherbourg, 4–7 Octobre 1990. Saint-Vaast-La-Hougue Musée Maritime de l'Ile Tatihou*, 1995, 325.

During the Peace of Amiens, trade resumed to normal after nearly ten years of war. But with warfare's return, difficulties also came back, bringing new changes to trade and navigation between Portugal and France. If Bordeaux managed to circumvent the effects of war by employing neutral ships, Rouen and Le Havre did not. Generally speaking, between 1803 and 1807, England imposed a moderate and prudent maritime blockade, according to François Crouzet, which allowed neutrals to trade.[30] Yet, Rouen and Le Havre do not fit this rule: the blockade there was more severe, and neutral vessels' navigation was minimal. In mid-1806, the British even completely blocked Le Havre by entering the Seine.[31] Several other French ports ended up obtaining cotton from Portugal, but three were crucial in 1806: Cherbourg, which received 18.3% of the cotton exported by Portugal; Nantes, which received 17.7%; and Caen, which received 13.0 % (Table 6.1 and Appendix C).

In order to clarify the abrupt rise of the ports of Cherbourg, Nantes, and Caen, it is essential to emphasize that due to the decline of outside markets, France shifted its focus home and endeavored to foster its own industry and market. Paris grew stronger throughout this period as money that had previously flowed to the ports that dealt with the Atlantic started to flow there.[32] Nantes was a preferred port for investors in Paris as it was not as affected by the British blockades and was the safest port with the lowest insurance rates. Cherbourg became of interest to merchants in Le Havre and Rouen, possibly because it was a well-protected military port and an unlikely location for naval raids by the British navy. Although close to Le Havre, Caen was a port not much affected by the English blockades, and cotton could be transported by barge to Rouen. Furthermore, part of the Brazilian cotton was used in the Calvados industry, as Caen experienced growth in its cotton industry during this period.

Cherbourg turned out to be the most important in the period. Some factors explain this. The proximity to Rouen was perhaps the most important. But Cherbourg had a deep and well-defended harbor. At the same time, it was virtually impossible for the British to secure a blockade north of the Cotentin because of the winds, currents, and reefs which are so dangerous to navigation. Shipping in Cherbourg was based on imports, and during the period of wars and blockades, the port acted more as a substitute port than an independent commercial port. Compared to 1790, the number of ships entering and leaving Cherbourg in 1806 increased significantly. At the same time, the number of

30 François Crouzet, "La ruine du grand commerce," in *Bordeaux au XVIIIe siècle*, ed. François-Georges Pariset (Fédération historique du Sud-Ouest, 1968), 497.

31 Daly, "Merchants and Maritime Commerce in Napoleonic Normandy," 35–37.

32 Butel, "Revolution and the Urban Economy," 40, 49.

vessels outfitted in Le Havre drastically decreased after the war in 1793. They grew again with the Peace of Amiens, but soon in 1803, they fell again.[33] Due to the blockade of Le Havre, trade was directed to Cherbourg. Consequently, merchant houses in Le Havre relocated their operations there.[34]

Calvados, the French department in Normandy, where Caen is located, saw a growing number of workshops and workers dedicated to cotton weaving, mainly between 1803 and 1806. The textile manufacturing sector was the most important in Calvados: wool and linen textiles were produced there but also cotton, including calicos. Yet, as early as the mid-eighteenth century, cotton overtook wool.[35] Cotton spinning and weaving in Calvados was concentrated in Falaise, Vire, and Caen. Despite Calvados's continued lag behind Rouen, the mechanization process from 1796 to 1800 facilitated the advancement of the cotton industry.[36] The sector of laces and bows (*dentelles*), which employed many women and children, was one of the most famous in the region. Initially, it was made with wool, but around 1800 to 1815, the production of dentelles made with cotton grew.[37] With successive bans on imports of cotton goods (whether in the form of yarn or cloth), this industry grew in France in 1806. Simultaneously, due to the continental blockade and the U.S. embargo, French industrialists escalated their acquisitions of cotton from the Levant. Due to all of these factors, there was an increase in cotton prices. The development of the industry was stopped in 1808, and if that was not enough, there was an "industrial crisis" in 1810–11 that re-emerged in 1812. The weaving sector recovered at the end of the year but fell again in 1813. Yet, despite these mishaps between 1806 and 1815, the cotton industry in Calvados grew, though other sectors did not.[38] Essentially, the Napoleonic period benefited the cotton industry but not the other textile industries. A third of the traffic with the port of Caen was

33 Dupré, "Les Difficultés Économiques Des Ports de La Manche Pendant La Révolution et l'Empire: L'apport Des Archives de La Marine," 320, 321, 323; see also Delobette, "Ces Messieurs du Havre," 863.

34 Daly, "Merchants and Maritime Commerce in Napoleonic Normandy," 35–37.

35 Alain Leménorel, "Le Calvados à l'époque napoléonienne (1800–1815). Tournant ou continuité? Première partie," *Annales de Normandie* 25, no. 1 (1975): 38, 48.

36 Leménorel, "Le Calvados à l'époque napoléonienne, Première partie," 48; Alain Leménorel, "Le Calvados à l'époque napoléonienne (1800–1815). Tournant ou continuité? Deuxième partie: Les facteurs "internes"", *Annales de Normandie* 25, no. 3 (1975): 196.

37 Leménorel, "Le Calvados à l'époque napoléonienne, Première partie," 40–41.

38 Leménorel, "Le Calvados à l'époque napoléonienne, Première partie," 49–50, 56; for commercial relations between France and the Levant, see Prasannan Parthasarathi, *Why Europe Grew Rich and Asia Did Not: Global Economic Divergence, 1600–1850* (Cambridge University Press, 2011), 26, 91, 97, 118, 138, 141.

carried out by neutral vessels between 1804 and 1805. Trade with Normandy was significantly impaired when measures were taken against the neutrals.[39]

Cherbourg and Caen were marginal ports for French overseas trade, and, to some extent, they became active and gained importance because of the blockades at Le Havre and Rouen. They thus differ from Nantes, a famous port for exporting *indiennes* and its vast involvement in the slave trade until the revolution in Saint-Domingue and the French Wars.[40] In addition to its port being well located on the Bay of Biscay, it was a crucial link with Paris, which ended up becoming a market for the purchase and sale of raw cotton coming from Lisbon and the United States through the neutrals, and which would then go on to manufacturing centers. Paris itself, even if briefly, developed its own cotton industry. Consequently, Paris firms established offices in Nantes, and dealers such as the Delesserts, originally from Le Havre, moved their subsidiary to the Atlantic port.[41] The *indiennage* sector was negatively affected during the period of the French Wars. However, despite the constraints in obtaining raw materials, the cotton industry did not stop developing in Nantes, with more evident progress in terms of industrial techniques.[42]

It was only in November 1806, with the Continental Blockade imposed by France, and after English retaliation forbidding any trade with France, that the neutral trade ended. What was the impact of this on Rouen and Le Havre? Almost none, as neutral trade with these ports was practically non-existent.[43] Neutral trade was fundamental for Rouen and Le Havre until the Peace of Amiens. After the Peace, this strategy no longer worked. Rouen and Le Havre circumvented the vicissitudes of war by resorting to the ports of Cherbourg,

---

39 Leménorel, "Le Calvados à l'époque napoléonienne, Deuxième partie," 198–99; see also M. J. C. Perrot, "L'industrie et Le Commerce de La Dentelle Dans La Région de Caen (Deuxième Moitié Du XVIIIe Siècle)," in *Actes Du 81e Congrès National Des Sociétés Savantes* (Presses Universitaires de France, 1956).

40 Paul Jeulin, *L'évolution Du Port de Nantes: Organisation et Trafic Depuis Les Origines* (Les presses universitaires de France, 1929), 345–81; Bernard Roy, *Une capitale de l'indiennage: Nantes* (Au musée des Salorges, 1948); Céline Cousquer, *Nantes, une capitale française des indiennes au XVIIIe siècle* (Coiffard Librairie e Editeur, 2002); Olivier Grenouilleau, *L'argent de La Traite: Milieu Négrier, Capitalisme et Développement, Un Modèle* (Aubier, 1996); Alan I. Forrest, *The Death of the French Atlantic: Trade, War, and Slavery in the Age of Revolution* (Oxford University Press, 2020).

41 Louis Bergeron, *L'épisode Napoléonien: Aspects Intérieurs, 1799–1815* (Éditions du Seuil, 1972), 191; David Pinkney, "Paris: Capitale Du Coton Sous Le Premier Empire," *Annales. Histoire, Sciences Sociales* 5, no. 1 (1950): 56–60.

42 Samuel Guicheteau, *La Révolution des ouvriers nantais: Mutation économique, identité sociale et dynamique révolutionnaire (1740–1815)* (Presses universitaires de Rennes, 2008), 75, 77–78, 93.

43 Daly, "Merchants and Maritime Commerce in Napoleonic Normandy," 38.

Caen, and Nantes. For these three new French ports that received cotton from Portugal, neutral shipping was also necessary.

If between 1793 and 1801 Portuguese vessels were cornered due to threats from French and Spanish privateers and left most of the navigation to Scandinavians and North Americans, between 1801 and 1807, they, now neutral, were protagonists in trade between Portugal and France: it was Portuguese navigation that, most of the time, guaranteed the "connections between the two countries." This was an exceptional moment. Perhaps for the first time in history, the Portuguese managed to carry out of Portugal the commodities they had brought from Brazil.[44] Following the conclusion of the Peace of Amiens, Portugal pursued a more amicable relationship with Napoleon. Consequently, France ceased its assaults on Portuguese vessels, both in Europe and the Atlantic, thereby favoring the neutral navigation of Portugal. Moreover, the cotton trade appeared to be dominated by Portuguese merchants in Lisbon, while French merchants were marginal (Table 6.5).

3 Jacome Ratton and Brazilian Cotton

From the perspective of the French mercantile community in Lisbon, the early nineteenth century remained dismal in comparison to the conditions of ten or twenty years prior. Only one French merchant, Philippe Roussac, was one of the leading exporters in 1806. Along with a French naturalized Portuguese, the well-known Jacome Ratton, they were probably the most important remains of the French merchant community in Lisbon on the eve of the royal family's flight to Brazil (see Appendix B). Very little is known about the biographical details of the French merchants in Lisbon. Ratton, however, despite being naturalized Portuguese, left several records that shed light on important micro aspects of Portuguese-French trade. He was not only a central figure in the reexport cotton trade, having been active in it from the beginning, but was also involved with trade in Brazil, with the slave trade, and was a chief figure in the industrialization of Portugal.[45] It is, therefore, worth following his trajectory closely.

44 Cruz, "Neutral Shipping and the Portuguese Economic Relations with the Atlantic World (1793–1814)," 331–32, 344; see also Hans Chr. Johansen, "Scandinavian Shipping in the Late Eighteenth Century in a European Perspective," *The Economic History Review* 45, no. 3 (1992): 479–93; Douglass C. North, *The Economic Growth of the United States, 1790–1860* (Prentice-Hall, 1961).

45 See Table 2.7 and Martins, "A Companhia Geral de Comércio Do Grão-Pará e Maranhão," 169.

Ratton's story actually begins with his father and reveals precious information on mercantile recruitment in the mid-eighteenth century. His father was an itinerant merchant who used to travel all over the Iberian Peninsula. At some point, he established himself in Porto, where he sold both wholesale and retail, but people who knew him defined him as a "poor packman" or "peddler."[46] Later, Ratton's parents came to Lisbon. They formed a partnership with Ratton's uncle, Jacome Bellon, who already had a trading house in Porto. By the 1755 earthquake, Ratton's father and uncle's merchant house had earned some reputation. He employed clerks but could still be seen retailing goods with his wife on the ground floor of his shop.[47]

Jacome Ratton was born on July 7, 1736 in the village of Monnestier of Briançon, Province Dauphine. When his parents moved to Lisbon, they left him in the care of his grandparents. He went to Lisbon in 1747 and was very early instructed in commercial practices. At the age of 17, he was admitted into a partnership with his father and uncle. The society was called Bellon, Rattons, and Sons and ended in 1758 when his parents and uncle left the business. But Jacome Ratton continued the enterprise through a new partnership with Paulo Bonifas in Lisbon and with João Baptista Bourgeois and Carlos Dubar in Porto. The company was named Ratton, Bonifas, and Company. The three partners did not subscribe to the company's capital. Instead, it was Ratton, his father, and uncle who underwrote large amounts of capital. The partnership ended in 1764, mainly because of losses from the unexpected peace of 1763 that ended the Seven Years' War.[48] In any case, as early as 1762, the Rattons' trading house was one of the most important of the French nation in Lisbon. In 1765, Ratton was classified by the French consul as "one of the best subjects the King has here: intelligent, zealous and wealthy,"[49] and he had also helped the consul to map the leading textiles made by the English that had good sales in Portugal so that the French could copy them.[50] It was during the Seven Years' War that Ratton was naturalized Portuguese, out of fear that the Portuguese king would confiscate the goods of the French. Although he was offered the option of going back to being French, he chose to remain Portuguese.[51]

Ratton tried several activities during his life, but it was around this time that he became interested in setting up textile industries in Portugal. In 1764

46 "pobre bufarinheiro" ou "mascate".

47 Labourdette, *La Nation française à Lisbonne*, 485–86; Ratton, *Recordações*, 7–8.

48 Ratton, *Recordações*, 7, 12.

49 "un des meilleurs sujets que le Roi ait ici: intelligent, zélé et riche." Labourdette, *La Nation française à Lisbonne*, 374.

50 Labourdette, *La Nation française à Lisbonne*, 374, 486.

51 Labourdette, *La Nation française à Lisbonne*, 32–33.

he wanted to set up a chintz printing factory on the outskirts of Lisbon and he was planning to call workers from Switzerland to do it. This would have been the first chintz printing factory in Portugal, but the plan did not work. Ratton did not manage to obtain authorization from the Treasury official, José Francisco da Cruz, who, like many other Portuguese, believed that industrial activities were despicable. Furthermore, foreign merchants also cautioned Ratton against investing in industries, since this may have potentially jeopardized his commercial company and negatively impacted other importers.[52] It was only 20 years later that a chintz printing factory was set up in Portugal. It was established in Vila Nogueira de Azeitão by Magalhães and Larcher, with state capital. The business did not thrive, and the factory was passed to Raimundo Pinto de Carvalho, a customs officer who was also unsuccessful in running the business. Another famous factory was that of Henrique Meuzon in Torres-Novas.[53]

Around 1788, now with support from the Queen and the Board of Trade—and with state money—Ratton started a cotton spinning factory in Vila de Tomár. The factory, they believed, would help reduce smuggling. Ratton called his "old friend" Timotheo Lecussan Verdier to join the company. Together they asked for a 20-year exemption from paying taxes on raw materials and manufacturing. The privilege was granted in 1789. It was a company with large capitals: Ratton subscribed 60 *contos de réis* and Verdier 40. Due to disagreements with his partner, Ratton decided to leave the company and sold his share to Verdier around 1794. In 1806, Ratton and his son joined a cotton spinning factory in Vila da Barca, in Minho, as interested parties. It was a business owned by Antônio Araújo de Azevedo, Secretary and Minister of State for Foreign Affairs and War.[54]

Ratton built the first private factory for fine hats in Portugal (there was another factory, but it was linked to the state-supported Royal Silk Factory, *Real Fábrica da Seda*, near Vila de Pombal). The factory was taken care of by João Baptista Alexis, a Frenchman. Ratton does not detail when he started his factory but wrote that he left it entirely to Alexis in 1785. In the same year, he bought Gabriel Milliet's hat factory in Lisbon on Formosa Street. It was common for fine hats to come from Paris, and from his father's time, Ratton was one of the biggest importers of this item. But Ratton reported that he was so fond of Portugal that he decided to risk capital in the industrial endeavor. Even before the Portuguese government banned the entry of fine hats in Portugal,

52 Ratton, *Recordações*, 28.
53 Ratton, *Recordações*, 28–29.
54 Ratton, *Recordações*, 34, 36, 37.

his factory was already making good profits. After his factory, others were built by other entrepreneurs, which reduced the smuggling of fine hats towards Portugal. Later, Ratton reported that his hat factory was "the biggest in Portugal."[55] Overall, Ratton attributes the industrialization of Portugal to the reign of D. José—and Pombal by extension—and this for several reasons: introduction of manufacturing arts, import exemption on raw materials, the export exemption for manufactured goods, tax exemption from goods entering overseas ports, prohibition of importing manufactures that competed with those of Portugal, and laws to crack down on smuggling. All of this, for Ratton, made it possible for the wealth to remain in Portugal and not be transferred abroad, which was reflected in Portugal's trade balance.[56]

It was also in the early 1760s that Ratton became involved in the raw cotton trade. By that moment, practically the only way to get fiber from Brazil was through the GCGPM. In his account, Ratton stated that, in 1762, he purchased 300 bales of cotton at the company's auctions. He had bought at a price below market, as the company owed him money: Ratton had sold goods to the company, so the company gave him a discount on cotton. He then shipped the cotton to Rouen—"which was the only market for that item at the time"[57]—but that deal caused him "great loss" because of the 1763 peace. When Ratton was writing his memoirs in the 1810s, the cotton trade underwent a lot of transformation, and at that time, it was necessary to send money to Maranhão to purchase cotton.[58]

In 1805, Napoleon doubled import taxes on woven cotton, and in 1806 he simply banned its importation. With import barriers, France's spinning and weaving industry prospered, and the famous Oberkampf began to invest in this branch of the cotton industry. Oberkampf's concern was to find contacts in France and abroad in search of raw material for cotton spinning. In 1806, he even contacted two merchants in Lisbon, recommended by the Mallet bank, to send him cotton, one of them being Ratton & Sons and the other *Pilaer et Vanwinghen*.[59] Oberkampf was particularly interested in cotton from Pernambuco and wanted the merchants to ship 300 bales to his factor in Nantes. In 1807, Oberkampf bought 4,000 bales of cotton from Lisbon, but 1,320 were somehow

55 Ratton, *Recordações*, 31, 283.

56 Ratton, *Recordações*, 95.

57 "que era o único mercado para aquele gênero naquele tempo." Ratton, *Recordações*, 181.

58 Ratton, *Recordações*, 181–82.

59 Jacome Ratton and his son Diogo Ratton started a company in 1785. Diogo had had commercial training in France and in the running of the trading house he had with his father. On June 15, 1791, Jacome gave permission for his son to trade for himself, see ANTT, 7º CNL, Ofício A, cx. 107, liv. 648, f.31–31v.

lost. At this time, Oberkampf was possibly speculating with the market, as his spinning mill would only start operating in 1810. Furthermore, through the *Chapeaurouge et Cie* in Hamburg, Oberkampf was planning to buy cotton from the United States.[60]

Oberkampf, living close to Paris, tried to obtain Brazilian cotton through Lisbon because it was of good quality and had long fiber. Ratton, who had contacts with several merchants on the European Atlantic coast, including Hamburg, and also with Protestant banks, was one of his best options. Oberkampf asked the merchant houses in Portugal to send him cotton, preferably through Nantes, as maritime insurance was cheaper there than in the English Channel ports, although transport costs to Paris would be expensive. If it was impossible to send it to Nantes, the houses in Lisbon could send it to Cherbourg or Caen. Caen had a slight advantage in that it was easy to ship the pieces of cotton to Rouen by barge.[61]

In Nantes, the cotton was to be sent to *Delaroche et Cie*, a branch of the Delessert bank. In Cherbourg, the cotton would have to be sent to Blanquet et Lanchon or Coussin-Despréaux. At Caen, cotton was to be consigned to Manoury-Lacour. Regardless of the port chosen, shipments should be made using neutral ships, preferably American or Portuguese. If insurance was too expensive, Oberkampf advised that exporters in Lisbon could waive insurance on condition that they distributed the goods in several vessels: a maximum of 100 bales per ship.[62] In the same way that Oberkampf asked the Mallet bank for contacts in Portugal to obtain cotton, he also requested merchants in London and Hamburg for contacts in the United States. Oberkampf ended up getting an agent there. Cotton shipments would be made directly to France, but merchants in London would make the payments.[63]

Throughout 1807, when Oberkampf ordered a few thousand bales of cotton from Ratton and *Pilaer et Vanwinghem* in Lisbon, he was anticipating good trading profits but only because there was English tolerance for neutral navigation. If the blockade would become generalized, he seriously considered passing the pieces of cotton overland through Bayonne and Spain. Ratton and *Pilaer et Vanwinghem* would be paid through payments from Oberkampf in Paris or could be paid by *Chapeaurouge et Cie* from Hamburg.[64]

60 Chapman and Chassagne, *European Textile Printers in the Eighteenth Century*, 163–64, 241.

61 Louis Bergeron, *Banquiers, Négociants et Manufacturiers Parisiens Du Directoire à l'Empire* (Ecole des hautes etudes en sciences sociales, 1978), 228, 238.

62 Bergeron, *Banquiers, Négociants et Manufacturiers*, 228–29.

63 Bergeron, *Banquiers, Négociants et Manufacturiers*, 239.

64 Bergeron, *Banquiers, Négociants et Manufacturiers*, 239, 370.

For the French to import cotton from Portugal in 1806, they had to use neutral vessels, pay insurance to companies in other countries, and still handle the costs of land transport, from cotton from Cherbourg and Caen to the mills in Rouen and its surroundings. The English, in turn, transported cotton in their own vessels and did not need to worry about such long land transports. As a result, the cost of raw cotton purchased in Lisbon was increased by 25% for the French and only 10–11% for the English. From 1807 to 1808, the price of cotton soared because of the loss of Lisbon as a supplier. In this scenario, the small spinners were unable to continue their business. However, the large spinners survived, as they managed to buy large quantities that supplied their industry for an extended period.[65]

4 The Continental Blockade and the Commercial Situation after the French Invasion of Portugal

The Continental Blockade was announced by France on November 21, 1806, prohibiting any trade on the Continent with England. Portugal did not obey, just as it had not accepted the blockade stipulated by the French in 1801 and 1803. Because of Napoleon's other military concerns in Eastern Europe, the Portuguese question was set aside but was examined again in July 1807. An ultimatum was given to the Portuguese Prince Regent to close Portuguese ports to British ships, and French troops were prepared to proceed to Lisbon to ensure the blockade's effectiveness. The fear of invasion was great as Napoleon was at the height of his power, having just defeated the Austrians, Prussians, and Russians.[66] Traditionally, Portuguese foreign policy has aimed for neutrality amid conflicts among European nations; however, the events of 1806–1807 necessitated a decisive alignment with one side. For Portuguese Minister António de Araújo e Azevedo, Portugal should join the French side. For Rodrigo de Sousa Coutinho, Portugal should go to war against France, and if it lost, should transfer the Portuguese Royal family to Brazil, a position obviously supported by the British.[67]

---

65 Daly, *Inside Napoleonic France*, 184.

66 Macedo, *O Bloqueio Continental*, 38–41; see also Jorge Miguel Pedreira and Fernando Dores Costa, *D. João VI: O Clemente* (Circulo de Leitores, 2006); Charles J. Esdaile, *The Peninsular War: A New History* (Penguin Books, 2003).

67 Macedo, *O Bloqueio Continental*, 38–41; see also Miguel Dantas da Cruz, *A Neutralidade Portuguesa Na Europa Da Revolução, 1792–1807: Dificuldades e Possibilidades* (Parede Tribuna da História, 2011); Jacques-Oliver Boudon, "Napoleão e a Europa depois de Tilsit," in *Portugal, Brasil e a Europa Napoleónica*, ed. José Luís Cardoso et al. (Imprensa

While Portugal was making up its mind, the cotton trade continued, both for France and England. When the Continental Blockade was proclaimed, the French consul in Lisbon already pointed out one of its possible flaws. France depended on neutral navigation, and until the imposition of the blockade, it was common for neutral vessels to be momentarily apprehended by the British. This by itself was not a problem, as they were soon released and resumed their way to France. Therefore, the idea contained in the decree of the Continental Blockade to not accept neutral vessels that came from England into France was not a good one. And both the consul and the minister who corresponded with him sought to show the French Minister of Finance that it would be wise to give a guarantee to traders in Lisbon so that they could ship their goods and that even if the English took the vessels, their merchandise would still be accepted in France.[68]

After the blockade decree, merchants in Lisbon were afraid of possible retaliation from the English, especially after the arrival of an English war vessel. The cautious traders, wanting to place orders for their correspondents, began looking for insurers to insure ships destined for France. Insurance rates for Caen were higher, and rates for Nantes were lower. But overall, they were high, at 5 to 12%, and insurers still charged an extra 8% fee if the English captured the vessel. These were costs that merchants in Portugal were unwilling to pay, and trade could be harmed as a result. A solution would only come if the Portuguese negotiated with the English to guarantee that France's commerce would continue. This perhaps explains why French manufacturers directly contacted Portuguese merchants to send them cotton: fearing a possible British retaliation in the form of interrupting shipping to France, the manufacturers wanted traders in Portugal to send cotton overland to them.[69]

Around March 14, 1807, an American vessel was carrying merchandise from Lisbon to Nantes. When the ship left the river Tagus, the captain was called by a captain of an English ship. The latter "wrote in his passport, that he warned him not to continue his voyage to France, nor to any port of the allies of France, or under the influence of France" and added, verbally, that if after this warning written in his passport, he were to be intercepted by another English ship, he would be stopped, taken to England and there imprisoned. The "frightened American" decided to return to Lisbon, where he reported

de Ciências Sociais, 2010); José Luís Cardoso, "Bloqueio Continental e desbloqueio marítimo: o Brasil no contexto global das Guerras Napoleónicas," in *Portugal, Brasil e a Europa Napoleónica*, ed. José Luís Cardoso et al. (Imprensa de Ciências Sociais, 2010).

68 Macedo, *O Bloqueio Continental*, 184.

69 Macedo, *O Bloqueio Continental*, 181–82, 190.

what had happened to the traders and the American consul. The Lisbon marketplace was "dismayed," "all operations were suspended," and it appeared that in retaliation for the French Continental Blockade, England had finally "declared all French ports in a state of blockade." Nevertheless, the British government had not issued any such orders, and the English envoy in Lisbon reassured the merchant community that the position of the British government remained unchanged. The English ship captain seemingly acted alone, yet the consequences of his actions reveal a great deal about the apprehension within the Lisbon market.[70]

Six months later, in September 1807, the British seized 18 Portuguese vessels heading towards France. By the end of the same month, Portuguese ships were no longer regarded as neutrals by the French, and all cotton cargoes on Portuguese vessels were transferred to American ships. Already in October, the British ceased to consider American vessels as neutral. It was left to Oberkampf—and to many other merchants and manufacturers in France—to resort to land transport, as he had planned in case the situation became even more problematic. However, the passage through Badajoz was hampered, and Junot, in Lisbon, had seized the pieces of cotton in the *Casa da Índia* as well as in the warehouses of private merchants. Oberkampf had to reach connections in Madrid to get someone to remove the cotton from Lisbon. Only in July 1808 did he receive news that some cotton was in "Valladolid and Yrem for lack of certificates of origin." In September, Oberkampf sent an agent to Spain to take care of these matters, his attorney Louis Katzenberger. Other Parisian businesspeople did the same. In December, he finally discovered the whereabouts of his properties: 254 bales were in Valladolid, 830 in Madrid, and 200 in Plasencia. Between the end of 1808 and the beginning of 1809, Katzenberger managed to send the bales to Bayonne in carriages. The passage of pieces of cotton through Spain was even more hampered by officials and rulers who demanded the payment of taxes and confiscated some bales as a form of payment.[71] Previously, when U.S. shipping carried out the cotton trade, Bayonne also played an important role: from Lisbon, the cotton was taken there and then followed in carts to Paris.[72]

An "Imperial Commission of Compensation" was created in Bayonne to consider the claims of French merchants harmed by events in Spain. Through

70 Macedo, *O Bloqueio Continental*, 186–87.

71 Bergeron, *Banquiers, Négociants et Manufacturiers*, 239–41.

72 Paul Butel, "Traditions and Changes in French Atlantic Trade between 1780 and 1830," *Renaissance and Modern Studies* 30, no. 1 (1986): 141; Butel, "Revolution and the Urban Economy," 42.

them it was possible to realize the significant transit of Brazilian cotton from Lisbon to France through Spain between 1808 and 1809. Generally, the French in France commanded the import and export business with Spain; in the latter country, they had agents who were also French. Cotton manufacturers throughout the French Empire were interested in cotton from Brazil. In 1808, after the blockade of Lisbon, thousands of bales of cotton were taken from Portugal to Spain and then to France. Buyers in Nantes, Rouen, Brussels, Rhénanie, Lille, Montpellier, Paris, and Mulhouse received or expected to receive the pieces of cotton that would pass through Badajoz, Trujillo, Salamanca, and Valladolid. In this type of negotiation, Oberkampf lost 2,684 bales, for a value he calculated at 2,934,919 francs.[73] As if that were not enough, another problem arose. In Bayonne, "the cotton that arrives from Spain is deposited at customs and is only distributed to owners when they prove their titles."[74] Only on May 1, 1808, after writing and appealing for help from various authorities, did Oberkampf discover that "1,447 bales were found in Spain and sent to Bayonne; 360 of them crossed the border. The fate of the rest – more than half – remains uncertain."[75] Other buyers such as Oberkampf were in Paris and had problems recovering their cotton bales: Charles Bazin et Marc Jennings, Bernard Daupias, Mardochée frères, Rousseau et Bertin and Barrillon.[76]

There were merchants in French ports who had cotton stocks and speculated on their prices. Manufacturers like Oberkampf also bought from these merchants, but the prices were very high, and manufacturers always tried to find ways to import raw cotton at their own risk, using merchant-importers as their agents working on commission. French manufacturers preferred cotton from Lisbon from 1808–1809 until approximately 1811, but because of this trade's recurrent complexities, they started to switch to cotton from the Levant.[77]

Thus, with the transfer of the head of the Portuguese government from Lisbon to Brazil, the Brazilian cotton trade to France would change once again. On October 20, 1807, after intense negotiations, the Prince Regent of Portugal

73 Abel Poitrineau, "Les Relations Économiques Franco-Espagnoles Vues à Travers Les Papiers de La Commission Impériale Des Indemnités de 1809–1810," *Actes Du 94e Congrès National Des Sociétés Savantes, Pau, 1969, Actes Du 94e Congrès National Des Sociétés Savantes. Tome 1* (1971), 283, 287–88, 290.

74 "les cotons arrivant d'Espagne sont entreposés en douane et ne sont distribués aux propriétaires qu'à mesure que ceux-ci justifient de leurs titres".

75 "1,447 balles ont été retrouvées en Espagne et mises en route vers Bayonne; 360 d'entre elles ont franchi la frontière. Le sort du reste—plus de la moitié—démeure incertain".

76 Bergeron, *Banquiers, Négociants et Manufacturiers*, 240–41, 371.

77 Bergeron, *Banquiers, Négociants et Manufacturiers*, 241–42.

surrendered to the threats, joined the French, and declared the Portuguese ports closed to British vessels. Yet, even before they were aware of this news, the French troops in Spain planned to march towards Portugal. And in early November, they actually started heading to Portugal. In other words, even after the Portuguese accepted the terms of the Continental Blockade, France was nevertheless trying to invade the country. This was the signal that the Portuguese should change sides, and this became even clearer on November 23 when the Prince Regent heard that the French were already in Portugal. On November 29, the Portuguese Royal family fled Lisbon with the help of the British Navy towards Rio de Janeiro.[78] On the eve of the invasion, cotton from Pernambuco in Paris doubled in price.[79]

In summary, it can be stated that, from a commercial perspective, the impact of the blockade on Portugal produced an outcome contrary to what the French anticipated. Instead of closing themselves off to England, the Portuguese established economic policies that were even more favorable to the British, namely in relations with the Brazil trade: its ports were opened to other nations in 1808, and England won a very advantageous trade agreement in 1810, including allowing the entry of British cotton goods into Brazil, something that was previously prohibited.[80] Between 1806 and 1814, Pernambuco cotton prices rose in the main centers of the cotton trade: London, Paris and Leipzig. However, the rise was more pronounced on the Continent.[81] In the end, Britain got a raw material source for its cotton factories and a consumer market in America.

According to Chassagne, Brazilian cotton ceased to enter France after the French invasion of Portugal. The commerce would only resume in 1812 but still through Germany.[82] Yet, it is known that, in mid-1812, England allowed the export of cotton to France. This was also due to licenses granted by the French government. Of the 299 permissions granted between July and October 1812, around 50 referred to vessels that left London for Rouen loaded with Brazilian cotton. Obviously, the situation was complicated in France. In early 1812, the raw cotton available was only sufficient for ten months and, besides, Pernambuco cotton was highly desired by French manufacturers because of its fine quality. Re-exporting raw cotton from England to France was nothing

78 Cruz, *A Neutralidade Portuguesa Na Europa Da Revolução, 1792–1807: Dificuldades e Possibilidades*; Macedo, *O Bloqueio Continental*, 43.

79 Heckscher, *The Continental System*, 169.

80 José Jobson de Andrade Arruda, *Uma Colônia Entre Dois Impérios: a Abertura dos Portos Brasileiros, 1800–1808* (Edusc, 2008).

81 Heckscher, *The Continental System*, 274.

82 Chassagne, *Oberkampf*, 188.

new: "on 19 May 1810 British East India merchants, who were as anxious to sell as Continental merchants were to buy, petitioned the Privy Council for permission to export cotton to France and Holland."[83] The smuggling that occurred with other goods probably included raw cotton.[84]

Obtaining raw cotton was something on Napoleon's agenda. One of the strategies was to import cotton from the Levant, but its low quality and short staple, added to the cost of transport, since it had to come via Genova or Marseille, hampered its sales.[85] Before, during, and after the Continental Blockade in 1806, Napoleon made efforts to grow cotton in France and Italy.[86] In fact, on March 6, 1807, a French minister asked the consul in Lisbon to send him good quality cotton seeds that could be sown in France.[87] The cessation of Brazil as a cotton supplier exacerbated the dire situation of the French cotton industry. The trade, which was already complicated before, carried out by neutral vessels destined for the ports of Cherbourg, Caen, Nantes, and other ports far from Rouen, would become even more complex. Direct commercial relations between Brazil and France were in theory prohibited and would remain so until the end of the war. The loss of Lisbon as a cotton supplier caused a severe crisis in Rouen. An important merchant there, *Berat fils*, went bankrupt because of his cotton that had never arrived from Lisbon.[88] With the flight of the Portuguese royal family to Rio de Janeiro, the importance of South America became even clearer for Napoleon. To hinder the British maritime trade, Napoleon had thought of several plans in the summer of 1808 to seize South American territory.[89] And English ministers were always afraid that France would attempt to found an empire in South America utilizing the Spanish colonies. French

83 Melvin, *Napoleon's Navigation System*, 263, 304, 327–28; see also Margrit Schulte Beerbühl, "Trading with the Enemy: Clandestine Networks during the Napoleonic Wars," *Quaderni Storici* 48, no. 143 (2) (2013): 541–65.

84 Gavin Daly, "English Smugglers, the Channel, and the Napoleonic Wars, 1800–1814," *Journal of British Studies* 46, no. 1 (2007): 30–46; José Luís Cardoso, "Lifting the Continental Blockade: Britain, Portugal and Brazilian Trade in the Global Context of the Napoleonic Wars," in *A Global History of Trade and Conflict since 1500*, ed. Lucia Coppolaro and Francine McKenzie (Palgrave Macmillan UK, 2013), 92.

85 Heckscher, *The Continental System*, 276.

86 Joseph Horan, "Napoleonic Cotton Cultivation: A Case Study in Scientific Expertise and Agricultural Innovation in France and Italy, 1806–1814," in *New Perspectives on the History of Life Sciences and Agriculture*, ed. Denise Phillips and Sharon Kingsland (Springer International Publishing, 2015).

87 Macedo, *O Bloqueio Continental*, 185.

88 Daly, *Inside Napoleonic France*, 182.

89 Martin Robson, *Britain, Portugal and South America in the Napoleonic Wars: Alliances and Diplomacy in Economic Maritime Conflict* (I.B. Tauris, 2011), 197, 199.

threats had been constant since the 1790s. In 1796, for example, France pressured Portugal to surrender part of Brazilian territory in the Amazon region,[90] and around the same time, the Brazilian coast was being threatened by French corsairs.[91] Between 1796 and 1800, seven projects were presented to the French government to attack Brazil, one of them specifically targeting Pernambuco. The aim was to undermine trade with the English.[92] The Treaty of Fontainebleau of October 1807 itself, on the eve of Junot's invasion of Portugal, stipulated that Portugal's colonies in America would be divided between France and Spain.[93]

Still, Napoleonic France found ways to obtain cotton. The loss of Brazilian cotton was partially offset by cotton imports from the Levant and to a lesser extent by cotton reexports from Italy and Grenada.[94] Official figures point out that France even imported cotton directly from Brazil after 1808, but it was very little compared to what it had imported between 1802 and 1807. Portugal actually imported more cotton from Maranhão than France between 1812 and 1821,[95] indicating an important French strategy to obtain cotton. Some knew that in 1810, cotton was leaving Portugal in the direction of Cádiz, and from there, it was smuggled to France.[96] As early as 1802–4, this was already happening, and Portuguese officials made accusations that Brazilian cotton was entering France thanks to the massive smuggling through Spain.[97] Portugal had trade surpluses with France for much of the period between 1802 and 1824, according to the official in charge of preparing the Portuguese trade balances. Still, according to him, it was Brazilian cotton, transported overland by the French, which was mainly responsible for the surpluses. Payments were made on the spot, and as the value of cotton was high, these transactions turned out to be an excellent deal for Lisbon merchants.[98] Ratton proceeded in a slightly different way. After 1808, he received gold coins from France—coming through the mail—to profit from exchange rates. He invested that money in cotton,

---

90 Robson, *Britain, Portugal and South America*, 263.

91 AHU, ACL, CU, 015, Cx. 188, Doc. 13038 and Cx. 194, Doc. 13377.

92 Mello, *A Outra Independência*, 26.

93 Cristina Moreira et al., "Portugal's French Wars: Cost, Loss, Missed Opportunities? 1793–1850," in *The Crucible of Revolutionary and Napoleonic Warfare and European Transitions to Modern Economic Growth*, ed. Patrick Karl O'Brien (Brill, 2022), 205.

94 Daly, *Inside Napoleonic France*, 182–83.

95 Lady Maria Callcott, *Journal of a Voyage to Brazil: And Residence There, During Part of the Years 1821, 1822, 1823* (Longman, Hurst, Rees, Orme, Brown, and Green, 1824), 332.

96 Macedo, *O Bloqueio Continental*, 58.

97 Arruda, *O Brasil no comércio colonial*, 295.

98 Weber, "Relações comerciais e acumulação mercantil," 385; Pedreira, *Estrutura industrial e mercado colonial*, 317–18.

which he sent to France, also by land. Although he admitted gains from this activity, he also wrote that he lost because of "thefts made by the Spanish guerrillas from the post office and burnt and lost cotton." Ratton had been deported from Portugal for conspiring against the regency of Portugal, and one of the accusations was precisely that of trading with the French enemy in times of war. He tried to defend himself by pointing to the fact that other commercial houses in Lisbon were doing the same.[99]

All things considered, and in spite of all the issues raised thus far, it appears that there were no significant issues with France's raw cotton supply after 1809.[100] This supports an argument made by Silvia Marzagalli: although foreign trade was visibly harmed in light of export and import numbers, there were "compensation mechanisms"—neutral navigation and smuggling—that made the scenario less tragic, and that enabled the French to circumvent the vicissitudes of wars. For her, the French Wars did not paralyze exchanges, and the fact that historically the French were already used to doing business in times of war helped in the continuation of trade, even if in a turbulent way.[101]

After 1815, no blockade or prohibition prevented France from buying cotton directly from Brazil. However, the treaty between Portugal and England signed in 1810, which charged only 15% import duty on English products, discouraged France and other nations from trading, as they would have to pay a 24% tax. This treaty was valid for 15 years, and on the eve of its expiration, the French consul in Brazil negotiated a Franco-Brazilian treaty that was signed in 1826 and was valid for six years.[102] The end of the 1810 treaty, which occurred in 1825, opened the doors for other nations to negotiate with Brazil, theoretically, on an equal footing with England.[103] However, at that time when there were no more wars or disadvantageous commercial treaties, the Brazilian cotton trade to France was already in decline. At that time, U. S. cotton dominated both the French and English markets.

99 Ratton, *Recordações*, 266–67.

100 Daly, *Inside Napoleonic France*, 182–83.

101 Marzagalli, "Le négoce maritime et la rupture révolutionnaire," 207; on the importance of neutral navigation, smuggling, and their impact on French mercantilism, see Silvia Marzagalli, "Was Warfare Necessary for the Functioning of Eighteenth-Century Colonial Systems? Some Reflections on the Necessity of Cross-Imperial and Foreign Trade in the French Case," in *Beyond Empires: Global, Self-Organizing, Cross-Imperial Networks, 1500–1800*, ed. Cátia Antunes and Amélia Polónia (Brill, 2016).

102 Jürgen Schneider, "Le commerce de la France avec le Brésil, et spécialement la position du commerce français sur les divers marchés du Brésil entre 1815 et 1848. Essai d'une analyse de la structure économique," in *L'Histoire Quantitative de Brésil de 1800 a 1930* (Editions du Centre National de la Recherche Scientifique, 1973), 232–33.

103 Schneider, "Le commerce de la France avec le Brésil," 242.

After the end of the French Wars, it was with Le Havre (and, by extension, Rouen) that the whole of Brazil had more commercial contacts in France and this was thanks to cotton. In terms of navigation, few vessels entered and left Le Havre to and from Brazil between 1815 and 1819, but the number of ships almost tripled in the period leading up to 1849.[104] In 1825, Brazil was Le Havre's second main trading partner, accounting for 11.3% of the vessels entering there, second only to the remaining French colonies in the Caribbean (Martinique and Guadeloupe), which together were responsible for 38% of the vessels.[105] The French-Brazilian treaty of 1826 still held a French mercantilist attitude, as it restricted the import of coffee and sugar from Brazil, goods that competed with those coming from the French colonies. This had negative implications, one of which was that Brazil reduced its supply of commodities that could interest France and consequently reduced its purchasing power to import French goods. Yet, France's policy concerning cotton from Brazil was the opposite: cotton import taxes were reduced.[106] As a result, France had a very active trade with the regions of Northern Brazil that grew cotton.[107]

One of the first negotiations involving France and Brazil was led by the trading house Delaroche, A. Delessert et Cie established first in Nantes and later in Le Havre. They had set up a vessel whose supercargo was Horace Emile Say, son of the famous economist Jean-Baptiste. As France's most industrialized and populous region, merchants and shipowners from Le Havre prevailed over trade with Brazil.[108] The Portuguese Mazza, probably the descendant of the Genoese J.M. Mazza in Lisbon from 1787 to 1792,[109] was in Le Havre and owned vessels that made voyages to Pernambuco and Bahia between 1826 and 1829. It seems that there was more significant contact between Le Havre and Pernambuco, as there were recurring transport services between the two places. In 1835, when France allowed the entry of coffee from Brazil, Rio de Janeiro figured as the leading Brazilian port in contact with France, Pernambuco was the third, and Maranhão the fifth.[110]

---

104 Schneider, "Le commerce de la France avec le Brésil," 234.

105 Dupré, "Les Difficultés Économiques Des Ports de La Manche Pendant La Révolution et l'Empire: L'apport Des Archives de La Marine," 325.

106 Schneider, "Le commerce de la France avec le Brésil," 232.

107 Horace Say, *Histoire des relations commerciales entre la France et le Brésil: et considérations générales sur les monnaies, les changes, les banques et le commerce extérieur* (Guillaumin, 1839), 63, 159.

108 Schneider, "Le commerce de la France avec le Brésil," 233.

109 Labourdette, *La Nation française à Lisbonne*, 425.

110 Schneider, "Le commerce de la France avec le Brésil," 234, 236.

Thanks to cotton, Pernambuco exported more than it imported from France between 1821 and 1825. However, with the gradual decline of this item, the circumstances have inverted: "in 1844–1845, Pernambuco's exports consisted of three-quarters of sugar and only 11.5% of cotton." Similarly, with the drop in raw cotton exports to France, Maranhão was no longer able to import French luxury products.[111] Between 1827 and 1836, raw cotton was the most important item France imported from Brazil, representing 35% to 45% of total imports. But from 1837 onwards, it dropped to moderate amounts that ranged from 3% to 18%. The decline in cotton exports was offset by the increase in coffee and sugar exports. Between 1827 and 1856, the main exports from France to Brazil were various fabrics, the most important being cotton goods.[112] But, overall, Brazilian cotton had already lost its importance to the French market by the end of the wars in 1815 or, at the latest, sometime around Brazil's independence in 1822. Like the British, French manufacturers would buy in bulk raw cotton from the U.S. South for the rest of the century.

5 The French Cotton Industry

It is well known that Portuguese reexports of Brazilian cotton had a significant role in the development of the European textile industry. Still, France's significance as a raw cotton buyer and the reasons behind its acquisition of so much Brazilian fiber were not sufficiently discussed. This section seeks to fill these gaps.

For England, Brazilian cotton was a sure way to get raw material that did not depend on the oscillations of U.S. suppliers. For France, it was convenient as it was easier to transport to its territory.[113] Although England imported more cotton from Portugal than France throughout the period 1782–1806, there were times when the French imported similar or even greater amounts than the English (Table 6.1). This points to similar industrial production conditions in both countries, and according to Chapman and Chassagne, France and England had very similar endogenous industrial production factors.[114] Although the 1790s were a troubled decade from a commercial point of view, the cotton industry was growing in France during the period. An example of

111 Schneider, "Le commerce de la France avec le Brésil," 238–39.
112 Schneider, "Le commerce de la France avec le Brésil," 236, 242–43.
113 Macedo, *O Bloqueio Continental*, 56.
114 Chapman and Chassagne, *European Textile Printers in the Eighteenth Century*, 214; see also Leon, "Structure du commerce," 407.

this is raw cotton imports. In 1789, France received 4,770,000 kilograms, and in 1803–04 imports reached 11 million. This massive inflow of cotton was also linked to Napoleon's incentives to the French domestic industry.[115]

Despite the efforts and progress made, even in 1806, the cotton industry in France was dispersed and relatively little mechanized. In the same year, five departments (*Seine-Inférieure, Maine-et-Loire* [department neighbouring Nantes], *Haut-Rhin* [on the Swiss border], *Rhône,* and *Nord*) employed 63% of workers in the cotton industry. There were 13,608 cotton workshops in France, employing 181,640 workers. Most of them were weaving workshops (9,307) employing 111,164 workers. Then came spinning and sock producers, with 1,980 and 2,193 manufacturers, employing 27,000 and 26,727 workers, respectively. The calico printing industries came last, accounting for 128 establishments employing 16,349 workers. The *Seine-Inférieure* was the leading cotton department in the Empire in 1805–6.[116]

Thus, when considering the manufacturing centres in France during the industrial revolution, Rouen, in the *Seine-Inférieure* department, is one of the first places that should come to mind. Before the French Revolution, Rouen was named as the "Manchester of France," and cotton from Brazil contributed to this fame. According to Daly, "Portugal remained the lifeline of the Rouen textile industry" because, until the French invasion of Portugal in 1807, the leading supplier of cotton in Rouen was Brazil. Before the events of 1791 and 1793, the primary source of raw cotton for France and *Haute-Normandie* in particular, except for the French Caribbean, was cotton coming from Portugal, the Low Countries, and the Levant.[117]

---

115 Jacques Godechot, "The Internal History of France During the Wars, 1793–1814," in *The New Cambridge Modern History: Volume 9: War and Peace in an Age of Upheaval, 1793–1830*, ed. C. W. Crawley, The New Cambridge Modern History (Cambridge University Press, 1965), 9: 300.

116 Serge Chassagne, "L'enquête, Dite de Champagny, Sur La Situation de l'industrie Cotonnière Française Au Début de l'empire (1805–1806)," *Revue d'histoire Économique et Sociale* 54, no. 3 (1976): 351–54, 358–61.

117 Daly, *Inside Napoleonic France*, 181; Ouvrage collectif, *La Révolution en Haute-Normandie*, 88. In July 1806, Champagny—the Minister of the Interior—wrote to Napoleon that "of all the neutral powers Portugal and America are those with whom since the Revolution our commercial relations have been the most active and the most important. They are very similar in nature, both of them—Portugal, especially—furnishing us the raw material for that one of our industries which has at present most activity, cotton: both of them, likewise, but America chiefly, feeding the consumption (become almost of first necessity) of colonial produce. In the trade of both the balance is to the disadvantage of France …"; see Melvin, *Napoleon's Navigation System*, 20.

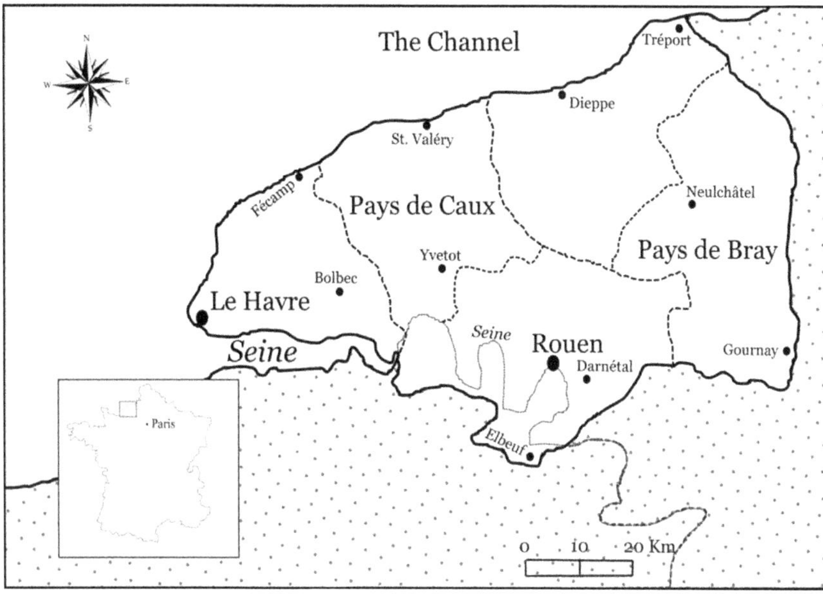

MAP 7.1 The Department of the Seine-Inférieure at the beginning of the nineteenth century
Source: Daly, *Inside Napoleonic France*, 13. Map prepared by the author.

The *Seine-Inférieure* department was where cotton industries were first established in France. There, cotton was spun, woven, and printed.[118] Since the Middle Ages, the region of Rouen was famous for producing woollen textiles, but by the end of the eighteenth century, wool had lost importance and was replaced cotton. Rouen produced *siamoises*, printed calicos, and *rouennerie*. The city of Rouen and its vicinities spun and wove cotton, but most of the cotton was manufactured inland, mainly in *Pays de Caux*. In the last quarter of the eighteenth century, two-thirds of the cotton fabrics traded in Rouen came from its hinterland.[119]

Generally speaking, the *Seine-Inférieure* department was based on small-scale spinning mills like the rest of France.[120] The largest spinning mills were found in the Seine Valley, close to small rivers and streams. In contrast, in

118 Serge Chassagne, *Le Coton et Ses Patrons: France, 1760–1840* (Editions de l'Ecole des hautes études en sciences sociales, 1991), 330; Daly, *Inside Napoleonic France*, 170–71; Jacqueline Jacqué, "Printed Textiles," in *French Textiles: From the Middle Ages through the Second Empire*, ed. Marianne Carlano and Larry Salmon (Wadsworth Atheneum, 1985).

119 Daly, *Inside Napoleonic France*, 26.

120 Daly, *Inside Napoleonic France*, 171–72; Henri Sée, *La France Économique et Sociale Au XVIIIe Siècle* (Colin, 1967), 97.

Rouen were concentrated factories a little smaller, driven by hand and horses but rarely by steam. In the Seine Valley, one of the biggest landowners was an English merchant, Valentin Rawle, who in 1806 employed 950 workers in his two factories that managed to spin 162,000 kilograms of cotton annually. In Rouen in the early nineteenth century, two of the main spinners were Jacques Levasseur, who employed 180 workers and produced 27,000 kilograms of cotton annually, and Le Bouvier, who yielded 41,000 kilograms.[121]

At *Pays de Caux*, in the *Yvetot arrondissement*, a wealthy grain production developed which partially fed the region. At the same time, many of its inhabitants engaged in spinning and weaving to supplement the income they obtained from agricultural activities. They did this predominantly through the "putting-out system" or "cottage industry," with merchants mainly in Rouen providing raw cotton or yarn to be spun and woven by farmworkers. Over the years, rural workers have been the target of disputes between the agricultural and manufacturing sectors.[122] The properties were smaller in *Pays de Bray*. On the coast and in the Seine Valley, due to the poverty of the soil, the industrial activity predominated. In the city of Rouen, a portion of the labor and land was allocated to the cotton textile industry precisely because of the poverty of its soil for agricultural activities. Most of the time, the *Seine-Inférieure* was unable to feed its population and depended on grain imports from adjacent departments.[123]

Before 1808, there were two great cotton importers from Portugal in Rouen: the Quesnel brothers and Frémery. The Quesnel family was one of the leading trading houses in Rouen, and they also invested in cotton manufactures, something that was not uncommon for French merchants at the time. Serge Chassagne, for example, found that 55% of France's manufacturers (82 out of a list of 148 spinners) had roots in commerce. The merchant François-Prosper Quesnel owned several properties in Rouen. Until his death in 1817, he had six houses in Rouen, a warehouse, a farm, a mansion, and several pieces of land and forests.[124] The merchants of Rouen played a crucial role as they generally

---

121 Daly, *Inside Napoleonic France*, 171.

122 Daly, *Inside Napoleonic France*, 14; Gay L. Gullickson, *The Spinners and Weavers of Auffay: Rural Industry and the Sexual Division of Labor in a French Village* (Cambridge University Press, 1986).

123 Daly, *Inside Napoleonic France*, 14, 18; Jean-Pierre Poussou, "Les Activités Urbaines En France Pendant La Révolution," *Revue Économique* 40, no. 6 (1989): 1063; Serge Chassagne, "La diffusion rurale de l'industrie cotonnière en France (1750–1850)," *Revue du Nord* 61, no. 240 (1979): 97–114.

124 Daly, "Merchants and Maritime Commerce in Napoleonic Normandy," 46–47; Chassagne, *Le Coton et Ses Patrons*, 274.

advanced the raw material to the villagers who spun and wove them and then transported the output to the Rouen market, from where it could have three destinations: cotton fabrics of inferior quality went to the French Caribbean to dress the enslaved people, and the fine fabrics were destined for the French domestic market or exported to other parts of Europe.[125]

With the loss of Saint-Domingue and the beginning of the war, everything changed. In general, these events delayed industrialization in France mainly by depriving it of raw materials and a broad consumer market. Furthermore, its isolation also made it challenging to import industrial technology, further delaying its manufactures. Still, the only sector that appears to have made progress was cotton textile manufacturing. From 1760 to 1790, France and England were not far apart in terms of "capital accumulation," and both were heavily dependent on foreign trade.[126] However, from 1790 to 1815, France took "a path not taken"[127] by England: the path of the state command, where it tried to control "undisciplined" workers, "encourage entrepreneurship," and "accelerate technical innovations". In England—with their *laissez-faire*—entrepreneurs had control over their workers, but this did not happen in France precisely because of the French Revolution. France reached its industrialization little by little and along crooked paths, but in the end, it was as productive as English industrialization.[128]

Simultaneously, the development of French industry served as a method of safeguarding the nascent republic from both internal and external dangers. However, in the context of a crisis triggered by revolution and war, relying solely on the market to ensure industrial growth would be challenging, therefore making it crucial for the state to establish guidelines. In theory, the state's role in French industrial growth should prioritize the promotion of technological advancements rather than the direct implementation of development programs. More precisely, "the state should focus on allowing the market to work more efficiently to encourage technological change."[129] Although more inclined towards a laissez-faire approach during the initial years of the French Revolution, the government leaned towards mercantilist interventionism

125 Daly, *Inside Napoleonic France*, 26.

126 Claude Fohlen, "France 1700–1914," in *The Emergence of Industrial Societies, Part One*, ed. Carlo M. Cipolla (Harvester Press, 1976), 4: 67–69.

127 Horn, *The Path Not Taken*.

128 Horn, *The Path Not Taken*, 5, 8–9; see also François Hincker, *La Révolution française et l'économie: décollage ou catastrophe?* (Nathan, 1989), 173; Réka Juhász, "Temporary Protection and Technology Adoption: Evidence from the Napoleonic Blockade," *American Economic Review* 108, no. 11 (2018): 3339–76.

129 Horn, *The Path Not Taken*, 186.

through the war years. Throughout this period, for example, it was encouraged that the French people only buy French clothes. This would be not only a patriotic act, but it would also help to beat the competition with English goods. Traditionally, French textiles were either luxury and destined for the domestic market or very cheap for colonies in the Caribbean. In the revolutionary period, what was searched for were French goods with fair prices to compete with English fabrics, which were still abundantly sold in France despite being forbidden.[130]

With England's declaration of War in 1793, and the law prohibiting imports of British goods in 1796, the French domestic market could be monopolized by its domestic industry. Nevertheless, English products, mainly cotton textiles, still entered France through smuggling, and it was such that, according to French officials, it exceeded smuggling before 1786. At the same time, spies and entrepreneurs acquired British machines making them enter France. British artisans and mechanics residing in Switzerland and the Netherlands also moved to France with their industry knowledge. The inventions and improvements made to machines in France, which were encouraged by the revolutionary state, began with machines brought from England or inspired by them. In the early 1790s, France found a provisional path to follow to preserve the Revolution: industrialization based on an economy run excessively by the state. After that, France found a path to follow that would be the definitive one: market deregulation, promotion of technological inventions, education and labor discipline, protection of the domestic market, and export of luxury products. This was the model of industrialization that allowed France, in the long run, to catch up with England. According to Horn, it was a slow but successful industrial revolution.[131]

---

130 Horn, *The Path Not Taken*, 185–91.

131 Horn, *The Path Not Taken*, 176–79; for Schmitd, the Revolution had very negative consequences for the cotton industry, which would only recover after 1800. See Charles Schmidt, "Les Débuts de l'industrie Cotonnière En France, 1760–1806," *Revue d'histoire Économique et Sociale* 7, no. 1/2 (1914): 31–34. For Fohlen, industrialization was interrupted in France because of the wars; see Fohlen, "France 1700–1914," 13, 19, 30. Dubuc argued similarly; see M. André Dubuc, "L'industrie Textile En Haute-Normandie Au Cours de La Révolution et de l'Empire," in *Le Textile En Normandie. Études Diverses* (Société Libre D'émulation de la Seine-Maritime, 1975). For a longer-term interpretation of the development of capitalism in France, see Sewell's work. For him, the production and consumption of fashionable goods in France during the eighteenth century are crucial elements that are generally left out of explanations about capitalism, usually focused on the work of factories in the nineteenth century; see William H. Sewell, "The Empire of Fashion and the Rise of Capitalism in Eighteenth-Century France," *Past & Present*, no. 206 (2010): 81–120.

At the center of this industrial movement was Normandy, the most industrially advanced French province.[132] Inside it was Rouen, one of the most important cities in France. Rouen was strategic because, touched by the river Seine, it was a sort of *entrepôt* between the sea and Paris. Up to Rouen, the river held large vessels weighing 300 tons, but after Rouen, the river narrowed, and boats were needed. In addition to Paris, Rouen was connected by roads with Caen to the south and Amiens to the north.[133] Rouen was strategic in two other ways: it was close to England and directly felt the effects of wars. At the same time, Rouen received more easily the technological progress and even English workers, who helped in the industrial development of the *Seine-Inférieure* in times of peace. John Holker of Lancaster, for example, introduced machines in Rouen.[134] However, the inventions of Hargrave (1765), Arkwright (1769), and Crompton (1779) were brought very slowly to Rouen, and even around the eve of the Revolution, spinning was still in its "infancy" in terms of mechanization.[135]

In fact, the mechanization of the cotton industry in Rouen was very precarious before 1800. In 1797, the industry was still based on the "spinning wheel." "Water frames" and "mule-jennies" were rarely used. However, hydraulic power-based spinning mills were being set up outside Rouen, in "Louviers, Malaunay, Charleval, Bolbec, and Gisors." It was during the Napoleonic era that the picture began to change, and mechanization surpassed the old cottage system. This was done mainly through government incentives, chiefly to compete with British products. Napoleon himself visited the cotton factories of Rouen, giving a kind of moral support to their owners. But the person who had direct interference in the development of the industry was the "prefect" of Rouen and his general council, which gave grants and prizes to those who invented or improved the machines. An Englishman from Manchester was also drawn to Rouen to set up two spinning mills, and other technicians from England could be found in Rouen supporting the cotton industry. Before the mechanization of cotton spinning, around ten spinners were needed to offer yarn to a weaver.

132 Horn, *The Path Not Taken*, 10.

133 Daly, *Inside Napoleonic France*, 18, 25.

134 André Rémond, *John Holker. Manufacturier et Grand Fonctionnaire En France Au XVIIIe Siècle, 1719–1786* (Librairie Marcel Rivière et Cie, 1946). See also John Raymond Harris, *Industrial Espionage and Technology Transfer: Britain and France in the Eighteenth Century* (Ashgate, 1998).

135 Daly, "Merchants and Maritime Commerce in Napoleonic Normandy," 18, 26; see also Jean Vidalenc, "Quelques remarques sur le rôle des Anglais dans la Révolution industrielle en France, particulièrement en Normandie, de 1750 à 1850," *Annales de Normandie* 8, no. 2 (1958): 273–90; Robert C. Allen, *The British Industrial Revolution in Global Perspective*, New Approaches to Economic and Social History (Cambridge University Press, 2009).

With mechanization, this ratio changed drastically, and more weavers were required to weave the enormous amount of yarn produced by the jennies. In 1782, there were about 20,000 weavers in the *Seine-Inférieure* region, and in 1808 they had jumped to 105,814. Like spinning, the weaving industry was also dispersed. Yet, while spinning became mechanized and increased the supply of yarn for weavers, weaving mills remained in the domestic system (cottage weaving) during the Napoleonic period.[136]

Thus, despite the obstacles in the Atlantic trade, the cotton industry flourished enormously during the Napoleonic period. According to Daly, "three main factors contributed to the cotton boom: mechanization, industry protection in the guise of the Continental Blockade, and widening continental market opportunities." Crouzet claimed that the blockades had a double positive effect: they protected the French market from the entry of manufactured goods from elsewhere and kept the French domestic market captive to consume the products of its own industry, the most successful of which was the cotton.[137]

Still, smuggling was constant throughout the period and what most worried the authorities and manufacturers in Rouen was the entry of textiles and cotton threads from England. Despite Normandy's enormous coastline, most smuggled goods arrived overland. British merchants sent goods, employing neutral vessels, to Antwerp, Amsterdam, Rotterdam, and Hamburg, which were introduced into France without interference by the French customs authorities. This trade required a sophisticated network of smugglers, but it was relatively well established, even relying on insurers and agents with fixed commissions. A commercial house in Rouen, *Bourgeois le jeune et compagnie*, proceeded as follows: in 1805, it employed an agent in Manchester who purchased cotton threads; then the yarn was shipped to Antwerp, and, with the help of a local merchant, the cotton was transported to France.[138] Due to the widespread use of the water-frame and the mule, Britain was a major exporter of warp yarn; the industry on the Continent was more focused on the production of weft yarns.[139]

---

136 Daly, *Inside Napoleonic France*, 169–74; see also Reddy, *The Rise of Market Culture*, 19–86.

137 Daly, *Inside Napoleonic France*, 167; François Crouzet, "Wars, Blockade, and Economic Change in Europe, 1792–1815," *The Journal of Economic History* 24, no. 4 (1964): 567–88; for Godechot, "industrial production was held back, especially with regard to cotton products, by the blockades." See Jacques Godechot, *L' Europe et l'Amerique a l'epoque Napoleonienne (1800–1815)* (Presses universitaires de France, 1967), 301; see also Louis Bergeron, "Problèmes économiques de la France napoléonienne," *Revue d'Histoire Moderne & Contemporaine* 17, no. 3 (1970): 469–505.

138 Daly, *Inside Napoleonic France*, 191–93; see also Marzagalli, *Les Boulevards de La Fraude*.

139 Richard Guest, *A Compendious History of the Cotton-Manufacture: With a Disproval of the Claim of Sir Richard Arkwright to the Invention of Its Ingenious Machinery* (J. Pratt, 1823), 33.

Textile manufacturers in Rouen preferred and favoured protectionist policies, as they were "unable" to compete with cheaper, better quality English yarns and fabrics. As such, they did not like the 1786 Treaty of Eden and, in a way, the blockades and Napoleonic trade policy were pleasing to them. Yet, although the continental blockade protected the French market, it also closed the door to the consumption of French textile abroad. In 1806 and 1811, for example, crises took place that essentially had to do with cotton goods that could not be sold because of the large supply.[140]

According to Jeff Horn, the historical literature tends to treat the case of English industrialization as the "true" path to productivity. This is an Anglo-centric view and suggests that all countries that did not follow England's footsteps carried out one type of industrialization that was not pure.[141] The case of France shows that cotton textile manufacturing grew, despite wars, smuggling, and a limited foreign market. Likewise, the raw cotton trade was also growing to support this booming industry. From France's point of view, cotton imports from Portugal had always been significant and increased between the second half of the eighteenth century and the beginning of the nineteenth century (Tables 7.2 and 7.3).

TABLE 7.2 Raw cotton imports into Rouen-Le Havre, 1755–1776

Years	French Colonies	Netherlands	Portugal	Other ports	Total
1755	1,339	19	20	-	1,378
1756	41	367	13	40	461
1757	-	1,010	12	112	1,134
1758	-	881	15	10	906
1759	-	890	48	37	975
1760	-	884	24	33	941
1761	-	-	-	-	-
1762	-	1,500	60	160	1,720
1763	633	611	91	135	1,470
1764	1,861	64	47	1	1,973
1765	-	-	-	-	-
1766	2,277	1	208	2	2,488
1767	2,436	31	315	-	2,782
1768	2,468	6	250	2	2,726

140 Daly, *Inside Napoleonic France*, 180, 185.
141 Horn, *The Path Not Taken*, 2.

TABLE 7.2 Raw cotton imports into Rouen-Le Havre, 1755–1776 (*cont.*)

Years	French Colonies	Netherlands	Portugal	Other ports	Total
1769	2,429	8	492	-	2,929
1770	2,101	12	702	-	2,815
1771	1,845	38	399	12	2,294
1772	1,770	10	365	1	2,146
1773	2,304	13	398	-	2,715
1774	2,302	26	1,228		3,556
1775	2,526	2	497	30	3,055
1776	1,894	-	271	8	2,173
Total (1766–1776)	24,352	147	5,125	55	

Sources and notes: Dardel, *Navires et Marchandises*, 561. Imports are given "en milliers de livres pesant." Table prepared by the author.

TABLE 7.3 Raw cotton imports into France, 1775–1790

Years	Portugal	Levant	French colonies	Total
1775	1,290,795	3,051,414	7,568,191	11,985,378
1776	679,475	10,206,941	5,887,003	16,846,023
1777	769,093	8,316,210	6,532,244	15,667,949
1778	1,364,355	4,527,150	5,658,743	11,718,182
1779	1,499,973	5,338,772	1,838,485	10,574,986
1780	4,206,930	7,206,250	775,390	13,227,378
1781	-	-	-	-
1782	2,532,000	-	-	8,681,897
1783	-	-	-	-
1784	-	-	-	-
1785	-	-	-	-
1786	2,290,000	-	-	-
1787	2,395,602	-	-	11,170,536
1788	2,367,000	-	-	-
1789	3,047,000	-	-	-
1790	1,222,369	-	-	-

Sources and notes: Labourdette, *La Nation française à Lisbonne*, 394. Imports are given "en livres tournois." The 'Total' column represents the total imported amount and does not correspond to the sum of the values in the preceding columns. Table prepared by the author.

According to data tabulated by Dardel, between 1766 and 1776, the French colonies were responsible for 82% of the supply of raw cotton to Le Havre-Rouen, followed by Portugal with 17%, and then Holland, Levant, and other ports.[142] From the 1770s onwards, raw cotton was the most important export item from Portugal to France. In 1786, for example, of all Portugal's exports to France (5,313,000 *livres tournois*), cotton was the main commodity (making up 2,290,000 *livres*). Cotton from Portugal represented 4–10% of total cotton imports into France before the United States War of Independence.[143] Imports stabilized at one-fifth after the conflict, but during the war, Portugal reached 31% of all French cotton imports.[144] Despite the commercial complications generated by the revolutionary wars, Portugal continued to export cotton to France, through ships and neutral ports and by way of smuggling. Brazilian cotton gained official prominence again during the French Consulate (1799–1804) and with the First French Empire (1804–1815). Cotton from Portugal was the most important import from France between 1800 and 1807, beating even U.S. cotton. In a report made in the context of preparations for the occupation of Portugal, the Minister of the Interior, Champagny, informed Napoleon on August 5, 1807, about the importance of raw Brazilian cotton. According to him, France bought about 52,000 bales of cotton from Portugal during 1806 and England 41,000. The share of cotton from the French colonies was marginal at this time: between 1805 and 1807, it did not even exceed 0.5% of total French cotton imports. It was a contrast with the situation in 1787, when cotton from the French colonies reached 70% of imports in value and those from Portugal only 6.4%.[145]

6 Conclusion

Between 1793 and 1815, trade towards France was constantly marred by abnormality. Brazilian cotton arrived at French ports and industrial centers for 22 years through neutral vessels, smuggling, and even by land. This reflected English maritime power, which prevented French expansion in the seas,

142 Dardel, *Navires et Marchandises*, 561.

143 Labourdette, *La Nation française à Lisbonne*, 346, 393–94.

144 Labourdette, *La Nation française à Lisbonne*, 394; for the history of French colonial trade, see Paul Butel and François Crouzet, "Empire and Economic Growth: The Case of 18th Century France," *Revista de Historia Economica – Journal of Iberian and Latin American Economic History* 16, no. 1 (1998): 177–93.

145 Chassagne, "L'enquête, Dite de Champagny, Sur La Situation de l'industrie Cotonnière Française Au Début de l'empire (1805–1806)," 342.

blocked ports, and allowed navigation through neutrals. The French cotton industry grew in the period—mainly relying on its protected internal market—and therefore, raw cotton inflows also grew. However, these were slow growths when compared with England. Despite the idiosyncrasies and difficulties, these were the years when Brazilian cotton entered France the most.

During these years, Lisbon's already weak French merchant community practically disappeared. It was the Portuguese, or French naturalized Portuguese, such as Ratton, who received orders from French manufacturers and merchants, took out insurance, and exported cotton employing neutral vessels. With Le Havre and Rouen blockaded, trade tended to be channeled to other ports. Cherbourg, Caen, and Nantes were the most preferred ports by traders, because they were safer as they were close to the *Seine-Inférieure* department. Furthermore, part of the raw cotton could be used by the manufacturers in the three ports.

Shipping services, at first, were offered by the Scandinavians and the United States and later by the Portuguese themselves. Hamburg and other ports with neutral status also played an important role. Cotton could be destined for northern Europe and then on to France. Another share of cotton was to supply the textile industry of Saxony. In these cases, trade and neutral navigation required a network of smugglers and false papers that were difficult to dismantle. With the Continental Blockade, the commercial system based on neutrals was severely compromised, so much so that the cotton trade started to be done by land after 1807–08. With it, new problems arose, such as loss of bales and extra fees charged by the Spanish authorities and intermediaries. This trade lasted a long time—even before the blockade came into force, it was already happening—and it was so relevant that, because of it, the Portuguese trade balance had surpluses in relation to France for many years. Thus, with the opening of Brazilian ports in 1808, Portugal still imported a great deal of cotton from Brazil and re-exported it in bulk to France. Because of its alliances with the Portuguese and the commercial treaty of 1810, England transported cotton directly to its country. However, part of the cotton in London could be shipped, subject to licenses, to French ports. After the wars ended and the treaty with England expired in the 1820s, the Brazilian cotton trade ceased to be relevant to French ports. Henceforth, for France and England, buying cotton from the United States was the best deal.

CHAPTER 8

The Brazilian Cotton Trade from Portugal to England

1 The Historical Trajectory of the English Factory and Its Institutions

It is understandable that the literature deals so much with commercial and diplomatic relations between Portugal and England. After all, the general interpretation is that Portugal became dependent on England as a form of recompensation to the British for having helped with the Portuguese independence from Spain in 1640. An economic dependence accompanied this political dependence through commercial treaties throughout the seventeenth and eighteenth centuries. Shipping services, purchases of Port wine, the wool trade and, above all, the Brazilian gold trade were dominated by the English. England had more solid commercial bases in Portugal than other foreigners.[1] This materialized in what is conventionally called—at the time and in the historical literature—the English factory in Portugal. The English who bought cotton in Lisbon—in bulk from the 1780s onwards—were members of this famous factory, which meant a group of merchants who lived abroad. Factors in Portugal were generally the agents of the principals in England; they took orders from abroad and were hired to buy cotton and other goods. Their remuneration could be a salary or commissions, but they could also be apprentices and/or merchants who traded on their own. The members of the factory did not necessarily need to be residents in Portugal. They could manage the business by proxy or through relatives in Portugal. The admission to the factory was conditioned by the merchant's social reputation and the quantity of goods he traded in. The English factory had its rules, its hospital, its cemetery, and its chapel. Membership brought social and economic benefits: it was a

1 The literature on these subjects is extensive; see for example Shillington and Chapman, *The Commercial Relations of England and Portugal*; C. R. Boxer, "English Shipping in the Brazil Trade, 1640–65," *The Mariner's Mirror* 37, no. 3 (1951): 197–230; Boxer, *The Golden Age of Brazil, 1695–1750*; Sandro Sideri, *Trade and Power: Informal Colonialism in Anglo-Portuguese Relations* (Rotterdam University Press, 1970); Carl A. Hanson, *Economy and Society in Baroque Portugal, 1668–1703* (University of Minnesota Press, 1981); Fisher, *The Portugal Trade*; Fisher, "Lisbon, Its English Merchant Community and the Mediterranean in the Eighteenth Century"; Costa, "Relações Económicas Com o Exterior

sign of social prestige, as well as commercial benefits such as reduced import taxes on English products and guaranteed spaces in the Lisbon customs area for unloading goods.[2] Even so, foreign merchants were reluctant to enter the customs house to clear out their products, as they found it disorderly and dirty, so much so that no "gentleman" could set foot there, so they left this task to others.[3]

The factory president was the consul, who was assisted by some vice-consuls spread across the Portuguese marketplaces. The figure of the consul, together with the judge conservator and the ambassador (and envoys), were institutions that sought to protect the foreign mercantile community in Portugal, and they—to a greater or lesser degree—ensured that the "fundamental problems of exchanges"—as coined by Avner Greif—were bypassed.[4] Of course, all foreign nations had similar institutions as I briefly explained with the French case in Chapter 6, yet the English community was the richest, and its consuls, judges, and diplomats tended to be the most important in Portugal.

Consuls regulated conflicts between members of their nation, intervened in the drawing up of inventories of assets, ratified notarial acts, issued passports to their nationals, and acted as intermediaries between vessel captains and local authorities. They were appointed by the British Crown and essentially settled disputes between the English merchant community with the Portuguese state. The judge conservator was chosen among the Portuguese judges, and the British factory paid him. As it was well remunerated, the position of judge conservator was sought after.[5] While the consul was responsible for taking care of commercial and navigation matters, the judge conservator was responsible for "defending private rights and interests" and ensuring that no part of the documentation produced by the foreign merchant fell into the hands of the public.

---

2 Shaw, *The Anglo-Portuguese Alliance*, 62–64; Lodge, "The English Factory at Lisbon," 225; on its historical roots and the role of factors in English foreign trade, see T. S. Willan, *Studies in Elizabethan Foreign Trade* (Manchester University Press, 1959), 1–33.

3 Fisher, "Lisbon as Port Town in the Eighteenth Century," 715; with the French invasion in 1807, all records of the English factory had to be removed from Portugal. However, according to Lodge, the ship carrying the documents sank in the Bay of Biscay; see Lodge, "The English Factory at Lisbon".

4 Avner Greif, "The Fundamental Problem of Exchange: A Research Agenda in Historical Institutional Analysis," *European Review of Economic History* 4, no. 3 (2000): 251–84. Merchants resorted to strategies to get around what we can call the fundamental problems of exchanges in long-distance trade. That is, how to ensure that someone miles away will comply with someone else's orders. See also Stephen A. Ross, "The Economic Theory of Agency: The Principal's Problem," *The American Economic Review* 63, no. 2 (1973): 134–39; Baskes, *Staying Afloat*.

5 Lodge, "The English Factory at Lisbon," 226–27.

The judge conservator "was a guardian of the private." He was knowledgeable about the law in the sphere of personal relationships, while the consul was knowledgeable about "commercial and maritime law." Because they had different jurisdictions, the judge conservator complemented the consular activity.[6] If the consul represented the king of his country to his nationals in foreign countries, the ambassador represented the king of his country for negotiations with the king of the country in which he resided.[7] The ambassador thus had a political function, but that did not prevent him from acting in favour of commercial affairs since it was through him that commercial treaties were negotiated.[8] Consuls, judge conservators, ambassadors (and commercial treaties) officially governed trade between nations in the eighteenth century. Still, as the consul was the one who had greater control and contact with the mercantile community, he was a central figure in the administration of trade within Portugal and toward his country of origin. Furthermore, much of what we know about the British community in Lisbon stems from consular correspondence.

The practices and fortunes of trade by the British community in Portugal varied over time. Anglo-Portuguese trade relations date back to the Middle Ages.[9] However, with the Portuguese Restoration in 1640, when Portugal needed English assistance to distance itself from Spain, the bond between the two countries became even closer and crystallized with the signing of commercial treaties. England took advantage of the agreements: the 1642 treaty, for example, allowed the British to access Portuguese colonial markets on the coast of Africa, on the Atlantic islands, and in Brazil. A 1654 treaty reiterated many clauses of the previous treaty, including English access to the Portuguese overseas market: the English nation acquired the right to have four families in Portugal who would trade with Portuguese domains overseas, both in Brazil and in Asia. Yet, this direct infiltration of the British into Portuguese colonial commerce remained a "dead letter," according to Kenneth Maxwell. Still, the treaty not only gave the "same liberties, privileges, and exemptions as the Portuguese in metropolitan and colonial commerce" but also gave freedom of creed and "prohibited the raising of customs duties on British goods above

6 Ana Crespo Solana, "El Juez Conservador ¿Una Alternativa al Cónsul de La Nación?," in *Los Cônsules de Extranjeros En La Edad Moderna y a Principios de La Edad Contempóranea* (Ediciones Doce Calles, 2013), 28–33.

7 Labourdette, *La Nation française à Lisbonne*, 309.

8 See, for example, John Methuen: Alan David Francis, "John Methuen and the Anglo-Portuguese Treaties of 1703," *The Historical Journal* 3, no. 2 (1960): 103–24; Alan David Francis, *The Methuens and Portugal, 1691–1708* (Cambridge University Press, 1966).

9 Shillington and Chapman, *The Commercial Relations of England and Portugal*.

twenty-three percent."[10] In 1703 came the Methuen treaty that abolished the ban on imports of English woollen cloth and at the same time guaranteed a market for Portuguese wines in England by taxing them below French wines.[11] With these treaties, England achieved several commercial and diplomatic advantages that would last to a lesser or greater degree until the beginning of the nineteenth century.[12] As much as the Portuguese were occasionally reluctant to comply with these agreements, they provided a formal guarantee that exchanges between the two nations would take place without much friction.

Treaties, of course, were not enough to attract foreign merchants without market opportunities. Thus, for most of the eighteenth century, English interests orbited, directly or indirectly, around the wealth of Portuguese overseas business. In the second half of the seventeenth century, the British entered the Portuguese economy mainly in the shipping sector: they were the ones who often carried out transport services with Portugal and with the Portuguese domains, and offered charter services on the coast of Portugal itself.[13] The development of the sugar industry in the British West Indies momentarily turned the British off from participating in the Brazilian sugar trade, even though they were still quite active in the import trade for the Portuguese market. The primary market for British products exported to Portugal was actually Brazil. From there, British goods could be illegally shipped to Spanish America to be exchanged for silver.[14] In any case, Portugal no longer had a commodity—as for instance sugar—to send to England to pay for its imports.[15]

Everything changed with the rise of Brazil's gold trade at the end of the seventeenth century. Gold revived the Portuguese economy and was the commodity responsible for giving pre-eminence to the English factory in Lisbon during the first half of the eighteenth century. During this period, the British shipped gold from Portugal to England in their vessels. Moreover, trade between Brazil and Portugal was pursued by the mercantile and financial interests

---

10 Lodge, "The English Factory at Lisbon," 213–15; Shaw, *The Anglo-Portuguese Alliance*, 15; Maxwell, "Pombal and the Nationalization of the Luso-Brazilian Economy," 613.

11 Lodge, "The English Factory at Lisbon," 221; Shaw, *The Anglo-Portuguese Alliance*, 18–19; John V. C. Nye, *War, Wine, and Taxes: The Political Economy of Anglo-French Trade, 1689–1900*, Princeton Economic History of the Western World (Princeton University Press, 2007).

12 Costa, "Relações Económicas Com o Exterior".

13 Shaw, *The Anglo-Portuguese Alliance*, 14; Boxer, "English Shipping in the Brazil Trade, 1640–65".

14 Shaw, *The Anglo-Portuguese Alliance*, 33.

15 Shaw, *The Anglo-Portuguese Alliance*, 33–36; see also Hanson, *Economy and Society in Baroque Portugal, 1668–1703*; Maximiliano M. Menz, "Reflexões sobre duas crises econômicas no Império Português (1688 e 1770)," *Varia Historia* 29, no. 49 (2013): 35–54.

of the British, who lent money to the Portuguese to do business in South America. According to Shaw, "trade between Portugal and Brazil remained largely in the hands of foreign merchants, and it was widely recognized that English merchants controlled trade more than the sum of other nations."[16] Mercator wrote in 1754 that the extraction of gold from Brazil was only possible thanks to foreign capital (commodities), mainly from Great Britain.[17]

2 The Debates about Pombal and the English

In this mid-century context, the role of the English emerges with some ambiguity in historiography. For Kenneth Maxwell, Pombal—the main Portuguese minister in charge of the political and economic decisions of Portugal—interpreted the Anglo-Portuguese trade as harmful to Portugal, which made him launch a program to make Portugal less dependent on England and English trade. This plan involved a series of regulations that ranged from creating monopoly companies to the transfer of commercial privileges to Portuguese merchants. The idea was to make the most of trade with the colonies and strengthen the Portuguese mercantile community so that it could replace the English. Ultimately the goal was to nationalize the Luso-Brazilian economy.[18]

This interpretation is largely supported by English consular and diplomatic records in Lisbon. The Board of Trade (*Junta do Comércio*), established by the King and Pombal in 1755, had a judge who superseded the judge conservator for the English, leading to complaints from the English regarding the Board's hindrance to foreign merchants. Furthermore, the establishment of the Pombaline companies (the GCGPM and the GCPP) further undermined the 1654 treaty as they, in addition to prohibiting the British trade to some areas of Brazil, also had judges who took precedence over the judge conservator of the British. With the loss of power of their judge, the commercial situation of the British was undermined. This was a turning point. According to Shaw, while

16 Shaw, *The Anglo-Portuguese Alliance*, 20, 37.

17 Fisher, "Lisbon as Port Town in the Eighteenth Century," 722; about Brazilian gold, see Virgílio Noya Pinto, *O ouro brasileiro e o comércio anglo-português: uma contribuição aos estudos da economia atlântica no século XVIII* (Companhia Editora Nacional, 1979); Michel Morineau, *Incroyables Gazettes et Fabuleux Métaux: Les Retours Des Trésors Américains d'après Les Gazettes Hollandaises (XVIe-XVIIIe Siècles)* (Cambridge University Press; Maison des sciences de l'homme, 1985); Donovan, "Commercial Enterprise and Luso-Brazilian Society During the Brazilian Gold Rush"; Furtado, *Homens de negócio*; Costa et al., *O ouro do Brasil*.

18 Maxwell, "Pombal and the Nationalization of the Luso-Brazilian Economy," 617.

in the past Portuguese kings sought to grant privileges for foreign merchants to trade with Portugal, Pombal did the opposite: he deliberately made life hard for foreign merchants to help domestic merchants. By 1769, the community of English factors in Portugal had greatly diminished, and by 1774 merchants in England were using the services of Portuguese agents. Shaw claimed that Pombal's policy of reducing the English presence was largely successful because the number of British merchants and the value of their trade was halved.[19]

The perception of the French consuls coincides with the reports of the English, especially concerning the Portuguese industrialization promoted by Pombal to replace not only English goods but also those from France.[20] The most recent Portuguese historiography goes in the same direction.[21] Pombal's desire to fight the English in Portugal arose when he had been an envoy in London in the early 1740s. There, he had seen first-hand the disadvantageous position of the Portuguese merchant community in relation to the English community in Portugal. His letters written around that time[22] would become, in the words of José Luís Cardoso, almost a kind of "forerunner and anticipation of his government plan" that took place between the 1750s and 1770s. How Pombal put this plan into practice varied according to "the contingent nature of the politics." Still, in general, it was a "program typically inserted in the mercantilist economic culture" of industrial promotion and protection of the domestic mercantile community.[23] According to Leonor Freire Costa, Pombal's policy had a positive effect since Portuguese commercial houses were more capable of operating abroad, and it is possible that the diversification of Portugal's commercial partners reached at the end of the eighteenth century had something to do with Pombal's "institutional war" against the British. The international political situation, though, also had its influence: the outcomes of the American War of Independence (1775–83), which drained British "naval resources," may have favored the Portuguese shipping sector in transporting cotton across Europe in the early 1780s.[24] Alan K. Manchester also argued that

---

19 Shaw, *The Anglo-Portuguese Alliance*, 91–93, 121–22, 133–34.

20 Labourdette, *La Nation française à Lisbonne*, 227–30, 354.

21 Pedreira, "A economia política do sistema colonial".

22 Sebastião José de Carvalho e Melo, *Escritos Economicos de Londres (1741–1742)* (Biblioteca Nacional, 1986).

23 José Luís Cardoso, "Política Económica," in *História Económica de Portugal, 1700–2000. Volume 1. O Século XVIII*, ed. Pedro Lains and Alvaro Ferreira da Silva (Imprensa de Ciências Sociais, 2005), 1: 356, 359, 362.

24 Costa, "Relações Económicas Com o Exterior," 288–90; see also Miguel Dantas da Cruz, "The Diversification of Portugal's Commercial Relations in the Late Eighteenth Century: Between Discourse and Praxis," *E-Journal of Portuguese History* 10, no. 1 (2012): 37–61.

Anglo-Portuguese relations were compromised because of Pombal. For him, it was Brazilian cotton and the French wars that made a rapprochement between the two countries possible.[25]

Richard Lodge took a different view on all of this. For him, Pombal knew of the unequal conditions of Portuguese traders based in England compared to English traders in Portugal. But Pombal did not intend to banish the English; he just wanted to reduce their participation so that they would be equalled under similar conditions to Portuguese merchants in England. For Lodge, what really damaged the English factory was the earthquake in Lisbon in 1755 since many goods had been lost and much of the credit given to the Portuguese was not paid, as the Portuguese also lost everything in the natural catastrophe.[26] England was indeed the most affected by the earthquake. They (including Ireland and Scotland) lost the equivalent of 160 million *livres tournois* in goods and money (for the purpose of comparison, Hamburg lost 40 million; Italy 25; the Netherlands 10; France 4; Sweden 3; and Germany, 2 million).[27] After 1755, the British factory never regained its former prosperity. England's export trade to Portugal fell sharply between 1758 and 1765 compared to the previous seven years. As if that were not enough, right after Pombal came the French Revolution, which further taught to the Portuguese the idea of nationality and then the fear of being invaded by the French. All this made it very difficult for foreign factors in general to be accepted in Portugal.[28]

Harold Fisher is inclined to another interpretation to explain the retraction of British interests in Portugal. Since the 1750s to 1760s, the entry of Brazilian gold into Lisbon was declining, and the English were naturally losing interest in trade with Portugal. At the same time, the price of grain transported by the British had risen so much in the producing regions that making sales in Portugal was difficult.[29] Thus, for Fisher, the explanation lies in economic reasons and not in Pombal's economic policy. It was because of gold that the English traded with Portugal (not only to procure metal but also because gold expanded the consumer market in America) and not because of commercial treaties such as the one signed in 1654.[30] In 1715, when gold was the main traded commodity, the English factory in Portugal reached 52 members. The impact

25 Manchester, *British Preeminence in Brazil*, 337.

26 Lodge, "The English Factory at Lisbon," 229, 235.

27 Ange Goudar, *Rélation historique du tremblement de terre survenu à Lisbonne le premier novembre 1755: Avec un détail contenant la perte en hommes, eglises, convens, palais, maisons, diamans, meubles, marchandises, &c* (Chez Philanthrope, à la Vérité, 1756), 215–16.

28 Lodge, "The English Factory at Lisbon," 235–36, 242.

29 Fisher, *The Portugal Trade*, 41–52.

30 Fisher, *The Portugal Trade*, 43–49.

of gold was so substantial that Lisbon had become one of the main ports in Europe by the mid-eighteenth century. Yet by the end of the century—despite trade with Asia and cotton from Brazil—Lisbon had lost its importance.[31] In times of depression, in the 1760s, the English factory had no more than 40 members. However, because of cotton and the growth of trade with Asia, the English merchants in Portugal rose again, reaching 59 members in 1794 and more than 80 in 1803 (see Appendix E).[32] Fisher claimed that Pombal's plan to strengthen the Portuguese mercantile community was not very successful, as the English were still present and fundamental to trade, both at the European level and with the colonies.[33] More specifically, the English shipping services that connected Portugal with the Mediterranean ports were lucrative for the English residing in Lisbon.[34]

Jorge Borges de Macedo similarly argued that Pombal did not pursue an anti-British policy. On the contrary, he even protected English commerce. Macedo concluded this by contrasting England and France in Pombal's strategy. In essence, there was a lack of commercial complementarity: for a long time, France only had things to sell to Portugal, and Portugal had nothing to offer France. Relations with England were still the most advantageous. Furthermore, during much of Pombal's government, the number of English vessels that entered Lisbon remained constant. If Pombal intended to reduce the presence of English commerce, he did not reach that goal from the shipping point of view. For Macedo, Pombal never wanted to exclude trade or capital from foreign nations. The Pombaline companies did not intend to take the English or any foreigners out of the picture as they allowed them to subscribe capital into the companies. What Pombal wanted, in fact, was to curb smuggling, which took place in an association between Portuguese merchants and foreigners (mainly with the English), as this illegal practice occurred primarily with Brazil. Hence the creation of monopoly companies (to protect the colonial market) and the suppression of travelling agents (Portuguese agents famously identified as smugglers, the *comissários volantes*).[35] All of this gave the impression that the target of the Pombaline policy was the English. French

31 Fisher, "Lisbon as Port Town in the Eighteenth Century," 728.

32 Fisher, "Lisbon, Its English Merchant Community and the Mediterranean in the Eighteenth Century," 24; A. R. Walford, *The British Factory in Lisbon & Its Closing Stages Ensuing Upon the Treaty of 1810* (Instituto britânico em Portugal, 1940), 71–74.

33 Fisher, "Lisbon as Port Town in the Eighteenth Century," 723–24.

34 Fisher, "Lisbon, Its English Merchant Community and the Mediterranean in the Eighteenth Century," 38.

35 On *comissários volantes*, see chapters 4 and 5.

merchants who constantly sought to obtain commercial advantages similar to those of the English became increasingly interested in buying legally from the GCGPM, the company that started the cultivation of cotton in Maranhão and which for many years (between 1755 and 1778) was the only one which transported cotton to Lisbon.[36]

What explains the fact that Portugal's cotton exports were primarily with France and not with their traditional and strongest English trading partner? The interpretations presented so far give us some clues. The British would probably not negotiate with the GCGPM, as the company's judge—who had precedence over the British judge conservator—discouraged them from trading with the company. For most of the Pombaline period, France ended up being the preferred market because it sought commercial benefits with Portugal and rarely associated with smuggling with Brazil, as was the case with the British. From the point of view of imports, why did France receive cotton from Portugal and not the British? Possibly for two reasons. First, cotton from Portugal paid the same rights in France as cotton coming from the French West Indies. The French consul in Lisbon expressed concern that this benefit should not be permitted, as the Portuguese imposed restrictions on cotton products from France.[37] Second, England was still well supplied by West Indian growers, and demand for raw cotton was still contained, possibly because Arkwright's patents had not expired, which would happen in 1785, and the mule was not yet being used more extensively. Moreover, cotton from the British colonies was "imported duty-free," while cotton from other places paid taxes in England for a long time.[38] In 1785, Britain reached a significant turning point by purchasing a greater amount of cotton in Lisbon compared to Portugal's other trading partners. During the early 1790s, Britain effectively acquired the majority of the cotton that was accessible in Lisbon (see Figure 8.1).

How the English in Portugal exported Brazilian cotton was based on old commercial organizations that the traditional gold and wine trades had set up. Furthermore, the export of cotton from Portugal was organized by wealthy foreigners' tax farmers of the period. The period between the 1770s and 1807 was also marked by changes in destination ports. London, the traditional port for trade between Portugal and England, was losing ground and in the late 1780s it was overtaken by the port of Liverpool. Yet, London's long pre-eminence

36 Jorge Borges de Macedo, *A Situação Económica No Tempo de Pombal: Alguns Aspectos*, 3a edição. (Gradiva, 1989), 89–95.

37 Labourdette, *La Nation française à Lisbonne*, 390–91.

38 Shillington and Chapman, *The Commercial Relations of England and Portugal*, 288.

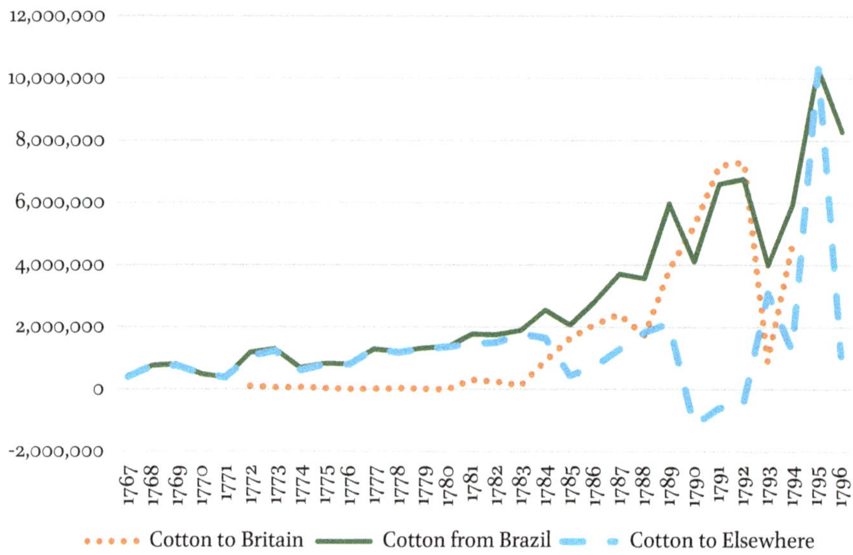

FIGURE 8.1 Cotton imports from Brazil and exports to Britain and elsewhere, 1767–1796
Notes and sources: Imports and exports are given in pounds. The figures for cotton imports from Brazil are underestimated, as they include only exports from Pernambuco and Maranhão. These two captaincies supplied approximately 90% of all cotton exported by Brazil; see The National Archives Kew (NA), Foreign Office (FO) 63/15. This helps to clarify why in some years Portugal exported more cotton to Europe than it imported from Brazil. Another explanation is the existence of huge stocks of cotton in Lisbon that accumulated from one year to the next. Be that as it may, England purchased almost all the cotton available in Lisbon at the beginning of the 1790s. For cotton imports from Brazil to Portugal, see Diego de Cambraia Martins and Felipe Souza Melo, "Cotton Exports from Brazil, 1758–1815 Dataset" (European University Institute, HEC, 2022), https://cadmus.eui.eu/handle/1814/74724. For cotton exports from Portugal to Britain, see NA, Board of Trade 6/62 and FO 63/14, 63/16, 63/17, 63/19, 63/20, and 63/26. Figure prepared by the author.

in the trade with Portugal explains that although Liverpool was the leading destination for Brazilian cotton, the Lisbon-based British merchants who handled the cotton trade were mainly from London. According to Alexey Krichtal, high competition from London firms discouraged Liverpool companies from settling in Portugal.[39] The following sections will explore some aspects of these trade organizations and some of their leading merchants.

39 Alexey Krichtal, "Liverpool and the Raw Cotton Trade: A Study of the Port and Its Merchant Community, 1770–1815" (Master's thesis, Victoria University of Wellington, 2013), 49.

3 From Gold to Cotton and from London to Liverpool

It was around the mid-1780s when exports of Brazilian cotton to England increased. As a result, the presence of British merchants in Lisbon also increased. Pressures from British manufacturers in the 1780s to grow more cotton in the British West Indies[40] must have resonated with merchants dealing with Portugal. From 9.2% of Portuguese cotton exports in 1782, England rose to more than 60% in 1789. The participation of the English in the group of leading exporters to England went from zero in 1782 to 43.01% of cotton *arrobas* exported in 1789. London, the primary English market for Brazilian cotton between 1770 and 1782[41] was superseded by Liverpool by 1789. In the 1790s, the concentration of exports in the hands of English merchants in Lisbon toward Liverpool became even more pronounced. Certainly, what favored the British was their already established commercial base in Portugal, which previously dealt with gold, wine, shipping services, and imports. These were firms primarily dealing with London but quickly reoriented themselves or were replaced by new companies with ties to Liverpool. In addition, the French wars favored this English domain, which made cotton shipments to France difficult. However, around 1806, afraid of the consequences of the war and a possible French invasion of Portugal, the British practically withdrew from the business. Consequently, the Portuguese began to export cotton in large quantities to Liverpool and French ports (Table. 6.6 and Appendix B and C).

Thus, even with the gold depression, the 1755 earthquake, and the Pombaline policy, the English never left Portugal. They still financed trade with Brazil and were the leading importers in Portugal. In addition, they offered shipping services, mainly to the Mediterranean, where they had a good relationship with pirates.[42] But after the end of the mining boom, the British had nothing substantial to buy in Portugal, except for wines. The rise of Brazilian cotton in the early 1780s changed this situation. It opened a new line of business that attracted old merchants in both England and Portugal and new young merchants such as Robert Spear. In the late 1770s or the beginning of the following decade, Spear, who came from a family of respectable linen drapers and who would become one of Manchester's biggest cotton dealers in the 1790s, was in Lisbon to buy raw cotton from Brazil. At that time, he was just a young apprentice working for the "cotton dealers of Manchester," Clegg and Kirkham, who, along with two other Manchester houses, had entrusted Spear with the

40 Edwards, *The Growth of the British Cotton Trade*, 79.

41 Carreira, *A Companhia Geral do Grão-Pará e Maranhão*, 2: 319.

42 Shaw, *The Anglo-Portuguese Alliance*, 36.

important mission "of making large purchases of Brazil cotton." Long after his trip to Portugal, he had a brief and frustrating partnership with Richard Arkwright in 1788. Nevertheless, he continued to be interested in cotton, traveling to the textile centres of France where he discovered the benefits of American cotton, more specifically the Sea-Island variety. From that moment, he started importing from the United States and employed an agent in Savannah to promote the cultivation of that type of cotton.[43] Spear's early trajectory is an excellent example of merchant recruitment in the eighteenth century. One of the strategies to become a merchant in England was to settle abroad, as the capital for that was low. So, some went to the British colonies, whilst others went to European ports. In the first half of the eighteenth century, an account of an insurance company director tells how he was considering sending one of his sons to Lisbon because there "a young man may begin busyness without any assistance from his master."[44]

Robert Spear probably had a quick stay in Portugal, unlike the merchant John Theodor Koster, who stayed for many years in Lisbon. During that time, he strengthened his position in the English factory, built ties with Portuguese society, bought large quantities of cotton from Brazil (see Appendix B), and with his commercial company was one of the biggest importers of raw cotton based in Liverpool.[45] We can trace Koster's relationship with Portugal and Brazil going back to 1772. From that year until 1776, he resided in London and received significant amounts of gold from Portugal. He moved to Lisbon in 1776 and remained in the city until 1801, where, in addition to being a major exporter of cotton, he also continued in the gold business, exporting it to England. In the meantime, he built social ties with the English and Portuguese communities. In 1778, Koster married Suzana Maria Carret, the daughter of another British merchant, Matheus Carret, with whom Koster had a business company. Matheus Carret gave 4,000,000 *réis* of dowry for his daughter. Although Koster kept the money, it was meant to be separated from the couple's other assets.[46] In the same year of the marriage, Matheus Carret made a trip to London, leaving Koster as his representative, giving him a power of attorney.[47] In 1785,

43 Memoirs of the Life and Character of the Late Robert Spear, Esq. of Manchester, William Bengo' Collyer, *The Investigator* (*or, Quarterly Magazine*) (Thomas and George Underwood, 1820), 1–5; about Richard Arkwright, see R. S. Fitton, *The Arkwrights: Spinners of Fortune* (Manchester University Press, 1989).

44 Walter E. Minchinton, "The Merchants in England in the Eighteenth Century," in *Explorations in Enterprise*, ed. Hugh G. J. Aitken (Harvard University Press, 1965), 282.

45 Krichtal, "Liverpool and the Raw Cotton Trade," 57, 61.

46 For the dowry contract, see ANTT, 7º CNL – Ofício A, Cx. 98, liv. 597, f. 44v–45.

47 For the power of attorney, see ANTT, 7º CNL – Ofício A, Cx. 98, liv. 597, f. 62v–63.

Koster became a member of the British Factory in Lisbon and, between 1793 and 1796, representative of the British Consulate in the same city.[48] He was also a member of the Lisbon Academy of Sciences.[49]

By the early 1790s, Koster admitted that gold was scarce in Lisbon and that Brazil's mines should already be in exhaustion. His business with gold from Brazil, in this particular type of operation, practically ceased by the end of the decade. What most probably must have taken place were operations with gold in the opposite direction. Koster sent gold to Pernambuco and Maranhão to buy cotton, as an account suggests.[50] Although Koster did not use this strategy for the period after 1801 when he had moved back to England, it was quite possible that he employed gold as a commodity to be traded for cotton during his time in Lisbon, a strategy used by the commercial community in Lisbon. According to Shillington and Chapman, "in 1791 it was recorded that London was sending gold to Lisbon, and Lisbon to Brazil."[51]

Koster returned to England in 1801, but instead of going to London he moved to Liverpool where he had good commercial connections. When Brazilian ports opened to other nations in 1808, Koster took advantage of the market he had known for a long time and was one of the largest importers of Brazilian cotton in Liverpool in the early 1810s. Due to his old age, Koster retired from business in 1819. He died in 1830 in Bordeaux, France. His wife, Suzana Maria, became responsible for managing his business and assets, until she died in Paris in 1842.[52] Her only son, Henry Koster, was born in Lisbon in 1793. Henry was also a merchant, and most likely worked as an agent for his father and other merchants in England, but most importantly, Henry travelled through the Brazilian Northeast, recording his experiences in the tropics in a book that would become one of the best reports about Brazilian society in the early nineteenth century. He died at the early age of 27 in Pernambuco in 1820.[53]

In the early days of his stay in Lisbon, John Koster's connections with Brazil were already bearing fruit. In 1782, Francisco José da Costa and his partner Feliciano Batista de Aguiar borrowed more than 5,000,000 *réis* in commodities from Koster, when one of them was in Lisbon. They were merchants who

48 About Koster at the Consulate, see Shaw, *The Anglo-Portuguese Alliance*, 48–49, 214.

49 For some biographical details of Koster, see S. G. Checkland, "John Koster, Anti-Bullionist," *The Manchester School* 20, no. 2 (1952): 174, 175, 176, 186.

50 Checkland, "John Koster, Anti-Bullionist," 181, 185.

51 Shillington and Chapman, *The Commercial Relations of England and Portugal*, 290.

52 Checkland, "John Koster, Anti-Bullionist," 183, 185, 199, 201; Krichtal, "Liverpool and the Raw Cotton Trade," 57–61.

53 Checkland, "John Koster, Anti-Bullionist," 184, 199; Koster, *Travels in Brazil*. See also The National Archives Kew, FO 63_206, f. 258, 266–267, and 271.

worked in the village of Goiana, 57 kilometers away from Recife. However, by 1787 the debtors had not yet paid Koster. He then tried to get his capital back by the traditional means, which consisted in sending an attorney to deal directly with the defaulters. Koster's attorney in Pernambuco even tried the local court; yet the debtors were "powerful" men in Goiana's village, and because of their influence as well as institutional failures of the local courts themselves, the recovery of capital was unfeasible. Koster complained that the judges in Goiana were "ignorant" people and that they, for the most part, assigned their work to advisers, and that these advisors, members of the court, were at the same time the lawyers of the two debtors. Koster also worried that, under the influence of the defaulters, they could "bribe" his attorneys in the village. Arguing this, Koster asked the Portuguese Queen for two things: first that the judicial process be transferred to the jurisprudence of the judge conservator of the British nation in Lisbon, and secondly that the case should pass to the responsibility of the *Ouvidor* of Pernambuco who was also a judge of mercantile causes. The provisional decision of the Queen and her advisers was that the *Ouvidor* of Pernambuco take charge of the judicial process.[54] It is unknown, however, whether Koster succeeded in recovering his money.

It was not the first time that Koster had given instruments of power to someone in Pernambuco to represent him. In 1784, on behalf of his firm, Carret, Koster and Company, he granted a power of attorney to the merchant Manuel Antônio Ferreira to represent his business house against his defaulters in Pernambuco.[55] In 1788, he did the same thing, but on behalf of his other firm, João Theodoro Koster and Company, appointing the attorney Bernardo Alemão de Cisneiros to collect their debtors in the same region.[56] This last firm of Koster was not only linked to the business with the captaincy of Pernambuco. His company also had an attorney in the captaincy of Bahia in 1786, Manuel Henriques, who was traveling to Brazil that year to collect the debtor Antônio José do Vale Viana.[57]

Koster was a very important merchant in the history of cotton. He not only traded between the Portuguese and British empires, but he had a sufficiently long lifespan that allowed him to exchange both with gold and cotton and with both colonial Brazil and the Brazil head of the Kingdom of Portugal after 1808. Koster also witnessed the change of the raw cotton market from London to Liverpool. In 1789, his firm Carret, Koster & Co. exported 4,957 *arrobas* to London

---

54 AHU, ACL, CU, 015, Cx. 160, Doc. 11524.
55 ANTT, 7º CNL – Ofício A, Cx. 102, liv. 620, f. 29–29v.
56 ANTT, 7º CNL – Ofício A, Cx. 105, liv. 636, f. 85–86v.
57 ANTT, 7º CNL – Ofício A, Cx. 104, liv. 629, f. 89.

and only 57 to Liverpool. Three years later, the scenario changed drastically: his company sent 8,987 *arrobas* to Liverpool and 2,430 to London. By 1806, all 11,621 *arrobas* of cotton that Koster's company bought in Lisbon were sent to Liverpool and nothing to London (see Appendix B). In addition to the large quantities exported from Lisbon, Koster's firm was headquartered in Liverpool and was one of the largest importers of raw cotton for the period 1784–1815.[58]

4 From Wine to Cotton

Merchants previously engaged in the wine trade, one of the few Portuguese products consumed in England, developed an interest in the lucrative cotton trade. One of them was George Sandeman. Originally from Perth, Scotland, he settled in London in 1790 to trade wine. He had a company, George Sandeman & Co, that operated in Portugal. As early as 1794, he was importing his first bales of cotton from Portugal on behalf of a London client, and between 1802 and 1805, he was responsible for about 9% of all Brazilian cotton imported into Liverpool, Glasgow, and Bristol.[59] Usually, "when British houses completed the purchase [of cotton] in Lisbon, Liverpool importers were expected to pay in full, usually giving instructions for the bill to be drawn on major London merchants and bankers." Evans, Offley & Sealy, one of the most important wine exporters in Porto[60] and one of the biggest cotton exporters in Lisbon (Appendix B), and Joseph Lyne & Co, were other firms with members in London and Lisbon. These companies took a 3% commission for their services to buy cotton in Portugal. The cotton exported by these Lisbon-based firms was destined for agents of dealers and manufacturers. These agents were responsible for taking the cotton to the textile centers.[61]

Other large spinners in England imported cotton from Lisbon and Porto. The London spinning firm of Bolders, Adey, Lustington, and Bolders was trying to contact merchants in Portugal for this. In Porto, they knew of the merchants Bearsley & Webb and in Lisbon of the Evans, Offley & Sealy company, where Sealy seemed to be solely responsible for actually buying cotton in Lisbon while Evans handled the company's capital. But in 1792, the firm in London asked to be informed of potential houses in Lisbon willing to ship cotton to

58 Krichtal, "Liverpool and the Raw Cotton Trade," 57, 61.

59 Krichtal, "Liverpool and the Raw Cotton Trade," 52, 54.

60 Norman R. Bennett, "The Golden Age of the Port Wine System, 1781–1807," *The International History Review* 12, no. 2 (1990): 221–48.

61 Krichtal, "Liverpool and the Raw Cotton Trade," 55–56.

England, possibly houses made up of men of "faithfulness and attention," as they used to refer to the firm Evans, Offley & Sealy.[62] This letter shows how important reputation was for gaining information and increasing connections. A reputable firm, such as Evans, Offley & Sealy, was asked not only for possible commercial deals but also to inform buyers in London about other potential business partners in Lisbon. About seven years later, in 1799, the English spinning firm was already buying raw cotton directly from Portugal, not through Lisbon but through George Sandeman & Co., based in Porto. Sandeman & Co. were under strict orders to buy 50 bales of cotton from Pernambuco and ship it through the port of Lisbon. Sandeman would also be responsible for arranging cotton insurance and sending the quotation of cotton prices in Lisbon to the firm in London for potential new orders. The wars with France made insurance an element of concern, so one of the clauses for continuing cotton imports from Portugal to England in 1801 was that Sandeman's firm always made insurance for the goods. If they agreed, they could send 150 bales of cotton—half from Pernambuco and the other half from Maranhão—to the firm's broker in two vessels. It was important that the commercial correspondence was precise and indicated concretely what the agents should do, but certain flexibility was necessary depending on the negotiation. The same 1801 letter, for example, left buyers in Lisbon a certain leeway: if they could not get cotton from Pernambuco, they could buy it from Maranhão, as long as the fibers were of "quality and clean." The letter also reveals that speed was essential to the industry. Stocks were low, so spinners needed more raw materials promptly. Therefore, they also asked to be informed as soon as possible whether the cotton purchases took place; otherwise, they would have to buy fibers in the marketplaces of Liverpool or London.[63]

Not many vessels were needed to carry cotton between Lisbon and Britain. The total number of English vessels that entered Lisbon in the late 1780s was around 350.[64] But only 68 vessels were enough to transport cotton in 1789: 32 to London, 29 to Liverpool, three to Cork, two to Dublin, one to Hull, and one to Leith. English shipping services were so abundant that they transported cotton to Genoa (six vessels) and Hamburg (three). Wars with France caused England to implement "regular naval convoys" to protect its merchant ships. This would facilitate trade and lower insurance premiums.[65] In the late 1790s and early

62 Fitton and Wadsworth, *The Strutts and the Arkwrights, 1758–1830*, 279.

63 Fitton and Wadsworth, *The Strutts and the Arkwrights, 1758–1830*, 279–82.

64 Serrão, *História de Portugal. Volume VI. O Despotismo Iluminado, (1750–1807)*, 428.

65 Redford, *Manchester Merchants and Foreign Trade, 1794–1858*, 26, 43–44; see also C. Northcote Parkinson, *The Trade Winds: A Study of British Overseas Trade During the French Wars,*

nineteenth century, the vessels that carried cotton to Great Britain increased in number: 40 to London, 14 to Liverpool, four to Cork, four to Hull, two to Greenock, one to Leith, and one to Bristol, between January and August 1801. Likewise, England increased the total number of vessels that entered Lisbon: English vessels made up 52% of the ships that entered Lisbon in 1799, eclipsing the Danes, who came in second with just 8.5% of entries (see Appendix D).[66]

5 Wealthy Tax Farmers and the Cotton Trade

Mellish and Devisme were other big English cotton merchants (Appendix B) who originated in the time when Brazil's gold was the backbone of the Portuguese economy. But for many years (from 1757 to 1784), Gerard Devisme and Joseph Mellish, together with the Swiss naturalized Englishman in 1735, David Purry, were the merchants who held the monopoly on the purchase of Brazilwood imported by Portugal and the only ones who could re-export it for Europe. The Brazilwood trade, as well as tobacco, was exclusively reserved for the Portuguese Crown, but the Crown yielded the selling right to tax farmers, the so-called *contratadores* (contractors). The primary market to which Purry, Mellish, and Devisme shipped Brazilwood (which released an excellent red dye for dyeing woolen and silk fabrics) was Marseille.[67] Brazilwood, however, was not the firm's only activity. They even bought diamonds from Brazil in the late 1750s.[68] They were also a company that owned some vessels that traded with France between the 1760s and 1790s.[69] And despite being English, they were very close to Pombal. While they were shareholders of the Pombaline companies, they also sold European products and bought colonial goods from them.[70]

1793–1815 (1948; Routledge, 2005); Patrick Crowhurst, *The Defence of British Trade, 1689–1815* (Dawson, 1977); Fitton and Wadsworth, *The Strutts and the Arkwrights, 1758–1830*, 284.

66 António Lopes et al., "As Frotas Do Brasil No Atlântico de Final Do Antigo Regime," *Actas Do Congresso Internacional Espaço Atlântico de Antigo Regime: Poderes e Sociedades* (2009), 12.

67 Thiago Alves Dias, "O negócio do pau-brasil, a sociedade mercantil Purry, Mellish and Devisme e o mercado global de corantes: escalas mercantis, instituições e agentes ultramarinos no século XVIII," *Revista de História*, no. 177 (May 2018): 25–26.

68 Dias, "O negócio do pau-brasil," 31; Tijl Vanneste, *Global Trade and Commercial Networks: Eighteenth-Century Diamond Merchants* (Pickering & Chatto, 2016), 55.

69 Labourdette, *La Nation française à Lisbonne*, 532.

70 Dias, "O negócio do pau-brasil," 25, 32; Agostinho Rui Marques Araújo, "Das Riquezas Do Brasil Aos Gastos e Gostos de Um Suíço Em Lisboa. David de Purry, Um Amigo de Pombal

Gerard Devisme, or *de Visme*, was born in London in 1726 and settled in Lisbon in 1746. His Huguenot family was originally from Picardy in France, and because of the revocation of the Edict of Nantes, they took refuge in England. He was educated at Westminster School and was probably apprenticed in the London trading house of his Dutch-born godfather, the merchant Gerard Vanneck. He went to Portugal at the age of 20, and in 1749 joined the company that had been established in 1740 by Purry and Mellish. The links between Purry and Devisme were probably facilitated and brokered by Vanneck, who in 1736 had financially helped Purry establish his first commercial company in Portugal.[71] Devisme made a fortune, and already in the Pombaline era, he was one of the country's most prominent merchants and tax farmers. He had a wide social circle in which he likely built a network of friends and acquaintances. Devisme had a good relationship with the French ambassador to Portugal, Bombelles, and preserved a certain admiration for the things of France. According to the ambassador: "there is no Englishman who shuns Anglicism and hatred of the French nation as Mr. Devisme. He likes the products of our industry [...] he uses our artists daily: the bronzes, the porcelain placed in his properties come from France".[72] The Huguenots, after a long time opposed by the French government, were allowed to enter as members of the French factory in Portugal around the middle of the eighteenth century. However, despite Devisme's admiration for the French, he and other merchants with French origins in Lisbon did not want to join this factory. Like Devisme, the "Auriol, Pratviel, Hoissard, des Minier, des Garnault, des Berthon, des Perrochon" chose to remain under the protection of England or the Netherlands.[73] Devisme was known for the parties he promoted, where important political figures joined, such as the Spanish and English ambassadors and members of the English mercantile community. He remained in Lisbon until 1792.[74] Likewise, Joseph Mellish came from a family of London merchants who began trading in the

---

(1709–1786)," *Revista Da Faculdade de Letras – Ciências e Técnicas Do Património*, I, vol. 2 (2003): 109–37; Melo, "O Negócio de Pernambuco," 108.

71 Gerald Luckhurst, "Gerard de Visme: 1755 and All That Came Afterwards," *The British Historical Society of Portugal* 44 (2017): 111–16.

72 "Il n'y a pas d'Anglais qui pousse l'anglicisme et la haine pour la nation française aussi loin que M. de Vismes. Il aime les produits de notre industrie [...] il a recours journellement à nos artistes: les bronzes, les porcelaines placés sans goût dans ses possessions viennent de France ...". Bombelles, *Journal d'un ambassadeur de France au Portugal, 1786–1788*, 93.

73 Labourdette, *La Nation française à Lisbonne*, 40.

74 A. R. Walford, "Gerard de Visme, Founder of the British Hospital (1793) and Member of the British Factory in Lisbon," *7th Annual Report of the British Historical Association* (1943).

early seventeenth century. Besides having business in Portugal, he was also involved in banking investment in London and was an associate of the Russia Company.[75] He was a member of the English parliament in the 1760s, and in addition to trading Brazilwood, he also exported grains from the United States to Portugal-based merchant Joaquim Pedro Quintela,[76] an important merchant of Brazilian diamonds[77] and one of the largest cotton exporters in Lisbon in 1782 (see Appendix B).

The interest of these British merchants in the cotton trade began at the time of the GCGPM. It was a very marginal business, though. Between 1760 and 1777, cotton only made-up 8% of everything they bought from the monopoly company. The bulk of Purry, Mellish, and Devisme's interests lay in obtaining cocoa from northern Brazil, making up 90% of their purchases. They bought colonial goods with money (about 71 million *réis*), but it is possible that part of this capital came from sales they made to the GCGPM: around seventeen million *réis* of goods were sold to the company, and among the products were armaments, gunpowder, and English and Asian textiles.[78] To a greater or lesser degree, other foreign firms proceeded in a similar way to Purry, Mellish, and Devisme in their dealings with the GCGPM. For example, the French brothers Paulo and Auriol Bonifas and the Dutch merchant Ludero Illius & Co sold and bought from the GCGPM, and there was still a particular preference for cocoa over cotton.[79] These merchants would remain in business after the GCGPM monopoly but not as the leading cotton merchants. Purry, Mellish, and Devisme apparently were not interested in exporting cotton in the early 1780s. It was only after the death of David Purry in 1786, with the firm renamed Mellish & Devisme, that they became keen on buying cotton in Lisbon and shipping it to European ports. In 1789 and 1792, Mellish & Devisme concentrated their shipments to Liverpool. Genoa was their second most important port, followed by London and Rouen. Furthermore, they were one of the few merchants that exported cotton directly to Leith (see Appendix B).

75 Records of the Archdeaconry of Nottingham, 1556–1942 – Papers of the Mellish Family of Hodsock, Nottinghamshire, c.1160–1991. https://mss-cat.nottingham.ac.uk/Calmview/Record.aspx?src=CalmView.Catalog&id=Me.

76 Dias, "O negócio do pau-brasil," 29.

77 Bernstein, *The Brazilian Diamond*, 63; Vanneste, *Global Trade and Commercial Networks*, 57.

78 Martins, "A Companhia Geral de Comércio Do Grão-Pará e Maranhão," 278–81.

79 Martins, "A Companhia Geral de Comércio Do Grão-Pará e Maranhão," 272–83.

6 Non-English Exporters and Consular Activity

Few non-Englishmen exported cotton in significant quantities to England. The British were pivotal to exports to England, but as Table 6.5 shows, they did not monopolize this trade. The only Portuguese with any relevance was João Pedro Manesch in 1799, who was one of the main dispatchers in the Lisbon customs, and thus someone in a privileged position, with vast knowledge of the import and export markets (Table 5.4). His main market was London. The German companies of Arnaldo Henrique and Bernardo Henrique Metzner were active in the cotton trade during most of the period. The growing merchant community of German immigrants in England likely facilitated the business of the two firms in Lisbon.[80] In addition to cotton exports to Liverpool and London, the two companies also did business with Hamburg, Amsterdam, Stockholm, Riga, Cádiz, Copenhagen, St. Petersburg, Bremen, Danzig, and even Montevideo.[81] Bernardo Henrique Metzner even had direct business with Brazil. In 1780, Antônio José Marques Guimarães, a resident of Maranhão, was indebted to him. Guimarães was also indebted to the French widow Frennelet.[82] Metzner delegated the task of charging Guimarães to José Vieira da Silva,[83] former administrator of the GCGPM in the colony and a famous planter in Itapecuru.[84] At the end of the same decade, Bernardo Henrique also did business with Bahia.[85]

Yet, one Dutchman in particular gained importance in the cotton trade, most likely due to his diplomatic and consular positions. Jacob Dohrman & Co. was a firm established by the brothers Jacob and Arnold Hendrik Dohrman. Arnold was probably the better known one of the two. He was born in 1748–1749, and until 1783 he lived in Lisbon, trading with Europe and the United States, where he had an agent. In the early 1780s, Portugal still did not recognize the independence of the United States of America, and Arnold was well-liked by the American government as he helped its citizens in Portugal. The fact that the Dutch merchants had a good relationship with all the belligerents encouraged Arnold to support the Americans. Moreover, Arnold actively participated in the revolutionary cause, as he financially helped the United States with war material and clothing. Additionally, besides money, he also helped

80 Chapman, *Merchant Enterprise in Britain*, 131.
81 Cunha, *Negociantes, mercadores e traficantes*, 196–209.
82 ANTT, 7° CNL, Ofício A, Cx. 100, liv. 604, f. 75v–76.
83 ANTT, 10° CNL, Cx. 19, liv. 101, f. 15–15v.
84 AHU, códice 598, f. 17v, f. 188v–189. Mota, "A Dinâmica Colonial," 29–30.
85 AHU, ACL, CU, 015, Cx. 192, Doc. 14042.

North American prisoners in Lisbon to return to their country. For these reasons, the American Congress appointed him an agent of the United States in Portugal around 1780. However, as his task was to assist the Americans, he came into conflict with the British in Portugal. With the end of the war, Arnold Dohrman was named consul of the United States in Portugal. In 1783, shortly before leaving Lisbon to the US, he established a company with his brother, Jacob. Arnold was the main partner, but he left the business in his brother's hands. As early as 1786, Jacob began trading alone, apparently dissolving the company while still retaining the Dohrman & Company name. For this new company, he had the help of his nephew, Daniel. Although they were no longer trading partners, Arnold appointed his brother as an agent of the United States in Portugal, and his task would be to assist Americans there.[86]

Soon after moving to the United States, Arnold began looking for new commercial contacts to expand the business. One of Arnold's attributes was his reputation for helping Americans in Portugal by providing them with housing, food, and clothing during the war. Although he did not do it for free—as the United States government reimbursed him for his expenses—Arnold used this argument to show potential business partners that he was a trustworthy person. While Arnold was trying to establish himself commercially in the US, Jacob and his other brother George were at odds with each other. Furthermore, Jacob went bankrupt in 1787 and, in debt, fled to Spain. George, who traded on his own, warned Arnold to appoint someone else to be the United States agent in Portugal as if they knew about Jacob's malpractices, this could harm Arnold in the United States. However, Arnold did not replace Jacob. He continued in his role as an agent of the United States, which was remunerated according to the payments that the captains of American ships paid him when they entered the Tagus River (these were the fees paid to the consul who was Arnold, but Jacob, as an agent, was the person receiving the money). The very next year, apparently recovered financially, Jacob informed Arnold that "incited by a well-known English house," John Bulkeley & Son, the ship captains were unwilling to pay the fees that had recently been raised. John Bulkeley & Son were also major cotton exporters in Lisbon (see Appendix B), and according to Arnold, it was a firm that had a "bad reputation" among New England merchants. The reason John Bulkeley & Son were conspiring against the Dohrman's, according to Arnold, was because the British firm wanted to rob him of the post of the consul of the Americans in Portugal or at least take the position of agent. This,

86 Jorge Martins Ribeiro, "Comércio e diplomacia nas relações luso-americanas: 1776–1822" (PhD diss., Universidade do Porto, 1997), 333–37.

however, did not happen; the Dohrmans continued to act as consuls of the Americans until 1793 when someone else replaced them.[87]

Probably the loss of this post was more severe for Jacob than for Arnold. A job at the American consulate, whether as consul, vice-consul, or agent, was an occupation that made it possible to increase his commission on sales of goods from the United States, as Jacob himself admitted in 1791. Arnold still had the refunds that Congress had given him for past services. With this money, he bought six ships that did business with various ports of Europe, bought land, and invested money in a bank and industry in the United States. But even during the 1790s, he was interested in trade with Portugal, as he repeatedly asked Jacob to send him copies of Portuguese mercantile newspapers.[88] Coincidentally or not, the period in which Jacob exported the most Brazilian cotton was when he was directly connected with the United States in 1792. In that year, the vast majority of the cotton he shipped went to Liverpool. By 1806, however, the volume of its exports had fallen, and England was no longer its primary market. Trieste and Marseille were where his main clients were, at a time when Napoleon was trying to put into practice the continental blockade against England (see Appendix B).

7 Cotton Purchases in Portugal

How did the English factory, or any other foreign merchant, buy cotton in Lisbon? Generally speaking, direct access to the first cotton sellers (the growers) or even the second (the merchants in colonial ports) was rare. There are a series of clues left by chroniclers and an interpretation deeply rooted in historiography that trade with Brazil was only allowed to Portuguese subjects.[89] Nevertheless, there are some hints that foreign merchants were trading directly with Brazil. The case of Koster, mentioned earlier in this chapter, is a good example. Like the Portuguese trading with Brazil, Koster probably aimed to recover the capital he had lent to merchants in Pernambuco through the goods (possibly sugar and cotton) that the debtors would send him from Brazil. It does not make a difference that this strategy went wrong because of the default of debtors in

87 Ribeiro, "Comércio e diplomacia nas relações luso-americanas," 340–42, 352.

88 Ribeiro, "Comércio e diplomacia nas relações luso-americanas," 347, 352. More information about the Dohrmans can be found at Tyson Reeder, *Smugglers, Pirates, and Patriots: Free Trade in the Age of Revolution* (University of Pennsylvania Press, 2019), 82–83.

89 Carrere, *A Picture of Lisbon, Taken on the Spot: Being a Description Moral, Civil, Political, Physical and Religious, of That Capital; with Sketches of the Government Character and Manners of the Portuguese in General …*, 38; Novais, *Portugal e Brasil*.

Pernambuco. What matters is that a foreign merchant could negotiate directly with Brazil. Yet, few foreigners imported cotton directly from Brazil. The biggest cotton importers in Lisbon were Portuguese (Chapter 5, Table 5.3). This obviously begs the question of why foreigners did not participate more fully in Brazil's imports.

Perhaps one answer to this question is to be found in French consular correspondence. In the context of the Seven Years' War, more specifically in 1762, trade between Portugal and France ceased, and all French people in Portugal were asked to become naturalized within 15 days; otherwise, they would be banned from the country, and their goods would be confiscated. Except for two French merchants who returned to France, the rest were naturalized Portuguese. After the war, and with the King of Portugal permitting French naturalized Portuguese to return to French citizenship, the newly appointed French consul in Portugal contemplated suggesting dual nationality for them. Thus, he suggested that they could engage in direct trade with Brazil, which would be beneficial for France. Nevertheless, the traders elucidated to the consul that this approach would be ineffective. To settle in Brazil, huge capital was needed, which French traders did not have, and even if they did, it would be a risky venture for four reasons: 1) The inhabitants and merchants of Brazil depended on long-term credits, which French creditors had to concede, as this was the custom; 2) This credit was in goods, and French goods were always in small quantities. If the French did not have this credit in Brazil, the "Brazilians" would seek it in Lisbon from the hands of other foreigners or even through the Portuguese; 3) There was no justice in Brazil to make debtors pay. They paid when they wanted; and 4) Finally, it was not favorable for the French to negotiate directly with Brazil because the payment when it came—came in the form of sugar, and the French did not need sugar, as they had their colonies in the West Indies that offered it in abundance.[90]

The arguments of the French merchants are supported by other evidence. Several Portuguese companies trading between Pernambuco and Lisbon depended on the capital of residents in Lisbon and not Brazil.[91] Thus, even if there were foreign merchant houses in Brazil, they would enter into serious competition with the houses in Lisbon regarding the supply of capital, that is, of European goods. The point raised by French merchants about Brazilians paying debts only when they wished is confirmed, as we have seen, by Koster's negotiation in the 1780s, which failed because of bad debtors. After the Brazilian gold cycle, what was left to be brought from Brazil was sugar, and

90 Labourdette, *La Nation française à Lisbonne*, 32–33.
91 Melo, "Hierarquias mercantis no Atlântico Português".

like the French, the English were not interested in this commodity either. In fact, the treaties signed between Portugal and England in the seventeenth century allowed the English to establish a very limited number of trading houses in Brazil. But according to Kenneth Maxwell, this was a "dead letter,"[92] an interpretation shared by Fernando Novais. One of the treaties signed with the British allowed four British families to settle in Salvador, then the capital of the State of Brazil. But the King of Portugal himself instructed the governor of Bahia in 1707 to try "with skill to give them so little shelter and favor that they dislike going to trade for the conquests because it will be very useful if our subjects will trade there." To Novais, it seems that the King's wishes came true, as the English did not settle in Salvador.[93] According to Vitorino Magalhães Godinho, there were even "foreign trading houses" in Brazil, but they were all expelled because of the smuggling of gold.[94] The French consul in Lisbon in 1778 stated that foreigners were not negotiating directly with Brazil.[95] Violet Mary Shillington and Annie Beatrice Wallis Chapman argued that the British negotiating directly with Brazil was so out of date that it became irrelevant. The English consul himself declared in 1787 that the British had no direct participation in trade with Brazil, but they contributed with capital.[96]

The foreign capital was used by traveling agents (*comissários volantes*) who went to Brazil or by Portuguese merchants based in Portugal who had business in Portuguese America. British factors sold products to them on the condition that they paid an upfront sum for the goods taken on credit. With this amount, the factors took their commission and still paid the principal merchants in England. According to Shaw, this system worked,[97] and when the debtors did not pay, the English lender could take the case to the courts. Since the treaty of 1654, the English were entitled to a special court in which they had their own judge. The judge conservator was accountable for collecting Portuguese debtors, and the British had designed this job precisely because they found the

92 Maxwell, "Pombal and the Nationalization of the Luso-Brazilian Economy," 613.

93 "com destreza fazer-lhes tão pouco agasalho e favor que eles se desgostem de ir comerciar às conquistas, porque será mui útil que se vão comerciar a elas os nossos vassalos." See Novais, *Portugal e Brasil*, 181–82.

94 Vitorino Magalhães Godinho, "Portugal, as frotas do açúcar e as frotas do ouro (1670—1770)," *Revista de História* 7, no. 15 (1953): 84.

95 Godinho, *Prix et monnaies au Portugal*, 339.

96 Shillington and Chapman, *The Commercial Relations of England and Portugal*, 283–85; see also Carlos Gabriel Guimarães, "A Inserção Dos Ingleses No Império Português: O Caso Da Família Gulston No Rio de Janeiro, c.1710-c.1720," in *A Segunda Escravidão e o Império Do Brasil Em Perspectiva Histórica*, ed. Mariana Muaze and Ricardo H. Salles (Casa Leiria, 2020).

97 Shaw, *The Anglo-Portuguese Alliance*, 119–20.

Portuguese institutions of justice too slow, corrupt, and at times prejudiced towards Protestants. According to Shaw, English merchants worked on small profit margins, and it was crucial that their debtors pay as quickly as possible so that the factors could pay their own creditors. That is why the figure of the judge conservator was essential to them.[98] However, the powers of the English judge conservator could not be extended to Brazil,[99] which perhaps further repelled the English in Portugal from doing direct trade with the Portuguese colonies. It remained for them to seal agreements with the Portuguese in Portugal, where they had more resources to recover their capital. British merchants, as creditors, were not obliged to comply with the moratoriums favorable to Portuguese debtors issued by the King of Portugal, for instance.[100] The French themselves acknowledged British infiltration through Portuguese intermediaries to trade with Brazil. Dumouriez even estimated that more than half of the trade with Brazil, from Lisbon, was in the hands of the British.[101]

Thus, the English, and foreigners in general, could even lend money to the Portuguese to trade with Brazil, but they were rarely interested in dealing directly with Portuguese America. According to data on imports of cotton from Brazil, it was the Portuguese who dominated this business (Appendix A, and Table 5.3). This indicates that the usual way for foreigners to obtain cotton in Lisbon was to buy it from Portuguese merchants. One of the biggest exporters of the English factory in Lisbon in 1789 and 1792, Daniel Bowden & Son, provides an interesting example of cotton purchases in Lisbon (Appendix B). The deal took place in early 1806. At that time, Daniel's firm was called Bowden & Co. A group of 18 Lisbon merchants had sold "huge amounts" of cotton bales to Bowden in mid-1805. Nevertheless, he failed to make the payment on time and dispatched the bales to England. For six months, Lisbon merchants were promised payments by Bowden that never came. But perhaps what worried them the most was a widespread rumor that Bowden was planning to move "secretly" to England.[102] The group of merchants urged the Portuguese Foreign Minister to ask the British envoy not to provide a passport for Bowden to return to England. The Portuguese minister replied that the case should go to the British judge conservator but that Bowden should be monitored so that he would not enter any vessel until he gave the creditors some kind of security—a

98 Shaw, *The Anglo-Portuguese Alliance*, 65, 82.

99 NA, FO 63/19, June 1794.

100 NA, FO 63/14, February 1791.

101 Charles François Du Périer Dumouriez, *An Account of Portugal, as It Appeared in 1766 to Dumouriez: Since a Celebrated General in the French Army* (C. Law, 1797), 36, 86, 200; Novais, *Portugal e Brasil*, 183.

102 "clandestinamente".

guarantor, for example—that he would pay the debts.[103] Apparently, Bowden left Lisbon as he did not appear as an exporter in 1806. Of the 18 merchants, only one was a foreigner, the French consul in Porto, one of the most prominent businessmen in Portugal, Bernardo Clamousse.[104] In addition to being a merchant, he also built a cotton factory, which he later turned into a tanning factory.[105]

Bowden's plan to flee Portugal may mean that he was avoiding paying his creditors. Still, it could also have been prompted by threats of a French invasion and possible confiscation of British property in the country. In fact, given the escalation of conflicts between France and England, many Englishmen may have withdrawn from Portugal before the invasion at the end of 1807.[106] Payment terms (*pagamento a prazo*) promised by Bowden to the group of 18 merchants in Portugal could have been a widespread tactic in the cotton trade and proof that he was only a factor (agent) and that he worked for the principals in England: he bought the cotton in Lisbon and was waiting for his bosses or clients to send him the capital to pay the Portuguese suppliers.

The interval between the arrival of cotton from Brazil and its sale outside Portugal could be long. As the Portuguese cotton textile industry was small compared to other countries, the vast majority of Brazilian cotton in Lisbon was exported. Between 1796 and 1807, Portugal imported 5,280,826 arrobas of cotton from Brazil, and out of these, it exported 4,640,225 abroad. In 11 years, only 640,601 arrobas (12% of the total imported) remained in Portugal or 53,383 arrobas in annual averages.[107] Cotton sales did not take place immediately after the fiber landed in Portugal: in some years, there was a build-up of stocks. Sales should occur as with other goods, through exchange of foreign products for cotton, or even payment in cash or opening an account with importers in Lisbon. Still, that merchants somehow retained cotton in Lisbon before being

---

103 ANTT. Ministério do Reino, mç. 956, proc. 37.

104 The other dealers, except for Clamouse and an illegible name, were José Alves Branco, Bento José Pacheco e Filhos, Felipe Ribeiro Figueiras, Manuel de Souza Freire e Companhia, Francisco José Bandeira e Companhia, José Pereira de Souza, Maria Luiza Potier, Manuel Ribeiro Guimarães, Joaquim Ramos de Araújo, Antônio José de Lemos, José Joaquim Barbosa, Antônio Esteves Costa e Irmão, Veríssimo Rodrigues Belo e Companhia, Francisco José de Souza, João Fernandes dos Santos, and Henrique José Gonçalves. See, ANTT. Ministério do Reino, mç. 956, proc. 37.

105 Pedreira, "Os Homens de Negócio Da Praça de Lisboa," 190, 366.

106 See Appendix E for the members of the English factory in Portugal at this time; some would move to Brazil and others to England.

107 Arruda, *O Brasil no comércio colonial*, 368–71.

promptly shipped abroad indicates that Lisbon's customs and merchants' warehouses served as significant venues for speculating on cotton prices.[108]

Although the law stipulated a time limit during which goods could stay in customs, it was such a long interval that it should not worry merchants in Lisbon too much: dry goods, like cotton, could stay up to three years there, counted from the moment vessels unloaded them. After the deadline, customs officials were supposed to post notices (*editais*) on the customs' doors warning the owners of the goods. If they did not come to pick up the goods within 30 days, customs' officials would auction them, and the costs of the auctions would be the owners' responsibility.[109] Auctions were also used in another way. It could happen that when a merchant died, his assets were auctioned off. This was the case of the deceased Antônio José dos Santos. In 1794, in his former house, at that time inhabited by Thomas Bellinge, an auction was carried out for more than 400 bales of cotton from Pernambuco, Paraíba, and Bahia.[110]

8 Shifts in the Trade Balance and Smuggling

The commercial growth achieved by Portugal at the end of the eighteenth century opened the doors to a new form of commercialization. If, on the one hand, the English factory had recovered the number of members it had lost with the Brazilian gold depression, on the other hand, the balance of trade between Portugal and England had changed radically.[111] Historically, Portugal has always had a trade deficit with England. But the situation began with reverse in the mid-1780s, and every year from 1790 to 1807, Portugal had a trade surplus with England. Broadly speaking, Portugal had a trade surplus with all foreign nations from 1797 to 1807. Concomitantly, Portugal had a trade deficit with Brazil. Overall, "the advantages of foreign trade outweighed the losses of colonial trade, and the general trend was surplus." The scenario from 1797 to 1807 was totally different from what happened in 1776, 1777, and 1787. In those three years, Portugal had a trade surplus with the colonies and a deficit with foreign

108 See, for example, the case of Bento José Pacheco and cotton sales within *Casa da Índia* in chapter 5.

109 Antonio Delgado Silva, *Collecção da legislação Portugueza desde a ultima compilação das ordenações: Legislação de 1802 a 1810* (Typ. Maigrense, 1826), 5: 253.

110 Manuel Lopes de Almeida, *Notícias Históricas de Portugal e Brasil* (*1751–1800*) (Coimbra Editora, 1964), 275, 285.

111 Fisher, "Lisbon, Its English Merchant Community and the Mediterranean in the Eighteenth Century," 24.

nations.[112] The weight of Brazil was tremendous for Portuguese trade: on average, "Brazil participated with 83.7% of Portuguese imports and received 78.4% of its exports from the colonies."[113] In turn, the weight of England was still substantial, despite the diversification of trade partners that Portugal reached at that time.[114] On average, considering all of Portugal's trading partners, England stood out, as 34% of Portuguese imports came from it, and about 39% of Portugal's exports were destined to England. Portugal had a trade surplus with England, as it had with Hamburg, Italy, France, Castile, and Denmark. Thus, to a large extent, "Portugal had a deficit in trade with the colonies due to the position of Brazil, and it had a surplus in foreign trade, at least in large part thanks to its exchange with England."[115] The way in which England paid for its imports was through the shipment of gold to Portugal. Therefore, Portugal, which three or four decades before was sending gold from Brazil to pay for its imports from England, was at the end of the century receiving gold from the English in exchange for cotton. Gold made its way to Brazil and the two largest cotton-growing regions, Maranhão and Pernambuco, were the two largest gold importers in Portuguese America.[116]

The very members of the English factory in Lisbon reported that "the old flow of gold from Brazil through Portugal to England was replaced by the flow of raw cotton." They said that "from less than one hundred thousand pounds sterling in 1785, the import of raw cotton from Portugal to England grew to over six hundred thousand pounds in value in 1791." Of all the "cotton exported from Lisbon in 1791, about 4,800,000 lbs. came from Pernambuco and about 3,000,000 from Maranhão. The rest came from Pará, Bahia, and Rio de Janeiro." Still in 1791, the balance of trade was favorable to Portugal, and England had to send gold to Lisbon—which would later go to Brazil—to buy cotton. Around 1806, the English envoy to Portugal, Strangford, even proposed an updated version of the Methuen treaty "by which Portugal should admit English manufactures of cotton at twenty percent ad valorem, while England would give preference to raw cotton from Brazil." But the treaty did not materialize.[117]

112 Novais, *Portugal e Brasil*, 289.

113 Novais, *Portugal e Brasil*, 290.

114 Costa, "Relações Económicas Com o Exterior"; Cruz, "The Diversification of Portugal's Commercial Relations in the Late Eighteenth Century".

115 Novais, *Portugal e Brasil*, 290–92.

116 Shillington and Chapman, *The Commercial Relations of England and Portugal*, 290–91; Alexandre, *Os sentidos do Império*, 68; Maximiliano M. Menz, *Entre impérios: formação do Rio Grande na crise do sistema colonial português (1777–1822)* (Alameda, 2009), 93.

117 Manchester, *British Preeminence in Brazil*, 52, 59.

Sixteen years prior, Robert Walpole, an ambassador and high-ranking diplomat in Portugal, posed a query to Luís Pinto de Sousa Coutinho, the Secretary of State for Foreign Affairs and War, on the crucial component of the Empire's political economy. Walpole found it highly peculiar that Portugal prohibited the importation of cotton fabrics from England while yet exporting significant amounts of raw cotton to his country. In addition, he found it intriguing that while Portugal aimed to grow its cotton textile industry, it simultaneously permitted the huge importation of cotton textiles from India. Why not ban these imports from Asia, and use Brazilian cotton in the Portuguese domestic industry or even allow the entry of cotton goods from England, increasing commercial complementarity between the two countries? Coutinho's response was succinct and lacking in detail, only stating that Portugal purchased cotton articles from India "to aid in navigation."[118] This was a clear statement of the "maritime vocation" of the Portuguese and their persistence in a "transport policy."[119]

Still according to Walpole, as England could not export cotton textiles (pure or mixed), they had to send gold to Portugal to pay for the imports.[120] And, as Brazil exported more items to Portugal than it imported, the resulting imbalance was also settled with money. However, Walpole argued that this had a detrimental outcome. When he wrote this, he thought that "money is the worst remittance that can be received from the Brazils; therefore, independent of any balance that may be due to the Colonies; it is sent in mercantile speculation back for the better purchasing of effects." Simply put, a portion of the money that was sent to Brazil was subsequently brought back to Portugal for the purpose of investing in the acquisition of products and engaging in speculative activities. According to Walpole, the situation had reached that point due to the exorbitant prices obtained for Brazilian commodities, namely sugar and cotton. Sugar was expensive because of the "failure of the crops in the French West Indies," which he attributed to "political convulsion" which resulted in the neglect of crops and also to hurricanes that had recently hit the region. Cotton was expensive because of the high demand from the British industry, mainly for cotton from Pernambuco. This cotton was paid for with money, as

118 NA, FO 63/12, May 1789.

119 António Sérgio, *Ensaios III* (Livraria Sá da Costa, 1974); Costa, *O transporte no Atlântico e a Companhia Geral do Comércio do Brasil, 1580–1663*, 1: 36.

120 The National Archives Kew, FO 63/15. Only with the treaty of 1810, Portugal would allow imports of cotton textiles from Britain; see Nuno Luís Madureira, *Mercado e Privilégios: A Indústria Portuguesa Entre 1750 e 1834* (Estampa, 1997), 314.

Portuguese/Brazilian sellers "know but little of foreign bills of Exchange; they always insist on ready Money for payment."[121]

As a result of this significant adjustment, there was an increase in the exchange rate against England. During most of the eighteenth century, the exchange rate for the *mil-réis* ranged from 65 to 66 pence. As the export of commodities from Portugal increased and the export of bullion decreased, the exchange rate naturally went up. Starting in 1786, there was consistent and ongoing growth. The value of the *mil-réis* in 1788 was calculated to be 66.5 d., 66.75 d. in 1789, 67 d. in 1790, and 67.5 d. in 1792. However, the previous rate mentioned was simply a nominal rate. The actual rate has been defined as 72. 5 d. Yet, this year appears to have been exceptionally unique. By 1798, the inherent exchange value per *mil-réis* had reverted back to 67.5 d.[122]

One of the reasons England never openly demanded direct trade with Brazil was because England always exported more to Portugal than it imported, and it had merchants in Portugal who were able to access markets in Brazil, at least through financing. But in the last decades of the eighteenth century, Portugal was in a "more egalitarian" situation with England.[123] This new scenario, most likely, boosted smuggling. With an eye on the Brazilian market, both for its cotton supply and for its consumer market, the illegal trade most likely increased.[124] According to Francisco José de Lima, an informant writing from England in 1799, there were "houses specializing in the business" of smuggling, working mainly in London and Liverpool. One of them was John Bammes, in London, which had more than eight ships dedicated solely to smuggling with Brazil. They were ships that left England armed, apparently to face the French, but which actually carried a series of goods (such as cotton cloth and gunpowder) to trade in Brazil. Traders could smuggle in two ways: 1) the English smugglers already had correspondents in Brazil prepared to do business; or 2) they were sailing along the Brazilian coast waiting for small boats from the coast loaded with colonial goods. It was also reported that there were Portuguese working for commissions in the smuggling business within these British ships. According to this informant, the most important Portuguese trading house in England was "Dias Santos." It was Dias Santos who had denounced to Francisco

121 NA, FO 63/14, October 13, 1791.
122 Shillington and Chapman, *The Commercial Relations of England and Portugal*, 290.
123 Shillington and Chapman, *The Commercial Relations of England and Portugal*, xi–xii.
124 Ernst Pijning, "Sources and Historiography: Conceptualizations of Contraband Trade in Colonial Brazil," *América Latina En La Historia Económica*, no. 24 (December 2005): 67–84.

José de Lima and the Portuguese consul in England the practice of smuggling.[125] Dias Santos was also a cotton trader but a small one.[126]

As factors, the English merchants in Lisbon were agents and not principals. This was the commercial arrangement that characterized the foreign trade of England and that can be observed as early as the Elizabethan era.[127] However, as some exporters in Lisbon were large merchants, it was quite possible that they acted as principals and had agents in England. Merchants in Brazil could also access English markets as principals, using merchants in Lisbon as their agents, who had connections in England to sell cotton.[128] Yet, it was unlikely that Portuguese merchants had a significant number of companies with headquarters in Liverpool. This was one of the great differences that distinguished the English, who kept companies with members in Lisbon or Porto and members in London or Liverpool.

9 Conclusion

The English merchant community in Portugal, comprised of consuls and factors, was the leading exporter of cotton from the mid-1780s until 1807. Historically, English merchants were the most powerful in Lisbon. Yet, their story faced moments of difficulties. To some extent, the decline in Brazilian gold shipments and the changes in the political economy spearheaded by Pombal scared the English away or significantly reduced their interests in Portugal and the Portuguese Empire between the mid-1750s and the mid-1780s.

With the growing need for raw materials to supply the cotton industry in Britain, mainly in the north of England, the English regained interest in the Portuguese Empire. Supplies from the West Indies were no longer enough in the mid-1780s. Soon after, Brazilian cotton gained even more importance: because of the loss of Saint-Domingue and the French wars in the 1790s—and the commercial difficulties that derived from the state of war—Lisbon became a center with abundant quantities of raw cotton. By the end of the 1780s, English merchants in Portugal were the main protagonists in the cotton trade.

Old and new merchants took part in the business. Indeed, there was a commercial advantage for the British. In addition to the centuries-old treaties with the Portuguese, English merchants used their longstanding connections

125 Revista do Instituto Histórico Geográfico Brasileiro, Tomo LXV, Parte 1, 1902, 299–300.
126 According to the Lisbon customs books.
127 Willan, *Studies in Elizabethan Foreign Trade*.
128 IAHGP, códice 171, f. 93–94.

inherited from the gold and wine trade, simply adapting them for the cotton trade. Wealthy English tax farmers and a few merchants from other nationalities with strategic positions (such as dispatchers from *Casa da Índia* and consular members) also took advantage of this scenario. Given that most of the merchants who imported cotton from Brazil were Portuguese, how the English and other nationalities bought cotton for re-export lay in the purchases made by the Portuguese merchant community in Lisbon. In this setting, credit sales and the role of the Lisbon customs office and the merchants' warehouses were ever-present elements.

With the growth of Brazilian cotton also came a reversal in the Portuguese trade balance with England. Previously in deficit, the Portuguese balance reached surpluses. The English paid for raw cotton with gold. This was apparently not enough: with Brazilian cotton's rise, smuggling was employed more forcefully in the final moments of colonization. As far as it is possible to observe, the English factors in Lisbon fulfilled orders placed by English manufacturers asking for Brazilian cotton. Thus, understanding the cotton trade necessarily involves analyzing merchants, companies, and consumer demands in England. The following section explores the place of Brazilian cotton in the British market, its trading mechanisms, and traders.

CHAPTER 9

The Place of Brazilian Cotton in British Industry: Ports, Commercial Organization, and Traders

1 London as a Financial and Commercial Center

In 1789, Great Britain received most of its raw cotton from the West Indies: 31% from its own colonies and 19% from the French ones. Next came cotton from Brazil, with 14.8%, and, right behind, Turkey, with 14.5%. American cotton was marginal, not even reaching 1% of British imports.[1] During the 1790s, Brazil was probably the biggest cotton supplier to Liverpool, overshadowing cotton from the West Indies.[2] From Great Britain's perspective, cotton from the United States gained primacy from 1806 to 1810, accounting for more than 53% of imports. In second came the British West Indies and in third Brazil with 16%. These years were the peak of the shares exported by Brazil and Portugal into Great Britain, considering the extended time frame from 1786 to 1883.[3] Thus, it is fair to say that the golden age of Brazilian cotton in England can be located between the 1790s and the 1810s. Yet there have been many changes in this short period, both concerning the British ports that imported raw cotton and the trading community responsible for bringing and distributing the fiber to the industrial centers in Great Britain. This chapter seeks to cover these aspects.

Various ports in England, Scotland, and Ireland imported cotton from Portugal (see Appendix C) and, after 1808, directly from Brazil. But two of them were, by far, the most relevant: London and Liverpool. The first was critical in the early years but was gradually overtaken by the northern port. This change reflects the growth and importance of Liverpool in serving the needs of the textile centers of Lancashire and the surrounding area. Furthermore, the development of provincial ports, such as Liverpool, partly contributed to the consumer revolution that was taking place in England. Increasingly, populations outside London required colonial products such as tobacco, sugar, and rum.[4]

1 R. Reid, *Glasgow, Past and Present* (D. Robertson, 1884), 3: 369–70.
2 Henry Smithers, *Liverpool, Its Commerce, Statistics, and Institutions: With a History of the Cotton Trade* (T. Kaye, 1825), 147.
3 Ellison, *The Cotton Trade of Great Britain*, 86.
4 Paul G. E. Clemens, "The Rise of Liverpool, 1665–1750," *The Economic History Review* 29, no. 2 (1976): 213; see also Jan de Vries, *The Industrious Revolution: Consumer Behavior and the*

Both ports were the leading destinations for raw cotton worldwide, not just Brazilian. For much of the eighteenth century, London was England's biggest importer. Although imports from the West Indies declined over the century, London continued to import cotton in bulk from the Levant, either directly from Salonica or Leghorn or via the Continent. The cotton brought by merchants from London could be "transhipped coastwise by Liverpool"[5] or it could be transported overland to Lancashire.[6] England had a well-developed canal system linking its major rivers, including a connection between the River Thames and the Mersey opened in 1805.[7] As one of the oldest marketplaces and as a supplier of fiber to spinners since the seventeenth century, London managed to dominate the raw cotton market until 1795. London developed a certain specialization with cotton from Brazil, from the Levant, and from India. Lancashire manufacturers and merchants bought cotton in London when prices there were lower than in Northwest England. Until 1803, for example, the Strutts—a family famous for spinning cotton in Northwest England—bought most of their raw cotton from London. It was common for London merchants to send cotton price quotations to spinners and merchants in Northwest England, but there were also partnerships between merchants from London and dealers in the Northwest. This type of partnership also made it possible for cotton textiles in the Northwest to be shipped to London. North-western spinners and dealers also came to London in the hope of buying raw cotton in bulk and cheap.[8] Still in 1812, most Brazilian cotton that arrived in England was stored in London.[9] Cotton would soon be transported to Liverpool, but as noted in Chapter 7, London's role as a supplier of Brazilian cotton to France during the French wars, whether through licenses or smuggling, should not be ignored.[10]

London's place in the industrial revolution is complex. Yet, there seems to be a consensus in the literature that its importance resided in the services and

---

Household Economy, 1650 to the Present (Cambridge University Press, 2008); Maxine Berg, "Consumption and Global History in the Early Modern Period," in *Global Economic History*, ed. Tirthankar Roy and Giorgio Riello (Bloomsbury Academic, 2019).

5 Wadsworth and Mann, *The Cotton Trade and Industrial Lancashire, 1600–1780*, 233.

6 Graham L. Rees, *Britain's Commodity Markets* (Elek, 1972), 85.

7 Parkinson, *The Trade Winds*, 49.

8 Edwards, *The Growth of the British Cotton Trade*, 107–9; see also Sarah Palmer, "The Eighteenth Century Ports of London and Liverpool: Private V. Corporate Promotion," in *I Porti Come Impresa Economica: Atti Della "Diciannovesima Settimana Di Studi, " 2–6 Maggio 1987*, ed. Simonetta Cavaciocchi (Le Monnier, 1988).

9 Chapman, *Merchant Enterprise in Britain*, 83.

10 Melvin, *Napoleon's Navigation System*, 263, 304, 327–28; Daly, "English Smugglers, the Channel, and the Napoleonic Wars, 1800–1814"; Cardoso, "Lifting the Continental Blockade," 92.

financing sectors as well as manufacturing.[11] In 1826–27 there were 1,224 textile manufacturing firms in London, employing 21,334 people. Of these, the silk industry, with 237 firms, was the most important. Conversely, there were no more than 87 firms manufacturing cotton. Textile finishing (such as dyeing and printing), famous in London at the beginning of the eighteenth century, lost importance at the end of the century. Apparently, one of the main reasons for this was the congestion of London's rivers. This critical energy source was abundant in Lancashire, where much of the textile finishing industry ended up going. Another part settled on the outskirts of London. Overall, trade, credit markets, and shipping services were more important to London than industry, making it a major import and export center for wholesale and retail.[12] In addition, London was one of the world's major financial hubs during the eighteenth century. This was one of the reasons the city hosted numerous trading houses of foreign merchants.

In Lancashire, the cotton industry was heavily financed by London credit, which meant that Manchester manufacturers and merchants had bank agents in London. From a standpoint of investment, the United States War of Independence was pivotal. London merchants and financiers who had provided capital to the American colonists faced bankruptcy due to defaults resulting from the war. This facilitated renowned Northern merchant manufacturers such as Livesey Hargreaves & Co., Peel, and Arkwright in getting capital from London, which was no longer flowing to America due to risk and warfare.[13] Londoners also settled in Manchester to become textile producers and employed agents in London to bring in raw cotton. For a long time, the manufacturers in Lancashire were dependent on the merchants and agents of

11 P. J. Corfield, *The Impact of English Towns, 1700–1800* (Oxford University Press, 1982), 71–72; P. J. Cain and A. G. Hopkins, "Gentlemanly Capitalism and British Expansion Overseas I. The Old Colonial System, 1688–1850," *The Economic History Review* 39, no. 4 (1986): 511; Christopher J. French, ""Crowded with Traders and a Great Commerce": London's Domination of English Overseas Trade, 1700–1775," *The London Journal* 17, no. 1 (1992): 30; see also Kocka, *Capitalism*, 61.

12 David C. Barnett, *London: Hub of the Industrial Revolution: A Revisionary History, 1775–1825* (Tauris Academic Studies, 1998), 3, 39, 55, 60, 87, 113; see also L. D. Schwarz, *London in the Age of Industrialisation: Entrepreneurs, Labour Force, and Living Conditions, 1700–1850* (Cambridge University Press, 1992), 226.

13 Chapman, *Merchant Enterprise in Britain*, 29, 38, 43, 52–53; Margrit Schulte Beerbühl, "Merchant Empires: Mercadores Hamburgueses Em Londres y Sus Redes de Comercio Internacional (1660–1815)," in *Comunidades Transnacionales: Colonias de Mercaderes Extranjeros En El Mundo Atlántico (1500–1830)*, ed. Ana Crespo Solana (Doce Calles, 2010), 105; see also Fernand Braudel, *Civilization and Capitalism, 15th-18th Century, Volume III: The Perspective of the World* (William Collins Sons & Co Ltd, 1984), 352–85.

London, but with "experience, capital, and connections," they gradually got rid of the Londoners and began "to open offices in the capital, selling to domestic consumers and to importers abroad."[14] Yet, London merchants never went out of business. Although Northern England's merchant manufacturers gained prominence, Londoners still had a share in the trade in cotton goods between 1760 and 1815. With the French wars, risks, bankruptcies, and tight profit margins, these Northern merchant manufacturers did not manage to stay in the trading business for a long time. As a result, London wholesalers again assumed the prominent role of sellers of cotton goods after 1815.[15] London, therefore, was always important to Lancashire: part of the raw material used by the textile industry in Northern England came from London, and part of the Lancashire production was sent to London.[16]

2 The Cotton Industry in Northern England and in the West of Scotland

As much as London received copious quantities of raw cotton for a long time, it was in the North of England that it would be used. The populous northern region of England (Lancashire, Cheshire, Derbyshire, and West Riding) concentrated 70% of the entire cotton industry at the end of the eighteenth century and 90% in 1835 (Map 9.1). In a way, this was the culmination of nearly two centuries of making cloth before the advent of water-powered factories and the other inventions and improvements in the second half of the eighteenth century. In this space of time, a capitalist class, specialized workers in the textile industry, and a working system (the domestic-system or putting out system) developed.[17] Between 1801 and 1821 a third of Lancashire's population was

14 Stanley D. Chapman, "The Commercial Sector," in *The Lancashire Cotton Industry. A History since 1700*, ed. Mary B. Rose (Lancashire County Books, 1996), 63–64, 72.

15 Chapman, *Merchant Enterprise in Britain*, 168–70, 175.

16 Chapman, *The Cotton Industry*, 11–12; Mary B. Rose, "Introduction: The Rise of the Cotton Industry in Lancashire to 1830," in *The Lancashire Cotton Industry. A History since 1700*, ed. Mary B. Rose (Lancashire County Books, 1996), 3; Chapman, "The Commercial Sector," 63.

17 Chapman, *The Cotton Industry*, 13, 19; see also Styles, "The Rise and Fall of the Spinning Jenny"; for other forms of industrial organization, see Maxine Berg, *The Age of Manufactures: Industry, Innovation, and Work in Britain, 1700–1820* (1985; Routledge, 1994). For proto-industrialisation, see Pat Hudson, *The Genesis of Industrial Capital: A Study of the West Riding Wool Textile Industry, c. 1750–1850* (Cambridge University Press, 1986); John K. Walton, "Proto-Industrialisation and the First Industrial Revolution: The Case of Lancashire," in *Regions and Industries a Perspective on the Industrial Revolution in Britain*, ed. Pat Hudson (Cambridge University Press, 1989); Franklin F. Mendels, "Proto-Industrialization: The First Phase of the Industrialization Process," *The Journal of Economic History*

MAP 9.1 Main districts for the cotton industry in the beginning of the nineteenth century
Sources: Chapman, *The Cotton Industry*, 13, 19. Wadsworth and Mann, *The Cotton Trade*, 218. Daniels, "Samuel Crompton's Census," 108. Farnie, *The English Cotton Industry*, 24. Map prepared by the author.

employed producing cotton goods.[18] By 1811, Manchester was England's leading cotton manufacturing center with over a million spindles, although it was to lose ground to neighbouring towns in the years to come.[19] For comparison pur-

32, no. 1 (1972): 241–61; Hans Medick, "The Proto-Industrial Family Economy: The Structural Function of Household and Family during the Transition from Peasant Society to Industrial Capitalism," *Social History* 1, no. 3 (1976): 291–315; Peter Kriedte, *Peasants, Landlords and Merchant Capitalists: Europe and the World Economy, 1500–1800* (1980; Berg Publishers, 1983); Sheilagh C. Ogilvie and Markus Cerman, eds., *European Proto-Industrialization* (Cambridge University Press, 1996).

18 Farnie, *The English Cotton Industry and the World Market, 1815–1896*, 24. For an overview of the industrial revolution and cotton, see Mokyr's introductory chapter on Joel Mokyr, ed., *The British Industrial Revolution: An Economic Perspective* (Westview Press, 1999), 1–127; Barbara Hahn, *Technology in the Industrial Revolution* (Cambridge University Press, 2020); Styles, "The Rise and Fall of the Spinning Jenny"; Peter Maw et al., "After the Great Inventions: Technological Change in UK Cotton Spinning, 1780–1835," *The Economic History Review* 75, no. 1 (2022): 22–55; Alexander Tertzakian, "Wages, Employment, and Technological Change in English Cotton Spinning, c.1780–1850" (Ph.D. diss., University of Cambridge, 2022).

19 John Langton and Robert John Morris, *Atlas of Industrializing Britain, 1780–1914* (Methuen, 1986), 108; G. W. Daniels, "Samuel Crompton's Census of the Cotton Industry in 1811," *Economic History* 2, no. 5 (1930): 108.

poses, France was far behind in the number of spindles at that time. In 1805, there were 800,000 spindles in France. Between 1843 and 1845, they jumped to 2,787,198, most of which were concentrated in the *Seine-Inférieure* and *Haut-Rhin* departments.[20]

The cotton industry was concentrated in Lancashire and found virtually no competitor within England. A series of factors favored this: the "poverty of natural resources," the "climate," the "water supply," the "textile tradition," the "mechanical inventions," and the access to labor and coal. The poverty of natural resources (few stones and wood for construction and the sterility of the soil) and the presence of mountains and marshy lands made Lancashire an isolated region from the rest of England with a low population density. At the same time, these conditions "also provided the great spur to the development of manufactures and the institutional framework for such development since it maintained the freedom of its communities from control by gild, corporation, or lord of the manor." The barrenness of the soil in East Lancashire and low land prices favored small-scale pastoral farming. In East Lancashire, the coarse woolen industry developed, controlled mainly by Yorkshire. In the west, the soil was better, and the flax industry grew under Ireland's influence. It was the "capitalist merchants" who organized these industries and sold their products. Very early, Lancashire was a region oriented not toward subsistence but toward the market.[21]

For centuries the British have been manufacturing textiles using materials such as wool, linen, and silk. The production techniques employed in these industries were similar to those used in cotton manufacturing. Furthermore, the presence of a production and commodification framework was already in progress. The old textile industries had established a robust production and marketing infrastructure that supported the rapidly growing cotton sector. This infrastructure included a production system centered around cottage-based manufacturing, importers with expertise in procuring raw materials, and exporters specializing in textile sales. The cotton business expanded due to the presence of consumer markets for textiles, both domestically in England and internationally.[22]

---

20 Chassagne, *Le Coton et Ses Patrons*, 268–69, 400.

21 Farnie, *The English Cotton Industry and the World Market, 1815–1896*, 46–47. See also Hudson, *The Industrial Revolution*; James Thomson, "Invention in the Industrial Revolution: The Case of Cotton," in *Exceptionalism and Industrialisation: Britain and Its European Rivals, 1688–1815*, ed. Leandro Prados de la Escosura (Cambridge University Press, 2004).

22 Deane, "The Industrial Revolution in Great Britain," 180. The wool industry also grew during the period of the first industrial revolution; see Phyllis Deane, "The Output of the British Woolen Industry in the Eighteenth Century," *The Journal of Economic History* 17,

The question of why mechanization took place in England and not in other countries has long been a topic of discussion in historical literature. The question of whether or not high salaries in the spinning industry influenced the development of labor-saving machinery has acquired significance in more recent times thanks to studies conducted by Robert C. Allen, Jane Humphries, and Benjamin Schneider.[23] While our understanding of spinning has significantly advanced via these efforts, it is undeniable that mechanization has led to a higher demand for raw materials. The spinning jenny, a creation of James Hargreaves in 1764, significantly enhanced spinning efficiency by enabling the involvement of children and young individuals in its operation. Nevertheless, the jenny was solely efficient in producing weft threads, and the spinners refrained from using it to create warp. Additionally, it was unsuitable for producing coarse yarn but exclusively good for fine yarn. In order for the jenny to function optimally, long-staple cottons sourced from the West Indies and Brazil proved to be more appropriate, while short-fiber cottons from the Levant were deemed unsuitable for this particular machine.[24] Conversely, the water-frame patented by Richard Arkwright in 1769 could spin warp threads yet was not suitable for making wefts. Cotton warps made with his machine were much cheaper than linen threads, which were the threads most used as warps up to that time. As a consequence, cotton cloths became cheaper.[25] Crompton, combining the principles of the frame and the jenny, invented his spinning mule in 1779. The mule was highly versatile since it had the ability to spin both

no. 2 (1957): 207–23; see also Parthasarathi, *Why Europe Grew Rich and Asia Did Not: Global Economic Divergence, 1600–1850*; Riello, "Cotton Textiles and the Industrial Revolution in a Global Context"; Jonathan P. Eacott, "Making an Imperial Compromise: The Calico Acts, the Atlantic Colonies, and the Structure of the British Empire," *The William and Mary Quarterly* 69, no. 4 (2012): 731–62.

23 Robert C. Allen, *The British Industrial Revolution in Global Perspective* (Cambridge University Press, 2009); Jane Humphries and Benjamin Schneider, "Spinning the Industrial Revolution," *The Economic History Review* 72, no. 1 (2019): 126–55; Robert C. Allen, "Spinning Their Wheels: A Reply to Jane Humphries and Benjamin Schneider," *The Economic History Review* 73, no. 4 (2020): 1128–36; Jane Humphries and Benjamin Schneider, "Losing the Thread: A Response to Robert Allen," *The Economic History Review* 73, no. 4 (2020): 1137–52.

24 Styles, "The Rise and Fall of the Spinning Jenny," 196, 217, 219; Hills, "Hargreaves, Arkwright and Crompton. Why Three Inventors?," 120.

25 Baines, *History of the Cotton Manufacture in Great Britain*, 163, 183; James A. Mann, *The Cotton Trade of Great Britain: Its Rise, Progress, & Present Extent, Based upon the Most Carefully Digested Statistics ...* (Simpkin, Marshall, 1860), 12; Arthur Young, *Annals of Agriculture, and Other Useful Arts*, XII (Bury St. Edmunds, 1789), 515.

warps and wefts, and was capable of producing yarns of varying coarseness, mediumness, and fineness.[26]

The jenny and the water-frame were capable of producing fustians, velverets, and calicoes, but neither machine had the ability to produce high-quality yarns needed for making muslins. However, the mule was ideally suited for producing it.[27] By 1793, every store sold British muslins that were visually indistinguishable from those of India but were priced at a discount of one-fourth or possibly more than one-third.[28] The muslin industry successfully captured a significant portion of the market that was previously dominated by fustians and silks. Muslins were highly sought after for summer clothing and nightwear, as well as various other garments including "gowns, petticoats, shawls, aprons, handkerchiefs, cravats, and waistcoats." The muslin trade had little importance until around 1785.[29] At that time, Brazil was the country that supplied the muslin and velveret trade with a portion of the higher-grade cotton wool that British merchants had unsuccessfully sought in the West Indies, India, and Africa.[30]

This high necessity for long staples—like those from Brazil but also from the West Indies—must have persisted until the 1810s. In the early nineteenth century, British spinners were satisfied with the medium fibers from the American South, the upland cotton. During the cotton supply crisis in 1813, spinners in England contended that their machinery was specifically tuned to spin upland cotton, making it difficult to attempt spinning other varieties. Nevertheless, certain spinners made adjustments to their machinery, specifically to accommodate the use of short fibers sourced from India. Therefore, it was possible to transition from one staple to another. Nevertheless, modifications were necessary, and the spinners were unwilling to be inconvenienced, thus favoring upland cotton over other options. In general, upland cotton proved to be more machine-friendly for spinning compared to similar types of Brazilian or West Indian cotton. Upland cotton possessed the most suitable qualities for manufacturing low-cost and medium-grade yarns, which were used in the creation of affordable calicoes and muslins.[31]

Another factor to be taken into account in the cotton business was the varying grades of yarn used for warps and wefts. Prior to the 1790s, the most sought-after fibers for spinning into warp yarns were long fibers from the

26 Maw et al., "After the Great Inventions," 25.

27 Edwards, *The Growth of the British Cotton Trade*, 5.

28 Baines, *History of the Cotton Manufacture in Great Britain*, 334; Farnie, "Cotton, 1780–1914," 723.

29 Edwards, *The Growth of the British Cotton Trade*, 37, 40–42.

30 Edwards, *The Growth of the British Cotton Trade*, 83.

31 Edwards, *The Growth of the British Cotton Trade*, 93, 103.

West Indies, Brazil, and the Sea Island. Cottons with short fibers, especially those originating from India and the Levant, were reserved for wefts. However, the introduction of medium upland cotton changed the market. The many varieties of upland cotton, characterized by their medium fiber length, could also be utilized for warps, though they were better suited for weaker warps. Russell states that spinners would have favored using long fiber for all warp threads and medium fiber for all weft threads. Still, due to the higher cost of long fibers, they resorted to using medium fibers for warp threads in lower-quality goods. In the mid-nineteenth century, the British industry had a high demand for specific types of medium staples, including Upland, Mobile, and New Orleans. By 1857, American cottons were predominantly utilized in the English cotton industry for both weft and warp production. During that year, the United States supplied 90 percent of the medium fiber cotton utilized in the industry. The remaining 10 percent consisted of a combination of long fiber and short fiber.[32] A century later, the textile industry had experienced minimal changes: long staple cottons "provide the textile industry with its highest qualities of cotton for use in the finest and strongest yarns, whilst the Upland types are the *bread-and-butter* cottons of commerce."[33]

Yet, even when American cotton was completely dominant, there were still distinct demands from British industry. During the 1830s, Ure observed that the raw cotton from Surat and Bengal, together with the inferior types of upland cottons, was utilized for producing coarse weft yarn. For high-quality muslins, it was necessary to use the finest fibers from Bahia, Demerara, New Orleans, and the lower-grade Sea-Island. The warps consisted of fibers sourced from New Orleans (or Louisiana), Egypt, Maranhão, Pernambuco, and Sea Island. However, during that period, the spinning industry had already achieved a high degree of complexity, enabling the blending of various grades of cotton.[34] The majority of the short fiber was used for the weft; however

32 Arthur W. Silver, *Manchester Men and Indian Cotton, 1847–1872* (Manchester University Press, 1966), 292–95; Edmund Russell, *Evolutionary History: Uniting History and Biology to Understand Life on Earth*, Studies in Environment and History (Cambridge University Press, 2011), 120.

33 E. Lord, "The Cotton Crop," in *Manual of Cotton Spinning, Volume 1*, ed. Alexander Frederick William Coulson (The Textile Institute, 1954), 89.

34 Andrew Ure, *The Cotton Manufacture of Great Britain: Systematically Investigated, and Illustrated by 150 Original Figures, Engraved on Wood and Steel; with an Introductory View of Its Comparative State in Foreign Countries, Drawn Chiefly from Personal Survey* (C. Knight, 1836), 2: 2; Andrew Ure, *The Cotton Manufacture of Great Britain: Systematically Investigated, and Illustrated by 150 Original Figures, Engraved on Wood and Steel; with an Introductory View of Its Comparative State in Foreign Countries, Drawn Chiefly from Personal Survey* (Knight, 1836), 1: lxx.

it could also be utilized for the coarsest type of warp if needed. It was typically blended with medium-fibered American cotton by spinners, but short fiber "could only be blended with it with much caution, and in very moderate proportions."[35] A considerable part of the warp threads made in Britain were exported, as it was common for spinners on the Continent to only make threads for wefts. According to Guest, "improvements in machinery and skill in the operative workmen are progressive, and in 1790 we [Britain] were in both so far advanced beyond all the continental nations put together, as to leave them scarcely the chance of success if they had attempted to rival us. By means of their agents sent over for the purchasing of twist [for warp], they have now acquired a knowledge of our machinery, and have many spinning factories; these are chiefly employed in making weft. The twist for their warps, which requires better machinery, and greater nicety and skill in spinning than weft, is supplied by the English."[36]

It is currently hard to determine which factors led to which: whether the upland cotton varieties adapted to the machines or whether the machine micro-inventions made it possible to use more medium fibers from the US. What is certain is that the influx of US cotton, in substantial volumes and at reduced prices, influenced a decline in the prices of all other cotton varieties traded in Great Britain. Prior to 1815, numerous price fluctuations occurred as a result of the repercussions of the French Wars on Atlantic trade and the challenges in accessing the blockaded ports in Europe (Figure 9.1). However, after the turbulent years of Napoleon had ended, the cotton industry in Europe still required long, fine fibers like those from Pernambuco, Sea Island from the United States, and the recently developed Jumel from Egypt. These cottons were indeed utilized less than upland cotton, yet were essential for the production of finer, luxurious fabrics. The cotton from Maranhão, being shorter in length than that from Pernambuco, suffered greater adverse effects, as it was readily substituted by cotton from the United States. This helps to explain why Pernambuco cotton did a little better in Brazil in the nineteenth century than Maranhão cotton.[37]

The high demand for cotton warps, initially driven by the production of velvet and later by the introduction of calico manufacturing by Arkwright,

35 Russell, *Evolutionary History* (Cambridge University Press, 2011), 120.

36 Guest, *A Compendious History of the Cotton-Manufacture*, 33–35.

37 Burlamaqui, *Monographia do algodoeiro*, 94–98; Soares, *Notas estatísticas sobre a produção agrícola e carestia dos gêneros alimentícios no Imperio do Brasil*, 266; Pereira, "The Cotton Trade and Brazilian Foreign Commerce," 154.

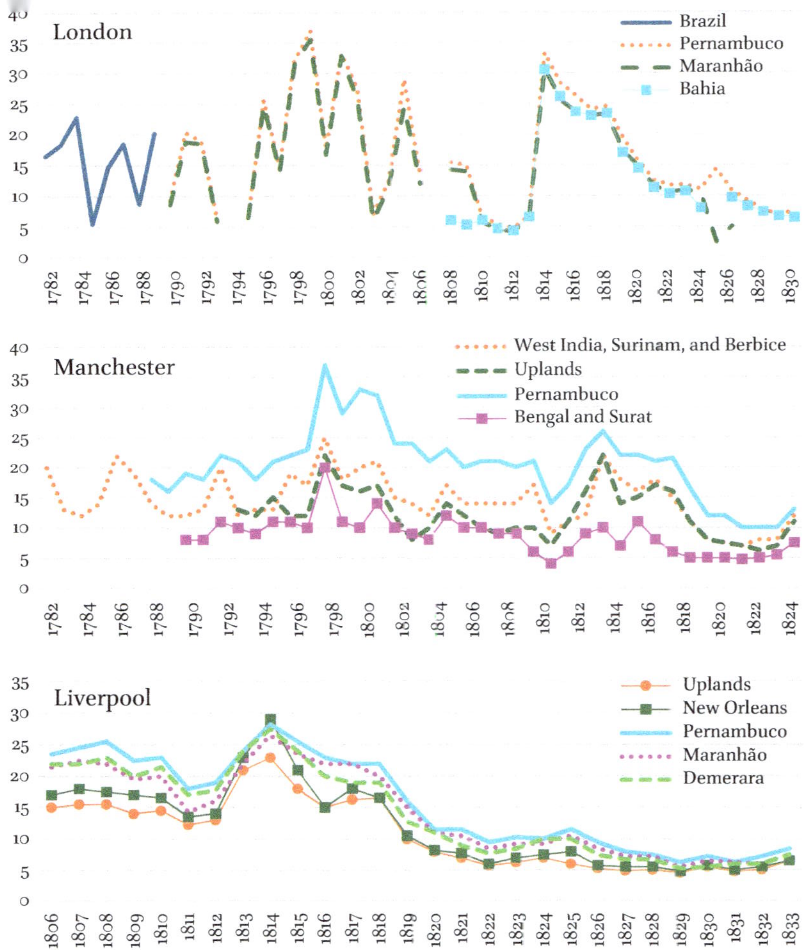

FIGURE 9.1
Prices of raw cotton in Great Britain, 1782–1833
Sources and notes: pence per pound. Price information at the time was generally given covering only the lowest and highest prices traded. The above charts are all based on averages of the lowest prices. London prices were obtained from multiple copies of the London Price Currents. From 1782 to 1785, and from 1813 to 1825, Guildhall Library, London. For 1786 and 1790, Beinecke Library, Yale University Library. From 1787 to 1789, and from 1796 to 1799, Seventeenth and Eighteenth Century Burney Newspapers Collection, British Library. For 1791 and 1792, Star and Evening Advertiser, Seventeenth and Eighteenth Century Burney Newspapers Collection. For 1793, *Some Information Respecting America* by Thomas Cooper, 1795. I was unable to locate any editions of the London Price Currents from 1794 and 1807. For 1795, American Antiquarian Society. From 1800 to 1806, and from 1826 to 1830, I collected prices from The British Newspaper Archive, on the following newspapers: Caledonian Mercury, Belfast News-Letter, Limerick Gazette, and Sheffield Independent. From 1808 to 1812, issues of the *Tradesman Or, Commercial Magazine*. Liverpool and Manchester prices were taken from Burn, *Statistics of the Cotton Trade Arranged in a Tabular Form: Also a Chronological History of Its Various Inventions, Improvements, Etc., Etc.* (Simpkin Marshall, 1847).
Figure prepared by the author.

provided a compelling incentive for small capitalists to invest in spinning jennies and warping mills.[38] "Colquhoun's estimates of 1789 indicate 310,000 water-frame spindles, 700,000 mule spindles, and 1,400,000 jenny spindles. By 1812, however, the mule had taken over with 4,209,570 spindles as against the 310,516 on water frames and only 158,880 on jennies."[39] In general, most cotton industries in the eighteenth century were relatively small in scale. It was the "growth and dispersion" of the Arkwright factory model that marked "the early development of the textile industry." On the whole, there were a few rich men who were the business magnates and many small businessmen who depended "on credit from merchants or merchant-manufacturers." But despite the presence of big figures in the business, "the cotton industry was never dominated by a handful of big capitalists." One of the big problems in expanding the cotton industry was capital. Even big firms found it difficult to raise capital to invest in new factories. As profitable as their industries were, spinners and weavers still needed capital to expand their business. One of the strategies was to borrow capital from a variety of sources, including family members, widows, retired merchants, attorneys, and people who had some savings and wanted to invest. Merchants and wholesalers in London could also lend credit to Northern manufacturers.[40]

Firms that performed vertical integration that is, carding, spinning, and weaving in one place were rare. The Peels and the Arkwrights were two of them. But most firms specialized in one of the stages of the textile industry. Large Manchester firms were able to place agents in commercial marketplaces to sell their yarn. But small spinners depended on brokers and merchants to market their products. Generally, the latter advanced the raw cotton to these small spinners in the form of credit and then bought the yarn.[41]

In the last quarter of the eighteenth century, Scotland had also become a significant hub for industry. The Scottish cotton industry was concentrated in the west, mainly in Glasgow, Renfrewshire, and Paisley. The region benefited from cheap labor from Ireland, access to raw materials arriving at ports on the

---

38 Wadsworth and Mann, *The Cotton Trade and Industrial Lancashire, 1600–1780*, 492.

39 Berg, *The Age of Manufactures*, 206.

40 Chapman, *The Cotton Industry*, 27–34. The origin of the capital used to finance the industrial revolution generated many debates; see for example François Crouzet, "Editor's Introduction," in *Capital Formation in the Industrial Revolution*, ed. François Crouzet (Methuen, 1972); B. L. Anderson, "The Attorney and the Early Capital Market in Lancashire," in *Capital Formation in the Industrial Revolution*, ed. François Crouzet (Methuen, 1972).

41 Chapman, *The Cotton Industry*, 39.

river Clyde (Glasgow and Greenock), resources of waterpower, and merchants with global connections. As in Lancashire, linen was the primary industry in Scotland in the mid-eighteenth century. Many of the techniques employed in flax would be transferred to the cotton industry. Likewise, the merchants who organized and financed the flax industry switched to cotton. Commercial connections with the American market, mainly because of the tobacco trade, were used for marketing raw cotton and cotton goods. Furthermore, part of the capital invested in the cotton industry stemmed from merchants who had enriched themselves from the tobacco trade with America and the West Indies. Around 1812, approximately 150,000 individuals were employed in cotton production, predominantly within their residences. Glasgow imported raw cotton, made cotton goods, and exported them. It differed from England, where Liverpool was just an import and export port, and Manchester, the region that produced cotton goods.[42]

Cotton from the British West Indies was the first fiber imported into Scotland and the first import of cotton from the United States to Liverpool occurred after the War of Independence ended in 1784.[43] It was probably around this time that Brazilian cotton reached Scotland. Its supply was partly guaranteed through Liverpool, Manchester, and London. Another part was imported directly to Glasgow or Greenock. In 1799, Scotland was one of Portugal's leading buyers of Brazilian cotton. Greenock was the third largest importer, buying 19.52% of Lisbon's cotton. By 1806, its share dropped to just under 5%, but Greenock managed to take fifth place as the main port of cotton purchases in Lisbon (Table 6.1. and Appendix C). Overall, however, the share of Brazilian cotton in Scotland's imports was small. For instance, Brazil was the minor cotton supplier to Scotland in 1810–11.[44] In both 1799 and 1806, the leading exporters to Scotland in Lisbon were members of the English factory: Parkers & Co., Mayne & Brown, and Offley, Sealy, and Son (Appendix B).

Regarding the cotton textile consumer market, the major outside markets during the first three-quarters of the eighteenth century were the United States, the West Indies, and Africa (where cottons were traded for Africans who were sold into slavery and sent to Virginia or the West Indies).[45] According to

42 Anthony Cooke, *The Rise and Fall of the Scottish Cotton Industry, 1778–1914: 'The Secret Spring'* (Manchester University Press, 2010), 3–6, 20–21, 28.

43 Reid, *Glasgow, Past and Present*, 3: 370; Chapman, "The Commercial Sector," 65.

44 Cooke, *The Rise and Fall of the Scottish Cotton Industry*, 23, 46, 49.

45 Kazuo Kobayashi, *Indian Cotton Textiles in West Africa: African Agency, Consumer Demand and the Making of the Global Economy, 1750–1850* (Palgrave Macmillan, 2019).

Wadsworth and Mann, by this time, it was the protection of overseas markets and not textile technology that made the cotton industry successful.[46] Relative to foreign markets, British cotton goods accounted for nearly half of total exports between the mid-1780s and mid-1840s. The European continent, North America, and the West Indies were the main destinations for textiles.[47] British cotton textiles were only allowed in Portugal and Brazil with the 1810 treaty, but before that they entered both territories through smuggling.[48]

According to Styles, in the beginning cotton was successful not because it was cheaper or stronger than other textiles but rather because of its "appearance" and "decorative properties."[49] Over time, England's production of cotton yarn and fabric became focused on producing low-quality items. Sandberg demonstrated the gradual deterioration of British cotton fabrics' general quality over the nineteenth century. This was mostly attributed to the significant increase in exports to Asian countries, particularly India, where there was a notable influx of low-cost items. The markets in Western Europe and the United States successfully assimilated higher grade textiles. While Lancashire did not primarily focus on the production of quality cottons, they nonetheless manufactured goods of this nature for targeted customers.[50] Lancashire textile goods were never intended for immediate sale to the end consumer as they were not finished products. Lancashire supplied cloth, but not clothing, with calico being one of the most important textile goods.[51]

3 The Role of Liverpool

Over the period, Liverpool became the main port to feed the Northern England cotton industry with raw materials. Between the mid-seventeenth and mid-eighteenth centuries, Liverpool's growth was linked to colonial markets,

---

46 Chapman, *The Cotton Industry*, 16; Wadsworth and Mann, *The Cotton Trade and Industrial Lancashire, 1600–1780*, 227–31.

47 Chapman, *The Cotton Industry*, 42–44; see also Davis, *The Industrial Revolution and British Overseas Trade*; Robert S. DuPlessis, *The Material Atlantic: Clothing, Commerce, and Colonization in the Atlantic World, 1650–1800* (Cambridge University Press, 2015); Riello, "Cotton Textiles and the Industrial Revolution in a Global Context".

48 Madureira, *Mercado e Privilégios: A Indústria Portuguesa Entre 1750 e 1834*, 314.

49 Styles, "What Were Cottons for in the Early Industrial Revolution?," 314.

50 Lars G. Sandberg, "Movements in the Quality of British Cotton Textile Exports, 1815–1913," *The Journal of Economic History* 28, no. 1 (1968): 2, 4, 9, 20.

51 Farnie, "Cotton, 1780–1914," 743.

mainly receiving tobacco and sugar, supplying servants to America, and organizing the Atlantic slave trade. Cotton was still irrelevant. However, during this period, key commercial relationships between Liverpool and the Chesapeake and West Indian markets were strengthened.[52] By the mid-eighteenth century, Liverpool was still in its infancy in procuring raw cotton on its own, although it was already the second most important port in England. By this time, cotton was arriving from the West Indies through direct or triangular trade. Vessels left Liverpool with cotton goods, went to Guinea, and traded them for enslaved Africans, which were then sent to the West Indies, where merchants exchanged them for colonial products, including raw cotton. Moreover, for Wadsworth and Mann, triangular trade was critical for Liverpool merchants to sell their cotton products and get raw cotton from the West Indies.[53]

Liverpool, curiously enough, developed very few cotton mills. According to Dumbell, the reasons for this are a mystery. Still, he conjectures that Liverpool lacked adequate manpower and a driving force for manufacturing, which made Liverpool industries lose competitiveness.[54] Liverpool, nevertheless, dominated the slave trade in England from the late 1740s until 1807, surpassing London and Bristol.[55] At the onset of the French Wars, Liverpool merchants possessed 572 vessels, of which slightly more than one hundred were utilized in the slave trade. The trade peaked in Liverpool in 1798, with 149 ships carrying 52,557 enslaved people across the Atlantic.[56]

In the 1780s, there was an unprecedented rise of Liverpool as a destination for raw cotton, and in the 1790s, Liverpool secured its place as the main port for cotton. This happened because of the port's proximity to the textile regions, and the cottons were easily transported overland between the port and factories scattered across the counties. Another factor that helped Liverpool as the main port for raw cotton was its contacts with merchants and planters in the U.S. South. Still, when wars and embargoes occurred, London and Glasgow gained a certain pre-eminence as they had greater contacts with suppliers who

52 Clemens, "The Rise of Liverpool, 1665–1750".

53 Wadsworth and Mann, *The Cotton Trade and Industrial Lancashire, 1600–1780*, 227–31; Stanley Dumbell, "Early Liverpool Cotton Imports and the Organisation of the Cotton Market in the Eighteenth Century," *The Economic Journal* 33, no. 131 (1923): 363–64.

54 Dumbell, "Early Liverpool Cotton Imports," 372.

55 French, "Crowded with Traders and a Great Commerce," 30.

56 A. C. Wardle, "Liverpool," in *The Trade Winds: A Study of British Overseas Trade During the French Wars, 1793–1815*, ed. C. Northcote Parkinson (1948; Routledge, 2005), 52, 62; see also David Richardson et al., eds., *Liverpool and Transatlantic Slavery* (Liverpool University Press, 2007).

brought cotton from Portugal/Brazil and the East.[57] Table 9.1 shows Liverpool concentrating more than half of the United Kingdom's cotton imports between 1802 and 1812. It also shows a large share of cotton entering England through other places. London was probably the other major port for raw cotton. In 1812, for example, almost all bales of Brazilian cotton in stock in the United Kingdom were in London. That year, Brazil was the second largest supplier of raw cotton (115,643 bales), second only to the United States (307,558 bales).[58]

For a long time, the British got a good share of raw cotton through trade with their settlements in West Indies and through the French and Spanish colonies. This was possible thanks to Jamaica, Dominica, and Grenada, which were allowed to function as free ports. Foreign vessels brought cotton from other colonies to the British West Indies, which were then transported to England. One-eighth of the cotton that arrived in Britain in 1789 came into the hands of the manufacturers that way. Saint-Domingue was one of the largest cotton growers and sent part of its output to the British colonies at the time of the free

TABLE 9.1 Raw cotton imported by the United Kingdom and Liverpool, 1802–1812

Year	Total importations of cotton into the U.K.	Importations of cotton into Liverpool	Liverpool (%)
1802	281,383	135,192	48.04
1803	238,898	140,291	58.72
1804	242,610	153,126	63.11
1805	252,620	177,508	70.26
1806	261,738	173,074	66.12
1807	282,667	196,467	69.50
1808	168,138	66,215	39.38
1809	440,382	267,283	60.69
1810	561,173	320,594	57.12
1811	326,231	174,132	53.37
1812	261,205	171,551	65.67

Source and notes: Edwards, *The Growth of the British Cotton Trade*, 111. Imports are given in bales and bags. Table prepared by the author.

57 Edwards, *The Growth of the British Cotton Trade*, 111.

58 Chapman, *Merchant Enterprise in Britain*, 83.

ports. Between 1783–1785 and 1787–1789, Saint-Domingue's cotton exports grew 31%. This growth was also supported by an increasing importation of enslaved people, in which England was one of the leading suppliers. However, after the slave revolution in Saint-Domingue in 1791, both the price of sugar and cotton rose in Europe, which encouraged growers in the United States and elsewhere to ship cotton to England.[59] The British West Indies could not keep up with the demands of British industry. Jamaica's land was not very suitable for growing cotton, and planters were still investing in sugar plantations. In Barbados and the Bahamas, there was a most successful conversion from sugar to cotton, but this was short-lived, from the mid-1780s until the early part of the next decade.[60] The slave revolution in 1791 again played an important role: sugar prices soared and the British West Indies turned more to sugar, thwarting plans to increase cotton production.[61]

Simultaneously, cotton sourced from the Southern region of the United States showed exceptional suitability in terms of both quality and quantity to meet the requirements of the British industry. The link between Liverpool and North American growers and merchants was very close precisely because of the magnitude of the trade between them. Different marketing methods could take place. The British merchant could go to the United States and there act as an agent for the planters, shipping their cottons to England. Merchants in Manchester or Liverpool were responsible for picking up the cotton bales and distributing them. There was a competition between the merchants of the two cities, but Manchester was losing importance to the detriment of Liverpool over time. In 1804, there were about 50 cotton merchants in Manchester, and none of them is on the list of the 90 merchants who operated in Liverpool in 1841. Liverpool was regarded as a highly competitive raw cotton market.[62] Southern growers also had at least three other commercialization possibilities: they could consign the cotton to an agent in Europe, sell the cotton at the nearest American port to a factor, or sell it inland to an intermediary.[63] In the last two methods, the factor was usually an American merchant, and the economic and social relations between planters and factors became known as the "cotton factorage system," where the factor not only commodified the crops but also

59 Edwards, *The Growth of the British Cotton Trade*, 79–80, 91; Drescher, *Econocide*, 62.

60 Edwards, *The Growth of the British Cotton Trade*, 79–80; Riello, *Cotton*, 187–210; see also Jaquay, "The Caribbean Cotton Production"; Ryden, "One of the Finest and Most Fruitful Spots in America".

61 Drescher, *Econocide*, 58; see also Chapman, *Merchant Enterprise in Britain*, 82.

62 Chapman, *The Cotton Industry*, 38–39.

63 Buck, *The Development of the Organisation of Anglo-American Trade, 1800–1850*, 67.

financed them.[64] According to Hall, in the early nineteenth century, most importers in Liverpool worked on commission, selling cotton owned by the Americans. But by the end of the nineteenth century, merchants in Liverpool acted more as principals than as commission agents to the Americans.[65] These were marketing methods that did not apply to the Brazilian cotton trade, simply because—most of the time—Portugal was in the way of Brazilian growers and British spinners.

During the 1780s to 1800s, several raw cotton growers across the globe sought to increase their production to supply the English market. To a large extent, the cotton industry had grown because there had been a steady increase in the supply of raw cotton to spinners. However, there were times when this growth in the supply of raw cotton was compromised, and it was not clear that the needed supplies would be met. In 1786, fustian manufacturers complained that cotton from the British West Indies was not imported in adequate quantities, particularly the fibers most suitable for making yarn of intermediate quality. Their desire was for more cotton to be produced in the British colonies, as English merchants and manufacturers had to import raw cotton from France.[66]

The request to plant more cotton was made to several islands in the British Caribbean. The response was quick. In 1788, a cotton gin was installed in the Bahamas. Soon, the mechanism spread to several islands and reached the South of the United States at the beginning of the 1790s. Another strategy employed by the British in the late 1780s was sending botanists to India to discover the best planting methods and the use of Persian seeds. They even considered the possibility of planting cotton in Africa. In the late 1780s, muslins manufacturers even asked the East India Company to stop importing textiles from India and only bring quality raw cotton to make the muslins in England. But this entailed two problems. First, the Company would have lost profits in Europe for not bringing in manufactured textiles. Second, the Indian luxury muslin producers themselves were unwilling to sell raw cotton to the Company to feed their competitors in England. The Company did ship raw cotton from India to England, but it was in small quantity and poor quality. Yet, probably because of land exhaustion caused by the great demand for raw cotton, mainly due to the "slash and burn" method of clearing the soil, cotton production in

64 Alfred Holt Stone, "The Cotton Factorage System of the Southern States," *The American Historical Review* 20, no. 3 (1915): 557–65; Woodman, *King Cotton and His Retainers*; Buck, *The Development of the Organisation of Anglo-American Trade, 1800–1850*, 68.

65 Hall, "Liverpool's Cotton Importers c. 1700 to 1914," 87–88.

66 Edwards, *The Growth of the British Cotton Trade*, 75–76.

the West Indies declined, and by the 1810s, the Caribbean lost its leading role in supplying the British cotton industry.[67]

By the early 1790s, fine cotton fabrics were all the rage and the West Indies could no longer satisfy this market. Moreover, the war in 1793 further complicated the situation by harming trade with the free ports in the West Indies, which still brought in some quality cotton to England. Around this time, from the late 1780s to the late 1790s, cotton from Brazil proved to be very suitable for manufacturers of chintz, calico, muslin, and velveret (or velveteen – cotton fabric similar to velvet), textiles that required better quality staple. But it was still a low amount of raw cotton. Manufacturers needed to produce high-quality cotton fabrics that were desirable to the middle and upper classes, rather than solely coarse fabrics for the lower classes. Consequently, they required sources of raw cotton at reasonable prices. During the 1790s, cotton production in the United States expanded, with Sea Island cotton emerging as the primary supplier for the English industry from 1799 to 1802. Sea Island cotton was sufficiently inexpensive to produce affordable intermediate fabrics such as calico and muslin. This variety of cotton was superior for the spinning process compared to Brazilian and West Indian cotton. In 1802, imports of cotton from the United States exceeded those from the West Indies, primarily due to upland cotton, which was more economical and yielded a stronger, more durable yarn, ultimately displacing other cotton varieties. Nevertheless, fibers from various regions continued to enter England, particularly during periods of low United States cotton exports.[68]

Embargoes and conflicts involving the United States and England benefited Brazilian cotton. In the context of the 1808 embargo, United States cotton was not reaching England, despite some American merchants sending cotton in vessels with "Spanish colors" and in British ships to Cádiz, Lisbon, and Fazal. The year 1814 was also marked by the great presence of Brazilian cotton in England. It was a good short period for Portuguese and perhaps Brazilian merchants: in 1813, Portuguese merchants in England (and others) even protested against the

---

67 Riello, *Cotton*, 202–3; Edwards, *The Growth of the British Cotton Trade*, 76–82.

68 On textile qualities, see Stanley D. Chapman, "Quantity Versus Quality in the British Industrial Revolution: The Case of Printed Textiles," *Northern History* 21, no. 1 (1985): 175–92; G. N. von Tunzelmann, "Technological and Organizational Change in Industry during the Industrial Revolution," in *The Industrial Revolution and British Society*, ed. Patrick O'Brien and Roland Quinault (Cambridge University Press, 1993); Maxine Berg, "Quality, Cotton and the Global Luxury Trade," in *How India Clothed the World: The World of South Asian Textiles, 1500–1850*, ed. Giorgio Riello and Tirthankar Roy (Brill, 2009). On the qualities of raw cotton fibers, see Russell, *Evolutionary History* (Cambridge University Press, 2011), 103–31; Edwards, *The Growth of the British Cotton Trade*, 83–84, 88–94.

entry of cotton from the United States. Yet, the war ended in December 1814, and there was a drop in cotton imports from Brazil (whose stocks were already high in England). When United States cotton arrived in England in small quantities, Brazilian cotton served as a substitute for upland cotton, but that never actually satisfied British manufacturers. Regardless of wars and embargoes, the cotton supply in England remained high to the point where stocks were built up and prices fell. As a result, the manufacturing industry could not consume all the raw cotton available on the market. It was the opposite scenario of what happened in 1792. In summary, the demands by British manufacturers to have an abundant source of cotton that would provide quality raw cotton were to some extent answered by the planting of upland cotton in the United States. Its high supply "exerted pressure on the price level of all cottons in the market" after 1800.[69]

If, from Portugal's point of view, England was an essential buyer, from the English perspective, cotton from Brazil was one of the main sources of raw material that fed its textile industry. Brazilian cotton made up more than 20% of Britain's total cotton imports in the late eighteenth century.[70] When we look at the inflows of goods into the port of Liverpool, we see that Brazil's cotton imports peaked in the 1790s. In this decade, Brazilian fiber beat that of the West Indies, until then the traditional supplier to the British, and became the main raw cotton imported into Liverpool. The period between 1801 and 1810 was marked by the meteoric growth of North American cotton cultivation, which displaced Brazilian cotton from the prime position. Yet, Brazilian cotton remained important as it ranked second and remained in that position at least until the end of the 1810s (Figure 9. 2).

4 Cotton Purchases from England

The cotton market in England differed significantly from the import market that Lisbon used to have with Brazil. Furthermore, it diverged from the

---

69 Edwards, *The Growth of the British Cotton Trade*, 98–106; Why upland cotton? "An upland crop, it was felt, could be twice as large as a Sea Island one, was less affected by adverse weather conditions, could be prepared for market in much less time because of the use of the Whitney gin, and always commanded a ready sale in Britain since it was the best cotton on the market for the production of the cheaper materials for which there was by far the greatest demand." G. W. Daniels, "American Cotton Trade with Liverpool under the Embargo and Non-Intercourse Acts," *The American Historical Review* 21, no. 2 (1916): 276–87.

70 Robson, *Britain, Portugal and South America*, 28.

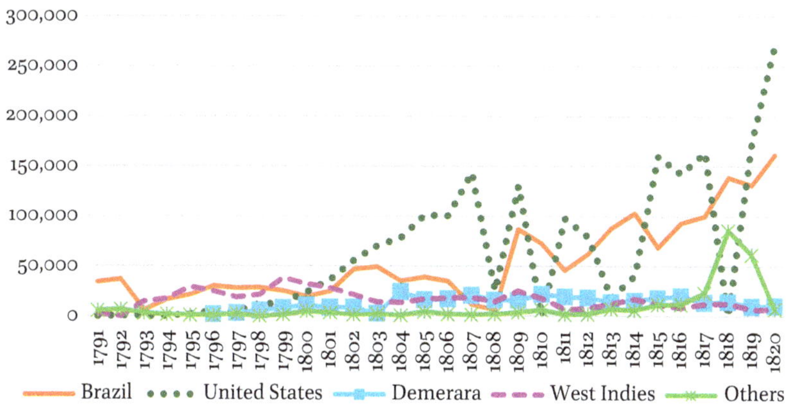

FIGURE 9.2 Liverpool Cotton Imports, 1791–1820
Source and notes: Smithers, *Liverpool, Its Commerce, Statistics, and Institutions*, 147. Imports are given in bales. Others = Suriname, East India, Ireland, Turkey, and Netherlands. Figure prepared by the author.

commerce that occurred between England and the United States. Given the intricate nature of the market, it is crucial to have a precise understanding of the commercial occupations in England that were involved in the distribution of cotton. There is a little amount of information available about London, but there is a significant amount of literature that discusses the cotton trade in Liverpool and the textile centres in Lancashire. In this section, I shall examine the five social groupings that had an interest in raw cotton: import merchants, commission agents, dealers, brokers, and spinners. The importing merchants and the commission agents were both importers. The only difference was that the former was the principal of the relationship, and the latter was the agent, most of the time working as a representative of exporters and planters from the West Indies and the United States. Dealers and brokers acted as intermediaries between importers/commission agents and spinners.

Once the importer or the commission agent received the cotton, he was unlikely to sell it directly to the spinners. The presence of an intermediary was expected, and one of these was the dealer. Dealers were mostly concentrated in Manchester. It was the dealer with his warehouse that made the connection between the port and yarn producers. The dealer could buy from the commission agent, or he could be an importer himself, as he could be involved in some kind of partnership with the importer. The purchase of cotton by the dealer could take place through "public or private auctions," when he would check the cotton directly in the warehouses. Dealers, in turn, could also sell cotton to spinners through "public auctions or private agreements." They "usually organized their public sales from a warehouse and advertised them in the local press. The auction was a quick method of sale since it took a large number of bidders, but some spinners were reluctant to buy there because they thought prices were kept artificially high." That was because some inexperienced spinners could make very high starting bids. In contrast, "the private treaty sale involved a simple contract between the dealer and the spinner. The dealer offered cotton for sale at his warehouse, or sent a sample, the spinner inspected it, and either bought it at the list price or submitted an offer. This was necessarily a slower method of sale than the auction, but it probably meant there were less violent fluctuations in the level of cotton prices." The dealer saved the time of the spinner and cotton importer, who could concentrate on their activities. Dealers sold cotton on credit, and spinners paid within a set amount of time that varied according to the size of their business. Larger spinner firms generally had more time to pay back debts. In this sense, dealers were essential for the expansion of the cotton industry. The dealer's figure emerges with great force, perhaps in the 1790s but certainly after the 1800s. His function "reflected the joint needs of the importer and the spinner. The latter required regular deliveries of special types of cotton, carefully sorted and graded; the importer looked for a quick sale of his consignments in order to please his shipper."[71]

The raw cotton trade was a business that tended towards specialization due to the enormous quantity of the product and the variety of fibers in the market. For instance, in 1801, at least 16 raw cotton types from different sources were traded in Liverpool, each of them classified into four levels: "ordinary, middling, good and fine." This enabled the creation of the figure of another intermediary, the broker. Brokers in Liverpool sent price quotes for all these cotton types to the spinners. One sales tactic used by brokers was not holding many auctions but selling directly to spinners or sending fiber samples to them. This was another element that favored Liverpool as the main port for cotton, as these techniques would have been difficult to achieve in London. There were two types of brokers: one to sell and one to buy. The first represented the importers and the second the spinners. In a way, the broker's employment was a refusal to use dealers' services, and over the years, brokers supplanted them. The difference was that the dealer still worked as an individual who advanced credit,

71 Edwards, *The Growth of the British Cotton Trade*, 113–17. See also Roger Lloyd-Jones and Myrddin John Lewis, *Manchester and the Age of the Factory: The Business Structure of Cottonopolis in the Industrial Revolution* (Croom Helm, 1988), 1–62; Sheryllynne Haggerty, "What's in a Price? The American Raw Cotton Market in Liverpool and the Anglo-American War," *Business History* 61, no. 6 (2018): 942–70.

and the price of raw cotton was higher in his hands. The broker did not extend credit—or at least that was not his function—and the cotton in his hands was cheaper. In addition, because he was at the port of Liverpool, the broker had more knowledge about the cotton market and types of cotton than the dealer, most of the time in Manchester. However, the dealer's decline is hardly noticeable in the early nineteenth century. Spinners still preferred dealers precisely because they provided credit.[72] Yet, the broker was an essential element in the trade and could accumulate money through brokerage fees. Despite his wealth, he did not enter into negotiations on his own, precisely because of the risks and because this activity, considered to be more speculative, could compromise his main enterprise of linking supply and demand for raw cotton. Furthermore, "the broker was strictly an agent for others and any transactions as principal tended to confuse relationships with buyer and seller and so provoke suspicion and misunderstanding of his motives." Over the years, the growth and wealth accumulated by brokers also allowed them to lend credit to Liverpool cotton importers.[73] In a way, the presence of brokers made the market and the cotton industry more efficient. The figure of the broker emerged at the end of the eighteenth century and gained prominence after 1815.[74] A broker who stood out in 1799 was Nicholas Waterhouse. He dealt with the large Liverpool cotton importers and the large fiber buyers, such as manufacturers (Strutt, Arkwright, and Peel were his clients) and the dealers in Manchester.[75]

A historical overview of the order of the functions involved in cotton trading in England shows that the "general merchant" or "general broker" imports the goods first, followed by the "cotton merchants," "cotton dealers," and "cotton broker." The West Indian cotton merchants, for example, tended to be the "general merchants" because the cargoes coming from the Caribbean were a miscellany of tropical products. For them, it was difficult to specialize in cotton. For other routes, more specifically towards the Mediterranean, English merchants were more specialized and could be called

72 Edwards, *The Growth of the British Cotton Trade*, 118–23; see also Nigel Hall, "The Business Interests of Liverpool's Cotton Brokers, c. 1800–1914," *Northern History* 41, no. 2 (2004): 339–55; Aldous and Coyle, "Examining the Role of a Private-Order Institution in Global Trade".

73 Francis E. Hyde et al., "The Cotton Broker and the Rise of the Liverpool Cotton Market," *The Economic History Review* 8, no. 1 (1955): 78, 80.

74 Hyde et al., "The Cotton Broker and the Rise of the Liverpool Cotton Market," 76.

75 Stanley Dumbell, "The Cotton Market in 1799," *The Economic Journal* 36, no. Supplement 1 (1926): 142; see also Aldous and Coyle, "Examining the Role of a Private-Order Institution in Global Trade".

cotton merchants.[76] This makes sense for the English trade with Portugal: vessels leaving Lisbon practically specialized in raw cotton, as the other less valuable cargoes were fruit and wine (Appendix D). However, it was still possible to see these characters and members blending and occupying two or more functions: a broker could be an importer and a dealer; and merchants could be manufacturers.

Cotton provided a commercial specialization that could hardly be achieved through another colonial good. The specialization in Liverpool took place, according to Stanley Dumbell, because of the high supply of cotton and high demand of the manufacturers, so a series of intermediaries were situated between the two points of the commercial chains. Essentially, the number of spinners had increased, as had their demand, which raised the need for more intermediaries to source raw cotton for them. Dealers and then brokers grew in importance as professionals with knowledge of the types of cotton suitable for the needs of their manufacturing clients. In other words, spinners needed these intermediaries to link the different kinds of raw cotton available on the market with the various cotton goods they could manufacture.[77]

These are mercantile arrangements that were pretty different from what was found in Lisbon. In the capital of the Portuguese empire, importing merchants did not have to supply local manufacturers. They simply sold cotton to other merchants. Importers in Lisbon could not be classified as "cotton merchants" as they traded in a myriad of goods coming from Brazil. The British case appears, at the same time, to be different from the French case. In Rouen, it seems that intermediaries such as brokers and dealers did not exist. For a long time, it was merchants in Rouen who advanced the fiber to small spinners in the interior of Upper Normandy.[78] However, this may have changed with the mechanization that took place between the 1790s and the Napoleonic period.

Few spinners went to Liverpool to buy raw cotton. Instead, they went to Manchester, where merchants and dealers brought in raw cotton from Liverpool and other parts of England, like London, Bristol, and Lancaster. There is evidence that merchants in Manchester could import cotton from Lisbon without the help of intermediaries in Liverpool in the 1790s. Spinners also bought cotton from merchants in Liverpool.[79] Thus, to some extent, there was a competition between the Liverpool and Manchester market. The small spinners sealed agreements with the intermediaries in Manchester, as these gave

76 Dumbell, "Early Liverpool Cotton Imports," 368; Rees, *Britain's Commodity Markets*, 86–87.
77 Dumbell, "Early Liverpool Cotton Imports," 364–70; see also Haggerty, "What's in a Price?".
78 Daly, *Inside Napoleonic France*, 14; Gullickson, *The Spinners and Weavers of Auffay*.
79 Dumbell, "Early Liverpool Cotton Imports," 366–69.

them credit. But the big spinners managed to buy from importers, dealers, and brokers in Liverpool.[80]

How were these occupations articulated to carry out the cotton trade from Portugal to England? Trade between Portugal and Liverpool tended to be organized through the operations of Lisbon-based merchants with dealers and large manufacturers in Lancashire rather than with importing merchants from Liverpool, even though these were also significant figures. Alexey Krichtal compiled a list of the 15 largest importers in Liverpool of cotton from Portugal between 1784 and 1802: seven were known to be brokers working for Lancashire dealers and manufacturers (Table 9.2). The importing merchants constituted another group that bought cotton at their own risk and sold it in Liverpool. Despite being different groups, companies and individuals could be brokers and merchants simultaneously: this was the case for Nicholas

TABLE 9.2 Top fifteen Liverpool cotton importers from Portugal, 1784–1802

Consignee	Occupation
Holt & Davis	Broker
Thomas & William Earle	Merchant
Geoffrey Goring	Broker
Ewart, Rutson & Co	Broker
Nicholas Waterhouse & Co	Merchant and broker
George Marsden	Merchant and broker
Iver McIver & Co	Merchant
Harrison & Nephew	Merchant
Henry Norris	Broker
Dauntsey Hulme & Co	Merchant
John Theodor Koster	Merchant
Thomas Smith & Nephew	Merchant
Daniel Whittaker	Broker
Pudsey & Richard Dawson	Merchant
Robert Jackson	Merchant

Source: Krichtal, *Liverpool and the Raw Cotton Trade*, 57. Table prepared by the author.

80 Dumbell, "The Cotton Market in 1799," 141.

Waterhouse & Co. and George Marsden. And like Lancashire dealers, Liverpool importers also had dealings with British firms in Lisbon to buy cotton there and ship it to England.[81]

According to Krichtal, Liverpool merchants did not have "large capital reserves," so few of them operated in the Liverpool-Portugal route. This important function of linking the two markets was carried out by the Lancashire dealers and manufacturers, who sealed agreements with British firms in Portugal to obtain cotton. Thus, Lancashire dealers and manufacturers deliberately sought to circumvent agreements with Liverpool importers. However, wars with France from 1793 on made the cotton trade riskier between Portugal and England, which forced Lancashire dealers and manufacturers to reduce their imports. Between 1803 and 1815, the group that brought cotton from Portugal had radically changed from the most prominent importers between 1784 and 1802 (Table 9.3), suggesting that Lancashire dealers and manufacturers were no longer the leading players, especially after the French invasion of Portugal in 1807.[82] George Sandeman's firm in Portugal, for instance, exported cotton mainly to Liverpool, but it also shipped bales to London and Hull. His customers in England numbered around 80 spinners. Between 1798 and 1806, Sandeman exported 30,967 bags, of which the Strutts ordered 950. Cotton from the Strutts was shipped to Nicholas Waterhouse or Samuel Hope in Liverpool.

TABLE 9.3 Top fifteen Liverpool cotton importers from Portugal and Brazil, 1803–1815

Consignee	Consignee
John Theodor Koster & Co*	Haworth & Peel
Lyne, Hathorn & Co*	A. Van Zellar & Co
John Hancock & Co	F. Haywood & Co
Costa, Guimarãens & Co	Stack, Lynch & Hore
Harrison & Latham	John & Robert Gladstone
Dyson Brothers & Co*	Antonio Martins Pedra & Co
George Roach & Co*	Samuel Holland & Co
Carvalho & Fortunatto	

Source: Krichtal, *Liverpool and the Raw Cotton Trade*, 61. * Known to be part of the Lisbon factory. Table prepared by the author.

81 Krichtal, *Liverpool and the Raw Cotton Trade*, 55–58.

82 Krichtal, *Liverpool and the Raw Cotton Trade*, 58, 60.

These agents could receive a commission of 0.5%. George Sandeman's firm also insured cotton for spinners who had purchased cotton from "other Portuguese houses." Those other houses were Evans & Co and Josh Lyne & Co.[83] The merchant that deserves to be stressed in the two tables (9.2 and 9.3) is John Theodor Koster, who, as we have seen, also had a branch of his company in Lisbon and was one of the biggest cotton exporters there (see Chapter 8 and Appendix B).

Large spinners in England were able to buy directly from exporters or planters. The Strutts, as seen, even bought cotton directly from Lisbon. However, Edwards claimed that this type of trade was very rare. According to him, "throughout this period it is the commission merchants and the importers who are most active in importing cotton into the British ports. Few spinners would have had the time, capital, or confidence, to have undertaken much importing on their own behalf."[84] However, this is open to interpretation. For Chapman, from the point of view of enterprises, two consequences emerged with the advent of the Industrial Revolution and wars. With the first, merchants began to invest in manufactures, and manufacturers began to be interested in trade, mainly in imports of raw materials and exports of their products. Both also invested in land and other activities. With the wars—the war against the colonies in America (1776–83) and the French wars (1793–1815)—many merchants went bankrupt, and others emerged. So, there was a great renewal of business and mercantile groups in that period,[85] which makes it difficult to specify who were the actors that dominated the raw cotton import business.

At the same time, London was still an important port. Before the consolidation of Sea Island cotton, South American cotton was the most requested one. For the most part, these cottons arrived in London and were later shipped to the north of England.[86] Between 1794 and 1817, the Strutts purchased 79,746 cotton bags from about 48 different places. Brazil—more specifically Pernambuco, Maranhão, Bahia, Ceará, and Pará—contributed 36,330 bags, 45.5% of the total, and was the largest cotton supplier to these famous English manufacturers.[87] There were constant complaints from the Strutts regarding the cleaning of cotton from South America that came with seeds and stones. Because of this, they asked for monetary compensation from the brokers who had sold them the bags. According to Fitton and Wadsworth, dirty cotton was due to the

83 Fitton and Wadsworth, *The Strutts and the Arkwrights, 1758–1830*, 282–84.
84 Edwards, *The Growth of the British Cotton Trade*, 124–25.
85 Chapman, *Merchant Enterprise in Britain*, 51, 58–61.
86 Fitton and Wadsworth, *The Strutts and the Arkwrights, 1758–1830*, 261.
87 Fitton and Wadsworth, *The Strutts and the Arkwrights, 1758–1830*, 264–67.

insufficient diffusion of "saw gin" throughout South America. As cotton came "dirty" from America, it needed to be cleaned mostly by women.[88]

In essence, the cotton trade between Portugal and England was, in many ways, different from the system of commissions that took place with the West Indies, where the principal was the Caribbean-based merchant or planter, and the agents were based in England.[89] For the Portuguese case, the trade could very well be made with principals in Lisbon sending cotton to agents to sell it in England, but what is striking is that there seemed to be a strong presence of residents in England (regardless of whether they were brokers, spinners, or import merchants) who were actively engaging in the cotton trade. They were the principals who gave agents (the English factory in Lisbon) orders to buy and ship cotton to England. This trade was easy due to the existence of companies that were headquartered in Portugal and England, like Koster.[90] From the point of view of English merchants standing in Lisbon, everything would change with the French invasion at the end of 1807, but merchants based in England would find means to continue purchasing cotton from Brazil in an even more efficient way.

5 The Trade after 1808

On January 16, 1808, Angelo Gonçalves Aires, a Portuguese merchant in Lisbon, dispatched a letter to George Roach to arrange his cotton shipments from Pernambuco to England. While not an important cotton exporter when he was in Lisbon, George Roach was a major importer in Liverpool (Table 9.3). Because of the threat of French invasion, George Roach, like many other Englishmen, had moved from Lisbon to London. Angelo would send a power of attorney to Roach to be responsible for the goods that arrived in England, sell them as he saw fit, and keep the sales capital until the war situation improved. When circumstances allowed, Roach was expected to send Angelo the money in bills. If this could not be done, he suggested an alternative: sending the value in another medium, such as flour produced in English America.[91] A few months later, rumors were spread—"dismal news; but without foundation, nor proof

88 Fitton and Wadsworth, *The Strutts and the Arkwrights, 1758–1830*, 270.

89 Krichtal, "Liverpool and the Raw Cotton Trade," 64.

90 Edwards, *The Growth of the British Cotton Trade*, 124–25; Shaw, *The Anglo-Portuguese Alliance*, 20, 37, 65, 82; Krichtal, *Liverpool and the Raw Cotton Trade*, 57, 61.

91 Letter of January 16, 1808. ANTT, Feitos Findos, Livros dos Feitos Findos, liv. 210.

of their being true"[92]—which, however, worried Angelo. Rumors said that all goods in England from inhabitants of Portugal and Brazil would be confiscated, if they did not go there to retrieve them. This worried Angelo and his son-in-law, who wrote again to Roach. They asked in the new letter to Roach to take hold of their properties. Angelo also wrote that he would send his son and partner to England to take care of these goods.[93]

The person who took the letter to Roach was Domingos Antônio Vaz Gloria. In May, Roach responded, saying that he could only find ten bales of cotton. But Angelo replied saying that this was not right, as according to Domingos Vaz Gloria—who was also in London looking for his own goods—he should have 150 bags in England, which came in several vessels loaded by Bento Antônio Domingues and José Bento Moreira in Pernambuco, in addition to other goods such as sugar and leather. According to Angelo, the Roach employee who looked into the matter did a poor job and requested a second check.[94] Dissatisfied with Roach's services, Angelo decided to contact Coltsmam & Stack, merchants who also left Portugal. According to Angelo, Roach was back in Lisbon in December 1808. When he returned to Portugal, Roach left to Lucena & Crowford the job of finding out what happened to Angelo's goods. They too did not seem to have satisfied Angelo's needs.[95] This imbroglio appeared to be an omen of how complicated the cotton trade between Brazil and England would become, being controlled at a distance by the Portuguese in Lisbon.

Shortly after that, the British started to operate from Brazil and would no longer need Portuguese or Brazilian intermediaries to bring cotton to England. Not only did the opening of Brazilian ports favor the arrival of the British, but on May 4, 1808, a judge conservator to the English was admitted in Brazil.[96] In 1810, a treaty was signed which allowed English goods to pay an import tax of 15% *ad valorem*, while Portuguese goods would pay 16%, and goods from other nations would pay 24%. This not only favored the British, but according to many (including Ratton) caused the end of the Portuguese industry that lost one of its main markets, Brazil.[97] Subsequently, merchants within the Portuguese Empire were granted the freedom to import cotton textiles from

92 "noticiais funestas; porém sem fundamento, nem prova de serem verdadeiras".
93 Letter of April 10, 1808. ANTT, Feitos Findos, Livros dos Feitos Findos, liv. 210.
94 Letter of September 20, 1808. ANTT, Feitos Findos, Livros dos Feitos Findos, liv. 210.
95 Letter of December 2, 1808. ANTT, Feitos Findos, Livros dos Feitos Findos, liv. 210.
96 Silva, *Collecção da legislação Portugueza desde a ultima compilação das ordenações*, 5: 499.
97 In parts of his recollections, Ratton mentions the 1810 treaty fraught with extreme disappointment; see Ratton, *Recordações*. However, goods coming from Portugal began to pay 15% of import duties from 1818 onwards; see Say, *Histoire des relations commerciales entre la France et le Brésil*, 55.

England.[98] After the 1810 treaty, a group of merchants in London founded the "Society of English Interested in Commerce in Brazil."[99] This pointed to the continued importance of London, even though the North of England was the main destination for Brazilian cotton.

John Luccock, a Yorkshire-born merchant, moved to Rio de Janeiro shortly after the opening of Brazilian ports in 1808. His marriage to a Lupton, a member of one of the most influential families in Yorkshire, gave him business contacts with the United States and Lisbon, the main marketplaces in which the Luptons had commerce. However, with the French invasion of Lisbon and the embargoes involving North America, business was threatened. Lisbon was an especially crucial port for the family who had business with the city for at least three-quarters of a century and had a member residing there: Francis Lupton was in Lisbon even before the earthquake, lost a great deal of money in the catastrophe, and was one of the English merchants who turned against Pombal in his policy of nationalizing the Portuguese economy.[100] His interest in cotton did not surface until the early 1790s, though. Between 1788 and 1792, Francis Lupton was associated with a company called Lupton, King & Lupton[101] and exported small quantities of cotton in 1792, only 351 arrobas.[102] In 1799, he was associated with the company Gonne, Harrison & Lupton, which exported 3,804 arrobas of cotton in nearly equal portions to Liverpool, Greenock, and London.[103] Perhaps fearful of an invasion by the French, he probably moved away from Lisbon in 1806, as he does not appear as an exporter in that year. Yet, his former colleague, Gonne, continued in the business and was one of the largest exporters not only in 1806 but in 1792 and 1799 (see Appendix B). To continue doing business with Brazilian products (and not just cotton) and take advantage of a large consumer market in South America, it seemed essential for the Luptons to send someone to Rio de Janeiro, and they appointed Luccock to the task. He would not be the only one; around a hundred English merchants settled in Rio after 1808, some coming directly from Lisbon, others from England.[104] Luccock's role was primarily to sell Lupton cloth, but he would also work on a commission basis for other manufacturers and merchants. As far as

98 Madureira, *Mercado e Privilégios: A Indústria Portuguesa Entre 1750 e 1834*, 314.

99 Viveiros, *História do Comércio do Maranhão 1612–1895*, 1: 120.

100 Herbert Heaton, "A Merchant Adventurer in Brazil 1808–1818," *The Journal of Economic History* 6, no. 1 (1946): 4.

101 The British Historical Society of Portugal, List of British Merchants in Lisbon 1788–1791, Report: HA 10, 1946–1950, 663.

102 According to my survey in the Lisbon customs books.

103 According to my survey in the Lisbon customs books.

104 Some names of British merchants in Lisbon who moved to Rio can be found in Appendix E.

the raw cotton trade is concerned, it appears that it was a business in which Luccock and the Luptons were directly and indirectly involved. They received requests from their bosses to export cotton bales from Brazil. When cotton supply from the United States was suspended or diminished, the demand for Brazilian fiber was so high that ships sailed from Liverpool in ballast directly to Pernambuco. In these scenarios, Luccock "shipped produce for British patrons, for Brazilian planters, and on his own account." When the United States normalized its shipments to England, surprisingly, "Brazil's boom continued a little longer, Luccock waxed rich, his planter friends made 500 percent on their shipments, and Pernambuco became so conscious of its economic importance that it staged an attempt to break free of Rio in 1817." Even when Luccock returned to England in 1818, he remained interested in Brazilian fiber, as he had left an assistant in Brazil who would sell his exported products and send him cotton in exchange.[105]

It was natural for foreign merchants to go to Rio, as it was the capital of the government, it had a larger consumer market, and it was possible to control trade with other parts of Brazil from there. Notwithstanding this, the British also went directly to the leading cotton growing and trading regions: Maranhão and Pernambuco. The British mercantile community in Maranhão, which after 1808 had restricted itself to only two merchants, increased considerably after the 1810 treaty (Table 9.4). In Pernambuco, perhaps one of the most

TABLE 9.4 British merchants in Maranhão in 1812

Wellstood & Bingham	Bolly Chavanes & Co.
Hesketh, Wilson & Co.	B. Hocart & Co.
Paterson, Lillie & Co.	W. Granger
Ely Hill, Henrique and João Moon & Co.	Setimus Sumnes
Haddon Clark & Co.	Joseph Willcox
Inglis Neilson & Co.	James Johnstone & Co.
Henrique Season, Ryder Gunston & Co.	George Turner & Co.
Fernando Bieber & Co.	

Source: Viveiros, *História do Comércio do Maranhão*, 122. Table prepared by the author.

105 Heaton, "A Merchant Adventurer in Brazil 1808–1818," 21–23. Luccock left a broad and rich account of his life in South America; see John Luccock, *Notes on Rio de Janeiro and the Southern Parts of Brazil* (printed for Samuel Leigh, 1820).

TABLE 9.5 British merchants in Pernambuco in 1817

Anthony J. Goring	Joseph Singlyhurst
Francis J. Howard	Robert Tod
George Thomas Mittchell	Samuel Handsman
Henry Koster	Samuel Preston
James Pech	Thomas Gardner
James Pincher	Thomas J. Granstone
James Stewart	Thomas Stewart
John Crowther	William Pelly

Source: NA, FO 63/206, f. 258, 266–267, and 271. Table prepared by the author.

famous traders was Henry Koster, son of John Koster, one of the leading raw cotton traders in Portugal and England (Appendix B and Tables 9.2 and 9.3). According to Henderson and British consular sources, there were 16 British merchants in Pernambuco around the end of the 1810s (Table 9.5).[106]

Yet according to the British consul in Maranhão, Robert Hesketh, only seven British houses actually traded.[107] Hesketh himself was one of the famous British merchants there. The companies were mostly made up of capital from London investors,[108] although the bulk of cotton's destination was still Liverpool. The Hesketh family is also a good example of merchants who successfully transitioned from the wine to the cotton trade, and from Portugal to Brazil. The family was from Lancashire. One of its prominent members, Robert Hesketh, was born in 1719 and inherited the business from his father who used to import wine from Porto. Robert got rich from this trade. Furthermore, he and his brother William, who was also a merchant, held public office in the city of Liverpool. In 1750, Robert sent his eldest son, John, to Porto to work as his agent. He exported a great deal of wine to his father but also to several other customers in England. In 1786, he formed a company with the famous wine merchant and major cotton exporter: Offley (see Appendix B). The firm was called Offley, Campion, Hesketh, & Co. and was dedicated to the wine trade. John married in Portugal, had nine children, and left for Liverpool when the French invaded Portugal in 1807. For most of their lives, John's children lived in Portugal, were

106 Henderson, *A History of the Brazil*, 390.
107 Ian Sargen, *Our Men in Brazil: The Hesketh Brothers Abroad* (Scotforth Books, 2009), 84.
108 Assunção, *De Caboclos a Bem-Te-Vis*, 253.

educated there, and they had a good knowledge of the Portuguese language. With the opening of Brazilian ports in 1808, and the promising Brazilian market, three of John's sons went to Brazil to pursue a career as merchants, just as their father and grandfather had done. Robert Hesketh, around 22 years old, was already in Maranhão in 1812. It was in that year that he was appointed British consul in Maranhão, Pará, and Ceará. Brothers William and Thomas joined Robert soon after. Thomas would later return to Liverpool, where he would act as a cotton merchant. He was an agent for his brothers, selling cotton and shipping manufactured goods to sell in Brazil.[109]

Of all that Brazil exported to England, raw cotton was the main commodity. Between 1807 and 1821, cotton accounted for 65.8% of exports to England (Table 9.6), and until at least 1835, cotton was the main Brazilian commodity exported to England.[110] During much of the 1810s, Portugal still received large

TABLE 9.6 Raw cotton exports to England in relation to total exports from Brazil, 1807–1821

Years	Total exports	Cotton exports	Cotton (%)
1807		15,000	
1808		165,337,000	
1809	1,227,038,000	582,920,000	47.51
1810	1,341,702,000	653,574,000	48.71
1811	1,083,194,000	623,751,000	57.58
1812	599,022,000	500,760,000	83.60
1813			
1814	1,190,337,000	740,793,000	62.23
1815	721,667,000	424,962,000	58.89
1816	869,539,000	650,613,000	74.82
1817	768,280,000	531,496,000	69.18
1818	1,030,251,000	807,495,000	78.38
1819	915,193,000	673,632,000	73.61
1820	1,245,748,000	942,857,000	75.69
1821	1,075,093,000	632,714,000	58.85

Source and notes: Arruda, *O algodão brasileiro*, 180. Exports are given in pounds. Table prepared by the author.

109 Sargen, *Our Men in Brazil*, 3–14.
110 Manchester, *British Preeminence in Brazil*, 207; Sturz, *A Review, Financial, Statistical, & Commercial, of the Empire of Brazil and Its Resources*, 97.

TABLE 9.7 Exports of cotton from Maranhão, 1812–1821

Years	Lisbon	Porto	England	France	United States	Other ports	Total
1812	17,591	2,997	196,154		827	185	217,754
1813	48,003	5,960	272,730				326,693
1814	65,045	6,351	166,459	10,527			248,382
1815	100,000	8,977	168,877			25	277,879
1816	105,448	10,822	214,538	19,413			350,221
1817	144,904	20,925	218,343	17,557			401,729
1818	88,488	18,595	267,164	27,488	205	853	402,793
1819	91,074	14,212	222,623	31,326		45	359,280
1820	67,730	12,493	268,736	16,502		1,732	367,193
1821	58,836	4,592	143,771	18,899			226,098
Total	787,119	105,924	2,139,395	141,712	1,032	2,840	

Source and notes: Callcott, *Journal of a Voyage to Brazil*, 332. Exports are given in arrobas. Table prepared by the author.

quantities of cotton and France—even after the end of the war in 1815—was importing small quantities directly from Brazil (Table 9.7). Yet, as noted in Chapter 7, there was an intense trade in cotton between Lisbon and France during the period.[111] In the mid-nineteenth century, France would become Brazil's second-largest cotton buyer.[112]

The British in Maranhão somehow monopolized cotton exports after the opening of the Brazilians ports in 1808. They also acquired a certain specialization in importing hardware, tableware, and fabrics. The Portuguese ended up dedicating themselves to exporting leather and rice, and the French apparently concentrated on the jewellery and bijoux trade.[113] Still, according to Gayoso, there seemed to be a special alliance between the Portuguese and the British to control the price of cotton. Writing in 1813, Gayoso claimed that after 1808, the number of cotton growers increased, and the number of buyers/exporters decreased, causing the price of cotton to fall. Intentionally, the Portuguese and British merchants "joined up"[114] to restrict competition and thus set cot-

111 See also Pedreira, *Estrutura industrial e mercado colonial*, 317–18; Weber, "Relações comerciais e acumulação mercantil," 385.

112 Burlamaqui, *Monographia do algodoeiro*, 88.

113 Viveiros, *História do Comércio do Maranhão 1612–1895*, 1: 130.

114 "se mancomunaram".

ton prices. They created, according to Gayoso, a monopoly and imposed low prices on farmers. Cotton production did not stop growing, but buyers were few from 1808. In 1812, with the lack of cotton from North America in Liverpool, the cotton prices of Maranhão were supposed to increase. However, they actually decreased because of the monopolists in Maranhão. Another strategy was to speculate: when other merchants came from abroad to buy cotton, the monopolists held the cotton until they got a favorable price.[115] Even the governor of Maranhão in 1822 pointed to the same problem with the monopolists.[116]

Gayoso explicitly stated that the reason for the lower price of cotton from Maranhão was the result of arbitrary procedures carried out by merchants. He also highlighted that such occurrences were not observed in Pernambuco, which therefore led to higher cotton prices in the latter region compared to Maranhão. Gayoso saw that the qualities of cotton from Maranhão and Pernambuco were similar, and he believed that the prices of the former were being deliberately reduced by English and Portuguese traders.[117] Nevertheless, this assumption is undermined when we examine the cotton prices exchanged in Brazil and Portugal. Prior until approximately 1787, cotton originating from Maranhão held a higher value compared to cotton from Pernambuco. However, subsequently, there was a change in the scenario, and cotton from Maranhão seldom surpassed the high standards of cotton from Pernambuco, both within Brazil and in Portugal.[118] Thus, even before the English settled in Maranhão, the price of cotton there was already lower than that of Pernambuco (Figure 9.3).

In 1816 Pernambuco exported over three-quarters of its cotton to England and Bahia, almost 89%.[119] Brazil's second-most important export between 1821 and 1830 was still cotton. In the following decade, it dropped to third place, behind coffee and sugar, and in the 1840s, it fell to fourth place, even behind hides and skins.[120] The English continued to be interested in cotton. In 1845, English merchants had 20 wholesale commercial houses in Recife. It was the second largest nationality, just behind the 27 Brazilian companies.[121]

115 Gayoso, *Compendio historico-politico*, 257–60, 262, 267.

116 Galves, "Ao Público Sincero e Imparcial," 117.

117 Gayoso, *Compendio historico-politico*, 311–12.

118 There is no explicit information about why Pernambuco cotton became more expensive in the 1780s compared to Maranhão cotton. My hypothesis is that European, primarily British, demand for finer, higher-quality yarns, coupled with the growing need for long-staple cotton, led to a rise in the value of Pernambuco cotton during this decade.

119 Manchester, *British Preeminence in Brazil*, 97.

120 Arruda, *O Brasil no comércio colonial*, 629.

121 José Antônio Gonsalves de Mello, *Ingleses Em Pernambuco: História Do Cemitério Britânico Do Recife e Da Participação de Ingleses e Outros Estrangeiros Na Vida e Na Cultura*

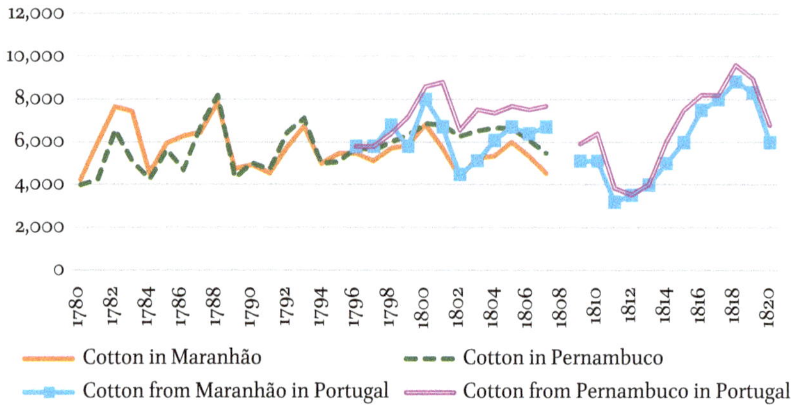

FIGURE 9.3 Cotton prices from Maranhão and Pernambuco in Brazil and Portugal, 1780–1820
Sources and notes: for prices in Brazil, see Martins and Melo, "Cotton Exports from Brazil, 1758–1815 Dataset" (European University Institute, HEC, 2022), https://cadmus.eui.eu/handle/1814/74724. For prices in Portugal, see Arruda, *O Brasil no Comércio colonial*, 368–369, and the Trade Balance records (*Balanças de Comércio*). Figure prepared by the author.

The French invasion at the end of 1807 represented the end of many things that had been happening for centuries. The colonial exclusive was one of them. Along with him, an entire mercantile community in Lisbon—foreign and national—that used to import and re-export Brazilian goods was broken up. Not only that, but the colonial market itself for exports from Portugal virtually disappeared or was seriously compromised after 1808. By 1750, Portugal received 15% of total British exports. In 1850, it received less than 1%.[122] It was the Empire that contributed to Portuguese consumption, not only because income in the metropolis increased due to colonial wealth[123] but because of the very fact that Brazil was an important consumer market for Portugal. The export level reached by Portugal in 1800 (5–7% of European exports) was the highest level achieved by the country in the nineteenth century.[124] The dismissal of Portugal as an entrepot was an excellent opportunity for the British;

de Pernambuco, No Período de 1813 a 1909 (Instituto Arqueológico, Histórico e Geográfico Pernambucano, 1972), 18.

122 Paul Bairoch, *Commerce Extérieur et Développement Économique de l'Europe Au XIXe Siècle* (Mouton, 1976), 266–67.

123 Costa et al., "The Great Escape?".

124 Bairoch, *Commerce Extérieur et Développement Économique de l'Europe Au XIXe Siècle*, 267.

not only did they have access to Brazilian cotton, but the consumer market for their products grew. In 1807, British goods sent to Brazil reached the amount of 1,200,000 pounds, and by 1812 they had jumped to 2,000,000 pounds.[125] Between the 1820s and 1830s, exports of British goods to Brazil reached a level equivalent to the values exported to the Caribbean.[126]

The end of the colonial exclusive was, in fact, favorable to England. Foreign trade was crucial to the British, not only because it generated income for England through taxes but also because it contributed to paying for the fight against Napoleon. To pay for the war against France, England relied on its income from trade, mainly from trade with the West Indies. With this money, they paid their army and navy and also earmarked monetary aid for other nations to fight France on the Continent. Another source was commercial rents with other European countries, such as Portugal. According to Robson, sustaining trade with Portugal (and by extension with Brazil) was essential for England to win the war against France.[127] From the end of 1807, "Britain did not have any strategic or commercial openings in Europe," and its relationship with the North Americans was also compromised. By 1808, England's intention was not "direct military intervention" but rather "to spread British commerce and influence" in South America. England had to face the Continental Blockade in Europe, its Continental allies being defeated, Lisbon being lost, the military unfeasibility of attacking Spanish possessions in America, and the United States declaring a trade embargo. At that moment, Brazilian marketplaces proved decisive for the British and had the potential to be an entrepot to access the markets of Spanish America. It was an illegal trade and one that took place well before the French wars, but with Brazil and Spain at war, the entry of smuggled English goods into Spanish America was jeopardized.[128]

---

125 Robson, *Britain, Portugal and South America*, 236.

126 Assunção, *De Caboclos a Bem-Te-Vis.*, 253. However, there is no consensus in the literature on the importance of the Brazilian consumer market for British interests; see D. C. M. Platt, *Business Imperialism, 1840–1930: An Inquiry Based on British Experience in Latin America* (Oxford University Press, 1977); Stephen H. Haber and Herbert S. Klein, "The Economic Consequences of Brazilian Independence," in *How Latin America Fell behind: Essays in the Economic Histories of Brazil and Mexico, 1800–1914*, ed. Stephen H. Haber (Stanford University Press, 1997); Pedreira, "From Growth to Collapse".

127 Parkinson, *The Trade Winds*; Robson, *Britain, Portugal and South America*, 263; William Nester, *The Coalitions Against Napoleon: How British Money, Manufacturing and Military Power Forged the Alliances That Achieved Victory* (Frontline Books, 2023).

128 Robson, *Britain, Portugal and South America*, 196–206. See also Rory Muir, *Britain and the Defeat of Napoleon, 1807–1815* (1996; Yale University Press, 2008); Michael Duffy, "World-Wide War and British Expansion, 1793–1815," in *The Oxford History of the British Empire:*

British imperialism did not exactly mean a territorial "conquest" but was rather driven by the commercial interests of the "largest merchant marine in the world and protected by the greatest naval force in the world." The proceeds from this trade would be directed toward funding the fight against Napoleon. That is why it was essential to open commerce with Brazil and get trade agreements that favored the English, and that is what happened in 1808 and 1810.[129] Raw cotton certainly played a big role in all of this. Most of the Brazilian exports to England between 1807 and 1821 were not made up of sugar or coffee, which suffered import restrictions by the British, but cotton.[130] The British were so interested in cotton from Brazil that they charged Brazilian vessels carrying the fiber the same fees as British vessels.[131] Yet, more important than raw cotton, the main responsible for England's commercial income and the primary items that demanded more market were cotton goods. From the early nineteenth century to the mid-1840s, "cotton represented 40 to 50 per cent of all British exports."[132] According to Hobsbawm, "it is not unfair to say" that Latin America "saved the British cotton industry in the first half of the nineteenth century, when it became the largest single market for it exports, mainly to Brazil."[133] In 1812, three-quarters of what England exported to Brazil comprised cotton textiles; in 1835, the picture was pretty much the same.[134]

With the loss of Brazil, the merchant community in Portugal was deprived of an important re-export item: raw cotton.[135] Perhaps the main ones affected were the Portuguese. The French in Lisbon had withdrawn from the export business long before 1808. It was the British who managed a successful transition from trade from Portugal to trade from Brazil. It was not preordained that it would be that way, though. Between the 1760s and early 1780s, the British were marginal players in cotton exports from Portugal. They also saw severe

---

Volume II: The Eighteenth Century, ed. P. J. Marshall and Alaine Low (Oxford University Press, 1998).

129 Robson, *Britain, Portugal and South America*, 202–3. See also Arruda, *Uma Colônia Entre Dois Impérios*.

130 José Jobson de Andrade Arruda, "O Algodão Brasileiro Na Época Da Revolução Industrial," *América Latina En La Historia Económica* 23, no. 2 (2016): 180.

131 Robson, *Britain, Portugal and South America*, 205.

132 Chapman, *Merchant Enterprise in Britain*, 6. According to Sturz, in the early 1830s Brazil consumed more British products than all the Spanish American republics combined and also more than all British exports to the African continent; see Sturz, *A Review, Financial, Statistical, & Commercial, of the Empire of Brazil and Its Resources*, 96.

133 Hobsbawm, *Industry and Empire: The Making of Modern English Society, 1750 to the Present Day*, 121.

134 Manchester, *British Preeminence in Brazil*, 97, 314.

135 Bairoch, *Commerce Extérieur et Développement Économique de l'Europe Au XIXe Siècle*, 267.

competition from French imports of raw cotton from Portugal in the early nineteenth century. In large part, the Anglo-Portuguese historical alliance explained British pre-eminence in the cotton trade from Portugal. This was guaranteed by commercial treaties, commercial and legal institutions (consuls and judges), and also because of the very strength and wealth of British merchants based in Portugal, who had strong connections with the commercial houses in England. These were things the French did not have in Portugal. But everything would change soon after 1815 and with even more intensity in the 1820s. Brazil, for several reasons, faced difficulties in growing cotton and did not manage to face the intense competition from U.S. cotton.

6 Conclusion

Brazilian cotton became important in terms of exports from Portugal/Brazil and imports from Britain between the mid-1780s and the conclusion of the 1810s. Much changed in these nearly three decades, though. London, the traditional port for Anglo-Portuguese trade, ceased to be the leading importer in the mid-1780s but continued to be important and sometimes stocked more cotton than Liverpool. However, spinners would consume Brazilian cotton in the north of England and the west of Scotland. As a result, London ended up assuming the role of a re-export port throughout the period, including sending raw Brazilian cotton to France. London merchants also financed industries in the north of England and sold cotton goods to domestic and overseas markets.

A series of factors favored the north of England and Scotland to become the leading textile centers in the world: the geographical settings, the agricultural structures, the organizational framework inherited from the spinning and weaving of flax and wool, cheap energy and high wages, the availability of capital (part of it coming from commerce), the marketing connections already established through other goods, good consumer markets in England and overseas, the protection of the British navy and the technological development in the cotton textile industry. The consequently increasing demand for raw cotton was met by the region's most important port, Liverpool. The way cotton was imported involved several intermediaries. Since several types of cotton fibers came from across the globe to Liverpool, and a tremendous variety of spinners were specializing in various kinds of yarns and cloths, intermediaries were needed with knowledge of the fiber import market and familiarity with the diverse demands of spinners. Two central figures in the cotton trade emerged: dealers and brokers, who operated in Manchester and Liverpool. However, the business of importing cotton from Portugal and Brazil was also done by traditional importers (or their agents) and could be done directly by spinners who had connections in Portugal.

With the French threatening to invade Portugal, the English merchant community in Portugal had to restructure itself to continue to buy Brazilian cotton and to sell cotton goods in South America, by far one of the main markets for the British in the first decades of the nineteenth century. They returned to London or Liverpool and sent their agents to Brazil, either to Rio de Janeiro or to the main Brazilian ports that exported cotton: Recife and São Luís. In the crucial years when United States cotton was having difficulty entering England (because of war and embargoes and the Continental blockade), Brazilian raw cotton and consumer markets for cotton goods in Portuguese and Spanish America proved to be of singular importance to the British economy. The monetary sources to fight Napoleon came from the export trade of manufactured goods, so it was crucial for the British to guarantee open overseas markets for their products.

Conclusion

And I asked my russet mule,
Carrying a load of cotton,
Where he was headed for.
"To work in the harvest home."

Sagarana, published in 1946, is one of the classics of Brazilian literature—a collection of stories that portray life in the Brazilian backlands (*sertão*). Interestingly, in the opening story, João Guimarães Rosa chooses to reproduce traditional verses about cotton, said to have been sung by the region's inhabitants. The phrase reproduced above is loaded with symbolism, though. Cotton is not exactly cotton but rather an allusion to something bigger: "the bale of life, the weight of the world, the existential burden." And the answer that the little donkey (or the mule) provides refers to the "will of destiny," to a role that the little donkey (who can actually be understood as a human being) had no way of escaping.[1] These words nevertheless illustrate the prominence of cotton in the Brazilian hinterlands—sufficiently popular to be incorporated into a song—over a century after its emergence during the Industrial Revolution. Brazilian raw cotton has a history, and one that has changed significantly in the last 200 years. Some legacies remained for a long time, such as the presence of cotton in Brazilian rural areas still in the mid-twentieth century like in *Sagarana* and its importance for poor populations. Others have changed significantly, such as the shift in Brazilian growing centers, agricultural technology, and the destination of exports that has been occurring since the late 1990s. The symbolic presence of cotton in *Sagarana* underscores its longstanding role in Brazilian society, not only as an economic commodity but also as a cultural reference embedded in collective memory. Such literary traces point to the persistence of cotton's significance well beyond its initial rise during the Industrial Revolution. To situate this cultural and social resonance within a broader historical framework, this conclusion seeks to retrace some of the key moments in the history of Brazilian raw cotton during the Industrial Revolution and extend the analysis into subsequent transformations.

1 João Guimarães Rosa, *Sagarana* (1946; Alfred A. Knopf, 1966), x–xi. Franklin de Oliveira wrote an introduction for the English edition (translated by Harriet de Onís), from which I derived the interpretation of the donkey song. This is the original song in Portuguese: "E, ao meu macho rosado, carregado de algodão, preguntei: p'ra donde ia? P'ra rodar no mutirão".

HTTPS://DOI.ORG/10.1163/9789004757561-015

This book sought to demonstrate that our understanding of cotton can be enriched by situating it within the agricultural structures of the Portuguese Empire and the diverse mercantile networks that sustained them, both of which underwent significant changes over time. Before U.S. cotton came to dominate global markets, Brazilian cotton played an important role in supplying European textile centers. While its importance to England is well established, its significance for France and other parts of the Continent has received far less scholarly attention. Moving beyond the classic framework that focuses on English textile centers, wage labor, and U.S. raw cotton tied to slave labor, this book highlighted a different perspective: one in which trade itself takes on central importance and where agricultural conditions within Brazil varied substantially. These differences—between Maranhão and the Northeast—invite a closer examination of diverse labor systems and the distinct qualities of cotton plants that shaped productivity. Through this comparative lens, the book offered the first global estimate of enslaved people engaged in the cotton sector alongside new data on cotton exports from these regions. The resulting production conditions generated abundant supplies of cotton for merchants, which means that without a strong production base, there could be no trade. At the same time, the history of Brazilian cotton cannot be understood apart from commerce. Exports began intensively only through a monopolistic trading company, a creation of Pombaline political economy, which stimulated investment in Maranhão and facilitated the African slave trade to northern Brazil. After the company's dissolution, independent merchants financed plantations, supplied enslaved labor, shipped cotton to Lisbon, and distributed fibers throughout Europe. Beyond domestic mercantile communities (that is, Portuguese), the cotton trade also relied heavily on foreign merchants. This book introduces original data and new arguments that underscore the need to consider the trans-imperial dimensions of Brazilian raw cotton exports, particularly the routes that carried cotton from Lisbon to Europe's major textile markets. Thus, without a comparative view of Brazil's main regions, an analysis of the Portuguese Empire's political economy, a nuanced understanding of mercantile communities, and a transnational perspective, the history of one of the Industrial Revolution's most important cotton suppliers cannot be fully understood.

If Brazilian cotton was so important, why has it not been examined comprehensively before? I believe several factors help explain this. First, while studies on Brazilian cotton do exist, they have typically focused on individual regions or on trade with England, without offering a broad picture. This fragmentation is partly due, I would argue, to the predominance of more traditional commodities in Brazilian economic history. The tendency to frame Brazil's trajectory as a straightforward transition from gold to coffee has diverted attention from cotton as a subject of serious historical inquiry. Furthermore, we could fairly argue that the raw cotton trade has been overlooked because historians traditionally focused on the finished goods of industrial capitalism (like textiles), technological innovation, and factory labor. The transatlantic circulation of raw cotton itself was seen as secondary, often absorbed into studies of slavery, plantation economies, or industrial growth, rather than examined as a distinct and central trade system.

What quickly became clear was that understanding a commodity like cotton requires much more than simply following bales of fiber across the ocean. The trade cannot be disentangled from slavery and plantation production, nor from imperial policies, financial credit systems, shipping infrastructures, or the rivalries of European powers. Markets did not operate as abstract spaces of supply and demand; they were historical arenas shaped by trust, networks, and institutions. To write this book, I had to hold all these factors together—the growers and enslaved laborers in Maranhão and Pernambuco, the Portuguese and foreign merchants in Lisbon, and the consumers and spinners in Rouen, Hamburg, and Manchester—and consider how their interactions transformed both sides of the Atlantic. The outcome of this book also brings us a deeper understanding of the quick changes that took place in a brief period: the commercial landscape changed rapidly, sometimes from one year to the next, making it difficult to treat the first phase of industrialization as a homogeneous period. Such factors, together with a more comprehensive understanding of the transformations undergone by raw cotton over time, would not have been possible without the use of a broad array of documents and historical sources. Customs records, consular reports, reports of colonial governors, trade balances, merchants' correspondence, different kinds of notarial records, court cases, parliamentary debates, and commercial newspapers all became indispensable. These sources allowed me to trace the movement of cotton from Brazilian plantations to Lisbon's warehouses, and from there to the spinning centers of France, Great Britain, and other places in Europe. They also helped me to identify the networks of growers, merchants, and intermediaries—sometimes hundreds of individuals at a time—who sustained this Atlantic trade.

This book points to three general conclusions. First, from the cultivation point of view, there is a certain consensus in old and current literature that cotton growing in Brazil was based on large slave plantations.[2] These big units of

2 Sven Beckert, *Empire of Cotton: A Global History* (Alfred A. Knopf, 2014), 94, 109–10; Caio Prado Júnior, *Formação do Brasil contemporâneo: colônia* (1942; 6. ed, Brasiliense, 1961),

agricultural production would be essential elements to complement the great manufacturing industries in Great Britain.[3] However, the new sources that I have used point to a more complex scenario. There were large plantations in Maranhão indeed, but cultivation in Northeastern Brazil was based on small slaveholding properties. And while the total numbers of enslaved people in the two regions were quite different, they produced cotton in similar quantities. Furthermore, this had an impact on trade: in Maranhão, the development of large plantations favored a group of wealthy growers to export cotton to Portugal; in the Northeast, where small cotton farms thrived, poor growers who used a small number of enslaved people had to sell their cotton bales to intermediaries and export-merchants on the coast.

Second, from the point of view of trade, the same literature has overemphasized the British demand, sidelining other markets, such as France, Genoa, and Hamburg. This book shows that France was the leading buyer of Brazilian cotton between the 1770s and the beginning of the 1780s. The English were scarcely interested in Brazilian cotton at the beginning of the Industrial Revolution. Years later, France was also important. Between 1800 and 1807, they bought more Brazilian cotton than the English. Between these two periods, England dominated as a destination for cotton exports from Lisbon, primarily because of the French Wars that posed a series of obstacles to trade with France. Yet, I show there were large inflows of Brazilian cotton into France through neutral vessels and smuggling. Hamburg was an important entrepôt for the illegal trade that linked Portugal and France during the wars. Genoa, in turn, was a chief port that brought cotton from Portugal, distributed it to the cotton mills in its surroundings, and shipped it to Switzerland.

Third, from the merchants' point of view, the literature has always taken for granted that the English trading community in Portugal was the strongest.[4] In effect, on many occasions, they were. Again, however, the configuration of

136–37; Thales Augusto Zamberlan Pereira, "The Cotton Trade and Brazilian Foreign Commerce during the Industrial Revolution" (PhD diss., Universidade de São Paulo, 2017), 12, 13, 40; Thales Augusto Zamberlan Pereira, "Poor Man's Crop? Slavery in Brazilian Cotton Regions (1800–1850)," *Estudos Econômicos (São Paulo)* 48, no. 4 (2018): 636.

3 Immanuel Wallerstein, *Historical Capitalism with Capitalist Civilization* (1983; Verso, 2011), 101–2; Jürgen Kocka, *Capitalism: A short history* (Princeton University Press, 2016), 66–67.

4 See for instance, L. M. E. Shaw, *The Anglo-Portuguese Alliance and the English Merchants in Portugal, 1654–1810* (Ashgate, 1998); Kenneth Maxwell, "Pombal and the Nationalization of the Luso-Brazilian Economy," *The Hispanic American Historical Review* 48, no. 4 (1968): 608–31; Harold Edward Stephen Fisher, "Lisbon, Its English Merchant Community and the Mediterranean in the Eighteenth Century," in *Shipping, Trade and Commerce: Essays in Memory of Ralph Davis*, ed. P. L. Cottrell and Derek Howard Aldcroft (Leicester University Press, 1981).

the mercantile communities that were importing and re-exporting cotton was more complex and changed over time. Cotton importers were a different group from the merchants who would ship the cotton bales to the rest of Europe: the group that received cotton from Brazil was mostly Portuguese, and the merchants who exported the fiber were of different nationalities with English traders dominating. Conversely, despite France being a key buyer, French merchants in Portugal were practically irrelevant in the business. The role of exporting cotton from Portugal to French ports was in the hands of other nationalities, mainly the Portuguese.

Basic institutions, such as the Portuguese legal and commercial framework that supported notarial acts, such as company contracts, obligation contracts, and powers of attorney, were essential parts of trade between Portugal and Brazil. Above this were what we might call the mercantilist institutions of the Portuguese Empire, particularly regarding navigation and the destination of vessels departing from Brazil: the owners of the vessels were mostly Portuguese, and trade between Brazil and any part of Europe outside of Portugal was prohibited. Thus, despite being a very old and criticized concept, mercantilism still carries some degree of validity, which has also been pointed out by others on various occasions.[5] In addition, mercantilism also provides a theoretical framework for understanding international relations between European nations, especially with regard to the nature of commercial treaties and the

5 Fernando A. Novais, *Portugal e Brasil na crise do antigo sistema colonial (1777–1808)* (Hucitec, 1979); Stanley L. Engerman, "Mercantilism and Overseas Trade, 1700–1800," in *The Economic History of Britain since 1700*, ed. Roderick Floud and Donald McCloskey, vol. 1 (Cambridge University Press, 1981); Evan Luard, *The Balance of Power: The System of International Relations, 1648–1815* (Macmillan, 1992); Nuala Zahedieh, "Making Mercantilism Work: London Merchants and Atlantic Trade in the Seventeenth Century," *Transactions of the Royal Historical Society* 9 (1999): 143–58; Leonor Freire Costa, "Relações Económicas Com o Exterior," in *História Económica de Portugal, 1700–2000*, ed. Pedro Lains and Alvaro Ferreira da Silva, vol. 1 (Imprensa de Ciências Sociais, 2005); Ronald Findlay and Kevin H. O'Rourke, *Power and Plenty: Trade, War, and the World Economy in the Second Millennium* (Princeton University Press, 2007); Philip J. Stern and Carl Wennerlind, eds., *Mercantilism Reimagined: Political Economy in Early Modern Britain and Its Empire* (Oxford University Press, 2013); Lars Magnusson, *The Political Economy of Mercantilism* (Routledge, 2015); Patrick O'Brien, "The Formation of States and Transitions to Modern Economies: England, Europe, and Asia Compared," in *The Cambridge History Capitalism*, Reprint edition, ed. Larry Neal, vol. 1 (Cambridge University Press, 2015); J. W. Horrocks, *A Short History of Mercantilism* (Taylor & Francis, 2017); Nuala Zahedieh, "Defying Mercantilism: Illicit Trade, Trust, and the Jamaican Sephardim, 1660–1730," *The Historical Journal* 61, no. 1 (2018): 77–102; Jacob Soll, "For a New Economic History of Early Modern Empire: Anglo-French Imperial Codevelopment beyond Mercantilism and Laissez-Faire," *The William and Mary Quarterly* 77, no. 4 (2020): 525–50; Eli F. Heckscher, *Mercantilism*, vol. 1 (1931; Routledge, 1994).

establishment of trading posts or factories. To a large extent, the English merchant community in Portugal enjoyed more favorable trading conditions than other nations because of agreements that had been established more than a century before Brazilian cotton arrived on the scene. Another idea associated with mercantilism, however, is mistaken. It is common to view trade between metropolises and colonies as exclusive to the subjects of their respective nations and barring foreign participation. What a thorough analysis of the Brazilian cotton trade reveals is that although the vast majority of merchants importing cotton from Lisbon were Portuguese, a small portion of foreigners were doing business directly with Brazil, while other foreign merchants used Portuguese courts to recover capital held by debtors in Brazil. Thus, foreigners were permitted in colonial trade with Brazil. The fact that they were not more important in this trade is what needs to be answered. This is a question worthy of further research. In this book, I have suggested some hypothetical ideas. It is possible that foreign merchants already had their hands full working in the re-export trade. Another factor was the recovery of debts from debtors in Brazil. This seemed to be a problem most foreigners preferred not to face. Therefore, they preferred to invest in Portuguese merchants in Portugal who did business with Brazil, as debt recovery was easier in this case.

The case of Brazilian cotton can also be useful for thinking about other overarching discussions. It can add for instance to an old conversation about the efficiency of slavery, a discussion that was partially resumed by the "New History of Capitalism" (NHC). Many years ago, U.S. southern slave plantations were compared to free northern farming to verify whether slavery was more efficient than free labor. The former, according to Fogel and Engerman, was more efficient than the latter.[6] More recently, the NHC, more specifically Baptist's thesis, argues that the U.S. cotton planting productivity augmented due to increased violence to enforce the labor demands on enslaved people.[7]

6 Robert William Fogel and Stanley L. Engerman, *Time on the Cross: The Economics of American Negro Slavery* (Wildwood House, 1976). Other scholars, however, have criticized this claim; see Paul A. David and Peter Temin, "Slavery: The Progressive Institution?," *The Journal of Economic History* 34, no. 3 (1974): 739–83; Paul A. David and Peter Temin, "Explaining the Relative Efficiency of Slave Agriculture in the Antebellum South: Comment," *The American Economic Review* (1979).

7 Edward E. Baptist, *The Half Has Never Been Told: Slavery and the Making of American Capitalism* (Basic Books, 2014), 121, 350. For criticisms regarding the New History of Capitalism, see Eric Hilt, "Economic History, Historical Analysis, and the "New History of Capitalism"", *The Journal of Economic History* 77, no. 2 (2017): 511–36; Alan L. Olmstead and Paul W. Rhode, "Cotton, Slavery, and the New History of Capitalism," *Explorations in Economic History* 67 (January 2018): 1–17; Gavin Wright, "Slavery and Anglo-American Capitalism Revisited," *The Economic History Review* 73, no. 2 (2020): 353–83; Trevor Burnard and Giorgio Riello, "Slavery and the New History of Capitalism," *Journal of Global History* 15, no. 2 (2020): 225–44.

However, this hypothesis is complicated to test.[8] Evidently, violence was an element that sustained the slave societies of the past, but the extent to which it impacted productivity is difficult to measure. From what has been presented so far, other factors impacted slave productivity (organization of slave labor, specialization in cash crop plantations, and the type of fiber being cultivated, for example) other than a single increase in coercion. The scenario certainly involved violence to make the enslaved people work, but it also comprised other incentives. In 1799, the farmer Manuel Arruda da Câmara wrote in his manual on how to plant cotton that the best way to make the enslaved people work well was to "combine punishment with reward": it was punishment when enslaved workers failed to meet the allotted harvest quota and extra remuneration when they exceeded what was asked of them.[9]

The history of Brazilian cotton, characterized by boom and bust, is inseparable from the broader history of U.S. cotton. With the end of the war in 1815, the cotton that would supply the French industry would become that of the United States, virtually putting an end to Brazilian cotton's relevance for the French cotton industry. If the interest of the French in raw Brazilian cotton disappeared with the end of the war, the British would still be interested in Brazilian fiber for a few more years. But overall, U.S. cotton showed clear signs of being the most advantageous to meet European cotton industry demands. What contributed to the continued British interest in Brazilian cotton was the possibility of penetrating South American consumer markets to sell their cotton textiles. Brazil remained the largest British market in the region until the mid-nineteenth century.[10] It was Latin America, and Brazil more specifically, that, according to Hobsbawm, saved the cotton textile industry in Great Britain, remembering that probably industrialization would not be possible without external markets.[11] Yet, a variety of factors contributed to the consolidation of U.S. pre-eminence, and a concise examination of the conditions that facilitated its growth is particularly pertinent to a deeper understanding of the trajectory of cotton in nineteenth-century Brazil. The precarious conditions of indigo and rice in Georgia and South Carolina, and tobacco in Virginia—the largest crops in the U.S. South until the 1790s—led

---

8 For criticisms of Baptist's argument, see Olmstead and Rhode, "Cotton, Slavery, and the New History of Capitalism"; Nuno Palma et al., "Slavery and Development in Nineteenth Century Brazil," *Capitalism: A Journal of History and Economics* 2, no. 2 (2021): 372–426.

9 Manuel Arruda da Câmara, *Memoria sobre a cultura dos algodoeiros e sobre o methodo de o escolher, e ensacar, etc.* (Na Officina da Casa Litteraria do Arco do Cego, 1799), 60–61.

10 D. C. M. Platt, *Latin America and the British Trade, 1806–1914* (Adam & Charles Black, 1972), 22, 29.

11 Eric J. Hobsbawm, *Industry and Empire: The Making of Modern English Society, 1750 to the Present Day* (Pantheon books, 1968), 121.

farmers to turn to a new crop, cotton, even relocating enslaved workers from the old crops to the new one.[12] Until 1811, Georgia and South Carolina were the leading cotton producers, accounting for three-quarters of total U.S. production. At the end of the same decade, they remained the leading cotton states, with an enslaved population that reached almost 40% of their total populations. After these states, cotton expanded to Alabama, Mississippi, and Louisiana.[13] The expansion of cotton production was largely a result of an expansion of cultivated areas. Similar to what happened in Brazil, as soon as one area lost its productivity, landowners moved to another. This was facilitated by the low price of land, making it more profitable to expand into new lands than to invest in fertilizers to utilize old lands.[14] The Louisiana Purchase (1803) and subsequent acquisitions extended the geographic reach of cotton.[15] The U.S. political and territorial expansion was equally critical: Federal policies facilitated the appropriation of Indigenous lands, opening millions of acres for cotton cultivation.[16] Furthermore, the South's warm climate, fertile soils, and long growing season offered advantages for the growing of cotton and other crops.[17] The cotton expansion, however, would not be possible without technological improvements. The 1793 invention of the cotton gin mechanized that process, rendering large-scale cultivation profitable in vast areas of the upland South.[18] More recently, Olmstead and Rhode explored how the technology used in seed selection played a role in explaining the increased yields of US cotton. Thus, not only was Whitney's gin relevant but so were the biological experiments that followed soon after.[19]

None of what has been said so far about U.S. cotton production would be possible without slave labor, which took on very peculiar characteristics. Not only was the transatlantic and interstate slave trade important, but also the

12 Curtis P. Nettels, *The Emergence of a National Economy, 1775–1815* (1962; Routledge, 2015), 183–84, 190.

13 Nettels, *The Emergence of a National Economy, 1775–1815*, 185–87.

14 Nettels, *The Emergence of a National Economy, 1775–1815*, 191.

15 John Elliott Cairnes, *The Slave Power: Its Character, Career, and Probable Designs: Being an Attempt to Explain the Real Issues Involved in the American Contest* (Macmillan, 1863), 209.

16 Claudio Saunt, *Unworthy Republic: The Dispossession of Native Americans and the Road to Indian Territory* (W. W. Norton & Company, 2020), 194.

17 F. V. Emerson, "Geographic Influences in American Slavery. Part II," *Bulletin of the American Geographical Society* 43, no. 2 (1911): 114.

18 Angela Lakwete, *Inventing the Cotton Gin: Machine and Myth in Antebellum America* (Johns Hopkins University Press, 2003).

19 Alan L. Olmstead and Paul W. Rhode, "Biological Innovation and Productivity Growth in the Antebellum Cotton Economy," *The Journal of Economic History* 68, no. 4 (2008): 1123–71.

very presence of a massive slave labor force, concentrated in the hands of a few planters, forced smallholders to the margins of this system. In this scenario, free wage labor found no place, and the Southern economy was almost entirely dependent on the labor of enslaved people.[20] The organization of work was also crucial, as much of the cotton plantations were based on the gang system where work was continuous and highly disciplined.[21] This arrangement, however, was sustained by coercion, not voluntary cooperation. Enslaved workers in this system labored more rigorously than free southern farmers or enslaved individuals on small plantations.[22] In the U.S. South, the abolition of the transatlantic trade in 1808 forced planters to rely on the natural growth of the enslaved population. More balanced sex ratios, slightly improved living conditions, and a labor regime that—although still brutal—allowed for longer life expectancy facilitated reproduction. In contrast, Brazilian slavery depended on continuous African imports until 1850. Sugar, cotton, and coffee plantations, as well as mining, imposed extreme workloads and high mortality. At the same time, extremely unequal gender ratios and precarious social and economic conditions discouraged family formation. For Brazilian planters, it was often cheaper to replace enslaved workers with newcomers than to support reproduction. As a result, the enslaved population in the U.S. grew rapidly through natural increase, reaching nearly four million by 1860. Brazil, despite having been the leader in the slave trade for many decades, at around the same time had about 1.5 million enslaved people.[23] The weight of the slave trade was so significant and the conditions for natural reproduction so precarious in Brazil that when the trade was abolished North of the Equator in 1815, the slave population in Maranhão began to decline significantly.[24]

Therefore, the year 1815 was a watershed moment. From that point on, upland cotton varieties flooded the market, causing other cotton prices around the world to plummet.[25] The impact of international market prices on Bra-

20 Nettels, *The Emergence of a National Economy, 1775–1815*, 192–93.

21 Fogel and Engerman, *Time on the Cross*, 204.

22 Robert William Fogel, *Without Consent or Contract: The Rise and Fall of American Slavery* (W. W. Norton & Company, 1989), 78–79, 197, 392.

23 Robert Edgar Conrad, *Children of God's Fire: A Documentary History of Black Slavery in Brazil* (Princeton University Press, 1994), xviii–xx; Herbert S. Klein and Francisco Vidal Luna, *Slavery in Brazil* (Cambridge University Press, 2010), 168.

24 Daniel B. Domingues da Silva, "The Atlantic Slave Trade to Maranhão, 1680–1846: Volume, Routes and Organisation," *Slavery & Abolition* 29, no. 4 (2008): 483.

25 Michael M. Edwards, *The Growth of the British Cotton Trade, 1780–1815* (Manchester University Press, 1967), 94–95; Douglas A. Farnie, *The English Cotton Industry and the World Market, 1815–1896* (Clarendon Press; Oxford University Press, 1979), 82–83; see also Rafael de Bivar Marquese and Marcelo Rosanova Ferraro, "The Political Economy of

zilian cotton agriculture had at least two important repercussions. Overall, from the 1820s to the 1840s, total Brazilian cotton exports declined slightly but began to grow again in the 1850s.[26] However, when we look at the two main producers, Maranhão and Pernambuco, their productions actually fell.[27] Consequently, before the U.S. Civil War, Brazil's general exports were already recovering but not through its traditional producers. It was the other provinces of Brazil that drove the growth, such as Alagoas, Paraíba, Ceará, Rio Grande do Norte, and Piauí. And perhaps the main characteristic of this period was the massive presence of free workers in the cotton fields, since the Atlantic slave trade to all of Brazil had already ended in 1850, with most of the enslaved population concentrated in the center-south. It is from this period that accounts indicate that cotton cultivation was a poor man's crop.[28] Indeed, it was, but for a long time before that, it was a crop worked by enslaved people.

Between the 1820s and the 1850s, Brazilian cotton experienced a decline in its share of the world market,[29] even as its cultivation stabilized and in some regions expanded. The fate of cotton following its heyday constitutes a subject for another inquiry. Here, however, it is pertinent to underscore the factors that contributed to its decline and to briefly trace its historical trajectory to the present. Such an approach can help underscore the long-term economic, social, and cultural legacies of a commodity that profoundly shaped the development of global capitalism. Cotton not only integrated Brazil into wider international markets but also intersected with the histories of slavery, industrialization, and international competition. Its enduring consequences remain evident today in persistent economic inequalities rooted in monoculture, in the racial hierarchies and social disparities inherited from the slave-based plantation system,

---

Brazilian Cotton in the Age of Industrial Capitalism," in *Colonial Commodities in Historical Capitalism: Brazil for Export.*, ed. Gustavo Acioli Lopes et al. (Routledge, 2026).

26 Stanley J. Stein, *The Brazilian Cotton Manufacture: Textile Enterprise in an Underdeveloped Area, 1850–1950* (Harvard University Press, 1957), 198.

27 Francisco de Assis Leal Mesquita, *Vida e morte da economia algodoeira do Maranhão: uma análise das relações de produção na cultura do algodão, 1850–1890* (Universidade Federal do Maranhão, 1987), 64–65; Sebastião Ferreira Soares, *Notas estatísticas sobre a produção agrícola e carestia dos gêneros alimentícios no Imperio do Brasil* (Typ. Imp. e Const. de J. Villeneuve e Comp., 1860), 261–62; John Casper Branner, *Cotton in the Empire of Brazil; the Antiquity, Methods and Extent of Its Cultivation, Together with Statistics of Exportation and Home Consumption* (Government Printing Office, 1885), 47.

28 See for instance, Joan Meznar, "Orphans and the Transition from Slave to Free Labor in Northeast Brazil: The Case of Campina Grande, 1850–1888," *Journal of Social History* 27, no. 3 (1994): 499–515; see also Pereira, "Poor Man's Crop?," 624.

29 Amy A. Quark, *Global Rivalries: Standards Wars and the Transnational Cotton Trade* (University of Chicago Press, 2013), 41.

and in global trade patterns that continue to situate former cotton-producing regions in dependent relationships with industrial centers.

It is problematic to pinpoint one major cause, but it is safe to say that several problems surrounded Brazilian fiber since its beginning. Already in the mid-1810s, Gayoso, a planter from Maranhão, listed five reasons for what we can classify as the germs of that decadence. First was the lack of land—because of the Native American threats—to expand the crops. Second was the high price of enslaved people. Third was the indebtedness of planters who were obliged to hand over their slaves as a form of payment. Fourth was the low price of cotton due to the merchants' monopoly in Maranhão. Fifth was the method of payment of taxes, more specifically tithes.[30] A little later, in the early 1820s, Lago enumerated six problems that were similar to those raised by Gayoso. The first was related to the low amount of land for farming, which reflected the archaic and soil-destroying way of agricultural methods of clearing the land done by the planters. The second was the danger of indigenous attacks. The third was the excessive taxes on producers. The fourth was the debt executions that took the planters' slaves. The fifth was the lack of proper roads in Maranhão to transport agricultural products. This resulted in the loss of properties along the precarious roads and sometimes discouraged even starting a plantation. Finally, the sixth reason was the obligation of owners to enlist in the militia, which kept them away from their plantations.[31]

In the 1830s, the French Horace Emile Say used to say that Brazilian cotton was "good and beautiful," but he also complained about the "difficult and expensive" conditions of overland transport and the lack of cleanliness in the cotton. Above all, however, Brazil (particularly Maranhão, Pernambuco, and Bahia) failed to "improve production and make it more economical" in order to compete with U.S. cotton. The failure was also linked to the series of revolts and wars that broke out in the North and Northeast of Brazil, creating "anarchy" and disorganizing the means of production and commerce. Consequently, in 1827 France imported 15 times more cotton from the U.S. than from Brazil, and this imbalance deepened in the years that followed. The problem was that cotton sales prices did not cover its costs, so production in Brazil was smaller and stagnant compared to the output in the U.S. According to him,

30 Raimundo Jose de Sousa Gayoso, *Compendio historico-politico dos principios da lavoura do Maranhão: suas producçoens, e progressos, que tem tido até ao prezente, entraves que a vão deteriorando; e meios que tem lembrado para desvanece-los, em augmento da mesma lavoura, e sem prejuizo do real patrimonio …* (P.N. Rougeron, Impressor, 1818), 227.

31 Antonio Bernardino Pereira do Lago, *Estatistica historica-geografica da Provincia do Maranhão oferecida ao Soberano Congresso das Cortes Geraes, extraordinarias, e constituintes da monarchia portugueza* (Academia Real das Sciencias, 1822), 58–60.

"Brazilians can only blame themselves. Its soil is more fertile than that of the U.S., its climate is healthier, its sun is more powerful; cotton grows easily in its privileged soil; always ripens well; fiber is fine and vigorous; the only fault then lies with those who do not know how to take advantage of the advantages that nature has squandered under their feet."[32]

The roots of the cotton depression between 1850 and 1890 in Maranhão were directly associated with the excessive indebtedness of producers, according to Mesquita. There were also excessive taxes, poor management by the planters, and a lack of modernization of agricultural methods. According to him, it was not the competition with U.S. cotton that caused the decline of cotton in Maranhão but the internal factors of the province itself.[33] In 1885, in his report to the U.S. government, John Branner thought that the main problems of Brazilian cotton agriculture were the lack of capital, good roads, and the incidence of pests that ruined from a quarter to a half the harvests. But one of Branner's main points was the culture's archaic character, which had changed little since colonial times. Still, like at the beginning of the century, there was the argument that cotton was excessively taxed.[34]

For Barbosa, Brazilian cotton failed in the nineteenth century because it was based on the production of small farmers, far from the coast (which increased transport costs), poor, and with little capital.[35] One of Barbosa's most important arguments is that the capital needed to expand Brazil's cotton production was being used elsewhere: growing sugar cane in the northeast and coffee in the southeast.[36] Absel indirectly helped to corroborate this argument showing that after the emancipation of enslaved people in the British West Indies, British tariff policies favored the increase in sugar production in the northeast (Bahia, Pernambuco, Paraíba, and Alagoas, in particular), mainly during the 1830s onwards.[37] Pereira supported the thesis that the fiscal policy of the Portuguese state after 1808 made the profitability of the cotton business fall. With independence, the centralization of Rio de Janeiro continued the policy of the

---

32 Horace Say, *Histoire des relations commerciales entre la France et le Brésil: et considérations générales sur les monnaies, les changes, les banques et le commerce extérieur* (Guillaumin, 1839), 157–58, 325.

33 Mesquita, *Vida e morte da economia algodoeira*, 232–34.

34 Branner, *Cotton in the Empire of Brazil; the Antiquity, Methods and Extent of Its Cultivation, Together with Statistics of Exportation and Home Consumption*, 7, 21.

35 Luiz Cordelio Barbosa, "Cotton in 19th Century Brazil: Dependency and Development" (PhD diss., University of Washington, 1989), 50–54, 58–60.

36 Barbosa, "Cotton in 19th Century Brazil," 78, 87, 111.

37 Christopher David Absell, "British Slave Emancipation and the Demand for Brazilian Sugar," *Cliometrica* 17, no. 1 (2023): 128–30.

Portuguese state. That is, while the central government in Rio took resources from the provinces through taxes, it did not replace them again so that regional governments could reduce production costs for cotton producers. What the central government did was to prohibit taxation by provincial authorities on imported products. And that directly harmed exports. After independence, the government relied on taxation of exportable products, sugar and cotton, the leading products in the first half of the nineteenth century, to support the growing state apparatus.[38] Marquese and Ferraro have recently critiqued Pereira's argument, emphasizing that it overlooks the significant roles played by labor shortages and high transportation costs.[39]

Brazil would produce substantial quantities again only during the American Civil War.[40] At that time, São Paulo joined the northeast and Maranhão as the leading suppliers; other growers also emerged during the nineteenth century, such as Minas Gerais, mostly supplying the Brazilian domestic market.[41] Exports increased between the 1860s and 1920s but rarely exceeding 30,000 metric tons. The growing Brazilian spinning industry consumed a good portion of the raw cotton at this juncture. At the beginning of the twentieth century, São Paulo (along with Paraná a little later) was a central cotton grower and where most factories were located. Yet, agricultural techniques were archaic, the fiber cultivated was short, and it was targeted at the manufacture of inferior-quality fabrics. The big leap came in the 1930s when the mark of 300,000 metric tons exported was surpassed.[42] The growth in the 1930s was directly related to the coffee crisis, which until then was Brazil's main export commodity. With the crisis, the lands in the center-south, previously intended for coffee, were sold and distributed to several small landowners in São Paulo and Paraná. Thus, the coffee crisis coincided with the cotton revival. It was a distinct growth from

38 Pereira, "The Cotton Trade and Brazilian Foreign Commerce," 17–18; Thales Augusto Zamberlan Pereira, "Taxation and the Stagnation of Cotton Exports in Brazil, 1800–60," *The Economic History Review* 74, no. 2 (2021): 522–45.

39 Marquese and Ferraro, "The Political Economy of Brazilian Cotton in the Age of Industrial Capitalism".

40 Sven Beckert, "Emancipation and Empire: Reconstructing the Worldwide Web of Cotton Production in the Age of the American Civil War," *The American Historical Review* 109, no. 5 (2004): 1405–38.

41 Alice Piffer Canabrava, *O desenvolvimento da cultura do algodão na Província de São Paulo (1861–1875)* (1951; 2. ed, Edusp, 2011); Douglas Cole Libby, "Proto-Industrialisation in a Slave Society: The Case of Minas Gerais," *Journal of Latin American Studies* 23, no. 1 (1991): 1–35; Télio Cravo, "Algodão, Política e Trabalho Compulsório: Notas Sobre a Dinâmica Econômica e a Construção Do Estado Nacional (1847–1861)," *Revista Biblioteca Brasiliana Mindlin* 3 (2022): 158–71.

42 Stein, *The Brazilian Cotton Manufacture*, 196–98.

what had occurred until then. There was technical progress, such as the use of fertilizers, insect and disease control, genetic improvements, and selection and storage of adequate seeds. They were developments primarily carried out by the State Agronomic Institute. In 1940 the center-south overtook the traditional cotton growers in the north and northeast of Brazil. Yet, until the 1960s, there was a geographic specialization of crops: the center-south producing short fibers and the north and northeast producing long ones. The technical progress made São Paulo highly productive, even with fragile international and domestic markets in the 1950s and 1960s.[43]

Since the end of the Second World War, the Brazilian government adopted measures to retain raw cotton within the national territory in order to supply the domestic industry. More drastic interventions—such as the export ban of 1973—initially curtailed cotton cultivation in the first half of the 1970s. Yet, with the subsequent recovery of the domestic market, cotton production expanded substantially in the latter half of the decade. This favorable phase, reinforced by the prohibition on cotton imports, persisted until the close of the 1980s.[44] With the so called "Brazilian economic opening" at the end of the 1980s, the cotton goods industry went into crisis because of competition and the absence of state protection. With it, the cultivation of cotton also suffered.[45] Between the 1970s and 1980s, Ceará, Paraíba, and Rio Grande do Norte were important cotton growers, and the aforementioned economic opening harmed them. At the same time, the spread of the boll weevil was perhaps even more destructive to farmers in the northeast of Brazil. From the mid-1990s, cotton recovered, and from there until today, the leading producers are found in Mato Grosso and Bahia.[46] Brazil is currently the fourth largest cotton producer in the world. China and India alternate between the first places, and the U.S. occupies the third position.[47]

43 José Sidnei Gonçalves and Soraia de Fátima Ramos, "Da Origem à Hegemonia e Crise Do Algodão Meridional Brasileiro No Século XX," *Informações Econômicas* 38, no. 2 (2008): 28–34; Christian Brannstrom, "Forests for Cotton: Institutions and Organizations in Brazil's Mid-Twentieth-Century Cotton Boom," *Journal of Historical Geography* 36, no. 2 (2010): 169–82.

44 Gonçalves and Ramos, "Da Origem à Hegemonia," 34–38.

45 Gonçalves and Ramos, "Da Origem à Hegemonia," 34–38.

46 Luis Cláudio Mattos et al., "A saga do algodão no semiárido nordestino: histórico, declínio e as perspectivas de base agroecológica," *Desenvolvimento e Meio Ambiente* 55 (December 2020): 562–63.

47 Data for the years 2010 to 2020, see: USDA, world agricultural supply and demand reports, https://www.ers.usda.gov/topics/crops/cotton-and-wool/cotton-sector-at-a-glance/. Brazilian cotton was also involved in a controversial and famous trade dispute with US

More than two centuries after the spectacular rise of raw cotton during the Industrial Revolution, dependence on foreign markets continues to shape the economic performance of global cotton producers. The principal markets are no longer Great Britain or France, nor the domestic industries of the United States and Brazil, but rather the textile centers of Asia. This shift has been accompanied by advances in technology and reductions in transportation costs, making cloth and clothing more affordable than ever before. Yet what appears as a triumph of modern consumer society also constitutes a profound crisis for textile workers, who endure low wages and degrading working conditions, as well as for the environment, increasingly strained by the dynamics of fast fashion. Today, as two centuries ago, the history of cotton remains a history of progress inseparable from the exploitation and precarious conditions under which it is produced. Some continuities, it seems, are remarkably persistent.

---

cotton; see Mark S. Langevin, *The Political Economy of Brazil's WTO Case Against the United States: Inside the Cotton Dispute* (Palgrave Macmillan, 2023).

Appendix A – Main Cotton Importers in Lisbon (1782–1806)

TABLE A1 Main cotton importers in Lisbon in 1782

Importers	Tax
Manuel Inácio Ferreira	665,955
The administrators of the GCGPM	500,712
Antônio José dos Santos Amorim	442,792
Mateus Poitier	361,104
Marcos José de Matos	290,376
Francisco da Fonseca Lemos	199,962
Manuel de Almeida Braga	173,544
Manuel Joaquim Rebelo	118,698
Miguel Pereira Guimarães	111,102
Manuel Pinto da Silva	109,680
Manuel José da Costa	104,148
Luis Antônio da Rocha	94,212
Padre Joaquim Inácio Betencourt	92,160
Total	3,264,445

Sources and notes: ANTT, "Alfândegas de Lisboa, Casa da Índia": books 223 and 291. The leading cotton importers were considered to be all those who, together, paid at customs in Lisbon more than half of the total import tax during the year. Import duties are in *réis*. Names in *italics* refer to merchants who appear in the other tables in this Appendix A. Table prepared by the author.

TABLE A2 Main cotton importers in Lisbon in 1789

Importers	Tax
Bento José Pacheco	1,473,624
Bernardo Clamousse e Companhia	854,100
José Duarte Guimarães	664,722
Francisco Xavier Fernandes Nogueira	547,296
Antônio Álves da Silva Basto	483,432
Antônio José dos Santos Amorim	387,084
Policarpo José Machado	380,048
João de Oliveira Guimarães	278,160
Paulo Jorge	264,312
Antônio Martins Pedra	248,328
Domingos Rodrigues Chaves	236,604
Antônio Afonço de Oliveira	235,332
Domingos Martins Chaves	225,504
José da Silva Obrens	206,304
Francisco Malaquias da Cunha	201,096
Aurélio Blanc	172,668
Constantino Soares de Melo	164,100
Pedro Antônio da Cruz e Companhia	152,280
Antônio José Ferreira	143,506
Manuel Raposo	138,208
Bernardo José da Costa	133,896
José Álves Viana	133,344
Antônio Pires Marinho	130,056
Carlos Lassence	124,236
Manuel de Almeida	123,372
Caetano Cordeiro de Araujo Feio	118,248
Manuel Nunes do Nascimento	112,116
Marcos José de Matos	112,080
Jerônimo José Chaves	111,300
Francisco José Bandeira	111,036
Total	**8,666,392**

Sources and notes: ANTT, "Alfândegas de Lisboa, Casa da Índia": books 314 and 315. The leading cotton importers were considered to be all those who, together, paid at customs in Lisbon more than half of the total import tax during the year. Import duties are in *réis*. Names in *italics* refer to merchants who appear in the other tables in this Appendix A. Table prepared by the author.

TABLE A3 Main cotton importers in Lisbon in 1792

Importers	Tax	Importers	Tax
Manuel de Souza Freire e Companhia	1,147,270	*José Álves Viana*	279,888
Bento José Pacheco e Filhos	860,899	*João de Oliveira Guimarães*	272,022
Antônio Álves da Silva Basto e Filho	772,793	Manuel José Duarte Guimarães	265,938
José da Silva Obrens	686,321		
Antônio Xavier	677,604	*José Pereira de Carvalho*	263,418
José Bento de Araújo	664,902	*João Antônio Viana*	249,030
José Antônio Pereira	638,754	*Manuel Isidoro de Almeida*	248,550
Bernardo Clamousse e Companhia	583,560	*Bernardo José da Costa*	245,442
Antônio Martins Pedra	441,000	*Marcos José de Matos*	233,316
João Teixeira de Barros	421,332	*Felipe Ribeiro Figueiras*	232,645
Tomé Ferreira da Costa	417,756	*Manuel Raposo*	229,092
Antônio José dos Santos Amorim	407,406	José Anacleto	220,811
Mateus Poitier	393,042	*Jerônimo José de Carvalho*	220,122
Francisco Xavier Fernandes Nogueira	374,280	*José Gomes da Costa*	206,542
Constantino Soares de Melo	348,780	Cristovão Manuel Digues	199,536
José Fernandes de Matos	321,599	Antônio Belford	159,372
Manuel José Machado	300,182	Francisco José de Souza	156,726
Antônio Francisco Machado e Companhia	295,260	**Total**	**13,435,190**

Sources and notes: ANTT, "Alfândegas de Lisboa, Casa da Índia": books 129 and 130. The leading cotton importers were considered to be all those who, together, paid at customs in Lisbon more than half of the total import tax during the year. Import duties are in *réis*. Names in *italics* refer to merchants who appear in the other tables in this Appendix A. Table prepared by the author.

TABLE A4 Main cotton importers in Lisbon in 1799

Importers	Tax	Importers	Tax
Antônio Xavier	1,050,051	*Francisco José de Serpa*	395,964
Jerônimo José de Carvalho	791,272	*Manuel Francisco Lavra*	390,252
José Álves Branco	710,580	*José Tavares*	385,260
José Bento de Araújo e Companhia	527,370	Antônio Simões da Costa	360,756
P, v A, Vanzeller	499,392	*José Gomes da Costa*	323,828
José da Silva Obrens	457,648	*José Antônio dos Anjos*	321,372
Felipe Ribeiro Figueiras	445,437	*Manuel de Souza Freire e Companhia*	311,652
Antônio José Batista de Sales	424,944		
Dias Santos e Carvalho	405,928	*Francisco José Pereira de Oliveira*	309,372

TABLE A4 Main cotton importers in Lisbon in 1799 (*cont.*)

Importers	Tax	Importers	Tax
José Antônio Pereira	302,076	*Luis Gonçalves Teixeira de Barros*	167,916
Manuel Antônio Teixeira da Silva	297,600	*Manuel José Machado*	166,920
José da Silva Ribeiro	293,532	*Luis Antônio Rodrigues Sete*	166,584
Bernardo Clamousse e Companhia	281,280	Manuel José de Almeida e Silva	161,304
Angelo Gonçalves Aires	259,260	Antônio Rodrigues Caldas	150,984
Manuel Isidoro de Almeida	253,584	*João de Oliveira Guimarães*	143,959
Manuel de Miranda Correa	252,528	*João Teixeira de Barros*	138,634
Francisco Antônio Durão	247,958	*Domingos de Meira Torres*	136,560
José Gonçalves Macieira	223,980	José Dioníssio Pereira	135,438
Antônio Esteves Costa	211,712	João Antônio Vieira Caldas	133,296
Correia, Viana e Companhia	210,944	Manuel José Machado de Sampaio	133,236
Caetano Cordeiro de Araujo Feio	202,008		
Domingos Álves Guerra	194,808	Joaquim José Vasques e Companhia	131,496
José Fernandes de Matos	188,832		
José Pereira de Carvalho	184,608	Domingos Antônio Vaz Gloria	128,450
Marcos José de Matos	184,488	*Manuel Ribeiro da Silva*	127,488
José Lopes de Abreu	182,460	*Francisco Hermano Vanzeller*	118,920
Antônio Henriques Castelão	174,024	**Total**	**14,397,945**

Sources and notes: ANTT, "Alfândegas de Lisboa, Casa da Índia": books 408, 410, and 411. The leading cotton importers were considered to be all those who, together, paid at customs in Lisbon more than half of the total import tax during the year. Import duties are in *réis*. Names in *italics* refer to merchants who appear in the other tables in this Appendix A. Table prepared by the author.

TABLE A5 Main cotton importers in Lisbon in 1806

Importers	Tax	Importers	Tax
Antônio Francisco Lisboa	2,393,425	*José Gomes da Costa*	866,404
Manuel Antônio Teixeira da Silva	2,375,925	*José da Silva Ribeiro*	854,150
Jerônimo José de Carvalho	1,908,380	*Antônio Esteves Costa e Irmão*	835,500
José Bento de Araújo	1,434,404	José da Silva Rego	813,775
Manuel de Souza Freire e Companhia	971,525	*Felipe Ribeiro Figueiras*	777,075
José da Silva Obrens	963,025	*Marcos José de Matos*	738,275
José Álves Branco	931,200	Veríssimo Rodrigues Belo	721,650
Manuel Francisco Lavra	924,180	*Manuel Ribeiro da Silva*	720,471
José Tavares	904,950	Manuel Fernandes	707,950
Teofilo de Oliveira Vale	867,700	*Francisco José de Serpa*	676,450

TABLE A5 Main cotton importers in Lisbon in 1806 (*cont.*)

Importers	Tax	Importers	Tax
Joaquim José de Almeida	666,650	Bento José Rodrigues	436,875
Manuel da Cruz	633,750	Caetano José Rodrigues	419,250
Joaquim José de Siqueira	626,625	*Correia, Viana e Companhia*	403,625
José Álves Viana	623,375	*Domingos de Meira Torres e Companhia*	402,725
Manuel Isidoro de Almeida	620,625	*Francisco Hermano Vanzeller*	377,175
Francisco Ribeiro da Cunha e Companhia	614,748	Fernando de Souza Machado	374,275
João José e Companhia	612,175	João Muniz Vieira	357,850
José Manuel da Cunha Oliveira	602,300	Félix José Antônio Viana	356,450
José Antônio dos Anjos	596,400	José Joaquim Ferreira Lobo	349,250
Luis Gonçalves Teixeira de Barros	575,600	*Francisco José Pereira de Oliveira*	346,425
Raimundo da Silva	557,165	*Domingos Álves Guerra*	342,450
Angelo Gonçalves Aires	551,675	Raimundo Inácio Lamas	338,675
Viúva Batista e Filhos	537,150	*José Antônio Pereira*	338,600
Bento José Pacheco e Filhos	520,825	Antônio Pires Leal	333,725
José Rodrigues	513,175	Manuel Caetano Veloso e Companhia	327,175
Antônio Francisco da Silva	498,025	Francisco Ricardo da Cruz	320,800
José Rodrigues Pereira dos Santos	496,175	Agostinho de Oliveira Guimarães	318,725
Tomás de Aquino e Souza	494,175	José Antônio de Oliveira Borges	313,600
José Pereira de Souza Caldas e Filho	485,200	José João	307,850
Antônio Álves de Carvalho	484,825	José João Barbosa	304,825
Santos Ferreira Loires	467,400	Isidoro de Almeida	302,675
João Antônio Viana e Filho	463,462	Manuel Barbosa de Carvalho	284,575
José Gonçalves Macieira	458,975	Manuel de Souza Lobo	282,600
Antônio José Batista de Sales	453,350	Salvador Moreira	282,100
Francisco José Moreira	448,080	José Bento Garces	276,425
Luis Antônio Rodrigues Sete	447,875	**Total**	**45,266,519**
João Antônio de Almeida	447,150		
Antônio Martins Pedra e Filho	446,775		
Bernardo Clamousse e Companhia	437,700		

Sources and notes: ANTT, "Alfândegas de Lisboa, Casa da Índia": book 1,475. The leading cotton importers were considered to be all those who, together, paid at customs in Lisbon more than half of the total import tax during the year. Import duties are in *réis*. Names in *italics* refer to merchants who appear in the other tables in this Appendix A. Table prepared by the author.

Appendix B – Main Cotton Exporters from Lisbon (1782–1806)

TABLE B1 Main cotton exporters from Lisbon in 1782

Name	Nationality	Genoa	Hamburg	Havre-de-Grâce	London	Rouen	Venice	Total
Hulse & Co.	Unknown	9,021				127	24	9,172
Bonifácio José Lamas	Portuguese			193	2,086	5,717		7,996
Boaventura Feliz	Portuguese	2,911				3,263		6,174
José Gonçalves	Portuguese	5,606				386		5,992
Marcos José de Matos	Portuguese	205		37		4,021		4,263
Joaquim de Souza Fonseca	Portuguese	2,569	103			720		3,392
Antônio José dos Santos Amorim	Portuguese			263		3,033		3,296
Bento José da Costa	Portuguese	319		964		1,683		2,966
Joaquim Pedro Quintela	Portuguese			96	2,561			2,657
Total		20,631	103	1,553	4,647	18,950	24	45,908

Sources: Arquivo Nacional Torre do Tombo (ANTT), "Alfândegas de Lisboa, Casa da Índia": books 138, 290, 288, 250, 249, 248, 247, 246, 139, 289, 140, and 141. For merchant nationalities see: The British Historical Society of Portugal, List of British Merchants in Lisbon 1788–1791, Report: HA 10, 1946–1950, 663 and The British Hospital, Lisbon, 1793, Report: HA 7 by A. R. Walford, 1943, 436–441. All names are taken from the Lisbon Almanach from 1788, 1789, 1790, 1791, and 1794. Labourdette, *La Nation française à Lisbonne de 1669 à 1790* and Cunha, *Negociantes, mercadores e traficantes no final da monarquia absoluta*. Cotton is given in arrobas. The main cotton exporters were considered to be all those who, together, exported more than half of the total each year. Table prepared by the author.

TABLE B2 Main cotton exporters from Lisbon in 1789

Name	Nationality	Amsterdam	Genoa	Hamburg	Liverpool	London	Marseille	Nantes	Rouen	Leith	Cork	North	France	Total
Lefevre Dittmer & Co.	French/ Hamburger	92	4,930	1,202	19,582	2,561	664	43	5,260					**34,334**
Melish & Devisme	English		3,914		10,564	3,850			539	1,001		137		20,005
Daniel Bowden & Son	English		231		14,715	2,524								**17,470**
João Daniel de Bruin & Jautard	Dutch/French		2,424		280	4,151		6	3,587				240	10,688
Widow Frenenlet	French		4,986			845			2,218					**8,049**
Thomas March & Co.	English				5,720	1,194					312			7,226
Bonifácio José Lamas	Portuguese					3,398			3,454					**6,852**

TABLE B2 Main cotton exporters from Lisbon in 1789 (*cont.*)

Name	Nationality	Amsterdam	Genoa	Hamburg	Liverpool	London	Marseille	Nantes	Rouen	Leith	Cork	North	France	Total
Carret, Koster & Co.	English				54	4,957			685					**5,696**
Arnaldo Henrique Metzener & Son	German		128		203	3,400			456					**4,187**
Camilo Pereira Soares Laroche	Portuguese					3,380			53					**3,433**
Total		**92**	**16,613**	**1,202**	**51,118**	**30,260**	**664**	**49**	**16,252**	**1,001**	**312**	**137**	**240**	**117,940**

Sources: Arquivo Nacional Torre do Tombo (ANTT), "Alfândegas de Lisboa, Casa da Índia": books 192, 193, 194, 195, 196, 311, 312, and 313. For merchant nationalities see: The British Historical Society of Portugal, List of British Merchants in Lisbon 1788–1791, Report: HA 10, 1946–1950, 663 and The British Hospital, Lisbon, 1793, Report: HA 7 by A. R. Walford, 1943, 436–441. All names are taken from the Lisbon Almanach from 1788, 1789, 1790, 1791, and 1794. Labourdette, *La Nation française à Lisbonne de 1669 à 1790* and Cunha, *Negociantes, mercadores e traficantes no final da monarquia absoluta*. Cotton is given in arrobas.
The main cotton exporters were considered to be all those who, together, exported more than half of the total each year. Table prepared by the author.

TABLE B3 Main cotton exporters from Lisbon in 1792

Name	Nationality	Liverpool	London	Rouen	Genoa	Hamburg	Cork	Dublin	Amsterdam	Greenock	Hull	Total
Daniel Bowden & Son	English	30,565						38			1,144	31,747
Lefevre, Dittmer & Co.	French/ Hamburger	14,451	284	7,129	3,262	1,695			223			27,044
Bellinge & M,e Mahon	English	25,707						244				25,951
Thomas March & Co.	English	15,716	3,444								144	19,304
Luis Stephens & Co.	English	14,808	1,221		135					48		16,212
Carret, Koster & Co.	English	8,987	2,430			9					377	11,803
Melish & Devisme	English	6,055		1,924	3,207							11,186
Jacob Dohrman & Co.	Dutch	8,547	869	558	284		237					10,495
Ricardo Sealy & Co.	English	9,672					305			203		10,180
Halford Gonne & Co.	English	6,019						163			122	6,304
Total		140,527	8,248	9,611	6,888	1,704	542	445	223	251	1,787	170,226

Sources: Arquivo Nacional Torre do Tombo (ANTT), "Alfândegas de Lisboa, Casa da Índia": books 133, 132, 131, 95, 94, and 97. For merchant nationalities see: The British Historical Society of Portugal, List of British Merchants in Lisbon 1788–1791, Report: HA 10, 1946–1950, 663 and The British Hospital, Lisbon, 1793, Report: HA 7 by A.R. Walford, 1943, 436–441. All names are taken from the Lisbon Almanach from 1788, 1789, 1790, 1791, and 1794. Labourdette, *La Nation française à Lisbonne de 1669 à 1790* and Cunha, *Negociantes, mercadores e traficantes no final da monarquia absoluta.* Cotton is given in arrobas. The main cotton exporters were considered to be all those who, together, exported more than half of the total each year. Table prepared by the author.

TABLE B4 Main cotton exporters from Lisbon in 1799

Name	Nationality	Liverpool	London	Greenock	Hamburg	Hull	Bristol	Barcelona	Copenhagen	Total
Holford Gonne & Co.	English	35,038	8,157	652		486				44,333
Bernardo Henrique Metzner & Co.	German	22,387	5,200							27,587
Parkers & Co.	English		1,583	15,131						16,714
Ricardo Sealy & Co.	English	9,900	2,243	832		3,409				16,384
Houston & Lindt	Unknown	4,104	2,617	7,133						13,854
Mayne & Brown	English	141		12,698						12,839
Carret, Koster & Co.	English	8,705	229							8,934
João Manuel Mahon & Co.	English	7,733	806							8,539
João Pedro Manesch	Portuguese		5,856		852		497	25	260	7,490
João Berthon	English	718	6,580							7,298
Total		88,726	33,271	36,446	852	3,895	497	25	260	163,972

Sources: Arquivo Nacional Torre do Tombo (ANTT). "Alfândegas de Lisboa, Casa da Índia": books 44, 45, 104, 162, 215, 407, 409, and 412. For merchant nationalities see: The British Historical Society of Portugal, List of British Merchants in Lisbon 1788–1791, Report: HA 10, 1946–1950, 663 and The British Hospital, Lisbon, 1793, Report: HA 7 by A. R. Walford, 1943, 436–441. All names are taken from the Lisbon Almanach from 1788, 1789, 1790, 1791, and 1794. Labourdette, *La Nation française à Lisbonne de 1669 à 1790* and Cunha, *Negociantes, mercadores e traficantes no final da monarquia absoluta.* Cotton is given in arrobas. The main cotton exporters were considered to be all those who, together, exported more than half of the total each year. Table prepared by the author.

TABLE B5 Main cotton exporters from Lisbon in 1806

Name	José Henriques Pinheiro	Francisco Anastacio Antunes	Bernardo Henrique Metzner & Co.	Manuel Teixeira Basto
Nationality	Portuguese	Portuguese	German	Portuguese
Amsterdam				295
Antwerp	2,879	917		
Bayonne (France)	43			
Belfast				
Caen	9,693	8,049		6,432
Cherbourg	12,922	7,252		7,767
Cork				
Glasgow				
Greenock				
Hamburg				
Hull				
Liverpool			17,810	63
Livorno			233	
London				
Marseille		218		
Nantes	4,733	9,720		1,706
Oneglia			1,492	
Rotterdam				
Trieste				958
Vila Franca				
Total	30,270	26,156	19,535	17,221

TABLE B5 Main cotton exporters from Lisbon in 1806 (*cont.*)

Name	Bras Francisco Lima	Maine & Browns	João Dowel M(e) Mahon	Carret, Koster & Co.	Jacome Ratton and Sons
Nationality	Portuguese	English	English	English	Portuguese
Amsterdam					
Antwerp	1,403				7,488
Bayonne (France)					
Belfast					
Caen	2,966				1,249
Cherbourg	12,341				190
Cork					
Glasgow		8,861			
Greenock					
Hamburg					
Hull					
Liverpool		3,410	8,238	11,621	
Livorno					
London			4,003		
Marseille					
Nantes					1,793
Oneglia					
Rotterdam					
Trieste					
Vila Franca	101				
Total	16,811	12,271	12,241	11,621	10,720

TABLE B5 Main cotton exporters from Lisbon in 1806 (*cont.*)

Name	Thomas F, Dyson & Co.	José Antônio dos Santos	Offley, Sealy and Son	Philippe Roussac	José Diogo de Bastos
Nationality	English	Portuguese	English	French	Portuguese
Amsterdam					191
Antwerp		704			2,071
Bayonne (France)					
Belfast			1,973		
Caen		1,839		2,224	
Cherbourg				2,747	2,781
Cork			20		
Glasgow		8,861			
Greenock	643	350	2,774		
Hamburg					626
Hull			1,045		
Liverpool	9,224	173	2,319		
Livorno					143
London					
Marseille					96
Nantes		5,221		2,793	
Oneglia					366
Rotterdam					435
Trieste					345
Vila Franca		172			
Total	9,867	8,459	8,131	7,764	7,054

TABLE B5 Main cotton exporters from Lisbon in 1806 (*cont.*)

Name	Jacob Dohrman & Co.	Holford Gonne and Lucas	Pirro Freitas e Silva	João Bulkeley and Son	City Total
Nationality	Dutch	English	Portuguese	English	
Amsterdam	781				1,267
Antwerp			345		15,807
Bayonne (France)					43
Belfast				3,029	5,002
Caen	207		1,992		34,651
Cherbourg	89		2,711		49,150
Cork					20
Glasgow					8,861
Greenock					3,417
Hamburg	19				645
Hull					1,045
Liverpool	344	6,930		2,717	62,849
Livorno	1,059				1,435
London					4,003
Marseille	1,991		412		2,717
Nantes			1,461		27,427
Oneglia	280				2,138
Rotterdam					435
Trieste	2,176				3,479
Vila Franca					273
Total	6,946	6,930	6,921	5,746	224,664

Source: Arquivo Nacional Torre do Tombo (ANTT), "Alfândegas de Lisboa, Casa da Índia": books 284, 106, 348, 517, 189, 207, 511, 329, 534, and 484. For merchant nationalities see: The British Historical Society of Portugal, List of British Merchants in Lisbon 1788–1791, Report: HA 10, 1946-1950, 663 and The British Hospital, Lisbon, 1793, Report: HA 7 by A. R. Walford, 1943, 436–441. All names are taken from the Lisbon Almanach from 1788, 1789, 1790, 1791, and 1794. Labourdette, *La Nation française à Lisbonne de 1669 à 1790* and Cunha, *Negociantes, mercadores e traficantes no final da monarquia absoluta*. Cotton is given in arrobas. The main cotton exporters were considered to be all those who, together, exported more than half of the total each year. The 'Total' 224,664 is the total exported from all cities combined. Table prepared by the author.

Appendix C – Ports That Imported Cotton from Lisbon (1782–1806)

TABLE C1 Ports that imported cotton from Lisbon in 1782

Ports	Arrobas	%
Rouen	37,317	49.10
Genoa	25,026	32.93
London	6,984	9.19
Havre-de-Grâce	6,058	7.97
Hamburg	255	0.34
Venice	159	0.21
Cork	99	0.13
Amsterdam	95	0.13
Ostend	3	0.00
Total	**75,996**	100

Sources: Arquivo Nacional Torre do Tombo (ANTT), "Alfândegas de Lisboa, Casa da Índia": books 138, 290, 288, 250, 249, 248, 247, 246, 139, 289, 140, and 141. Table prepared by the author.

TABLE C2 Ports that imported cotton from Lisbon in 1789

Ports	Arrobas	%
Liverpool	56,895	31.80
London	51,199	28.61
Rouen	37,698	21.07
Genoa	25,032	13.99
Hamburg	1,652	0.92
Cork	1,418	0.79
Dublin	1,252	0.70
Leith	1,001	0.56
Marseille	835	0.47
France	624	0.35

TABLE C2 Ports that imported cotton from Lisbon (*cont.*)

Ports	Arrobas	%
Nantes	444	0.25
Ireland	263	0.15
Sant-Valery	220	0.12
North	177	0.10
Waterford	120	0.07
Amsterdam	92	0.05
Bremen	13	0.01
Total	**178,934**	100

Sources: Arquivo Nacional Torre do Tombo (ANTT), "Alfândegas de Lisboa, Casa da Índia": books 192, 193, 194, 195, 196, 311, 312, and 313. Table prepared by the author.

TABLE C3 Ports that imported cotton from Lisbon in 1792

Ports	Arrobas	%
Liverpool	164,195	64.88
London	26,765	10.58
Genoa	25,857	10.22
Rouen	20,709	8.18
Greenock	5,023	1.98
Hull	2,592	1.02
Cork	2,521	1.00
Dublin	2,219	0.88
Hamburg	1,832	0.72
Havre-de-Grâce	780	0.31
Amsterdam	357	0.14
Leith	238	0.09
Total	**253,088**	100

Sources: Arquivo Nacional Torre do Tombo (ANTT), "Alfândegas de Lisboa, Casa da Índia": books 133, 132, 131, 95, 94, and 97. Table prepared by the author.

TABLE C4 Ports that imported cotton from Lisbon in 1799

Ports	Arrobas	%
Liverpool	146,237	49.77
London	71,195	24.23
Greenock	57,371	19.52
Hamburg	7,554	2.57
Hull	4,470	1.52
Dublin	2,897	0.99
Cork	1,020	0.35
Amsterdam	885	0.30
Bristol	525	0.18
North	380	0.13
Barcelona	378	0.13
Glasgow	356	0.12
Copenhagen	260	0.09
Livorno	166	0.06
Altona	71	0.02
Naples	35	0.01
Gothenburg	30	0.01
Venice	5	0.00
Bilbao	4	0.00
Total	**293,839**	100

Sources: Arquivo Nacional Torre do Tombo (ANTT), "Alfândegas de Lisboa, Casa da Índia": books 44, 45, 104, 162, 215, 407, 409, and 412. Table prepared by the author.

TABLE C5 Ports that imported cotton from Lisbon in 1806

Ports	Arrobas	%	Ports	Arrobas	%
Liverpool	123,582	27.47	Glasgow	2,778	0.62
Cherbourg	82,440	18.33	Amsterdam	2,352	0.52
Nantes	79,581	17.69	Hull	1,145	0.25
Caen	58,616	13.03	Cork	717	0.16
Greenock	22,109	4.91	Bordeaux	646	0.14
London	18,205	4.05	Dublin	560	0.12
Antwerp	17,599	3.91	Rotterdam	435	0.10
Hamburg	6,641	1.48	Vila Franca	330	0.07
Trieste	6,579	1.46	Bilbao	229	0.05
Belfast	6,388	1.42	Toningem	217	0.05
Livorno	5,187	1.15	Waterford	141	0.03
Barcelona	4,946	1.10	Ancunes	120	0.03
Marseille	4,148	0.92	Sweden	109	0.02
Oneglia	3,957	0.88	Bayonne	94	0.02
Total				449,851	100

Sources: Arquivo Nacional Torre do Tombo (ANTT), "Alfândegas de Lisboa, Casa da Índia", books 284, 106, 348, 517, 189, 207, 511, 329, 534 and 484. Table prepared by the author.

Appendix D – Vessels Leaving Lisbon in 1789 and 1801

TABLE D1 Vessels that transported cotton and vessels that went to Africa in 1789

Vessel	Captain	Flag	Destination	Cotton	Wine	Fruit	Leather	Tobacco	Sugar
Minerva	Jean Thuillier	French	Bilbao	x					
S. Macario e Minerva	Joaquim José Torquato	Portuguese	Bissau, Cacheu, and Maranhão						
Amável Donzela	José de Oliveira	Portuguese	Cabo Verde						
Betsy	Thomas Donald	English	Coast of Africa					x	
Elisabeth & Nancy	William Browne	English	Cork	x					
Mary	George Maybury	English	Cork	x					
Elisabeth & Ann	John Julian	English	Cork	x					
Favourite	John Farrie	English	Dublin	x	x	x			
James	Richard Webb	English	Dublin	x	x				
Cecilia	Jean Vollett	French	Genoa	x			x		x
Lindenholf	Douwe Eeltje Hofker	Dutch	Genoa	x			x	x	
Jonge Folkert	Okke Benjamin Bakker	Dutch	Genoa	x			x	x	
Jonge Sybrand	Gaspar Schmerkel	Dutch	Genoa	x			x		
Jonge Cornelis	Jan Tennes Swart	Dutch	Genoa	x			x	x	x
Henrick	Tjerk Jans Clapper	Dutch	Genoa	x			x	x	x
Uriendschap	Peter Jacob Rotgans	Dutch	Genoa	x			x	x	x

TABLE D1 Vessels that transported cotton and vessels that went to Africa in 1789 (*cont.*)

Vessel	Captain	Flag	Destination	Cotton	Wine	Fruit	Leather	Tobacco	Sugar
Juffrouw Elisabeth % Maria	Gerret Boift	Dutch	Genoa	x			x	x	x
Jonge Daniel	Symon Wybrands	Dutch	Genoa	x			x	x	x
Jonge Sybrand	Gaspar Schmerkel	Dutch	Genoa	x					x
Firth	Joseph Bonnell	English	Genoa	x			x	x	
Chance	Thomas Spark	English	Genoa	x			x		x
Martha	Henry Cole	English	Genoa	x			x	x	x
Helen	Christopher Chapman	English	Genoa	x				x	x
Friends Adventure	George Denholm	English	Genoa	x			x	x	x
Foster	Andrew Hodgson	English	Genoa	x			x	x	x
Reverfau	Jean Fermon	French	Guinea					x	
Le Patriote	Louis Huet Dekchu	French	Guinea					x	
La Ville de Bale	Antoine Burgine	French	Guinea					x	
La Demoiselle	Victor Coupey	French	Guinea					x	
Tolerance	Nicolas Delalie	French	Guinea					x	
Le Comte de Turville	Nicolas le Roux	French	Guinea					x	
Centurion	François Cotte	French	Guinea					x	
Principe Negro	Louis Alexandre Jacques	French	Guinea					x	
O Agradavel	Aleixo Michel	French	Guinea					x	
Le Saint Espirite	Nicolas Julien Legue	French	Guinea					x	

TABLE D1 Vessels that transported cotton and vessels that went to Africa in 1789 (*cont.*)

Vessel	Captain	Flag	Destination	Cotton	Wine	Fruit	Leather	Tobacco	Sugar
La Nymphe	Jean Jacques Lucadou	French	Guinea					x	
Le Baron de Bender	Toussaint le Forestien	French	Guinea					x	
L'Etoile	Jean Horquelard	French	Guinea					x	
La Jeune Elisabeth	Pierre Jacques Guenet	French	Guinea					x	
Cegogne	Alexander Cary	French	Guinea					x	
Merdiano	Denis Lamee	French	Guinea					x	
La Ebene	Joseph Munier	French	Guinea					x	
L'Abeille	Guillaume Dubois	French	Guinea					x	
Le Duc de Normandie	Charles Michel Chouteau	French	Guinea					x	
Le Marquis de Bouille	Leonard Julien Guirouard	French	Guinea					x	
Le Conte de Montemorim	Clement Duchesne	French	Guinea					x	
Elisabeth	Pierre Lartioga	French	Guinea					x	
Les Ceeurs Unis	Louis Bennes	French	Guinea					x	
Sartine	Jacques Papin	French	Guinea					x	
Le Citoyen	Bafilie le Ray	French	Guinea					x	
Le Duc de Normandie	Pierre Patrovilhau	French	Guinea					x	
Hinde	Thamas Harvey	English	Guinea					x	
Fly	David Mac Leary	English	Guinea					x	
Ranger	John Carran	English	Guinea					x	

TABLE D1 Vessels that transported cotton and vessels that went to Africa in 1789 (*cont.*)

Vessel	Captain	Flag	Destination	Cotton	Wine	Fruit	Leather	Tobacco	Sugar
Gambia	John Proudfoot	English	Guinea					x	
Prince	John Gillan	English	Guinea and Jamaica					x	
N. Senhora de Belém	José das Neves Leão	Portuguese	Guinea and Maranhão						
S. Pedro e S. Paulo	José Antônio de Vargues	Portuguese	Guinea and Maranhão						
Urouw Geertruyda	Harme Lubbes Priem	Dutch	Hamburg	x					x
Jacobus Albertus	Age Doedas Van Sraverin	Dutch	Hamburg	x			x	x	x
Antelope	David Boyter	English	Hamburg	x					
Margaret	Robert Gray	English	Hamburg	x		x		x	x
Sarah	George Straker	English	Hamburg	x				x	x
Brothers	Spragg Browne	English	Hull	x	x	x			
N. S. da Vitória, S. Antônio e Almas	Francisco José Campina	Portuguese	Ilha da Madeira and Cabo Verde						
Rebecca	Joseph Shelton	English	Leith	x	x	x			
Sally	Nathaniel Letherland	English	Liverpool	x	x	x			
Hannah	Arthur Smith	English	Liverpool		x	x			
Fanny	John Withers	English	Liverpool	x	x	x			
Apollo	John Holdgate	English	Liverpool	x					
Peggy	Robert Frew	English	Liverpool	x		x			
Oliver Tree	John Richardson	English	Liverpool	x	x				
Maxwell	Thomas Tempelton	English	Liverpool	x					
Mary	William Young	English	Liverpool	x					
Lisbon Packet	William Padmore	English	Liverpool	x					
Hannach	Arthur Hearding	English	Liverpool	x	x	x			

TABLE D1 Vessels that transported cotton and vessels that went to Africa in 1789 (*cont.*)

Vessel	Captain	Flag	Destination	Cotton	Wine	Fruit	Leather	Tobacco	Sugar
Mary	George Maybery	English	Liverpool	x					
Industry	James Hacket	English	Liverpool	x					
Brothers	Patrick Devereus	English	Liverpool	x					
Leopard	John Harding	English	Liverpool	x	x				
Friends Adventure	Silvanus Hanglin	English	Liverpool	x					
Resolution	Connolly Mac Causland	English	Liverpool	x					
Oliver Tree	John Richardson	English	Liverpool	x					
Neptune	Philip Wilkinson	English	Liverpool	x					
Lark	Stephen Newport	English	Liverpool	x					
Fanny	William Roe	English	Liverpool	x					
Good Intent	John Clark	English	Liverpool	x	x				
Newgrove	David Baxter	English	Liverpool	x					
Liberty	John Row	English	Liverpool	x	x	x			
Mary	James March	English	Liverpool	x					
Hannah	Arthur Harding	English	Liverpool	x	x				
Mary	William Young	English	Liverpool	x					
Lively	George Smith	English	Liverpool	x					
Betsy	Gerrald Forrestal	English	Liverpool	x		x			
Fanny	John Best	English	Liverpool	x		x			
Friendship	Robert Perrey	English	London	x		x			
Lion	Sinclair Halcrous	English	London	x	x	x			
London	William Dawson	English	London	x	x	x			
Venus	John Quinton	English	London	x	x				
Jemima	Stephen Redman	English	London	x	x	x			

TABLE D1 Vessels that transported cotton and vessels that went to Africa in 1789 (*cont.*)

Vessel	Captain	Flag	Destination	Cotton	Wine	Fruit	Leather	Tobacco	Sugar
Svern	Thomas Stone	English	London	x	x	x			
Astley	James Hutchings	English	London	x	x				
Sheperds	George Brander	English	London	x	x	x			
Lisbon Packet	Samuel Haire	English	London	x	x	x			
Saint George	Archibald Hill	English	London	x	x	x			
Valentine	John Cobb	English	London	x	x	x			
Juno	George Kennedy	English	London	x	x	x			
Balmer	Joseph Coles	English	London	x		x			
Queen	William Mopett	English	London	x	x	x			
Betsy	Michael Firth	English	London	x	x	x			
Saint George	James Williamson	English	London	x	x	x			
Saint George	Archibald Hill	English	London	x	x	x			
Rochedale	Edward Lake	English	London	x	x				
Sheperds	George Brander	English	London	x	x	x			
Betsy	William Nichols	English	London	x		x			
Harriot	Alexander Philips	English	London	x	x	x			
Queen	William Mopett	English	London	x		x			
Mercury	James Frank	English	London	x	x	x			
Chatty	Marcus Whit Seager	English	London	x		x			
Dublin	Charles Todd	English	London	x		x			
Friendship	Robert Terrey	English	London	x		x			
Minerva	James Cobby	English	London	x		x			
Valentin	John Cobb	English	London	x	x	x			
Ann	John Cockburn	English	London	x	x	x			

TABLE D1 Vessels that transported cotton and vessels that went to Africa in 1789 (*cont.*)

Vessel	Captain	Flag	Destination	Cotton	Wine	Fruit	Leather	Tobacco	Sugar
Realto	Thomas Kibett	English	London	x		x			
Christiana Frances	Thomas Fowman	English	London	x		x			
Rochedale	George Lightfoot	English	London	x		x			
Le jeune Victoire	Joseph Guyot	French	Marseille	x			x		
Le Saint Christophe	Olivier le Parlouer	French	Marseille	x			x		
Le Turbot	Pierre Gafton	French	Nantes	x			x		
Uriendschap	Wilhelm Bragges	Dutch	Ostend	x		x		x	
La Nouvelle Alliance	Jean Baptiste Moulard	French	Rouen	x		x	x		
Dolphin	Jacques François Boiemar	French	Rouen	X		X			
Le Neptune	Nicolas Rock	French	Rouen	x		x			
Le Deux Seeurs	Jean Jacques Thomas Pilastre	French	Rouen	x		x			
Marianne Cherie	Charles Etienne Bien	French	Rouen	x		x	x		
Les Deux Freres	Yves le Biller	French	Rouen	x					
Alerte	Jacques Guillaume Gremont	French	Rouen	x					
Momus	Auguste Daniel Bouthard	French	Rouen	x		x	x		
La Nouvelle Alliance	Jean Baptiste Moulard	French	Rouen	x		x	x		
Saint Charles	Joseph Marie Homom	French	Rouen	x		x			
Alliance	Jean Hargous	French	Rouen	x		x	x		
Minerva	Jean Michel le Roux	French	Rouen	x	x	x			

TABLE D1 Vessels that transported cotton and vessels that went to Africa in 1789 (*cont.*)

Vessel	Captain	Flag	Destination	Cotton	Wine	Fruit	Leather	Tobacco	Sugar
Delphin	Jacques François Boiemar	French	Rouen	x			x		
S. Jean Baptiste	Pierre Le Biller	French	Rouen	x			x		
Mariana Querida	Jean Nicolas Topsent	French	Rouen	x			x		
La Belle Marianne	Joseph Guezenec	French	Rouen	x					
Les Deux Freres	Yves le Biller	French	Rouen	X		X			
Auguste	François Collard Descheres	French	Rouen	x					
L'Alerte	Jacques Guillaume Gremont	French	Rouen	x		x			
O Senhor do Bom Fim e N. S. do Rosário	Silvestre Fernandes de Mello	Portuguese	Rouen	x					
Bom Fim e N. S. do Rosário	Silvestre Fernandes de Mello	Portuguese	Rouen	x					

Source: ANTT, Junta do Comércio, mç. 310, cx. 620 – Relações de entrada e saída dos navios do porto de Lisboa em 1789. Table prepared by the author.

TABLE D2 Vessels that transported cotton between January and August 1801

Vessel	Captain	Flag	Destination	Cotton	Wine	Fruit	Leather	Tobacco	Sugar
Ceres	Nicolax Niffen	Danish	Altanar	x					x
Sophia Beata	Andreas Liberg	Swedish	Bremen	x					x
Samuel & Thomaz	John Cowlter	English	Bristol	x	x				
Pennsylvania	Francis Knox	American	Cherbourg	x			x		x
Sussana	John Hodgson	English	Cork	x	x				
Betsey	André Harrison	English	Cork	x	x				
L'Cherry	William Murphy	English	Cork	x	x				
L'Haron	John Murphy	English	Cork	x	x				
Hilton	William Lamacraft	English	Greenock	x	x				
Wadstray	William Way	English	Greenock	x					
Ofter Grefon	Peter Oftlund	Swedish	Greenock	x		x			
Die Frau Rebecca	Hinrich Eytman	Hamburger	Hamburg	x					x
Leopoldo Segundo	Rickmer Peter Krohu	Hamburger	Hamburg	x					x
Elisabeth	Peter Dyer	American	Hamburg	x					
Lelia-Byrd	William Forfyth	American	Hamburg	x					
Magdalena e Ana	Jens Temmereeg	Danish	Hamburg	x					
Anna & Lifeth	Frans Jochim Schroder	Danish	Hamburg	x					x
Maria Dorothea	Gerard Henrique Glafemeyer	Lubeck	Hamburg	x					x
Die Gutt Erwarring	Peter Hendrik Sckomaker	Lubeck	Hamburg	x					x
Senhora Teckla	Harman William Lange	Papenburg	Hamburg	x					
Vrouw Hintzen	Gerrit van Noort	Prussian	Hamburg	x					x

TABLE D2 Vessels that transported cotton between January and August 1801 (*cont.*)

Vessel	Captain	Flag	Destination	Cotton	Wine	Fruit	Leather	Tobacco	Sugar
Phenis	Cristopher Johnson	English	Hull	x	x				
Prince of Brazil	George Cammel	English	Hull	x	x				
Brothers	Henry Brown	English	Hull	x	x				
Thorley	George Stephenson	English	Hull	x	x				
Ann	Andrew Alles	English	Leith	x	x				
Beaver	Richard Saunder	English	Liverpool	x					
Elisa	Thomas Ashford	English	Liverpool	x					
Belle	John Dunly	English	Liverpool	x					
Amazona	Thomaz Fuber	English	Liverpool	x					
Catherine	Daniel Smarth	English	Liverpool	x		x			
De Fiance	Thomaz Nichols	English	Liverpool	x					
Brothers	John Barclay	English	Liverpool	x					
Apollo	Daniel Aubone	English	Liverpool	x					
Robert & Sarah	John Garmen	English	Liverpool	x					
Bridget	Daniel Thomaz	English	Liverpool	x					
Lede	John Hall	English	Liverpool	x					
Bee	James Tullock	English	Liverpool	x	x				
Thetis	David Rutherford	English	Liverpool	x	x				
Carr	William Colwett	English	Liverpool	x	x				
Experiment	John Gowing	English	London	x	x	x			
Blenhaim	Alexander Webster	English	London	x	x	x			
Swift	Henry Webster	English	London	x	x	x			
John Mac Douald	William Head	English	London	x	x	x			
Blakeney	Thomas Warwick	English	London	x	x	x			

TABLE D2 Vessels that transported cotton between January and August 1801 (*cont.*)

Vessel	Captain	Flag	Destination	Cotton	Wine	Fruit	Leather	Tobacco	Sugar
Isca	John Moore	English	London	x	x	x			
Betsey	Charles Costanche	English	London	x	x	x			
Concord	Thomas Crows	English	London	x		x			
Eolus	John Forrester	English	London	x		x			
Blandford	Stephen Baker	English	London	x	x				
Three Brothers	William Red	English	London	x	x				
Hero of the Nile	Alexander Philip	English	London	x	x				
Nautilius	George Thew	English	London	x	x				
Edgel	Daniel Carrol	English	London	x	x				
Ann	Thomaz Hernaman	English	London	x	x				
Commerce	Joseph Befant	English	London	x	x				
Hope	Hefekeah Martins	English	London	x	x				
Friends	Peter Ridland	English	London	x	x				
Betsey	Benjamin Eynon	English	London	x	x				
Alert	Thomaz Hill	English	London	x	x				
Venus	Lowis Humphtries	English	London	x	x				
William	William Hill	English	London	x	x				
Sprigty	John White	English	London	x	x				
Harriot	John Pearson	English	London	x	x				
Rochdale	John Penant	English	London	x	x				
Pomona	John Street	English	London	x	x				
Nancy	Edward Stanwarth	English	London	x	x				
Bulbury	Richard Miller	English	London	x	x				
Emelina	William Horswell	English	London	x	x				
Elisabeth	J. R. Stephens	English	London	x	x				
Harriot	Thomas Syms	English	London	x	x				
Hannah	Thomaz Tilbury	English	London	x	x				

TABLE D2 Vessels that transported cotton between January and August 1801 (*cont.*)

Vessel	Captain	Flag	Destination	Cotton	Wine	Fruit	Leather	Tobacco	Sugar
Fame	Anthony Harrison	English	London	x	x				
George	William Atkins	English	London	x	x				
Albion	William Gammon	English	London	x	x				
Longston	John Webster	English	London	x	x				
Favorie	George Logster	English	London	x	x				
Elisabeth	Lucas Quinton	English	London	x	x				
Sommerset	Thomaz Foreman	English	London	x	x				
Mentor	Tunstall Simpson	English	London	x	x				
Swenkfund	Issac Roding	Swedish	Nantes	x					x

Source: ANTT, Junta do Comércio, mç. 311, cx. 621 – Relações de entrada e saída dos navios do porto de Lisboa em 1801. Table prepared by the author.

Appendix E – Members of the English Factory in Portugal between 1788 and 1820

Name	Residence	Years	Date of admission to the factory	Note
Abel Worth	Rua da Caldeira	1788, 1789, 1790, and 1791		
Allen Brownlie & Co	Rua Bela Vista e Rua da Caldeira	1788, 1789, 1790, 1791, and 1794		
Ambrose Goddard	Wilts.	1803	February 2, 1756	
Andrew James Morrough	Rua do Alecrim	1788, 1789, 1790, 1791, and 1794		
Archibald Brown	Lisbon		August 23, 1804	In Rio de Janeiro in 1815
Archibald Brownlie	Ribeira Nova	1788, 1789, 1790, 1791, 1794, and 1803	March 31, 1790	In Madeira in 1815
B. M. Adamson	Lisbon		July 14, 1804	
Bellinge, Mordaunt & Mahon	Travessa dos Remolares	1788, 1789, 1790, and 1791		
Brander & Co	S. Paulo	1794		
Buller & Stephens	Cais do Santarém	1788, 1789, 1790, 1791, and 1794		
Carret, Koster & Co	Lisbon (Rua dos Fanqueiros) and Liverpool	1794 and 1803	August 29, 1785	
Chambers Kendall	Lisbon		March 12, 1811	
Charles Borlean	London	1803	December 9, 1750	
Charles Boucher	Great Britain	1803	October 20, 1751	
Charles Higgs	Lisbon		March 6, 1811	

(*cont.*)

Name	Residence	Years	Date of admission to the factory	Note
Charles Ironside	Lisbon		January 23, 1818	
Charles Lyne	Lisbon	1803	May 13, 1795	In London in 1815
Charles Manoel Allen & Co	Rua da Caldeira	1788, 1789, 1790, 1791, and 1794		
Charles Russell	Lisbon and Rio de Janeiro	1803	January 11, 1798	
Christopher Hake & Co	As Chagas	1788, 1789, 1790, and 1791		
Connel & Morony	Rua Fresca	1788, 1789, 1790, 1791, and 1794		
Daniel Bowden & Son	Travessa dos Remolares	1788, 1789, 1790, 1791, and 1794		
Daniel Parminster	Lisbon	1803	June 4, 1773	
David Dyson	England	1803	March 5, 1764	
Devisme & Co	Rua Formosa	1788, 1789, 1790, 1791, and 1794		
Edward Ellerton	Lisbon and England		April 26, 1814	
Edward Forest	Rua Nova de S. Francisco	1788, 1789, 1790, and 1791		
Edward Joyce	Rua da Caldeira	1788, 1789, 1790, and 1791		
Edward Maine	Lisbon	1803	March 19, 1778	In Scotland in 1815
Edward Perechon (Vice Consul in Lisbon)		1788, 1789, 1790, and 1791		
Edward Turner Eyton	Lisbon and England		January 19, 1815	

(*cont.*)

Name	Residence	Years	Date of admission to the factory	Note
Evans, Offley, & Sealy	Pedras Negras	1788, 1789, 1790, 1791, and 1794		
Fitz-Gibbon & French	Rua Nova d'El Rei	1788, 1789, 1790, 1791, and 1794		
Francis Arbouin	Rua Bela Rainha	1794 and 1803	January 10, 1754	
Francis Graham	Bica Grande	1788, 1789, 1790, and 1791		
Francis Lupton	Lisbon	1803	June 16, 1791	In London in 1815
Francis Morrogh	Rua das Flores	1788, 1789, 1790, 1791, and 1794		
George J. Sealy	Lisbon		July 14, 1804	In Bahia in 1815
George Koster	Lisbon and London	1803	January 9, 1788	
George Roach	Lisbon (Rua Madalena) and Liverpool	1794 and 1803	January 21, 1789	
George Thomas Bulkeley	Lisbon (Rua do Arsenal) and England	1788, 1789, 1790, 1791, 1794, and 1803	May 29, 1767	
George Warden	England	1803	January 10, 1782	
Gerald Gould	Rua das Flores	1788, 1789, 1790, 1791, and 1794		
Gerorge Allen	Travessa dos Remolares	1788, 1789, 1790, and 1791		
Henry Gallwey & Co	Rua da Emenda	1788, 1789, 1790, 1791, and 1794		
Holford, Gonne & Co	Pedras Negras e na Quintinha	1788, 1789, 1790, 1791, and 1794		

(*cont.*)

Name	Residence	Years	Date of admission to the factory	Note
Holford, Marshall & Holford	Pedras Negras	1788, 1789, 1790, and 1791		
Horn & Still	As necessidades	1788, 1789, 1790, 1791, and 1794		
Hudson, Harrison & Gonne	Pedras Negras	1788, 1789, 1790, 1791, and 1794		
Hugh Goodair	Largo de S. Paulo	1794 and 1803	April 3, 1794	
Hugh Parker	Ribeira Nova e Rua do Carvalho	1788, 1789, 1790, and 1791		
Hugh Skeys	Dublin	1803	February 20, 1782	
J. & B. Illius Ficke	S. Julião	1788, 1789, 1790, 1791, and 1794		
J. T. Forrest	Pedras Negras	1794		
James Alton	Lisbon (Rua dos Retrozeiros) and Western Islands	1794 and 1803	January 19, 1791	
James Bell	Lisbon		August 23, 1804	In Gibraltar in 1815
James Bowness	Lisbon		April 26, 1814	
James Brander & Co	Behind the Convent of S. Francisco de Paula	1788, 1789, 1790, 1791, and 1803	May 13, 1766	
James Burn & Sons	Lisboan (Rua da Rosa das Partilhas) and London	1788, 1789, 1790, 1791, 1794, and 1803	March 5, 1764	
James Finnie	Lisbon		July 24, 1817	
James Forest	Rua Nova de S. Francisco	1794		

(*cont.*)

Name	Residence	Years	Date of admission to the factory	Note
James Graham	Lisbon		January 11, 1820	
James Houston	Great Britain	1803	February 19, 1766	
James Joyce	Rua da Caldeira	1794		
James Little	Tenerife	1803	July 27, 1787	
James Mac Gibbon	Stirling	1803	March 19, 1778	
James Mc. Andrew	London	1803	August 18, 1791	
James Milne	Lisbon	1803	January 11, 1798	
James Philips & Co	A Buenos Aires	1788, 1789, 1790, 1791, 1794, and 1803	January 10, 1793	
James Slack & Co	Corpo Santo	1794		
Jedediah Stephens	Lisbon and Rio de Janeiro	1803	June 4, 1773	
Jeremy & Thomas Dyson	Lisbon (Calçada da Madalena) and England	1788, 1789, 1790, 1791, 1794, and 1803	March 19, 1778	
John B. Vivien & Herbert	Rua Nova d'El Rei	1788, 1789, 1790, 1791 and 1794		
John Bell & Co	Lisbon (Rua dos Douradores) and Rio de Janeiro	1788, 1789, 1790, 1791, 1794, and 1803	December 15, 1774	
John Berthon	Lisbon	1803	March 6, 1767	
John Bulkeley & Sons	Aos Remolares	1788, 1789, 1790, 1791, and 1794		
John Chrispin	Lisbon	1803	January 14, 1802	Consul at Porto in 1815
John Crawford	London	1803	August 25, 1772	
John Cuffin	Corpo Santo	1794		
John Edwards	Rua do Arsenal	1788, 1789, 1790, 1791, 1794, and 1803	January 28, 1767	In England in 1815

(*cont.*)

Name	Residence	Years	Date of admission to the factory	Note
John Fredk Worthington	Lisbon	1803	January 20, 1803	In Rio de Janeiro in 1815
John French	Largo de S. Paulo	1788, 1789, 1790, and 1791		
John Garnault	Lisbon	1803	March 5, 1764	
John Gooch	London	1803	March 6, 1767	
John Hitchcock (Vice Consul in Figueira and Aveiro)		1788, 1789, 1790, 1791, and 1794		
John Josiah Holford	London	1803	October 27, 1786	
John King	Great Britain	1803	October 20, 1751	
John Leigh	Lisbon	1803	May 13, 1795	
John Lempriére (Vice Consul in Faro)		1788, 1789, 1790, 1791, and 1794		
John March	Lisbon	1803	May 4, 1786	
John Matthew Bulkeley	Lisbon		October 26, 1804	In London in 1815
John McKean	Lisbon		July 21, 1819	
John Parley	London	1803	May 20, 1763	
John Robins	Lisbon	1803	June 6, 1798	In Jersey in 1815
John Skies	Lisbon (Boa Hora) and Rio de Janeiro	1788, 1789, 1790, 1791 and 1803	June 4, 1773	
John Stanley	S. Catarina e ao Chiado	1788, 1789, 1790, 1791, and 1794		
John Thomas Forest	Rua dos Algibebes	1788, 1789, 1790, and 1791		

(*cont.*)

Name	Residence	Years	Date of admission to the factory	Note
John Turner	Rua dos Douradores	1788, 1789, 1790, 1791, 1794, and 1803	March 21, 1767	
John Watts Garland	Lisbon		April 26, 1814	
John Whitehead (Vice Consul in Oporto)		1788, 1789, 1790, 1791, and 1794		
John Wilby	Lisbon		April 26, 1814	
Johnn Elias Perochon	London	1803	November 2, 1769	
Joseph Axtill	Chiado	1794 and 1803	March 19, 1778	
Joseph Coles		1803	June 4, 1773	In America in 1807
Joseph Edmonds	Lisbon		August 23, 1804	
Joseph Edwards	Great Britain	1803	March 21, 1767	
Joseph Lyne	Lisbon	1803	May 13, 1795	In London in 1815
Joseph Penwarin	Lisbon	1803	May 13, 1795	
Joseph Sill	Great Britain	1803	February 6, 1769	
Josiah Holford	London	1803	February 17, 1749	
Lawrence Fowke		1803	June 8, 1771	In Ireland in 1815
Lawrence Ormerod	Lisbon and Oporto		April 26, 1814	
Long & Murphy	Largo de S. Paulo	1788, 1789, 1790, and 1791		
Luiz Stephens & Co	Rua Nova d'El Rei	1788, 1789, 1790, 1791, and 1794		
Lupton, King & Lupton	Rua dos Fanqueiros	1788, 1789, 1790, and 1791		
Matheson, Anthony	Rua do Arsenal	1788, 1789, 1790, and 1791		

(*cont.*)

Name	Residence	Years	Date of admission to the factory	Note
Mathew Taylor	Travessa dos Remolares	1788, 1789, 1790, 1791, and 1794		
May, Coppendale & Co	S. João da Praça e Cais de Santarém	1788, 1789, 1790, 1791, and 1794		
Mayne & Brown	A Lapa	1788, 1789, 1790, 1791, and 1794		
Mellish & Devisme	Rua Formosa	1788, 1789, 1790, and 1791		
Mordaunt & Co	Ribeira Nova	1788, 1789, 1790, 1791, and 1794		
Nathaniel Bowden	Lisbon	1803	May 13, 1795	
Nicolas Conolly	Rua de S. Bento	1788, 1789, 1790, 1791, and 1794		
Parker & Co	Ribeira Nova ao Pé do Arco	1794		
Parminster, Farquhar & Co	Rua da Emenda	1788, 1789, 1790, 1791, and 1794		
Pasley Little & Co	Rua da Caldeira	1788, 1789, 1790, and 1791		
Patrick Caffery & Son	Cais da Ribeira Nova	1788, 1789, 1790, 1791, and 1794		
Paul Berthon	Lisbon	1803	December 13, 1798	
Peter Berthon	London	1803	November 7, 1759	
Powe & Co	Rua do Alecrim	1788, 1789, 1790, 1791, and 1794		

(*cont.*)

Name	Residence	Years	Date of admission to the factory	Note
Power & Horton	Ribeira Nova	1788, 1789, 1790, and 1791		
Richard Allen (Vice Consul in Viana)		1788, 1789, 1790, 1791, and 1794		
Richard Buller	Lisbon	1803	November 6, 1754	
Richard Goodall	Lisbon	1803	January 11, 1798	
Richard Hake	London	1803	December 12, 1787	
Richard Sealy	Lisbon and Rio de Janeiro	1803	December 15, 1774	
Richard Stert	London	1803	August 31, 1771	
Robert Lucas	Lisbon		January 27, 1807	
Robert Munro	Lisbon		January 11, 1820	
Robert Noble	A Buenos Aires	1788, 1789, 1790, and 1791		
Robert Slack & Co	Campolide	1788, 1789, 1790, 1791, and 1794		
Robert Wilson	England	1803	May 21, 1795	
Robert Young	Lisbon	1803	April 3, 1794	In England in 1815
Roger Bidgood Whitney	Lisbon		April 26, 1814	
Samuel Acton	Lisbon		August 23, 1804	
Samuel Fowke	Cork	1803	November 12, 1764	
Samuel Waterhouse	Lisbon		May 23, 1815	
Sir John Hort (Consul)	Rua da Bela Vista	1788, 1789, 1790, and 1791		
Sir Robert Walpole (Ambassador)	Santa Martha	1788, 1789, 1790, and 1791		
Slack & Connor	Corpo Santo	1788, 1789, 1790, and 1791		

(*cont.*)

Name	Residence	Years	Date of admission to the factory	Note
Stephen Geradot	London	1803	December 15, 1751	
Stephen Skinner Barnett	Lisbon	1803	February 26, 1802	
Stert, Amies & De La Rue	As portas do mar	1794		
Thomas Allen (Vice Consul in Caminha)		1794		
Thomas Arthur	Ribeira Nova	1788, 1789, 1790, 1791, and 1794		
Thomas Barker	Lisbon		July 14, 1804	
Thomas Coppendale	Lisbon and England	1803	January 28, 1768	
Thomas Custance	Lisbon		April 26, 1814	
Thomas Finnemore Hill	Lisbon and England		April 26, 1814	
Thomas Garland	Lisbon		February 14, 1810	
Thomas Herbert	Lisbon	1803	May 13, 1795	In London in 1815
Thomas Lempriere	Hamburg and Bordeaux	1803	November 8, 1787	
Thomas March & Co	Rua Áurea	1788, 1789, 1790, and 1791		
Thomas O'Brien	Ribeira Nova	1788, 1789, 1790, and 1791		
Thomas Rice	Rua da Caldeira	1788, 1789, 1790, 1791, and 1794		
Thomas Shannon	Lisbon		January 22, 1820	
Timothy Goodall	Boa Hora	1788, 1789, 1790, 1791, and 1794		

(*cont.*)

Name	Residence	Years	Date of admission to the factory	Note
Valentine French	Largo de S. Paulo	1788, 1789, 1790, and 1791		
Walter Grossett & Co	Behind Conceição Velha	1788, 1789, 1790, 1791, and 1794		
William & John James Stephens	Lisbon (Rua das Flores) and Rio de Janeiro	1788, 1789, 1790, 1791, 1794, and 1803	December 12, 1776	
William Armitage	Rua dos Algibebes	1788, 1789, 1790, and 1791		
William Brown	Lisbon	1803	October 27, 1786	
William Burn	London	1803	January 4, 1772	
William Carruthers	Lisbon		January 11, 1820	
William Cossart	Lisbon	1803	January 11, 1798	In Madeira in 1815
William D. McAndrew	Lisbon		January 11, 1820	
William Davenport	Rua Augusta	1788, 1789, 1790, 1791, 1794, and 1803	December 10, 1772	
William Farquhar	London	1803	November 24, 1785	
William Gonne	London	1803	November 8, 1787	
William Henry Pinson	Lisbon		February 14, 1810	In England in 1815
William Kempe	Lisbon and Liverpool		January 24, 1804	
William Lucas	Rua dos Fanqueiros	1788, 1789, 1790, and 1791		
William March	Lisbon	1803	October 14, 1801	In Rio in 1807
William Morgan	Lisbon and London		September 13, 1804	

(*cont.*)

Name	Residence	Years	Date of admission to the factory	Note
William Newman	Lisbon and England		February 28, 1811	
William Oxenford	Lisbon	1803	December 19, 1799	In London in 1815
William Plaxton Allcock	Lisbon and England		July 14, 1804	
William Sill	Lisbon	1803	April 3, 1794	In Scotland in 1815
William Stephens	Lisbon	1803	July 17, 1752	
William Tonkin	Rua Larga de S. Roque	1788, 1789, 1790, 1791, and 1794		
William Williamson (Vice Consul in Setúbal)		1788, 1789, 1790, 1791, and 1794		
William Young	Lisbon		August 23, 1804	In Rio de Janeiro in 1815

Sources: The British Historical Society of Portugal, List of British Merchants in Lisbon 1788–1791, Report: HA 10, 1946–1950, 663 and The British Hospital, Lisbon, 1793, Report: HA 7 by A. R. Walford, 1943, 436–441. The 1803 list, which was updated to 1820, was taken from A. R. Walford, *The British Factory in Lisbon & Its Closing Stages Ensuing Upon the Treaty of 1810* (Instituto británico em Portugal, 1940), 71–74.

Sources and Bibliography

Manuscript Sources

AHU – Arquivo Histórico Ultramarino, Lisboa (Overseas Historical Archive)

AHU, ACL, CU, 009, Cx. 28, Doc. 2880.
AHU, ACL, CU, 009, Cx. 36, Doc. 3597.
AHU, ACL, CU, 009, Cx. 36, Doc. 3603.
AHU, ACL, CU, 009, Cx. 37, Doc. 3699.
AHU, ACL, CU, 009, Cx. 52, Doc. 5014.
AHU, ACL, CU, 009, Cx. 52, Doc. 5020.
AHU, ACL, CU, 009, Cx. 54, Doc. 5123.
AHU, ACL, CU, 009, Cx. 57, Doc. 5321.
AHU, ACL, CU, 009: Cx. 58, Doc. 5353.
AHU, ACL, CU, 009, Cx. 59, Doc. 5432.
AHU, ACL, CU, 009, Cx. 60, Doc. 5495.
AHU, ACL, CU, 009, Cx. 60. Doc. 5515.
AHU, ACL, CU, 009, Cx. 61, Doc. 5562.
AHU, ACL, CU, 009, Cx. 61, Doc. 5563.
AHU, ACL, CU, 009, Cx. 64, Doc. 5688.
AHU, ACL, CU, 009, Cx. 64, Doc. 5729.
AHU, ACL, CU, 009, Cx. 64, Doc. 5730.
AHU, ACL, CU, 009, Cx. 66, Doc. 5832.
AHU, ACL, CU, 009, Cx. 67, Doc. 5843.
AHU, ACL, CU, 009, Cx. 67, Doc. 5844.
AHU, ACL, CU, 009, Cx. 68, Doc. 5938.
AHU, ACL, CU, 009, Cx. 68, Doc. 5939.
AHU, ACL, CU, 009, Cx. 70, Doc. 6112.
AHU, ACL, CU, 009, Cx. 73, Doc. 6272.
AHU, ACL, CU, 009, Cx. 73, Doc. 6292.
AHU, ACL, CU, 009, Cx. 73, Doc. 6284.
AHU, ACL, CU, 009, Cx. 73, Doc. 6324.
AHU, ACL, CU, 009, Cx. 74, Doc. 6389.
AHU, ACL, CU, 009, Cx. 75, Doc. 6429.
AHU, ACL, CU, 009, Cx. 75, Doc. 6495.
AHU, ACL, CU, 009, Cx. 77, Doc. 6567.

AHU, ACL, CU, 009, Cx. 79, Doc. 6718.
AHU, ACL, CU, 009, Cx. 79, Doc. 6746.
AHU, ACL, CU, 009, Cx. 80, Doc. 6775.
AHU, ACL, CU, 009, Cx. 81, Doc. 6868.
AHU, ACL, CU, 009, Cx. 81, Doc. 6882.
AHU, ACL, CU, 009, Cx. 84, Doc. 7042.
AHU, ACL, CU, 009, Cx. 84, Doc. 7093.
AHU, ACL, CU, 009, Cx. 86, Doc. 7178.
AHU, ACL, CU, 009, Cx. 89, Doc. 7404.
AHU, ACL, CU, 009, Cx. 90, Doc. 7457.
AHU, ACL, CU, 009, Cx. 92, Doc. 7604.
AHU, ACL, CU, 009, Cx. 93, Doc. 7680.
AHU, ACL, CU, 009, Cx. 93, Doc. 7684.
AHU, ACL, CU, 009, Cx. 93, Doc. 7702.
AHU, ACL, CU, 009, Cx. 96, Doc. 7859.
AHU, ACL, CU, 009, Cx. 97, Doc. 7887.
AHU, ACL, CU, 009, Cx. 102, Doc. 8250.
AHU, ACL, CU, 009, Cx. 108, Doc. 8499.
AHU, ACL, CU, 009, Cx. 114, Doc. 8842.
AHU, ACL, CU, 009, Cx. 134, Doc. 9861.
AHU, ACL, CU, 009, Cx. 154, Doc. 11057.
AHU, ACL, CU, 009, Cx. 155, Doc. 11113.
AHU, ACL, CU, 009, Cx. 158, Doc. 11370.
AHU, ACL, CU, 013, Cx. 40, Doc. 3199.
AHU, ACL, CU, 013, Cx. 42, Doc. 4151.
AHU, ACL, CU, 013, Cx. 50, Doc. 4873.
AHU, ACL, CU, 013, Cx. 50, Doc. 4897.
AHU, ACL, CU, 013, Cx. 51, Doc. 4663.
AHU, ACL, CU, 013, Cx. 51, Doc. 4917.
AHU, ACL, CU, 014, Cx. 30, Doc. 2178.
AHU, ACL, CU, 014, Cx. 35, Doc. 2510.
AHU, ACL, CU, 014, Cx. 36, Doc. 2617.
AHU, ACL, CU, 014, Cx. 41, Doc. 2890.
AHU, ACL, CU, 015, Cx. 9. Doc. 873.
AHU, ACL, CU, 015, Cx. 17, Doc. 1711.
AHU, ACL, CU, 015, Cx. 21, Doc. 1967.
AHU, ACL, CU, 015, Cx. 42, Doc. 3767.
AHU, ACL, CU, 015, Cx. 44, Doc. 3940.
AHU, ACL, CU, 015, Cx. 44, Doc. 4004.

AHU, ACL, CU, 015, Cx. 83, Doc. 6913.
AHU, ACL, CU, 015, Cx. 95. Doc. 7501.
AHU, ACL, CU, 015, Cx. 95. Doc. 7502.
AHU, ACL, CU, 015, Cx. 95. Doc. 7503.
AHU, ACL, CU, 015, Cx. 136. Doc. 10156.
AHU, ACL, CU, 015, Cx. 139, Doc. 10311.
AHU, ACL, CU, 015, Cx. 146, Doc. 10688.
AHU, ACL, CU, 015, Cx. 152, Doc. 11023.
AHU, ACL, CU, 015, Cx. 158, Doc. 11423.
AHU, ACL, CU, 015, Cx. 159, Doc. 11475.
AHU, ACL, CU, 015, Cx. 160, Doc. 11524.
AHU, ACL, CU, 015, Cx. 162, Doc. 11607.
AHU, ACL, CU, 015, Cx. 178, Doc. 12472.
AHU, ACL, CU, 015, Cx. 188, Doc. 13038.
AHU, ACL, CU, 015, Cx. 194, Doc. 13377.
AHU, ACL, CU, 015, Cx. 199, Doc. 13653.
AHU, ACL, CU, 015, Cx. 202, Doc. 13809.
AHU, ACL, CU, 015, Cx. 192, Doc. 14042.
AHU, ACL, CU, 015, Cx. 207, Doc. 14139.
AHU, ACL, CU, 015, Cx. 223, Doc. 15104.
AHU, ACL, CU, 015, Cx. 230, Doc. 15543.
AHU, ACL, CU, 015, Cx. 251, Doc. 16832.
AHU, ACL, CU, 015, Cx. 255, Doc. 17592.
AHU, ACL, CU, 015, Cx. 269, Doc. 17903.
AHU, ACL, CU, 015, Cx. 270, Doc. 18008.
AHU, ACL, CU, 015, Cx. 274, Doc. 18319.
AHU, ACL, CU, 015, Cx. 255, Doc. 18523.
AHU, ACL, CU, 015, Cx. 274, Doc. 18650.
AHU, ACL, CU, 015, Cx. 274, Doc. 18726.
AHU, ACL, CU, 023–01, Cx. 54, Doc. 4144, São Paulo Alfredo Mendes Gouveia.
AHU, ACL, CU, 005, Cx. 93, Doc. 18282, Bahia Eduardo de Castro e Almeida.
AHU, Códice 256.
AHU, Códice 598.
AHU, Códice 599.

ANTT – Arquivo Nacional Torre do Tombo, Lisboa (Institute of the National Archives – Torre do Tombo)

CGGPM. Cartas aos administradores do Maranhão, livro 215.
CGGPM. Copiador de cartas para o Maranhão, livro 230.
CGPP. Copiador de Pernambuco. N.º 1 – liv. 382. 1759–1773.

Feitos Findos, Juízo da Índia e Mina, mç. 7, n.º 14, cx. 273.
Feitos Findos, Juízo da Índia e Mina, mç. 40, n.º 5, cx. 227.
Feitos Findos, Juízo da Índia e Mina, mç. 35, n.º 22, cx. 35.
Feitos Findos, Juízo da Índia e Mina, mç. 17, n.º 11, cx. 204.
Feitos Findos, Juízo da Índia e Mina, mç. 14, n.º 28 cx. 381
Feitos Findos, Juízo da Índia e Mina, mç. 12, n.º 10, cx. 199.
Feitos Findos, Juízo da Índia e Mina, mç 52, n.º 7, cx. 239.
Feitos Findos, Juízo da Índia e Mina, mç. 38, n.º 9, cx. 225.
Feitos Findos, Juízo da Índia e Mina, mç. 3, n.º 15, cx. 269.
Feitos Findos, Juízo da Índia e Mina, mç. 27, n.º 13, cx. 214.
Feitos Findos, Juízo da Índia e Mina, mç. 55, n.º 3, cx. 242.
Feitos Findos, Juízo da Índia e Mina, mç. 68, n.º 16, cx. 255.
Feitos Findos, Juízo da Índia e Mina, mç. 82, n.º 19, cx. 82.
Feitos Findos, Juízo da Índia e Mina, mç. 26, n.º 12, cx. 26.
Feitos Findos, Juízo da Índia e Mina, Justificações Ultramarinas, Brasil, mç. 113, n.º 12
Feitos Findos, Juízo da Índia e Mina, Justificações Ultramarinas, Brasil, mç. 13, n.º 13.
Feitos Findos, Juízo da Índia e Mina, Justificações Ultramarinas, Brasil, mç. 341, n.º 11.
Feitos Findos, Juízo da Índia e Mina, Justificações Ultramarinas, Brasil, mç. 45, n.º 3.
Feitos Findos, Juízo da Índia e Mina, Justificações Ultramarinas, África, mç. 19, n.o 10, cx. 34.
Feitos Findos, Conservatória da Companhia Geral de Pernambuco e Paraíba, mç. 15, n.º 1, cx. 19.
Feitos Findos, Registo Geral de Testamentos, liv. 306, f. 151v-152v.
Feitos Findos, Conservatória Geral do Comércio, cx. 53, mç. 12, nº 7.
Feitos Findos, Livros dos Feitos Findos, liv. 210.
Arquivo do Arquivo, Avisos e Ordens, mç. 5, n.o 36, 1801.
Mesa da Consciência e Ordens, Habilitações para a Ordem de Cristo, Letra B, mç. 7, n.º 5.
Mesa da Consciência e Ordens, Habilitações para a Ordem de Cristo, Letra M, mç. 30, n.º 35.
Conselho da Fazenda, Justificações do Reino, Letra D, mç. 4, n.º 4.
Ministério do Reino, mç. 853, proc. 4.
Ministério do Reino, mç. 956, proc. 37
Alfândega de Lisboa, Casa da Índia, import books: 223, 291, 314, 315, 129, 130, 408, 410, 411, and 1,475.
Alfândega de Lisboa, Casa da Índia, export books: 138, 290, 288, 250, 249, 248, 247, 246, 139, 289, 140, 141, 192, 193, 194, 195, 196, 311, 312, 313, 133, 132, 131, 95, 94, 97, 44, 45, 104, 162, 215, 407, 409, 412, 284, 106, 348, 517, 189, 207, 511, 329, 534, and 484.
Alfândega de Lisboa, Casa da Índia, liv. 1,841. Registo das leis, ordens, condições dos contratos e fábricas.
Junta do Comércio, Registro Geral, Liv. 121 and 122.

Junta do Comércio, mç. 10 (cx. 38) Correspondência recebida das autoridades ultramarinas.
CNL – Cartório Notarial de Lisboa (*Notary Office of Lisbon*)
2º CNL, Cx. 132, liv.626, f. 88v–90.
2º CNL, Cx. 134, liv.635, f. 15.
3º CNL, Cx. 152, liv. 711, f. 53–53v.
3º CNL, Cx. 154, liv. 723, f. 77–77v.
3º CNL, Cx. 154, liv. 726, f. 56v–57.
6º CNL, Cx. 21, liv. 104, f. 66–68v.
6º CNL, Cx. 25, liv. 122, f. 79–80.
6º CNL, Cx. 25, liv 124, f. 52v–53v.
6º CNL, Cx. 26, liv. 126, f. 10–11.
6º CNL, Cx. 27, liv. 132, f. 26v–28v, and 61–61v.
6º CNL, Cx. 27, liv. 135, f. 75v–76.
10º CNL, Cx. 27, liv. 144, f. 97–97v.
7º CNL, Ofício A, Cx. 98, liv. 597, f. 44v–45.
7º CNL, Ofício A, Cx. 100, liv. 604, f. 75v–76.
7º CNL, Ofício A, Cx. 102, liv. 620, f. 29–29v.
7º CNL, Ofício A, Cx. 104, liv. 629, f. 89.
7º CNL, Ofício A, Cx. 105, liv. 636, f. 85–86v.
7º CNL, Ofício A, Cx. 105, liv. 640, f. 57–58v.
7º CNL, Ofício A, cx. 107, liv. 648, f. 31–31v.
7º CNL, Ofício A, Cx. 110, liv. 667, f. 88v.
7º CNL, Ofício A, Cx. 112, liv. 680, f. 39v.
10º CNL, Cx. 19, liv. 101, f. 15–15v.
10º CNL, Cx. 21, liv. 114, f. 12v–13.
10º CNL, Cx. 25, liv. 134, f. 52v–53v.
10º CNL, Cx. 26, liv. 141, f. 50–51v.
10º CNL, Cx. 30, liv. 164, f. 103.
10º CNL, Cx. 31, liv. 171, f. 19.
10º CNL, Cx. 36, liv. 190, f. 130v–131.
10º CNL, Cx. 37, liv. 199, f. 29v.
BNRJ – Biblioteca Nacional do Rio de Janeiro.
Mapas Estatísticos de Pernambuco, 1763, BN, 03,01,038.

IEB – Instituto de Estudos Brasileiros

Alberto Lamego. AL-050-012.
IAHGP – Instituto Arqueológico Histórico Geográfico Pernambucano.
Códice 169.
Códice 171.

APEJE – Arquivo Público Estadual Jordão Emerenciano

Correspondência com a Corte, 03.
Correspondência com a Corte, 09.

BNP – Biblioteca Nacional de Portugal

Plano geral da cidade de Lisboa em 1785, Francisco D. Milcent.

BNE – Biblioteca Nacional de España

Planta da Cidade de Lisboa Novamente edeficada della Ruina que padeceó no Terramoto do Primeiro de Novembro del Anno 1755.

NA – the National Archives Kew

FO 63/12, 63/19, 63/206.

Printed Sources

Almanách de Lisboa: para o anno ... 1788 1800, 1805. Typog. da Academia Real das Sciencias.

Antonil, André João. *Cultura e opulencia do Brazil, por suas drogas e minas, com varias noticias curiosas do modo de fazer o assucar.., Obra de André João Antonil*. 1837. http://digital.bbm.usp.br/handle/bbm/7461.

Bombelles, Marquis de. *Journal d'un ambassadeur de France au Portugal, 1786–1788*. Presses universitaires de France, 1979.

Branner, John Casper. *Cotton in the Empire of Brazil; the Antiquity, Methods and Extent of Its Cultivation, Together with Statistics of Exportation and Home Consumption*. Government Printing Office, 1885.

Burlamaqui, Frederico Leopoldo Cesar. *Monographia do algodoeiro*. Typ. de N.L. Vianna e filhos, 1863.

Callcott, Lady Maria. *Journal of a Voyage to Brazil: And Residence There, During Part of the Years 1821, 1822, 1823*. Longman, Hurst, Rees, Orme, Brown, and Green, 1824.

Câmara, Manuel Arruda da. *Memoria sobre a cultura dos algodoeiros e sobre o methodo de o escolher, e ensacar, etc*. Na Officina da Casa Litteraria do Arco do Cego, 1799.

Carrere, Joseph-Barthélemy-François. *A Picture of Lisbon, Taken on the Spot: Being a Description Moral, Civil, Political, Physical and Religious, of That Capital; with Sketches of the Government Character and Manners of the Portuguese in General ...* Printed for Henry Colburn, 1809.

Collyer, William Bengo'. *The Investigator (or, Quarterly Magazine)*. Thomas and George Underwood, 1820.

Dumouriez, Charles François Du Périer. *An Account of Portugal, as It Appeared in 1766 to Dumouriez: Since a Celebrated General in the French Army*. C. Law, 1797.

Ellison, Thomas. *The Cotton Trade of Great Britain: Including a History of the Liverpool Cotton Market and of the Liverpool Cotton Brokers' Association*. Effingham Wilson, Royal Exchange, 1886.

Gardner, George. *Travels in the Interior of Brazil: Principally Through the Northern Provinces, and the Gold and Diamond Districts, During the Years 1836–1841*. Reeve, brothers, 1846.

Gayoso, Raimundo Jose de Sousa. *Compendio historico-politico dos principios da lavoura do Maranhão: suas producçoens, e progressos, que tem tido até ao prezente, entraves que a vão deteriorando; e meios que tem lembrado para desvanece-los, em augmento da mesma lavoura, e sem prejuizo do real patrimonio ...* P.N. Rougeron, Impressor, 1818.

Goudar, Ange. *Rélation historique du tremblement de terre survenu à Lisbonne le premier novembre 1755: Avec un détail contenant la perte en hommes, eglises, convens, palais, maisons, diamans, meubles, marchandises, &c.* Chez Philanthrope, à la Vérité, 1756.

Henderson, James. *A History of the Brazil*. Longman, 1821.

'Ideia Da População Da Capitania de Pernambuco, e Das Suas Anexas, Extensão de Suas Costas, Rios e Povoações Notáveis, Agricultura, Número Dos Engenhos, Contratos, e Rendimentos Reaes, Aumento Que Estes Tem Tido, Etc, Etc, Desde o Ano de 1774 Em Que Tomou Posse Do Governo Das Mesmas Capitanias o Governador e Capitam General Jozé Cezar de Menezes'. *Anais Da Biblioteca Nacional Do Rio de Janeiro, Volume XL* (1918): 1–112.

'Informação Geral Da Capitania de Pernambuco, 1749 – Anais Da Biblioteca Nacional Do Rio de Janeiro, Volume XXVIII.' 1906.

Koster, Henry. *Travels in Brazil*. Longman, Hurst, Rees, Orme, and Brown, 1816.

Lago, Antonio Bernardino Pereira do. *Estatistica historica-geografica da Provincia do Maranhão oferecida ao Soberano Congresso das Cortes Geraes, extraordinarias, e constituintes da monarchia portugueza*. Academia Real das Sciencias, 1822.

Luccock, John. *Notes on Rio de Janeiro and the Southern Parts of Brazil*. Printed for Samuel Leigh, 1820.

Melo, Sebastião José de Carvalho e. *Escritos Economicos de Londres (1741–1742)*. Biblioteca Nacional, 1986.

Ratton, Jacome. *Recordações de Jacome Ratton sobre ocorrências do seu tempo, de maio de 1747 a setembro de 1810. 2. ed. revista cuidadosamente por J.M. Teixeira de Carvalho*. Imprensa da Universidade, 1920.

Reid, R. *Glasgow, Past and Present*. Vol. 3. 3 vols. D. Robertson, 1884.

Say, Horace. *Histoire des relations commerciales entre la France et le Brésil: et considérations générales sur les monnaies, les changes, les banques et le commerce extérieur*. Guillaumin, 1839.

Silva, Antonio de Moraes. *Diccionario Da Lingua Portugueza – Recompilado Dos Vocabularios Impressos Ate Agora, e Nesta Segunda Edição Novamente Emendado e Muito Acrescentado, Por Antonio de Moraes Silva.* Typographia Lacerdina, 1789.

Silva, Antonio Delgado. *Collecção da legislação Portugueza desde a ultima compilação das ordenações: Legislação de 1750 a 1762.* Vol. 1. Typ. Maigrense, 1830.

Silva, Antonio Delgado. *Collecção da legislação Portugueza desde a ultima compilação das ordenações: Legislação de 1763 a 1774.* Vol. 2. Typ. Maigrense, 1829.

Silva, Antonio Delgado. *Collecção da legislação Portugueza desde a ultima compilação das ordenações: Legislação de 1775 a 1790.* Vol. 3. Typ. Maigrense, 1828.

Silva, Antonio Delgado. *Collecção da legislação Portugueza desde a ultima compilação das ordenações: Legislação de 1802 a 1810.* Vol. 5. Typ. Maigrense, 1826.

Smithers, Henry. *Liverpool, Its Commerce, Statistics, and Institutions: With a History of the Cotton Trade.* T. Kaye, 1825.

Sturz, Johann Jakob. *A Review, Financial, Statistical, & Commercial, of the Empire of Brazil and Its Resources: Together with a Suggestion of the Expediency and Mode of Admitting Brazilian and Other Foreign Sugars Into Great Britain for Refining and Exportation.* E. Wilson, 1837.

Tollenare, Louis-François de. *Notas dominicaes tomadas durante uma residencia em Portugal e no Brasil nos annos 1816, 1817 e 1818.* Empreza do Jornal do Recife, 1905.

Secondary Sources

Aaslestad, Katherine. "Paying for War: Experiences of Napoleonic Rule in the Hanseatic Cities." *Central European History* 39, no. 4 (2006): 641–75.

Acioli, Vera Lúcia Costa. *Jurisdição e conflitos. Aspectos da administração colonial: Pernambuco, século XVII.* EDUFPE, 1997.

Adams, Julia. "Principals and Agents, Colonialists and Company Men: The Decay of Colonial Control in the Dutch East Indies." *American Sociological Review* 61, no. 1 (1996): 12–28.

Albuquerque, Débora de Souza Leão, Flávio Rabelo Versiani, and José Raimundo Oliveira Vergolino. "Financiamento e Organização Do Tráfico de Escravos Para Pernambuco No Século XIX." *EconomiA* 14, no. 1A (2013): 211–25.

Alcochete, Nuno Daupias d'. "As Casas de Morada de Bernardo Clamouse." *Boletim Cultural Da Câmara Municipal Do Porto* 17, nos. 1–2 (1954): 216–44.

Alden, Dauril. "Late Colonial Brazil, 1750–1808." In *The Cambridge History of Latin America. Volume 2: Colonial Latin America,* edited by Leslie Bethell. Cambridge University Press, 1984.

Alden, Dauril. "Manoel Luís Vieira: An Entrepreneur in Rio De Janeiro during Brazil's Eighteenth Century Agricultural Renaissance." *The Hispanic American Historical Review* 39, no. 4 (1959): 521–37.

Alden, Dauril. *Royal Government in Colonial Brazil, with Special Reference to the Administration to the Marquis of Lavradio, Viceroy, 1769–1779*. University of California, 1968.

Aldous, Michael, and Christopher Coyle. "Examining the Role of a Private-Order Institution in Global Trade: The Liverpool Cotton Brokers' Association and the Crowning of King Cotton, 1811–1900." *Business History Review* 95, no. 4 (2021): 671–702.

Alegre, Maria Sylvia Porto. "Vaqueiros, agricultores, artesãos: origens do trabalho livre no Ceará Colonial." *Revista de Ciências Sociais* 20/21 (1989): 1–29.

Alexandre, Valentim. *Os sentidos do Império: questão nacional e questão colonial na crise do Antigo Regime português*. Edições Afrontamento, 1993.

Allen, Robert C. "Spinning Their Wheels: A Reply to Jane Humphries and Benjamin Schneider." *The Economic History Review* 73, no. 4 (2020): 1128–36.

Allen, Robert C. *The British Industrial Revolution in Global Perspective*. New Approaches to Economic and Social History. Cambridge University Press, 2009.

Allen, Robert C. *The British Industrial Revolution in Global Perspective*. Cambridge University Press, 2009.

Almanách: para o anno ... 1788. Typog. da Academia Real das Sciencias, 1788.

Almeida, Manuel Lopes de. *Notícias Históricas de Portugal e Brasil (1751–1800)*. Coimbra Editora, 1964.

Amaral, Luciano. "Institutions, Property, and Economic Growth: Back to the Passage from the "Ancien Régime" to Liberalism in Portugal." *Análise Social* 47, no. 202 (2012): 28–55.

Anderson, B. L. "The Attorney and the Early Capital Market in Lancashire." In *Capital Formation in the Industrial Revolution*, edited by François Crouzet. Methuen, 1972.

Andrade, Manuel Correia de. *A Terra e o Homem no Nordeste*. Brasiliense, 1963.

Antonil, André João. *Cultura e opulencia do Brazil, por suas drogas e minas, com varias noticias curiosas do modo de fazer o assucar.., Obra de André João Antonil*. 1711, 1837. http://digital.bbm.usp.br/handle/bbm/7461.

Antunes, Cátia. "Free Agents and Formal Institutions in the Portuguese Empire: Towards a Framework of Analysis." *Portuguese Studies* 28, no. 2 (2012): 173–85.

Antunes, Cátia. *Globalisation in the Early Modern Period: The Economic Relationship between Amsterdam and Lisbon, 1640–1705*. Aksant, 2004.

Antunes, Cátia, ed. *Pursuing Empire: Brazilians, the Dutch and the Portuguese in Brazil and the South Atlantic, c.1620–1660*. Brill, 2022.

Antunes, Cátia, and Karwan Fatah-Black, eds. *Explorations in History and Globalization*. Routledge, 2016.

Antunes, Cátia, and Amélia Polónia. *Beyond Empires: Global, Self-Organizing, Cross-Imperial Networks, 1500–1800*. Brill, 2016.

Araújo, Agostinho Rui Marques. "Das Riquezas Do Brasil Aos Gastos e Gostos de Um Suíço Em Lisboa. David de Purry, Um Amigo de Pombal (1709–1786)." *Revista Da Faculdade de Letras – Ciências e Técnicas Do Património*, I, vol. 2 (2003): 109–37.

Armytage, Frances. *The Free Port System in the British West Indies. A Study in Commercial Policy, 1766–1822.* Longmans, Green and Co., 1953.

Arruda, José Jobson de Andrade. "A Produção Econômica." In *Nova História Da Expansão Portuguesa*, edited by Joel Serrão and António Henrique R. de Oliveira Marques, VIII. Editorial Estampa, 1986.

Arruda, José Jobson de Andrade. "Decadence or Crisis in the Luso-Brazilian Empire: A New Model of Colonization in the Eighteenth Century." *Hispanic American Historical Review* 80, no. 4 (2000): 865–78.

Arruda, José Jobson de Andrade. "O Algodão Brasileiro Na Época Da Revolução Industrial." *América Latina En La Historia Económica* 23, no. 2 (2016): 167–203.

Arruda, José Jobson de Andrade. *O Brasil no comércio colonial.* Editora Ática, 1980.

Arruda, José Jobson de Andrade. *Uma Colônia Entre Dois Impérios: a Abertura dos Portos Brasileiros, 1800–1808.* Edusc, 2008.

Ashton, Thomas Southcliffe. *The Industrial Revolution, 1760–1830.* 1948; Oxford University Press, 1968.

Assunção, Matthias Röhrig. *De Caboclos a Bem-Te-Vis. Formação Do Campesinato Numa Sociedade Escravista: Maranhão 1800–1850.* Annablume, 2015.

Assunção, Matthias Röhrig. "Elite Politics and Popular Rebellion in the Construction of Post-Colonial Order. The Case of Maranhão, Brazil (1820–41)." *Journal of Latin American Studies* 31, no. 1 (1999): 1–38.

Assunção, Matthias Röhrig. "Exportação, mercado interno e crises de subsistência numa província brasileira: o caso do Maranhão, 1800–1860.| *Estudos Sociedade e Agricultura* 14 (2000): 32–71.

Aston, T. H., and C. H. E. Philpin, eds. *The Brenner Debate: Agrarian Class Structure and Economic Development in Pre-Industrial Europe.* Cambridge University Press, 1985.

Azevedo, Dannylo de. "O Fazendeiro do Brasil: manuais agrícolas no Brasil colonial em finais do século XVIII." Master's thesis, Universidade de São Paulo, 2018.

Azevedo, João Lúcio de. *O marquês de Pombal e a sua época.* A. M. Teixeira, 1909.

Bailey, Ronald. "The Other Side of Slavery: Black Labor, Cotton, and Textile Industrialization in Great Britain and the United States." *Agricultural History* 68, no. 2 (1994): 35–50.

Baines, Edward. *History of the Cotton Manufacture in Great Britain.* H. Fisher, R. Fisher, and P. Jackson, 1835.

Bairoch, Paul. *Commerce Extérieur et Développement Économique de l'Europe Au XIXe Siècle.* Mouton, 1976.

Bairoch, Paul. "L'économie Française Dans Le Contexte Européen à La Fin Du XVIIIe Siècle." *Revue Économique* 40, no. 6 (1989): 939–64.

Banaji, Jairus. *A Brief History of Commercial Capitalism.* Haymarket Books, 2020.

Barbosa, Luiz Cordelio. "Cotton in 19th Century Brazil: Dependency and Development." PhD diss., University of Washington, 1989.

Barman, Roderick J. *Brazil: The Forging of a Nation, 1798–1852*. Stanford University Press, 1988.

Barnett, David C. *London: Hub of the Industrial Revolution: A Revisionary History, 1775–1825*. Tauris Academic Studies, 1998.

Barry, Boubacar. *Senegambia and the Atlantic Slave Trade*. 1988; Cambridge University Press, 1998.

Baskes, Jeremy. *Staying Afloat: Risk and Uncertainty in Spanish Atlantic World Trade, 1760–1820*. Stanford University Press, 2013.

Bauss, Rudy. "A Legacy of British Free Trade Policies: The End of the Trade and Commerce between India and the Portuguese Empire, 1780–1830." *Calcutta Historical Journal* 6, no. 2 (1982): 81–115.

Baxter, William T. "Observations on Money, Barter and Bookkeeping." *The Accounting Historians Journal* 31, no. 1 (2004): 129–39.

Beckert, Sven. *Empire of Cotton: A Global History*. Alfred A. Knopf, 2014.

Beckert, Sven, Ulbe Bosma, Mindi Schneider, and Eric Vanhaute. "Commodity Frontiers and the Transformation of the Global Countryside: A Research Agenda." *Journal of Global History* 16, no. 3 (2021): 435–50.

Beer, George Louis. *The Old Colonial System, 1660–1754*. With unknown library. Vol. 1. The Macmillan Company, 1912.

Beerbühl, Margrit Schulte. "Merchant Empires: Mercadores Hamburgueses Em Londres y Sus Redes de Comercio Internacional (1660–1815)." In *Comunidades Transnacionales: Colonias de Mercaderes Extranjeros En El Mundo Atlántico (1500–1830)*, edited by Ana Crespo Solana. Doce Calles, 2010.

Beerbühl, Margrit Schulte. "Trading with the Enemy: Clandestine Networks during the Napoleonic Wars." *Quaderni Storici* 48, no. 143 (2) (2013): 541–65.

Benedict, C. R., H. L. Lewis, and R. J. Kohel. "Cotton Fiber Quality." In *Cotton: Origin, History, Technology, and Production*, edited by C. Wayne Smith and J. Tom Cothren. John Wiley & Sons, 1999.

Bennett, Norman R. "The Golden Age of the Port Wine System, 1781–1807." *The International History Review* 12, no. 2 (1990): 221–48.

Berg, Maxine. "Consumption and Global History in the Early Modern Period." In *Global Economic History*, edited by Tirthankar Roy and Giorgio Riello. Bloomsbury Academic, 2019.

Berg, Maxine. "Quality, Cotton and the Global Luxury Trade." In *How India Clothed the World: The World of South Asian Textiles, 1500–1850*, edited by Giorgio Riello and Tirthankar Roy. Brill, 2009.

Berg, Maxine. *The Age of Manufactures: Industry, Innovation, and Work in Britain, 1700–1820*. 1985; Routledge, 1994.

Bergeron, Louis. *Banquiers, Négociants et Manufacturiers Parisiens Du Directoire à l'Empire*. Ecole des hautes etudes en sciences sociales, 1978.

Bergeron, Louis. *L'épisode Napoléonien: Aspects Intérieurs, 1799–1815*. Éditions du Seuil, 1972.

Bergeron, Louis. "Problèmes économiques de la France napoléonienne." *Revue d'Histoire Moderne & Contemporaine* 17, no. 3 (1970): 469–505.

Bernardes, Denis. "Notícia Sobre a Cultura Do Algodoeiro Na Província de Pernambuco Pelo Chancelier Boilleau (1826)." *Revista Do Instituto Arqueológico, Histórico e Geográfico Pernambucano,* LI (1979): 301–12.

Bernardes, Denis. *O patriotismo constitucional: Pernambuco, 1820–1822*. Editora Hucitec, 2006.

Bernstein, Harry. *The Brazilian Diamond in Contracts, Contraband, and Capital*. University Press of America, 1988.

Bettencourt, José de Sá. *Memória Sobre a Plantação Dos Algodões, e Sua Exportação: Sobre a Decadencia Da Lavoura de Mandiocas, No Termo Da Villa de Camamú, Comarca Dos Ilhéos, Governo Da Bahia …* Officina de Simão Thaddeo Ferreira, 1798.

Bivar Marquese, Rafael de, and Marcelo Rosanova Ferraro, "The Political Economy of Brazilian Cotton in the Age of Industrial Capitalism," in *Colonial Commodities in Historical Capitalism: Brazil for Export,* edited by Gustavo Acioli Lopes, Leonardo Marques, and Felipe Souza Melo. Routledge, 2026.

Blackburn, Robin. *The Making of New World Slavery: From the Baroque to the Modern, 1492–1800*. Verso, 1998.

Blau, Peter M., and W. Richard Scott. *Formal Organizations: A Comparative Approach*. Stanford University Press, 1962.

Bohorquez, J., and Maximiliano M. Menz. "State Contractors and Global Brokers: The Itinerary of Two Lisbon Merchants and the Transatlantic Slave Trade during the Eighteenth Century." *Itinerario* 42, no. 3 (2018): 403–29.

Bohorquez, Jesús. "Globalizar el sur: la emergencia de ciudades globales y la economía política de los imperios portugués y español: Rio de Janeiro y La Habana durante la era de las revoluciones." PhD diss., European University Institute, 2016.

Bombelles, Marquis de. *Journal d'un ambassadeur de France au Portugal, 1786–1788*. Presses universitaires de France, 1979.

Botelho, Tarcísio R. "A população brasileira em 1850: uma estimativa." *Revista Economia e Políticas Públicas* 7, no. 2 (2019): 135–66.

Botelho, Tarcísio R. "A População Da América Portuguesa Em Finais Do Período Colonial (1776–1822): Fontes e Estimativas Globais." *Anais de História de Além-Mar,* no. 16 (January 2015): 79–106.

Boudon, Jacques-Oliver. "Napoleão e a Europa depois de Tilsit." In *Portugal, Brasil e a Europa Napoleónica,* edited by José Luís Cardoso, Nuno Gonçalo Monteiro, and José Vicente Serrão. Imprensa de Ciências Sociais, 2010.

Boxer, C. R. "English Shipping in the Brazil Trade, 1640–65." *The Mariner's Mirror* 37, no. 3 (1951): 197–230.

Boxer, Charles Ralph. *Portuguese Society in the Tropics: The Municipal Councils of Goa, Macao, Bahia, and Luanda, 1510–1800*. University of Wisconsin Press, 1965.

Boxer, Charles Ralph. *The Golden Age of Brazil, 1695–1750: Growing Pains of a Colonial Society*. University of California Press, 1962.

Boxer, Charles Ralph. *The Portuguese Seaborne Empire 1415–1825*. Hutchinson, 1969.

Boyajian, James C. *Portuguese Trade in Asia Under the Habsburgs, 1580–1640*. Johns Hopkins University Press, 2008.

Branner, John Casper. *Cotton in the Empire of Brazil; the Antiquity, Methods and Extent of Its Cultivation, Together with Statistics of Exportation and Home Consumption*. Government Printing Office, 1885.

Braudel, Fernand. *Civilization and Capitalism, 15th-18th Century, Volume II: The Wheels of Commerce*. William Collins Sons & Co Ltd, 1982.

Braudel, Fernand. *Civilization and Capitalism, 15th-18th Century, Volume III: The Perspective of the World*. William Collins Sons & Co Ltd, 1984.

Brenner, Robert. *Merchants and Revolution: Commercial Change, Political Conflict, and London's Overseas Traders, 1550–1653*. 1993; Verso, 2003.

Brilli, Catia. "Coping with Iberian Monopolies: Genoese Trade Networks and Formal Institutions in Spain and Portugal during the Second Half of the Eighteenth Century." *European Review of History: Revue Européenne d'histoire* 23, no. 3 (2016): 456–85.

Brilli, Catia. "La Nación Genovesa de Lisboa y Sus Cónsules En El Último Cuarto Del Siglo XVIII." In *Los Cônsules de Extranjeros En La Edad Moderna y a Principios de La Edad Contempóranea*. Ediciones Doce Calles, 2013.

Brinton, Mary C., and Victor Nee. *The New Institutionalism in Sociology*. Russell Sage Foundation, 1998.

Britton, Karen Gerhardt. *Bale o' Cotton: The Mechanical Art of Cotton Ginning*. Texas A&M University Press, 1992.

Brown, Larissa Virginia. "Internal Commerce in a Colonial Economy: Rio De Janeiro and Its Hinterland, 1790–1822." PhD diss., University of Virginia, 1986.

Browning, Oscar. "The Treaty of Commerce Between England and France in 1786." *Transactions of the Royal Historical Society* 2, no. 4 (1885): 349–64.

Brubaker, C. L., F. M. Bourland, and J. F. Wendel. "The Origin and Domestication of Cotton." In *Cotton: Origin, History, Technology, and Production*, edited by C. Wayne Smith and J. Tom Cothren. John Wiley & Sons, 1999.

Buck, Norman Sydney. *The Development of the Organisation of Anglo-American Trade, 1800–1850*. 1925; David & Charles, 1969.

Buescu, Mircea. *História Econômica Do Brasil. Pesquisas e Análises*. APEC, 1970.

Bulferetti, Luigi, and Claudio Costantini. *Industria e commercio in Liguria nell'età del Risorgimento* (*1700–1861*). Banca commerciale italiana, 1966.

Burlamaqui, Frederico Leopoldo Cesar. *Monographia do algodoeiro*. Typ. de N.L. Vianna e filhos, 1863.

Burnard, Trevor, and John Garrigus. *The Plantation Machine: Atlantic Capitalism in French Saint-Domingue and British Jamaica*. University of Pennsylvania Press, 2016.

Burns, E. Bradford. "The Enlightenment in Two Colonial Brazilian Libraries." *Journal of the History of Ideas* 25, no. 3 (1964): 430.

Burns, E. Bradford. "The Role of Azeredo Coutinho in the Enlightenment of Brazil." *The Hispanic American Historical Review* 44, no. 2 (1964): 145–60.

Buron, Edmond. "Statistics on Franco-American Trade, 1778–1806." *Journal of Economic and Business History* (1932): 571–80.

Butel, Paul. "Revolution and the Urban Economy: Maritime Cities and Continental Cities." In *Reshaping France: Town, Country, and Region during the French Revolution*, edited by Alan I. Forrest and Peter Jones. Manchester University Press, 1991.

Butel, Paul. "Traditions and Changes in French Atlantic Trade between 1780 and 1830." *Renaissance and Modern Studies* 30, no. 1 (1986): 124–45.

Butel, Paul, and François Crouzet. "Empire and Economic Growth: The Case of 18th Century France." *Revista de Historia Economica – Journal of Iberian and Latin American Economic History* 16, no. 1 (1998): 177–93.

Butterworth, James. *A Complete History of the Cotton Trade: Including Also, That of the Silk, Calico-Printing, & Hat Manufactories; with Remarks on Their Progress in Bolton, Bury, Stockport, Blackburn, and Wigan, to Which Is Added, an Account of the Chief Mart of These Goods, the Town of Manchester*. J.W. Leake, printer, 1823.

Cahen, Léon. "Une Nouvelle Interprétation Du Traité Franco-Anglais De 1786–1787." *Revue Historique* 185, no. 2 (1939): 257–85.

Cain, P.J., and A. G. Hopkins. "Gentlemanly Capitalism and British Expansion Overseas I. The Old Colonial System, 1688–1850." *The Economic History Review* 39, no. 4 (1986): 501–25.

Çalışkan, Koray. *Market Threads: How Cotton Farmers and Traders Create a Global Commodity*. Princeton University Press, 2010.

Callcott, Lady Maria. *Journal of a Voyage to Brazil: And Residence There, During Part of the Years 1821, 1822, 1823*. Longman, Hurst, Rees, Orme, Brown, and Green, 1824.

Câmara, Manuel Arruda da. *Memoria sobre a cultura dos algodoeiros e sobre o methodo de o escolher, e ensacar, etc.* Na Officina da Casa Litteraria do Arco do Cego, 1799.

Cardoso, José Luís. "Bloqueio Continental e desbloqueio marítimo: o Brasil no contexto global das Guerras Napoleónicas." In *Portugal, Brasil e a Europa Napoleónica*, edited by José Luís Cardoso, Nuno Gonçalo Monteiro, and José Vicente Serrão. Imprensa de Ciências Sociais, 2010.

Cardoso, José Luís. "Lifting the Continental Blockade: Britain, Portugal and Brazilian Trade in the Global Context of the Napoleonic Wars." In *A Global History of Trade and Conflict since 1500*, edited by Lucia Coppolaro and Francine McKenzie. Palgrave Macmillan UK, 2013.

Cardoso, José Luís. "Política Económica." In *História Económica de Portugal, 1700–2000. Volume 1. O Século XVIII.*, edited by Pedro Lains and Alvaro Ferreira da Silva, vol. 1. Imprensa de Ciências Sociais, 2005.

Cariello, Rafael, and Thales Zamberlan Pereira. *Adeus, senhor Portugal: crise do absolutismo e a Independência do Brasil.* Companhia das Letras, 2022.

Carlos, Ann M., and Stephen Nicholas. "Agency Problems in Early Chartered Companies: The Case of the Hudson's Bay Company." *The Journal of Economic History* 50, no. 4 (1990): 853–75.

Carlos, Ann M., and Stephen Nicholas. "Theory and History: Seventeenth-Century Joint-Stock Chartered Trading Companies." *The Journal of Economic History* 56, no. 4 (1996): 916–24.

Carrara, Angelo Alves. *Minas e currais: produção rural e mercado interno em Minas Gerais 1674–1807*. UFJF, 2007.

Carrara, Angelo Alves. "O crédito no Brasil no período colonial: Uma revisão historiográfica." *Varia Historia* 36, no. 70 (2020): 15–51.

Carrara, Angelo Alves, Maximiliano M. Menz, Felipe Souza Melo, and Rodrigo da Costa Dominguez. "The Brazilian Economy During the Old Regime Crisis (c. 1750–1807)." *Revista de Historia Economica – Journal of Iberian and Latin American Economic History* 41, no. 1 (2023): 119–46.

Carreira, António. *A Companhia Geral do Grão-Pará e Maranhão. (O comércio monopolista. Portugal-África-Brasil na segunda metade do século XVIII)*. Vol. 1. Companhia Editora Nacional, 1988.

Carreira, António. *A Companhia Geral do Grão-Pará e Maranhão. (O comércio monopolista. Portugal-África-Brasil na segunda metade do século XVIII)*. Vol. 2. Companhia Editora Nacional, 1988.

Carreira, António. *As companhias pombalinas: de Grão-Pará e Maranhão e Pernambuco e Paraíba*. 2a. ed. Editorial Presença, 1983.

Carrere, Joseph-Barthélemy-François. *A Picture of Lisbon, Taken on the Spot: Being a Description Moral, Civil, Political, Physical and Religious, of That Capital; with Sketches of the Government Character and Manners of the Portuguese in General ...* Printed for Henry Colburn, 1809.

Carvalho, Carlos Jesus de. *Ascensão e Crise Da Lavoura Algodoeira No Maranhão (1760–1910)*. Eduema, 2018.

Carvalho, Marcus J. M. de. *Liberdade: Rotinas e Rupturas Do Escravismo No Recife, 1822–1850*. Editora Universitária da UFPE, 2010.

Carvalho, Rómulo de. "O Recurso a Pessoal Estrangeiro No Tempo de Pombal." *Revista de História Das Ideias*. Tomo I (1982): 91–115.

Castro, Antonio Barros de. "Escravos e senhores nos engenhos do Brasil: um estudo sobre os trabalhos do açúcar e a política econômica dos senhores." *Estudos Econômicos (São Paulo)* 7, no. 1 (1977): 177–220.

Chambouleyron, Rafael. "Conquistas diferentes e de diferentes climas: o Maranhão, o Brasil e a América portuguesa (séculos XVII e XVIII)." *Esboços: histórias em contextos globais* 26, no. 41 (2019): 84–103.

Chambouleyron, Rafael. *Povoamento, Ocupação e Agricultura na Amazônia Colonial.* Editora Açai, 2010.

Chapman, Stanley D. *Merchant Enterprise in Britain: From the Industrial Revolution to World War I.* Cambridge University Press, 1992.

Chapman, Stanley D. "Quantity Versus Quality in the British Industrial Revolution: The Case of Printed Textiles." *Northern History* 21, no. 1 (1985): 175–92.

Chapman, Stanley D. "The Commercial Sector." In *The Lancashire Cotton Industry. A History since 1700*, edited by Mary B. Rose. Lancashire County Books, 1996.

Chapman, Stanley D. *The Cotton Industry in the Industrial Revolution.* 1972. Second Edition. Macmillan Education, 1987.

Chapman, Stanley D., and Serge Chassagne. *European Textile Printers in the Eighteenth Century: A Study of Peel and Oberkampf.* Heinemann Educational: Pasold Fund, 1981.

Chase, Jeanne. "War on Trade and Trade in War: Stephen Jumel and New York Maritime Commerce (1793–1815)." *Bulletin Du Centre d'histoire Des Espaces Atlantiques* 4 (1988): 111–61.

Chassagne, Serge. "Calico Printing in Europe Before 1780." In *The Cambridge History of Western Textiles*, edited by David Jenkins. Cambridge University Press, 2002.

Chassagne, Serge. "La diffusion rurale de l'industrie cotonnière en France (1750–1850)." *Revue du Nord* 61, no. 240 (1979): 97–114.

Chassagne, Serge. *Le Coton et Ses Patrons: France, 1760–1840*. Editions de l'Ecole des hautes études en sciences sociales, 1991.

Chassagne, Serge. "L'enquête, Dite de Champagny, Sur La Situation de l'industrie Cotonnière Française Au Début de l'empire (1805–1806)." *Revue d'histoire Économique et Sociale* 54, no. 3 (1976): 336–70.

Chassagne, Serge. *Oberkampf: Un grand patron au siècle des Lumières.* 1980; Aubier, 2015.

Checkland, S. G. "John Koster, Anti-Bullionist." *The Manchester School* 20, no. 2 (1952): 174–202.

Clair, Kassia St. *The Golden Thread: How Fabric Changed History.* Liveright Publishing, 2019.

Clauder, Anna Cornelia. *American Commerce as Affected by the Wars of the French Revolution and Napoleon, 1793–1812.* 1932; Augustus M. Kelley, 1972.

Clemens, Paul G. E. "The Rise of Liverpool, 1665–1750." *The Economic History Review* 29, no. 2 (1976): 211–25.

Clément, Alain. ""Du bon et du mauvais usage des colonies": politique coloniale et pensée économique française au XVIIIe siècle." *Cahiers d'économie Politique* (Paris) 56, no. 1 (2009): 101–27.

Collyer, William Bengo. *The Investigator (or, Quarterly Magazine)*. Thomas and George Underwood, 1820.

Cooke, Anthony. *The Rise and Fall of the Scottish Cotton Industry, 1778–1914: 'The Secret Spring'*. Manchester University Press, 2010.

Coornaert, E. L. J. "European Economic Institutions and the New World; the Chartered Companies." In *The Cambridge Economic History of Europe. Vol. IV. The Economy of Expanding Europe in the Sixteenth and Seventeenth Centuries*, edited by E. E. Rich and C. H. Wilson. Cambridge University Press, 1967.

Corfield, P. J. *The Impact of English Towns, 1700–1800*. Oxford University Press, 1982.

Costa, Francisco Augusto Pereira da. *Anais Pernambucanos. Vol. VII*. FUNDARPE, 1983.

Costa, Hipólito da. *Correio Braziliense Ou Armazém Literário, Issue 4*. W. Lewis, Paternoster. Row, 1810.

Costa, Leonor Freire. "Entre o Açúcar e o Ouro: Permanência e Mudança Na Organização Dos Fluxos (Séculos XVII e XVIII)." In *Nas Rotas Do Império. Eixos Mercantis, Tráfico e Relações Sociais No Mundo Português*, edited by João Fragoso. EDUFES, 2006.

Costa, Leonor Freire. *O transporte no Atlântico e a Companhia Geral do Comércio do Brasil, 1580–1663*. Vol. 1. Comissão Nacional para as Comemorações dos Descobrimentos Portugueses, 2002.

Costa, Leonor Freire. "Relações Económicas Com o Exterior." In *História Económica de Portugal, 1700–2000*, edited by Pedro Lains and Alvaro Ferreira da Silva, vol. 1. Imprensa de Ciências Sociais, 2005.

Costa, Leonor Freire, Pedro Neves, and Tomás Pinto de Albuquerque. "Democracia e plutocracia nas companhias coloniais pombalinas, 1757–1777." *Ler História*, no. 82 (June 2023): 82.

Costa, Leonor Freire, Nuno Palma, and Jaime Reis. "The Great Escape? The Contribution of the Empire to Portugal's Economic Growth, 1500–1800." *European Review of Economic History* 19, no. 1 (2015): 1–22.

Costa, Leonor Freire, Maria Manuela Rocha, and Tanya Araújo. "Social Capital and Economic Performance: Trust and Distrust in Eighteenth-Century Gold Shipments from Brazil." *European Review of Economic History* 15, no. 1 (2011): 1–27.

Costa, Leonor Freire, Maria Manuela Rocha, and Rita Martins de Sousa. *O ouro do Brasil*. Imprensa Nacional-Casa da Moeda, 2013.

Cousquer, Céline. *Nantes, une capitale française des indiennes au XVIIIe siècle*. Coiffard Librairie e Editeur, 2002.

Coutinho, Rodrigo de Souza. *Textos Políticos, Económicos e Financeiros, 1783–1811. Tomo I*. Banco de Portugal, 1993.

Crafts, N. F. R. *British Economic Growth during the Industrial Revolution*. Clarendon Press; Oxford University Press, 1985.

Crouzet, François. "Editor's Introduction." In *Capital Formation in the Industrial Revolution*, edited by François Crouzet. Methuen, 1972.

Crouzet, François. "La ruine du grand commerce." In *Bordeaux au XVIIIe siècle*, edited by François-Georges Pariset. Fédération historique du Sud-Ouest, 1968.

Crouzet, François. "Les Conséquences Économiques de La Révolution Française: Réflexions Sur Un Débat." *Revue Économique* 40, no. 6 (1989): 1189–203.

Crouzet, François. "Wars, Blockade, and Economic Change in Europe, 1792–1815." *The Journal of Economic History* 24, no. 4 (1964): 567–88.

Crowhurst, Patrick. *The Defence of British Trade, 1689–1815*. Dawson, 1977.

Crowhurst, Patrick. *The French War on Trade: Privateering, 1793–1815*. Scolar Press, 1989.

Cruz, Mariléia dos Santos, Érica de Lima de Matos, and Ediane Holanda Silva. ""Exma. Sra. D. Maria Firmina Dos Reis, Distinta Literária Maranhense": A Notoriedade De Uma Professora Afrodescendente No Século XIX." *Notandum*, no. 48 (n.d.): 151–66.

Cruz, Miguel Dantas da. *A Neutralidade Portuguesa Na Europa Da Revolução, 1792–1807: Dificuldades e Possibilidades*. Parede Tribuna da História, 2011.

Cruz, Miguel Dantas da. "Neutral Shipping and the Portuguese Economic Relations with the Atlantic World (1793–1814)." In *Neutres et Neutralité Dans l'espace Atlantique Durant Le Long XVIIIe Siècle (1700–1820). Une Approche Globale. Neutrals and Neutrality in the Atlantic World during the Long Eighteenth Century (1700–1820). A Global Approach*, edited by Éric Schnakenbourg. Editions Les Perséides, 2015.

Cruz, Miguel Dantas da. "The Diversification of Portugal's Commercial Relations in the Late Eighteenth Century: Between Discourse and Praxis." *E-Journal of Portuguese History* 10, no. 1 (2012): 37–61.

Cunha, Carlos Guimarães da. *Negociantes, mercadores e traficantes no final da monarquia absoluta: a burguesia mercantil em Portugal, dos anos finais do século XVIII até ao início da Revolução Liberal*. Edições Colibri, 2014.

Cunha, Elba Monique Chagas da. "O Diretório dos Índios como projeto de "civilização" portuguesa para os sertões pernambucanos." *Revista Latino-Americana de História-UNISINOS* 3, no. 12 (2014): 85–116.

Curto, Diogo Ramada. "Vitorino Magalhães Godinho e a questão da escravatura." In *Vitorino Magalhães Godinho, Estrutura da antiga sociedade portuguesa*. Edições 70, 2019.

Daly, Gavin. "English Smugglers, the Channel, and the Napoleonic Wars, 1800–1814." *Journal of British Studies* 46, no. 1 (2007): 30–46.

Daly, Gavin. *Inside Napoleonic France: State and Society in Rouen, 1800–1815*. Ashgate, 2001.

Daly, Gavin. "Merchants and Maritime Commerce in Napoleonic Normandy." *French History* 15, no. 1 (2001): 26–50.

Daniels, G. W. "American Cotton Trade with Liverpool under the Embargo and Non-Intercourse Acts." *The American Historical Review* 21, no. 2 (1916): 276–87.

Daniels, G. W. "Samuel Crompton's Census of the Cotton Industry in 1811." *Economic History* 2, no. 5 (1930): 107–10.

Dardel, Pierre. *Commerce, Industrie et Navigation a Rouen et au Havre au XVIIIe siècle: rivalité croissante entre ces deux ports, la conjoncture*. Société libre d'émulation de Seine-Maritime, 1966.

Dardel, Pierre. *Navires et Marchandises Dans Les Ports de Rouen et Du Havre Au XVIIIe Siècle*. SEVPEN, 1963.

Davis, Lance E., and Stanley L. Engerman. *Naval Blockades in Peace and War: An Economic History since 1750*. Cambridge University Press, 2006.

Davis, Ralph. *The Industrial Revolution and British Overseas Trade*. Leicester University Press, 1979.

Dean, Warren. *With Broadax and Firebrand: The Destruction of the Brazilian Atlantic Forest*. University of California Press, 1995.

Deane, Phyllis. "The Industrial Revolution in Great Britain." In *The Fontana Economic History of Europe. The Emergence of Industrial Societies, Part One*, edited by Carlo M. Cipolla, vol. 4. Harvester Press, 1973.

Deane, Phyllis. "The Output of the British Woolen Industry in the Eighteenth Century." *The Journal of Economic History* 17, no. 2 (1957): 207–23.

Delobette, Edouard. "Ces Messieurs du Havre. Negociants, commissionnaires et armateurs de 1680 a 1830." Ph.D., Université de Caen, 2005.

Dias, Manuel Nunes. *Fomento e Mercantilismo: A Companhia Geral Do Grão Pará e Maranhão (1755–1778)*. Vol. 1. Universidade Federal do Pará, 1970.

Dias, Maria Odila Leite da Silva. *A interiorização da metrópole e outros estudos*. Alameda, 2005.

Dias, Thiago Alves. "Dinâmicas Mercantis Coloniais: Capitania Do Rio Grande Do Norte (1760–1821)." Master's thesis, Universidade Federal do Rio Grande do Norte, 2011.

Dias, Thiago Alves. "O negócio do pau-brasil, a sociedade mercantil Purry, Mellish and Devisme e o mercado global de corantes: escalas mercantis, instituições e agentes ultramarinos no século XVIII." *Revista de História*, no. 177 (May 2018): 01–39.

Disney, A. R. *A Decadência Do Império Da Pimenta. Comércio Português Na Índia No Início Do Século XVII*. Edições 70, 1981.

Donaghay, Marie Martenis. "The Anglo-French Negotiations of 1786–1787." Ph.D. diss., University of Virginia, 1970.

Donovan, Bill M. "Commercial Enterprise and Luso-Brazilian Society During the Brazilian Gold Rush: The Mercantile House of Francisco Pinheiro and the Lisbon to Brazil Trade, 1695–1750." PhD diss., Johns Hopkins University, 1990.

Drescher, Seymour. *Econocide: British Slavery in the Era of Abolition*. University of Pittsburgh Press, 1977.

Dubuc, M. André. "L'industrie Textile En Haute-Normandie Au Cours de La Révolution et de l'Empire." In *Le Textile En Normandie. Études Diverses*. Société Libre D'émulation de la Seine-Maritime, 1975.

Duffy, Michael. "World-Wide War and British Expansion, 1793–1815." In *The Oxford History of the British Empire: Volume II: The Eighteenth Century*, edited by P. J. Marshall and Alaine Low. Oxford University Press, 1998.

Duguid, Paul. "Introduction: The Changing Organization of Industry." *Business History Review* 79, no. 3 (2005): 453–66.

Dumbell, Stanley. "Early Liverpool Cotton Imports and the Organisation of the Cotton Market in the Eighteenth Century." *The Economic Journal* 33, no. 131 (1923): 362–73.

Dumbell, Stanley. "The Cotton Market in 1799." *The Economic Journal* 36, no. Supplement 1 (1926): 141–48.

Dumouriez, Charles François Du Périer. *An Account of Portugal, as It Appeared in 1766 to Dumouriez: Since a Celebrated General in the French Army*. C. Law, 1797.

Dunn, Richard S. *Sugar and Slaves: The Rise of the Planter Class in the English West Indies, 1624–1713*. The University of North Carolina Press, 1973.

DuPlessis, Robert S. *The Material Atlantic: Clothing, Commerce, and Colonization in the Atlantic World, 1650–1800*. Cambridge University Press, 2015.

Dupré, Philippe. "Les Difficultés Économiques Des Ports de La Manche Pendant La Révolution et l'Empire: L'apport Des Archives de La Marine." In *Les Normands et La Mer XXVè Congrès Des Sociétés Historiques et Archéologiques de Normandie, Communauté Urbaine de Cherbourg, 4–7 Octobre 1990. Saint-Vaast-La-Hougue Musée Maritime de l'Ile Tatihou* (1995), 318–26.

Eacott, Jonathan P. "Making an Imperial Compromise: The Calico Acts, the Atlantic Colonies, and the Structure of the British Empire." *The William and Mary Quarterly* 69, no. 4 (2012): 731–62.

Edwards, Michael M. *The Growth of the British Cotton Trade, 1780–1815*. Manchester University Press, 1967.

Ellison, Thomas. *The Cotton Trade of Great Britain: Including a History of the Liverpool Cotton Market and of the Liverpool Cotton Brokers' Association*. Effingham Wilson, Royal Exchange, 1886.

Eltis, David. *The Rise of African Slavery in the Americas*. Cambridge University Press, 1999.

Engerman, Stanley L. "Mercantilism and Overseas Trade, 1700–1800." In *The Economic History of Britain since 1700*, edited by Roderick Floud and Donald McCloskey, vol. 1. Cambridge University Press, 1981.

Ensminger, Jean. "Reputations, Trust, and the Principal Agent Problem." In *Trust in Society*, edited by Karen S. Cook. Russell Sage Foundation, 2001.

Erikson, Emily. *Between Monopoly and Free Trade: The English East India Company, 1600–1757*. Princeton University Press, 2014.

Erikson, Emily, ed. *Chartering Capitalism: Organizing Markets, States, and Publics*. Emerald, 2015.

Esdaile, Charles J. *The Peninsular War: A New History*. Penguin Books, 2003.

Falcon, Francisco José Calazans. *A época pombalina: política econômica e monarquia ilustrada*. Editora Ática, 1982.

Farnie, Douglas A. "Cotton, 1780–1914." In *The Cambridge History of Western Textiles.*, edited by David Jenkins. Cambridge University Press, 2002.

Farnie, Douglas A. *The English Cotton Industry and the World Market, 1815–1896*. Clarendon Press; Oxford University Press, 1979.

Farnie, Douglas A. "The Role of Merchants as Prime Movers in the Expansion of the Cotton Industry, 1760–1990." In *The Fibre That Changed the World: The Cotton Industry in International Perspective, 1600–1990s*, edited by Douglas A. Farnie and David J. Jeremy. Oxford University Press, 2004.

Farr, James R. *The Work of France: Labor and Culture in Early Modern Times, 1350–1800*. Rowman & Littlefield Publishers, 2008.

Felipe, Mariely de Albuquerque Mello. "E a natureza os entregou ao jogo dos tempos: a seca de 1791 na capitania de Pernambuco e suas anexas." Master's thesis, Universidade de São Paulo, 2020.

Ferlini, Vera Lúcia Amaral. *Terra, trabalho e poder: o mundo dos engenhos no Nordeste colonial*. Brasiliense, 1988.

Filho, Lycurgo de Castro Santos. *Uma Comunidade Rural Do Brasil Antigo: (Aspectos Da Vida Patriarcal No Sertão Da Bahia Nos Séculos XVIII e XIX)*. Ed. Nacional, 1956.

Filho, Oswaldo Munteal. "O Príncipe D. João e o Mundo de Queluz: Despotismo Ministerial, Tensões Estamentais e Sacralização Do Estado Na Crise Do Antigo Regime Português." *Anais Do Museu Histórico Nacional* 31 (1999): 9–34.

Findlay, Ronald, and Kevin H. O'Rourke. "Commodity Market Integration, 1500–2000." In *Globalization in Historical Perspective*, edited by Michael D. Bordo, Alan M. Taylor, and Jeffrey G. Williamson. University of Chicago Press, 2003.

Findlay, Ronald, and Kevin H. O'Rourke. *Power and Plenty: Trade, War, and the World Economy in the Second Millennium*. Princeton University Press, 2007.

Fine, Ben, and Ellen Leopold. *The World of Consumption*. Routledge, 1993.

Fisher, Harold Edward Stephen. "Lisbon as Port Town in the Eighteenth Century." In *I Porti Come Impresa Economica: Atti Della "Diciannovesima Settimana Di Studi," 2–6 Maggio 1987*, edited by Simonetta Cavaciocchi. Le Monnier, 1988.

Fisher, Harold Edward Stephen. "Lisbon, Its English Merchant Community and the Mediterranean in the Eighteenth Century." In *Shipping, Trade and Commerce: Essays in Memory of Ralph Davis*, edited by P. L. Cottrell and Derek Howard Aldcroft. Leicester University Press, 1981.

Fisher, Harold Edward Stephen. *The Portugal Trade: A Study of Anglo-Portuguese Commerce, 1700–1770*. Methuen, 1971.

Fitton, R. S. *The Arkwrights: Spinners of Fortune*. Manchester University Press, 1989.

Fitton, R. S., and A. P. Wadsworth. *The Strutts and the Arkwrights, 1758–1830: A Study of the Early Factory System*. Manchester University Press, 1968.

Fligstein, Neil, and Luke Dauter. "The Sociology of Markets." *Annual Review of Sociology* 33, no. 1 (2007): 105–28.

Flory, Rae Jean Dell. "Bahian Society in the Mid-Colonial Period: The Sugar Planters, Tobacco Growers, Merchants, and Artisans of Salvador and the Recôncavo, 1680–1725." PhD diss., University of Texas at Austin, 1978.

Fogel, Robert William. *Without Consent or Contract: The Rise and Fall of American Slavery*. W. W. Norton & Company, 1989.

Fogel, Robert William, and Stanley L. Engerman. *Time on the Cross: The Economics of American Negro Slavery*. Wildwood House, 1976.

Fohlen, Claude. "France 1700–1914." In *The Emergence of Industrial Societies, Part One*, edited by Carlo M. Cipolla, vol. 4. Harvester Press, 1976.

Forrest, Alan I. *The Death of the French Atlantic: Trade, War, and Slavery in the Age of Revolution*. Oxford University Press, 2020.

Fragoso, João Luís Ribeiro. *Homens de Grossa Aventura: Acumulação e Hierarquia Na Praça Mercantil Do Rio de Janeiro, 1790–1830*. 1992; Civilização Brasileira, 1998.

Francis, Alan David. "John Methuen and the Anglo-Portuguese Treaties of 1703." *The Historical Journal* 3, no. 2 (1960): 103–24.

Francis, Alan David. *The Methuens and Portugal, 1691–1708*. Cambridge University Press, 1966.

French, Christopher J. ""Crowded with Traders and a Great Commerce": London's Domination of English Overseas Trade, 1700–1775." *The London Journal* 17, no. 1 (1992): 27–35.

Frutuoso, Eduardo, Paulo Guinote, and António Manuel Barreto Lopes. *O Movimento Do Porto de Lisboa e o Comércio Luso-Brasileiro, 1769–1836*. Comissão Nacional para as Comemorações dos Descobrimentos Portugueses, 2001.

Fulcher, James. *Capitalism: A Very Short Introduction*. Oxford University Press, 2004.

Furtado, Celso. *Formação Econômica Do Brasil*. 1959; Companhia das Letras, 2007.

Furtado, Júnia Ferreira. *Homens de negócio: a interiorização da metrópole e do comércio nas minas setecentistas*. Editora Hucitec, 1999.

Gallo, Marzia Cataldi. *Mezzari and the Cotton Route. I Mezzari e La via Del Cotone*. San Giorgio Editrice, 2007.

Gallo, Marzia Cataldi. "Tessuti Genovesi: Seta, Cotone Stampato e Jeans." In *Atti Della Società Ligure Di Storia Patria, Nuova Serie, XLIV/2*, edited by Dino Puncuh. Società Ligure di Storia Patria, 2004.

Galloway, J. H. "Agricultural Reform and the Enlightenment in Late Colonial Brazil." *Agricultural History* 53, no. 4 (1979): 763–79.

Galves, Marcelo Cheche. ""Ao Público Sincero e Imparcial": Imprensa e Independência Do Maranhão (1821–1826)." Ph.D., Universidade Federal Fluminense, 2010.

Games, Alison. "Atlantic History: Definitions, Challenges, and Opportunities." *The American Historical Review* 111, no. 3 (2006): 741–57.

Gardner, George. *Travels in the Interior of Brazil: Principally Through the Northern Provinces, and the Gold and Diamond Districts, During the Years 1836–1841*. Reeve Brothers, 1846.

Gayoso, Raimundo Jose de Sousa. *Compendio historico-politico dos principios da lavoura do Maranhão: suas producçoens, e progressos, que tem tido até ao prezente, entraves que a vão deteriorando; e meios que tem lembrado para desvanece-los, em augmento da mesma lavoura, e sem prejuizo do real patrimonio …* P.N. Rougeron, Impressor, 1818.

Gereffi, Gary, Miguel Korzeniewicz, and Roberto P. Korzeniewicz. "Introduction: Global Commodity Chains." In *Commodity Chains and Global Capitalism*, edited by Gary Gereffi and Miguel Korzeniewicz. Praeger, 1994.

Gervais, Pierre. "Capitalism and (or) Age of Commerce: The Peculiarities of Market Exchange in the Early Modern Era." *XVII–XVIII. Revue de La Société d'études Anglo-Américaines Des XVIIe et XVIIIe Siècles*, no. 77 (December 2020).

Gervais, Pierre. "Neither Imperial, nor Atlantic: A Merchant Perspective on International Trade in the Eighteenth Century." *History of European Ideas* 34, no. 4 (2008): 465–73.

Godechot, Jacques. *L'Europe et l'Amerique a l'epoque Napoleonienne (1800–1815)*. Presses universitaires de France, 1967.

Godechot, Jacques. "The Internal History of France During the Wars, 1793–1814." In *The New Cambridge Modern History: Volume 9: War and Peace in an Age of Upheaval, 1793–1830*, edited by C. W. Crawley, vol. 9. The New Cambridge Modern History. Cambridge University Press, 1965.

Godinho, Vitorino Magalhães. *Estrutura da antiga sociedade portuguesa*. 1971; Edições 70, 2019.

Godinho, Vitorino Magalhães. "Portugal, as frotas do açúcar e as frotas do ouro (1670—1770)." *Revista de História* 7, no. 15 (1953): 69–88.

Godinho, Vitorino Magalhães. *Prix et monnaies au Portugal: 1750–1850*. Armand Colin, 1955.

Goebel, Dorothy Burne. "The "New England Trade" and the French West Indies, 1763–1774: A Study in Trade Policies." *The William and Mary Quarterly* 20, no. 3 (1963): 332–72.

Goldin, Claudia Dale. "The Economics of Emancipation." *The Journal of Economic History* 33, no. 1 (1973): 66–85.

Gorender, Jacob. *O Escravismo Colonial.* 1978; Fundação Perseu Abramo, 2010.

Goudar, Ange. *Rélation historique du tremblement de terre survenu à Lisbonne le premier novembre 1755: Avec un détail contenant la perte en hommes, eglises, convens, palais, maisons, diamans, meubles, marchandises, &c.* Chez Philanthrope, à la Vérité, 1756.

Graeber, David. *Debt: The First 5,000 Years.* Melville House, 2011.

Grafe, Regina. "On the Spatial Nature of Institutions and the Institutional Nature of Personal Networks in the Spanish Atlantic." *Culture & History Digital Journal* 3, no. 1 (2014): 1–11.

Granovetter, Mark S. "Economic Action and Social Structure: The Problem of Embeddedness." *American Journal of Sociology* 91, no. 3 (1985): 481–510.

Granovetter, Mark S. *Society and Economy: Framework and Principles.* The Belknap Press of Harvard University Press, 2017.

Granovetter, Mark S., and Richard Swedberg. *The Sociology of Economic Life.* Third edition. Westview Press, 2011.

Grassby, Richard. *The Idea of Capitalism before the Industrial Revolution.* Rowman & Littlefield, 1999.

Greif, Avner. *Institutions and the Path to the Modern Economy: Lessons from Medieval Trade.* Cambridge University Press, 2006.

Greif, Avner. "The Fundamental Problem of Exchange: A Research Agenda in Historical Institutional Analysis." *European Review of Economic History* 4, no. 3 (2000): 251–84.

Grenouilleau, Olivier. *L'argent de La Traite: Milieu Négrier, Capitalisme et Développement, Un Modèle.* Aubier, 1996.

Guest, Richard. *A Compendious History of the Cotton-Manufacture: With a Disproval of the Claim of Sir Richard Arkwright to the Invention of Its Ingenious Machinery.* J. Pratt, 1823.

Guicheteau, Samuel. *La Révolution des ouvriers nantais: Mutation économique, identité sociale et dynamique révolutionnaire (1740–1815).* Presses universitaires de Rennes, 2008.

Guimarães, Carlos Gabriel. "A Inserção Dos Ingleses No Império Português: O Caso Da Família Gulston No Rio de Janeiro, c.1710-c.1720." In *A Segunda Escravidão e o Império Do Brasil Em Perspectiva Histórica,* edited by Mariana Muaze and Ricardo H. Salles. Casa Leiria, 2020.

Gullickson, Gay L. *The Spinners and Weavers of Auffay: Rural Industry and the Sexual Division of Labor in a French Village.* Cambridge University Press, 1986.

Haber, Stephen H., and Herbert S. Klein. "The Economic Consequences of Brazilian Independence." In *How Latin America Fell behind: Essays in the Economic Histories of Brazil and Mexico, 1800–1914,* edited by Stephen H. Haber. Stanford University Press, 1997.

Haggerty, Sheryllynne. "Structural Holes and Bad Ideas: Liverpool's Atlantic Trade Networks in the Early-Eighteenth Century." In *Merchants and Trade Networks in the*

Atlantic and the Mediterranean, 1550–1800, edited by Manuel Herrero Sánchez and Klemens Kaps. Routledge, 2016.

Haggerty, Sheryllynne. "What's in a Price? The American Raw Cotton Market in Liverpool and the Anglo-American War." *Business History* 61, no. 6 (2018): 942–70.

Hahn, Barbara. *Technology in the Industrial Revolution*. Cambridge University Press, 2020.

Halimi, Serge. "When Market Journalism Invades the World." *Le Monde Diplomatique*, 1 May 1997. https://mondediplo.com/1997/05/globalsation3158.

Hall, Nigel. "Liverpool's Cotton Importers c. 1700 to 1914." *Northern History* 54, no. 1 (2017): 79–93.

Hall, Nigel. "The Business Interests of Liverpool's Cotton Brokers, c. 1800–1914." *Northern History* 41, no. 2 (2004): 339–55.

Hancock, David. *Oceans of Wine: Madeira and the Emergence of American Trade and Taste*. Yale University Press, 2009.

Hanson, Carl A. *Economy and Society in Baroque Portugal, 1668–1703*. University of Minnesota Press, 1981.

Harris, John Raymond. *Industrial Espionage and Technology Transfer: Britain and France in the Eighteenth Century*. Ashgate, 1998.

Harvey, Mark. "Slavery, Indenture and the Development of British Industrial Capitalism." *History Workshop Journal* 88 (October 2019): 66–88.

Hawthorne, Walter. *From Africa to Brazil: Culture, Identity, and an Atlantic Slave Trade, 1600–1830*. Cambridge University Press, 2010.

Heaton, Herbert. "A Merchant Adventurer in Brazil 1808–1818." *The Journal of Economic History* 6, no. 1 (1946): 1–23.

Heckscher, Eli F. *Mercantilism*. Vol. 1. 1931; Routledge, 1994.

Heckscher, Eli F. *The Continental System: An Economic Interpretation*. Clarendon Press, 1918.

Hemming, John. *Red Gold: The Conquest of the Brazilian Indians*. Harvard University Press, 1978.

Henderson, James. *A History of the Brazil*. Longman, 1821.

Henderson, W. O. "The Anglo-French Commercial Treaty of 1786." *The Economic History Review* 10, no. 1 (1957): 104–12.

Hills, R. L. "Hargreaves, Arkwright and Crompton. Why Three Inventors?" *Textile History* 10, no. 1 (1979): 114–26.

Hincker, François. *La Révolution française et l'économie: décollage ou catastrophe?* Nathan, 1989.

Hobsbawm, Eric J. *Industry and Empire: The Making of Modern English Society, 1750 to the Present Day*. Pantheon books, 1968.

Holanda, Sérgio Buarque de. *Caminhos e Fronteiras*. 1956; Companhia das Letras, 2001.

Hopkins, Terence K., and Immanuel Wallerstein. "Commodity Chains in the World-Economy Prior to 1800." *Review (Fernand Braudel Center)* 10, no. 1 (1986): 157–70.

Horan, Joseph. "Napoleonic Cotton Cultivation: A Case Study in Scientific Expertise and Agricultural Innovation in France and Italy, 1806–1814." In *New Perspectives on the History of Life Sciences and Agriculture*, edited by Denise Phillips and Sharon Kingsland. Springer International Publishing, 2015.

Horn, Jeff. *The Path Not Taken: French Industrialization in the Age of Revolution, 1750–1830*. MIT Press, 2006.

Horrocks, J. W. *A Short History of Mercantilism*. Taylor & Francis, 2017.

Hudson, Michael. *The Lost Tradition of Biblical Debt Cancellations*. Research Paper Presented at the Hentry George School of Social Science. 1992. https://michael-hudson.com/wp-content/uploads/2010/03/HudsonLostTradition.pdf.

Hudson, Pat. *The Genesis of Industrial Capital: A Study of the West Riding Wool Textile Industry, c. 1750–1850*. Cambridge University Press, 1986.

Hudson, Pat. *The Industrial Revolution*. 1992; Hodder Arnold, 2005.

Humphries, Jane, and Benjamin Schneider. "Losing the Thread: A Response to Robert Allen." *The Economic History Review* 73, no. 4 (2020): 1137–52.

Humphries, Jane, and Benjamin Schneider. "Spinning the Industrial Revolution." *The Economic History Review* 72, no. 1 (2019): 126–55.

Hyde, Francis E., Bradbury B. Parkinson, and Sheila Marriner. "The Cotton Broker and the Rise of the Liverpool Cotton Market." *The Economic History Review* 8, no. 1 (1955): 75–83.

'Ideia Da População Da Capitania de Pernambuco, e Das Suas Anexas, Extensão de Suas Costas, Rios e Povoações Notáveis, Agricultura, Número Dos Engenhos, Contratos, e Rendimentos Reaes, Aumento Que Estes Tem Tido, Etc, Etc, Desde o Ano de 1774 Em Que Tomou Posse Do Governo Das Mesmas Capitanias o Governador e Capitam General Jozé Cezar de Menezes.' *Anais Da Biblioteca Nacional Do Rio de Janeiro, Volume XL* (1918): 1–112.

Jacobini, Maria Lucia de Paiva. "O jornalismo econômico e a concepção de mercado: uma análise de conteúdo dos cadernos de economia da Folha de S.Paulo e O Estado de S.Paulo." *Brazilian journalism research* 4, no. 2 (2008): 190–209.

Jacqué, Jacqueline. "Printed Textiles." In *French Textiles: From the Middle Ages through the Second Empire*, edited by Marianne Carlano and Larry Salmon. Wadsworth Atheneum, 1985.

Jaquay, Barbara Gaye. "The Caribbean Cotton Production: An Historical Geography of the Region's Mystery Crop." Ph.D., Texas A&M University, 1997.

Jenkins, David. *The Cambridge History of Western Textiles*. Cambridge University Press, 2002.

Jensen, Michael C., and William H. Meckling. "Theory of the Firm: Managerial Behavior, Agency Costs and Ownership Structure." *Journal of Financial Economics* 3, no. 4 (1976): 305–60.

Jeulin, Paul. *L'évolution Du Port de Nantes: Organisation et Trafic Depuis Les Origines*. Les presses universitaires de France, 1929.

Johansen, Hans Chr. "Scandinavian Shipping in the Late Eighteenth Century in a European Perspective." *The Economic History Review* 45, no. 3 (1992): 479–93.

Johnson, Walter. *River of Dark Dreams: Slavery and Empire in the Cotton Kingdom*. Belknap Press of Harvard University Press, 2013.

Jones, S. R. H., and Simon P. Ville. "Efficient Transactors or Rent-Seeking Monopolists? The Rationale for Early Chartered Trading Companies." *The Journal of Economic History* 56, no. 4 (1996): 898–915.

Juhász, Réka. "Temporary Protection and Technology Adoption: Evidence from the Napoleonic Blockade." *American Economic Review* 108, no. 11 (2018): 3339–76.

Jung, Danielle F., and David A. Lake. "Markets, Hierarchies, and Networks: An Agent-Based Organizational Ecology." *American Journal of Political Science* 55, no. 4 (2011): 972–90.

Kaps, Klemens. "Small but Powerful: Networking Strategies and the Trade Business of Habsburg-Italian Merchants in Cadiz in the Second Half of the Eighteenth Century." *European Review of History: Revue Européenne d'histoire* 23, no. 3 (2016): 427–55.

Killick, John R. "Bolton Ogden & Co.: A Case Study in Anglo-American Trade, 1790–1850." *The Business History Review* 48, no. 4 (1974): 501–19.

Killick, John R. "Risk, Specialization and Profit in the Mercantile Sector of the Nineteenth Century Cotton Trade: Alexander Brown and Sons 1820–80." *Business History* 16, no. 1 (1974): 1–16.

Kobayashi, Kazuo. *Indian Cotton Textiles in West Africa: African Agency, Consumer Demand and the Making of the Global Economy, 1750–1850*. Palgrave Macmillan, 2019.

Kocka, Jürgen. *Capitalism: A short history*. Princeton University Press, 2016.

Koster, Henry. *Travels in Brazil*. Longman, Hurst, Rees, Orme, and Brown, 1816.

Krichtal, Alexey. "Liverpool and the Raw Cotton Trade: A Study of the Port and Its Merchant Community, 1770–1815." Master's thesis, Victoria University of Wellington, 2013.

Kriedte, Peter. *Peasants, Landlords and Merchant Capitalists: Europe and the World Economy, 1500–1800*. 1980; Berg Publishers, 1983.

Labourdette, Jean-François. *La Nation française à Lisbonne de 1669 à 1790: entre Colbertisme et libéralisme*. Fondation Calouste Gulbenkian, Centre culturel portugais, 1988.

Lago, Antonio Bernardino Pereira do. *Estatistica historica-geografica da Provincia do Maranhão oferecida ao Soberano Congresso das Cortes Geraes, extraordinarias, e constituintes da monarchia portugueza*. Academia Real das Sciencias, 1822.

Lakwete, Angela. *Inventing the Cotton Gin: Machine and Myth in Antebellum America.* Johns Hopkins University Press, 2003.

Langton, John, and Robert John Morris. *Atlas of Industrializing Britain, 1780–1914.* Methuen, 1986.

Lee, C. H. *A Cotton Enterprise, 1795–1840: A History of M'Connel & Kennedy Fine Cotton Spinners.* Manchester University Press, 1972.

Leménorel, Alain. "Le Calvados à l'époque napoléonienne (1800–1815). Tournant ou continuité? Deuxième partie: Les facteurs "internes"". *Annales de Normandie* 25, no. 3 (1975): 187–202.

Leménorel, Alain. "Le Calvados à l'époque napoléonienne (1800–1815). Tournant ou continuité? Première partie." *Annales de Normandie* 25, no. 1 (1975): 33–59.

Lemire, Beverly. "Fashioning Cottons: Asian Trade, Domestic Industry and Consumer Demand, 1660–1780." In *The Cambridge History of Western Textiles*, edited by David Jenkins. Cambridge University Press, 2002.

Lemire, Beverly. "Revising the Historical Narrative: India, Europe, and the Cotton Trade, c.1300–1800." In *The Spinning World: A Global History of Cotton Textiles, 1200–1850*, edited by Giorgio Riello and Prasannan Parthasarathi. Oxford University Press, 2009.

Lemire, Beverly. "Transforming Consumer Custom: Linen, Cotton and the English Market, 1660–1800." In *The European Linen Industry in Historical Perspective*, edited by Brenda Collins and Philip Ollerenshaw. Oxford University Press, 2003.

Lenk, Wolfgang. *Guerra e Pacto Colonial. A Bahia Contra o Brasil Holandês (1624–1654).* Alameda, 2013.

Leon, Pierre. "Structure du commerce exterieur et evolution industrielle de la France a la fin du XVIIIe siècle." In *Conjoncture économique, structures sociales: Hommage à Ernest Labrousse*, edited by Fernand Braudel. Mouton, 1974.

Leonzo, Nanci. "As Instituições." In *Nova História Da Expansão Portuguesa. O Império Luso-Brasileiro, 1750 1822. Volume VIII*, 1a. edição, edited by Joel Serrão, António Henrique de Oliveira Marques, and Maria Beatriz Nizza da Silva. Editorial Estampa, 1986.

Lévy, Robert. *Histoire économique de l'industrie cotonnière en Alsace: étude de sociologie descriptive.* Librairie Félix Alcan, 1912.

Linhares, Maria Yedda Leite. "Pecuária, alimentos e sistemas agrários no Brasil (séculos XVII e XVIII)." Arquivos Do Centro Cultural Calouste Gulbenkian. *Arquivos do Centro Cultural Calouste Gulbenkian*, no. 34 (1995): 585–99.

Linhares, Maria Yedda Leite, and Francisco Carlos Teixeira Silva. *História da agricultura brasileira: combates e controvérsias.* Brasiliense, 1981.

Lisboa, Breno Almeida Vaz. "Engenhos, açúcares e negócios na Capitania de Pernambuco (c.1655– c.1750)." *CLIO: Revista de Pesquisa Histórica* 32, no. 1 (2014): 196–214.

Lloyd-Jones, Roger, and Myrddin John Lewis. *Manchester and the Age of the Factory: The Business Structure of Cottonopolis in the Industrial Revolution.* Croom Helm, 1988.

Lodge, Richard. "The English Factory at Lisbon: Some Chapters in Its History." *Transactions of the Royal Historical Society* 16 (1933): 211–47.

Lopes, António, Eduardo Frutuoso, and Paulo Guinote. "As Frotas Do Brasil No Atlântico de Final Do Antigo Regime." *Actas Do Congresso Internacional Espaço Atlântico de Antigo Regime: Poderes e Sociedades* (2009): 1–28.

Lopes, Gustavo Acioli. *A Fênix e o Atlântico: a Capitania de Pernambuco e a Economia-Mundo Europeia*. Alameda Editorial, 2018.

Lopes, Gustavo Acioli. "O Saco de batatas colonial? Considerações sobre o uso do conceito de campesinato na historiografia do Brasil colônia." *Clio – Revista de Pesquisa Histórica* 1, no. 29 (2011).

Lopes, Gustavo Acioli, Leonardo Marques, and Felipe Souza Melo, eds. *Colonial Commodities in Historical Capitalism: Brazil for Export*. Routledge, 2026.

Lopes, Luis Seabra. "Sistemas Legais de Medidas de Peso e Capacidade, do Condado Portucalense ao Século XVI." *Portvgalia* XXIV (2003): 113–64.

Lopez, Robert, and Irving Woodworth Raymond. *Medieval Trade in the Mediterranean World: Illustrative Documents*. Columbia University Press, 1961.

Lord, E. "The Cotton Crop." In *Manual of Cotton Spinning, Volume 1*, edited by Alexander Frederick William Coulson. The Textile Institute, 1954.

Luard, Evan. *The Balance of Power: The System of International Relations, 1648–1815*. Macmillan, 1992.

Luccock, John. *Notes on Rio de Janeiro and the Southern Parts of Brazil*. Printed for Samuel Leigh, 1820.

Luckhurst, Gerald. "Gerard de Visme: 1755 and All That Came Afterwards." *The British Historical Society of Portugal* 44 (2017): 111–16.

Lugar, Catherine. "The Merchant Community of Salvador, Bahia, 1780–1830." PhD diss, State University of New York at Stony Brook, 1980.

Macedo, Jorge Borges de. *A Situação Económica No Tempo de Pombal: Alguns Aspectos*. 3a edição. Gradiva, 1989.

Macedo, Jorge Borges de. *O Bloqueio Continental: Economia e Guerra Peninsular*. Gradiva, 1990.

Macedo, Jorge Borges de. *Problemas de História Da Indústria Portuguesa No Século XVIII*. Quero, 1982.

Madureira, Nuno Luís. *Mercado e Privilégios: A Indústria Portuguesa Entre 1750 e 1834*. Estampa, 1997.

Magalhães, Joaquim Romero. "Sebastião José de Carvalho e Melo e a economia do Brasil." In *Labirintos brasileiros*, edited by Joaquim Romero Magalhães. Alameda, 2015.

Magnusson, Lars. *The Political Economy of Mercantilism*. Routledge, 2015.

Manchester, Alan K. *British Preeminence in Brazil, Its Rise and Decline. A Study in European Expansion*. 1933; Octagon Books, 1964.

Mann, James A. *The Cotton Trade of Great Britain: Its Rise, Progress, & Present Extent, Based upon the Most Carefully Digested Statistics …* Simpkin, Marshall, 1860.

Marcondes, Renato Leite, and Lélio Luiz de Oliveira. "Renascimento açucareiro: importações de açúcar brasileiro pelo Porto, 1762–1801." *Ler História*, no. 81 (December 2022): 117–41.

Marcos, Rui Manuel Figueiredo. *As Companhias Pombalinas: Contributo Para a História das Sociedades por Acções em Portugal.* Almedina, 1997.

Martins, Diego de Cambraia. "A Companhia Geral de Comércio Do Grão-Pará e Maranhão e Os Grupos Mercantis No Império Português (c.1755 – c.1787)." PhD diss, Universidade de São Paulo, 2019.

Martins, Diego de Cambraia, and Felipe Souza Melo. "Cotton Exports from Brazil, 1758–1815 Dataset." European University Institute, HEC, 2022. https://cadmus.eui.eu/handle/1814/74724.

Marzagalli, Silvia. "Establishing Transatlantic Trade Networks in Time of War: Bordeaux and the United States, 1793–1815." *Business History Review* 79, no. 4 (2005): 811–44.

Marzagalli, Silvia. "Le négoce maritime et la rupture révolutionnaire: un ancien débat revisité." *Annales historiques de la Révolution française*, no. 352 (June 2008): 184–207.

Marzagalli, Silvia. *Les Boulevards de La Fraude: Le Négoce Maritime et Le Blocus Continental, 1806–1813: Bordeaux, Hambourg, Livourne.* Presses universitaires du Septentrion, 1999.

Marzagalli, Silvia. "Was Warfare Necessary for the Functioning of Eighteenth-Century Colonial Systems? Some Reflections on the Necessity of Cross-Imperial and Foreign Trade in the French Case." In *Beyond Empires: Global, Self-Organizing, Cross-Imperial Networks, 1500–1800*, edited by Cátia Antunes and Amélia Polónia. Brill, 2016.

Mauro, Frédéric. *Portugal, o Brasil e o Atlântico, 1570–1670.* Vol. 1. 1983; Editorial Estampa, 1997.

Maw, Peter, Peter Solar, Aidan Kane, and John S. Lyons. "After the Great Inventions: Technological Change in UK Cotton Spinning, 1780–1835." *The Economic History Review* 75, no. 1 (2022): 22–55.

Maxwell, Kenneth. *Conflicts and Conspiracies: Brazil and Portugal, 1750–1808.* 1973; Routledge, 2004.

Maxwell, Kenneth. "Pombal and the Nationalization of the Luso-Brazilian Economy." *The Hispanic American Historical Review* 48, no. 4 (1968): 608–31.

Maxwell, Kenneth. *Pombal: Paradox of the Enlightenment.* Cambridge University Press, 1995.

Mazzaoui, Maureen Fennell. *The Italian Cotton Industry in the Later Middle Ages, 1100–1600.* Cambridge University Press, 1981.

McCulloch, John Ramsay. *A Dictionary, Practical, Theoretical, and Historical, of Commerce and Commercial Navigation: Illustrated with Maps and Plans*. Vol. 1. Longman, Orme, Brown, Green, and Longmans, 1839.

Medick, Hans. "The Proto-Industrial Family Economy: The Structural Function of Household and Family during the Transition from Peasant Society to Industrial Capitalism." *Social History* 1, no. 3 (1976): 291–315.

Mello, Evaldo Cabral de. *A Fronda dos Mazombos: Nobres Contra Mascates, Pernambuco, 1666–1715*. Editora 34, 2003.

Mello, Evaldo Cabral de. *A Outra Independência: o federalismo pernambucano de 1817 a 1824*. Editora 34, 2004.

Mello, Evaldo Cabral de. *Frei Joaquim do Amor Divino Caneca*. Editora 34, 2001.

Mello, Evaldo Cabral de. *O Bagaço da Cana*. Penguin, 2012.

Mello, Evaldo Cabral de. *Olinda Restaurada: guerra e açúcar no Nordeste, 1630–1654*. Editora 34, 2007.

Mello, Evaldo Cabral de. *Rubro Veio. O Imaginário Da Restauração Pernambucana*. Alameda, 2008.

Mello, Evaldo Cabral de. *Um Imenso Portugal. História e Historiografia*. Editora 34, 2008.

Mello, José Antônio Gonsalves de. *Ingleses Em Pernambuco: História Do Cemitério Britânico Do Recife e Da Participação de Ingleses e Outros Estrangeiros Na Vida e Na Cultura de Pernambuco, No Período de 1813 a 1909*. Instituto Arqueológico, Histórico e Geográfico Pernambucano, 1972.

Mello, José Antônio Gonsalves de. "Nobres e Mascates Na Câmara Do Recife, 1713–1738." *Instituto Arqueológico, Histórico e Geográfico Pernambucano* 53 (1981): 113–262.

Melo, Felipe Souza. "A movimentação comercial de um negociante em Pernambuco no final do século XVIII: o diário de escrituração de Bento José da Costa." *Faces da Historia* 5, no. 1 (2018): 179–97.

Melo, Felipe Souza. *Financiando o Negócio de Pernambuco: Produção Colonial, Comércio Ultramarino e a Economia Do Transporte No Atlântico Português (Século XVIII)*. Hucitec; ABPHE, 2021.

Melo, Felipe Souza. "Hierarquias mercantis no Atlântico Português: as relações de agência no comércio entre Portugal e Brasil, 1780 a 1807." *Revista de História*, no. 180 (April 2021): 1–43.

Melo, Felipe Souza. "O Negócio de Pernambuco: Financiamento, Comércio e Transporte Na Segunda Metade Do Século XVIII." Master's thesis, Universidade de São Paulo, 2017.

Melo, Felipe Souza. "The Fleet System and the Troubled Shipping Institutions in the Portuguese Atlantic (Seventeenth and Eighteenth Centuries)." *Colonial Latin American Review* 32, no. 3 (2023): 345–68.

Melo, Felipe Souza, and Diego de Cambraia Martins. "Reassessing the Productivity of Enslavement on Large-Scale Plantations and Small Farms in Brazilian Cotton Production (c. 1750 – c.1810)." *Historical Research* 96, no. 272 (2023): 193–221.

Melo, Sebastião José de Carvalho e. *Escritos Economicos de Londres (1741–1742)*. Biblioteca Nacional, 1986.

Melvin, Frank Edgar. *Napoleon's Navigation System: A Study of Trade Control during the Continental Blockade*. D. Appleton and company, 1919.

Menard, Russell R. "Law, Credit, the Supply of Labour, and the Organization of Sugar Production in the Colonial Greater Caribbean: A Comparison of Brazil and Barbados in the Seventeenth Century." In *The Early Modern Atlantic Economy*, edited by John J. McCusker and Kenneth Morgan. Cambridge University Press, 2001.

Mendels, Franklin F. "Proto-Industrialization: The First Phase of the Industrialization Process." *The Journal of Economic History* 32, no. 1 (1972): 241–61.

Menz, Maximiliano M. "A Companhia de Pernambuco e Paraíba e o Funcionamento Do Tráfico de Escravos Em Angola (1759–1775/80)." *Afro-Ásia*, no. 48 (December 2013): 45–76.

Menz, Maximiliano M. "Domingos Dias da Silva, o último contratador de Angola: a trajetória de um grande traficante de Lisboa." *Tempo* 23, no. 2 (2017): 383–407.

Menz, Maximiliano M. *Entre impérios: formação do Rio Grande na crise do sistema colonial português (1777–1822)*. Alameda, 2009.

Menz, Maximiliano M. "Reflexões sobre duas crises econômicas no Império Português (1688 e 1770)." *Varia Historia* 29, no. 49 (2013): 35–54.

Menz, Maximiliano M. *Senhor Da Morte: Capitalismo, Guerra e Tráfico de Escravos. Portugal, Angola e Brasil (1640–1771)*. HUCITEC, 2024.

Mesquita, Francisco de Assis Leal. *Vida e morte da economia algodoeira do Maranhão: uma análise das relações de produção na cultura do algodão, 1850–1890*. Universidade Federal do Maranhão, 1987.

Metzer, Jacob. "Rational Management, Modern Business Practices, and Economies of Scale in the Ante-Bellum Southern Plantations." *Explorations in Economic History* 12, no. 2 (1975): 123–50.

Miller, Joseph C. *Way of Death: Merchant Capitalism and the Angolan Slave Trade, 1730–1830*. University of Wisconsin Press, 1988.

Milward, Alan S., and S. B. Saul. *The Economic Development of Continental Europe 1780–1870*. 1973; Routledge, 2013.

Minchinton, Walter E. "The Merchants in England in the Eighteenth Century." In *Explorations in Enterprise*, edited by Hugh G. J. Aitken. Harvard University Press, 1965.

Mintz, Sidney W. *Sweetness and Power: The Place of Sugar in Modern History*. Penguin Books, 1986.

Mistler, Jean. "Hambourg Sous l'occupation Française: Observation Au Sujet Du Blocus Continental." *Francia* 1 (1973): 451–66.

Mokyr, Joel, ed. *The British Industrial Revolution: An Economic Perspective*. Westview Press, 1999.

Mont Serrath, Pablo Oller. "O Império Português no Atlântico: poderio, ajuste e exploração (1640–1808)." PhD diss, Universidade de São Paulo, 2013.

Montgomery, Florence M. *Textiles in America: 1650–1870. A Dictionary Based on Original Documents, Prints and Paintings, Commercial Records, American Merchants' Papers, Shopkeepers' Advertisements, and Pattern Books with Original Swatches of Cloth.* W.W. Norton & Company, 1984.

Moore, John Hebron. "Cotton Breeding in the Old South." *Agricultural History* 30, no. 3 (1956): 95–104.

Moore, John Hebron. *The Emergence of the Cotton Kingdom in the Old Southwest: Mississippi, 1770–1860*. Louisiana State University Press, 1988.

Morais, Ana Lunara da Silva. "Senhores de engenho e lavradores de cana-de-açúcar da capitania de Pernambuco: Conflitos e direitos de propriedade, América portuguesa, século XVIII." *Historia Agraria* 83 (April 2021): 73–95.

Moreira, Cristina, and Jari Eloranta. "Importance of "Weak" States during Conflicts: Portuguese Trade with the United States during the Revolutionary and Napoleonic Wars." *Revista de Historia Economica – Journal of Iberian and Latin American Economic History* 29, no. 3 (2011): 393–423.

Moreira, Cristina, Jaime Reis, and Rita Martins de Sousa. "Portugal's French Wars: Cost, Loss, Missed Opportunities? 1793–1850." In *The Crucible of Revolutionary and Napoleonic Warfare and European Transitions to Modern Economic Growth*, edited by Patrick Karl O'Brien. Brill, 2022.

Morgan, Philip D. "Task and Gang Systems: The Organization of Labor on New World Plantations." In *Critical Readings on Global Slavery*, edited by Damian Alan Pargas and Felicia Roşu. Brill, 2017.

Morineau, Michel. *Incroyables Gazettes et Fabuleux Métaux: Les Retours Des Trésors Américains d'après Les Gazettes Hollandaises (XVIe-XVIIIe Siècles)*. Cambridge University Press; Maison des sciences de l'homme, 1985.

Mota, Antonia da Silva. "A Dinâmica Colonial Portuguesa e as Redes de Poder Local Na Capitania Do Maranhão." PhD diss, Universidade Federal de Pernambuco, 2007.

Mota, Antonia da Silva, and Daniel Souza Barroso. "Economia e demografia da escravidão no Maranhão e no Grão-Pará: uma análise comparativa da estrutura da posse de cativos (1785–1850)." *Revista de História*, no. 176 (January 2017): 1–41.

Mota, Antonia da Silva, and Maísa Faleiros da Cunha. "No âmago da africanização: pessoas negras e de cor nos mapas populacionais do Maranhão colonial (1798–1821)." *Revista Brasileira de Estudos de População* 34, no. 3 (2017): 465–84.

Mota, Carlos Guilherme. *Nordeste 1817: Estruturas e Argumentos*. Perspectiva, 1972.

Muir, Rory. *Britain and the Defeat of Napoleon, 1807–1815*. 1996; Yale University Press, 2008.

Muldrew, Craig. "Credit and the Courts: Debt Litigation in a Seventeenth-Century Urban Community." *The Economic History Review* 46, no. 1 (1993): 23–38.

Nardi, Jean-Baptiste. *O fumo brasileiro no período colonial: lavoura, comércio e administração*. Brasiliense, 1996.

Nester, William. *The Coalitions Against Napoleon: How British Money, Manufacturing and Military Power Forged the Alliances That Achieved Victory*. Frontline Books, 2023.

Niephaus, Heinz-Theo. *Genuas Seehandel von 1746–1848: die Entwicklung der Handelsbeziehungen zur Iberischen Halbinsel, zu West- und Nordeuropa sowie den Überseegebieten*. Böhlau, 1975.

North, Douglass C. *The Economic Growth of the United States, 1790–1860*. Prentice-Hall, 1961.

Nouveau Dictionnaire d'histoire naturelle, appliquee aux arts: Principalement à l'Agriculture et à l'Economie rurale et domestique. VI. Crapelet, 1803.

Novais, Fernando A. "A proibição das manufaturas no Brasil e a política econômica Portuguesa do fim do século XVIII." *Revista de História* 33, no. 67 (1966): 213–37.

Novais, Fernando A. *Portugal e Brasil na crise do antigo sistema colonial (1777–1808)*. Hucitec, 1979.

Nye, John V. C. *War, Wine, and Taxes: The Political Economy of Anglo-French Trade, 1689–1900*. Princeton Economic History of the Western World. Princeton University Press, 2007.

O'Brien, Patrick. "The Formation of States and Transitions to Modern Economies: England, Europe, and Asia Compared." In *The Cambridge History Capitalism*, Reprint edition, edited by Larry Neal, vol. 1. Cambridge University Press, 2015.

Ogilvie, Sheilagh C., and Markus Cerman, eds. *European Proto-Industrialization*. Cambridge University Press, 1996.

Olmstead, Alan L., and Paul W. Rhode. "Biological Innovation and Productivity Growth in the Antebellum Cotton Economy." *The Journal of Economic History* 68, no. 4 (2008): 1123–71.

Olmstead, Alan L., and Paul W. Rhode. "Cotton, Slavery, and the New History of Capitalism." *Explorations in Economic History* 67 (January 2018): 1–17.

O'Rourke, Kevin H. "The Worldwide Economic Impact of the French Revolutionary and Napoleonic Wars, 1793–1815." *Journal of Global History* 1, no. 1 (2006): 123–49.

O'Rourke, Kevin H., and Jeffrey G. Williamson. "When Did Globalisation Begin?" *European Review of Economic History* 6, no. 1 (2002): 23–50.

Ouvrage collectif. *La Révolution en Haute-Normandie: 1789–1802*. Editions du P'tit Normand, 1988.

Palacios, Guillermo. "Peasantry and Slavery in Brazil: A Contribution to the History of the Free Poor Planters from the General Captaincy of Pernambuco, 1700–1817. Volume II." Ph.D., Princeton University, 1993.

Palacios, Guillermo. "Peasantry and Slavery in Brazil: A Contribution to the History of the Free Poor Planters from the General Captaincy of Pernambuco, 1700–1817. Volumes I." Ph.D., Princeton University, 1993.

Palma, Nuno, Andrea Papadia, Thales Pereira, and Leonardo Weller. "Slavery and Development in Nineteenth Century Brazil." *Capitalism: A Journal of History and Economics* 2, no. 2 (2021): 372–426.

Palmer, Sarah. "The Eighteenth Century Ports of London and Liverpool: Private V. Corporate Promotion." In *I Porti Come Impresa Economica: Atti Della "Diciannovesima Settimana Di Studi," 2–6 Maggio 1987*, edited by Simonetta Cavaciocchi. Le Monnier, 1988.

Pares, Richard. *Merchants and Planters*. Economic History Review Supplement, 4. Cambridge University Press, 1960.

Parkinson, C. Northcote. *The Trade Winds: A Study of British Overseas Trade During the French Wars, 1793–1815*. 1948; Routledge, 2005.

Parthasarathi, Prasannan. *Why Europe Grew Rich and Asia Did Not: Global Economic Divergence, 1600–1850*. Cambridge University Press, 2011.

Pedreira, Jorge Miguel. "A economia política do sistema colonial." In *O Brasil Colonial: Volume 3*, edited by João Fragoso and Maria de Fátima Gouvêa. Civilização Brasileira, 2014.

Pedreira, Jorge Miguel. "A Indústria." In *História Económica de Portugal, 1700–2000. Volume 1. O Século XVIII.*, edited by Pedro Lains and Alvaro Ferreira da Silva, vol. 1. Imprensa de Ciências Sociais, 2005.

Pedreira, Jorge Miguel. "Brasil, Fronteira de Portugal: Negócio, Emigração e Mobilidade Social (Séculos XVII e XVIII)." In *Do Brasil à Metrópole, Efeitos Sociais (Séculos XVII–XVIII). Anais Da Universidade de Évora, n. 8–9*, edited by Mafalda Cunha. 1998.

Pedreira, Jorge Miguel. "Custos e Tendências Financeiras Do Império Português, 1415–1822." In *A Expansão Marítima Portuguesa, 1400–1800*, edited by Francisco Bethencourt and Diogo Ramada Curto. Edições 70, 2010.

Pedreira, Jorge Miguel. *Estrutura industrial e mercado colonial: Portugal e Brasil (1780–1830)*. DIFEL, 1994.

Pedreira, Jorge Miguel. "From Growth to Collapse: Portugal, Brazil, and the Breakdown of the Old Colonial System (1750–1830)." *Hispanic American Historical Review* 80, no. 4 (2000): 839–64.

Pedreira, Jorge Miguel. "Os Homens de Negócio Da Praça de Lisboa de Pombal Ao Vintismo (1755–1822). Diferenciação, Reprodução e Identificação de Um Grupo Social." PhD diss, Universidade Nova de Lisboa, 1995.

Pedreira, Jorge Miguel, and Fernando Dores Costa. *D. João VI: O Clemente*. Circulo de Leitores, 2006.

Pereira, Thales Augusto Zamberlan. "Poor Man's Crop? Slavery in Brazilian Cotton Regions (1800–1850)." *Estudos Econômicos (São Paulo)* 48, no. 4 (2018): 623–55.

Pereira, Thales Augusto Zamberlan. "Taxation and the Stagnation of Cotton Exports in Brazil, 1800–60." *The Economic History Review* 74, no. 2 (2021): 522–45.

Pereira, Thales Augusto Zamberlan. "The Cotton Trade and Brazilian Foreign Commerce during the Industrial Revolution." PhD diss., Universidade de São Paulo, 2017.

Perrot, M. J. C. "L'industrie et Le Commerce de La Dentelle Dans La Région de Caen (Deuxième Moitié Du XVIIIe Siècle)." In *Actes Du 81e Congrès National Des Sociétés Savantes*. Presses Universitaires de France, 1956.

Picard, Charles. *Saint-Quentin: de son commerce et de ses industries*. Vol. 1. J. Moureau, 1865.

Piccinno, Luisa, and Andrea Zanini. "Genoa: Colonizing and Colonized City? The Port City as a Pole of Attraction for Foreign Merchants (16th-18th Centuries)." In *Reti Marittime Come Fattori Dell'integrazione Europea (Atti Della Settimana Di Studio Datini)*, edited by Giampiero Nigro. Firenze University Press, 2019.

Pietschmann, Horst. "Introduction: Atlantic History – History between European History and Global History." In *Atlantic History: History of the Atlantic System 1580–1830 : Papers Presented at an International Conference, Held 28 August-1 September, 1999, in Hamburg*, edited by Horst Pietschmann. Vandenhoeck & Ruprecht, 2002.

Pijning, Ernst. "Controlling Contraband: Mentality, Economy and Society in Eighteenth-Century Rio de Janeiro." PhD diss., Johns Hopkins University, 1997.

Pijning, Ernst. "Sources and Historiography: Conceptualizations of Contraband Trade in Colonial Brazil." *América Latina En La Historia Económica*, no. 24 (December 2005): 67–84.

Pinkney, David. "Paris: Capitale Du Coton Sous Le Premier Empire." *Annales. Histoire, Sciences Sociales* 5, no. 1 (1950): 56–60.

Pinto, Virgílio Noya. *O ouro brasileiro e o comércio anglo-português: uma contribuição aos estudos da economia atlântica no século XVIII*. Companhia Editora Nacional, 1979.

Platt, D. C. M. *Business Imperialism, 1840–1930: An Inquiry Based on British Experience in Latin America*. Oxford University Press, 1977.

Poitrineau, Abel. "Les Relations Économiques Franco-Espagnoles Vues à Travers Les Papiers de La Commission Impériale Des Indemnités de 1809–1810." *Actes Du 94e Congrès National Des Sociétés Savantes, Pau, 1969, Actes Du 94e Congrès National Des Sociétés Savantes. Tome 1* (1971): 283–91.

Pombo, Nívia. *Dom Rodrigo de Sousa Coutinho: pensamento e ação político-administrativa no Império Português (1778–1812)*. Hucitec, 2015.

Poussou, Jean-Pierre. "Les Activités Urbaines En France Pendant La Révolution." *Revue Économique* 40, no. 6 (1989): 1061–77.

Powell, Walter. "Neither Market Nor Hierarchy: Network Forms of Organization." *Research in Organizational Behaviour* 12 (January 1990): 295–336.

Prado Júnior, Caio. *Formação do Brasil contemporâneo: colônia*. 1942. 6. ed. Brasiliense, 1961.

Prado Júnior, Caio. *História Econômica do Brasil*. 1945. 41st ed. Brasiliense, 1994.

Price, Jacob M. "Transaction Costs. A Note on Merchant Credit and the Organization of Private Trade." In *The Political Economy of Merchant Empires. State Power and World Trade, 1350–1750*. Cambridge University Press, 1991.

Puntoni, Pedro. *A mísera sorte a escravidão africana no Brasil holandês e as guerras do tráfico no Atlântico Sul, 1621–1648*. Hucitec, 1999.

Quark, Amy A. *Global Rivalries: Standards Wars and the Transnational Cotton Trade*. University of Chicago Press, 2013.

Ragatz, Lowell Joseph. *The Fall of the Planter Class in the British Caribbean, 1763–1833: A Study in Social and Economic History*. 1928; Octagon, 1977.

Ratton, Jacome. *Recordações de Jacome Ratton sobre ocorrências do seu tempo, de maio de 1747 a setembro de 1810. 2. ed. revista cuidadosamente por J.M. Teixeira de Carvalho*. Imprensa da Universidade, 1920.

Reddy, William M. *The Rise of Market Culture: The Textile Trade and French Society, 1750–1900*. Cambridge University Press, 1984.

Redford, Arthur. *Manchester Merchants and Foreign Trade, 1794–1858*. Manchester University Press, 1934.

Reeder, Tyson. *Smugglers, Pirates, and Patriots: Free Trade in the Age of Revolution*. University of Pennsylvania Press, 2019.

Rees, Graham L. *Britain's Commodity Markets*. Elek, 1972.

Reid, R. *Glasgow, Past and Present*. Vol. 3. D. Robertson, 1884.

Rémond, André. *John Holker. Manufacturier et Grand Fonctionnaire En France Au XVIIIe Siècle, 1719–1786*. Librairie Marcel Rivière et Cie, 1946.

Ribeiro, Jorge Martins. "Comércio e diplomacia nas relações luso-americanas: 1776–1822." PhD diss., Universidade do Porto, 1997.

Ribeiro Júnior, José. "A Economia Algodoeira Em Pernambuco. Da Colônia à Independência." *Revista Brasileira de História* 1, no. 2 (September 1981): 235–42.

Ribeiro Júnior, José. *Colonização e monopólio no nordeste brasileiro: a Companhia Geral de Pernambuco e Paraíba, 1759–1780*. 1976; HUCITEC, 2004.

Ribeiro, Vítor. "Privilégios Dos Estrangeiros Em Portugal (Ingleses, Franceses, Alemães, Flamengos e Italianos)." *História e Memórias Da Academia Das Sciências de Lisboa* XIV (1922): 229–84.

Richardson, David, Suzanne Schwarz, and Anthony Tibbles, eds. *Liverpool and Transatlantic Slavery*. Liverpool University Press, 2007.

Ricupero, Rodrigo. "O estabelecimento do Exclusivo Comercial Metropolitano e a conformação do Antigo Sistema Colonial no Brasil." *História (São Paulo)* 35 (2016).

Riello, Giorgio. "Cotton Textiles and the Industrial Revolution in a Global Context." *Past & Present* 255, no. 1 (2021): 87–139.

Riello, Giorgio. *Cotton: The Fabric That Made the Modern World.* Cambridge University Press, 2013.

Robson, Martin. *Britain, Portugal and South America in the Napoleonic Wars: Alliances and Diplomacy in Economic Maritime Conflict.* I.B. Tauris, 2011.

Rodney, Walter. *A History of the Upper Guinea Coast, 1545–1800.* 1970; Monthly Review Press, 1980.

Rodrigues, Lúcia Lima, Alvaro Ricardino, and Sofie Tortelboom Aversari Martins. ""Corporate Governance Regulations": A New Term for an Ancient Concern? The Case of Grão Pará and Maranhão General Trading Company in Portugal (1754)." *Accounting History*, 2 November 2009.

Rodríguez, Manuel Bustos. *El Consulado de cargadores a Indias en el siglo XVIII (1700–1830).* Editorial UCA, 2017.

Röhr, Julius Philipp Benjamin von. *Observations sur la culture du coton, rédigées par ordre de S. M. le Roi de Danemarck, pour l'utilité des colonies danoises dans les Indes Occidentales ; par J.-P.-B. de Rohr, directeur et inspecteur de l'Agriculture dans l'île de Sainte-Croix, etc. Avec un préface de M. L. D. Philippe-Gabriel Hensler, professeur de médecine, à Kiel. Traduit de l'allemand.* 1793; Imprimerie-Librairie de Madame Huzard, 1807.

Roland de la Platière, Jean-Marie. *L'art du fabricant de velours de coton précédé d'une dissertation sur la nature, le choix et la préparation des matières et suivi d'un traité de la teinture et de l'impression des étoffes de ces matières.* Moutard, 1780.

Ronfeldt, David. *Tribes, Institutions, Markets, Networks: A Framework About Societal Evolution.* RAND Corporation, 1996.

Rose, J. Holland. "The Franco-British Commercial Treaty of 1786." *The English Historical Review* 23, no. 92 (1908): 709–24.

Rose, Mary B. *Firms, Networks and Business Values: The British and American Cotton Industries since 1750.* Cambridge University Press, 2000.

Rose, Mary B. "Introduction: The Rise of the Cotton Industry in Lancashire to 1830." In *The Lancashire Cotton Industry. A History since 1700*, edited by Mary B. Rose. Lancashire County Books, 1996.

Ross, Stephen A. "The Economic Theory of Agency: The Principal's Problem." *The American Economic Review* 63, no. 2 (1973): 134–39.

Roy, Bernard. *Une capitale de l'indiennage: Nantes.* Au musée des Salorges, 1948.

Ruders, Carl Israel. *Viagem em Portugal, 1798–1802.* Vol. 1. Biblioteca Nacional, 2002.

Russell, Edmund. *Evolutionary History: Uniting History and Biology to Understand Life on Earth.* Cambridge University Press, 2011.

Ryden, David Beck. ""One of the Finest and Most Fruitful Spots in America": An Analysis of Eighteenth-Century Carriacou." *The Journal of Interdisciplinary History* 43, no. 4 (2013): 539–70.

Salvucci, Linda K. "Atlantic Intersections: Early American Commerce and the Rise of the Spanish West Indies (Cuba)." *Business History Review* 79, no. 4 (2005): 781–809.

Sandberg, Lars G. "Movements in the Quality of British Cotton Textile Exports, 1815–1913." *The Journal of Economic History* 28, no. 1 (1968): 1–27.

Sargen, Ian. *Our Men in Brazil: The Hesketh Brothers Abroad.* Scotforth Books, 2009.

Say, Horace. *Histoire des relations commerciales entre la France et le Brésil: et considérations générales sur les monnaies, les changes, les banques et le commerce extérieur.* Guillaumin, 1839.

Schammas, Carole. "The Revolutionary Impact of European Demand for Tropical Goods." In *The Early Modern Atlantic Economy*, edited by John McCusker and Philip Morgan. Cambridge University Press, 2000.

Schmidt, Charles. "Les Débuts de l'industrie Cotonnière En France, 1760–1806." *Revue d'histoire Économique et Sociale* 7, no. 1/2 (1914): 26–55.

Schneider, Jürgen. "Le commerce de la France avec le Brésil, et spécialement la position du commerce français sur les divers marchés du Brésil entre 1815 et 1848. Essai d'une analyse de la structure économique." In *L'Histoire Quantitative de Brésil de 1800 a 1930*. Editions du Centre National de la Recherche Scientifique, 1973.

Schwartz, Stuart B. "Colonial Brazil, c. 1580–c. 1750: Plantations and Peripheries." In *The Cambridge History of Latin America. Volume 2: Colonial Latin America*, edited by Leslie Bethell. Cambridge University Press, 1984.

Schwartz, Stuart B. "Patterns of Slaveholding in the Americas: New Evidence from Brazil." *The American Historical Review* 87, no. 1 (1982): 55–86.

Schwartz, Stuart B. *Slaves, Peasants, and Rebels: Reconsidering Brazilian Slavery.* University of Illinois Press, 1992.

Schwartz, Stuart B. *Sugar Plantations in the Formation of Brazilian Society: Bahia, 1550–1835*. Cambridge University Press, 1985.

Schwarz, L. D. *London in the Age of Industrialisation: Entrepreneurs, Labour Force, and Living Conditions, 1700–1850*. Cambridge University Press, 1992.

Scott, John. "Commodity Chains." In *A Dictionary of Sociology*. Oxford University Press, 2015.

Sée, Henri. *La France Économique et Sociale Au XVIIIe Siècle.* Colin, 1967.

Sérgio, António. *Ensaios III.* Livraria Sá da Costa, 1974.

Serrão, Joaquim Veríssimo. *História de Portugal. Volume VI. O Despotismo Iluminado, (1750–1807)*. Editorial Verbo, 1982.

Sewell, William H. "The Empire of Fashion and the Rise of Capitalism in Eighteenth-Century France." *Past & Present*, no. 206 (2010): 81–120.

Shaw, L. M. E. *The Anglo-Portuguese Alliance and the English Merchants in Portugal, 1654–1810*. Ashgate, 1998.

Sheaves, Mark. "The Anglo-Iberian Atlantic as a Hemispheric System? English Merchants Navigating the Iberian Atlantic." In *Entangled Empires: The Anglo-Iberian*

Atlantic, 1500–1830, edited by Jorge Cañizares-Esguerra. University of Pennsylvania Press, 2018.

Shillington, Violet Mary, and Annie Beatrice Wallis Chapman. *The Commercial Relations of England and Portugal*. G. Routledge & sons, 1907.

Sideri, Sandro. *Trade and Power: Informal Colonialism in Anglo-Portuguese Relations*. Rotterdam University Press, 1970.

Silva, Andrée Mansuy Diniz. "Portugal and Brazil: Imperial Re-Organization, 1750–1808." In *The Cambridge History of Latin America. Volume 1: Colonial Latin America*, edited by Leslie Bethell. Cambridge University Press, 1984.

Silva, Angélica de Vasconcelos. "Closing Doors (1780–1813): The Liquidation Process at General Company of Pernambuco and Paraíba." PhD diss., Universidade de São Paulo, 2016.

Silva, Antonio de Moraes. *Diccionario Da Lingua Portugueza – Recompilado Dos Vocabularios Impressos Ate Agora, e Nesta Segunda Edição Novamente Emendado e Muito Acrescentado, Por Antonio de Moraes Silva*. Typographia Lacerdina, 1789.

Silva, Antonio Delgado. *Collecção da legislação Portugueza desde a ultima compilação das ordenações: Legislação de 1750 a 1762*. Vol. 1. Typ. Maigrense, 1830.

Silva, Antonio Delgado. *Collecção da legislação Portugueza desde a ultima compilação das ordenações: Legislação de 1763 a 1774*. Vol. 2. Typ. Maigrense, 1829.

Silva, Antonio Delgado. *Collecção da legislação Portugueza desde a ultima compilação das ordenações: Legislação de 1775 a 1790*. Vol. 3. Typ. Maigrense, 1828.

Silva, Antonio Delgado. *Collecção da legislação Portugueza desde a ultima compilação das ordenações: Legislação de 1802 a 1810*. Vol. 5. Typ. Maigrense, 1826.

Silva, Daniel B. Domingues da. "The Atlantic Slave Trade to Maranhão, 1680–1846: Volume, Routes and Organisation." *Slavery & Abolition* 29, no. 4 (2008): 477–501.

Silva, Daniele Ferreira da. "Colonialismo e fiscalidade na capitania de Pernambuco (1770–1793)." Master's thesis, Universidade Federal de Pernambuco, 2011.

Silva, Luís Antônio Vieira da. *História Da Independência Da Província Do Maranhão, 1822–1828*. 1862; Companhia Editora Americana, 1972.

Silva, Maria Beatriz Nizza da. *Elites Pernambucanas Do Fim Do Período Colonial*. Editora Singular, 2018.

Silver, Arthur W. *Manchester Men and Indian Cotton, 1847–1872*. Manchester University Press, 1966.

Smelser, Neil J., and Richard Swedberg. *The Handbook Of Economic Sociology*. 2 edizione. Princeton Univ Press, 2005.

Smithers, Henry. *Liverpool, Its Commerce, Statistics, and Institutions: With a History of the Cotton Trade*. T. Kaye, 1825.

Soares, Sebastião Ferreira. *Notas estatísticas sobre a produção agrícola e carestia dos gêneros alimentícios no Imperio do Brasil*. Typ. Imp. e Const. de J. Villeneuve e Comp., 1860.

Solana, Ana Crespo. "El Juez Conservador ¿Una Alternativa al Cónsul de La Nación?" In *Los Cônsules de Extranjeros En La Edad Moderna y a Principios de La Edad Contempóranea*. Ediciones Doce Calles, 2013.

Soll, Jacob. "For a New Economic History of Early Modern Empire: Anglo-French Imperial Codevelopment beyond Mercantilism and Laissez-Faire." *The William and Mary Quarterly* 77, no. 4 (2020): 525–50.

Souza, George Félix Cabral de. "Comerciantes de Escravos Em Pernambuco (c. 1660 – c. 1760): Aproximação a Um Grupo Mercantil Colonial." *CLIO: Revista de Pesquisa Histórica* 37, no. 2 (2019): 2.

Souza, George Félix Cabral de. *Elites e Exercício de Poder No Brasil Colonial: A Câmara Municipal Do Recife, 1710–1822*. Editora UFPE, 2015.

Spix, Johann Baptist von, and Carl Friedrich Philipp von Martius. *Viagem Pelo Brasil (1817–1820)*. Vol. 2. 1828; Senado Federal, 2017.

Stampp, Kenneth M. *Peculiar Institution: Slavery in the Ante-Bellum South*. Vintage, 1956.

Stein, Robert Louis. *The French Sugar Business in the Eighteenth Century*. Louisiana State University Press, 1988.

Stein, Stanley J. *The Brazilian Cotton Manufacture: Textile Enterprise in an Underdeveloped Area, 1850–1950*. Harvard University Press, 1957.

Stern, Philip J., and Carl Wennerlind, eds. *Mercantilism Reimagined: Political Economy in Early Modern Britain and Its Empire*. Oxford University Press, 2013.

Stone, Alfred Holt. "The Cotton Factorage System of the Southern States." *The American Historical Review* 20, no. 3 (1915): 557–65.

Strum, Daniel. "Institutional Choice in the Governance of the Early Atlantic Sugar Trade: Diasporas, Markets, and Courts." *Economic History Review* 72, no. 4 (2019): 1202–28.

Strum, Daniel. *O Comércio do Açúcar: Brasil, Portugal e Países Baixos, 1595–1630*. Versal, 2012.

Sturz, Johann Jakob. *A Review, Financial, Statistical, & Commercial, of the Empire of Brazil and Its Resources: Together with a Suggestion of the Expediency and Mode of Admitting Brazilian and Other Foreign Sugars Into Great Britain for Refining and Exportation*. E. Wilson, 1837.

Styles, John. "The Rise and Fall of the Spinning Jenny: Domestic Mechanisation in Eighteenth-Century Cotton Spinning." *Textile History* 51, no. 2 (2020): 195–236.

Styles, John. "What Were Cottons for in the Early Industrial Revolution?" In *The Spinning World: A Global History of Cotton Textiles, 1200–1850*, edited by Giorgio Riello and Prasannan Parthasarathi. Oxford University Press, 2009.

Subrahmanyam, Sanjay. "Rural Industry and Commercial Agriculture in Late Seventeenth-Century South-Eastern India." *Past & Present*, no. 126 (1990): 76–114.

Swedberg, Richard. *Principles of Economic Sociology*. 1st edition. Princeton University Press, 2007.

Tertzakian, Alexander. "Wages, Employment, and Technological Change in English Cotton Spinning, c.1780–1850." Ph.D. diss., University of Cambridge, 2022.

Thompson, Grahame. *Between Hierarchies and Markets: The Logic and Limits of Network Forms of Organization*. Oxford University Press, 2003.

Thompson, Grahame, Jennifer Frances, Rosalind Levacic, and Jeremy Mitchell, eds. *Markets, Hierarchies, and Networks: The Coordination of Social Life*. SAGE, 1991.

Thomson, James. "Invention in the Industrial Revolution: The Case of Cotton." In *Exceptionalism and Industrialisation: Britain and Its European Rivals, 1688–1815*, edited by Leandro Prados de la Escosura. Cambridge University Press, 2004.

Tollenare, Louis-François de. *Notas dominicaes tomadas durante uma residencia em Portugal e no Brasil nos annos 1816, 1817 e 1818* [*Notes dominicales: prises pendant un voyage en Portugal et au Brésil en 1816, 1817 et 1818*]. Empreza do Jornal do Recife, 1905.

Tomaz, Fernando. "As Finanças Do Estado Pombalino, 1762–1776." In *Estudos e Ensaios Em Homenagem a Vitorino Magalhães Godinho*. Sá da Costa, 1988.

Tunzelmann, G. N. von. "Technological and Organizational Change in Industry during the Industrial Revolution." In *The Industrial Revolution and British Society*, edited by Patrick O'Brien and Roland Quinault. Cambridge University Press, 1993.

Turner, A. *Manual Do Plantador d'algodão*. Officina Typ. do Frias, 1859.

Ure, Andrew. *The Cotton Manufacture of Great Britain: Systematically Investigated, and Illustrated by 150 Original Figures, Engraved on Wood and Steel; with an Introductory View of Its Comparative State in Foreign Countries, Drawn Chiefly from Personal Survey*. Vol. 1. Knight, 1836.

Ure, Andrew. *The Cotton Manufacture of Great Britain: Systematically Investigated, and Illustrated by 150 Original Figures, Engraved on Wood and Steel; with an Introductory View of Its Comparative State in Foreign Countries, Drawn Chiefly from Personal Survey*. Vol. 2. C. Knight, 1836.

Valadares, Virgínia Maria Trindade. *A sombra do poder: Martinho de Melo e Castro e a administração da capitania de Minas Gerais* (*1770–1795*). Hucitec, 2006.

Vanneste, Tijl. *Global Trade and Commercial Networks: Eighteenth-Century Diamond Merchants*. Pickering & Chatto, 2016.

Veloso, José Mariano da Conceição. *O Fazendeiro do Brazil, Tomo 5, Filatura*. Na Impressam Regia, 1806.

Verger, Pierre. *Fluxo e Refluxo Do Tráfico de Escravos Entre o Golfo Do Benin e a Bahia de Todos Os Santos Dos Séculos XVII a XIX*. 1968. 3ª edição. Corrupio, 1987.

Versiani, Flávio Rabelo, and José Raimundo Oliveira Vergolino. "Posse de escravos e estrutura da riqueza no agreste e sertão de Pernambuco: 1777–1887." *Estudos Econômicos* (*São Paulo*) 33, no. 2 (2003): 353–93.

Vesme, Carlo Baudi di. "Il Portogallo Nell'epoca Di Pombal (1755–1777) Secondo Alcune Relazioni Contemporanee Con Un Excursus Sui Rapporti Tra Il Portogallo e Genova Nel Medesimo Periodo." In *Genova, La Liguria e l'oltremare Tra Medioevo Ed Eta' Moderna – Studi e Ricerche d'archivio*, edited by Raffaele Belvederi, III. Pubblicazioni dell'Istituto di scienze storiche, Università di Genova, 1979.

Vidalenc, Jean. "Quelques remarques sur le rôle des Anglais dans la Révolution industrielle en France, particulièrement en Normandie, de 1750 à 1850." *Annales de Normandie* 8, no. 2 (1958): 273–90.

Vilhena, Luís dos Santos. *Recompilação de Notícias Brasílicas Contidas Em Três Cartas*. Salvador, Bahia, 1802.

Viveiros, Jerônimo de. *História do Comércio do Maranhão 1612–1895*. Vol. 1. Associação Comercial do Maranhão, 1954.

Vries, Jan de. *The Industrious Revolution: Consumer Behavior and the Household Economy, 1650 to the Present*. Cambridge University Press, 2008.

Wadsworth, A. P., and J. D. L. Mann. *The Cotton Trade and Industrial Lancashire, 1600–1780*. 1931; Manchester University Press, 1965.

Walford, A. R. "Gerard de Visme, Founder of the British Hospital (1793) and Member of the British Factory in Lisbon." In *7th Annual Report of the British Historical Association*. 1943.

Walford, A. R. *The British Factory in Lisbon & Its Closing Stages Ensuing Upon the Treaty of 1810*. Instituto britânico em Portugal, 1940.

Walker, C. E. "The History of the Joint Stock Company." *The Accounting Review* 6, no. 2 (1931): 97–105.

Wallerstein, Immanuel. *Historical Capitalism with Capitalist Civilization*. 1983; Verso, 2011.

Wallerstein, Immanuel Maurice. *The Modern World-System. Capitalist Agriculture and the Origins of the European World-Economy in the Sixteenth Century*. Vol. 1. 1974; University of California Press, 2011.

Walton, John K. "Proto-Industrialisation and the First Industrial Revolution: The Case of Lancashire." In *Regions and Industries a Perspective on the Industrial Revolution in Britain*, edited by Pat Hudson. Cambridge University Press, 1989.

Wardle, A. C. "Liverpool." In *The Trade Winds: A Study of British Overseas Trade During the French Wars, 1793–1815*, edited by C. Northcote Parkinson. 1948; Routledge, 2005.

Weber, Adelir. "Relações comerciais e acumulação mercantil: Portugal, Hamburgo e Brasil entre a colônia e a nação." Ph.D., Universidade de São Paulo, 2008.

Westerfield, Ray Bert. *Middlemen in English Business: Particularly between 1660 and 1760*. 1915; David & Charles, 1968.

Wheeler, James Talboys. *Hand-Book to the Cotton Cultivation in the Madras Presidency*. Virtue bros. & co., 1863.

Willan, T. S. *Studies in Elizabethan Foreign Trade*. Manchester University Press, 1959.

Williams, D. M. "Liverpool Merchants and the Cotton Trade, 1820–1850." In *Liverpool and Merseyside: Essays in the Economic and Social History of the Port and Its Hinterland*, edited by John Raymond Harris. Frank Cass and Company, 1969.

Williams, Eric. *Capitalism and Slavery*. 1944; University of North Carolina Press, 1994.

Williamson, Oliver E. *Markets and Hierarchies, Analysis and Antitrust Implications: A Study in the Economics of Internal Organization*. Free Press, 1975.

Wood, Ellen Meiksins. *The Origin of Capitalism: A Longer View*. 1999; Verso, 2002.

Woodman, Harold D. *King Cotton and His Retainers: Financing and Marketing the Cotton Crop of the South, 1800–1925*. 1968; University of South Carolina Press, 1990.

Woolf, Stuart. "L'impact de l'occupation Française Sur l'économie Italienne (1796–1815)." *Revue Économique* 40, no. 6 (1989): 1097–117.

Woronoff, Denis. "L'industrialisation de La France de 1789 à 1815. Un Essai de Bilan." *Revue Économique* 40, no. 6 (1989): 1047–59.

Wright, Gavin. *The Political Economy of the Cotton South: Households, Markets, and Wealth in the Nineteenth Century*. W. W. Norton & Company, 1978.

Young, Arthur. *Annals of Agriculture and Other Useful Arts*. X. Bury St. Edmunds, 1788.

Young, Arthur. *Annals of Agriculture, and Other Useful Arts*. XII. Bury St. Edmunds, 1789.

Zahedieh, Nuala. "Defying Mercantilism: Illicit Trade, Trust, and the Jamaican Sephardim, 1660–1730." *The Historical Journal* 61, no. 1 (2018): 77–102.

Zahedieh, Nuala. "Making Mercantilism Work: London Merchants and Atlantic Trade in the Seventeenth Century." *Transactions of the Royal Historical Society* 9 (1999): 143–58.

Index

www.ingramcontent.com/pod-product-compliance
Ingram Content Group UK Ltd.
Pitfield, Milton Keynes, MK11 3LW, UK
UKHW022228051026
15624UKWH00002B/412

9 789004 757554